Biographical Directory of the Governors of the United States 1789-1978

Volume III
(Montana-Pennsylvania)

Biographical Directory of the Governors of the United States 1789-1978

Volume III
(Montana-Pennsylvania)

Edited by
Robert Sobel and John Raimo

MECKLER BOOKS
A Division of Microform Review Inc.
520 Riverside Ave.
Westport, CT 06880

Library of Congress Cataloging in Publication Data

Main entry under title:

Biographical directory of the governors of the United
   States, 1789-1978.

   1. Governors—United States—Biography. I. Sobel,
Robert, 1931 (Feb. 19)- II. Raimo, John W., 1946 (Dec. 28)-
E176.B573   973'.0992 [B]   77-10435

ISBN 0-930466-00-4

ISBN 0-930466-01-2 (Vol. I); -02-0 (Vol. II); -03-9 (Vol. III); -04-7 (Vol. IV)

Meckler Books, *A Division of Microform Review Inc.*
520 Riverside Avenue
P.O. Box 405 Saugatuck Station
Westport, Conn. 06880
Printed in United States of America

CONTENTS

Volume Three

Index to Volumes I-IV follows Pennsylvania

Volume Four

Index to Volumes I-IV follows Wyoming

PREFATORY NOTE

Of the approximately 2,000 men and women who served as a State Governor,* the great majority of these have not been the subject of full-scale, published biographies. While some have appeared as major figures in the lives of other individuals, little is known about many Governors who held office during the nation's first half century. For some, information hitherto could be found only through an archival search. Now this data will be more readily accessible.

The Biographical Directory of the Governors of the United States, 1789-1978 is arranged alphabetically by states; within each state, the order of biographical entries is chronological. Biographies of those who served more than one term of office as Governor are situated within the years of first gubernatorial term. Inserts, listing the Governor's name and terms of office, have been included in the chronological sequence in order to preserve the recording of the continuity of the governorship within each state. The general index, appearing at the end of each volume, cites the volume number and first page of each biographical entry.

Each biography has been written by an expert, usually a researcher in a state or local historical society, a librarian, or a professor of history. Wherever possible, such basic information as dates of birth and death, ancestry and family, religion and political affiliation, electoral results, and political and private careers, have been included. In addition, the biographies contain bibliographic guides for further research; many also indicate where the Governor's papers are located.

For the original thirteen states, the biographical entries begin with the Governor taking office in 1789, the year in which the new Federal Constitution was implemented, rather than in 1776, the year the American colonies declared their independence from Great Britain. Although this decision has meant that some Governors, who served both under the Articles of Confederation and the Federal Constitution, are here discussed primarily in terms of developments during their gubernatorial careers after 1788; they, and the remaining governors of the colonial period (1607 to 1789), will be subsequently treated in a single volume scheduled to appear in the near future.

Robert Sobel
New College, Hofstra University

John W. Raimo
Editor

*The actual number is a matter of some dispute, for some states do not include individuals who served as Acting Governor on their lists. All those who took the oath of office from 1789 have been included in this work, which means that several who served less than a week are to be found here.

The following individuals have contributed entries to *The Biographical Directory of the Governors of the United States, 1789-1978*:

Elizabeth S. Adams, Michigan Historical Commission
Thomas Appleton, University of Kentucky
Mrs. Thomas H. Baird, Western Kentucky Museum
Willard Barnes, University of Idaho
Rodney E. Bell, South Dakota State University
Arthur W. Bergeron, Jr., Louisiana Archives & Records Service
W.C. Bethea, Arkansas Historical Commission
Aaron Berman, New York City, New York
Bob L. Blackburn, Oklahoma State University
Richard Bland, University of Kentucky
Warren M. Blankenship, University of Oregon
Susan Blain, Rhode Island Historical Society
Frank Boles, Bentley Library, University of Michigan
Ruth B. Bordin, Bentley Library, University of Michigan
Roger Bridges, Illinois State Historical Library
Larry Brooks, New York City, New York
Eugene T. Carroll, Denver, Colorado
Loren B. Chan, San Jose State University
Steven Channing, University of Kentucky
Russell J. Clemens, University of Missouri-Columbia
Len G. Cleveland, Georgia Department of Archives and History
David R. Colburn, University of Florida
Bridget Collier, Vermont Historical Society
James F. Cook, Floyd Junior College
David Crosson, University of Wyoming
Phyllis David, Alaska Historical Library
Michael D'Innocenzo, Hofstra University
Richard M. Doolen, Bentley Library, University of Michigan
Michael W. Everman, Oklahoma State University
Tomas Felt, New York Office of State History
Kenny A. Franks, Oklahoma Historical Society
John A. Fribley, University of Wyoming
Russell W. Fridley, Minnesota Historical Society
Patricia C. Gaster, Nebraska State Historical Society
Christopher C. Gibbs, University of Missouri-Columbia
Judith Gildner, *Annals of Iowa*
Steven K. Gragert, Oklahoma State University
David B. Gracy, III, Texas State Library
Larry Gragg, University of Missouri-Columbia
C.L. Grant, Georgia State University
James W. Hammack, Jr., Murray State University
Mac R. Harris, Oklahoma Historical Society
Lowell Harrison, Western Kentucky University
Gordon O. Hendrickson, University of Wyoming
Patricia Hickin, Richmond, Virginia
Ann Hinckley, Utah Division of State History

Zaneta Hirst, Montana Historical Society
Melvin G. Holli, University of Illinois at Chicago Circle
James Larry Hood, Kentucky Historical Society
Hazel Hopper, Indiana State Library
Millicent S. Huff, Texas State Library
H. Draper Hunt, University of Maine at Portland
Peter Iverson, University of Wyoming
Michael Kass, Massapequa, New York
Gregory Kendrick, University of Wyoming
Tevis L. Kimball, Rhode Island Historical Society
Philip Klein, Pennsylvania State University
James C. Klotter, Kentucky Historical Society
Stanford J. Layton, Utah Division of State History
Linda Lotridge Levin, Rhode Island Historical Society
Foy Lisenby, University of Central Arkansas
Nena B. Lovinger, University of Oregon
Robert M. McBride, Tennessee Historical Quarterly
Ursula McFarland, Rhode Island Historical Society
H. Brett Melendy, University of Hawaii at Manoa
Howard L. Meredith, Oklahoma Historical Preservation Review Commission
Frank C. Mevers, New Hampshire Historical Society
Mary L. Montanye, Anna Maria College
Waddy Moore, University of Central Arkansas
Miriam Murphy, Utah Division of State History
Keith A. Murray, Western Washington State College
Alan S. Newell, Historical Research Associates
Warren H. Onken, Jr., University of Wyoming
Ruth C. Page, New Hampshire Historical Society
John C. Paige, Wyoming State Archives and Historical Department
Betsy Peters, University of Wyoming
Marsha Peters, Rhode Island Historical Society
Robert Peters, University of Oregon
Steven L. Piott, University of Missouri-Columbia
John O. Pohlman, California State College at Dominguez Hills
A. Kent Powell, Utah Division of State History
Thomas E. Powers, Bentley Historical Library, Michigan Historical Collections
George E. Pozzetta, University of Florida
Harry Readnour, University of Central Arkansas
Patrick Reed, Northern Virginia Community College
Robert W. Righter, University of Wyoming
Leonard Rogoff, University of North Carolina
John Rusmandel, Freeport, New York
A. Bower Sageser, Kansas State University
Robert K. Scher, University of Florida
Paul Alan Schmidt, Stratford, Connecticut
Robert F. Sexton, University of Kentucky
T. McNeal Simpson, University of Tennessee
J.M. Skaggs, Wichita State University
James M. Smallwood, Oklahoma State University

John David Smith, Lincoln Library and Museum
John S.H. Smith, Utah State Historical Society
Homer E. Socolofsky, Kansas State University
Stuart Sprague, Morehead State University
Michael Starr, Hiram College
Vicki Sullivan, Oklahoma Historical Society
Hambleton Tapp, Kentucky Historical Society
Linda Thatcher, Utah Division of State History
Shirley Thayer, Maine State Library
Melvina K. Thurman, Oklahoma Historical Society
Carrie M. Townley, University of Nevada-Reno
Joseph G. Tregle, Jr., University of New Orleans
Len Tucker, Massachusetts Historical Society
Louis Tucker, New York Office of State History
Kirby O. Turner, University of Oklahoma
Carl N. Tyson, Oklahoma State University
Bruce Udolf, Boston, Massachusetts
Robert M. Warner, Bentley Library, University of Michigan
Gary D. Williams, Historical Research Associates
Sylvia Wrobel, University of Kentucky
B. Michael Zuckerman, Rhode Island Historical Society
Timothy A. Zwink, Oklahoma State University

INTRODUCTION

The office of American Governor is of central significance in the structure of American political parties. Since parties are organized on a statewide rather than a national basis, the Governor is the central personality in the state party of which he is a member. His leadership position automatically makes him the key spokesman on political matters within his state. A Governor who knows how to exploit effectively the media can develop insurmountable advantages of incumbency, often guaranteeing not only himself but also his party effective dominance within his state. The wealth of patronage appointments at the disposal of the Governor further strengthens the role of his party. It is not too much to say that an effective Governor is responsible for his party's performance on the national level. His organizational effectiveness lays the foundation for both state and national performance.

No less significantly, the program that a Governor pursues on a statewide level can be a testing of its effectiveness on a nationwide basis. Typical of this process was the performance of Robert M. La Follette, whose governorship of Wisconsin between 1901-1906 was marked by innovative programs of reform that emphasized the importance of expert knowledge in the shaping of public policy. His parallel efforts to make the selection process for candidates and campaign expenditures less vulnerable to corruption turned Wisconsin into a laboratory for progressive reform. The opportunities to make a statewide mark have often made the governorship a stepping stone to the presidency. A classic instance was the incumbency of Woodrow Wilson between 1911 and 1913 in New Jersey, where his highly visible reform program gave him national exposure. In a sense, the state provides a microcosmic testing of the man and program before they are applied to the macrocosmic stage of the nation.

In addition, the health of a party depends in substantial measure on its ability to elect Governors and members of State Legislatures. A party defeated on the national level can still sustain itself so long as it holds a significant proportion of governorships and state offices. But if it fails to maintain itself on the statewide level, the party begins to atrophy and runs the serious risk of its demise. No better evidence of this consequence is to be found than the fate of either the Federalist or Whig Party, each of which disintegrated when it could no longer win governorships and state offices. This fact permits the assertion that the basic unit of American politics is the state. It is there that the critical decisions which ultimately shape national politics are made. Therefore, to understand the dynamics of American politics, one must understand its functioning on the state level. Given the importance of the governorship, it is safe to say that an understanding of the gubernatorial office, and the men and women who have held it, is a key to such dynamics. From the *Biographical Directory of the Governors of the United States, 1789-1978*, a wealth of detail can be extracted that explains the origins and nature of the office, how it has evolved over time, and how it has shaped American history. In addition, by describing the people who have held the office, one obtains not only an insight into the nature of American politicians but also a striking perception of the nature of the American electorate who have chosen them.

The office of State Governor has its roots in the colonial governorship. As such, it is the oldest executive office in the United States. Prior to the Revolution, the governorship resembled in many ways the role of the King in the parliamentary system. It had extensive appointive powers, the authority to convene and dissolve colonial assemblies, the right to veto legislation, as well as the ability to serve as commander of the colonial militia. Outside of Connecticut and Rhode Island, the Governors were chosen by the crown; in these two New England colonies, they were elected. Since many colonial grievances prior to the Revolution were directed against the exercise of executive power, one of the major results of the Revolution was a major redefinition of the power of the governorship. The principle of an elective governorship, chosen either directly or indirectly from and by the citizenry, became accepted practice. To assure a responsive governorship, terms of office of one year became commonplace. The concern for the separation of powers was apparent in the care with which the Governor was distinguished from the legislature. Public determination to keep the executive subordinate to the legislative authority was reflected in the numerous limitations that circumscribed early gubernatorial powers. Nonetheless, despite these limitations, the Governor was clearly recognized as the head of the state, as well as the commander of the state militia. In addition the dimensions of the power assigned to the post-revolutionary Governors varied from state to state. In the old charter states of Connecticut and Rhode Island, the Governor continued to be popularly elected, and remained essentially independent of the legislature. In sharp contrast was the legislatively appointed Governor of South Carolina. In the states of New York and Massachusetts, a strong Governor possessed a suspensive veto power and extensive appointive authority. For a brief time, in states such as Georgia and Vermont, the Governor did little more than preside over an executive council which exercised the powers of the executive. Whatever the dimensions of their power, by 1792, all state chief executives were known as Governor.

The emphasis on a one-year term was originally common, with the exception of New York and Delaware which gave their chief executives three-year terms, and South Carolina which authorized a two-year term. The seven states of Pennsylvania, Delaware, Maryland, Virginia, North and South Carolina, and Georgia placed limits on the re-eligibility of an incumbent Governor. The most striking restriction was in Georgia which limited the term to one single year in a three-year period. Interestingly, the modern constitution of Georgia limits an incumbent to a single term in an eight-year period, a restriction that is also true in North and South Carolina, Virginia, Tennessee and Mississippi. The one-year term restriction did not prevent the repeated election of incumbent Governors. William Livingston, the first Governor of the State of New Jersey, was elected to fourteen successive terms between 1776 and 1790. Yet the effort to keep Governors responsive to the electorate was an overriding concern in keeping the terms brief.

More important to the development of a democratically chosen governorship was the shift to a popularly elected Governor. Outside of the original thirteen states, only Kentucky and Louisiana failed immediately to establish direct gubernatorial elections, but even these two quickly reverted to popular choice. Of the original thirteen states, all but South Carolina had abandoned legislative choice of the Governor before the Civil War, and in 1865, the "Palmetto State" fell into line. A number of states made the additional requirement of either a runoff election or a legislative choice between the two top candidates when no candidate won a clear majority. Today only the southern states of Georgia, Mississippi, Arkansas, Alabama, Florida, Louisiana, North Carolina, Oklahoma, South Carolina, Texas and Virginia provide for a runoff; the other states have settled for a plurality choice. The power of the popular choice was never more strikingly demonstrated than in the 1839 election by a single vote of Marcus Morton to the governorship of Massachusetts.

Not all gubernatorial contests have been settled as peacefully. Rhode Island teetered on the edge of Civil War in 1842, as two factions, led by Thomas W. Dorr and Samuel W. King, both claimed the office. Federal intervention assured King's incumbency, but the source of the original dispute, Dorr's effort to broaden the suffrage to all whites, was resolved in 1843 with the adoption of a new constitution incorporating liberalized suffrage provisions. A more spectacular controversy erupted in Kentucky in 1899 when a bitterly fought election reached a climax when the Democratically controlled legislature chose the anti-railroad reformer William Goebel to replace the Republican William S. Taylor. Taylor was removed on the grounds that his narrow victory had been fraudulently won. Tension exploded on January 30, 1900, when Goebel was shot outside the State Capitol. The legislature then proclaimed Goebel Governor, and upon his death four days later, his Lieutenant Governor, J.C.W. Beckham, succeeded him. Eventually the Kentucky courts upheld the choice of Beckham. Taylor escaped prosecution for complicity in the assassination by fleeing to Indiana, but the Republican Secretary of State, as well as an aide, were eventually convicted and sentenced to life imprisonment. A more recent dispute was settled in Rhode Island in 1956, when the State Supreme Court invalidated some 5,000 absentee votes to assure Dennis Joseph Roberts a fourth term by a bare 711 votes. Invariably, these disputed elections have reflected the existence of deeply felt internal divisions within states.

A further complication in the choosing of Governors has been the time period during which gubernatorial candidates have been chosen. Over the years arguments have been made that candidates should be chosen at elections other than those involving presidential candidates. Obviously, so long as most Governors were chosen for one or two years, their elections would coincide with that of Presidents. But as a four-year term became the more common period, efforts were made to switch gubernatorial choices to off-year elections. This process has arrived at the point that presently only the Governors of Arkansas, Delaware, Indiana, Missouri, Montana, New Hampshire, North Carolina, North Dakota, Rhode Island, Utah, Vermont and West Virginia are to be chosen in the year of presidential election. The present Governor of Illinois, James R. Thompson, was elected to a two-year term in 1976 in order to provide for a shift to an off-year four year sequence. The five states of Kentucky, Louisiana, Mississippi, New Jersey and Virginia have futher lessened the chance that state and national issues might be confused by electing their Governors at times when no member of the federal government is being voted on.

The choosing of gubernatorial candidates during the nineteenth and well into the twentieth century had been made at conventions. The colorful, often corrupt, nature of the convention process resulted in a developing backlash that steadily displaced the convention by the direct primary system. With its compulsory application to party choices in Wisconsin in 1903, the direct primary became a central focus of Progressive political reform. Ironically, in one party states, such as those in the South, the primary election which resulted in the choice of the designated Democratic Party candidate became the key election. Once the party candidates were chosen in the primary, despite reform expectations, the election tended to attract party workers and zealots in far larger proportions than regular voters. This gave a decided advantage to candidates who had strong party worker support. In states such as California, which until 1959 allowed a candidate to cross-file for nomination by more than one party, it was possible for a candidate like Earl Warren to win both the Republican and the Democratic gubernatorial nomination in 1946. Most states have since adopted the "closed" primary that generally restricts voting in primaries to registered members of the parties. The last of the fully convention states, Indiana, has since 1976 switched to a primary. Connecticut still uses the convention method of choosing its candidates, but any losing candidate, who in convention gets 25 percent of the delegate vote, can call for a primary; Delaware also still uses conventions to select candidates. In most primaries, the plurality winner gets the nomination, a process that allowed Brendan Byrne of New Jersey to win renomination in 1977 with barely 30 percent of the vote.

The path to nomination as Governor was once considerably more difficult. In the formative stages of the republic, many states required that a Governor own substantial amounts of property. The largest amount required was in South Carolina, which specified that the candidate own no less than a £10,000 debt-free freehold. In contemporary terms that would be tantamount to requiring a Governor to be a millionaire. Most states originally placed precise requirements on the Governor's religious belief. Typical of this was New Jersey's requirement that the Governor be a member of a Protestant sect. More in line with contemporary practice, Virginia started out with neither property nor sectarian requirements. But over time, the original restrictions were steadily modified. The religious test was finally terminated in 1961 when the United States Supreme Court found a Maryland statute requiring state officials to declare their belief in Christianity, or in a future existence where the sinful were punished and the believer rewarded, an unconstitutional violation of freedom of religion. Some requirements still remain. Most Governors must be at least thirty years of age, and all are required to be American citizens and residents of the states of which they are Governor. The requirement that a Governor be a native-born United States citizen ceased in 1955 when Maine deleted that requirement from its Constitution. Similarly, gubernatorial qualifications specifically designate the conviction for certain kinds of crime as an immediate disqualification.

The question of qualification has occasionally resulted in a serious conflict over the eligibility of a gubernatorial candidate. In 1924, Miriam A. Ferguson, the Democratic candidate for the Texas governorship, was challenged on the grounds of her sex, the fact that she was married, and that her husband, James E. Ferguson, had been previously removed from the Texas governorship by impeachment. The courts decided in her favor and she went on to be elected. In the middle 1930s, William Langer of North Dakota was forced to relinquish the Governor's post on the grounds that his conviction for a felony made him ineligible to hold the office.

But given the number of past Governors, the most remarkable fact is the relatively few controversies that have surrounded gubernatorial qualifications.

An analysis of the governorship over a span of time indicates certain constants in the character of the individuals who have held the post. Most immediately, the candidates have been overwhelmingly male, with the inclusion of only five women, Nellie Tayloe Ross of Wyoming, Miriam A. Ferguson of Texas, Lurleen Wallace of Alabama, Ella Grasso of Connecticut and Dixy Lee Ray of Washington (all Democrats.) A study of the proportion of party representation finds that 35.5 percent of all Governors have been Republican; 45.1 percent Democrats; 7.9 percent Democratic-Republican, i.e. Jeffersonian Republicans, the predecessor of the Democratic Party; 6.5 percent Whigs; 2.8 percent Federalists; and the remaining 2.2 percent from a scattering of parties. The average age at which Governors have been first elected is 48.2 years. A surprising difference is found between Democrats who have averaged 46.5 years and Republicans who have averaged 50.1 years. Overwhelmingly, by 97.6 percent to 2.4 percent, Governors have been married, with Democrats, by a two to one margin, likely to be the unmarried. However, few Governors have matched the marital record of Jonas Galusha of Vermont who married and buried four wives.

Generally Governors have reflected the population composition of their home states. The preponderance of the Protestant faith is reflected in the fact that 87.5 percent of all Governors have belonged to a Protestant sect. Of the remainder, 12.1 percent were Roman Catholic, .1 percent Jewish, and the final .3 percent have noted no religion. The latter fact strongly suggests that gubernatorial candidates have found it advantageous to identify with some religious sect. Interesting evidence of recent change is the fact that among incumbent Governors, 65 percent are Protestant, 30.5 percent are Roman Catholic, 4 percent are Jewish, and .5 percent are Greek Orthodox. With regard to discernible ethnic origin, the overwhelming preponderance of incumbents have been of British, German, Irish and Scandinavian origin. More recently, candidates of Italian, Slavic, Hispanic, i.e. Mexican, and Japanese ancestry have been elected. The presence of a given group in a state, particularly if it is numerous, is no guarantee that one of its number will be quickly elected to the governorship. For example, the first Jewish Governor of New York State, Herbert Lehman, was not elected until 1932, although Idaho, Oregon and New Mexico, with negligible Jewish populations, elected the first modern Jewish Governors, Moses Alexander (1915), Julius L. Meier (1930) and Arthur Seligman (1930), respectively.[1] Similarly, New Jersey, whose Roman Catholic population approaches 40 percent, did not elect a Roman Catholic Governor (Richard J. Hughes) until 1961, while Connecticut, with its sizeable Italian population, elected its first Governor of Italian origin (Ella Grasso) in 1974. It is worth noting that no black has ever been elected to a governorship, although Pinckney B.S. Pinchback, a black, served briefly in 1872-1873 as Governor of Louisiana, when the white incumbent was impeached.

The most significant determinant in the choice of gubernatorial candidate has been his prior service in state government. No fewer than 71.3 percent of all Governors have served in the state legislature previous to their election. This strongly suggests that the connections one makes through state service have played

---

1. David Emanuel, Governor of Georgia (1801), was the first Jewish Governor.

a significant role in party nominations. A gubernatorial candidate with such credentials has the immense advantage of being a predictable quantity for the party leadership. It also means that an outsider, such as Woodrow Wilson was when nominated by New Jersey Democrats in 1910, is an exceptional development. Almost 14 percent of all Governors have served in either the Senate or the House of Representatives. The latter office is more likely to be held before the governorship, while the former is more likely to be held subsequently. In addition, no fewer than 31.1 percent have served on the federal level in other than Congress. Among the latter were fourteen future Presidents, a number that indicates that gubernatorial service has been an impressive advantage in seeking the presidency.[2] An odd fact was the election of the Confederate Vice President, Alexander Stephens, after the Civil War to the governorship of Georgia. In the category of the unusual fact, only Sam Houston served as Governor in more than one state, i.e. Tennessee (1827-29) and Texas (1859-61). However, a number of Governors held previous state offices in states other than those that had elected them Governor. Some examples are Ninian Edwards, an Illinois Governor, who had served in the Kentucky House of Representatives, as well as being that state's Chief Justice; George Thomas Wood of Texas who had served in the Georgia legislature; William Erskine Stevenson of New Mexico who had sat in the Pennsylvania Legislature; Arthur Calvin Mellette of South Dakota who had been a member of the Indiana House of Representatives; and William John McConnell of Idaho who had also been an Oregon State Senator.

The portrait of Governors would not be complete without noting their educational, professional, and military attainments. Although it is difficult to draw effective comparisons between contemporary and past educational facilities, it is safe to deduce that the average Governor has had a significantly more extensive educational background than his constituents. It seems that 76.8 percent of all Governors have attended colleges or universities. Interestingly, all present 50 incumbents in state governorships had received higher education, and Oklahoma's David Boren was a Rhodes scholar. Approximately 66 percent of all Governors have been practicing lawyers, a dominant characteristic of all elected officials on both the state and federal level. Among present Governors the percentage of lawyers is 52 percent. This decline in the number of lawyers has resulted in an interesting diversification of occupations among present Governors. Seven have been active in business; two have been dentists, and the present Governor of Indiana is still a practicing medical doctor; four are farmers or ranchers; one was a commercial fisherman and air taxi operator, and another a high school teacher and coach; while Dixy Lee Ray of Washington State is an oceanographer. The steady broadening of the occupational range of Governors in the past four decades reflects the widening of political parameters in the United States. One can assume that the traditional dominance in politics of lawyers will continue to decline, although as a group they are likely to remain the largest single component. Equally as striking is the fact that 68.1 percent of Governors have given military service. Americans have traditionally honored their veterans, a fact illustrated by South Dakota's election of Congressional Medal of Honor winner Joseph Foss after World War II.

2. Jefferson (VA); Monroe (VA); Van Buren (NY); Tyler (VA); Polk (TN); A. Johnson (TN); Hayes (OH); Cleveland (NY); McKinley (OH); T. Roosevelt (NY); Wilson (NJ); Coolidge (MA); F.D. Roosevelt (NY); Carter (GA).

One limitation on gubernatorial candidacy has been the inescapable expense of running for the office. It is safe to assume that the vast mass of Governors have come from solid middle class circumstances. Most Governors can expect to receive presently a salary approximating that of a middle range business executive. In addition to their salaries, they may receive the use of the Governor's residence and other perquisites of office, such as a limousine and a private plane. However, a large proportion of Governors are likely to find that an independent outside income is an essential ingredient to surviving the expenses of office. Since its earliest origins, the post has carried with it the implied idea that compensation is secondary to the distinction of the office. As a result, most governorships pay substantially less than equivalent federal offices. Present salaries range from a high of $85,000 in New York State to a low of $10,000 in Arkansas. Most Governors are paid between $25,000 and $50,000 annually. The combination of heavy campaign costs and comparatively low salaries has resulted in most candidates being people of independent means who have further access to substantial campaign contributions.

Once in office Governors have found that their office resembles the national presidency in both its structure and power. Like the President, the Governor is both the Chief Executive and Party Chief within his political bailiwick. He also is Commander-in-Chief of the state armed forces and will be expected to call them into action if circumstances dictate their use. When the Governor is sworn into office, he is expected to deliver an inaugural address that forecasts the general policies that his administration will follow. Normally, the Governor delivers an annual "state of the state" address which spells out unsettled problems and their proposed solution. Since many state responsibilities are likely to affect directly the daily lives of the average citizen, any failure to provide effective service is likely to focus criticism against the Governor. The result is that the gubernatorial post is more likely to see frequent changes in incumbents than congressional posts. Typically it can result in the Republicans, as was true in 1968, holding 31 of the 50 governorships and the Democrats in 1978 holding 36 of the posts. The vulnerability of Governors, combined with the frequent limits imposed on their terms of office, has meant that few Governors hold their offices for longer than eight years. Nonetheless, strong Governors have the power to guide their legislatures to implement legislative programs that are needed.

At the outbreak of the Civil War, Indiana's Republican Governor, Oliver P. Morton, used the State Militia to disband the Democratically controlled State Legislature. More generally, the Governor is likely to maintain good relations with the legislature by working carefully with the legislative leadership. Obviously this process is simplified if the leadership is of the Governor's party, but even a legislature dominated by the opposition is likely to deal cautiously with an incumbent Governor. They are well aware that as Chief Executive, he is in a powerful position to depict the legislature as "obstructionist." In every state but North Carolina, the Governor possesses an executive veto, a weapon that can be used to embarrass the legislature. This is particularly true since more than half the states provide the Governor with the additional time of a month or more to deal with legislation reaching him at the end of a legislative session. Since most legislation is passed in the closing days of a session, this permits the Governor to use wide-ranging consultations before he approves a measure. Only a most inept Governor is likely to fail to invoke a powerful backing before he issues his veto.

Once a veto is made, most states require that three-fifths or two-thirds of the full legislative membership vote to override it, and Alaska requires a three-fourths vote to override a veto of a money bill. In addition, in New Jersey, Massachusetts, Virginia and Alabama, the Governor can return a bill with suggestions on specific amendments that would make a bill satisfactory to him. The power of the veto is indicated by the fact that less than 2 percent of bills vetoed by Governors are presently overridden. Ironically, the public perception of this increased gubernatorial power has resulted in its holding Governors responsible for failure to meet public problems.

The final public control that can be exerted over the governorship is removal from office. With the exception of Oregon, every state provides for an impeachment procedure similar to that in the federal constitution, and even in Oregon, a Governor can be removed by a trial conducted in a manner similar to other criminal trials. In addition, Wisconsin, Michigan, California, Oregon, Arizona, Colorado, Idaho, Nevada, Washington, Louisiana, North Dakota and Kansas provide for the recall of a Governor. However, these removal procedures are used infrequently. It is as if Americans understand that removal from office involves awesome implications and must be used with care, less it degenerate into potential abuse. This is a fear that was reenforced during the Reconstruction when two Southern Governors were removed by impeachment, a third forced to resign under the threat of impeachment, and three other Southern incumbents impeached but not tried.

More recently in the twentieth century, the New York Legislature removed William Sulzer on charges that he was contemptuous of its powers. The Texas Legislature removed James E. Ferguson for abusing his appointive, fiscal and pardoning powers. A number of Governors have been removed after their conviction on criminal charges, involving most recently, in 1977, governor Marvin Mandel of Maryland. Perhaps the most extraordinary example of gubernatorial corruption was exposed when Vice President Spiro Agnew was obliged to relinquish his office in 1973 on charges that arose out of corruption dating from his prior governorship of Maryland. But given the number of past Governors, it is apparent that the process of removal is as sparingly used as in the federal executive.

Without question, the American governorship provides a profound insight into the nature of the American executive. In sheer number, Governors are the largest single component of executive power on the political level. To understand how they achieved their political position is to come to understand the vast structure of state political organization that is the hidden side of the federal system. The changes that have occurred in the shape of the American governorship during the past two centuries are the key to understanding how the American political system has evolved into an increasingly centralized democratic republic. Finally, the Governors are a reflection of the extraordinary diversity that has characterized state politics. Within the constant of one republic, the state polity has provided Americans with the opportunity to diverge from their sister states, and to experiment on a scale that allows them to confine the original risks to one state, while making subsequent benefits available to all states. In these four volumes, the reader is given an introduction to a side of the American political experiment that has been hidden — and the Governors whose biographies are contained here are the actors in that shadowed experiment.

James P. Shenton
Columbia University

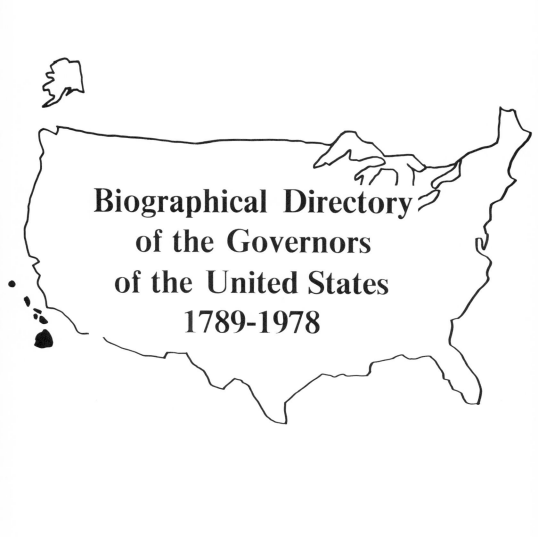

Biographical Directory
of the Governors
of the United States
1789-1978

MONTANA

MONTANA

TOOLE, Joseph Kemp, 1889-1893, 1901-1908

Born on May 12, 1851 in Savannah, Missouri, son of Edwin, a farmer, and Lucinda (Porter) Toole; one of ten children. Raised in Savannah and St. Joseph. Graduated from public school; enrolled in Western Military Institute in Newcastle, Kentucky, graduating with high honors in 1867. Studied law with a Newcastle firm; served as a member of local Court of Appeals; moved to Helena, Montana in 1869 and continued study in the firm of his brother Edwin W. Toole; admitted to the Montana Bar in 1872. Married Lilly Rosencrans, May 6, 1890; father of Rosencrans, Edwin Warren and Joseph Porter. Toole was first elected to public office as a Democratic candidate for District Attorney in 1872, securing reelection without opposition in 1874. In 1880, he won election to Montana's Twelfth Legislative Assembly from Lewis and Clark County, and served as President of the Council. Four years later, Lewis and Clark voters elected him to the State Constitutional Convention; however, the United States Congress failed to sanction this constitution. In November of 1884 and 1886, Toole was elected Territorial Delegate to Congress, where he worked successfully to secure passage of an Enabling Act for statehood. He declined reelection to Congress in 1888, but became a delegate to the 1889 Constitutional Convention. In 1889, voters elected him Montana's first state Governor, over Republican Thomas C. Power, 19,564 votes to 18,988. Although a brilliant orator and well-liked by both parties, Toole's first year in office proved unsuccessful when political issues so divided the first Legislative Assembly that no laws were passed. In 1891, Toole helped achieve political accord; during the second Legislature, statutes were passed which formed the basis for Montana's civil and criminal codes. Toole did not run for reelection in 1892, returning to private law practice. In 1900, he again entered politics and won election as Governor, defeating Republican David S. Folsom, 31,419 votes to 22,691. Toole presided over the dedication of Montana's Capitol in 1902, and attempted to reduce political and economic tensions in a state deeply divided by struggles between competing copper magnates. Toole defeated Republican William Lindsay in 1904, 35,377 votes to 26,957, for his third term in the governor's office. He advocated and secured the creation of a Board of Railroad Commissioners during this term. Toole resigned on April 1, 1908, for reasons of health. He retired to San Francisco, California, returning to Montana frequently. Toole died in Helena on March 11, 1929, and was buried in Resurrection Cemetery there. Bibliography: M. A. Leeson, *History of Montana, 1739-1885* (Chicago, 1885); Joaquin Miller, *An Illustrated History of the State of Montana* (Chicago, 1894); A. W. Bowen and Company, *Progressive Men of the State of Montana* (Chicago, 1902). Papers of Toole on deposit at the Montana State Archives, Helena.

RICKARDS, John Ezra, 1893-1897

Born on July 23, 1848 in Delaware City, Delaware, son of David Townsend Rickards, a merchant, farmer and local preacher, and Mary (Wellington) Rickards; a Methodist. Married Lizzie M. Wilson on July 5, 1876; father of three sons, Homer C., Earl M., and Steward A. His first wife died in 1881, and he married Eliza A. Boucher on June 18, 1883. Rickards had five children by his second marriage, three of whom survived, Howard B., Carlisle, and Rachel. Rickards attended school in Middletown, Delaware, before moving to Philadelphia, where he engaged in business. After a move to Colorado in 1870 and San Francisco in 1878, he settled in Butte, Montana in 1882. He was involved in the oil business while living in that city. Rickards was elected City Alderman of Butte in 1885, and traveled to the Territorial Legislature in 1887 as a Republican from Silver Bow County. In 1889, he was a member of the Montana Constitutional Convention. A Republican, Rickards became the state's first lieutenant governor in 1889, serving under Democratic Governor Joseph K. Toole. During Rickards' term as lieutenant governor, he participated in a dispute involving conflicting election returns from the Thirty-fourth Precinct in Silver Bow County. A disagreement over those returns dead-locked the first State Assembly, and was finally resolved when Rickards ruled that senators present, but not voting, could not be considered absent. A quorum was established and a joint session of the legislature was called. Rickards ran as a Republican for the governorship of Montana in 1892. He defeated his Democratic opponent, Timothy E. Collins, by a vote of 18,187 to 17,650, and became Montana's second state governor. Early in his term in office, Governor Rickards entered another political battle, this one involving the Marcus Daly-William A. Clark political feud. Clark desperately wanted an appointment, as a Democrat, to the United States Senate, but was blocked by Daly supporters and Republicans. At a critical moment in the voting, after it appeared that Clark had won, a Daly spokesman arose in the Montana State Senate to charge Clark with corrupt practices. The session ended with Clark's defeat, and Governor Rickards seized the opportunity to appoint Republican Lee Mantle to fill the U.S. Senate vacancy. The U.S. Senate later refused to seat Mantle for a period of two years. Aside from taking advantage of political squabbles, Rickards also was active in establishing state government in Montana. He directed the adoption of a state code, and appointed a State Board of Education which founded the state university system. Rickards also supervised passage of an Anti-Gambling Act. He left office in 1897, and retired to California. John E. Rickards died on December 26, 1927 in California. Bibliography: Joaquin Miller, *An Illustrated History of the State of Montana* (Chicago, 1894); *Progressive Men of the State of Montana* (Chicago, 1902); Montana State Historical Society Library, "Vertical File," Rickards, John E. Papers of Rickards on deposit in the Montana State Historical Society in Helena, Montana.

SMITH, Robert Burns, 1897-1901

Born in Hickman County, Kentucky on December 29, 1854, the eldest of nine children of Dewitt C., a farmer, and Eliza (Hughes) Smith. Completed his education in Mayfield, Kentucky, studying law under Edward Crossland; admitted to the

Kentucky Bar in 1877. Married Catherine Crossland on April 9, 1878; father of Mary H. and Edward C. Moved to Dillon, Montana in September, 1882, where he practiced law. In 1884, Beaverhead County residents elected Smith as a Democratic delegate to the unsuccessful constitutional convention of that year. President Grover Cleveland appointed Smith the United States District Attorney for Montana in 1885, a post he resigned on March 4, 1889, after Benjamin Harrison's election as president. During the fall of 1889, Smith moved to Helena and the next year became City Attorney. Smith became involved with the People's (Populist) Party in 1892, becoming an early and life-long supporter of William Jennings Bryan, on whose behalf he campaigned in 1896, 1900 and 1908. In 1894, Smith was the unsuccessful candidate of the People's Party for Congress, losing to Republican Charles S. Hartman, 23,140 votes to 15,240, but finishing 5,000 votes ahead of the Democratic nominee, Hal S. Corbett. By 1896, Smith had forged an alliance among Montana's Democratic and Populist elements, defeated the Republican gubernatorial nominee, A. C. Botkin, 36,688 to 14,993, and, thereby helped Bryan carry the Montana presidential vote by a 4:1 margin. Smith also took an active part in the successful campaign to make Helena the permanent site of the state capital over its rival Anaconda. During his single term, Smith succeeded in securing legislation to improve roads in Montana's rural areas; to create a state university in Missoula; and to establish the School of Mines in Butte. Also under his administration, construction began on Montana's Capitol. Declining to run for reelection in 1900, Smith resumed the practice of law, this time in Butte. He was stricken by kidney disease and retired to Flathead County, where he operated a fruit orchard. Smith died in Kalispell on November 16, 1908, and was buried in the C. E. Conrad Cemetery there. Bibliography: M. A. Leeson, *History of Montana, 1739-1885* (Chicago, 1885); *Progressive Men of the State of Montana* (Chicago, 1902); Vera L. McCarthy, ed., *Proceedings of the Montana Bar Association, 1903-1914* (Helena, 1914). Papers of Smith on deposit in the Montana State Archives, Helena.

TOOLE, Joseph Kemp, 1889-1892, 1901-1908

NORRIS, Edwin L., 1908-1913

Born on August 15, 1865 in Cumberland County, Kentucky, son of W. W., a farmer, and Martha (Nunn) Norris, both of whom were Presbyterians. Attended school at Southern Normal College, graduating in 1886. Married Bettie J. Wilkins of Bowling Green, Kentucky on April 19, 1892. Norris taught school for two years in Kentucky. In 1888, he moved to Dillon, Montana, read law in the office of Robert B. Smith, and was admitted to the Montana Bar in 1889. He was a Democratic State Senator from Beaverhead County from 1896 to 1900, and in 1899 was elected President Pro Tempore of the Montana Senate. He was elected to the lieutenant governorship in 1904 and in April, 1908, became Governor, following the resignation of Joseph K. Toole. Later in 1908, Norris was elected to the governorship of Montana by a plurality of 1,490 votes over his Republican opponent. The votes were cast as follows: Edwin Norris, 32,282 votes, Republican

Edward Donlan, 30,792 votes, and Socialist Harry Hazelton, 5,112 votes. During his administration, Norris continued his earlier efforts to reform the life insurance industry in the state. He succeeded in enacting laws prohibiting rebates and discrimination by life insurance companies. Governor Norris also supported the non-partisan nomination of judges and worked at securing employee compensation from coal mine operators in Montana. Norris returned to the practice of law in Great Falls after his retirement from the governorship in 1913. He continued in that occupation until his death in 1924. He was buried in Great Falls. Bibliography: Robert Raymer, *Montana: The Land and the People* (Chicago and New York, 1930); Tom Stout, *Montana, Its Story and Biography* (Chicago, 1913); *Progressive Men of the State of Montana* (Chicago, 1902). Papers of Norris on deposit in the Montana State Historical Society in Helena, Montana.

STEWART, Samuel Vernon, 1913-1921

Born on August 2, 1872 in Monroe County, Ohio, son of John Wilson, a farmer, and Maria (Carle) Stewart; a Baptist. Brother of William R.C., Harold M., Sallie W., and one other who died in childhood. Married Stella Baker on April 27, 1905 in Booneville, Missouri, who bore him three daughters, Emily, Marjorie and Leah. After training at the Kansas Normal College and the State Normal College, he entered the University of Kansas in Lawrence, where he received a Bachelor of Law degree in 1898. Upon graduation, Stewart went to Virginia City, Montana and established a law practice that eventually enabled him to become City Attorney and later County Attorney. In 1902, Stewart was defeated in a bid for the State Senate. He became Democratic State Central Committee Chairman in 1910, a position he held until 1912, when he resigned to run for the governorship. Stewart defeated Republican challenger Harry L. Wilson by a vote of 25,381 to 22,950 votes; the Progressive candidate, Frank J. Edwards, polled 18,881 votes, while the Socialist, Lewis J. Duncan, garnered 12,556. He won reelection in 1916 by over 9,000 votes, defeating Edwards, who ran on the Republican ticket. Stewart entered office as Montana's fifth governor on January 1,1913. Governor Stewart's administration saw numerous changes in state government, including; the formation of the State Highway Commission; railroad, tax and public service commissions; state boards for entomology; commissioners for the insane; examiners for nurses; a fish and game law; and dairy and athletic commissions. During his administration, the Montana Supreme Court was given an additional two justices, raising the number to five. Stewart called a special session of the legislature in 1919 to establish the Irrigation Commission and to bring the Railroad and Public Service Commissions together in a cooperative effort to adjust prices following World War I. Early in his period as governor, Stewart was called upon to deal with labor problems in Butte. These troubles forced him to call out the National Guard in 1914. In 1921, Stewart resumed private law practice with John Greist Brown in Helena. He remained with that firm for ten years, five of which were spent as City Attorney. In 1928 and 1936, Stewart was an unsuccessful candidate for the Democratic nomination for the U.S. Senate, but on November 4, 1930, Stewart won election to the Montana House of Representatives for a one-year term. In 1932, he successfully ran for the post of Associate Justice of the Montana Supreme Court. Stewart was serving his second term with that body when he died on September 15, 1939. Bibliography: Merrill G. Burlingame and K. Ross Toole, *History of Montana* (New York, 1957); Jules Karlin, *Joseph M. Dixon of Montana* (Missoula, 1974); Tom Stout, *Montana: Its Story and Biography* (Chicago, 1921); Butte Newswriters Association, *Men of Affairs and Representative Institutions of the State of Montana* (Butte, 1914); Montana State Historical Society Library, "Vertical File," Stewart, Samuel V. Papers of Stewart on deposit in the Montana State Historical Society in Helena, Montana.

DIXON, Joseph Moore, 1921-1925

Born on July 31, 1867 in Snow Camp, North Carolina, son of iron foundry owner Hugh W. and Flora A. (Merchison) Dixon; Attended Earlham College, Richmond, Indiana, and graduated from Guilford College, North Carolina in May, 1889. Moved to Missoula, Montana, 1891; admitted to the bar, December, 1892; Assistant Prosecuting Attorney, Missoula County, 1893-1895; Prosecuting Attorney, 1895-1897. Married Carolyn Worden on March 12, 1896; father of Betty, Dorothy, Florence, Mary Jo, Peggy and Virginia. Dixon was elected to Montana's Seventh Legislative Assembly as a Republican in 1900; between March 4, 1903 and March 3, 1907, he served in the United States House of Representatives during the Fifty-eighth and Fifty-ninth Congresses. In 1906 he was elected United States Senator from Montana. In Congress Dixon was active in securing larger homesteads, long and short haul rate regulation of railroads, and the opening of the Flathead and Crow Reservations in Montana to settlement by non-Indians. He continually advocated both federal funds for irrigation and women's suffrage. In 1912, Dixon served as Chairman of the National Progressive Convention, and was manager for Theodore Roosevelt's unsuccessful "Bull Moose" presidential campaign. The same year, Dixon ran for reelection to the Senate as a Progressive, but lost to Democrat Thomas J. Walsh, 28,421 votes to 22,161. Dixon returned to his law practice in 1913, edited a Missoula newspaper, and managed a dairy farm in the Flathead Valley. Dixon returned to politics in 1920 with a successful campaign for Governor. Running as a Republican, he defeated his Democratic opponent, Burton K. Wheeler, 111,113 to 74,875. During his single term he brought reform to state government, including a highly controversial modification in the means of taxing Montana's large copper mining industry. Largely because of his progressive programs, Dixon faced corporate opposition and lost his bid for reelection in 1924 to Democrat J. E. Erickson, 88,801 votes to 74,126. Returning to his business interests, Dixon ran for the Senate once more in 1928, losing to Burton K. Wheeler, 103,655 to 91,185. In 1929, President Herbert Hoover appointed Dixon First Assistant Secretary of the Interior, a position which he filled until 1933. Dixon died in Missoula, May 22, 1934, and was buried in the city cemetery. Bibliography: *Progressive Men of the State of Montana* (Chicago, 1902); Tom Stout, *Montana, Its Story and Biography* (Chicago, 1921); Jules A. Karlin, *Joseph M. Dixon of Montana* (Missoula, 1974). Papers of Dixon in the University of Montana Archives, Missoula.

ERICKSON, John Edward, 1925-1933

Born on March 14, 1863 in Stoughton, Dane County, Wisconsin to Eric and Lena (Amble) Erickson; both Lutherans, who settled in a homestead in Greenwood County, Kansas shortly after John's birth. Eldest of seven children. Married Grace Vance on June 27, 1898 in Salt Lake City, Utah and raised three children: Vance, Elene and John Cooper. Erickson attended Washburn College in Topeka, Kansas and received a B.A. degree from that institution in 1890. He edited the *Chronicle* in Burlingame, Kansas and studied law at the offices of Clagston and Fuller until he was admitted to the Kansas Bar in 1891. In 1893, Erickson began a legal practice in Chouteau, Teton County, Montana. He served as County Attorney from 1897 to 1905, Judge for Montana's Eleventh Judicial District from 1905 to 1915, and returned to private practice in Kalispell, Montana in 1916. In 1920, he was a delegate to the Democratic National Convention in San Francisco, after which he served as chairman of the Democratic State Central Committee until 1924. On November 4, 1924, he defeated Republican Joseph M. Dixon by a vote of 88,801 to 74,126 to become Montana's seventh state governor. He won reelection twice, in 1928 and 1932. With legislative approval, Governor Erickson imposed a license tax on the annual gross profits of mining operations in the state, enacted a new banking code, revised state land and corporation laws, and helped financially burdened rural schools by establishing an equalization fund. During his second term, Erickson signed into law a gasoline tax, with the proceeds going toward highway construction. In 1933, John Erickson resigned as governor and was appointed United States Senator from Montana, filling the vacancy created by the death of Thomas J. Walsh. His appointment embittered many Montanans. He served until November 6, 1934, when he failed to receive his party's nomination in an election to fill the post. Erickson returned to private law practice in Helena, Montana, and died in that city on May 25, 1946, with burial in the Conrad Memorial Cemetery in Kalispell. Bibliography: Jules Karlin, *Joseph M. Dixon of Montana* (Missoula, 1974); Helen Fitzgerald Sanders, *A History of Montana* (Chicago, 1902); "Governor John E. Erickson of Montana," *The Westerner* (July 6, 1929); Montana State Historical Society Library, "Vertical File," Erickson, John E. Papers of Erickson on deposit in the Montana State Historical Society in Helena, Montana.

COONEY, Frank H., 1933-1935

Born on December 31, 1872 in Norwood, Ontario, Canada, son of John W., a nurseryman, and Mary (O'Callaghan) Cooney, both Roman Catholics. Brother of Byron, Percival and Howard Cooney. Married Emma May Poindexter on December 27, 1899; father of seven children: Frances H., John Phillip, May Margaret, Walter, Tyler Thompson, Virginia Elizabeth and Gage Rodman. Cooney attended Catholic schools in Ontario, but never enrolled in college. He moved to Butte, Montana in 1891, where he founded Cooney Brokerage Company, a retail grocery business. Cooney also engaged in mining activities in Butte and in the livestock business in the Bitterroot Valley. He opened Montana's first cannery in 1913 at Stevensville. Between 1898 and 1900, Cooney was a public administrator for Silver Bow County. After running for Lieutenant Governor on the Democratic ticket in

1924 and 1928 and losing both times, he was elected to that post in 1932. Cooney became Governor of Montana in 1933, upon the resignation of John E. Erickson. After assuming the post of governor, Frank Cooney immediately appointed former Governor Erickson to the U.S. Senate seat vacated by the death of Thomas J. Walsh. The "Erickson-Cooney Deal" was a major embarrassment to the state Democratic Party. It diminished the popularity of both men and created tension within the party. As governor, Cooney was a progressive. He was able to secure the resignation of conservative State Relief Director T. C. Spaulding, and to appoint a number of liberal members to the Relief Commission. Cooney also encouraged programs of water conservation and flood water utilization. In 1934, he survived an attempt by conservative opponents to impeach him. Cooney's career as governor abruptly ended in December, 1935, when he died of heart failure in Great Falls, Montana. He was buried in Missoula. Bibliography: Tom Stout, *Montana, Its Story and Biography* (Chicago, 1921); Helen Fitzgerald Sanders, *A History of Montana* (Chicago, 1913); Larry D. Quinn, *Politicians in Business: A History of the Liquor Control System in Montana* (Missoula, 1970); Butte Newswriters Association, *Men of Affairs and Representative Institutions of the State of Montana* (Butte, 1914); Michael P. Malone, "Montana Politics And The New Deal," *Montana Magazine of Western History*, vol. 21, no. 1 (January, 1971); Montana State Historical Society (Helena), "Vertical File," Cooney, Frank H. Papers of Cooney on deposit at the Montana State Historical Society in Helena, Montana.

HOLT, William Elmer, 1935-1937

Born on October 14, 1884, in Savannah, Missouri, son of Benjamin King and Susan (Brooks) Holt, both of whom were Methodists. Married Lora Howe on September 10, 1910, and had two children, Lora Berta and Benjamin. Holt's family had moved to Miles City, Montana when he was young, and he learned the cowboy's craft on his father's ranch; he also learned the value of land in Montana. In 1902, he graduated from the University of Nebraska, but he returned to Montana to engage in the real estate business. Holt was in charge of land interests for the Northern Pacific Railroad during the early 1900s. In 1912, Holt was elected as a Democrat to the Montana House of Representatives. From 1932-1935, he was a State Senator from Custer County. In 1935, Holt, as President Pro Tempore of the Senate, was next in line for succession to the governorship of Montana. The death of Governor Frank Cooney in that year and the absence of a lieutenant governor, made Holt the chief executive. During his term as governor, Holt was involved in relief work as a member of the Montana Relief Commission. He also initiated a modest reform in Montana's Liquor Control Board by requiring vendors and employees of the board to resign from their jobs before filing for political office. This requirement prevented state liquor stores from becoming campaign headquarters. Governor Holt entered the Democratic primary for governor in 1936. He lost to challenger Roy E. Ayers by a vote of 43,822 to 39,397. Holt left office in January, 1937. Holt left Montana after his term of office and moved to Seattle, Washington, where he was Western General Land Agent for the Northern Pacific Railroad. He died in Seattle on March 1, 1945. Bibliography: Michael Malone, "Montana Politics and The New Deal," *Montana Magazine of Western History*, vol. 21, no. 1 (January,

1971); Larry D. Quinn, *Politicians in Business: A History of the Liquor Control System in Montana* (Missoula, 1970); Montana State Historical Society Library, "Vertical File," Holt, W. Elmer. Papers of Holt on deposit at the Montana State Historical Society in Helena, Montana.

AYERS, Roy Elmer, 1937-1941

Born on a ranch in Fergus County, Montana on November 9, 1882, son of George W., a pioneer cattleman, and Mary E. (Sullenger) Ayers; eldest of six children. Married Ellen Simpson on June 7, 1905 in Lewistown, Montana and had three children: Eleanor, Arthur and Donald. Attended Lewiston High School and graduated with a law degree from Valparaiso University in 1903. Ayers began a legal practice in Lewistown and continued his ranching interests. He was elected County Attorney for Fergus County in 1904 and served from 1905 to 1909. From 1908 to 1912, he served as a member of the Montana Board of Education and as the elected judge of the Fergus County District Court. Ayers was reelected to two additional four-year terms to that post in 1912 and 1916. He received some notoriety in 1914 when he dismissed the Butte mayor and the Silver Bow County sheriff for refusing to order men under their authority to fire on crowds who were destroying property. From January to November, 1922, Ayers served on the Montana Supreme Court, resigning that position to resume private law practice in Lewistown. Chosen as a delegate to every Montana State Democratic Convention between 1906 and 1940, Ayers was also selected for the 1920 and 1940 National Democratic Conventions. He lost the 1928 primary election for Governor to Democratic incumbent John Erickson by a vote of 24,304 to 23,665. In 1932, Ayers was elected to the United States House of Representatives from the Second Montana Congressional District, and was reelected in 1934. On November 3, 1936, Democratic gubernatorial candidate Ayers defeated his Republican opponent, Frank Hazelbaker, by a vote of 115,310 to 108,914 to become the first native-born Montanan to attain the post of governor. Governor Ayers took office on January 4, 1937, and held the position for a four-year term which expired on January 6, 1941. A fiscal conservative, his leading accomplishment while chief executive was to present the state with a balanced budget for the years 1938-1940. He managed this by reducing the interest rate on state bonds and by settling old bond and warrant debts to effect lower costs on new state loans. Ayers retired from politics after completing his four-year term as governor. He moved to a 6,000 acre ranch near Grassrange, Montana, where he raised livestock until his final retirement in 1952. Ayers died on May 23, 1955 in Lewistown, Montana, and was buried in Lewistown City Cemetery. Bibliography: Helen Fisk Sanders, *A History of Montana* (Chicago and New York, 1913); Tom Stout, *Montana: Its History and Biography* (Chicago and New York, 1921); Butte Newswriters Association, *Men of Affairs and Representative Institutions of the State of Montana* (Butte, 1914); Montana State Historical Society Library, "Vertical File," Ayers, Roy. Papers of Ayers on deposit at the Montana State Historical Society in Helena, Montana.

FORD, Samuel Clarence, 1941-1949

Born on November 7, 1882 in Albany, Kentucky, son of a lumberman and farmer, William, and Glenora (Snow) Ford, both of whom were Baptists. The Fords raised six children: Sallie, James P., Samuel C., Iva, Charles F. and Bina. Married Mary L. Shobe in Helena, Montana on November 24, 1910; they had four daughters: Dorothy, Isabelle, Elizabeth and Mary Margaret. Attended primary and secondary school in Ivanhoe and Garden City, Kansas. Graduated in 1906 with LL.B. degree from the University of Kansas Law School. Began law practice in Helena in 1906. From 1908 to 1914, he served as Assistant U.S. Attorney for Montana. Elected as a Republican to a four-year term as Montana Attorney General in 1916. In 1920, Ford made his first bid for the Montana governorship, but placed third in the Republican primary. He continued his law practice in Helena until 1928, when he was elected Associate Justice of the Montana Supreme Court. Ford lost an attempt at reelection to the Supreme Court in 1932. In 1940, he defeated five other Republican primary candidates to gain his party's nomination for Governor. On November 5, 1940, Ford defeated incumbent Democratic Governor Roy Ayers by a vote of 124,435 to 119,453. He won reelection to the position in 1944, outdistancing the Democratic challenger, Leif Erickson, by 116,461 votes to 89,224. During his eight years as Montana's chief executive, Ford earned a reputation for fiscal conservatism and non-partisan fairness in state appointments. His "pet project" was the development of the Missouri River to provide both cheap electricity for industry, and irrigation water for Montana's farmers. He was a member of the Missouri Basin Inter-Agency Committee and chairman of the Missouri River State Committee. World War II delayed work on many of his river projects. In 1948, Governor Ford received his party's nomination for a third term, but lost the election to Democrat John W. Bonner by a vote of 124,267 to 97,792. Ford resumed his law practice in Helena, Montana and did not run for any other political office. Ford died in his Helena home on November 25, 1961; he was buried in Forestvale Cemetery. Bibliography: *Progressive Men of the State of Montana* (Chicago, 1902); Tom Stout, *Montana: Its Story and Biography* (Chicago, 1921); Michael Leeson, *History of Montana* (Chicago, 1885); Montana State Historical Society Library, "Vertical File," Ford, Samuel C. Papers of Ford on deposit at the Montana State Historical Society in Helena, Montana.

BONNER, John Woodrow, 1949-1953

Born in Butte, Montana on July 16, 1902, son of Patrick J., a rancher, and Kathleen (Kelly) Bonner, both of whom were Roman Catholics. Married Josephine A. Martin on February 6, 1929 in Butte; they had five children, Josephine, Jacqueline, Patricia, Wilma and Thomas. Bonner was educated in the Butte public schools, taught grade school in Perma, Montana, and directed athletics at Camas Prairie Junior High School from 1921-1923. In 1928, he graduated from Montana State University with the A.B. and LL.B. degrees. Bonner was admitted to the Montana Bar in 1928 and began private practice in Butte. From 1929 to 1936, he was an attorney for the Montana Highway Commission, and between 1936 and 1940 he filled the same position for the Railroad and Public Service Commission. Bonner served as secretary treasurer of the State Democratic Central Committee and as chairman of the Lewis and Clark County Democratic Central Committee. He entered politics in 1940 as a Democratic candidate for State Attorney General, defeating Republican candidate S. R. Foot by a vote of 138,550 to 89,988. Particularly active in protecting Montana's water rights while Attorney General, Bonner resigned that post in 1942 to serve in the United States Army as a Major in the Judge Advocate General's Department. He attained the rank of Colonel before leaving the army with decorations which included the Bronze Star, Croix de Guerre (France), and the Legion of Merit. Bonner returned to Montana and began a law practice in Helena. On July 20, 1948, he defeated four other candidates in the Democratic primary for Governor of Montana. Bonner went on to beat his Republican rival, incumbent Sam C. Ford, in the general election by a vote of 124,267 to 97,792. As governor, Bonner supported funding for state institutions, which resulted in the construction of the Pioneer Veterans Memorial Building and the State Home for the Senile Aged. He signed a Veterans' Preference Law and increased the funding for programs aiding the aged, the blind, dependent children, and injured workers. Bonner reorganized the Department of Labor, Industry and Agriculture by creating a separate Department of Agriculture. During his administration, highway construction received high priority. On November 4, 1952, Governor Bonner lost a reelection bid to Republican challenger J. Hugo Aronson by 134,423 votes to 129,369. Bonner retired to private law practice in Helena, but sought the Democratic nomination for the United States Senate in 1960. He finished second among four challengers, losing the nomination to Lee Metcalf. In 1968, Bonner was elected Associate Justice of the Montana Supreme Court. Failing health hindered Bonner's efforts on the Supreme Court from 1969 until his death in Helena on March 28, 1970. Bibliography: Robert Raymer, *Montana: The Land and the People* (Chicago and New York, 1930); University of Montana Library, "Vertical File," Bonner, John; Montana State Historical Society, "Vertical File," Bonner, John. Papers of Bonner on deposit at the Montana State Historical Society in Helena, Montana.

ARONSON, J. Hugo, 1953-1961

Born on September 1, 1891 in Gallstad, Sweden, son of Aron, a tenant farmer, and Fredricka (Ryding) Johanson, both of whom were Lutherans. Brother of Anna, Karl, Erik and Julia. He attended school through the eighth grade in Sweden and emigrated to the United States in 1911. Aronson became a U.S. citizen on February 13, 1914. He wandered throughout the West for a period of years before filing on a homestead in Powell, Wyoming. During World War I, Aronson served with the U.S. Army, 20th Engineers in France. There he met and married Matilda Langane on June 3, 1919. She died in 1936, and Aronson married Rose McClure in 1944, fathering one child in 1945, Rika Bertha. Aronson was primarily in the oil business although his interests ranged from trucking to ranching and banking. While in the oil rig construction business, Aronson founded three towns in north-central Montana: Oilmont, Gallop City and Santa Rita. He sold his oil field trucking service and rig building business in 1946, and began farming on the Blackfeet Indian Reservation, west of Cut Bank, Montana. Aronson began his political career in 1934, when he was elected Alderman of Cut Bank. In 1938 and 1940, he won election as a Republican to the Montana House of Representatives, and was a State Senator between 1944 and 1952. In 1952, he was a successful Republican primary candidate for Governor, defeating his opponent, Leonard C. Young, by a vote of 56,391 to 21,904. Aronson went on to defeat John W. Bonner in the general election by a vote of 134,423 to 129,369. Governor Aronson was reelected to office in 1956, when he defeated his Democratic opponent, Arnold Olsen, 138,878 to 131,488. Governor Aronson's main interest while in office was in prison reform. He supervised the purchase of a 330,000 acre ranch at Deer Lodge, Montana, for use in the rehabilitation of prison inmates. Ironically, a serious prison riot occurred at Deer Lodge State Prison in April, 1959, in which the deputy warden and three prisoners were killed. Aronson called up the National Guard to quell the disturbance. Governor Aronson also directed his administration toward securing federal highway funds for the state and in extending the leasing period for state-owned oil and gas reserves. He also succeeded in reorganizing the State Forestry Office. In 1961, J. Hugo Aronson retired from public service. He remained active in the Republican Party and served as Richard Nixon's honorary Montana Campaign Chairman in the 1968 presidential race. Aronson's wife, Rose, died in 1968; he now lives in Columbia Falls, Montana. Bibliography: J. Hugo Aronson and L. O. Brockmann, *The Galloping Swede* (Missoula, 1970); Merrill G. Burlingame and K. Ross Toole, *A History of Montana* (New York, 1957); University of Montana, "Vertical File," Aronson, J. Hugo; Montana State Historical Society, "Vertical File," Aronson, J. Hugo. Papers of Aronson on file at the Montana State Historical Society in Helena, Montana.

NUTTER, Donald Grant, 1961-1962

Born on November 28, 1915 in Lambert, Montana, son of C. E., a merchant, and Anne Grant (Wood) Nutter, both of whom were Congregationalists. Married Maxine Trotter on April 16, 1938 and had one son, John. Educated at North Dakota State School of Science in Wahpeton from 1933-1935 and graduated with a law degree from Montana State University in 1954. Nutter served from 1937 to 1938 as the deputy clerk of the District Court in Richland County, Montana, and as undersheriff of that county from 1938 to 1939. He was employed by the Tractor and Equipment Company of Sidney, Montana, from 1938-1942 and from 1945-1947. In 1942, Nutter joined the Army Air Force and served as a B-24 pilot during World War II, accumulating sixty-two combat missions before his discharge in 1945. After World War II, Nutter returned to Sidney and opened his own implement business in 1947. He sold that business in 1950 and entered law school. Nutter was admitted to the Montana Bar in 1954. He was elected to the Montana Senate from Richland County in 1950 and reelected to a second four-year term in 1954. Nutter chaired the Montana Republican Central Committee from 1958-1960, when he resigned to run for the office of Governor. He defeated Republican challenger Wesley D'Ewart in the primary by 33,099 votes to 32,538 votes, and won the general election over his Democratic opponent, Paul Cannon, by a vote of 154,122 to 125,438. Nutter entered the office of governor in 1961, declaring his intention to improve the business climate in Montana, to increase the tax base by encouraging new industry and to end deficit spending by the state legislature. He found the governor's position a weak one, due to the power vested in the Board of Examiners, of which the governor was only a member. During Nutter's brief term in office, he sought legislative approval for gubernatorial control of state boards and commissions. On January 25, 1962, Governor Nutter, two aides, and three crew members died in the crash of a C-47 National Guard airplane in the mountains near Wolf Creek, Montana. The governor's party was en route to a meeting of the U.S. Highway 2 Association, when Nutter became the first elected Montana governor to die while in office. Nutter was buried on January 29, 1962 in Sidney, Montana. Bibliography: Judith Rollins, "Governor Donald G. Nutter and the Montana Daily Press," Unpublished Master's Thesis, University of Montana, Missoula, 1963; Donald Nutter, *State of the State Message* (Helena, 1961); University of Montana, "Vertical File," Nutter, Donald G.; Montana State Historical Society Library, "Vertical File," Nutter, Donald. Papers of Nutter on deposit at the Montana State Historical Society in Helena, Montana.

BABCOCK, Tim, 1962-1969

Born on October 27, 1919 in Little Fork, Minnesota to Erwin H. and Olive Babcock; Presbyterian. Moved to Glendive, Montana in early 1920; graduated in 1939 from Dawson County High School in Glendive. Married Betty Ruth Lee, September 21, 1941; father of Lorna Lee and Marla Kay. Combat infantryman in the United States Army during World War II; entered the petroleum trucking business in Miles City with his father-in-law in 1945. Babcock began his career in politics in 1953 when he won a seat in the State House of Representatives from Custer County. In 1955 he moved his family and trucking firm to Billings, and was elected to the Montana House of Representatives for Yellowstone County in 1957 and 1959. In 1960 he was successful in his bid for Lieutenant Governor, defeating Democrat Henry Anderson, 145,942 votes to 129,895. Babcock became Governor on January 26, 1962, after the death of Governor Donald Nutter in a plane crash. In 1964 he ran for Governor against Roland Renne and won by a margin of 144,113 to 136,862. While retaining his position as governor, he ran for U.S. Senator in 1966, but was defeated by Democrat Lee Metcalf, 138,166 to 121,697. As governor he formed the Department of Administration, the Department of Institutions, and the University System of higher education. In 1968 Babcock ran for reelection against Democrat Forrest Anderson and was defeated, 150,481 votes to 116,432, notably because of a sales tax which he advocated for Montana. After his defeat, he assumed an executive position with Occidental Petroleum and purchased a Helena radio and television station; he also began construction of the Colonial Hilton Hotel in Helena, which he still owns and operates. His wife, Betty, was a member of Montana's 1972 Constitutional Convention and was a Republican member of the State House of Representatives from Lewis and Clark County in 1975. Bibliography: Jerry R. Holloron, "The Montana Daily Press and the 1964 Gubernatorial Campaign," Unpublished M.A. Thesis, University of Montana, 1965. Montana Historical Society, "Vertical File," Babcock, Tim. Papers of Babcock in the Montana State Historical Society Archives.

ANDERSON, Forrest Howard, 1969-1973

Born on January 30, 1913 in Helena, Montana, son of Oscar, a merchant, and his wife, Nora (O'Keefe) Anderson; a Methodist. Married Margaret Evelyn Samson on January 24, 1941 in Dillon, Montana; father of three children: Margaret Louise, Arlee Joan and Newell Burke. Graduated from Helena High School and spent one year at Montana State University before transferring to Columbus (American) University in Washington, D.C.; obtained a law degree in 1938. He practiced law in Helena from 1938 to 1952. Anderson was elected to a term in the Montana State Legislature in 1943. From 1945-1947, he was the County Attorney for Lewis and Clark County. Between 1947-1949, Anderson served as special counsel for the state's industrial accident fund. He was elected Associate Justice of the Montana Supreme Court in 1952, resigning that post in 1956 to run for the office of Attorney General. In 1968, Forrest Anderson defeated Leroy Anderson in the Democratic primary to become his party's nominee for Governor. When incumbent Governor Tim Babcock based his campaign on support for a sales tax which Anderson had firmly opposed, Anderson won the general election with a vote of 150,481 votes to 116,432, the largest plurality since 1920. His victory ended the Republican Party's sixteen-year control of the Montana chief executive's office. Governor Anderson's administration was noted for attempts at reorganization of the state's bureaucratic structure, with notable success in the Department of Administration, the Board of Investments, and the Departments of Agriculture, Livestock, and Business Regulation. He consolidated the functions of numerous agencies into only a few. He also upgraded the state prison system through non-partisan appointments, and secured a considerable amount of federal funding for counties suffering from the impact of short-term military construction projects. In April, 1971, Anderson announced his intention to run for a second term as governor, but, for reasons of health, renounced that attempt in October. Forrest Anderson retired from active political life after his term as governor ended. He resides in Helena, Montana. Bibliography: University of Montana Library, "Vertical File," Anderson, Forrest B.; Montana State Historical Society Library, "Vertical File," Anderson, Forrest. Papers of Anderson on deposit at the Montana State Historical Society Library in Helena, Montana.

JUDGE, Thomas L., 1973-

Born on October 12, 1934 in Helena, Montana to contractor Thomas P. and Blanche (Guillot) Judge; a Roman Catholic. One brother, Terry; graduated from Helena High School in 1953; B.A. in Journalism, University of Notre Dame; graduate work and certificate in advertising in 1959 from University of Louisville, Louisville, Kentucky. Served as an officer in U.S. Army Adjutant General Corp, 1958-1959, and currently Captain in U.S. Army Reserve. Married on January 22, 1966 to Carol Anderson; father of Tommy and Patricia. Owner of a Helena advertising and public relations firm. His political career began in 1961 when he went to the State Legislature as a Representative from Lewis and Clark County. Returned to the House in 1963 and 1965. In 1967, he was elected to the State Senate from Lewis and Clark County. Elected Lieutenant Governor in 1968 when he defeated Republican Tom Selstad, 146,527 votes to 124,322. Became Governor in 1972 by defeating Republican Ed Smith, 172,523 to 146,231. Won reelection for Governor in 1976 by defeating former Attorney General Robert Woodahl, a Republican, 195,420 to 115,848. During his first term as governor, Judge reorganized the structure of state government, and under his administration a new State Constitution was passed. He also instituted a statewide referendum on property tax relief in 1976, and succeeded in securing its enactment during the state's 1977 Legislative Assembly. Bibliography: Legislative Biography File, Montana Historical Society, Helena; Montana Historical Society, "Vertical File," Judge, Thomas L.

NEBRASKA

NEBRASKA

BUTLER, David C., 1867-1871

Born on December 15, 1829 near Bloomington, Monroe County, Indiana, son of George W. Butler, a farmer, and Nancy Christy Butler. Brother of Joseph, Thomas C., Mary A., William H., Eliza J., James H., George W., Andrew B., and Cinthia E. Married to Mary Paulina Smith on April 22, 1852; remarried to Lydia Story on January 25, 1860; father of Violet Nancy, George Ozias, Violet Eliza, Olive, Ozias, David Seth, Darius, and Paul. Intermittent primary education. Indiana farmer and cattle trader until his 1858 arrival in Nebraska Territory, where he established himself in Pawnee City as a cattle trader, merchant, and lawyer. Elected to lower house, Territorial Legislature on the Republican ticket in 1861, and to upper house, Territorial Council, in 1863. In 1866 as the Republican candidate for Governor, Butler ran against Democrat J. Sterling Morton, and won by a popular vote of 4,093 to 3,948; sworn into office on March 27, 1867. He was reelected in 1868, defeating Democrat James R. Porter by a popular vote of 8,576 to 6,349; and in 1870, he defeated Democrat John H. Croxton by a popular vote of 11,126 to 8,648. His 1869 bid for election by the State Legislature to the U.S. Senate failed. As the first governor of Nebraska, Butler encouraged immigration and internal improvements. He stimulated railroad building and helped shape early state railroad policy. He influenced removal of the state capital from Omaha to Lincoln in 1867 and promoted lot sales in the new capital city. Proceeds from these sales were used to erect public buildings in Lincoln. Butler was impeached before completing his third term as governor and was formally removed from office on June 2, 1871, for allegedly appropriating state money for his own use. Secretary of State William H. James served as acting governor until the election of Robert W. Furnas in 1873. After his removal from office, Butler returned to stock raising near Pawnee City. On February 15, 1877, all record of his impeachment was officially expunged from the legislative record. In 1882 Butler was elected to the State Senate as an Independent from Nebraska's Third District. In 1888 he ran for a fourth term as governor on the Union Labor ticket, but received fewer popular votes (3,941) than either the Republican winner John M. Thayer (103,983) or Democrat John A. McShane (85,420). Butler died, May 25, 1891, on his farm near Pawnee City. Bibliography: "Necrology [of David Butler]," *Nebraska State Historical Society Proceedings and Collections*, Series II, vol. I (1894-95); Theodore Hodwalker, "Public Career of David Butler, First Governor of Nebraska," Unpublished Manuscript, Nebraska State Historical Society, Lincoln, 1938; "Nebraska 200," *Lincoln Sunday Journal Star*, (June 27, 1976); "Obituary," *Omaha Daily Bee*, (May 26, 1891); Joseph L. Edwards, *Centennial History of Pawnee County, Nebraska* (Pawnee City, 1876); *Biennial Report of the Secretary of State of the State of Nebraska* (Lincoln, 1893), *U.S. Census for Indiana, 1850*. Papers of Butler on deposit at the Nebraska State Historical Society Archives, Lincoln.

JAMES, William Hartford, 1871-1873

Born on October 16, 1831 in Marion Ohio, son of Isaac Evan James, a tanner, and Betsy (Bates) James; a Protestant. Brother of ten: Eliza, Isabella, John C., Alfred, Isaac Evan, Jr., Isabelle Ann, Martin Van Buren, Walter, Mary and George. Married to Louisa Epler on February 12, 1857; father of Frank Evan, Mary Luella James Chase, Ida James Doolittle, and Helen Bates James. Primary education in local public schools, supplemented by two years at Marion Academy. As a young man, he was engaged in farming, clerking, and reading law. In 1853 James moved to Des Moines, Iowa; in 1855 he was admitted to the Iowa Bar, and moved to Sergeant Bluff, where he established a legal practice. In 1857 James settled in Dakota County, Nebraska, where he had filed on a claim, and engaged in surveying and practicing law. Active in civic and political affairs, he was elected president of a Democratic County Convention, 1857; appointed a Dakota City trustee, 1858; elected Dakota City alderman, 1859; appointed Justice of the Peace, Dakota Precinct, 1860; appointed Dakota County Attorney, 1861, and reelected, 1863; and appointed Registrar, United States Land Office, Dakota County, 1864. In 1870 James was elected Secretary of State on the Republican ticket; he was appointed State Librarian in 1871. Following the impeachment and removal from office of Governor David C. Butler, Secretary of State James served as Acting Governor from June 2, 1871 to January 13, 1873. He also served concurrently as an *ex-officio* member of the University of Nebraska Board of Regents. Acting Governor James completed Butler's unfinished term of office amidst great hostility between the legislative and executive branches of state government. A number of new counties were organized by the legislature; James was often called upon to arbitrate disputed elections and to appoint various officers as these new counties established governmental organizations. He delivered his only message to the legislature on January 10, 1873, and was succeeded in office by Robert Wilkinson Furnas on January 13, 1873. Upon leaving the governor's office, James moved to West Point, Nebraska. in 1877 he was appointed Registrar, United States Land Office, Colfax County, Washington and moved there, taking a homestead near Colfax. William H. James died on February 1, 1920, and was buried at Colfax. Bibliography: *Messages and Proclamations of the Governors of Nebraska*, Works Progress Administration Official Project no. 165-1-81-317 (Lincoln, 1941); M.M. Warner, *Warner's History of Dakota County, Nebraska* (Lyons, 1893); "Obituary," *Nebraska History*, vol. III, no. 2 (April-June, 1920); "Obituary," *Colfax Gazette*, (February 6, 1920); "Obituary," *Spokane Chronicle*, (February 2, 1920); Alfred T. Andreas, ed., *History of the State of Nebraska* (Chicago, 1882); Thomas Weston Tipton, *Forty Years of Nebraska at Home and in Congress* (Lincoln, 1902); R.L. Polk & Co., *Whitman, Garfield and Latah Counties Directory, 1921-22*. Papers of James on deposit at the Nebraska State Historical Society Archives, Lincoln.

FURNAS, Robert Wilkinson, 1873-1875

Born on May 5, 1824 near Troy Ohio, son of William Furnas, a farmer, and Martha (Jenkins) Furnas, both of Quaker descent. A younger sister, Rachel, and a twin brother died before reaching adulthood. Married to Mary Elizabeth McComas on October 29, 1845; father of William Edward, Fillmore Taylor, Arthur Wilkinson, George Gilbert, John Somerville Inskip, Mollie Furnas Weeber, Celia Hensley Furnas Lowman, and

Robert. His first wife died on April 1, 1897; Furnas was married for a second time on December 25, 1899 to Mrs. Susannah (Emswiler) Jameson. Intermittent primary education. As a young man, Furnas held a variety of jobs: farm worker, general store helper, tinsmith's and printer's apprentice, jewelry and insurance salesman, railroad and postal employee, printer, editor, and Troy City Clerk, 1852-55. Following his 1856 arrival in Brownville, Nebraska Territory, he founded the *Nebraska Advertiser* and promoted local education, agriculture, and railroad construction. Furnas, a former Whig, proclaimed himself a Democrat in 1857. Elected to Territorial Council, 1856, 1858. Author of common school law for Nebraska Territory, and of bill creating a Territorial Board of Agriculture. Named Public Printer for Nebraska Territory, 1857; and Chief Clerk of Territorial Council, 1861. Following the outbreak of the Civil War in 1861, Furnas, a Colonel in the territorial militia, was promoted to Brigadier General, Second Brigade, Nebraska Volunteers. He later served as Colonel, First Regiment, Indian Home Guards, 1862; and Colonel, Second Nebraska Cavalry Regiment, 1862-63. Indian agent for the Omaha tribe, 1864-66. By c.1860 Furnas had switched from the Democratic to the Republican Party. Served on the University of Nebraska Board of Regents, 1869-73, and later *ex-officio* member during his 1873-75 term as governor. He failed to obtain the Republican nomination for Governor in 1870, but did secure the nomination in 1872 and defeated Democrat Henry C. Lett by a popular vote of 16,543 to 11,227; inaugurated on January 13, 1873. As governor Furnas was beset by administrative problems and state-wide economic hardship, caused by drought and grasshopper plague, which necessitated various relief measures. At the expiration of his single term, he retired to his farm and nursery near Brownville. Furnas served for several years as an employee of the Pension Office, Department of the Interior, and as an agent for the United States Department of Agriculture, reporting agricultural statistics and related information to Washington. In 1878, he headed the revitalization of the Nebraska State Historical Society and served as its president, 1878-91, 1902-05. As president (1869-74) and secretary (1884-1905) of the Nebraska State Board of Agriculture, he gathered and published valuable agricultural data and encouraged the development of an annual Nebraska State Fair. Commissioner to several national and international expositions, including the New Orleans Cotton Centennial, 1884-85. Furnas died in Lincoln on June 1, 1905, and was buried at Brownville. Bibliography: Tanzy R. Furnas, *Genealogy of the Furnas Family* (Dayton, n.d.); *Messages and Proclamations of the Governors of Nebraska*, Works Progress Administration Official Project No. 165-1-81-317 (Lincoln, 1941); Robert C. Farb, *Robert W. Furnas of Nebraska* (Lincoln, 1949); Robert C. Farb, "The Military Career of Robert W. Furnas," *Nebraska History*, vol. XXXIII, no. 1 (March, 1951); John L. McKinley, *The Political Career of Robert W. Furnas* (Lincoln, 1927); Myron B. Jenkins, *Robert Wilkinson Furnas, Biographical Notes* (Lincoln, 1940?). Papers of Furnas on deposit at the Nebraska State Historical Society in Lincoln.

GARBER, Silas, 1875-1879

Born on September 21, 1833 in Logan County, Ohio, son of Martin Garber and Madaline (Mohler) Garber, both of whom were Dunkards. Brother of John, Madaline, Samuel, Jacob, Mary Garber Mohr, Abram, Joseph, Isaac, Martha Garber Dunning, Hannah Garber Hall, Benjamin, Martin (d. 1826), and Martin (d. 1903). Married to Roselle Dana on March 25, 1857; father of William Seward Garber. Following the death of his first wife, Garber was married for a second time on July 1, 1875 to Lyra C. Wheeler. Attended local public schools and at the age of seventeen moved to Clayton County, Iowa and engaged in farming. After the outbreak of the Civil War, Garber enlisted as a private, 3rd Missouri Regiment; he later served as Lieutenant, and then Captain, of Company D, 27th Iowa Infantry. At the end of the war, Garber moved to California and engaged in stock trading. In 1870 he homesteaded in Webster County, Nebraska, on the modern site of the town of Red Cloud; Garber operated a general merchandise store, and played an active role in the organization of Webster County government. He was elected the first Webster County Probate Judge, 1871; elected to House of Representatives, Nebraska Legislature, 1872; appointed Registrar. United States Land Office, Lincoln, 1873. In 1874 he was chosen the Republican gubernatorial nominee, in response to rising demand from the new western counties of Nebraska for additional representation. He defeated Democrat Albert Tuxberry by a popular vote of 21,568 to 8,025 (Jonathan F. Gardner received 4,159, and J.S. Church, 1,346). Sworn into office on January 12, 1875. *Ex-officio* member, University of Nebraska Board of Regents, 1875-76. Reelected Governor in 1876, defeating Democrat Paren England by a popular vote of 31,947 to 17,219, with Jonathan F. Gardner receiving 3,022. Garber's two terms as governor coincided with an important period in the development and settlement of Nebraska. After years of effort, the constitution of 1875 was adopted. Despite the grasshopper plagues of the 1870's, Garber stressed the continued importance of immigration and agriculture and did much to promote settlement of the state. Following the expiration of his second term as governor, Silas Garber returned to Webster County and engaged in merchandising, banking and stock raising. Garber died on January 12, 1905, and was buried at Red Cloud. Bibliography: *Messages and Proclamations of the Governors of Nebraska*, Works Progress Administration Official Project No. 165-1-81-317 (Lincoln, 1941); Cora Garber Dunning, *Genealogy of the Ludwig Mohler Family in America* (Lincoln, 1921); Cheryl L. Henderson, "The Life and Times of Silas Garber," *Webster County Histories*, I (1974?); "Funeral of Ex-Governor Garber," *Webster County Histories*, I (1974?); *Biennial Report of the Secretary of State of the State of Nebraska* (Lincoln, 1893); "Obituary," *Nebraska State Journal*, (January 13, 1905); Thomas Weston Tipton, *Forty Years of Nebraska at Home and in Congress* (Lincoln, 1902). Papers of Garber on deposit at the Nebraska State Historical Society Archives, Lincoln.

NANCE, Albinus, 1879-1883

Born on March 30, 1848 at La Fayette, Illinois, son of Hiram Nance, a doctor and member of the Christian Church, and Sarah (Smith) Nance, a Congregationalist. Brother of Adella Nance Shilton, Hiram Irving, Sarah Belle Nance Castle, Roswell S., Roy, Burton F., Charles H., and Willis Orville. Married to Sarah White on September 30, 1875 father of Helen Marie Nance Anderson. Received his early schooling at La Fayette and Kewanee, Illinois; enlisted at the age of sixteen as a private in the 9th Illinois Cavalry and served until the close of the Civil War. After his return from the army, he attended Knox College, Galesburg, Illinois for a year, studied law, and was admitted to the Illinois Bar in 1870. In 1871 he homesteaded in Polk County, Nebraska and later settled in Osceola, where he practiced law. Elected to the House of Representatives, Nebraska Legislature, 1874; reelected, 1876, and chosed Speaker of the House. Chairman, Nebraska delegation to 1876 Republican National Convention in Cincinnati. In 1878 as Republican candidate for Governor, Nance defeated Democrat W.H. Webster by a popular vote of 26,469 to 13,473; Levi C. Todd received 9,475 votes. Renominated by acclamation in 1880 and defeated Democrat Thomas W. Tipton by a popular vote of 55,237 to 28,167, with O.T.B. Williams receiving 3,898 votes. Nance was widely known as the "Boy Governor" because he was only thirty years of age when first elected to the governorship. Despite his use of the Nebraska National Guard to quell an 1882 labor disturbance, he enjoyed a relatively tranquil administration. Nebraska was beginning to emerge from the economic depression of the mid 1870|s| caused by drought and grasshopper plagues, and entering a period of growth and prosperity marked by his conservative administration of state fiscal affairs. His second administration also saw the passage of the 1881 Slocumb Liquor Law, designed to regulate the granting of liquor licenses in Nebraska. Upon the expiration of his second term, Nance returned to his private law practice in Osceola. He later became a banker and broker, handling railroad stocks and bonds, in Lincoln and Chicago. Albinus Nance died on December 7, 1911 in Chicago. Bibliography: *Messages and Proclamations of the Governors of Nebraska*, Works Progress Administration Official Project No. 165-1-81-317 (Lincoln, 1941); George W. Nance, *The Nance Memorial* (Bloomington, Illinois, 1904); Osceola Centennial Book Committee, *Osceola, 1871-1971* (Lincoln, 1972); Mildred Newman Flodman, *Early Days in Polk Country* (Lincoln, 1966); *Biennial Report of the Secretary of State of the State of Nebraska* (Lincoln, 1893); Thomas Weston Tipton, *Forty Years of Nebraska at Home and In Congress* (Lincoln, 1902); "Out of Old Nebraska," Nebraska State Historical Society newspaper release, November 13, 1949. Papers of Nance on deposit at the Nebraska State Historical Society Archives, Lincoln.

DAWES, James William, 1883-1887

Born on January 8, 1844 in McConnelsville, Morgan County, Ohio, son of Edward M. Dawes, a farmer and physician, and Caroline (Dana) Dawes; a Congregationalist. Brother of Benjamin Dana, Eunice, John Winchester, Mary Caroline, and Charlotte Eliza Dawes McCue. Married to Francis Anna Dawes, a cousin, on May 11, 1871. Moved in 1856 with his family to Port, Wisconsin, where he worked on the family farm and attended school. He spent two terms at Western Reserve College in Ohio, and six months at Milwaukee Business College. After four years (1864-68) of clerking in a Kilbourn City mercantile establishment, Dawes entered the law office of a cousin, John H. Dawes, at Fox Lake and was admitted to the Wisconsin Bar, 1871. Later that year he moved to Crete, Nebraska, where he first entered the mercantile business and later practiced law. He was actively engaged in Republican Party politics from the time of his arrival in the state. Dawes was a member of the 1875 State Constitutional Convention; and in 1876 was elected to the Nebraska Senate. Party positions included: chairman, Republican State Central Committee, 1876-82; delegate, 1880 Republican National Convention; and for the next four years, Nebraska representative on Republican National Committee. In 1882 as Republican candidate for Governor, Dawes defeated Democrat J. Sterling Morton by a popular vote of 43,495 to 28,562; E. P. Ingersoll received 16,991. He was sworn into office on January 4, 1883 and again reelected in 1884. Dawes|with 72,835 votes, defeated Morton and James G. Miller with 57,634 and 3,075 votes respectively. Dawes' two terms as governor coincided with part of the period of Nebraska's greatest growth and development. More than 11 million acres of public land within the state were claimed, and agricultural and industrial production increased dramatically. Dawes was much interested in the progress of Nebraska's state institutions and in the education of its youth. During his administration and throughout his political career (from 1872-1912), Dawes served on the Board of Trustees of Doane College, Crete, Nebraska. Upon the expiration of his second term as governor, Dawes resumed his Crete law practice and dealt in real estate. In 1898 he was appointed paymaster in the United States Army with the rank of Major for the duration of the Spanish-American War. Later his commission was made permanent and Dawes was stationed in Cuba and the Philippines until his retirement from the Army in 1909. The remainder of his life was spent near Milwaukee, Wisconsin, where he died on October 8, 1918; he was buried in Forest Home Cemetery. Bibliography: *Messages and Proclamations of the Governors of Nebraska*, Works Progress Administration Official Project No. 165-1-81-317 (Lincoln, 1941); *Biennial Report of the Secretary of State of the State of Nebraska* (Lincoln, 1893); "Out of Old Nebraska," Nebraska State Historical Society newspaper release, December 11, 1949; "Obituary: James William Dawes," *Crete News*, (October 10, 1918); Thomas Weston Tipton, *Forty Years of Nebraska at Home and in Congress* (Lincoln, 1902); John Brenneman, *et al.*, *History of Doane College, 1872 to 1912, Crete, Nebraska* (Crete, 1957); Henry W. Holland, *William Dawes and His Ride with Paul Revere* (Boston, 1878).

THAYER, John Milton, 1887-1891, 1891-1892

Born on January 24, 1820 in Bellingham, Massachusetts, son of Elias Thayer, a farmer, and Ruth (Staples) Thayer, both of whom were Baptists. Brother of Lyman Wheelock, Hannah Ellis, Ruth Daniels, Mary Blake, Elias, Julia Ann, Susan, and Elias Nelson. Married to Mary Torrey Allen on December 17, 1842, and father of Milton Bertrand, George Dana, Walter Allan, Rollin, Herbert, and John Milton Jr. Taught in local schools before entering Brown University in 1837; graduated in 1841. He became a lawyer, an editor of the *Worcester Magazine and Historical Journal*, [Massachusetts], and a Lieutenant in the Massachusetts Militia. After his 1854 relocation in Nebraska Territory, Thayer farmed and practiced law; he was also appointed Brigadier General (1855) and Major General (1856) of the Territorial Militia. He was defeated in both the 1855 race for the Territorial House of Representatives and in an 1857 bid to become delegate to Congress. In 1858, appointed Treasurer, Territorial Board of Agriculture. Originally a Democrat, he became a Republican, but failed in 1859 and again in 1860 to receive the Republican nomination for delegate to Congress. In 1860 he was elected a member of a proposed constitutional convention, which never met; he was also elected to the Territorial Council. With the outbreak of the Civil War in 1861, Thayer was commissioned Colonel of the First Nebraska Infantry Regiment and in 1862 was promoted to Brigadier General. Later he was placed in command of five Iowa regiments and the 3rd Illinois Cavalry. Breveted Major-General of Volunteers, March, 1865. Resigned his commission in July and returned to Nebraska, where he helped secure its admission into the Union in 1867. U.S. Senator from Nebraska, 1867-71; later his Senatorial attempts in 1871, 1875, and 1883 failed. He became the Governor of Wyoming Territory, 1875-79. In 1886 as Republican candidate for Governor, Thayer defeated Democrat James E. North by a popular vote of 75,956 to 52,656, with Harvey Wesley Hardy receiving 8,175, and Jabez Burrows, 1,422. He was sworn into office on January 6, 1887 and was reelected in 1888, defeating Democrat John A. McShane by a popular vote of 103,983 to 85,420; George E. Bigelow received 9,511, and David Butler, 3,941. Thayer's two terms in office saw much farm and labor agitation for increased railroad regulation. During the last months of his administration, he organized relief boards to care for drought-stricken Nebraska counties. His second term should have expired on January 8, 1891, but Thayer's contention that Governor-Elect James E. Boyd was ineligible to serve delayed the transition until January 15. Following the Nebraska Supreme Court's ruling that Boyd was indeed ineligible, Thayer served as governor from May 5, 1891 to February 8, 1892, when Boyd again assumed the office after the United States Supreme Court had ruled him eligible. Thayer, seventy-two years of age when he stepped down as governor, returned to his private law practice. In June, 1902, the University of Nebraska conferred upon him the honorary degree of LL.D. John M. Thayer died on March 19, 1906, and was buried in Wyuka Cemetery, Lincoln. Bibliography: *Messages and Proclamations of the Governors of Nebraska*, Works Progress Administration Official Project No. 165-1-81-317 (Lincoln, 1942); E.G. Curtis, "John Milton Thayer, I-II," *Nebraska History*, vol. XXVIII, no. 4 (October-December, 1947); E.G. Curtis, "John Milton Thayer, III-IV," *Nebraska History*, vol. XXIX, no. 1 (March, 1948); E.G. Curtis, "John Milton Thayer, V-VII," *Nebraska History*, vol XXIX, no. 2 (June, 1948); *Biennial Report of the Secretary of the State of Nebraska* (Lincoln, 1893); Edgar S. Dudley, "Notes on the Early Military History of Nebraska," *Transactions and Reports of the Nebraska State Historical Society* (Lincoln, 1887); Bezaleel Thayer, *Memorial of the Thayer Name* (Oswego, 1874). Papers of Thayer on deposit at the Nebraska State Historical Society Archives, Lincoln.

BOYD, James E., 1891, 1892-1893

Born on September 9, 1834 in County Tyrone, Ireland, son of Joseph, a miller and farmer, and Margaret Boyd; both were Episcopalians. Brother of John., Eliza, Thomas F., Samuel, Joseph, Isabella, Mary, John Wilson, and Catherine Boyd Taylor. Married to Anna H. Henry on August 22, 1858; father of Margaret Boyd Clark, Eleanora Boyd Bierbower, James E., Jr., and two other children who died in infancy. Emigrated with his family to Belmont County, Ohio, 1844; relocated near Zanesville, 1847. Common school education; later a grocery store employee and carpenter. In 1856 he moved west, first to Des Moines, Iowa, and then to Omaha, Nebraska Territory, where he worked as a carpenter and contractor. Elected Douglas County clerk, 1857. Moved to Buffalo County, 1858, and engaged in farming and ranching, merchandising, and commercial freighting. In 1866 he was elected to the Nebraska House of Representatives. Following his 1868 return to Omaha, Boyd became prominent in business and financial circles, and began a distinguished political career: Douglas County delegate to state constitutional conventions in 1871, 1875; president, Omaha City Council, 1880; Mayor of Omaha, 1881-83, 1885-87; delegate to Democratic National Conventions of 1884, 1888, 1892; Democratic National Committeeman from Nebraska, 1884-92. An 1883 bid for the U.S. Senate failed. In 1890 as Democratic candidate for Governor, Boyd defeated Republican Lucius D. Richards by a popular vote of 71,331 to 68,878; John H. Powers received 70,187, and Bartlett L. Paine, 3,676. Boyd took the governor's oath of office on January 8, 1891, but previous Governor John M. Thayer's contention that he was not a U.S. citizen and therefore ineligible to serve, delayed the transition until January 15. Following the Nebraska Supreme Court's ruling that Boyd was indeed ineligible,

Thayer reassumed the office, serving as governor from May 5, 1891 to February 8, 1892, when Boyd was reinstated by order of the United States Supreme Court, which had declared him eligible. During his fragmented term of office, agrarian agitation for increased railroad regulation continued. Boyd's 1891 veto of the Newberry Railroad Bill, which would have reduced freight rates in Nebraska, angered many. He was not nominated to run for a second term. After retiring as governor in 1893, Boyd managed his grain commission offices in Omaha, St. Louis and Chicago. An 1893 try for the U.S. Senate failed, as did an 1894 bid for the U.S. House of Representatives from Nebraska's Second Congressional District. Retired from business, 1902; chairman, Omaha's first Municipal Water Board. 1903. James E. Boyd died in Omaha on April 30, 1906, and was buried in Prospect Hill Cemetery, Omaha. Bibliography: *Messages and Proclamations of the Governors of Nebraska*, Works Progress Administration Official Project No. 165-1-81-317 (Lincoln, 1942); *Biennial Report of the Secretary of State of the State of Nebraska* (Lincoln, 1893); "Nebraska Congressmen," *Morning World Herald* [Omaha] (November 8, 1894); Alfred T. Andreas, ed., *History of the State of Nebraska* (Chicago, 1882); *U.S. Census for Ohio, 1850*; "Obituary," *Omaha Daily Bee* (May 1, 1906); "Joseph Boyd, the Mayor's Father Comes to See his Children in Omaha," *Omaha Daily Herald* (March 8, 1882). Papers of Boyd on deposit in the Nebraska State Historical Society Archives, Lincoln.

THAYER, John Milton, 1887-1891, 1891-1892

BOYD, James E., 1891, 1892-1893

CROUNSE, Lorenzo, 1893-1895

Born on January 26, 1834 in Sharon, Schoharie County, New York, son of John Crounse, a tanner, and Margaret (Van Aernam) Crounse, both of whom were Lutheran. Brother of John Quincy Adams, Ann Eliza Crounse Zoller, Henry Van Aernam, Jane Ann Crounse Gilbert, and Jacob Alexander. Married to Mary E. Griffiths in 1860; father of Gretchen Crounse McIntyre, William Griffiths, Marie Crounse Bowen, and Jessie Crounse Hitchcock. Common school education supplemented by several summer terms at New York Conference Seminary. Began teaching school in 1851; four years later he took up the study of law and was admitted to the bar in 1857 at Fort Plain, New York, where he later practiced. With the outbreak of the Civil War in 1861, Crounse raised Battery K, First Regiment, New York Light Artillery; served as its Captain until injuries compelled his honorable discharge in 1862, whereupon he returned to his Fort Plain law practice. Following his 1864 arrival in Nebraska Territory, Crounse practiced law; filed on a homestead near Rulo, 1865; and began his political career. He served in the lower house territorial legislature, 1866, where he helped draft a state constitution and worked for its adoption by Nebraska voters. His political activities included: Associate Justice, Nebraska Supreme Court, 1867-73; appointed Reporter, Nebraska Supreme Court, 1873; U.S. Representative from Nebraska, 1873-77; an 1876 bid for the

U.S. Senate (unsuccessful); appointed Internal Revenue Collector for Nebraska, 1879; chairman, Nebraska delegation, 1880 Republican National Convention; appointed Assistant Secretary of U.S. Treasury, 1891. In 1892 the Republicans nominated Crounse for Governor as a compromise candidate to unite the party in Nebraska. He defeated Populist nominee Charles H. Van Wyck by a popular vote of 78,426 to 68,617; Democrat J. Sterling Morton received 44,195 and C.E. Bentley, 6,235; he was inaugurated on January 13, 1893. During his administration Crounse emphasized economy, retrenchment, rigid accountability for expenditures of public money, and strict adherence to rules of conduct by all state officials. Attempts were made to eliminate corruption and mismanagement in state institutions, and impeachment proceedings were begun against several officials for misuse of state funds. Crounse refused to be a candidate in 1894. Following his retirement from the governorship, Crounse returned to Washington County, where he had settled after his 1866 election to the Nebraska Supreme Court. Elected to Nebraska Senate, 1900. A 1901 bid for the U.S. Senate failed. Lorenzo Crounse died on May 13, 1909 in Omaha and was buried at Fort Calhoun, Washington County. Bibliography: *Messages and Proclamations of the Governors of Nebraska*, Works Progress Administration Official Project No. 165-1-81-317 (Lincoln, 1942); "Obituary," *Omaha Bee* (May 14, 1909); "Obituary," *Morning World Herald* [Omaha] (May 14, 1909); "Lorenzo Crounse Descendants Still Prominent," *Sunday World Herald*, [Omaha], (July 7, 1957); *Biennial Report of the Secretary of State of the State of Nebraska* (Lincoln, 1896); Records of St. John's Evangelical Lutheran Church, Sharon, New York; Vreeland Y. Leonard, "The Crounse Family of Albany County, State of New York and Its Descendants," Manuscript, 1946, in New York State Library, Albany; Papers of Crounse on deposit at the Nebraska State Historical Society Archives, Lincoln.

HOLCOMB, Silas Alexander, 1895-1899

Born on August 25, 1858 in Gibson County, Indiana, son of John Cook Holcomb, a farmer and teacher, and Lucinda Reavis (Skelton) Holcomb, both of whom were Baptists. Brother of Stephen Howard, Lizzie Belle, Wilbur Walter, Effie May, Estella E. Holcomb Kirkpatrick, Erasmus, and Birdie L.; half-brother of James Bennett, Joseph Elihu, and Charles Hume. Married to Alice Brinson on April 13, 1882; father of Harold, Nettie Holcomb Hohl, and Marian Holcomb Wyman. Common school education supplemented by normal school course; farm worker and teacher. In 1879 Holcomb relocated in Hamilton County, Nebraska, where he farmed and taught school. After reading law in Grand Island, he was admitted to the bar in 1882; the next year he opened a law office in Broken Bow and homesteaded nearby. Active in local politics, Holcomb soon became prominent in the agrarian-based Populist movement. Elected Nebraska 12th District Judge, 1891; an 1893 race for the Nebraska Supreme Court failed, but the resulting recognition did gain him the 1894 Populist nomination for Governor. With the support of William Jennings Bryan and other Silver Democrats, Holcomb ran on a fusion ticket and defeated Republican Thomas J. Majors by a popular vote of 97,815 to 94,613. Sworn into office on January 3, 1895. He was reelected in 1896, defeating Republican John H. MacColl by a popular vote of 116,415 to 94,723. Holcomb's victories in 1894 and 1896 forced the dominant Republican Party in Nebraska to adjust some of its policies and to realign its leadership; as a result, many voters abandoned their traditional political allegiances and became independents. His administration provided some aid for stricken Nebraskans during the drought and depression years following 1893. Holcomb opposed the graft and corruption in the state treasury system and introduced changes in state land and fiscal policy, and in the management and administration of state institutions. He did not run for reelection in 1898. After Holcomb left the governor's office in 1899, he served on the Nebraska Supreme Court for six years (1900-06), the last two as Chief Justice. Following his retirement from the bench, he spent several years in Seattle, Washington; he later returned to Broken Bow and resumed his law practice. Chairman, Board of Commissioners of State Institutions (later the Board of Control), 1913-19. After retiring from the Board because of poor health, Holcomb moved to Bellingham, Washington. Silas Holcomb died on April 25, 1920, at Bellingham, and was buried at Broken Bow. Bibliography: Hannah Elizabeth McPherson, *The Holcombes, Nation Builders* (Washington, 1947); *Messages and Proclamations of the Governors of Nebraska*, Works Progress Administration Official Project No. 165-1-81-317 (Lincoln, 1942); N.C. Abbott, "Silas A. Holcomb," *Nebraska History*, vol XXVI, no. 4 (October-December, 1945); N.C. Abbott, "Silas A. Holcomb (Part Two)," *Nebraska History*, vol XXVII, no. 1 (January-March, 1946); *Biennial Report of the Secretary of State of the State of Nebraska* (Lincoln, 1896); "Obituary," *Custer County Chief* (April 29, 1920); "Obituary," *Custer County Republican* (April 29, 1920); W.L. Gaston and A.R. Humphrey, *History of Custer County, Nebraska* (Lincoln, 1919). Papers of Holcomb on deposit at the Nebraska State Historical Society Archives, Lincoln.

POYNTER, William Amos, 1899-1901

Born on May 29, 1848 in Wooford County, Illinois, son of William Chapman Poynter, minister and pioneer Illinois settler, and Huldah Jane (Watkins) Poynter, both of whom were Church of Christ members. Brother of John W. and Daniel J. Married to Maria Josephine McCorkle on October 12, 1869; father of Charles W. M. Poynter and Josephine Mary Poynter Bickford. Graduated from Eureka College in 1867. Poynter taught school for several years and then entered the grocery and hardware business. In 1879 he moved to Boone County, Nebraska, near Albion, where he farmed and raised livestock. Active in local politics, he was elected in 1884 to the Nebraska House of Representatives. Elected to the Nebraska Senate, 1890, and chosen President Pro Tempore. A race in 1892 as the Populist candidate for Congress from Nebraska's Third District failed, when he was defeated by Republican George D. Meiklejohn. Interested in the advancement of agriculture, Poynter helped organize the Boone County Agricultural Society and served on the State Board of Agriculture; in 1895 he was elected first vice-president and a member of the Board of Managers. Nominated and elected Governor in 1898 as the fusion candidate of the Populists, Democrats, and Silver Republicans, defeating Republican Monroe L. Hayward by a popular vote of 95,703 to 92,982. Inaugurated on January 5, 1899. During Poynter's single term as governor, a hostile state legislature prevented the enactment of much of his program, which was concerned primarily with railroad regulation. He did sign a bill permanently locating the state fair at Lincoln. Poynter was renominated for Governor by the fusionists in 1900, but was narrowly defeated by Republican Charles H. Dietrich by a popular vote of 113,879 to 113,018. After retiring from the governorship in 1901, Poynter continued to live in Lincoln, where he participated actively in public affairs. He lectured widely, engaged in the insurance business, and helped to organize the Security Savings and Loan Association of Lincoln, serving as its president until his death. William A. Poynter died on April 5, 1909 in Lincoln, and was buried in Wyuka Cemetery, Lincoln. Bibliography: *Messages and Proclamations of the Governors of Nebraska*, Works Progress Administration Official Project No. 165-1-81-317 (Lincoln, 1942); "Obituary of William Chapman Poynter," *Argus* [Albion] (December 29, 1899); "Obituary of William Amos Poynter," *Argus* [Albion] (April 10, 1909), and *Daily Star* [Lincoln] (April 5, 1909); *Nebraska Statistical Handbook, 1974-75* (Lincoln, 1975); Theron E. Sedgwick, *York County, Nebraska, and Its People* (Chicago, 1921). Papers of Poynter on deposit at the Nebraska State Historical Society Archives, Lincoln.

DIETRICH, Charles Henry, 1901

Born on November 26, 1853 in Aurora, Illinois, youngest of ten children of John Leonard, a shoemaker, and Wilhelmina (Stein) Dietrich; an Episcopalian. Brother of Wilhelmina Dietrich Meyer, his only sibling who survived into adulthood. Married to Elizabeth Slaker on May 4, 1878; father of Gertrude Elizabeth Dietrich Knox Smith, and a son who died in infancy. His first wife died in February of 1887; Dietrich was married a second time to Margretta Shaw Stewart on October 27, 1909. He left Aurora public schools at the age of twelve, and as a young man engaged in a variety of occupations: farm and store worker, and blacksmith, Aurora; hardware store employee, St. Joseph and Chicago; city railway employee, Chicago, St. Louis, and Memphis; timber cutter, Laconia Circle, Arkansas. Attracted to the Black Hills of South Dakota in 1875 by gold discoveries, he became a merchant and prospector, and located the Aurora mine in 1877. The next year, after a brief venture in sheep raising near San Antonio, Texas, Dietrich settled in Hastings, Nebraska, entered business, and began to promote vigorously the town's development, which included his presidency of the German National Bank from 1887 to 1905. As a prominent Republican businessman, Dietrich was nominated for Governor in 1900 by the Republican State Convention, and subsequently defeated fusion candidate William A. Poynter by a popular vote of 113,879 to 113,018. In his inaugural address of January 3, 1901, Dietrich recommended a change in the number of district and supreme court judges in Nebraska; codification of state laws; and the creation of a Board of Control to manage state institutions. On March 28, he was elected by the Nebraska Legislature as a compromise candidate to fill out the unexpired term of deceased U.S. Senator Monroe L. Hayward, and he resigned the governorship on May 1. Dietrich was succeeded by Lieutenant Governor Ezra P. Savage. Following his resignation from the governorship, Dietrich served in the U.S. Senate (1901-1905), where he encouraged an enlarged homestead bill for Nebraska, and promoted reclamation and the American beet sugar industry. After the expiration of his term in 1905, he retired to Hastings where he spent his last years. Charles H. Dietrich died on April 10, 1924, and was buried at Parkview Cemetery, Hastings. Bibliography: *Messages and Proclamations of the Governors of the State of Nebraska*, (Lincoln, 1942); Dorothy Weyer Creigh, ed., *Adams County: The People* (Hastings, 1971); Margretta S. Dietrich, "Senator Charles H. Dietrich," *Publications of the Nebraska State Historical Society* (Lincoln, 1975); "Obituary," *Hastings Daily Tribune* (April 14, 1924); William R. Burton, ed., *Past and Present of Adams County, Nebraska* (Chicago, 1916). Papers of Dietrich on deposit at the Nebraska State Historical Society Archives, Lincoln.

SAVAGE, Ezra Perin, 1901-1903

Born on April 3, 1842 in Connorsville, Indiana, son of Benjamin Warren and Hanna (Perin) Savage; a Mason. Brother of Delphine Savage Kelly, Frances, Del, and B.A. Savage. Married to Anna C. Rich on October 11, 1866; father of Harold S., Howard P., Edmund C., Charles C., Jessie R., and Emily W. Married to Elvira Hess on April 9, 1896; remarried to Julia McCullough on September 26, 1900. Moved from Indiana to Lyons, Iowa with his family late in 1842. He was a farm worker and wood cutter while attending Davenport High School and later, Iowa College, Davenport, which he left before completing his studies. Savage entered the U.S. Army in August, 1861, and was shortly afterward discharged for disability; however, during the Civil War he went south with his company as a scout. After the end of the war, Savage entered the seed grain and implement business in Lyons; turned to cattle raising in Crawford County, Iowa, 1873; and was admitted to the Iowa Bar about 1875. In the 1870s Savage settled in Custer County, Nebraska upon a claim now part of the town site of Sargent. He was elected to the Nebraska House of Representatives, 1883, and superintended concurrently for a time the University of Nebraska's agricultural farm in Lincoln. Following the expiration of his term in the Legislature, Savage entered the stock commission business in Omaha. He took part in the incorporation of South Omaha and was chosen president of its first board of trustees in 1886. He was elected first Mayor of South Omaha, 1877; appointed City Councilman, 1888; elected presidential elector, 1892. In the 1890s he returned to Custer County to farm and raise livestock. In 1900 Savage was elected Lieutenant Governor on the Republican ticket. Following Governor Charles H. Dietrich's resignation from the governorship on May 1, 1901 to enter the U.S. Senate, Savage succeeded to the post. Savage served as Acting Governor until the end of Dietrich's term in January, 1903. He represented the state at the laying of the keel of the battleship *Nebraska* in Seattle in 1902. The most memorable act of his administration was the parole, and later pardon, of former State Treasurer Joseph C. Bartley, convicted and imprisoned for embezzling state funds. The resulting barrage of criticism caused Savage to withdraw as a contender in the 1902 Republican gubernatorial race. Following his retirement from the governorship, Savage moved to Tacoma, Washington to enter the lumber business. Ezra P. Savage died on January 8, 1920 at Tacoma. Bibliography: *Messages and Proclamations of the Governors of Nebraska*, Works Progress Administration Official Project No. 165-1-81-317 (Lincoln, 1942); Obituaries: *Sargent Leader* (January 15, 1920); *Custer County Republican*, (January 15, 1920), *Custer County Chief* (January 15, 1920); Albert Watkins, *History of Nebraska* (Lincoln, 1913); James W. Savage and John T. Bell, *History of the City of Omaha, Nebraska, and South Omaha* (New York and Chicago, 1894); *U.S. Census for Iowa, 1850*. Papers of Savage on deposit at the Nebraska State Historical Society Archives, Lincoln.

MICKEY, John Hopwood, 1903-1907

Born on September 30, 1845 near Burlington, Iowa, son of Oliver Perry, a farmer, and Betsy Ann Davison Mickey, both of whom were Methodists. Brother of George F., Adaline T., Albert P., Weston, Basil S., Thomas B., William O., and Iona Ann. Married to Morinda McCray on September 10, 1867; father of Harlan A., Oliver Edward, Evan S., Bertha E. Mickey Smith, Marie Nain, John and Warren. Following the death of his first wife in 1886, he re-married to Flora Cinderella Campbell on December 8, 1887; they were the parents of Benjamin Hopwood, James Harold, Ralph D., Flora Elizabeth, and Norma Adaline. He had early primary education in Louisa County, Iowa, district schools and served in 8th Iowa Cavalry, 1863-65. With the end of the Civil War, he attended Wesleyan College, Mount Pleasant, Iowa for several years; later farmed and taught school. In 1868 he homesteaded near Osceola, Polk County, Nebraska, where he soon became prominent in local affairs. He was elected County Treasurer, 1870; promoted county settlement as Union Pacific Railroad land agent; established first Osceola bank, 1879; an active member of the Methodist Episcopal Church; named president of the Board of Trustees, Nebraska Wesleyan University, Lincoln, in 1879; participated actively in church affairs throughout his life, and elected to Nebraska House of Representatives, 1880. Mickey's nomination for the governorship by the Republicans in 1902 came on the thirteenth ballot after a heated convention battle with John B. Dinsmore of Sutton. He subsequently defeated fusion candidate William H. Thompson by a popular vote of 96,471 to 91,116, and was inaugurated on January 8, 1903. Reelected in 1904, defeating fusion candidate George W. Berge by a popular vote of 111,711 to 102,558. Mickey's two terms as governor were marked by rising prosperity in Nebraska. He urged adoption of the direct primary (established during his successor's administration), and established a more efficient state auditing system. A memorable feature of his administration was his record-breaking use of his executive clemency powers in granting pardons and commutations. After the expiration of his term as governor, Mickey returned to Osceola, and resumed banking, farming, and stock raising. John H. Mickey died on June 2, 1910, and was buried in Osceola. Bibliography: *Messages and Proclamations of the Governors of Nebraska*, Works Progress Administration Official Project No. 165-1-81-317 (Lincoln, 1942); J. Sterling Morton, *Illustrated History of Nebraska* (Lincoln, 1907); *U.S. Census for Iowa, 1850*; "Obituary: John H. Mickey," *Osceola Record* (June 9, 1910); "Obituary: Betsy Ann Mickey," *Osceola Record* (June 1, 1899); Osceola Centennial Book Committee, *Osceola, 1871-1971* (Lincoln, 1972); *Nebraska Statistical Handbook, 1974-75* (Lincoln, 1975); "Out of Old Nebraska," Nebraska State Historical Society newspaper release, August 20, 1950. Papers of Mickey on deposit at the Nebraska State Historical Society Archives, Lincoln.

SHELDON, George Lawson, 1907-1909

Born on May 31, 1870 in Nehawka, Nebraska, son of Lawson Sheldon, pioneer farmer, mill owner, and political figure of Cass County, and Julia Ann Pollard, both of whom were Episcopalians. Brother of Florence Sheldon Todd, Gertrude S. Sheldon Wolph, Frank P., Vilas P., and an unnamed child who died in infancy. Married to Rose Higgins on September 4, 1895; father of George Lawson, Jr., Mary Ellen Sheldon House, Anson Hoisington, and Julia Pollard Sheldon Griffin. Early education at Nehawka; graduated from University of Nebraska, Lincoln, 1892, and Harvard, 1893. After leaving Harvard, Sheldon returned to Nehawka to enter the family business of farming and cattle raising. Captain, 3rd Nebraska Volunteer Infantry, Spanish-American War, 1898-99. Sheldon's public career began in 1902 with his election to the Nebraska Senate; reelected, 1904. As a member of the progressive wing of the Republican Party who had actively supported reform legislation, Sheldon was nominated on the Republican ticket for Governor in 1906. Defeated Democrat Ashton C. Shallenberger by a popular vote of 97,858 to

84,885, and was inaugurated January 3, 1907. First native born Nebraskan to serve as governor of the state. Shallenberger defeated Sheldon at the next gubernatorial election in 1908 by a popular vote of 132,960 to 125,976. Sheldon's 1906 campaign attacked railroad domination of state politics, and his single term as governor was characterized by his opposition to special interest groups. Free railroad passes were abolished, passenger fares reduced to two cents per mile, and a State Railway Commission was created. A mandatory statewide direct primary law was enacted. As one of Nebraska's delegates-at-large to the Republican National Convention of 1908, he was a possible vice-presidential running mate for William Howard Taft. Following his retirement from the governorship in 1909, Sheldon moved to Mississippi and entered the cotton and cattle business on his Washington County plantation. Served in Mississippi House of Representatives, 1920-24; ran several times as a Republican candidate for Governor and Congressman, and revitalized the Republican Party in Mississippi. Collector of Internal Revenue for Mississippi, 1930-33. Moved to Clinton, 1939. George L. Sheldon died on April 4, 1960 in Jackson, Mississippi, and was buried at Greenville. Bibliography: *Messages and Proclamations of the Governors of Nebraska*, Works Progress Administration Official Project No. 165-1-81-317 (Lincoln, 1942); J. Sterling Morton, *Illustrated History of Nebraska* (Lincoln, 1907); "Ideal Home Life and Public Activity of George Lawson Sheldon," *Omaha Bee* (October 14, 1906); Virginia Speich, "The Political Career of George L. Sheldon 1907-1909," *Nebraska History*, vol. 53, no. 3 (Fall, 1972); "Nebraska's First Native Son Governor" *Lincoln Sunday Journal and Star* (July 30, 1950); Obituaries: *Lincoln Star* (April 5, 1960), and *Nebraska State Journal* (April 5, 1960). Papers of Sheldon on deposit at the Nebraska State Historical Society Archives, Lincoln.

SHALLENBERGER, Ashton Cockayne, 1909-1911

Born on December 23, 1862 in Toulon Illinois, son of Martin Shallenberger, lawyer, and Eliza Jane (Hall) Shallenberger; a Congregationalist. Brother of Thomas M., Onslow P., Eugene, Herman G., Percy H., Matilda Shallenberger Higgins, and Pauline Shallenberger Ragan. Married to Eliza Zilg on May 24, 1885; father of Martin Conrad, Grace Pauline, and Dorothy Eliza Shallenberger Thoeney. Following his early education in the Toulon public schools, Shallenberger attended the University of Illinois for several years. Arrived in Nebraska about 1881 and worked as a general store clerk in Stromsburg and shortly thereafter in Osceola, where he started his own business, 1885. Moved to Alma, 1887; operated a general store, and organized the Bank of Alma, 1887, of which he became first cashier and later president. Elected on the Democratic ticket to the U.S. House of Representatives from Nebraska's 5th District, 1900. Defeated for reelection by George W. Norris, 1902. The Democratic nominee for Governor in 1906, he was defeated by Republican George L. Sheldon by a popular vote of 97,858 to 84,885. Nominated again in 1908, Shallenberger defeated Sheldon by a popular vote of 132,960 to 125,976. He was defeated for renomination in the 1910 Democratic primary by James C. Dahlman. During Shallenberger's single term as a State Bank Guarantee of Deposits Law was enacted. The "Oregon Plan" of expressing a preference for U.S. Senators in the direct primary was also adopted in Nebraska. Shallenberger's signing of the controversial "daylight saloon" measure, requiring saloons to close at 8 p.m. daily, was a factor in his defeat for the 1910 Democratic gubernatorial nomination. After leaving the governor's office in 1911,

Shallenberger devoted himself to politics, farming, and livestock raising. In 1912 he was nominated for U.S. Senator in the Democratic primary, but lost to George W. Norris in the first preferential vote under the "Oregon Plan" at the following election. Served in the U.S. House of Representatives, 1915-19, 1923-29, and 1931-35, six terms from the Fifth District and one from the Fourth District, created after the 1930 census. As a member of Congress, he promoted reclamation, irrigation, a rural credit system, and a federal bank deposit guarantee system. Ashton C. Shallenberger died on February 22, 1938 in Franklin, Nebraska, while on a speaking engagement, and was buried in Alma. Bibliography: *Messages and Proclamations of the Governors of Nebraska*, Works Progress Administration Official Project No. 165-1-81-317 (Lincoln, 1942); Albert Watkins, *History of Nebraska* (Lincoln, 1913); Eliza Jane (Hall) Shallenberger, *Stark County and Its Pioneers* (Cambridge, Illinois, 1876); "Obituary: Onslow P. Shallenberger," *Imperial Republican* (January 6, 1922); "Obituary: Ashton C. Shallenberger," *Nebraska State Journal* (February 23, 1938); Osceola Centennial Book Committee, *Osceola 1871-1971* (Lincoln, 1972); *Nebraska Statistical Handbook 1974-1975* (Lincoln, 1975); Theron E. Sedgwick, *York County Nebraska and Its People* (Chicago, 1921). Papers of Shallenberger on deposit at the Nebraska State Historical Society Archives, Lincoln.

ALDRICH, Chester Hardy, 1911-1913

Born on November 10, 1862 near Pierpont, Ohio, eldest of four sons and one daughter of George W. Aldrich, a farmer, and Sophronia Hardy Aldrich, who were practicing Methodists. Brother of Charles G., Charlie S., Harley H. and Grace E. Married to Sylvia Stroman on June 4, 1889; father of George Stroman, Frederick S., Chester Hardy, Jr., John B., and Lee. Attended Pierpont High School and at the age of eighteen entered Hillsdale (Michigan) College; taught school intermittently to pay for his three-year preparatory course. Graduated from Ohio State University, 1888. Later that year, Aldrich came to Ulysses, Nebraska, where he became principal of the high school and read law. Admitted to the Nebraska Bar, 1890. Practiced law in 1891 in David City. He also raised livestock and soon became prominent in local affairs, serving on the School Board, City Council, and as Mayor. Elected to the Nebraska Senate on the Republican ticket, 1906. Chairman, Committee on Constitutional Amendments and Federal Relations; author of Aldrich commodity freight rate law, which reduced rates on most articles shipped in Nebraska, and of a Railway Commission Law. Lost 1908 race for the U.S. House of Representatives to C.H Sloan. In 1910 he was nominated for Governor in the open Republican primary and defeated Democrat James C. Dahlman by a popular vote of 123,070 to 107,760. Though renominated for a second term, Aldrich was defeated in 1912 by Democrat John H. Morehead by a popular vote of 123,997 to 114,075. During Aldrich's single term as governor, he was often at odds with the legislature, which was controlled by the Democrats. His veto of a telephone merger bill passed by the legislature prevented for several years the Bell Telephone Company and other interests from establishing territorial divisions to regulate telephone service in Nebraska. Enacted during his administration were an initiative and referendum measure and a Commission Plan of Government Bill for towns having over 5,000 residents. Recognizing the rising importance of the automobile, Aldrich recommended, in his outgoing message to the legislature, the improvement of Nebraska's system of roads. After the expiration of his term as governor, Aldrich practiced law in Lincoln. Elected

Associate Justice, Nebraska Supreme Court, 1918. Chester H. Aldrich died on March 10, 1924 in Superior, after a prolonged illness that had prevented his service on the Nebraska Supreme Court since June of 1923. Burial in Evergreen Cemetery, Superior. Bibliography: *Messages and Proclamations of the Governors of Nebraska*, Works Project Administration Official Project No. 165-1-81-317 (Lincoln, 1942); *Nebraska Statistical Handbook 1974-1975* (Lincoln, 1975); Albert Watkins, *History of Nebraska* (Lincoln, 1913); "Out of Old Nebraska," Nebraska State Historical Society newspaper release, November 12, 1950; Theron E. Sedgwick, *York County Nebraska and Its People* (Chicago, 1921); Obituaries: *Superior Express* (March, 13, 1924), *Lincoln Star* (March 11, 1924). Papers of Aldrich on deposit at the Nebraska State Historical Archives, Lincoln.

MOREHEAD, John Henry, 1913-1917

Born on December 3, 1861 in Columbia, Iowa, son of Andrew, a farmer, and Frances Amelia (Cooper) Morehead. Of Scottish-Presbyterian background, Andrew joined a Christian Union group in Iowa. Brother of Charles, Ludlow Halstead, William, Mary Morehead Duckworth, Lavina Morehead Smith, and Elizabeth Morehead Dorrell. Married to Minnie Weisenreder on February 17, 1886; father of Dorothy Lee and Edwin J. Attended local district schools; a private school in Knoxville, Iowa, until seventeen years of age; and then Shenandoah Business College. Following his arrival in Nemaha County, Nebraska in the early 1880s, he taught school and worked as a farm hand for several years, before opening a general merchandise store at Barada in adjoining Richardson County. As the business prospered, Morehead invested in farm land and livestock, and entered banking at Barada and nearby Falls City. Elected Richardson County Treasurer on the Democratic ticket, 1895; reelected 1897. Single term Mayor of Falls City. Delegate to 1908 Democratic National Convention. Elected in 1910 to Nebraska Senate. Following the death of Lieutenant Governor M. R. Hopewell in May 1911, Morehead, as Presidnt Pro Tempore of the Senate, became the Lieutenant Governor. In 1912 he was nominated for Governor in the Democratic primary and defeated Republican Chester H. Aldrich by a popular vote of 123,997 to 114,075. Reelected in 1914, defeating Republican R. Beecher Howell by a popular vote of 120,206 to 101,229. He did not seek a third term. During his two terms as governor, He was known as a fiscal conservative, and reduced the state's indebtedness. He appointed members of the first Board of Control, which was to govern state institutions. Enacted during his administration were a Workmen's Compensation Law and in 1915 the first Budget Law, which made the governor chief budget officer. Morehead was also interested in state banking laws and in improvement of Nebraska's roads. After leaving the governor's office in 1917, Morehead continued to participate actively in politics. In 1918, as a Democratic nominee for the U.S. Senate, he campaigned unsuccessfully against Republican Senator George W. Norris. Defeated in the 1920 gubernatorial race by Republican Samuel R. McKelvie by a popular vote of 152,863 to 130,433. U.S. Representative, First Congressional District, 1923-35. After retiring from the House, he returned to farming, stock raising, banking, and the real estate business. Chairman, Nebraska delegation to 1940 Democratic National Convention. John H. Morehead died on May 30, 1942 in St. Joseph, Missouri; buried at Steele Cemetery, Falls City. Bibliography: *Messages and Proclamations of the Governors of Nebraska*, Works Progress Administration Official Project No. 165-1-81-317 (Lincoln, 1942); Lewis C.

Edwards, *History of Richardson County, Nebraska* (Indianapolis, 1917); Obituaries: *Falls City Journal* (June 1, and June 4, 1942); Theron E. Sedgwich, *York County, Nebraska and Its People* (Chicago, 1921); *Nebraska Statistical Handbook, 1974-1975* (Lincoln, 1975); "Out of Old Nebraska," Nebraska State Historical Society newspaper release, December 3, 1950. Papers of Morehead on deposit at the Nebraska State Historical Society Archives, Lincoln.

NEVILLE, M. Keith, 1917-1919

Born on February 25, 1884 in North Platte, Nebraska, son of William, a lawyer, and Mollie Ann (Kieth) Neville, an Episcopalian. Half-brother of Irene Thecla Neville Reynolds, daughter of William Neville's second wife, Irene Morrison Rector Neville. Married to Mary Virginia Neill on October 21, 1908; father of Frances Neville Newberry, Mary Neville Sieman, Irene Neville Bystrom, and Virginia Neville Robertson. Graduated from St. John's Academy, 1901, and from St. John's College, 1905, both in Annapolis, Maryland. In 1906 Neville became manager of the family ranch near North Platte, and in 1910 he was named a director of the First National Bank at North Platte; he later became president of the institution in 1931, and chairman of the board in 1951. Though young and without political experience, Neville in 1916 defeated Charles W. Bryan in a bid for the Democratic gubernatorial nomination. In the general election, he defeated Republican Abraham L. Sutton by a popular vote of 143,564 to 136,811. Defeated for reelection in 1918 by Republican Samuel R. McKelvie by a popular vote of 120,888 to 97,886. The first major problem of Neville's administration was the implementation of a 1916 prohibition amendment to the state constitution. Following America's entry into World War I in 1917, Neville was commissioned as Colonel, 7th Nebraska Infantry, but was never called into service. The governor's program to promote the war effort in Nebraska, including measures on sabotage, sedition, and the teaching of foreign languages in the public schools, was a factor in the failure of his 1918 bid for reelection. After retiring from the governorship in 1919, Neville returned to North Platte to manage his banking, ranching, and real estate interests. Active in local civic and political affairs, Neville served on the North Platte school board and city council, and on the Platte Valley Public Power and Irrigation District board of directors, 1933-39. He also continued to play an important role in the state Democratic Party. He was elected Democratic State Central Committee chairman, 1922, and Democratic National Committeeman in 1934. He was the National Recovery Act director in Nebraska in 1933. A bid for the 1940 Democratic gubernatorial nomination failed, as did a 1954 try for the U.S. Senate against Republican Carl T. Curtis. M. Keith Neville died on December 4, 1959 in North Platte, and was buried in the North Platte Cemetery. Bibliography: *Messages and Proclamations of the Governors of Nebraska*, Works Progress Administration Official Project No. 165-1-81-317 (Lincoln, 1942); Ira L. Bare and Will H. McDonald, ed., *An Illustrated History of Lincoln County, Nebraska, and Her People* (Chicago and New York, 1920); *Keith Neville at Home* (North Platte, n.d.), campaign brochure on file at Nebraska State Historical Society Archives, Lincoln; Obituaries: *Lincoln Star* (December 5, 1959), *North Platte Telegraph-Bulletin* (December 4, 1959); *Nebraska Statistical Handbook 1974-1975* (Lincoln, 1975). The Neville Papers are in the possession of Mrs. Keith Neville and Mrs. Irene Neville Bystrom, North Platte, Nebraska.

McKELVIE, Samuel Roy, 1919-1923

Born on April 15, 1881 near Fairfield, Nebraska, son of Samuel, a farmer and stock breeder, and Jennie (Glandon) McKelvie; a Methodist. Brother of Homer L., Otis Albert, Othello, Jennie Maude McKelvie Schleuter, Hiram Claude, Pearl G., Florence T. McKelvie Brown, and Floyd. Married to Flossie (Martha) Groves DeArnold on June 19, 1904; father of Dorothy and Josephine McKelvie Berks (an adopted daughter?). Attended University of Nebraska, Lincoln, 1899-1900, and graduated from Lincoln Business College in 1901. Advertising solicitor for the *Twentieth Century Farmer* of Omaha, 1902-05; became editor of the *Nebraska Farmer*, Lincoln, in 1905, and its principal owner and publisher in 1908. His political career began with a term on the Lincoln City Council, 1908-09. Elected to Nebraska House of Representatives, 1910. Elected Lieutenant Governor on the Republican ticket in 1912. Nominated for the governorship in 1918, McKelvie defeated Democrat M. Keith Neville by a popular vote of 120,888 to 97,886. Reelected in 1920, defeating Democrat John H. Morehead by a popular vote of 152,863 to 130,433. He did not seek a third term. McKelvie's two terms as governor were marked by many important changes in Nebraska government. The state administrative system was reorganized by the adoption of the Civil Administrative Code, the state accounting system revised, and the first executive budget introduced. Highway improvement programs were organized, and a system of state parks established. A constitutional convention was held, 1919-20, and forty-one amendments to the state constitution were adopted. Also the current Nebraska capitol building was authorized and construction begun. Following his retirement from the governor's office, McKelvie returned to publishing the *Nebraska Farmer*. He declined appointment as Secretary of Agriculture under President Herbert Hoover, but did serve on the Federal Farm Board, 1929-31. Delegate to Republican National Conventions of 1928, 1932, and 1936. Owner of the "By The Way Ranch" near Valentine, he engaged in stock raising and promoted the Nebraska cattle industry. Samuel R. McKelvie died on January 6, 1956 at his winter home near Mesa, Arizona. Burial at Wyuka Cemetery, Lincoln. Bibliography: *Messages and Proclamations of the Governors of Nebraska*, Works Progress Administration Official Project No. 165-1-81-317 (Lincoln, 1942); Bruce H. Nicoll and Ken R. Keller, *Sam McKelvie, Son of the Soil* (Lincoln, 1954); *Samuel McKelvie Honor Dinner*, Block and Bridle Club (Lincoln, 1938); *Nebraska Statistical Handbook 1974-1975* (Lincoln, 1975); "Obituary," *Lincoln Star* (January 7, 1956); "Out of Old Nebraska," Nebraska State Historical Society newspaper release, February 18, 1951. Papers of McKelvie on deposit at the Nebraska State Historical Archives, Lincoln.

BRYAN, Charles Wayland, 1923-1925, 1931-1935

Born on February 10, 1867 in Salem, Illinois, son of Silas Lillard, a farmer, lawyer, circuit judge, and a Baptist; and of Mariah Elizabeth (Jennings) Bryan, Methodist and later Baptist. Brother of Virginia Ann, John Henshen, Hiram Lillard, William Jennings, Russell Jones, Frances Maria Bryan Millson (later Baird), Nancy Lillard, and Mary Elizabeth Bryan Allen. Married to Mary Louise Brokaw on November 29, 1891; father of Silas Millard, Virginia, and Mary Louise Bryan Harnsberger. Attended University of Chicago and Illinois College, Jacksonville. Farmer until his 1891 move to Lincoln, Nebraska. After jobs in Lincoln and Omaha, including those of insurance salesman and tobacco broker, Bryan in 1897 became political secretary and business manager for his brother, William Jennings Bryan; publisher and associate editor of *The Commoner*, 1901-23. Member of governor's staff with the rank of Colonel, 1897-1902. Elected to Lincoln City Commission, 1915, 1921; Mayor of Lincoln, 1915-17, 1935-37. Defeated for the gubernatorial nomination in the Democratic primaries of 1916 and 1918. In 1922 Bryan defeated Republican Charles H. Randall by a popular vote of 214,070 to 163,735. Renominated for a second term, Bryan withdrew to accept the 1924 Democratic vice-presidential nomination; he and presidential nominee John W. Davis were defeated by Republicans Calvin Coolidge and Charles G. Dawes. Defeated in the 1926 gubernatorial race by Republican Adam McMullen by a popular vote of 201,120 to 202,688, and in 1928 by Republican Arthur J. Weaver, 308,262 to 230,640. In 1930 Bryan gained the Nebraska governorship for a second time, defeating Weaver by a popular vote of 222,161 to 215,615. In 1932, Bryan defeated Dwight Griswold, 296,117 to 260,888. Bryan in all served three terms as governor, 1923-25, 1931-33, and 1933-35. He was a strong advocate of economy in government, and in his first term he reduced state taxes and expenditures. During his second term a deadlock developed between Bryan and the legislature over state appropriations; the legislature adjourned, and a special session had to be called by Governor Bryan in June of 1931 to resolve the issue. Following his retirement from the governorship in 1935, Bryan remained active in politics. A 1934 bid for the Democratic nomination for the U.S. Senate failed. In 1938 Bryan, as an independent candidate for Governor, received 76,258 votes, trailing Democrat Robert L. Cochran (218,787) and Republican Charles J. Warner (201,898). A 1940 race for the U.S. House of Representatives also failed. In 1942 Bryan made his ninth and last try for the governorship, and was defeated by Republican Dwight Griswold, 283,271 to 95,231. Charles W. Bryan died on March 4, 1945 in Lincoln, and was buried in Wyuka Cemetery. Bibliography: *Messages and Proclamations of the Governors of Nebraska*, Works Progress Administration Official Project No. 165-1-81-317 (Lincoln, 1942); Paolo E. Coletta, "The Youth of William Jennings Bryan—Beginnings of a Christian Statesman," *Nebraska History*, vol. XXXI, no. 1 (March, 1950); Phyllis H. Winkelman, "Notes on the Bryan Family" (1963), unpublished manuscript on file, Nebraska State Historical Society Library, Lincoln; "Obituary," *Lincoln Star* (March 5, 1945); *Nebraska Statistical Handbook 1974-1975* (Lincoln, 1975); Paolo E. Coletta, "Silas Bryan of Salem," *Journal of the Illinois State Historical Society*, vol. XLII, no. 1 (March, 1949); Harry R. Swanson, *Official Report of the Nebraska State Canvassing Board* (Lincoln, 1938). Papers of Bryan on deposit at the Nebraska State Historical Society Archives, Lincoln.

McMULLEN, Adam, 1925-1929

Born on June 12, 1872 in Wellsville, New York, son of John H., railroad engineer, machinist, and later grocer, and Mary (Harbison) McMullen; Episcopalian. Brothers: Alexander, James J., Paul, John F.P., Moses P., Matthew; sisters: Mary E., Jane, Marge (Marget). Married to Cordelia Greenwood on June 5, 1901. Accompanied his family from New York to Wymore, Nebraska in 1883. Graduated from the University of Nebraska, Lincoln in 1896, and from George Washington University, Washington, D.C. in 1899. While in Washington, he served as secretary to Nebraska Congressman Jesse B. Strode and later to Senator Charles H. Dietrich. Upon his return to Nebraska in

1902, McMullen was admitted to the state bar and established a law practice in Wymore. His political career began in 1904, when he was elected to the Nebraska House of Representatives; reelected in 1906. Mayor of Wymore; member of Wymore school board, 1916-20; and was elected to the Nebraska Senate in 1916. In 1920 he unsuccessfully contested the renomination of Governor Samuel R. McKelvie in the Republican primary. In 1924, however, he was nominated and elected Governor, defeating Democrat John N. Norton by a popular vote of 229,067 to 183,709. Reelected in 1926, defeating Democrat Charles W. Bryan, 206,120 to 202,688. He did not seek a third term. Governor McMullen's two terms were characterized by his active promotion of an adequate state highway system, and by improvements in agriculture and irrigation. He advocated sound economy in government, and during his second term the floating state debt was eliminated by levying a special tax. McMullen was the first governor to occupy offices in the present state capitol building. In 1928 he led a delegation of Midwest governors to the Republican National Convention to demand a strong farm program to aid the depressed agricultural economy. After leaving the governorship in 1929, McMullen returned to Beatrice, where he had established himself after leaving Wymore about 1920, to manage his Gage County farm properties and Oklahoma oil interests. Beatrice Postmaster, 1932; delegate, Republican National Convention in 1932. Unsuccessful candidate for Republican nomination to U.S. Senate, 1940. He split with the Republicans in 1956 over farm policy, and campaigned against Dwight D. Eisenhower's farm program in 1956 and 1958. Adam McMullen died on March 2, 1959 in Beatrice and was buried in Wymore. Bibliography: *Messages and Proclamations of the Governors of Nebraska*, Works Progress Administration Official Project No. 165-1-81-317 (Lincoln, 1942); "Obituary: John H. McMullen," *Beatrice Daily Sun* (September 12, 1923); "Obituary: Mary (Harbison) McMullen." *Beatrice Daily Express* (October 4, 1909); "Obituary: Adam McMullen," *Lincoln Star* (March 3, 1959); *Nebraska Statistical Handbook 1974-1975* (Lincoln, 1975); "Out of Old Nebraska," Nebraska State Historical Society newspaper release, April 22, 1951; *Nebraska State Census Records, 1885*. Papers of McMullen on deposit at the Nebraska State Historical Society Archives, Lincoln.

WEAVER, Arthur J. 1929-1931

Born on November 18, 1873 near Falls City, Nebraska, son of Archibald Jerrard Weaver, lawyer, district judge, and U.S. Congressman, and Martha A. (Meyers) Weaver; a Methodist. Brother of Archibald J., Harriet Blanche, Ruth M. Weaver Dennis, Lawrence M., and Paul B. Married in 1897 to Persa Morris, who died in January, 1906; remarried to Maude E. Hart on September 2, 1908; father of Maude Harriet Weaver Hutchins, Dorothy Jane Weaver Morgan, Arthur J., Jr., Ruth Jean Weaver Young, Phillip Hart, and Josephine Miranda Weaver Gates. Graduated from Wyoming Seminary, Kingston, Pennsylvania in 1892; from the University of Nebraska, Lincoln in 1895; and from the University of Nebraska College of Law in 1896. Established a law practice in Falls City and entered politics. Elected to Nebraska House of Representatives in 1898; City Attorney for Falls City, 1899-1901; Richardson County Attorney, 1901-03; member, City Council of Falls City, 1910-16; and elected Falls City Mayor, 1915. President, Nebraska Constitutional Convention of 1919-20, chairman, Nebraska Electoral College, 1920, and of Republican State Convention, 1924. In 1925 Weaver was widely supported for the position of U.S. Secretary of Agriculture but did not receive the post. While pursuing an active political career, Weaver also engaged in farming, stock raising, fruit growing, and banking; he also promoted the development of inland waterways and the agricultural, recreational, and historical resources of Nebraska. In 1928 Weaver ran for Governor on the Republican ticket, defeating Democrat Charles W. Bryan by a popular vote of 308,262 to 230,640. Defeated in a 1930 bid for reelection by Bryan, 222,161 to 215,615. During Weaver's single term as governor, he instituted the current practice of submitting the biennial state budget in two parts: one for the appropriation of revenue from general taxation, and for the appropriation of revenue received from federal grants, gasoline taxes, and miscellaneous fees. A major problem during his administration was the inability of the state bank guarantee system to cover losses to depositors after the failure of many state banks in 1929; a special session of the legislature in 1930 ended the system. Following his retirement from the governorship in 1931, Weaver returned to Falls City. He was the Chairman of the Nebraska delegation to the Republican National Convention, 1932, and president of the Nebraska State Historical Society from 1939 to 1941. He was defeated by Hugh Butler in a 1940 attempt for the Republican nomination for U.S. Senator. Arthur J. Weaver died on October 17, 1945 in Falls City and was buried in Steele Cemetery. Bibliography: *Messages and Proclamations of the Governors of Nebraska*, Works Progress Administration Official Project No. 165-1-81-317 (Lincoln, 1942); Lewis C. Edwards, *History of Richardson County, Nebraska* (Indianapolis, 1917); "Six Children See Mrs. Weaver Proclaimed Nebraska Mother," *Lincoln Star* (May 2, 1952); *Nebraska Statistical Handbook, 1974-1975* (Lincoln, 1975); "Obituary: Arthur J. Weaver," *Falls City Journal* (October 18, 1945); "Obituary: Archibald J. Weaver," *Falls City Journal* (April 21, 1887). Papers of Weaver on deposit at the Nebraska State Historical Society Archives, Lincoln.

BRYAN, Charles Wayland, 1923-1925, 1931-1935

COCHRAN, Robert LeRoy, 1935-1941

Born on January 28, 1886 near Avoca, Nebraska, son of Charles Austin, farmer, and Jane Wilkinson Cochran; an Episcopalian. Brother of Cyrus and Mabel Cochran Norris. Married to Aileen Gantt on March 18, 1919; father of Mary Aileen Cochran Grimes and Robert LeRoy, Jr. Graduated from Brady High School, 1906, and in 1910 from the University of Nebraska with a degree in civil engineering. The young Cochran practiced his skills with the Lincoln County Surveyor in 1910, and worked as surveyor, Atchison, Topeka, and Santa Fe Railroad in 1911. Elected Lincoln County Surveyor in 1911. Appointed State Bridge Inspector in 1915, and Deputy State Engineer in 1917. With America's entry into World War I, Cochran enlisted during August of 1917 in the U.S. Army and served as First Lieutenant, and later Captain, of Artillery; he was discharged in 1919. District Engineer, Nebraska Department of Public Works, 1919-22, State Engineer, 1923-34. In 1934 Cochran was nominated and elected Governor on the Democratic ticket, defeating Republican Dwight P. Griswold by a popular vote of 284,095 to 266,707. Reelected in 1936, defeating Griswold by a popular vote of 333,412 to 257,267. Reelected in 1938 for an unprecedented third consecutive term, defeating Republican Charles J. Warner 218,787 to 201,898. Cochran was the first governor to work with a unicameral legislature elected on a non-partisan basis, and with the newly-established legislative council. His "pay as you go" approach to state government had discouraged deficit spending and bonded indebtedness. In compliance with federal acts, his administration did enact a state social security plan in 1935, and unemployment insurance in 1937. Chairman, Conference of State Governors, and president, Council of State Governments, 1937-39. A 1940 try for the U.S. Senate on the Democratic ticket failed, when he was defeated by Republican Hugh Butler. After retiring from the governorship, Cochran served as commanding officer with the rank of Colonel at Camp Leonard Wood near Rolla, Missouri, 1941-42. Assistant commissioner, 1942-43, and commissioner, 1943-44, Federal Public Housing Authority; and liaison officer for the United Nations Relief and Rehabilitation Administration in North Africa and Europe, 1944-45. Employed by the Civil Works Division of the U.S. Bureau of the Budget, and later special assistant in the field of water resources, 1945-56. For seven months in 1947 Cochran served as deputy chief under Dwight Griswold of the American Mission for Aid to Greece. Following his retirement in 1956, he did consulting engineering work; served briefly as state engineer, 1959. Robert L. Cochran died on February 23, 1963, in Lincoln and was buried in Lincoln Memorial Park. Bibliography: *Messages and Proclamations of the Governors of Nebraska*, Works Progress Administration Official Project No. 165-1-81-317 (Lincoln, 1942); "Obituary: Charles A. Cochran," *Brady Vindicator* (December 10, 1914); "Obituary," *Lincoln Star* (February 24, 1963); *Nebraska Statistical Handbook, 1974-1975* (Lincoln, 1975); James F. Pedersen and Kenneth D. Wald, *Shall the People Rule* (Lincoln, 1972); "Former Governor Cochran Retires Next Month," *Lincoln Star* (December 25, 1955); Ted Landale, "Busy Roy Cochran," *Sunday World Herald of the Midlands* (February 8, 1959). Papers of Cochran on deposit at the Nebraska State Historical Society Archives, Lincoln.

GRISWOLD, Dwight Palmer, 1941-1947

Born on November 27, 1893 in Harrison, Nebraska, son of Dwight Hubbard, merchant and banker, and Clarissa (Palmer) Griswold; a Presbyterian. Brother of Vera Ellen and Florence Clarissa Griswold Barker. Married to Erma Elliott on September 25, 1919; father of Dwight Elliott and Dorothy Helen Griswold Gayer. Graduated from Kearney Military Academy, 1910. Attended Nebraska Wesleyan University, Lincoln, 1910-12, and was graduated from the University of Nebraska, Lincoln in 1914. Clerk, First National Bank of Gordon, for several years following graduation. Sergeant, 4th Nebraska Infantry in the Mexican border conflict, 1916-17. First Lieutenant, and later Captain, 127th Field Artillery, U.S. Army, 1917-18. After the war, Griswold returned to the First National Bank of Gordon as assistant cashier, cashier, and later director. Editor and co-owner, *Gordon Journal*, 1922-40. Elected to the Nebraska House of Representatives in 1920 but defeated for reelection in 1922. Elected to the Nebraska Senate, 1924, 1926, 1928. Resigned, 1929, to become state commander of the American Legion. In 1932 Griswold ran for Governor on the Republican ticket and was defeated by Democrat Charles W. Bryan by a popular vote of 296,117 to 260,888. In a second try for the governorship in 1934, Griswold was defeated by Democrat Robert L. Cochran, 284,095 votes to 266,707. Defeated in the 1936 gubernatorial race by Cochran, 333,412 to 257,267. In 1940, in his fourth attempt for the governorship, Griswold defeated Democrat Terry Carpenter, 365,638 votes to 235,167. Reelected in 1942, defeating

Democrat Charles W. Bryan, 283,271 to 95,231; and in 1944, defeated Democrat George W. Olsen, 410,136 to 128,760. A 1946 bid for the U.S. Senate failed when Griswold was defeated in the Republican primary by incumbent Hugh Butler. During his three terms as governor, Griswold was largely occupied with Nebraska's participation in the national war effort and in postwar reconstruction. However, his administration did see the enactment of some progressive measures: the legal interest rate in Nebraska was reduced from 19 to 13 percent; the maximum old age assistance allowance was raised; the state Workmen's Compensation Law was broadened to include occupational diseases; and a merit system for hiring state employees was instituted. Following his service as governor, Griswold in 1947 was appointed Director, Internal Affairs and Communications Division, Military Government of Germany, and later Chief of the American Mission for Aid to Greece, 1947-48. Following his service in Greece, Griswold resumed his banking career and settled in Scottsbluff, Nebraska. He was a member of Nebraska Board of Regents from 1951 to 1952. With the death of U.S. Senator Kenneth S. Wherry in 1951, Griswold entered the race for the unexpired term and won the 1952 election. Dwight P. Griswold died on April 12, 1954 in Bethesda, Maryland, while serving as a U.S. Senator. Buried in Fairview Cemetery, Scottsbluff. Bibliography: *Messages and Proclamations of the Governors of Nebraska* Works Progress Administration Official Project No. 165-1-81-317 (Lincoln, 1942); Ruth Van Ackeren, ed., *Sioux County, Memoirs of Its Pioneers* (Harrison, 1967); Ted Landale, "He Doesn't Believe in Pushing People Around," *Omaha Sunday World Herald Magazine* (February 22, 1953); *Nebraska Statistical Handbook 1974-1975* (Lincoln, 1975); *Dwight Palmer Griswold, Late a Senator from Nebraska. Memorial Addresses Delivered in Congress* (Washington, D.C. 1954); "Obituary," *Lincoln Star* (April 13, 1954). Papers of Griswold on deposit at the Nebraska State Historical Society Archives, Lincoln.

PETERSON, Frederick Demar Erastus, 1947-1953

Born on July 18, 1903 in Oakland, Nebraska, son of Henry Christian, railroad station agent, and Hermanda (Swanberg) Peterson, both of whom were Lutherans. Brother of Norma Dagmar Peterson Rubrecht Kern, Thelma Linea Peterson Launt, Carl Thorvald, Paul Bjorn, Frederick Norden, and Evar Pershing. Married to Elizabeth Howells Pleak on June 6, 1929. His degrees include an A.B., Wayne State College, Wayne, 1927, and an A.M. from the University of Nebraska, Lincoln, 1931. Teacher, Carroll, 1925-26; Madison, 1927-29 and Kimball, 1929-30. Graduate student and instructor at the University of Nebraska, 1931-33. Superintendent of Schools, Elgin, 1933-39; and publisher of the *Elgin Review*, 1936-46. Manager of Republican Hugh Butler's successful campaign for the U.S. Senate in 1940. Secretary and administrative assistant to Nebraska Governor Dwight Griswold, 1941-42. Peterson entered the Army Air Corps in May, 1942, and had attained the rank of Lieutenant Colonel when he was discharged in 1946. Elected Governor on the Republican ticket in 1946, defeating Democrat Frank Sorrell by a popular vote of 249,468 to 131,367; reelected in 1948, defeating Sorrell, 286,119 votes to 190,214. Elected for a third term in 1950, defeating Democrat Walter R. Raecke, 247,081 to 202,638; he did not seek a fourth term until 1966. During Peterson's three terms as governor, Nebraska suffered a series of natural disasters, including the historic blizzard of 1949. His sponsorship of the ten year 1.1 mill institutional building levy improved facilities at state institutions. Highway revenue measures advocated by

Peterson were enacted into law, but later defeated by referendum. During his term of office, the governor supported the Missouri River basin development; chairman, Conference of State Governors; and president, Council of State Governments, 1952. He was an unsuccessful contender against incumbent Hugh Butler for the 1952 Republican senatorial nomination. Following his retirement from the governorship in 1953, Peterson served as: administrative assistant to President Dwight Eisenhower; Federal Civil Defense Administrator, 1953-57; and U.S. Ambassador to Denmark, 1957-60. After his return from Denmark, Peterson settled in Hastings, Nebraska and served with the N.M. McDonald Company; he later entered banking at Hastings and Wayne. He was on the University of Nebraska Board of Regents, 1963-66. In a 1966 bid for a fourth term as governor, Peterson was defeated in the Republican primary by Norbert Tiemann. He was the U.S. Ambassador to Finland, 1969-73. In Finland, he served as American host to the U.S.—Soviet Strategic Arms Limitations Talks (SALT). Following his return from Finland, Peterson settled in Wayne, Nebraska, and served as resource coordinator for Nebraska Congressman Charles Thone, 1973-74. Peterson is presently Distinguished Professor of Political Science and Political Affairs, Wayne State College. Bibliography: "Val Peterson File," Republican State Headquarters, Lincoln; "Peterson to Return to Politics, Writing," *Lincoln Evening Journal* (April 26, 1973); *Nebraska Statistical Handbook, 1974-1975* (Lincoln,1975);"From the Capitol: Peterson, Soon to be an Ex-governor, Reminisces," *Lincoln Sunday Journal and Star* (January 4, 1953); "Peterson Files for Governor," *Lincoln Evening Journal* (January 26, 1966); "Star Profile: Gov. Val Peterson," *Lincoln Star* (March 29, 1952); " 'Country Boy' Val Peterson Comes Home to Academic Atmosphere," *Omaha World Herald* (September 30, 1973). Family records in possession of Val Peterson, Wayne.

CROSBY, Robert Berkey, 1953-1955

Born on March 26, 1911 in North Platte, Nebraska, son of Mainard E., a lawyer, and Cora May (Berkey) Crosby, both of whom were Presbyterians. Brother of Horace E., and Lucy Anne Crosby Kline. Married to Elizabeth Daisy Ehler on November 29, 1934; father of Robert Mainard and Susan Mary Crosby Smith. Following the death of his first wife in January of 1971, Crosby married for a second time to La Von Kehoe Stuart on May 22, 1971. After graduation from North Platte High School, Crosby attended Hastings College, Hastings, 1927-29; he was graduated from the University of Minnesota, 1931. Received his LL.B. from Harvard University Law School in 1935; practiced law in North Platte for several months, 1935; and in Omaha, 1935-37. Entered his father's law firm in North Platte, 1937. Elected to the Nebraska Unicameral, 1940; and reelected, 1942. Chosen Speaker of the Unicameral, 1943. Lieutenant, U.S. Navy, 1944-46. While still in the Navy, Crosby filed for the office of Lieutenant Governor, whereupon he secured the Republican nomination and was elected. He recommended to the 1947 session of the Unicameral that the office be abolished and refused to become a candidate again in 1948. Returned to private law practice and served as assistant state chairman of the Republican Party until 1950, when he acted as campaign manager for the Republican gubernatorial nominee, Val Peterson. In 1952 Crosby was nominated and elected Governor on the Republican ticket, defeating Democrat Walter R. Raecke by a popular vote of 366,009 to 229,700. He did not seek a second term. After Crosby took office in January of 1953, the Nebraska Supreme Court handed down a decision mandating equalization of tax assessments. The governor's subsequent efforts on behalf of tax equalization culminated in "Operation Honesty," a controversial public campaign to reduce fraudulent state personal property tax reports. During his single term Crosby encouraged location of new industry in Nebraska; he was the first Nebraska governor to appoint three U.S. Senators to complete unexpired terms. Crosby was defeated in a 1954 bid for the Republican senatorial nomination by Carl T. Curtis. After he left the governorship in 1955, Crosby returned to private law practice in Lincoln. He has served as a lobbyist in the Nebraska Unicameral. Active in Republican politics, he has served as a member of the platform committee in the National Republican Conventions of 1956, 1960, and 1964. Bibliography: Ted Landale, "Gov.-Elect Crosby," *Omaha Sunday World Herald Magazine* (January 4, 1953); "Mrs. Stuart Weds E.-Gov. Crosby in Cathedral Rite," *Omaha Sunday World Herald* (May 23, 1971); *Nebraska Statistical Handbook, 1974-1975* (Lincoln, 1975); "M.E. Crosbys, Parents of Former Nebraska Governor, Wed 50 Years," *Lincoln Sunday Journal and Star* (September 6, 1959); "I Led With My Chin—Crosby," *Lincoln Sunday Journal and Star* (January 2, 1955). Papers of Crosby on file at the Nebraska State Historical Society Archives, Lincoln.

ANDERSON, Victor Emanuel, 1955-1959

Born on March 30, 1902 in Havelock, (now part of Lincoln), Nebraska, son of Ernest Emanuel, machinist and hardware merchant, and Maria Sophia (Larson) Anderson, both of whom were Lutherans. Brother of Elsa Margaret Anderson Sallee and Eva Victoria Anderson Allan. Married to Elizabeth May on December 27, 1941 and father of Roger Lee. Following graduation from Havelock High School in 1920, Anderson attended the University of Nebraska until 1924, when he left school to become a partner in his father's plumbing and hardware business in Havelock. Anderson's political career began in 1936, with his appointment as trustee of Lancaster County Sanitary District No. 1. He formed the Victor E. Anderson Bottle Gas and Propane Company, 1946; and entered banking in Havelock. Elected to the Nebraska Unicameral, 1948; resigned in 1950 to accept the appointment of Mayor of Lincoln to complete the unexpired term of his predecessor. Elected for a complete term as mayor, 1952. With a reputation as an efficient business and government administrator, Anderson in 1952 sought the Republican nomination for Governor, but was defeated by Robert Crosby. Anderson did secure the nomination in 1954 and subsequently defeated Democrat William F. Ritchie by a popular vote of 250,080 to 164,753; reelected in 1956, defeating Democrat Frank Sorrell, 308,293 to 228,048. In 1958 Anderson was defeated in his bid for a third term by Democrat Ralph G. Brooks, 211,345 to 209,705. During his two terms as governor, Anderson became known for his "hard tack" budget policy. He sought to keep taxes and spending in check, issues which he emphasized in his campaigns. At the same time, he greatly improved mental health care in the state. His firm handling of an inmates' revolt at the Nebraska Penitentiary in March, 1955 attracted national attention. Following his retirement from the governorship in 1959, Anderson was named by President Dwight Eisenhower as a U.S. delegate to the NATO-sponsored Atlantic Congress in London. A director of the Standard Reliance Insurance Company, Anderson in 1961 was one of the founders of Life Investors of Nebraska, an all-Nebraska corporation which included a life insurance company and a locally-owned investment firm. He was on the Board of Trustees of Nebraska Wesleyan University, 1955-61. At the time of his death, he was planning a two-month trip around the world for briefings at each of the nation's command posts as a member of the Defense Orientation Conference Association, to which he had been appointed by Air Force Chief of Staff Curtis LeMay. Victor E. Anderson died on August 15, 1962 in Lincoln, and was buried in Wyuka Cemetery. Bibliography: O.M. Nelson, *Swedes in Lincoln and Vicinity* (1936); Ted Landale, "Businessman Governor," *Omaha Sunday World Herald Magazine* (January 9, 1955); *Nebraska Statistical Handbook, 1974-1975* (Lincoln, 1975); "Anderson Devoted Lifetime to State," *Lincoln Star* (August 16, 1962); "Anderson's Investment Was Himself," *Lincoln Star* (October 24, 1971); "Obituary," *Lincoln Star* (August 16, 1962). Papers of Anderson on deposit at the Nebraska State Historical Society, Lincoln.

BROOKS, Ralph Gilmour, 1959-1960

Born on July 6, 1898 in Eustis, Nebraska, son of Adam Hansford, merchant and farmer, and Tina S. Olson Brooks, both of whom were Methodists. Brother of William H. and Raymond P. Married in 1924 to Opal E. Gembler (they were divorced in 1930); father of LaVonne Marie Brooks Regehr; remarried on December 24, 1934 to Darlene L. Day. Following his graduation from Sargent High School in 1916, Brooks taught school in Cherry and Custer counties before entering Nebraska Wesleyan University, Lincoln in 1920. While attending college, he was for a time associate editor of *Nebraska Monthly Report* published by the State Department of Public Works. After interrupting his schooling with a year of teaching at Superior High School, 1923-24, Brooks graduated in 1925, and attended the University of Nebraska College of Law, 1925-26. Admitted to the Nebraska Bar in 1930. Received an M.A. in school administration, University of Nebraska in 1932. His teaching positions included: Cedar Rapids, 1926-29; Hartington, 1929-34; Wymore, 1934-45; and Audubon, Iowa, 1945-47. In 1947 Brooks settled in McCook, Nebraska where he served as Superintendent of Schools and president of McCook Junior College. Brooks' first venture into politics was an unsuccessful race as the Democratic candidate in 1942 for the U.S. House of Representatives from Nebraska's First District; he lost to Republican Carl T. Curtis. In 1958 Brooks was drafted to run for Governor, and subsequently defeated Republican Victor E. Anderson by a popular vote of 211,345 to 209,705. Brooks took office in 1959 on a slim margin of victory that resulted in the second gubernatorial recount in Nebraska history. As the first Democratic governor in eighteen years, he faced a hostile majority in the predominantly Republican Unicameral. A number of controversial issues soon emerged: the requested resignation or dismissal by the governor of several state officials; his personal epousal of an increase in the assessed value of railroad properties in Nebraska and his endorsement of a proposed state labor relations bill; interstate highway difficulties over routing and construction priorities; and Democratic intra-party struggles. During his administration Brooks promoted an intensive traffic safety program and aggressive industrial expansion in the state. He did not seek the Democratic gubernatorial nomination in 1960, but at the time of his death had entered the race for the U.S. Senate seat of incumbent Republican Carl T. Curtis. Lieutenant Governor Dwight W. Burney succeeded to the governorship after Brooks' death in office on September 9, 1960; Brooks was buried in Lincoln Memorial Park. Bibliography: "Obituary," *Lincoln Star* (September 10, 1960); "Obituary," *McCook Daily Gazette* (September 10, 1960); Ted Landale, "Ex-Highways Man in Governors' Seat," *Omaha Sunday World-Herald Magazine* (January 4, 1959); James F. Pedersen and Kenneth D. Wald, *Shall the People Rule* (Lincoln,

1972); *Nebraska Statistical Handbook* (Lincoln, 1975). Papers of Brooks on deposit at the Nebraska State Historical Society Archives, Lincoln.

BURNEY, Dwight Willard, 1960-1961

Born near Hartington, Nebraska on January 7, 1892, son of Willard H., a farmer, and Julia (Jones) Burney, who were Congregationalists. Brother of Blanche Burney Jones, Sadie Burney Parks, George, Quay, and Lenyce Burney Marsh. Married to Edna Wales on December 2, 1914; father of Donald Eugene, Willard Wales, Dwight W., Jr., and Howard Keith. Burney's first wife died in 1962; he was married for a second time to Grayce Stevens Hahn on January 1, 1965. He graduated from Hartington High School in 1910, and attended the University of South Dakota, Vermillion from 1910 to 1912. He was a school teacher in Turton, South Dakota from 1912 to 1914 and entered the farming and livestock business near Hartington in 1915. Active in local school affairs and 4-H Club work; elected in 1944 to the Nebraska Unicameral, and reelected in 1946, 1948, 1950, 1952, and 1954. While participating in six consecutive sessions of the Unicameral, Burney served as: chairman of the Legislative Education Committee in 1949; chairman of the Legislative Council in 1951; chairman of the Inter-Governmental Co-operative Committee in 1953; Speaker in 1955. He became known for his advocacy of a state sales tax and an improved road system. He was the Lieutenant Governor from 1957 to 1965. Burney succeeded to the governorship upon the death of Governor Ralph Brooks, September 9, 1960, and served until the inauguration of the state's next elected governor, Frank B. Morrison, on January 5, 1961. During his brief period as Acting Governor, Burney, with few exceptions, continued the programs of former Governor Ralph Brooks, and conducted state affairs in a conservative manner. The 1960 dismissal of the Nebraskan Aeronautics Department Director Jack Obbink was one of the governor's few controversial actions. A long-time proponent of a state sales tax, Burney continued his advocacy of a broadened tax base to lighten the property tax load. Following his retirement from the governorship in 1961, Burney continued as lieutenant governor until 1965. In 1964 he ran for Governor on the Republican ticket and was defeated by Democrat Frank B. Morrison, 347,026 to 231,029. Burney retired in 1965 and resides in Polk. Bibliography: Dwight W. Burney, *Nebraska's Farmer Governor* (1967); *Nebraska Statistical Handbook, 1974-1975* (Lincoln, 1975); "Burney's Career Marked by 17 Election Victories," *Lincoln Evening Journal* (September 10, 1960); "Dwight Burney, Chief of State," *Lincoln Star* (September 10, 1960); Grayce Stevens Burney and Mildred Stevens Anderson, *Polk Memoirs* (Polk, 1974). Papers of Burney on deposit at the Nebraska State Historical Society Archives, Lincoln.

MORRISON, Frank Brenner, 1961-1967

Born on May 20, 1905 in Golden, Colorado, son of Frank, an irrigation engineer, and Viva Brenner Morrison; a Methodist. Brother of Hope Morrison Hunter and Hazel Morrison Sparrow. Married to Maxine Elizabeth Hepp on June 28, 1936; father of Frank Brenner, Jr., David Jon, and Jean Marie Morrison Galloway. Received his B.S. from Kansas State University, Manhattan, Kansas, in 1927; school superintendent in Farwell, Nebraska from 1928 to 1929. Received his LL.B., from the University of Nebraska

College of Law in 1931; teacher at the Nebraska School of Agriculture in Curtis from 1931 to 1932. Lawyer in Maywood, and later in Stockville; settled in McCook in 1942. With prior experience as County Attorney in Frontier and Red Willow counties, Morrison ran for Congress unsuccessfully as a Democrat from Nebraska's First Congressional District in 1948, and again in 1954. Unsuccessful contender for Democratic gubernatorial nomination in 1950; defeated in 1956 by Republican Dwight W. Burney in a race for Lieutenant Governor. Leader in the "New Life" movement within the state Democratic Party and manager of the Nebraska presidential campaigns of Senator Estes Kefauver in 1952 and 1956. Morrison was defeated in his race for the U.S. Senate by Republican Roman Hruska in 1960. In 1960 Morrison sought and received the Democratic gubernatorial nomination, subsequently defeating Republican John R. Cooper, 311,344 to 287,302. Reelected in 1962, defeating Republican Fred A. Seaton, 242,669 votes to 221,885. Elected for a third term in 1964, defeating Republican Dwight W. Burney, 347,026 votes to 231,029. Defeated by incumbent Republican Carl T. Curtis in a try for the U.S. Senate in 1966. While Morrison shared the traditional low tax views of his Democratic predecessors in office, some innovations in state government were made during his administration: substitution of gubernatorially-responsive state departments for the Board of Control; revised procedures for handling executive budgeting and accounting; a state employees' retirement system; the first water resources study program; a state-wide educational television system; and enactment of a state income tax bill, which became law without the governor's signature. After he left the governor's office in 1967, Morrison practiced law in Omaha. Appointed AID (Agency for International Development) Food Consultant to India, 1968. He was defeated by Republican incumbent Roman Hruska in a 1970 race for the U.S. Senate; in 1971 he was appointed to the Nebraska Commission on Social and Judicial Reform. He was also appointed Douglas County Public Defender to complete an unexpired term in 1971, and was elected for a full term in 1972. A 1974 race for the Nebraska attorney general's office was unsuccessful. Morrison is currently practicing law, and maintains offices in Omaha and Whitefish, Montana. Bibliography: James Denney, "Governor-Elect's Aim: To Play It By Ear," *Sunday World Herald Magazine of the Midlands* (December 18, 1960); "Obituary: Mrs. Viva Brenner Morrison," *McCook Daily Gazette* (June 29, 1964); James F. Pedersen and Kenneth D. Wald, *Shall the People Rule* (Lincoln, 1972); "Morrison Picks Governor Race," *Lincoln Journal and Star* (October 24, 1954); *Nebraska Statistical Handbook, 1974-1975* (Lincoln, 1975); "Morrison Going to India as AID Food Consultant," *Lincoln Evening Journal* (April 24, 1968); "Morrison Aims at Defender Job," *Lincoln Star* (February 15, 1972); "Morrison Leads Study on Reform," *Lincoln Star* (December 18, 1971); "Morrison Runs for Attorney General," *Lincoln Evening Journal* (January 4, 1974). Papers of Morrison on file at the Nebraska State Historical Society Archives, Lincoln.

TIEMANN, Norbert Theodore, 1967-1971

Born on July 18, 1924 in Minden, Nebraska, son of Martin William, a Lutheran minister, and Alvina (Rathert) Tiemann. Brother of A.E. Tiemann and Lorna. Married to Lorna Lou Bornholdt on July 19, 1950; father of Mary Catherine, Norbert Theodore, Jr., Lorna Christine, and Amy Eileen. After his graduation from Campbell High School in 1942, Tiemann entered the University of Nebraska College of Agriculture in Lincoln. Summoned to active duty in 1943, Tiemann served with the U.S. Army in the Pacific and served in Korea with the occupation forces after Japan's surrender. Discharged, 1946, as a Staff Sergeant. Tiemann then resumed his education at the University of Nebraska and graduated in 1949. Assistant Dawes County agent, Lexington, 1949-50; assistant manager, Nebraska Hereford Association, Central City, 1950. Tiemann was recalled to active military duty as a Second Lieutenant, 1950, and served in occupied Germany until 1952. Executive secretary, National Livestock Feeders Association, Omaha, 1952; director of industry relations, National Livestock and Meat Board, Chicago, 1952-54. In 1954 Tiemann left Chicago to become cashier of the Commercial State Bank in Wausa, Nebraska; became bank president, 1957. As the business prospered, Tiemann turned his attention to politics; he served as: Mayor of Wausa, 1956-62; chairman, Knox County Republican Central Committee; member state Republican Budget and Finance Committee; president, Nebraska Bankers Association, 1964, 1965; chairman, Nebraska Heart Fund, 1964; and finance director for Republican gubernatorial candidate Dwight W. Burney in 1964. In 1966 Tiemann secured the Republican gubernatorial nomination and subsequently defeated Democrat Philip C. Sorensen, 299,245 votes to 186,985. In 1970, Tiemann was defeated in a bid for reelection by Democrat J. James Exon, 248,552 votes to 201,994. Tiemann was the first governor in Nebraska history to serve a four year, instead of a two year term. His administration was noted for a number of progressive measures: state sales and income taxes to replace the property tax levy; state aid to local school districts; introduction of daylight savings time; a modern state telecommunications system; and a new Department of Economic Development to lure industry to the state. Tiemann's aggressive support of a broadened tax base cost him some of his initial popularity, and was undoubtedly a factor in his defeat in the 1970 gubernatorial contest. After leaving the governorship in 1971, Tiemann became a vice-president of First Mid America, Inc., a Lincoln investment banking firm. In 1973 he was named Federal Highway Administrator. He is currently with the firm Henningson, Durham, and Richardson, and resides in McLean, Virginia. Bibliography: "Tiemann Stayed in Tomb to Survive Typhoon," *Omaha World Herald* (December 29, 1966); "Just Like Cinderella, This Grandmother is Going to the Ball," *Lincoln Sunday Journal and Star* (December 11, 1966); "Tiemann Comments:'If I Fail Then I Should Have Remained Banker'," *Omaha World Herald* (December 30, 1966); *Nebraska Statistical Handbook, 1974-1975* (Lincoln, 1975); James Denney, "1967 Midlands Man of the Year—Governor Tiemann," *Sunday World Herald Magazine of the Midlands* (December 31, 1967); James Denney, "Nobby Tiemann—Private Citizen," *Sunday World Herald Magazine of the Midlands* (April 25, 1971); "Tiemann Is Delighted To Be 'Road Builder'," *Omaha World Herald* (April 14, 1973); Personal Communication from Norbert Tiemann, May 31, 1977. Papers of Tiemann on deposit at the Nebraska State Historical Society Archives, Lincoln.

EXON, John James, 1971-

Born on August 9, 1921 in Geddes, South Dakota, son of John James, abstractor and businessman, and Luella Johns Exon; both Episcopalians. Brother of Virginia. Married to Patricia Ann Pros on September 18, 1943; father of Stephen James, Pamela Ann Exon Bricker, and Candace Lee. Following graduation from Lake Andres (South Dakota) High School in 1939, Exon entered the University of Omaha. In 1941 he left school to enter the U.S. Army Signal Corps, and served in New Guinea, the Philippines, and Japan; he was discharged in 1945 as a Master Sergeant. After leaving the Army, Exon began working in Fremont for the Universal Finance Corporation, and entered politics there, supporting several Democrats for City Council offices and for mayor. In 1950 Exon was put in charge of the company's Lincoln office, and in 1954 he started his own office equipment supply company. Although he had worked for several Democratic candidates in the early 1950s (especially for Frank B. Morrison in his 1952 congressional race), Exon first established a statewide reputation in Ralph Brooks' successful campaign for the governorship in 1958. He also directed Frank B. Morrison's successful campaign for the governor's office in 1960, and served on the state committees for Congressman Clair Callan and Lieutenant Governor Philip Sorensen. Exon rapidly moved upward in the party organization: member, Executive Committee, Nebraska Democratic Party in 1964; Nebraska State Coordinator for the Lyndon Johnson — Hubert Humphrey campaign in 1964; delegate to the Democratic National Convention in 1964; vice-chairman of the Nebraska State Democratic Central Committee from 1964 to 1968; and Democratic National Committeeman from 1968 to 1969. In 1970 Exon secured the Democratic gubernatorial nomination and went on to defeat incumbent Republican Norbert T. Tiemann, 248,552 votes to 201,994. In 1974 Exon ran for a second term and defeated Republican Richard Marvel, 267,012 votes to 159,780. Widely regarded as a fiscal conservative, Exon had pledged during his 1970 campaign to hold the line on state sales and income tax rates and to control state spending. He also favored abolition of the state sales tax on food and the encouragement of agriculture. His victory in that year was viewed as a repudiation of some of the fiscal policies of his predecessor, Norbert Tiemann. Exon has also stated that strengthening Nebraska's Democratic Party would be one of his goals while in office. Bibliography: "Politics, Respect for Dollar Shaped Exon's Life," *Lincoln Star* (December 22, 1970); "J.J. Exon's Fiscal Conservatism Has Roots in 1930 Depression," *Lincoln Star* (December 23, 1970); Duane Hutchinson, *Exon, Biography of a Governor* (Lincoln, 1971); *Nebraska Statistical Handbook, 1974-1975* (Lincoln, 1975); James F. Pedersen and Kenneth D. Wald, *Shall the People Rule* (Lincoln, 1972); Election statistics on file, Nebraska Secretary of State, Lincoln; "Exon Looks Into Past, Future, *Lincoln Evening Journal* (May 6, 1972); "Governor J. James Exon," on file, Nebraska Governor's Office, Lincoln. Papers of Exon are in the possession of J. James Exon, Lincoln.

NEVADA

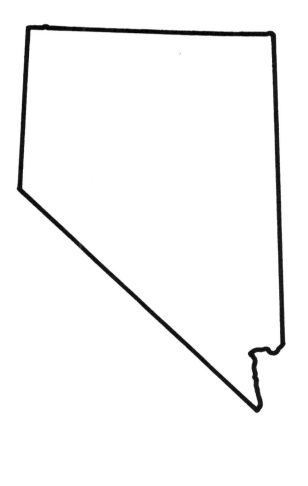

NEVADA

BLASDEL, Henry Goode, 1864-1871

Born on January 20, 1825 near Lawrenceburg, Indiana, son of Jacob and Elizabeth Blasdel; a Methodist. Married to Sara Jane Cox on December 5, 1845; father of Henry G., Shelly W. and Lillian. He attended public school, but left before graduating due to his father's death. He took up farming, mining, real estate and produce shipping. Moved to California in 1852 and opened up a produce commission house in San Francisco. Moved to Territory of Utah, present-day Nevada, to mine. In 1864 represented Nevada on the committee from the National Union League which informed President Lincoln of his renomination. In 1864 Blasdel was nominated unanimously to run for Governor of Nevada for a two-year term on the Republican ticket. He ran against D.E. Buell, a Democrat, winning by a vote of 9,834 to 6,555. He was reelected in 1866 to serve a four-year term, defeating John D. Winters, a Democrat, by 5,125 votes to 4,105. As governor, Blasdel set up the state government for Nevada and supervised the changeover from territory to statehood. He helped add two sections of land to Nevada; advised on the construction of the state capitol building; met with the Shoshoni Indians in 1864 to quell an uprising; led a party of government officials across the state to new mines of Lincoln County, crossing desert areas previously avoided by travellers. Blasdel chose not to run for another term, and returned to his mining interests. Blasdel died on July 26, 1900 in Fruitvale, California and was buried there. Bibliography: Myrtle Tate Myles, *Nevada's Governors* (Sparks, Nevada, 1972). A few of Blasdel's Papers are on deposit in the Nevada Historical Society in Reno, Nevada.

BRADLEY, Lewis Rice, 1871-1879

Born on February 18, 1805 in Madison County, Virginia, son of Sally Hancock and Reuben Bradley, a tobacco raiser. Married to Virginia Hode Willis in 1835; father of John Reuben, Sarah Watts and Virginia Hode. Attended public school for a few years, but left due to his father's death and took up mule trading, farming and cattle raising. Moved to California in 1852; moved to Nevada in 1862, where he continued in the cattle business. He was the first to introduce the Texas Longhorn to Nevada, hence his nickname, "Old Broadhorns." He was nominated by the Democratic Party for Governor of Nevada in 1870, and ran against F.A. Tritle, a Republican, winning by a vote of 7,200 to 6,148. He was reelected in 1874, defeating J.C. Hazlett, a Republican, by a vote of 10,310 to 7,785. During his terms as governor, Bradley established the University of Nevada, and succeeded in removing control of the state prison system from Lieutenant Governor Frank

Denver, who had refused to relinquish his position to the warden appointed by the legislature. He also insured that all groups and elements in the state received fair treatment, and gave no special concessions to the mining interests. He ran for a third term in 1878, but lost to John H. Kinkead, a Republican, by a vote of 9,747 to 9,252. Bradley later returned to his cattle raising, and died on March 21, 1879 in Elko, Nevada. He was buried there in the Odd Fellows Cemetery. Bibliography: Myrtle Tate Myles, *Nevada's Governors* (Sparks, Nevada, 1972); Victor Goodwin, "Lewis Rice Bradley: Nevada Cattleman and Governor," *Nevada Historical Society Quarterly*, vol. XIV no.4 (Winter 1971) *Morning Appeal* [Carson City] (March 22, 1879); *Elko Independent* (March 30, 1879). Some of Bradley's Papers are on deposit in the Nevada Historical Society in Reno, Nevada.

KINKEAD, John Henry, 1879-1883

Born on December 10, 1826 in Somerset County, Pennsylvania, son of a bridge builder. Married to Elizabeth (Lizzie) Fall in 1856; no children. He graduated from Lancaster High School, Lancaster, Pennsylvania; entered the mercantile and livestock business; moved to Nevada in 1860, where he established a mercantile firm in Carson City and later in Unionville, where he also had mining interests. Elected Territorial Treasurer of the Territory of Nevada in 1862; served as a member of both State Constitutional Conventions; became involved in national problems and in obtaining Alaska from Russia. Appointed postmaster of Sitka, the first appointed official in Alaska, and later became the town's Mayor. Elected Governor of Nevada in 1878 on the Republican ticket, defeating Lewis R. Bradley, a Democrat, by a vote of 9,747 to 9,252. Kinkead helped to promote the Virginia and Truckee Railroad, toll roads, and mining in Nevada. He left office at the end of his term in 1883, declining his party's offer of renomination. He returned to Alaska, where he was appointed first Territorial Governor of Alaska by President Chester Arthur in 1884. After his service, he returned to Carson City, Nevada, and resumed his mercantile and mining interests. Kinkead died in Carson City on August 25, 1904 and was buried in the Lone Mountain Cemetery there. Bibliography: Myrtle Tate Myles, *Nevada's Governors* (Sparks, Nevada, 1972). Some of Kinkead's Papers are on deposit in the Nevada State Archives in Carson City, Nevada.

ADAMS, Jewett William, 1883-1887

Born on August 6, 1835 on South Hero Island, Grand Isle, Vermont, son of William and Nancy Adams. Married to Emma Lee in 1878. Received a district school education. An inventor, he engaged in the mercantile business, freighting, cattle raising, and gambling. He served as a Major in the Nevada militia. A Democrat, Adams ran for Lieutenant Governor in 1874, defeating John Bowman, a Republican, and A.J. Hatch, by 9,529 votes to 7,930 and 601, respectively. He was reelected in 1878, defeating H.R. Mighels, a Republican, by a vote of 9,877 to 9,021. In 1882 he was elected Governor, defeating Enoch Strother, a Republican, by a vote of 7,770 to 6,535. During his term as governor, Adams was faced with the problems caused by the growing concern about the railroads and silver. Also he had the University of Nevada moved from Elko to Reno. He ran for reelection in 1886, but lost to Charles Clark Stevenson, the Republican candidate, by 5,869 votes to 6,463. After leaving office, Adams returned to stock raising. In 1894 he was appointed Superintendent of the United States Mint in Carson City by Grover Cleveland, serving until 1898. He moved to San Francisco, California in 1915. Adams died in San Francisco on June 18, 1920 and was buried there. Bibliography: Myrtle Tate Myles, *Nevada's Governors* (Sparks, Nevada, 1972); Orville Holderman, "Jewett W. Adams and W.N. McGill, Their Lives and Ranching Empire," Unpublished Masters Thesis, University of Nevada, Reno, 1963; Reno *Evening Gazette* (June 19, 1920); *Daily Appeal* [Carson City] (June 19, 1920). There are no papers relating to Adams in Nevada repositories.

STEVENSON, Charles Clark, 1887-1890

Born in 1826 in Ontario County, New York, brother of Edward A. Stevenson, Territorial Governor of Idaho, 1885-89. Moved with his parents to Canada at the age of four, then to Michigan. Married (wife unknown); father of Jessie L. and Edward G.; divorced; remarried to Ellen M. Frame. Little formal education. In 1859, moved to Gold Hill, Nevada, where he engaged in mining, milling and agriculture. Elected State Senator from Storey County in 1866, 1868 and 1872. Elected delegate to the Republican National Convention at Philadelphia in 1872 and at Chicago in 1884. In 1885, elected Chairman of the Nevada Silver Convention held in Carson City. Member of the Board of Regents of the State University from 1875 to 1887. In 1876 represented Nevada at the Philadelphia Centennial Exposition as state commissioner. A Republican, Stevenson in 1886 defeated Jewett William Adams, the incumbent Democratic governor, by a vote of 6,463 to 5,869. As governor, Stevenson reorganized the State University, upgrading it from the level of a preparatory school to that of a university. Under his guidance, a bill was passed establishing Stewart Indian School for Nevada's Indians. Holding office during the Twenty Year Depression in Nevada, Stevenson initiated many programs to aid the agricultural and livestock industries, which helped keep the state solvent during that period. His administration passed several acts to encourage new railroad construction. Also attempts were made to solve the problems of reclamation and irrigation in the state. Stevenson died in office on September 21, 1890 in Carson City. He was buried in Mountain View Cemetery in Carson City. Bibliography: Myrtle Tate Myles, *Nevada's Governors* (Sparks, Nevada, 1972); *Morning Appeal* [Carson City, Nevada] (September 23, 1890). Some of Stevenson's Papers are on deposit in the Nevada Historical Society in Reno, Nevada and some are deposited in the Nevada State Archives in Carson City, Nevada.

BELL, Francis Jardine, 1890-1891

Born in Toronto, Canada on January 28, 1840, parents unknown; a Congregationalist. Married to Mary Poore in 1872; father of Agnes and Fernald. Little formal education. At age eighteen, was superintendent of the construction of the telegraph line called "Bee's Grapevine Line," running from Placerville, California to Genoa,

Nevada. Supervised the building of telegraph lines from Salt Lake Valley, Utah, to Sacramento, California, in the early 1860s, and in the late 1860s supervised the construction of the telegraph lines running parallel to the Central Pacific Railroad. Telegraphed the Nevada Constitution to President Lincoln in October, 1864, to speed the entry of the state into the Union. Introduced the telephone into the state in 1876, just after the first successful demonstration by a distant cousin, Alexander Graham Bell. Bell's first telephone installation in Nevada was in the Consolidated Virginia Mine in Virginia City in 1876. Served as Warden of the State Prison from 1883 to 1887. Governor Stevenson appointed Bell to fill the vacancy of Lieutenant Governor in 1889. When Stevenson filed a certificate of disability due to illness on September 1, 1890, Bell became Acting Governor; Bell, a Republican, was elevated to the governor's chair after Stevenson's death on September 21, 1890. During his few months in office, Bell carried on the policies established by Stevenson. He chose not to run for election. After his gubernatorial service Bell continued to work in the field of telegraph and telephone communications as well as with his mining interests and investments. He was active in the Freemasons, holding the top office in the state. Served as warden of the State Prison from 1893 to 1895 and as a Justice of the Peace from 1907 to 1909. Bell died in Oakland, California on February 13, 1927 and was buried in the Masonic Cemetery in Reno, Nevada. Bibliography: Myrtle Tate Myles, *Nevada's Governors* (Sparks, Nevada, 1972); *Nevada State Journal* [Reno, Nevada] (February 14, 1927). No papers relating to Bell exist in state repositories.

COLCORD, Roswell Keyes, 1891-1895

Born in North Searsport, Maine, on April 25, 1839, son of a miner, James Colcord; a Methodist. Married to Mary F. Hopkins on April 25, 1868; father of Stella, Ethel and Harry. Completed a mechanical engineering program in Searsport public schools; worked as a ship's carpenter until 1856; came west, and in 1863, settled in Nevada where he built bridges and mills, and managed several mines. Served as commissioner from Nevada to the Paris Exposition of 1889. In the 1890 gubernatorial contest, Colcord, a Republican, defeated Theodore Winters, a Democrat, by a vote of 6,791 to 6,601. As governor, Colcord tightened the state budget, put the state on a cash basis, and developed financial programs which helped to bring about Nevada's secure economic position. He created the first State Board of Equalization, which attempted to place property assessment under state control; initiated a State Board of Health; established the mechanical engineering department of the University of Nevada; and introduced the Australian, or secret, ballot into state elections. Also he was the first Nevada governor to fight for equal suffrage for women. He chose not to run for a second term. On October 14, 1898, President McKinley appointed Colcord Superintendent of the Carson City Mint, which no longer coined money, but which operated as an assay office and shipping place for bullion. After thirteen years in this position he retired in 1911. Colcord died in Carson City on October 30, 1939, the oldest living ex-governor in the nation and the oldest active Mason in Nevada. He was buried in Lone Mountain Cemetery in Carson City. Bibliography: Myrtle Tate Myles, *Nevada's Governors* (Sparks, Nevada, 1972); *Daily Appeal* [Carson City, Nevada] (October 30, 1939); *Reno*

Evening Gazette (October 30, 1939). Colcord's Papers are on deposit in the Nevada State Archives in Carson City and the Bancroft Library in Berkeley, California.

JONES, John Edward, 1895-1896

Born in Montgomeryshire, Wales, on December 5, 1840, son of a farmer. Married to Elizabeth Weyburn on November 25, 1880; father of Edith and Parvin. Graduated from Iowa State University in 1865. Worked as a teacher, miner and farmer until 1867, when he worked on the construction of the Union Pacific Railroad. Came to Nevada in 1869, settling in Eureka. Was an organizer of the state militia in 1876, holding the rank of Major until his death. Appointed United States Deputy Internal Revenue Collector in 1883. Elected Surveyor-General of Nevada in 1886 and 1890, and served until 1894, when he ran for Governor. Jones ran on the Silver Party ticket, defeating A.C. Cleveland, a Republican, who received 3,861 votes; George E. Peckham, a Populist, who received 711 votes; and Theodore Winters, a Democrat, who received 678 votes. Jones was elected with 5,223 votes. Jones spent only a short time as governor, promoting reclamation and irrigation while in office. In the fall of 1895, he went to California to try to regain his health. On November 19, 1895, Lieutenant Governor Reinhold Sadler assumed the duties of governor. Jones died of cancer on April 10, 1896 in San Francisco, California. His body lay in state at the Capitol in Carson City, followed by an ecumenical service and the largest military funeral in Nevada up to that time. A Mason, he was buried in the Masonic section of Lone Mountain Cemetery in Carson City. Bibliography: Myrtle Tate Myles, *Nevada's Governors* (Sparks, Nevada, 1972); *Morning Appeal* [Carson City] (April 14,1896); *Nevada State Journal* [Reno, Nevada] (April 14, 1896). Some of Jones' Papers are on deposit in the Nevada State Archives in Carson City.

SADLER, Reinhold, 1896-1903

Born in Czarnikau, Prussia on January 10, 1848, son of a toolsmith and merchant. Brother of Herman Sadler. Married to Louise Zadow in 1875; father of Edgar, Alfred, Bertha, Clarence and Minnie. Little formal education. Worked as a merchant, stockman, and was engaged in mining and milling. Elected Treasurer of Eureka County, as a Democrat, in 1880; in 1882 ran for State Treasurer as a Democrat, but was defeated by George Tufly, a Republican, by a vote of 7,654 to 6,635. Ran as a Democrat for State Controller in 1886, and lost to J.F. Hallock, a Republican, by a vote of 6,364 to 5,957. Ran for Lieutenant Governor on the Silver Party ticket in 1894, defeating J.F. Emmitt, a Republican, by a vote of 5,967 to 4,088. On November 19, 1895, Sadler assumed the duties of governor because of the illness of Governor John E. Jones. He became Governor upon the death of Jones, on April 10, 1896. Sadler ran for a second term in 1898 on the Silver Party ticket, defeating J.B. McCullough, the People's Party candidate, (833 votes); William McMillan, a Republican (3,548 votes); and George Russell, a Democrat

(2,057 votes). Sadler received 3,570 votes. As governor, he began to advertise the state nationally. He also instituted the State Board of Assessors; upgraded public health measures; supported reclamation measures and acts; and began the first Farmers' Institute in the state; and started a movement to end pollution by upstream industry of the Truckee River. He did not run for reelection. When his term was over, Sadler returned to eastern Nevada to manage his extensive business and livestock interests. In 1904 he ran for the United States Congress on the Stalwart-Silver Party ticket, but was defeated, receiving 572 votes. C.D. Van Duzer received 5,525 votes, running on the Silver-Democrat Party ticket, and J.A. Yerington, a Republican, received 5,301 votes. Sadler died on January 29, 1906 in Eureka and was buried in the Masonic section of the Lone Mountain Cemetery in Carson City. Bibliography: Myrtle Tate Myles, *Nevada's Governors* (Sparks, Nevada, 1972); *Morning Appeal* [Carson City] (January 30, 1906). Sadler's Papers are on deposit in the Nevada Historical Society in Reno and the State Archives in Carson City.

SPARKS, John, 1903-1908

Born in Mississippi on August 30, 1843, son of Mary Deal and Samuel Sparks, a stockman. One of ten children; a Baptist. Married to Rachel Knight in 1872; father of one daughter, Maud; remarried to his wife's sister, Nora Knight, in 1879; father of Benton H., Charles and Leland. Little formal education; began in the cattle business at age fourteen, and later introduced the first Hereford cattle to Nevada. Moved to Texas in his youth, where he was a Texas Ranger and served in the Confederate Army during the Civil War. Sparks, a Silver-Democrat, defeated A.C. Cleveland, a Republican, in the 1902 gubernatorial contest, by 6,540 to 4,778 votes. In 1906 Sparks was reelected, defeating James F. Mitchell, a Republican, who received 5,556 votes, and Thomas B. Casey, a Socialist, who received 815 votes. Sparks received 8,686 votes. During his administration, irrigation laws were enacted; the office of State Engineer was established; a state railroad commission was set up; and an eight-hour day for mine workers was declared. Sparks also requested that federal troops be sent to Goldfield because of labor troubles; as a result, the Nevada State Police was created. While Sparks was governor, several new state buildings were constructed, housing the newly-created Board of Bank Commissioners and the Nevada Historical Society. In addition, the public school system was reorganized, and a state superintendent of education was put in charge of all state public schools. The town of Sparks was named after him. He died in office. Sparks died on May 22, 1908 at his Alamo Ranch near Reno. He was buried in the Masonic Cemetery in Reno. Bibliography: Myrtle Tate Myles, *Nevada's Governors* (Sparks, Nevada, 1972); *Reno Evening Gazette* [Carson City] (May 22, 1908); Velma Stevens Truett, "From Longhorns to Herefords," *Nevada Highways and Parks* (special centennial issue, 1964). Sparks' Papers are on deposit in the Nevada Historical Society in Reno and the State Archives in Carson City.

DICKERSON, Denver Sylvester, 1908-1911

Born in Millville, California, on January 24, 1872, the son of Harvey Franklin and Catherine (Bailey) Dickerson; a Christian. Married to Una Reilly on April 23, 1904; the father of eight children: Harvey, Norinne, June, Donald, Denver, Belford, Barbara and George Dickerson. Attended public school in Millville. First Sergeant, Troop D, 2nd United States Volunteer Cavalry, Idaho, 1898-1899. Newspaperman. Printer's assistant, *Ketchum Keystone,* Idaho, 1883-1885; owner, White Pine, Nevada, *News,* 1904-1905; owner, Ely, Nevada, *Expositor,* 1906-1913. County clerk, White Pine County, Nevada, 1903; county recorder, White Pine County, Nevada, 1904-1906; Lieutenant Governor, Nevada, 1907-1908. Mason. As the lieutenant governor, Dickerson was elevated to the governor's office on May 22, 1908, after the death of Governor John Sparks. A progressive Democrat, Dickerson attempted to implement reform legislation during his term of office, supporting such programs as reorganization of the state prison system; reform of the state mental hospitals; and strengthening of the State Railroad Commission. However, because of the brevity of Dickerson's term and because he had succeeded to the office rather than being elected, few of his proposals were successful. Dickerson sought election in 1910 and was the Democrat candidate for Governor. However, he was defeated in the general election by progressive Republican Tasker L. Oddie, 8,798 votes to 10,435. He left office on January 2, 1911. Returning to private life, Dickerson resumed control of his newspaper in Ely, Nevada. He was warden of the Nevada State Prison from 1913 to 1919; and from 1919 to 1923 he was Superintendent of Federal Prisons. In 1923 he again became the warden of the Nevada State Prison, a position which he held until his death on November 28, 1925. Bibliography: James Scrugham, ed., *Nevada: A Narrative of the Conquest of a Frontier Land,* 3 vols. (Chicago, 1935); Richard G. Lillard, *Desert Challenge: An Interpretation of Nevada* (New York, 1942); Gilman M. Ostrander, *Nevada: the Great Rotten Borough, 1859-1964* (New York, 1966); John Koontz, ed., *Political History of Nevada* (Carson City, 1965).

ODDIE, Tasker Lowndes, 1911-1915

Born on October 24, 1870 in Brooklyn, New York, son of Henry Meigs Oddie (1837-1898), senior partner in the New York Stock Exchange firm of Turner, Manuel and Company, and Ellen Gibson Prout Oddie, both of whom were Protestants. Brother of Grace, Walter, Sarah, Clarence, Anna Siebert and Ethel. Married to Claire Gardner MacDonald on December 2, 1903; divorced on November 15, 1904; remarried to Daisy Rendall MacKeigan on November 30, 1916; no children. Attended Metropolis Law School (which later became the Night Law School of New York University) and graduated with his LL.B degree in 1895. Employed by the Woodbridge Company, a New York real estate concern with investments in Nevada, where he was sent in 1898. Elected District Attorney of Nye County, 1900. Concurrently served in managerial capacities for the Tonopah, Tonopah-Belmont, and Tonopah Midway mining companies. Was a member of the State Senate from 1905 to 1909. Ran for the governorship in 1910 as a progressive Republican. He gained the nomination by winning Nevada's first primary election, defeating William A. Massey of Reno, by a vote of 3,109 to 2,950. Afterwards, Oddie triumphed in the general election, defeating the Democratic candidate, Acting Governor Denver S. Dickerson, by a vote of 10,435 to 8,798. As governor, Oddie sponsored progressive legislation dealing with workmen's compensation, mining safety, and the eight-hour work day. He opposed the legalization of gambling and easy divorces. Oddie sought reelection in 1914, but was defeated by Democratic challenger Emmet D. Boyle, by a vote of 8,537 to 9,623. From 1915 to 1920, Oddie engaged in mining and real estate speculation, as well as politics. In 1918, his bid to make a political comeback was thwarted when he was again defeated by Boyle for the governorship. In 1920, Oddie ran for the United States Senate, and successfully challenged the Democratic incumbent, Charles B. Henderson. He received 11,550 votes to Henderson's 10,402. Six years later, he was reelected to a second term. As a United States Senator, Oddie helped his party in passing the Fordney-McCumber Tariff (1922), and was instrumental in securing legislation of benefit to Nevada, including federal funds for highway construction and appropriations for the United States Naval Ammunition Depot in Hawthorne. When he sought a third term in the Senate in 1932, he was defeated by the Democratic candidate, Patrick A. McCarran, by a vote of 19,706 to 21,398. Returning to private life in 1933, Oddie resumed his activities as a mining entrepreneur. He served as president of the Gold Mining Association of America and the Nevada Mine Owners' Association. He made his last attempt to recapture his old Senate seat in 1938, but McCarran defeated him by receiving 27,406 votes to Oddie's 19,078. Oddie died on February 17, 1950 and was buried in the Lone Mountain Cemetery in Carson City, Nevada. Bibliography: C.B. Glasscock, *Gold in Them Hills* (Indianapolis, 1932); Marjorie Moore Brown, *Lady in Boomtown: Miners and Manners on the Nevada Frontier* (Palo Alto, Calif., 1968); Loren B. Chan, *Sagebrush Statesman: Tasker L. Oddie of Nevada* (Reno, 1973). The Oddie Papers are on deposit in the Nevada State Division of Archives, Carson City; the Nevada State Historical Society, Reno; and the Henry E. Huntington Library and Art Gallery, San Marino, California.

BOYLE, Emmet Derby, 1915-1923

Born in Virginia City, Nevada, on July 26, 1879, the son of Edward Dougherty and Sarah (Donoghue) Boyle; a Presbyterian. Married to Vida Margaret McClure on September 28, 1903. Attended public school in Virginia City, Nevada; graduated, University of Nevada, 1889; graduated, University of Nevada, Master of Engineering, 1903. Engineer; foreman, La Compania la Esperanza y Anexas, El Oro, Mexico, 1900-1901; manager, North Rapidan Mines, Como, Nevada, 1902-1907; independent consulting mining and mechanical engineer, Reno, Nevada, 1907-1910. State engineer, Nevada, 1910-1911; member, Nevada State Tax Commission, 1913-1914. Member, American Institute of Mining and Metallurgical Engineers; American Academy of Political and Social Science; National Tax Association. Sigma Alpha; Phi Kappa Kappa. As a Democrat, Boyle was elected Governor of Nevada in 1914 with 9,623 votes, defeating incumbent Republican Tasker Oddie, who had 8,537, and Socialist candidate W.W. Morgan, who had 3,391. He took office on January 4, 1915. Boyle fought for fiscal conservatism in the state, and during his administration the state was placed on a sound economic footing, which was achieved through a revision of the state tax system. Also enacted during his tenure were measures increasing workmen's compensation; increasing teacher retirement benefits; and strengthening the protections for orphans. Also, the State Highway Department was created. During World War I, Governor Boyle acted as the chairman of a convention representing several silver producing states, which discussed negotiations for sales of the mineral to the Department of the Treasury. Boyle was reelected in 1918, defeating Republican Tasker Oddie. Boyle had 12,875 votes to Oddie's 11,845. He did not seek a third term in 1922, leaving office on January 1, 1923. Boyle lived in Reno, Nevada, until his death on January 3, 1926. Bibliography: J.E. Wier, "The Mystery of Nevada," in Thomas C. Donnelly (ed.), *Rocky Mountain Politics* (Albuquerque, 1940); James Scrugham, ed., *Nevada: A Narrative of the Conquest of a Frontier Land,* 3 vols. (Chicago, 1935); John Koontz, ed., *Political History of Nevada* (Carson City, 1965); Gilman M. Ostrander, *Nevada: The Great Rotten Borough, 1859-1964* (New York, 1966).

SCRUGHAM, James Graves, 1923-1927

Born in Lexington, Kentucky, on January 19, 1880, the son of James Grinstead and Theodotia (Allen) Scrugham; a Methodist. Married to Julia McCann on August 4, 1904; father of James G. and Martha Scrugham. Graduated from the University of Kentucky, Bachelor of Mechanical Engineering, 1900; M.E., 1906. Lieutenant Colonel, United States Army, 1918; Lieutenant Colonel, United States Army Reserve. Businessman; educator; engineer, Creaghead Engineering Company, Cincinnati, Ohio, 1899; engineer, Metropolitan West Side Elevated Railway Company, Chicago, 1899-1901; engineer, Abner Doble Company, San Francisco, 1901-1903; professor of mechanical engineering, University of Nevada, 1903-1914; dean, College of Engineering, University of Nevada, 1914-1917; state engineer, Nevada, 1917-1923. Public service commander, Nevada, 1919-1923. Tau Beta Phi; Sigma Chi; Phi Kappa Phi; Mason; Elk. A Democrat, Scrugham was elected Governor of Nevada in 1922 with 15,437 votes, defeating Republican challenger John H. Miller, who received 13,215 votes. He took office on January 1, 1923. Scrugham was elected at the end of the Democratic Party's dominance in Nevada, and in 1924, only one year after he was sworn into office, the opposition gained control of the State Legislature. Although Scrugham supported comprehensive programs, including increased appropriations for higher education, he was unsuccessful because of the waning strength of his party. He sought reelection in 1926, but was defeated by Fred Balzar. Scrugham received 14,521 votes to the Republican's 16,374. He left office on January 3, 1927. After leaving office, Scrugham was a special advisor to the Secretary of the Interior in 1927. He was a member of the United States House of Representatives from 1933 to 1943, and was elected to the United States Senate in 1942. He died on June 2, 1945, before the expiration of his term. Bibliography: James Scrugham, ed., *Nevada: A Narrative of the Conquest of a Frontier Land* (Chicago, 1935); John Koontz, ed., *Political History of Nevada* (Carson City, 1965); Russell R. Elliott, *History of Nevada* (Lincoln, 1973); Elmer Rusco, *Voting Behavior in Nevada* (Reno, 1966).

BALZAR, Frederick Bennett, 1927-1934

Born in Virginia City, Nevada, on June 15, 1880, the son of Serafino and Minnie (Bennett) Balzar; a Christian Scientist. Married to Idelle Edna Sinnamon on November 11, 1907; father of one daughter, Phylis Rae Balzar. Graduated Polytechnic High School, San Francisco, California. Mining engineer; independent miner, 1899 to 1904. Member, Nevada State Assembly, 1905-1909; member, Nevada State Senate, 1909-1917; Sheriff and County Assessor, Mineral County, Nevada, 1917-1927; chairman, Mineral County Draft Board, 1918; chairman, Nevada Republican Party, 1924. Mason. As a Republican, Balzar was elected Governor of Nevada in 1926 with 16,374 votes, defeating Democratic incumbent James G. Scrugham, who received 14,521 votes. He took office on January 3, 1927. The major event of Balzar's administration was the beginning of the Great Depression. The economic disruption severely damaged Nevada's financial basis, because of its reliance on mineral wealth. The state's plight was eased by the influx of federal funds for highway construction and for the Boulder Canyon Project, which resulted in the building of Hoover Dam. Also, a major aid to the state's economy came during Governor Balzar's administration with the legalization of gambling in 1931. In addition, the state's liberal divorce laws were approved during his term. The initiation of gambling and liberal divorce laws sharply increased Las Vegas and Reno's population and tax bases; however the new wealth did not stop the widespread failure of banks across the state in 1932. The economic troubles caused a rebirth of the silver issue—the coinage of silver at a sixteen to one ratio to gold—that had been raised during the last decade of the nineteenth century. Balzar was reelected in 1930, defeating C.L. Richards, a Democrat, by 18,442 votes to 16,192. Balzar's career was cut short when he died on March 21, 1934, while still in office; he was succeeded by Lieutenant Governor Morley I. Griswold. Bibliography: Ralph Simmons, comp., *Boulder Dam and the Great Southwest* (Los Angeles, 1936); James T. Patterson, *The New Deal and the States: Federalism in Transition* (Princeton, 1969); Gilman M. Ostrander, *Nevada: The Great Rotten Borough, 1859-1964* (New York, 1966); John Koontz, ed., *Political History of Nevada* (Carson City, 1965).

GRISWOLD, Morley, 1934-1935

Born in Elko, Nevada, on October 10, 1890, the son of Chauncey Warner and Mary Ellen (Dakin) Griswold; an Episcopalian. Married to Marianne Williamson on August 4, 1920; father of Mary Louise and Morley Williamson Griswold. Graduated from the University of Michigan, A.B., 1913; LL.B., 1915. First Lieutenant, American Expeditionary Force, 1917-1918. Attorney, Reno, 1915-1926. Lieutenant Governor, Nevada, 1926-1934. Mason, American Legion. After the death of Governor Fred Balzar, Lieutenant Governor Griswold became Acting Governor of Nevada. A Republican, Griswold took office on March 21, 1934, and served the remainder of Balzar's term. Although Griswold's administration was brief, he worked to relieve the plight of Nevadans trapped by the economic disruption of the Great Depression. His most important success was the increase in funds for highway construction which he secured from the federal government. Griswold sought the governorship in 1934, but was defeated by Democrat Richard Kirman. Griswold received 14,778 votes to Kirman's 23,088. He left office on January 7, 1935. After leaving office, Griswold returned to his law practice in Reno, Nevada. He died on October 3, 1951. Bibliography: John A. Brennan, *Silver and the First New Deal* (Reno, 1969): Gilman Ostrander, *Nevada: the Great Rotten Borough, 1859-1964* (New York, 1966); United States Bureau of Reclamations, *The Story of Hoover Dam* (Washington, D.C., 1961); Elmer Rusco, *Voting Behavior in Nevada* (Reno, 1966).

KIRMAN, Richard, 1935-1939

Born on January 14, 1877 in Virginia City, Nevada, son of Richard Kirman, a farmer and businessman; a Protestant. Married to Mabelle Jean King on January 19, 1898; father of Claire and Richard Kirman, Jr. Attended the public schools of Virginia City and San Francisco. Employed as a bookkeeper in the Bullion Exchange Bank of Carson, Nevada; was one of the founders of the Farmers and Merchants Bank of Reno, Nevada, serving as its president until 1934; served as an assemblyman from Ormsby County, Nevada in 1899, regent of the University of Nevada from 1902 to 1904, and Mayor of Reno from 1907 to 1909. As the Democratic gubernatorial candidate, Kirman was elected Governor of Nevada by popular vote on November 6, 1934, defeating the Republican candidate, Governor Morley Griswold, by a vote of 23,088 to 14,778. He was inaugurated on January 7, 1935. During his administration, construction of Boulder (now Hoover) Dam was completed; numerous gambling establishments were initiated; and a conservative and "businesslike" government was created. Declining to be a candidate for renomination, Kirman left office on January 2, 1939 upon the inauguration of Edward P. Carville. Afterwards, he returned to his business interests among which was the J.R. Bradley Company, a hardware firm, of which he was president from 1905 to 1952 and the cattle and ranching business in the Jacks Valley area, south of Carson, Nevada. Member of the Masons, the Independent Order of Odd Fellows, Rebecca Lodge and Order of the Eastern Star. Kirman died on January 19, 1959 and was interred at Odd Fellows Cemetery in Reno, Nevada. Bibliography: *Evening Gazette* [Reno, Nevada] (January 19, 1959) *Nevada State Journal* [Reno, Nevada] (January 20, 1959): Myrtle Tate Myles, *Nevada's Governors* (Sparks, Nevada, 1972); Roy Glashan, *American Governors and Gubernatorial Elections, 1775-1975* (Stillwater, Minnesota, 1975).

CARVILLE, Edward Peter, 1939-1945

Born in Mound Valley, Nevada, on May 14, 1885, the son of Edward and Emily Ellen (Porcher) Carville; a Catholic. Married to Irma M. Callahan in August 1910; father of Edward, Richard and Robert Thomas Carville. Attended public school in Elko County, Nevada; graduated Notre Dame, 1909. Attorney; law practice, Elko County, Nevada, 1909-1912. District Attorney, Elko County, Nevada, 1934-1938. A Democrat, Carville was elected Governor of Nevada in 1938 with

28,528 votes, defeating the Republican candidate, John A. Fulton, who received 17,586 votes. He took office on January 2, 1939. As Governor of Nevada during World War II, Carville's most important accomplishment in office was the work he did to prepare the state to aid in the war effort; Nevada was particularly important as a source of magnesium and other minerals needed for fighting. Governor Carville's strong support for the many Japanese-Americans in Nevada, and his public statements that the people of the state should not persecute loyal citizens, earned him the enmity of many individuals. Carville was reelected in 1942 with 24,505 votes, defeating Republican A.V. Tallman, who received 16,164. However, he did not complete his term in office. When Senator James Scrugham died in office, Carville resigned from the governorship in order to be appointed to his unexpired term. He left office on July 24, 1945. Carville unsuccessfully sought election to the United States Senate in 1946, but was defeated, and left the Senate on January 3, 1947. He then returned to his law practice in Reno, Nevada. He died on June 27, 1956. Bibliography: Elmer Rusco, *Voting Behavior in Nevada* (Reno, 1966); John Koontz, ed., *Political History of Nevada* (Carson City, 1965); Gilman Ostrander, *Nevada: the Great Rotten Borough, 1859-1964* (New York, 1966); Russell R. Elliott, *History of Nevada* (Lincoln, 1973).

PITTMAN, Vail Montgomery, 1945-1951

Born in Vicksburg, Mississippi, on September 17, 1883, the son of William Buckner and Catherine (Key) Pittman; an Episcopalian. Married to Ida Brewington on May 20, 1919. Attended the University of South Dakota; attended business college, Kansas City, Missouri. Businessman; newspaperman; manager and co-owner, cotton plantation, Louisiana, 1900-1903; owner and manager, coal business, Tonopah, Nevada, 1904-1907; manager and co-owner, Placer Mining Company, Round Mountain, Nevada, 1911; managing editor, *Tonopah Miner,* Tonopah, Nevada, 1913-1919; owner, Ely, Nevada, *Daily Times,* 1920-1951; vice-president, White Pine Building and Loan Association, White Pine, Nevada, 1925-1928; owner, *Ely Record,* Ely, Nevada, 1946-1951. Under-sheriff, Tonopah, 1907-1911; Sergeant-at-Arms, Nevada State Senate, 1911; member, Nevada State Senate, 1925-1929; Lieutenant Governor, Nevada, 1942-1945. Sigma Delta Chi; Rotary. A Democrat, Pittman assumed the office of governor when Edward P. Carville left the position on July 24, 1945. He was elected Governor in 1946 with 28,655 votes, defeating Republican Melvin E. Jepson, who received 21,247. Although Pittman was successful in his quest for the governorship, his party was severely divided during his administration, and little was accomplished because of the Republican Party's strength in the legislature. Unfortunately, this inaction by the state government laid the groundwork for economic depression in Nevada in the late 1940s and early 1950s. The division within the Democratic Party was partially responsible for Pittman's failure to gain reelection in 1950. He collected 26,164 votes, but lost to Republican Charles H. Russell, who received 35,609. He left office on January 1, 1951. After leaving office Pittman returned to his private business interests. He became a member of the Democratic National Committee in 1960, after failing in his attempt to become governor in 1954. He died in Reno, Nevada, on January 29, 1964. Bibliography: Eric Moody, *Southern Gentleman of*

Nevada Politics: Vail M. Pittman (Reno, 1974); Elmer Rusco, *Voting Behavior in Nevada* (Reno, 1966); Gilman Ostrander, *Nevada: the Great Rotten Borough, 1859-1964* (New York, 1966); John Koontz, ed., *Political History of Nevada* (Carson City, 1965).

RUSSELL, Charles H., 1951-1959

Born in Lovelock, Nevada, on December 27, 1903, the son of James and Ellen D. (Ernest) Russell; an Episcopalian. Married to Marjorie Ann Guild in 1939; father of five children, Clark G., Virginia, Robert Craig, Charles David, and James Todd. Attended public school in Lovelock and Deeth, Nevada, and in Oakland, California; graduated from Elko County High School, Nevada, 1922; graduated from University of Nevada, 1926. Teacher, high school, Ruby Valley, Nevada, 1927; rancher, Elko County, Nevada, 1928; foreman, Kennecott Copper Corporation, Ruth, Nevada, 1929; editor, Ely, Nevada, *Ely Record,* 1929-1946. Member, Nevada State Assembly, 1934-1941; member, Nevada State Senate, 1941-1946, member, United States House of Representatives, 1947-1949; agent, Joint Committee on Foreign Economic Cooperation of Congress, 1949-1950. Lions Club; Rotary Club; Elks; Sigma Delta Chi; Masons; Royal Arch Masons; Shrine; Consistory. A Republican, Russell was elected to the governorship of Nevada in 1950, defeating Democratic incumbent Vail Pittman. Russell collected 35,609 votes to Pittman's 26,164. He took office on January 1, 1951. His administration witnessed record-setting population growth for Nevada, making it the fastest growing state in the Union. Also, legalized gambling spread during his terms, sharply increasing the state's tax base. The most noteworthy accomplishment of his career as the state's chief executive came in 1957, when the Governor vetoed a measure which would have removed most of the controls on gambling in the state. Although the bill was backed by numerous leaders in both of the state's major parties, Russell's veto was upheld by the State Senate by a vote of eleven to six. Russell was reelected in 1954, with 41,665 votes, again defeating Vail Pittman, who collected 36,797. Russell ran for a third term in 1958; however, he was defeated in the general election by Democratic challenger Grant Sawyer. Russell collected 34,025 votes to Sawyer's 50,864. He left office on January 5, 1959. After leaving office, Russell worked for the Mercury Institute until October 1959, when he was named the Chief of the United States AID Mission to Paraguay. He served in this capacity until he was appointed Assistant to the President of the University of Nevada in August of 1963. He retired on January 1, 1968. He now lives in Carson City, Nevada. Bibliography: Joseph F. McDonald, "Gambling in Nevada," *Annals of the American Academy of Political and Social Science* (May, 1950); Oscar Lewis, *Sagebrush Casinos: The Story of Legal Gambling in Nevada* (Garden City, New York, 1953); Elmer Rusco, *Voting Behavior in Nevada* (Reno, 1966); Frank Johnson, "The Man Who Brought Gambling in Nevada," *Nevada Centennial Magazine* (Las Vegas, 1964).

SAWYER, Grant, 1959-1967

Born in Twin Falls, Idaho, on December 14, 1918, the son of Harry W. and Bula (Cameron) Sawyer; a Methodist. Married to Bette Hoge on August 1, 1948; father of Gail Sawyer. Attended Linfield College in McMinnville, Oregon, 1938-1939; graduated from the University of Nevada, B.A., 1941; attended George Washington Law School, 1941-1942; graduated Georgetown University Law School, 1948. First Lieutenant, United States Army, 1942-1946. Attorney; law practice, Elko, Nevada, 1948-1958. District Attorney, Elko County, Nevada, 1950-1958; chairman, Nevada Democratic Party, 1955; delegate, Democratic National Convention, 1956, 1960, 1964. American Legion; Veterans of Foreign Wars; Nevada Chamber of Commerce. A Democrat, Sawyer was elected Governor of Nevada in 1958 with 50,864 votes, defeating Republican incumbent Charles H. Russell, who received 34,025. He took office on January 5, 1959. The most significant accomplishments of Sawyer's administration were the passage of a new gambling control law; the establishment of a human rights commission in the state; and the reorganization of the state government. Also, some headway was made toward the congressional reapportionment of Nevada. In 1962 Sawyer was easily reelected with 64,784 votes, defeating Republican Oran K. Gragson, who received 32,145. However, in 1966 Sawyer was defeated in his attempt to win a third term, collecting 65,870 votes, but losing to Republican Paul Laxalt, who received 71,807 votes. He left office on January 2, 1967. After leaving office, Sawyer returned to his private law practice in Carson City, Nevada. Bibliography: Elmer Rusco, *Voting Behavior in Nevada* (Reno, 1966); John Koontz, ed., *Political History of Nevada* (Carson City, 1965); Gilman Ostrander, *Nevada: the Great Rotten Borough, 1859-1964* (New York, 1966); Russell R. Elliott, *History of Nevada* (Lincoln, 1973).

LAXALT, Paul, 1967-1971

Born in Reno, Nevada, on August 2, 1922, the son of Dominique and Theresa (Alpetche) Laxalt; a Catholic. Married to Jackalyn Ross on June 23, 1946; father of six children, Gail, Sheila, John, Michelle, Kevin and Kathleen. Attended Santa Clara University, 1940-1943; graduated from the University of Denver, B.S., LL.B, 1949. Served, United States Army, 1943-1945. Businessman; attorney; admitted to the Nevada Bar, 1949; law practice, Carson City, Nevada, 1949-1951; member Laxalt, Ross and Laxalt, 1954-1962. District Attorney, Ormsby County, Nevada, 1954-1955; Lieutenant Governor, Nevada, 1962-1966. American Legion; Veterans of Foreign Wars. A Republican, Laxalt was elected Governor of Nevada in 1966 with 71,807 votes, defeating Democratic incumbent Grant Sawyer, who received 65,870 votes. Laxalt took office on January 2, 1967. The major accomplishments of his administration were the passage of increased sales tax measures; higher appropriations for public education; increased gambling taxes; a bill allowing corporations to be permitted gambling licenses; and an enlargement of the Nevada Supreme Court from three to five justices. In 1969 Governor Laxalt proposed the largest biennial budget in the state's history. Funds for public education were allowed to increase their gasoline taxes. In 1970 Laxalt declined to run for a second term. He left office on January 4, 1971. After leaving office Laxalt returned to his law practice, becoming the senior partner in Laxalt, Barry, and Allison in Carson City. In 1972 he became General Manager and President of the Ormsby House Hotel and Casino in Carson City. He left both positions in 1974 to run for the United States Senate. He was elected to the Senate and is still a member of the body. Bibliography: *Nevada State Journal* (April 26, 1969); Elmer Rusco, *Voting Behavior in Nevada* (Reno, 1966); Gilman Ostrander, *Nevada: the Great Rotten Borough, 1859-1964* (New York, 1966); Russell R. Elliott, *History of Nevada* (Lincoln, 1973).

O'CALLAGHAN, Mike, 1971-

Born in LaCrosse, Wisconsin, on September 10, 1929, the son of Neil T. and Olive (Berry) O'Callaghan; a Roman Catholic. Married to Carolyn Randall on August 25, 1954; father of five children, Michael Neil, Mary Colleen, Teresa Marie, Brian Jack and Timothy Joe O'Callaghan. Graduated, University of Idaho, B.S., M.Ed., LL.D.; postgraduate, University of Nevada, Colorado State University, Georgetown University, Claremont Graduate School; graduated, University of Nevada at Las Vegas, LL.D., 1972; attended St. Martin's College, Olympia, Washington, 1973. Served, United States Marine Corps, 1946-1948; United States Air Force, 1950-1952; United States Army, 1952-1953; recipient, Purple Heart; Silver Star; Bronze Star. Social worker; teacher, Henderson, Nevada, High School, 1956-1961; chief probation officer and director of court services, Clark County, Nevada, 1961-1963; director, Nevada Department of Health and Welfare, 1963-1964; project management director, Job Corps Conservation Centers, 1964-1966; regional director, Office of Emergency Planning, San Francisco, 1967-1969. Lions. A Democrat, O'Callaghan was elected Governor of Nevada in 1970, defeating Republican Ed Fike. O'Callaghan collected 70,697 votes to Fike's 64,400. He took office on January 4, 1971. The primary accomplishments of O'Callaghan's administration have been the passage of a fair housing law; strong anti-pollution measures; and a bill to reapportion the legislature. He has also pushed for stronger laws to control the gambling interests in Nevada. O'Callaghan was reelected in 1974 with 114,114 votes to defeat Republican Shirley Crumpler, who had 28,959 and Independent James Ray Houston who received 26,285. Bibliography: Don W. Driggs, *The 1970 Election in Nevada, Governmental Research Newsletter* (Reno, 1971); Eleanore Bushnell, *Commentary on the Legislature—1971, Governmental Research Newsletter* (Reno, 1971); Elmer Rusco, *Voting Behavior in Nevada* (Reno, 1966); Russell R. Elliott, *History of Nevada* (Lincoln, 1973).

NEW HAMPSHIRE

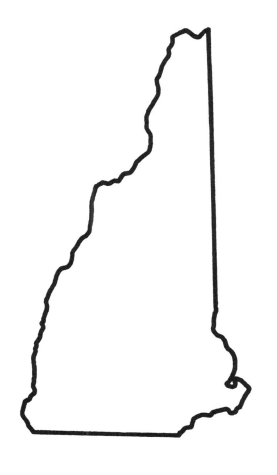

NEW HAMPSHIRE

SULLIVAN, John, 1789-1790

Born on February 17, 1740, in Somersworth, New Hampshire, son of John Sullivan, a schoolmaster, and Margery (Brown) Sullivan, both of whom emigrated to America c. 1731 from Ireland, probably as redemptioners. Brother of Benjamin, Daniel, James, Ebenezer and Mary Sullivan Hardy. Married to Lydia Remick Worster of Kittery, Maine, in 1760; father of Lydia, John, James, George and two daughters (both named Margery), who died in infancy. Educated by his father; read law at Portsmouth, New Hampshire; with Samuel Livermore. Practiced law in Berwick, Maine, before settling in Durham, New Hampshire, about 1763. Commissioned as Major in the militia in 1772, and in 1774 chosen as a delegate to the Continental Congress. Appointed a Brigadier General and served in Washington's army from July, 1775 to November 1779, when, as a Major General, he was forced to resign because of ill health. Returned briefly to the practice of law; served in Congress, 1780-81. Member of the New Hampshire Constitutional Convention in 1782 and 1783, and State Attorney General, 1782-86. Entered race for the presidency (governorship) of the state in February 1785, but was defeated. Became Speaker of the House, and one of the president's five advisory councillors. Elected President (Governor) in 1786, with 4,309 votes to John Langdon's 3,600. Reelected in 1787; although Langdon received more votes than Sullivan in this election, he did not have a majority, and the Senate decided in favor of Sullivan. Defeated by Langdon in the election of 1788 by a vote of 4,421 to 3,664. Ran again in 1789, gaining a plurality of 3,657 votes over John Pickering's 3,488; selected by the Senate and inaugurated on June 9, 1789. As president (governor) of the state, Sullivan saw the need to encourage manufacturing; support the actions of the national Congress; and maintain a good military force. In the summer and fall of 1786, he faced a monetary crisis, but succeeded in firmly putting down the paper money rioters. He was a leader in the movement for a stronger union of the states, and President of the New Hampshire Convention in 1788, which ratified the new Federal Constitution. In October of 1789 he was appointed a Federal Judge for the District of New Hampshire. His dual role as president (governor) and judge was objectionable to the legislature, however, and Sullivan resigned from office shortly before the expiration of his term in June 1790. During his last years Sullivan was ill and debt-ridden. He was physically unable to serve as judge after May of 1792, but never resigned the post. Sullivan died in Durham on January 23, 1795, and was buried in the family plot overlooking the Oyster River. Bibliography: Otis G. Hammond, ed., *Letters and Papers of Major-General John Sullivan*, 3 vols. (Concord, N.H., 1930, 1931, 1939); Charles P. Whittemore, *A General of the Revolution, John Sullivan of New Hampshire* (New York, 1961); Jere Daniell, *Experiment in Republicanism, New Hampshire Politics and the American Revolution, 1741-1794* (Cambridge, Massachusetts, 1970). The Sullivan Papers are, in large part, deposited in the New Hampshire Historical Society.

BARTLETT, Josiah, 1790-1794

Born on November 21, 1729, in Amesbury, Massachusetts, son of Stephen Bartlett, a cobbler, and Hannah (Webster) Bartlett, both of whom were Congregationalists. Brother of Stephen, Joseph, Simeon, Levi, and Hannah. Apprenticed in Amesbury and set up a medical practice in Kingston, New Hampshire, in 1751. Married to Mary Bartlett, a cousin, on January 15, 1754; father of Mary, Lois, Miriam, Rhoda, Levi, Ezra, Josiah and Sarah. Practiced medicine and trained apprentices in Kingston; in 1757 was first chosen selectman of the town. Entered the New Hampshire Legislature in 1765 as a representative from Kingston, having formed a medical partnership with his neighbor, Dr. Amos Gale. Held positions as Justice of the Peace for Rockingham County and militia Colonel under commission from the royal governor. Attended the first four of New Hampshire's provincial congresses in 1774 and 1775, and served as a delegate to the Continental Congress in 1775, 1776 and 1778. Signed the Declaration of Independence and the Articles of Confederation for New Hampshire. Sat on the State Executive Council from 1776 to 1782, and served as a Justice on the Rockingham County Inferior Court of Common Pleas from 1776 to 1782. Sat on the New Hampshire Superior Court from 1782 to 1790, and was appointed Chief Justice in 1790; member of the State Committee of Safety throughout the Revolution. He was also a member and temporary chairman of New Hampshire's convention to consider ratification of the United States Constitution in 1788. In December 1788 Bartlett declined appointment to the United States Senate for reasons of ill health. When no candidate emerged with a majority of votes for president of the state in 1790 (Bartlett came in third with a vote of 1,676 in a field of four candidates), the House and Senate selected Bartlett; he was sworn into office on June 5, 1790. In 1791 Bartlett garnered 8,679 votes against 288 for his several opponents, and in 1792 he repeated the success, winning by 8,092 votes to 297. Amendments to the State Constitution in 1792 created the separate executive position of governor, a position which Bartlett won easily in the 1793 election. Bartlett neither sought votes through active campaigning nor held membership in any organized political party or faction. While Bartlett was Governor, New Hampshire was recovering politically and economically from the Revolution. The bitter political disputes of the 1780s seemed to be disappearing, however, and when a State Superior Court judge—Woodbury Langdon—was impeached by the House of Representatives, Bartlett urged that the Senate accept the judge's belated resignation from office. Bartlett helped to structure the constitutional amendments of 1792, involved lawmakers and the public more deeply in civil and military appointments, and helped the legislature to serve the state efficiently and economically. He worked actively to secure the charter of the New Hampshire Medical Society, of which he was the first president from 1791 to 1793. Bartlett retired to his home at the end of his term in 1794, and died on May 19, 1795; he was buried in the old cemetery in Kingston, New Hampshire. Bibliography: Jere R. Daniell, *Experiment in Republicanism: New Hampshire and the American Revolution, 1741-1794* (Cambridge, Mass., 1970); Frank C. Mevers, "Josiah Bartlett: Dedicated Physician, Sterling Patriot," in George E. Gifford, Jr., ed., *Physician Signers of the Declaration of Independence* (New York, 1976); Elwin L. Page, "Josiah Bartlett and the Federation," *Historical New Hampshire* (October, 1947); Levi Bartlett, *Sketches of the Bartlett Family* (Lawrence, 1876); [Levi Bartlett], "Memoir of Governor Josiah Bartlett," MS., New Hampshire Historical Society (1820). The extant Bartlett Papers have been compiled in the microfilm edition of the "Papers of Josiah Bartlett," 7 rolls (Concord, N. H., 1976).

GILMAN, John Taylor, 1794-1805, 1813-1816

Born on December 19, 1753, in Exeter, New Hampshire, son of Nicholas Gilman, a shipbuilder, merchant and state treasurer during the Revolution, and Ann (Taylor) Gilman, both of whom were Congregationalists. Brother of Nicholas, Nathaniel, Elizabeth, Samuel, Daniel and Joseph. Married to Deborah Folsom on January 13, 1776; after her death on February 20, 1791, remarried to Mary Adams on July 5, 1792; and after her death on October 15, 1812, remarried to Mrs. Charlotte (Peabody) Hamilton on December 29, 1814; father of John Taylor (1779-1808), Ann Taylor, Dorothy, Mary (1786-1813), and Elizabeth. Educated at common schools in Exeter; received an honorary A.M. degree from Dartmouth College in 1794, and an honorary LL.D. degree from Dartmouth in 1799. Entered his father's mercantile business, served briefly in the militia in 1775, and clerked under his father in the state treasury office during the war. Member of the State Legislature from 1779 to 1781, and concurrently a member of the State Committee of Safety; several times elected to the Continental Congress, but attended only in 1782-83. Selected to be State Treasurer after his father's death in 1783, and served until 1788. Voted with the Federalists in the 1788 State Convention that ratified the Federal Constitution, and was State Treasurer again, 1791-94. Received only 708 votes in his first gubernatorial campaign in 1793, losing to Josiah Bartlett. Won the governorship annually beginning in 1794 (7,629 votes opposed to a scattering of 2,841). Reelected in 1795 (9,340 opposed to 100); 1796 (7,809 opposed to 2,966); 1797 (9,625 to 1,198); 1798 (9,379 to Republican Oliver Peabody's 1,189, Timothy Walker's 734, and John Langdon's 364); 1799 (10,138 to 1,600); 1800 (10,362 to Republican Timothy Walker's 6,039); 1801 (10,898 to Walker's 5,249); 1802 (10,377 to Republican John Langdon's 8,753); 1803 (12,263 to Langdon's 9,011); and 1804 (12,246 to Langdon's 12,009). As governor, Gilman presided over routine matters in a state enjoying a prosperous economy. He approved of and the legislature endorsed the Jay Treaty of 1795; he was also an ardent advocate of states' rights, and oversaw the refurbishing of Fort William and Mary, renamed Fort Constitution. During his first period in office, the *Crescent* was built at Portsmouth and was sailed to the Mediterranean, where it was presented to the Dey of Algiers; Dartmouth College also added a medical school in 1798. Gilman's banking policy aroused strong political opposition in 1799-1800, when he objected to any further incorporation of banks in the state: he was then president of the New Hampshire Bank in Portsmouth, the state's only chartered bank. The Alien and Sedition Acts, although unpopular in New Hampshire, did not destroy Gilman and the Federalist Party. Gilman eventually lost to Langdon in the elections of 1805, 1806, and 1808, but returned to the legislature in 1810 and 1811, and became a Presidential Elector in 1812. He won the most votes in the 1812 gubernatorial election but lost to William Plumer in the legislature. He defeated Plumer in 1813 (18,107 to 17,410), 1814 (19,695 to 18,794), and 1815 (18,357 to 17,799). During his final years as governor, Gilman spent much time strengthening the defenses of Portsmouth harbor to meet federal requirements, although he did not approve of the War of 1812. He served for many years as a trustee of Phillips Exeter Academy and from 1807 was a trustee of Dartmouth College. In 1813, at the beginning of his second period of office, the legislature revised the state court system, abolishing superior and inferior courts, and putting in a Supreme Court and a Circuit Court of Common Pleas. After leaving the governor's office in 1816, Gilman retired to his home in Exeter. He remained neutral in the Dartmouth College Case, and, once it was settled to his satisfaction in 1819, resigned from the college's board of trustees. Gilman died on August 31, 1828, at Exeter, and was buried in Exeter Cemetery. Bibliography: Arthur Gilman, *The Gilman Family* (Albany, N.Y., 1869); Alexander W. Gillman, *Searches into the History of the Gillman or Gilman Family* (London, 1895); Charles H. Bell, *History of the Town of Exeter* (Exeter, N. H:, 1888); W. F. Whitcher, "New Hampshire in the Continental Congress and in the Congress of the Confederation," *The Granite Monthly*, VI (June 1883); Arthur K. Smart, "When New Hampshire Laid the Foundations for Our United Nations," *Historical New Hampshire*, V (March 1949); Mark D. Kaplanoff, "Religion and Righteousness: A Study of Federalist Rhetoric in the New Hampshire Election of 1800," *Historical New Hampshire*, XXIII (Winter 1968). Collection of approximately 70 items in the archives of the Dartmouth College Library, Hanover, N. H.

LANGDON, John, 1805-1809, 1810-1812

Born on June 26, 1741, in Portsmouth, New Hampshire, son of John Langdon, a farmer, and Mary Hall Langdon. Brother of Woodbury, Mary, Elizabeth, Abigail and Martha. Married to Elizabeth Sherburne on February 3, 1776; father of Elizabeth and John, who died in infancy. Educated at Hale's Latin Grammar School; began business as an employee of Portsmouth merchant Daniel Rindge in 1760; took first command of a merchant vessel in 1763; in 1773 actively opposed the Tea Act; served under John Sullivan during the raid on Fort William and Mary in 1774; equipped John Stark's brigade for the Battle of Bennington, 1777. Served in the State Legislature 1775, 1777-81, 1786-87 (as Speaker), and 1801-05 (as Speaker 1803-05); attended the Continental Congress, 1775-76; appointed Continental Naval Agent, and supervised the construction of *Raleigh, Ranger,* and *America*; served in Congress again from 1783 to 1784, and in the New Hampshire State Senate from 1784 to 1785; President (i.e., Chief Executive) of New Hampshire in 1785, but lost in 1786 and 1787 to John Sullivan. Supported legislation allowing real or personal property to be sufficient for payment of debts in lieu of cash. Langdon attended the Federal Constitutional Convention in 1787; he signed the Constitution, and supported it in New Hampshire's state ratifying convention. In 1788 Langdon (4,421 votes) defeated Sullivan (3,364) for president, but resigned to serve in the United States Senate. He was a member of the Senate from 1789 to 1801, and its first President Pro Tempore. As a Democratic-Republican, Senator Langdon supported the funding system and the creation of the Bank of the United States, but opposed assumption of state debts by the federal government. After the end of his period in the Senate, he returned to New Hampshire and unsuccessfully ran for Governor against John Taylor Gilman in 1802, 1803 and 1804. However, he defeated Gilman in 1805 by 16,097 votes to 12,287. Except for 1809, when he lost to Jeremiah Smith, Langdon was reelected Governor annually until 1811. In 1806 he polled 15,277 votes to Timothy Farrar's 1,720, Gilman's 1,553, Smith's 902, and Oliver Peabody's 866; in 1807 he received 13,912 votes, with 2,949 scattered among a number of opponents; in 1808 he beat Gilman, 12,641 to 1,261; and in 1810 and 1811 he defeated Smith by counts of 16,325 to 15,166, and 17,554 to 14,477. As governor, Langdon induced the legislature to select a permanent seat of government (Concord), and secured laws prohibiting the importation of slaves, regulating the manufacture and sale of bread, ordering the inspection of beef, and prohibiting the issuing of private notes as currency. He defended Jefferson's embargo of 1807-09. Langdon was offered the post of Secretary of the Navy by Jefferson, but declined the opportunity and retired to his home in Portsmouth. He also refused a chance to run for Vice President of the United States in 1812. Late in life he became interested in religion, and was the founder of the New Hampshire Bible Society. Langdon died on September 18, 1819, in Portsmouth, and was buried in the North Burying Ground. Bibliography: Lawrence Shaw Mayo, *John Langdon of New Hampshire* (Concord, N.H., 1937); Jere R. Daniell, *Experiment in Republicanism: New Hampshire Politics and the American Revolution, 1741-1794* (Cambridge, Mass., 1970); Lynn W. Turner, *William Plumer of New Hampshire, 1759-1850* (Chapel Hill, 1962); Charles W. Brewster, *Rambles About Portsmouth*, 2nd ed. (Portsmouth, 1873 and 1971); John Langdon Elwyn, "Some Account of John Langdon," *Early State Papers of New Hampshire*, XX (1891); William F. Whitcher, "New Hampshire in the Continental Congress and in the Congress of the Confederation," *Granite Monthly*, VI (1883). There is a collection of Langdon Papers in the New Hampshire Historical Society, but most have apparently been lost.

SMITH, Jeremiah, 1809-1810

Born on November 29, 1759, in Peterborough, New Hampshire, son of William Smith, an immigrant farmer from Northern Ireland, and Elizabeth (Morison) Smith, both of whom were Scotch-Irish Presbyterians. Brother of William, James, Robert, Elizabeth, John, Hannah, Jonathan and Samuel. Married to Elizabeth Ross on March 8, 1797 (d. 1827), in Bladensburg, Maryland; father of Ariana, William and Jeremiah; remarried after his wife's death in 1827, to Elizabeth Hale on September 20, 1831. Volunteered to serve under General John Stark and was wounded at the Battle of Bennington, Vermont, in August 1777. Entered Harvard in 1777, but moved to New Jersey and was graduated from Queens College (Rutgers) in 1780. Read law for five years in Massachusetts, and was admitted to the New Hampshire Bar in 1786; set up a practice in Peterborough. Member of the State Legislature, 1787-90, where he conducted the impeachment of Judge Woodbury Langdon and chaired the committee that presented the revised statutes from the State Constitutional Convention in 1791-92. Won a seat in the United States Congress beginning in 1791, but resigned in 1797 to accept appointment as United States District Attorney; served briefly as Judge of Probate for Rockingham County, and as an Adams appointee to the United States Circuit Court in 1801-02; Chief Justice of the State Superior Court, 1802-09; as a Jeffersonian Republican, defeated Federalist John Langdon for the governorship in 1809 by a vote of 15,610 to 15,241. Governor Smith devoted most of his first address to the legislature to a plea for reform of the state's weak judicial system, asking especially that compensation be made more equal to the duties and responsibilities required of a judge. The plea was ignored, however, since Federalist lawmakers were still in the majority. Nevertheless, despite the disadvantage of a hostile legislature, Smith was able to secure a significant addition to the medical school facilities of Dartmouth College. He lost the elections of 1806, 1810 and 1811 to Langdon. Smith returned to his Exeter law practice, and became Chief Justice of the State Supreme Court between 1813 and 1816. He joined with Daniel Webster and Jeremiah Mason in representing Dartmouth College in its famous case of 1819. He also collected manuscripts of law cases, served as president of an Exeter bank, received honorary LL.D. degrees from Dartmouth in 1804 and Harvard in 1807, and was treasurer and trustee of Phillips Exeter Academy between 1828 and 1842. Smith died on September 21, 1842, in Dover, where he had recently moved, and was buried in Winter Street Cemetery in Exeter. Bibliography: John H. Morison, *Life of the Hon. Jeremiah Smith, LL.D.* (Boston, 1845); Charles H. Bell, *The Bench and Bar of New Hampshire* (Boston, 1894); Albert Smith, *History of the Town of Peterborough* (Boston, 1876); Jonathan Smith, *The Home of the Smith Family in Peterborough, New Hampshire, 1749-1842* (Clinton, Mass., 1900); Jeremiah Smith, Jr., ed., *Smith's Decisions: Reports of Cases Decided in the Superior and Supreme Judicial Courts of New Hampshire from 1802 to 1816* (Boston, 1879). The Smith Papers on deposit in the New Hampshire Historical Society at Concord.

LANGDON, John, 1805-1809, 1810-1812

PLUMER, William, 1812-1813, 1816-1819

Born on June 25, 1759, in Newburyport, Massachusetts, son of Samuel Plumer, a cordwainer and farmer, and Mary (Dole) Plumer. Brother of Rebecca, Mary, Samuel, Daniel and Hannah. Married to Sally Fowler on February 13, 1788; father of William, Sarah, Samuel, George Washington, John Jay and Quintus. Educated at the South Writing School of Newburyport and then at a common school in Epping, New Hampshire. Formal education ended at seventeen; read law between 1786 and 1788 under John Prentice of Londonderry, New Hampshire. Was drawn strongly to the Baptist faith in 1779, but by 1781 had been converted to Deism, and had permanently abandoned organized religion. Admitted to the bar in 1787. Entered politics in 1783 as a town elder of Epping; elected to the State Legislature in 1785, and then annually from 1788 to 1791, when he was Speaker, and again from 1797 to 1801; a leader of the State Constitutional Convention of 1791-92. In 1802 the State Senate chose Plumer, a Federalist, to fill the vacancy in the United States Senate caused by the resignation of James Sheafe. Served until 1807, when he converted to Jeffersonian Republicanism. Returned to the State Senate in 1810 and 1811; challenged Federalist John Taylor Gilman for the governorship in 1812; although Plumer only won 15,492 votes to Gilman's 15,613, a scattered vote of 877 cast for other candidates deprived Gilman of a majority, and the election was decided in the State Legislature, where Plumer won by a small margin. During his first term as governor, Plumer presided over a revision of the penal code and a reapportionment for purposes of taxation. He also called up troops from the first militia brigade for the War of 1812, and oversaw the building of a new state prison. Plumer lost to John Taylor Gilman in the elections of 1813 (17,410 to 18,107), 1814 (18,794 to 19,695), and 1815 (17,799 to 18,357). He won, however, in 1816 (20,338) over Federalist James Sheafe (17,994); in 1817 (19,088) over Federalists James Sheafe (12,029) and Jeremiah Mason (3,067), and Independent Josiah Bartlett (539); and in 1818 (18,674) over Federalists Jeremiah Mason (6,850) and William Hale (5,019). During his second period as governor, the United States Supreme Court, in *Trustees of Dartmouth College v. Woodward*, decided against Plumer in his attempt to control the administration of the college by means of a state-appointed board of trustees. Plumer also presided over a revision of the state's judicial system, selected the site for New Hampshire's present State House, and supported relief for the non-imprisonment of debtors. He lost a contest for the United States Senate in 1819, and in December 1820, cast the only electoral vote in the nation opposing the Monroe-Tompkins ticket. Plumer then retired to his farm in Epping, where he wrote for newspapers under the pseudonyms of "Veritas," "Aristides," "Columbus" and "Cincinnatus." He was a member of many organizations, including the Massachusetts Historical Society and the New Hampshire Historical Society, of which he was a founder and the first president in 1823. Plumer died on December 22, 1850, in Epping. He was buried in the family cemetery there. Bibliography: Lynn W. Turner, *William Plumer of New Hampshire, 1759-1850* (Chapel Hill, 1962); William Plumer, Jr., *Life of William Plumer* (Boston, 1856); Everett S. Brown, ed., *William Plumer's Memorandum of Proceedings in the United States Senate, 1803-1807* (New York, 1923); Sidney Perley, *The Plumer Genealogy* (Salem, Mass., 1917); Lynn W. Turner, "The Electoral Vote Against Monroe in 1820, an American Legend," *Mississippi Valley Historical Review*, XLII (September 1955); William G. McLoughlin, "The Bench, The Church, and The Republican Party in New Hampshire, 1790 to 1820," *Historical New Hampshire*, XX (Summer, 1965); Albert S. Wait, "The Life, Character, and Public Services of Governor William Plumer," New Hampshire Historical Society *Proceedings*, III (1902). Major collections of Plumer's papers are housed at the Library of Congress, the N. H. State Library, the N. H. Historical Society, and Dartmouth College.

GILMAN, John Taylor, 1794-1805, 1813-1816

PLUMER, William, 1812-1813, 1816-1819

BELL, Samuel, 1819-1823

Born on February 9, 1770, in Londonderry, New Hampshire, son of John Bell, a farmer and state political figure, and Mary Ann (Gilmore) Bell, both of whom were Presbyterians. Brother of James, Ebenezer, Jonathan, John, Elizabeth, Susannah, Mary, Mary Ann and three who died in infancy. Married to Mehitable Bowen Dana on November 26, 1797; father of Samuel Dana, John (d. 1830), James, Luther V. and Mary Ann; after his wife's death in 1827, remarried on July 4, 1828, to Lucy G. Smith; father of George, John, Charles and Louis. Educated in common schools of Londonderry, and graduated from Dartmouth College in 1793; read law with Samuel Dana of Amherst, New Hampshire, admitted to the bar in Hillsborough County in 1796, and set up a practice in Francestown, New Hampshire. Moved to Amherst, and was president of the Hillsborough Bank, which operated from 1806 until about 1810—the only bank in New Hampshire to fail between 1792 and 1840. Entered politics as a Democratic-Republican member of the State House of Representatives, 1804-07, and became its Speaker from 1805 to 1807; member and President of the State Senate, 1807-09, and member of the Executive Council, 1809-11. Trustee of Dartmouth College, 1808-11; moved to Chester, New Hampshire, in 1812; held seat on Superior Court, 1816-19; won nomination for Governor in 1819, and defeated Federalist William Hale, 13,761 votes to 8,660. Won against only token opposition in 1820 (22,212 to 2,559); 1821 (22,582 to 1,866); and 1822 (22,934 to 1,046). Governor Bell supported the repeal of the Toleration Act in 1819, thus ending the power of towns to tax individuals for support of the clergy. He advocated and won legislation conferring chancery powers on the Superior Court in matters affecting trusteeship of charitable foundations, demanded a stricter licensing system to fight intemperance, and supported the federal tariff, urging the development of manufacturing and economic diversification in the state. He also took an interest in reports on the number and treatment of deaf persons and paupers in the state, and endeavored to locate the causes of crime in New Hampshire. In 1823 Bell won appointment to the United States Senate, where he served until 1835; while in the Senate, he supported the compromise tariff of 1833. He opposed Andrew Jackson's bank policy, however, and joined the Whig Party in 1834. Bell eventually retired to his farm at Chester, where he died on December 23, 1850; he was buried in the village cemetery. Among his other honors, he received an honorary LL.D. degree from Bowdoin College in 1821. Bibliography: *The Bell Family in America* (New York, 1913); Benjamin Chace, *History of Old Chester, From 1719 to 1869* (Auburn, N. H., 1869); Edward L. Parker, *The History of Londonderry* (Boston, 1851); Charles H. Bell, *The Bench and Bar of New Hampshire* (Boston, 1894); Norman W. Smith, "The 'Amherst Bubble,' Wildcat Banking in Early Nineteenth Century New Hampshire," *Historical New Hampshire*, XX (Spring 1965).

WOODBURY, Levi, 1823-1824

Born on December 22, 1789, in Francestown, New Hampshire, son of Peter Woodbury, a merchant and farmer, and Mary (Woodbury) Woodbury. Brother of Mary, Peter Perkins, Anstriss, Martha, Hannah, James Trask, Harriet, Jesse, Adeline and George Washington. Married to Elizabeth Williams Clapp in June 1819; father of Charles Levi, Mary Elizabeth, Frances A., Virginia L. and Ellen Carolina DeQuincey. Educated at Atkinson Academy and graduated from Dartmouth College in 1809; read law with Jeremiah Smith in Exeter, Samuel Dana in Boston, and at Litchfield Law School in Connecticut; was admitted to the bar and began practice in Francestown in 1812. Chosen clerk of the State Senate in 1816, and received appointment to the bench of the Superior Court; moved to Portsmouth in 1819. In 1823 the Democratic-Republican Party nominated Samuel Dinsmoor for the governorship. Since the Federalists no longer functioned as a party in New Hampshire, Woodbury, although also a Democratic-Republican, challenged Dinsmoor by running as an independent. Woodbury won by a vote of 16,985 to 12,718. By 1824 Woodbury was a Jacksonian Democrat; he lost a close election for governor in that year, when the State Legislature chose David L. Morril. Governor Woodbury presided over a session of the legislature which had as its principal aim the incorporation of the New Hampshire Historical Society as a private, non-profit organization formed to preserve the state's heritage. Woodbury served as the Society's first vice president, and succeeded William Plumer as its president. He endeavored to improve the adminstration of justice in the state, and to improve New Hampshire's public transportation facilities. After the end of his gubernatorial term, Woodbury returned to his law practice. In 1825 he was elected to the State Legislature and became its Speaker. He also served in the United States Senate from 1825 to 1831, as Secretary of the Navy from 1831 to 1834, and as Secretary of the Treasury from 1834 to 1841. During his career in national politics, Woodbury opposed the policies of the Bank of the United States. He returned to the United States Senate in 1841, and in 1845, having declined the ambassadorship to the Court of St. James, he was appointed an Associate Justice on the United States Supreme Court. He received honorary LL.D. degrees from Dartmouth College and Wesleyan University. Woodbury died on September 4, 1851, at his home in Portsmouth, and was buried in Harmony Grove Cemetery. Bibliography: Vincent J. Capowski, "The Making of a Jacksonian Democrat: Levi Woodbury, 1789-1831," Ph.D. Dissertation, Fordham University, 1966; Charles H. Bell, *The Bench and Bar of New Hampshire* (Boston, 1894); Charles Levi Woodbury, *Genealogical Sketches of the Woodbury Family* (Manchester, N. H., 1904); *Writings of Levi Woodbury, LL.D.*, 3 vols. (Boston, 1852); Vincent J. Capowski, "The Era of Good Feelings in New Hampshire: The Gubernatorial Campaigns of Levi Woodbury, 1823-1824," *Historical New Hampshire*, XXI (Winter 1966); H. B. Fant, "Levi Woodbury's Week in Vermont," *Vermont History*, XXXIV (January 1966); Robert Rantoul, Jr., *Eulogy on the Hon. Levi Woodbury* (Portsmouth, 1852). The papers of Woodbury are housed in the Library of Congress and in the Dartmouth College Library.

MORRIL, David Lawrence, 1824-1827

Born on June 10, 1772, in Epping, New Hampshire, son of the Reverend Samuel Morril, pastor of the Congregational Church in Epping, and Ann (Lawrence) Morril. Brother of Samuel. Married to Jane Wallace on September 23, 1794; after her death on December 14, 1823, remarried to Lydia Poore on August 3, 1824; father of David Lawrence (b. June 25, 1825, d. June 10, 1826), David Lawrence, Jr., Samuel and William H., all by his second marriage. Received preparatory education in theology from his grandfathers, Rev. Isaac Morril and Rev. David Lawrence, and training in medicine from his stepfather, Dr. Timothy Johnson; entered Phillips Exeter Academy in November 1790, and received a teaching certificate in 1791; received honorary A.M. and M.D. degrees from Dartmouth College while Governor, and an LL.D. degree from the University of Vermont; went to Natick, Massachusetts, to study and practice medicine with his uncle, Dr. Isaac Morril; practiced medicine in Epsom, New Hampshire, 1793-1800; returned to the study of theology, and was ordained pastor of the Presbyterian-Congregational Church in Goffstown, New Hampshire, on March 2, 1802; resumed medical career in 1807, and asked for dismissal from his church at Goffstown in 1809; continued as a physician until 1830. Published a number of sermons, orations and controversial pamphlets, and served as president of the New Hampshire Medical Society in 1823-24. Entered politics in 1808 as Goffstown's representative to the State Legislature; annually reelected until 1817, and became Speaker in 1816; chosen to the United States Senate in 1816, and served until 1823; returned to the State Senate in 1823, and chosen its President. As a Democratic-Republican and supporter of John Quincy Adams, Morril won the governorship in 1824 with 14,899 votes, as opposed to Democrat Levi Woodbury's 11,741. In 1825 Morril ran virtually unopposed, obtaining 29,166 votes out of a total of 29,752. In 1826 he polled 17,679 votes to defeat Benjamin Pierce, a Jacksonian Democrat, who received 12,287. As governor, Morril endorsed a program of state internal improvements, by showing a strong interest in road construction and the promotion of education. He advocated but failed to obtain the establishment of a state university for New Hampshire. The highlight of his term was his reception of Lafayette on the occasion of the Frenchman's visit to New Hampshire in 1825. Morril ran for a fourth time in 1827, but was overwhelmingly defeated by Pierce by a vote of 23,695 to 2,529. Morril retired to his medical practice after his term as governor, but in 1831 he moved to Concord, New Hampshire, where he edited the *Religious Observer* for two years. During his later years, he was vice president of the American Bible Society, and was active in the Sunday School Union and the Home Missionary Society. Morril died on January 28, 1849, at Concord, where he was buried in the Old North Cemetery. Bibliography: Annie Morrill Smith, *Morrill Kindred in America*, 2 vols. (New York, 1914-31); Nathan F. Carter, *The Native Ministry of New Hampshire* (Concord, N. H., 1906); George P. Hadley, *History of the Town of Goffstown, 1733-1920*, 2 vols. (1922-24); *New England Historical and Genealogical Register*, III (Boston, 1849); Hamilton S. Putnam, ed., *The New Hampshire Medical Society: A History, 1791-1966* (Milford, N. H., 1966); William H. Brown, "David Lawrence Morril," *Historical New Hampshire*, XIX (Summer, 1964). Morril's diary for 1799-1810 and some other papers are in the New Hampshire Historical Society in Concord.

PIERCE, Benjamin, 1827-1828, 1829-1830

Born on December 25, 1757, in Chelmsford, Massachusetts, son of Benjamin Pierce, a farmer (who died young and left Benjamin to be brought up by an uncle, Robert Pierce), and Elizabeth (Merrill) Pierce. Brother of Rebecca, Jesse, Phebe, Lydia, Leafey, Susannah, Ester and Merrill. Married to Elizabeth Andrews on May 24, 1787; father of Elizabeth; after his wife's death in 1788, remarried to Anna Kendrick on February 1, 1790; father of Benjamin Kendrick, Nancy M., John S., Harriet B., Charles Grandison, Franklin, Charlotte and Henry Dearborn. Farmed in Chelmsford, and left farming after learning of the British raids on Lexington and Concord; served in the Battle of Bunker Hill, and continued on active duty until resigning as a Captain in 1784; remained in the New Hampshire militia, achieving the rank of Brigadier General by 1805. Began farming in Hillsborough in 1786. Elected as a Democrat to the General Court, 1789-1802; served on the Executive Council, 1803-09 and 1814-18; High Sheriff of Hillsborough County, 1809-14 and 1818-23. Ran for Governor in 1826 as a Jackson Democrat, but lost to David L. Morril; defeated Morril in 1827 by a vote of 23,695 to 2,529; lost in 1828 to John Bell; won in 1829, beating Bell by a vote of 22,615 to 19,583. Governor Pierce called for a return to personal self-denial by New Hampshire's citizens as a means of improving the state's economy. He was also a strong advocate of better transportation facilities for the state. During his administration the Hopkinton Academy was established in 1827, and the state began to develop mining and quarry industries. Pierce retired to his farm after his years as governor had ended. He also served as vice president of the Massachusetts Society of the Cincinnati from 1836. Pierce died on April 1, 1839, in Hillsborough, and was buried in the Pine Hill Cemetery. Bibliography:

Frederick C. Pierce, *Pierce Genealogy* (Worcester, 1882); Roy F. Nichols, *Franklin Pierce: Young Hickory of the Granite Hills* (Philadelphia, 1931); George W. Browne, *The History of Hillsborough, New Hampshire, 1735-1921*, 2 vols. (Manchester, N. H., 1921-22); Donald B. Cole, *Jacksonian Democracy in New Hampshire, 1800-1851* (Cambridge, Mass., 1970); "Memoir of Benjamin Pierce," *The New England Historical and Genealogical Register*, VII (January 1853). The Benjamin Pierce Papers are on deposit in the New Hampshire Historical Society.

BELL, John, 1828-1829

Born on July 20, 1765, in Londonderry, New Hampshire, son of John Bell, a farmer and public official during the Revolution, and Mary Ann (Gilmore) Bell, both of whom were Presbyterians. Brother of James, Ebenezer, Jonathan, (Governor) Samuel, Elizabeth, Susannah, Mary, Mary Ann and three others who died in infancy. Married to Persis Thom on December 25, 1803; father of Mary Anne Persis, Eliza Thom, John, Susan Jane, Harrietta Adelia, Jane Gibson, Caroline, Christopher Sergeant, James Isaac and (Governor) Charles Henry. Engaged in profitable trade with Canada. Entered politics as a legislator from Londonderry, 1799-1800, moving soon thereafter to Chester, New Hampshire; was a State Senator from 1803 to 1804; a Councillor from 1817 to 1823, and Sheriff of Rockingham County from 1823 to 1828. Running as an Adams Democrat, he won the governorship in 1828 over Benjamin Pierce, 21,149 votes to 18,672. Governor Bell urged experimentation by the state in farming and agriculture and pressed for the institution of formal agricultural education. During his term of office, a number of significant manufacturing companies around the state were incorporated, the academies at Lee and Boscawen were established, and the Exeter Savings Bank was chartered. Bell lost the gubernatorial election of 1829 to Benjamin Pierce. Bell then retired to his home in Chester, where he resumed his business and farming activities. Bell died on March 22, 1836, in Chester. He was buried in the village cemetery. Bibliography: *The Bell Family in America* (New York, 1913); Benjamin Chace, *History of Old Chester, From 1719 to 1869* (Auburn, N. H., 1869); Edward L. Parker, *The History of Londonderry* (Boston, 1851); Ezra S. Stearns, *Genealogical and Family History of the State of New Hampshire*, vol. IV (New York, 1908). There are some Bell Papers on deposit in the New Hampshire Historical Society.

PIERCE, Benjamin, 1827-1828, 1829-1830

HARVEY, Matthew, 1830-1831

Born on June 21, 1781, in Sutton, New Hampshire, son of Matthew Harvey, a farmer and legislator, and Hannah (Sargeant) Harvey. Brother of Jonathan, Philip, John, Benjamin W., Susan and Hannah. Married to Margaret Rowe of Newburyport, Massachusetts on September 21, 1811; father of Frederick Rowe and Margaret Elizabeth. Received general preparation for college from the Rev. Samuel Wood of

Boscawen, New Hampshire; graduated from Dartmouth College in 1806; read law with John Harris of Hopkinton, New Hampshire, and began a practice there in 1809. Originally a Baptist, but in 1806 confirmed in the Episcopal Church. As a Democratic-Republican he was a member of the legislature, 1814-20 (as Speaker, 1817-20); won election to the United States Congress in 1821 and 1823; served in the State Senate 1825-28 (as President, 1826-28); on the Executive Council, 1828-30; won election as Governor in 1830 over Timothy Upham, 23,214 votes to 19,040. Governor Harvey pointed out clearly the evils inherent in the custom of imprisonment for debt, but it took another decade for the legislature to abolish the practice. He called attention to overcrowded prison conditions and advocated giving a small amount of money to each prisoner after his release. Harvey resigned on February 28, 1831, to become Judge of the United States District Court for New Hampshire, leaving the governor's office to Senate President Joseph M. Harper. Harvey, who remained on the bench until his death, moved to Concord, New Hampshire, in 1850. He was one of the early trustees of Hopkinton Academy (founded in 1827), president of the New Hampshire Historical Society from 1832 to 1834, and the recipient of an honorary LL.D. degree from Dartmouth College in 1855. Harvey died on April 7, 1866, in Concord, and was buried in the Old North Cemetery. Bibliography: Charles H. Bell, *The Bench and Bar of New Hampshire* (Boston, 1894); Augusta H. Worthen, *The History of Sutton, New Hampshire* (Sutton, N.H., 1890 and 1975); C. C. Lord, *Life and Times in Hopkinton, N. H.* (Concord, N. H., 1890); William L. Foster, *A Sketch of the Life and Character of Honorable Matthew Harvey* (Concord, N. H., 1867); C. C. Lord, "Matthew Harvey," *The Granite Monthly*, X (1887); obituary, *The New England Historical and Genealogical Register*, XX (July 1886).

HARPER, Joseph Morrill, 1831

Born on June 21, 1787, in Limerick, Massachusetts, (now Maine), son of Samuel Harper, a farmer and soldier, and Sarah (Godfrey) Harper. Brother of Susan, Betsey, Sukey, Abigail, Eunice, Ezekiel, Hannah, Samuel and Clarissa. Married to Elizabeth Clough on June 6, 1816; father of Joseph Clough, Charles Augustus and Sarah Elizabeth. Received a general education at Fryeburg Academy, and began the study of medicine in 1808 under Dr. Jonathan Kittredge of Canterbury, New Hampshire; set up a practice in Sanbornton, New Hampshire, in 1810, and in 1811 returned to Canterbury; continued his successful practice in Canterbury and became a fellow of the New Hampshire Medical Society, which had been incorporated during the gubernatorial term of Dr. Josiah Bartlett. Joined the army in 1813 as Second Surgeon of the 4th Infantry, and remained on active duty until the War of 1812 ended in 1815. Entered politics as a Democratic legislator from Canterbury in 1826, and was a member of the Lower House until 1828; won election to the State Senate in 1829, and became its President in 1830-31. When Governor Matthew Harvey resigned to accept a judgeship on the United States District Court for New Hampshire in February 1831, Harper, as President of the Senate, inherited the governor's chair. The legislature had no routine or emergency reason to meet during Harper's brief tenure; consequently, he was able to accomplish little while he remained Governor. In 1831 Harper won election to the United States Congress, where he sat for two terms as a staunch supporter of measures put forward by

President Andrew Jackson. In 1835 he returned to his farm and medical practice in Canterbury. He held positions as Justice of the Peace, 1835-65, and president of Mechanics Bank in Concord, New Hampshire, 1847-56. Harper died on January 15, 1865, in Canterbury, where he was buried in the village cemetery. Bibliography: James O. Lyford, *History of the Town of Canterbury, New Hampshire, 1727-1912* (Canterbury, N. H., 1912 and 1973); M. T. Runnels, *History of Sanbornton, New Hampshire*, 2 vols. (Boston, 1882); Donald B. Cole, *Jacksonian Democracy in New Hampshire, 1800-1851* (Cambridge, Mass., 1970); Philip A. Grant, "The Bank Controversy and New Hampshire Politics, 1834-1835," *Historical New Hampshire*, XXIII (Autumn 1968); "Biography of Hon. Joseph M. Harper," *The Farmer's Monthly Visitor*, XIII (April, 1853).

DINSMOOR, Samuel, 1831-1834

Born on July 1, 1766, in Windham, New Hampshire, son of William Dinsmoor, a farmer, and Elizabeth (Cochran) Dinsmoor, both of whom were Scotch-Irish Methodists. Brother of Janet, Robert, John, William, Margaret, Mary, Isaac, Elizabeth and Annis. Married to Mary Boyd Reid in 1798 at Londonderry, New Hampshire; father of Governor Samuel Dinsmoor, Jr., Mary Eliza, George Reid and William. Graduated from Dartmouth College in 1789; taught school for several years, and settled in Keene, New Hampshire, in 1792, where he read law under Peleg Sprague. Admitted to the bar in 1795, and set up his own practice. Organized the Keene light infantry militia unit in 1804, and as a Major General was its commander for many years; appointed Keene Postmaster in 1808; served in the United States Congress from 1811 to 1813, where, as a "War Hawk," he voted in favor of war with Great Britain. Served as a Presidential Elector in 1820; appointed Collector of the Direct Tax, State Councillor in 1821, and Judge of Probate for Cheshire County, 1823-31; lost the governorship in 1823 to Levi Woodbury, and was on the 1825 commission to settle the boundary between New Hampshire and Massachusetts. In 1831, as a Jacksonian Democrat, Dinsmoor won the gubernatorial race with 23,503 votes, defeating Democratic-Republican Ichabod Bartlett, who polled 18,681; he repeated his victory over Bartlett in 1832 (24,167 to 14,920 votes); in 1833 he defeated Democratic-Republican Arthur Livermore (28,277 to 3,959). As governor, Dinsmoor advocated establishment of a hospital for the insane, but it was ten years before the state developed such an institution. He called for strengthened defenses for the state, although militia discipline had already begun to decline steadily. On Dinsmoor's advice, the legislature appointed a committee to investigate the number and condition of blind persons in the state. During his administration the first free public library in the United States was founded in Peterborough, New Hampshire; the state's banks prospered; railroads were becoming financially sound investments; the constitution of the "Indian Stream Republic" along the Canadian border of New Hampshire was rewritten and submitted to the legislature; and many new businesses were incorporated, including the Amoskeag Manufacturing Company, the Sullivan Manufacturing Company, and the Winnipiseogee Lake Cotton and Woolen Manufacturing Company. Dinsmoor had become president of the Ashuelot Bank in Keene in 1833, and he took up this position when he retired from the governorship. Dinsmoor died on March 15, 1835, in Keene. He was buried in the Washington Street Cemetery. Bibliography: Charles H. Bell, *The Bench and Bar of New*

Hampshire (Boston, 1894); S. G. Griffin, *A History of the Town of Keene* (Keene, N. H., 1904); Leonard A. Morrison, *The History of Windham* (Boston, 1883); Leonard A. Morrison, *The Earliest History and Genealogy of the Dinsmoor-Dinsmore Family* (Lowell, Mass., 1891); Donald B. Cole, *Jacksonian Democracy in New Hampshire, 1800-1851* (Cambridge, Mass., 1970); Vincent J. Capowski, "The Era of Good Feelings in New Hampshire: The Gubernatorial Campaigns of Levi Woodbury, 1823-1824," *Historical New Hampshire*, XXI (Winter 1966).

BADGER, William, 1834-1836

Born on January 13, 1779, in Gilmanton, New Hampshire, son of Joseph Badger, Jr., a farmer, public official and army officer during the Revolution, and Elizabeth (Parsons) Badger. Brother of Joseph, Hannah, Sarah, Elizabeth and Ebenezer. Married on May 1, 1803 to Martha Smith; father of John and Martha; after his wife's death in January 1810, married Hannah Pearson Cogswell on January 12, 1814; father of Joseph and William. Educated in common schools and attended Gilmanton Academy. Early life devoted to business; was chiefly responsible for the construction of a cotton cloth factory, a sawmill and a grist mill for the town of Gilmanton; elected a trustee of Gilmanton Academy in 1804, and eventually became President of the Board. Served as an Aide-de-Camp to Governor Langdon with the rank of Colonel. Entered the legislature as a representative for Gilmanton in 1810, and won reelection in 1811 and 1812; elected to the State Senate in 1814, 1815 and 1816, serving as its President, 1816-17; became an Associate Justice on the Court of Common Pleas, 1816-20, moderator of town meetings, 1817-23 and 1825-26, High Sheriff of Strafford County, 1820-30, and a Presidential Elector in 1824, 1836 and 1844. Large wealth and many civic honors made Badger a strong Democratic candidate for Governor in 1834; he won handily, receiving 28,542 of the 30,173 votes cast. In 1835 Badger (25,767 votes) defeated the Whig candidate, Joseph Healey (14,825). Governor Badger called attention for the first time to the advisability of dispensing with capital punishment, suggesting solitary confinement and hard labor as a substitute punishment, and demonstrated his feeling by postponing a hanging for as long as possible. His term witnessed the high point of the crisis centering on the "Indian Stream Republic:" Badger delivered a special message in June 1835 urging the legislature to maintain possession of the territory. The legislature complied by ordering General Joseph Low's 24th Militia Regiment to assist the county sheriff in maintaining control. Badger also induced the legislature to endorse President Jackson by attacking the United States Bank; encouraged the state's lawmakers in 1834 to bolster the militia; and signed a bill providing for direct methods of preventing smallpox in New Hampshire's towns. Badger retired to his business and civic interests in Gilmanton after his period as governor, but remained an active member of the state Democratic Party. Badger died on September 21, 1852, in Gilmanton. Bibliography: John C. Badger, *Giles Badger and His Descendants* (Manchester, N. H., 1909); *The New England Historical and Genealogical Register*, VII (1853); Daniel Lancaster, *The History of Gilmanton* (Gilmanton, N.H., 1845); D. Hamilton Hurd, ed., *History of Merrimack and Belknap Counties* (Philadelphia, 1885); Edgar Aldrick, "Our Northern Boundary: The Provisional Government of the Indian Stream Territory, 1832-35," New Hampshire Historical Society, *Proceedings*, II (1895), and *The Granite Monthly*, XVII (October, 1894);

Philip A. Grant, Jr., "The Bank Controversy and New Hampshire Politics, 1834-1835," *Historical New Hampshire*, XXIII (Autumn 1968).

HILL, Isaac, 1836-1839

Born on April 6, 1788, in Cambridge, Massachusetts, son of Isaac Hill, a farmer, and Hannah Russell Hill; Episcopalian. Brother of Walter Russell, Hannah Russell Cushing, Sultina Townsend, Susan Wellington Hastings, Mary Adams Moore, George Washington, Horatio and Rebecca Russell Reding. Married to Susanna Ayer on February 2, 1814; father of William Pickering, John McClary, Georgiana Toscan and Isaac Andrew. Family moved to newly purchased farm in Ashburnham, Massachusetts, in 1798. Isaac was educated in the district schools, worked on the family farm, and in 1802 was apprenticed to Joseph Cushing, publisher of the *Amherst Cabinet* in Amherst, New Hampshire. Moved to Concord, New Hampshire, where he purchased the *American Patriot,* changing its name to the *New Hampshire Patriot* and publishing his first issue in May 1809; continued publication for twenty years. Entered politics as clerk of the N. H. State Senate, 1819 and 1825, and was elected to the Senate in 1820, 1821, 1822 and 1827. In 1829 President Andrew Jackson appointed Hill Second Comptroller of the United States Treasury. The United States Senate in April 1830 refused to confirm this "kitchen cabinet" appointment of Jackson's, and the New Hampshire State Legislature responded by electing Hill to the United States Senate. He sat for five years, resigning in 1836 to accept the governorship of New Hampshire. Out of a total vote of 30,924 in 1836, Hill received 24,903, Joseph Healey 2,566, and George Sullivan 2,344, with 1,111 going to other candidates. In 1837 Hill received 22,361 out of a total vote of 24,532, with Healey polling 557, Sullivan 458, and 1,156 scattered among others. Hill repeated the success in 1838, obtaining 28,697 out of 54,570 votes to defeat James Wilson, Jr. Wilson received 25,675 votes, and 198 were scattered. Hill was a popular and successful governor. An enthusiastic advocate of railroads, he and his brother Horatio were leaders in bringing the railroad to Concord, New Hampshire. He believed in public responsibility for the care of the insane; defended economy in government; urged rotation in office; was on of the first public officials to advocate the preservation of early state records; and denounced the tariff, the United States Bank, and the use of federal funds for internal improvements. In 1840 President Van Buren appointed Hill to the subtreasury in Boston, a post he held until March 1841. He was removed by the Harrison administration. In 1840, with his two oldest sons, he established *Hills New Hampshire Patriot,* which merged in 1847 with the original *New Hampshire Patriot.* Hill also edited and published the *Farmer's Monthly Visitor* for ten years, and during the last fifteen years of his life was actively involved in the promotion of agricultural improvements. Hill was a success in both his publishing enterprises and in his role as owner of the Franklin Bookstore in Concord. He invested large sums in real estate, and helped to organize the New Hampshire Savings Bank, the third bank in the state. Hill died on March 22, 1851, and was buried in Blossom Hill Cemetery, Concord, New Hampshire. Bibliography: Cyrus Parker Bradley, *Biography of Isaac Hill of New Hampshire* (Concord, 1835); *Manual of the General Court of New Hampshire* (Concord, 1891); Ezra S. Stearns, *Genealogy and Family History of the State of New Hampshire*, 4 vols. (Chicago, 1908); Elwin L. Page, *Printing in Concord, New Hampshire* (Concord, 1938);

Donald B. Cole, *Jacksonian Democracy in New Hampshire* (Cambridge, Mass., 1970); Daniel F. Secomb, *History of the Town of Amherst, New Hampshire* (Somersworth, 1972). Hill's papers are on deposit in the New Hampshire Historical Society, Concord, and Dartmouth College, Hanover.

PAGE, John, 1839-1842

Born on May 21, 1787, in Haverhill, New Hampshire, son of John Page, a farmer and sutler, and Hannah Royce Green Page. Brother of William Green, Stephen Royce and Samuel. Married to Hannah Merrill in 1812; father of John Alfred, Nathaniel Merrill, Edward Livingstone, Sarah Hazen, Frederick William, Henry Harrison, Stephen Royce, George Washington and George Brackett. Attended common schools with the intention of entering college, but had to end formal education at the age of fifteen to assist his father financially. Although his mother was a Baptist, he became strongly attached to the Methodist Episcopal Church. Served on New Hampshire's frontier as a Lieutenant under Captain Ephraim H. Mahurin at Stewartstown between July 27, 1812 and January 27, 1813. Built a house on his farm at Haverhill in 1812. Entered politics as a selectman and served fourteen terms; became a United States tax assessor for the district in 1815, a Democratic legislator from 1818 to 1820 and in 1835, and the Register of Deeds for Grafton County in 1827 and 1829-35. Selected in 1835 over Franklin Pierce on the fifth ballot to fill the unexpired term of United States Senator Isaac Hill, and served until March 1837, when he lost the seat to Pierce; won election to the Executive Council in 1835 and 1838, and in 1839 won as the Democratic gubernatorial candidate (30,518 votes) over the Whig James "Long Jim" Wilson, Jr., of Keene (23,928); repeated victory in 1840 (29,521 votes) over Whig Enos Stevens (20,716); in 1841 received 29,116 votes to defeat Stevens (21,230) and Free Soil candidate Daniel Hoit (1,273). While governor, Page promoted agriculture and arranged for the geological survey of the state by Dr. Charles T. Jackson of Boston. Page opposed the granting of additional bank charters, believing that twenty-eight commercial banks were more than enough for the state's needs. He convinced the legislature of the need for the new independent United States Treasury, cautioned against excessive and special legislation, approved an appropriation for education of the blind, signed legislation abolishing imprisonment for debtors, and presided during the controversy over the boundary between Maine and Canada that led to the Webster-Ashburton Treaty of 1842. After his years as governor, Page retired to his farm and used his influence to achieve the construction of the Boston, Concord and Montreal Railroad. He moved over to the Free Soil Party during the Texas controversy, and later became an organizer of the state Republican Party. Page died on September 8, 1865, in Haverhill, and was buried in Ladd Street Cemetery. Bibliography: William F. Whitcher, *History of the Town of Haverhill, New Hampshire* (n. p., 1919); John Q. Bittinger, *History of Haverhill, N. H.* (Haverhill, N. H., 1888); Chandler E. Potter, *The Military History of the State of New Hampshire, 1623-1861*, part 2 (Baltimore, 1972 [originally published in 1869]); Hamilton Child, *Gazetteer of Grafton County, N. H., 1709-1886* (Syracuse, N. Y., 1886); Donald B. Cole, *Jacksonian Democracy in New Hampshire, 1800-1851* (Cambridge, Mass., 1970); Roy F. Nichols, *Franklin Pierce: Young Hickory of the Granite Hills*, 2nd ed. rev. (Philadelphia, 1958). There is a small collection of Page Papers in Dartmouth College.

HUBBARD, Henry, 1842-1844

Born on May 3, 1784, in Charlestown, New Hampshire, son of John Hubbard, a farmer, and Prudence Stevens Hubbard; Unitarian. Brother of Nancy, Laura, John, Jr., Elizabeth and Richard. Married to Sally Walker Dean on November 30, 1813; father of Henry, Sarah Dean, Nathaniel Dean, Richard and Aaron Dean. Received private tutoring locally and graduated from Dartmouth College in 1803. Read law under Jeremiah Mason at Portsmouth, New Hampshire, was admitted to the bar in 1806, and set up practice in Charlestown; Appointed Judge Advocate of the 5th Militia Brigade under the Militia Law of 1820. Entered politics as town moderator in 1810, and was a selectman in 1819, 1820 and 1828; elected to the legislature in 1812, 1813, 1814, 1819, 1820, 1823 and 1824, and served as Speaker of the House between 1825 and 1827 in place of Levi Woodbury, who had been elected to the United States Senate; served concurrently as Solicitor for Sullivan County, 1823-28; and as Probate Judge for the County, 1827-29; originally a Federalist, but had become a Democrat when he won election to the United States Congress in 1831; reelected to Congress, and served as Speaker Pro Tempore in 1834, staunchly supporting Jackson and his bank policy; member of the United States Senate, 1835-41. Won the 1842 gubernatorial election with 26,831 votes over Whig Enos Stevens (12,234), Independent Democrat John H. White (5,869), and Free Soiler Daniel Hoit (2,812); repeated victory in 1843, garnering 23,050 votes to Whig Anthony Colby's 12,551, White's 5,497, and Hoit's 3,402. Governor Hubbard favored lowering United States tariff rates rather than distributing among the states the revenue from sales of public lands: he felt that a high tariff would hurt the consumer in order to protect a few manufacturers. He also advocated public financial support to defray the defense costs of indigent citizens on trial, and recommended that acquitted defendants not be compelled to bear the entire cost of their trials. Hubbard denounced capital punishment, urged legislation making corporations responsible so that stockholders could not recklessly enrich themselves at the expense of the public, and advised that the property of females, up to a certain limit, not be taxed, since they lacked earning power equal to that of men. Hubbard lived in Boston, Massachusetts, from 1846 to 1849, where he was a Sub-Treasurer during the Polk administration. In 1849 he returned to his law practice in Charlestown, New Hampshire. Hubbard died on June 5, 1857, in Charlestown, and was buried in Forest Hill Cemetery. Bibliography: Edward W. Day, *One Thousand Years of Hubbard History* (New York, 1895); Henry H. Saunderson, *History of Charlestown, New Hampshire, The Old No. 4* (Claremont, N. H., 1876); Charles H. Bell, *The Bench and Bar of New Hampshire* (Boston, 1894); Donald B. Cole, *Jacksonian Democracy in New Hampshire, 1800-1851* (Cambridge, Mass., 1970); Philip A. Grant, Jr., "The Bank Controversy and New Hampshire Politics, 1834-1835," *Historical New Hampshire*, XXIII (Autumn 1968).

STEELE, John Hardy, 1844-1846

Born on January 4, 1789, in Salisbury, North Carolina, son of an immigrant brick maker from Northern Ireland; orphaned at an early age. Moved to Peterborough, New Hampshire in 1811 with Nathaniel Morison, a carriage maker, who met Steele while on a visit to Fayetteville, North Carolina. Married to Jane Moore on November 5, 1816; after her death in 1831, married her sister, Nancy Moore, on January 8, 1833; father of five sons by his first marriage—Edwin, John, Henry, George and Hardy—and one son by his second marriage—Charles. Became skilled as a machinist and set up the first power loom in New Hampshire in 1817; erected the Union Manufacturing Company's cotton mill at West Peterborough in 1824, and managed it until 1845; also owned and managed a family farm in Peterborough. Under the militia reorganization of 1830, Steele was made an Aide-de-Camp to Governor Matthew Harvey. Entered politics through his election to the legislature as a Democrat in 1829. Served as town moderator, 1830-38; sat on the Governor's Council, 1840-42; made a business trip to England in 1842; chosen as the Democratic gubernatorial nominee in 1844, and won with 25,986 votes, over Whig Anthony Colby (14,750), Free Soiler Daniel Hoit (5,767), and Independent Democrat John H. White (1,988); won again in 1845 with 23,406 votes, to defeat Colby (15,579) and Hoit (5,786). As governor, Steele supported the policies of the Democratic administration in Washington. He stressed that the purpose of corporations was to serve the public interest, and that their number ought to be limited; he also preferred a low tariff; and advocated the annexation of Texas and the maintenance of the nation's claim to Oregon, blaming existing friction on the British government. After the completion of the state geological survey during Steele's term, businesses were established to exploit the ores discovered in the state. Steele signed a new railroad act in November 1844, establishing the State Railroad Commission as the agency required to force unwilling farmers to sell land along surveyed railway routes. Steele retired to his Peterborough farm at the end of his period as governor, and indulged in some agricultural experimentation. He was elected a town selectman in 1846, and was an active Freemason, serving as district Deputy Grand Master from 1838 to 1851. Steele died on July 3, 1865, in Peterborough. He was buried in the village cemetery. Bibliography: Albert Smith, *History of the Town of Peterborough* (Boston, 1876); Gerald D. Foss, *Three Centuries of Freemasonry in New Hampshire* (Concord, N. H., 1972); Chandler E. Potter, *The Military History of the State of New Hampshire, 1623-1861*, part 2 (Baltimore, 1972 [originally published, 1869]); Richard H. Sewell, *John P. Hale and the Politics of Abolition* (Cambridge, Mass., 1965); John Lindenbusch, "Journal Kept by John H. Steele on a Journey from Peterborough, N. H. to Salisbury, North Carolina in the Months of November & December 1838," *Historical New Hampshire*, XVIII (December, 1963).

COLBY, Anthony, 1846-1847

Born on November 13, 1792, in New London, New Hampshire, son of Joseph Colby, a farmer and legislator, and Anna (Heath) Colby. Brother of Joseph, Sarah and Judith. Married to Mary Everett on November 24, 1814; after her death in June 1837, married Mrs. Eliza (Messenger) Richardson; father of Daniel Everett, Susan Farnum and Robert. Member of the Baptist Church. Educated in the common schools, and became involved in manufacturing. Built a grist mill in New London; established a stage line on the road from Hanover, New Hampshire, to Lowell, Massachusetts, in 1832; was associated with the establishment of the scythe industry in New Hampshire. Appointed an Ensign in the militia in 1814, and rose to Captain in 1819, Major in 1825, Lieutenant Colonel in 1825, Colonel in 1825, Brigadier General in 1834, and Major General in 1837. Became a town moderator, and entered politics as a legislator, winning annually, 1828-32 and 1837-39; ran as a Whig candidate for the United States Congress in 1833 and 1835, but lost both times to his Democratic opponent; became the Whig candidate for governor in 1843, 1844 and 1845, but lost each year to the Democratic candidate; won nomination again in 1846, and polled 17,707 votes to Democrat Jared W. Williams' 26,740, and Independent Democrat Nathaniel S. Berry's 10,379. When the election went to the legislature for a decision, however, the Independent Democrats joined with the Whigs to elect Colby. As governor, Colby presided over the state during the Mexican War. Resolutions approving the war were defeated in 1846, and passed only by a small majority in 1847, but the 9th Regiment of United States Infantry was raised within the state under the leadership of Franklin Pierce. Colby supported the tariff as a means of protecting manufacturers and raising wages, and called for a broader distribution of dividends. One result of Colby's election was a temporary decline in New Hampshire's Democratic Party, permitting the abolitionist and Free Soil Party candidate John Parker Hale to win election to the United States Senate. Colby was renominated in 1847, but lost decisively to Democrat Jared W. Williams. After leaving the governor's office, Colby returned to New London, where he established and endowed Colby Academy (now Colby-Sawyer College). He received an honorary A.M. degree from Dartmouth College in 1850, and served as a trustee of Dartmouth from 1850 to 1870. Colby served again in the State Legislature in 1860-61, and was appointed State Adjutant General by Governor Berry in 1861; he resigned in 1863. Colby died on July 13, 1873, in New London. He was buried in Old Main Street Cemetery. Bibliography: Mary B. Lord, *A History of the Town of New London* (Somersworth, N. H., 1899 and 1972); Henry K. Rowe, *A Centennial History, 1837-1937; Colby Academy-Colby Junior College* (New London, N. H., 1937); Chandler E. Potter, *The Military History of the State of New Hampshire, 1623-1861,* part 2 (Baltimore, 1972 [originally published, 1869]); Lucy Lowden, "The People's Party: The 'Heirs of Jackson' and the Rise of the Republican Party in New Hampshire," Ph.D. Dissertation, Western Illinois University, 1971; Philip M. Marston, "Amos Tuck and the Beginning in New Hampshire of the Republican Party," *Historical New Hampshire,* XV (November, 1960).

WILLIAMS, Jared Warner, 1847-1849

Born on December 22, 1796, in West Woodstock, Connecticut, son of Captain Andrew Williams and Sarah (Skinner) Williams. Married to Sarah Hawes Bacon in 1824 in Woodstock, Connecticut; father of George Canning and Jared Irving. Attended Brown University, graduating in 1818. Studied law at Litchfield, Connecticut, and received an LL.D. degree from Brown University in 1852. Admitted to the bar in 1822, and set up a practice in Lancaster, New Hampshire. Williams, a Democrat, was elected to the State Legislature in 1830 and 1835 as a representative, and in 1833 and 1834 as a senator, serving as president of the Senate in 1834-35. He was Register of Probate for Coos County from 1832 to 1837, and won election to the United States Congress in 1837 and 1839. In the election of 1846, Williams received the largest vote total for Governor (26,740) but lost to Anthony Colby (17,707) when the election was decided in the legislature. In 1847 he received 30,806 votes to defeat Free Soiler Nathaniel S. Berry (8,531) and Whig Anthony Colby (21,109). Williams repeated the success in 1848, defeating Berry by a vote of 32,245 to 28,829. Governor Williams presided while the State Legislature passed resolutions supporting the Mexican War. He witnessed the legislative defeat of a bill designed to impose regulations of property ownership on a spouse who joined the Shakers, and signed a bill reducing to six months the waiting period required for a spouse to obtain a divorce from an individual who had joined that religious sect. Williams advocated the acceptance of the Wilmot Proviso, advised the State Legislature to restrict the powers of corporations, recommended a well-ordered militia, and received President Polk during Polk's visit to New Hampshire in July 1847. Williams returned to serve as Judge of Probate for Coos County in 1852. He was also appointed to the United States Senate in 1853 to fill part of the unexpired term of Charles G. Atherton. In 1864 he served as a delegate to the Democratic National Convention. Williams died on September 29, 1864, and was buried in the Summer Street Cemetery of Lancaster. Bibliography: Amos N. Somers, *History of Lancaster, New Hampshire* (Concord, 1899); Donald B. Cole, *Jacksonian Democracy in New Hampshire, 1800-1851* (Cambridge, Mass., 1970); *History of Coos County* (Syracuse, 1888); Charles H. Bell, *The Bench and Bar of New Hampshire* (Boston, 1894); Richard F. Upton, "Franklin Pierce and the Shakers: A Subchapter in the Struggle for Religious Liberty," *Historical New Hampshire*, XXIII (Summer 1968).

DINSMOOR, Samuel, Jr., 1849-1852

Born on May 8, 1799, in Keene, New Hampshire, son of Governor Samuel Dinsmoor and Mary (Reid) Dinsmoor; brother of Mary Eliza, George Reid and William. Married to Ann Eliza Jarvis of Weathersfield on September 11, 1844; remarried to Mrs. Catharine Pickman (Abbot) Fox, widow of Charles James Fox of Nashua, New Hampshire, in May 1853; father of two sons from the first marriage. Entered Dartmouth College in 1810 at the age of eleven, and graduated in 1814; received an honorary LL.D. from Dartmouth in 1851. Read law with his father and was admitted to the bar in 1818. Accompanied gubernatorial appointee General James Miller to the Arkansas Territory in 1819, where he was Miller's legal assistant for several years. Set up his own law practice in Keene in 1823. Entered politics through a clerkship in the State Senate, which he held in 1826, 1827, 1829 and 1830. During this period, many a journey to France on family financial business, became familiar with the French language and customs, and was one of two commissioners appointed to meet and escort Lafayette through New Hampshire in 1825. After 1830 Dinsmoor was cashier of the Ashuelot Bank in Keene, becoming president when his father died in 1835. His business prominence made him a leading contender for the Democratic nomination in 1849. He won a clear majority (30,107 votes) over Free Soil candidate Nathaniel S. Berry (7,045) and Whig Levi Chamberlain (18,764). His popularity continued in 1850, when (with 30,751 votes) he again defeated Berry (6,472) and Chamberlain (18,512). Dinsmoor chose not to run in 1851, but was prevailed upon to accept the nomination. He received only 27,425 votes against Free Soiler John Atwood's 12,049 and Whig Thomas E. Sawyer's 18,458, thus throwing the election to the Democratic-dominated legislature, assuring Dinsmoor's election. As governor, Dinsmoor presided over significant revisions in the state militia system as enacted by each of the three legislatures which met during his administration. The revisions called for enrollment of all white males between the ages of eighteen and forty-five, but dismissed required active duty except in the case of war, invasion or other public emergency. Dinsmoor sat as governor during the State Constitutional Conventions of 1850 and 1851; he also supported the principle that the state that makes corporations has the right to control them, and called for complete and open financial disclosures from the state's railroads. After his retirement Dinsmoor returned to business and civic affairs in Keene. Dinsmoor died on February 24, 1869, in Keene, New Hampshire. Bibliography: Charles H. Bell, *The Bench and Bar of New Hampshire* (Boston, 1894); Hamilton Child, *Gazetteer of Cheshire County, New Hampshire, 1736-1885* (Syracuse, N. Y., 1885); George T. Chapman, *Sketches of the Alumni of Dartmouth College* (Cambridge, Mass., 1867); Chandler E. Potter, *The Military History of the State of New Hampshire*, part 2 (Baltimore, 1972 [originally published in 1869]); S. G. Griffin, *A History of the Town of Keene* (Keene, 1904); Thomas C. Rand, "The Gem of the Ashuelot Valley: A Sketch of Keene," *The Granite Monthly*, XVIII (1895).

MARTIN, Noah, 1852-1854

Born on July 26, 1801, in Epsom, New Hampshire, son of Samuel Martin, a shoemaker of Scotch-Irish descent, and Sally (Cochran) Martin. Brother of Mary, Thomas, James, Elizabeth, Caroline and Nancy. Married to Mary Jane Woodbury on October 25, 1825; father of Elizabeth A. and Caroline M. Apprenticed under physicians in Pembroke, N.H. and Deerfield, N.H. for three years. Attended Dartmouth College Medical School, and was graduated in the class of 1824. Practiced in Pembroke, 1824-1825, in Great Falls, 1825-1834, and in Dover from 1834. Was a member of the New Hampshire Medical Society, and its president in 1858. Founder and first president of the Dover Medical Association, 1849-50. As a Jacksonian Democrat he was elected to the New Hampshire House of Representatives in 1830, 1832 and 1837, and to the State Senate in 1835 and 1836. Running as a Democrat, Martin won the governorship in 1852 with 30,800 votes, defeating John Atwood of the Free Soil Party (9,497), Thomas E. Sawyer, a Whig (19,857) and others (269). In 1853 he won (30,934 votes) over John F. White, Free Soil (7,995), James Bell, Whig (17,590), and others (47). Governor Martin proposed a state agricultural commission, and urged that agriculture come under the supervision of state educational institutions. He cautioned the legislature against chartering competitive railroad lines when there was enough business to support only one; urged the legislature to make railroads legally responsible for loss of life or injury through carelessness; advocated private rather than state ownership of public utilities and natural resources. In 1852, while he was governor, New Hampshire refused to abolish the religious test. As governor during the presidency of New Hampshire's Franklin Pierce, he advocated the enforcement of the national Fugitive Slave Law. The state under Martin generally enjoyed the prosperity and economic expansion which the nation was experiencing as a whole. At the end of his gubernatorial service, Martin returned to his medical practice in Dover, and kept aloof from further political involvement. Martin died on May 28, 1863, in Dover. Bibliography: D. Hamilton Hurd, ed., *History of Merrimack and Belknap Counties, New Hampshire* (Philadelphia, 1855); Hamilton S. Putnam, ed., *The New Hampshire Medical Society: A History* (Milford, N.H., 1966); John Randolph Ham, M. D., *The Dover*

(N.H.) Physicians (Concord, 1879); "Noah Martin," *The New England Historical and Genealogical Register*, XVIII (1864); *Dover Centennial Celebration, 1855-1955* (Dover, 1955); "Gov. Noah Martin," *The Granite Monthly*, vol. 1 (n.s.)(June, 1888).

BAKER, Nathaniel Bradley, 1854-1855

Born on September 29, 1818, in Henniker, New Hampshire, son of Abel Baker, a carder of wool, and Nancy (Bradley) Baker. Married to Lucretia M. Tenbroeck on May 10, 1843; father of four children, whose names are unknown. Attended Phillips Exeter Academy; graduated from Harvard in 1839. Studied law under Franklin Pierce in Concord, New Hampshire; set up his own practice in 1842. Joint proprietor and editor of the *New Hampshire Patriot*, 1841-1845. Appointed chief engineer of the Concord Fire Department in 1851. Entered politics as Democratic clerk of the Court of Common Pleas in 1845; transferred to clerkship of the Superior Court for Merrimack County in 1846. Elected to the State Legislature in 1850, served as Presidential Elector in 1852, and became a trustee of St. Paul's School in Concord. Won the Democratic nomination for governor in 1854 and in the general election received 29,788 votes, defeating Free Soil candidate Jared Perkins (11,080) and Whig candidate James Bell (16,941). As governor, Baker witnessed heated debates in the legislature over resolutions denouncing the Kansas-Nebraska Bill and the Missouri Compromise, with the resolutions finally failing to pass. He also appointed John S. Wells to the United States Senate in 1855 following the death of Sen. Moses Norris, Jr., and signed acts that required the filing of notices of marriage intentions with town clerks and that empowered married women to make wills. During his term many new banks were incorporated, and new businesses (i.e., the Manchester Locomotive Works, Claremont Railroad Company, Abbot Coach Company) and organizations (i.e., New Hampshire State Teachers' Association) were chartered. Baker ran for governor in 1855, but lost (27,055 votes) to Ralph Metcalf (32,769). Baker then moved to Clinton, Iowa, where he established a law practice. He won election as a Republican to Iowa's State Legislature in 1859, and served as that state's Adjutant General from July 1861 until his death. Baker died on September 11, 1876, and was buried in Des Moines, Iowa. Bibliography: Leander W. Cogswell, *History of the Town of Henniker, New Hampshire* (Somersworth, 1973); Charles H. Bell, *The Bench and and Bar of New Hampshire* (Boston, 1894); Roy F. Nichols, *Franklin Pierce: Young Hickory of the Granite Hills*, 2nd ed., rev. (Philadelphia, 1958); H.H. Metcalf, "Last Year of the Old Regime," *Granite Monthly*, LV (1923); Edward J. Gallagher, "Luther Roby, Early New Hampshire Publisher," *Historical New Hampshire*, II (September, 1946).

METCALF, Ralph, 1855-1857

Born on November 21, 1798, in Charlestown, New Hampshire, son of John Metcalf, a lumberman and farmer, and Ruby (Converse) Metcalf. Married to Lucretia Ann Bingham in January 1835; after her death in 1836, married Martha Ann Gilmore on November 10, 1843; father of Ralph and Frances E. by his second marriage. Studied at the academy in Chester, Vermont, and entered Dartmouth in 1819, but left in 1821 to teach at the Literary Scientific and Military Academy in Norwich, Vermont; rejoined his Dartmouth class in 1822 and graduated in 1823. Studied law at Charlestown in the offices of Henry Hubbard, and later under Richard Bartlett of Concord, New Hampshire, and George B. Upham of Claremont, New Hampshire. Admitted to the bar in 1826, and practiced in Newport, New Hampshire, until 1828, then in Binghamton, New York, until 1830, when he returned to Claremont. Entered politics as New Hampshire's Secretary of State, 1831-36; clerked for Secretary of the Treasury Levi Woodbury in Washington, D. C., 1838-40. Returned to his law practice in Newport, 1841-45, and was Register of Probate for Sullivan County, 1845-51. Chaired a special committee to compile state laws in 1850, and represented Newport in the legislature in 1852 and 1853. As the first gubernatorial candidate of the "Know-Nothing" or American Party in 1855, he received 32,769 votes defeat Free Soiler Asa Fowler (1,237), Whig James Bell (3,436), and Democrat Nathaniel B. Baker (27,055). In 1856 Metcalf garnered 32,119 votes for a narrow lead over the Democrat John S. Wells (32,031). However, Whig candidate Ichabod Goodwin's 2,360 votes threw the election to the State Legislature, and since that body was dominated by the "Know-Nothing" Party, Metcalf was elected over Wells by a vote of 175 to 150. Governor Metcalf advocated the prohibition of public liquor sales, and signed a legislative enactment to that effect. He also took a strong stand against the extension of slave territory, and denounced the assault on Charles Sumner by Preston Brooks in the United States Senate; the State Legislature eventually issued a statement condemning Brooks' action. Metcalf's "Know-Nothing" principles were evident in his approval of a legislative resolution which instructed New Hampshire's federal congressmen to enact a new naturalization law requiring immigrants to reside in the United States for twenty-one years before becoming eligible for citizenship. Metcalf also denounced Roman Catholicism. Metcalf's retirement to his law practice in Claremont was brief, and he died on August 26, 1858, in Claremont. Bibliography: Charles H. Bell, *The Bench and Bar of New Hampshire* (Boston, 1894); George T. Chapman, *Sketches of the Alumni of Dartmouth College* (Cambridge, Mass., 1867); Henry H. Saunderson, *History of Charlestown, New Hampshire* (Claremont, 1876); Edmund Wheeler, *The History of Newport, New Hampshire* (Concord, N. H., 1879); Otis F. R. Waite, *History of the Town of Claremont, New Hampshire* (Manchester, N. H., 1895).

HAILE, William, 1857-1859

Born in May 1807 in Putney, Vermont, son of John and Eunice (Henry) Haile, both of whom were Protestants. Married to Sabrina Shaw Walker in 1828 in Chesterfield, New Hampshire; father of William Henry and three daughters. Received little formal education, but was awarded an honorary M.A. degree by Dartmouth College in 1857. Entered business in 1823 as a clerk in the Chesterfield store of Ezekiel Pierce, into whose family he had moved at about the age of fifteen; opened his own store at Centre Village in 1828; moved to and opened a business in Hinsdale, New Hampshire, in 1835, and set up a lumber business there in 1846. Formed in 1849 the firm of Haile & Todd (later Haile, Frost & Co.), manufacturers of cashmerettes. Began political career as a representative of Hinsdale in the State Legislature, 1846-50, and 1853; chosen to the State Senate in 1854, and as its President in 1855; returned to the State Legislature in 1856. Won election as Republican candidate for Governor in 1857 with 34,216 votes to defeat Democrat John S. Wells (31,214). Haile repeated the success in 1858 by defeating Democrat Asa P. Cate, 36,326 votes to 31,679. Governor Haile opposed the further extension of slavery, the sale of intoxicating liquor, unlimited immigration, and the Dred Scott Decision of the United States Supreme Court. He strongly recommended the establishment of a state normal school, but did not see that proposal accepted until 1870. He also supported the purchase of a farm which had been owned by General John Stark as a site for a state reform school, and by 1858 the school had been established with a building to accommodate one hundred and fifty children. At the end of his period as governor, Haile returned to his business in Hinsdale. He moved to Keene, New Hampshire in 1873, where he continued his general merchandising business. Haile died on July 22, 1876, in Keene. Bibliography: John M. Comstock, *Dartmouth Necrology: Obituary Record of the Graduates of Dartmouth College* (Hanover, 1877); William R. Cutter, *Genealogical and Personal Memoirs Relating to the Families of the State of Massachusetts*, vol. 3 (New York, 1910); D. Hamilton Hurd, ed., *History of Cheshire and Sullivan Counties, New Hampshire* (Philadelphia, 1886); Philip M. Marston, "Amos Tuck and the Beginning in New Hampshire of the Republican Party," *Historical New Hampshire*, XV (November, 1960).

GOODWIN, Ichabod, 1859-1861

Born on October 8, 1794, in North Berwick, Maine, son of Samuel Goodwin, a farmer, and Anna Thompson (Gerrish) Goodwin, both of whom were Congregationalists. Brother of Anna Thompson, Joseph Gerrish, Samuel, Hannah Jane, Mary Elizabeth, Sarah Elliot, Olive Jordan and Daniel Rayne, who was president of Trinity College and later of the University of Pennsylvania. Married to Sarah Parker Rice of Portsmouth, New Hampshire on September 3, 1827; father of Abby Rice, Hope, Sarah Parker Rice, Georgette Cumming, Samuel, Frank and Susan Boardman, who married Admiral George Dewey. Attended the academy in South Berwick, Maine; received an honorary M.A. degree from Dartmouth College in 1857. Entered business as a clerk for Samuel Lord of Portsmouth; later became master and part owner of several sailing vessels. Had become a successful merchant by 1832, engaging in various financial and civic enterprises. President of two railroad lines, two banks, and the Portsmouth Steam Factory, which manufactured textiles. Entered the New Hampshire General Court in 1838, and served in 1843, 1844, 1850, 1854 and 1856. Initially a Whig, he attended national party conventions in 1844, 1848 and 1852. Member of the State Constitutional Conventions in 1850 and 1876. Became the last Whig candidate for governor, receiving 2,360 votes in 1856; joined the Republicans, and in 1859 was nominated and defeated Asa P. Cate, the Democrat, 36,296 votes to 32,802. Governor Goodwin presided over the reorganization of the state judiciary. The courts of common pleas were abolished and their business transferred to the State Supreme Court during his tenure. Goodwin supported a state legislative resolution opposing the extension of slavery, and endorsed acts aimed at regulating railroads and defining powers of police courts to suppress intemperance. In 1860 Goodwin was renominated by acclamation and was reelected, polling 38,037 votes to Cate's 33,544. When the first call for Civil War volunteers came in May 1861, Goodwin acted immediately by borrowing money on his own initiative to outfit two regiments, an action ratified at the June legislative session. In 1861 Goodwin was considered for renomination, but lost to Nathaniel S. Berry. Goodwin then returned to his business and civic enterprises in Portsmouth. His house is today part of Strawbery Banke, Portsmouth. Goodwin died in Portsmouth on July 4, 1882, and was buried in South Church Cemetery. Bibliography: William Best Hesseltine, *Lincoln and the War Governors* (New York, 1948); Chandler E. Potter, *The Military History of the State of New Hampshire, 1623-1861,* 2 parts (Concord, 1869; reprint ed., 1972); Otis F. R. Waite, *New Hampshire in the Great Rebellion* (Claremont, N. H., 1870); John Samuel Goodwin, *The Goodwins of Kittery, York County, Maine* (Chicago, 1898); John M. Comstock, *Dartmouth Necrology: Obituary Record of the Graduates of Dartmouth College* (Hanover, 1883); Frank Goodwin, "Hon. Ichabod Goodwin," *Granite Monthly,* III (May, 1880). The Goodwin Family Papers are at Strawbery Banke, Portsmouth, with a few on deposit in the New Hampshire Historical Society, Concord.

BERRY, Nathaniel Springer, 1861-1863

Born on September 1, 1796, in Bath, Maine, son of Abner Berry, a shipbuilder who was killed when Nathaniel was six years old, and Betsey (Springer) Berry. One of four children. Married to Ruth Smith (1800-57) on January 26, 1821; father of William Augustus and Emeline Smith, who married Charles E. Morse. Apprenticed as a tanner in Bath, New Hampshire; received an honorary M.A. degree from Dartmouth College in 1861. Joined the Methodist Church in 1823, and was a delegate to its General Conference in 1872. After his first wife's death, married Mrs. Louise Farley of Andover, Massachusetts in January 1860. Served as Lieutenant, Captain, and Lieutenant Colonel of the 34th Regiment of state militia. Was a tanner in Bristol, New Hampshire, 1820-36, and in Hebron, New Hampshire, 1836-57, when he gave up the business. Won election to the State Legislature as a representative from Bristol in 1828, 1833, 1834 and 1837, and from Hebron in 1854; chosen to the State Senate in 1835 and 1836; chosen as a delegate to the Democratic National Convention in 1840. Served as an Associate Justice on the Court of Common Pleas for Grafton County, 1841-50; Judge of Probate for Grafton County, 1856-61; and Justice of the Peace for twenty-three years. A Democrat until 1840, he became an organizer of the Free Soil Party; chosen as Free Soil nominee for Governor in 1846 (received 10,379 votes), in 1847 (8,531), in 1848 (28,829), in 1849 (7,045), and in 1850 (6,472). Nominated by the Republicans in 1861 and won over George Stark, 35,467 votes to 31,452. Berry defeated Stark again in 1862, polling 32,150 votes to Stark's 28,566. As governor, Berry was concerned principally with issues stemming from the Civil War. His government enlisted and equipped fifteen regiments of infantry, three companies of sharpshooters, four companies of cavalry, and one of heavy artillery. Berry also presented to President Lincoln an address, prepared by the twenty-two governors attending the Altoona Conference in Pennsylvania, which expressed their support for Lincoln's administration. After his years as governor had ended, Berry retired to Andover, Massachusetts, where he lived until 1878; he lived with his daughter in Milwaukee, Wisconsin until 1883, and then returned to Bristol, New Hampshire. Berry died in Bristol on April 27, 1894. Bibliography: Richard W. Musgrove, *History of the Town of Bristol,* 2 vols.

(Bristol, N. H., 1904); J. W. Robinson, "Nathaniel Springer Berry," *Granite Monthly*, XV (1893); Otis F. R. Waite, *New Hampshire in the Great Rebellion* (Claremont, N. H., 1870); William B. Hesseltine, *Lincoln and the War Governors* (New York, 1948); James O. Lyford, *Life of Edward H. Rollins* (Boston, 1906); John M. Comstock, *Dartmouth Necrology: Obituary Record of the Graduates of Dartmouth College, 1893-94* (Hanover, 1894).

GILMORE, Joseph Albree, 1863-1865

Born on June 10, 1811, in Weston, Vermont, son of Asa Gilmore, a textile manufacturer, and Lucy (Dodge) Gilmore. Brother of Granville, Asa, Hugh H., Lucy Gilmore Dodge, Susanna W. Gilmore Benton, Charles H., Mariah C. Gilmore Harrington, Lucius, Lucia Gilmore Wiley, Nancy J. Gilmore Adams, Addison and Abigail W. Gilmore Gray. Married to Ann Page Whipple of Dunbarton, New Hampshire, on July 10, 1832; father of Joseph Henry, Ann Caroline, who married William E. Chandler, Maria Thomas Barrett, Elizabeth Augusta, Franklin Adams, Edward Everett, Frank Whipple, Mary A., John Leach, Emma Lincoln and Addison. Attended common school; professed adherence to the Baptist religion. Kept a store in Boston by the age of twenty-one; later moved to Concord, New Hampshire; where he opened a wholesale grocery store in 1842; became a construction agent on the Concord and Claremont Railroad in 1848, and Superintendent of the Concord Railroad and 175 miles of related lines in 1856. Gilmore was originally a Whig, but by 1858 he had been elected to the State Senate as a Republican. Reelected in 1859, and became President of the Senate. Gilmore ran for Governor in 1863, receiving 29,035 votes as opposed to Democrat Ira A. Eastman's 22,833 votes and Independent Walter Harriman's 4,372 votes. The election went for a decision to the legislature, where Gilmore won over Eastman by a count of 192 votes to 133, with Harriman receiving only one vote. Gilmore was reelected in 1864, defeating Democrat Edward W. Harrington by a vote of 37,006 to 31,340. As governor during the Civil War, Gilmore raised and equipped the 18th Regiment of N. H. Infantry, the 1st Regiment of N. H. Cavalry, and the 1st Regiment of N. H. Heavy Artillery, making New Hampshire's total commitment 33,258, a number 1,814 in excess of the state's quota. He oversaw the raising of a loan of $1.5 million to provide bounties for soldiers, and arranged furloughs and free transportation for soldiers to vote, but vetoed a bill permitting soldiers to vote in the field, fearing that it would be unconstitutional. Gilmore also supported New Hampshire's ratification of the Thirteenth Amendment to the United States Constitution. During his term the State House was enlarged. Gilmore retired from office in poor health. He died on April 17, 1867, in Concord. Bibliography: Otis F. R. Waite, *New Hampshire in the Great Rebellion* (Claremont, N. H., 1870); William B. Hesseltine, *Lincoln and the War Governors* (New York, 1948); Leon B. Richardson, *William E. Chandler, Republican* (New York, 1940); James O. Lyford, *Life of Edward H. Rollins* (Boston, 1906); Frank S. Osgood, "Robert and James Gilmore . . . and Their Descendants," MS, New Hampshire Historical Society. The Gilmore Papers are in two collections at the New Hampshire Historical Society—the Gilmore Papers and the William E. Chandler Papers.

SMYTH, Frederick, 1865-1867

Born on March 9, 1819, in Candia, New Hampshire, son of Stephen Smyth, a farmer, and Dolly (Rowe) Smyth, both of whom were Congregationalists. Brother of Gilman Chase, Sarah, Sophia and Abraham Calvin. Married to Emma Lane on December 11, 1844; after her death in 1884, married Marion Cossar in Scotland in 1886. Smyth left no children. He attended one term at Phillips Academy in Andover, Massachusetts, and received an honorary M.A. degree from Dartmouth College in 1865. Entered into business in Manchester, New Hampshire; became president of the First National Bank, treasurer of the Merrimack River Savings Bank, and president of the Concord Railroad. Also treasurer of the New Hampshire Agricultural Society and vice-president of the American Pomological Society. He entered politics in 1849 as city clerk of Manchester, and became Mayor of Manchester, 1852-54 and 1864; a Republican state legislator, 1857-58; a contender in the gubernatorial race of 1859; and president of the State Republican Convention at Manchester in 1860, where Smith surprised even Abraham Lincoln by introducing him as the next president of the United States. Smyth officially represented the nation at the London International Exhibit in 1861. His success as Manchester's Mayor in 1864 made him the outstanding candidate for Governor in 1865, a position he won over the Democrat Edward W. Harrington by a vote of 34,145 to 28,017. The following year, 1866, Smyth again defeated the Democrat candidate, John G. Sinclair, by a count of 35,136 to 30,484. Governor Smyth devoted much of his energy to a full-scale effort at reforming the state's finances. He borrowed $1.2 million to fund the state war debt, settled all claims against the federal government on terms advantageous to the state, and put New Hampshire's credit on as sound a footing as that of any other state. He also mustered out the remaining soldiers from the war units, oversaw a revision of the state's statutes; supported the Fourteenth Amendment to the United States Constitution; reorganized the state militia; took steps to restore fish to certain state rivers; and launched a program designed to publish the state's papers. Smyth retired to business and civic affairs at the end of his gubernatorial service. Between 1866 and 1878 he sat on the Board of Trustees of the National Home for Disabled Volunteer Soldiers, and in 1878 he went to Paris as President Hayes' appointed honorary commissioner to the International Exposition. Smyth died on April 22, 1899, in Hamilton, Bermuda. Bibliography: Benjamin Perley Poore and F. B. Eaton, *Sketches of the Life and Public Services of Frederick Smyth of New Hampshire* (Manchester, N. H., 1885); Otis F. R. Waite, *New Hampshire in the Great Rebellion* (Claremont, N. H., 1870); James O. Lyford, *Life of Edward H. Rollins* (Boston, 1906); F. B. Eaton, "Hon. Frederick Smyth," *Granite Monthly*, III (1880); Lucy Lowden, "The Granite State for Lincoln," *Historical New Hampshire*, XXV (Spring 1970). Papers of Smyth on deposit in the Manchester Historic Association, Manchester, N.H.

HARRIMAN, Walter, 1867-1869

Born on April 8, 1817, in Warner, New Hampshire, son of Benjamin E. Harriman, a farmer, and Hannah (Flanders) Harriman; Universalist. Brother of Henry H., Benjamin F., David D., Elkanah W., Augustine W., Leonidas, Hannah, Helen and

Frank P. Married to Apphia K. Hoyt in September 1841; after her death in 1843, married Almira R. Andrews in October 1844; father of Georgia, Walter Channing and Benjamin E. Married a third time, to Jessie B. Farmer in April 1879. Educated at Hopkinton and Henniker Academies in New Hampshire; received an honorary M.A. degree from Dartmouth College in 1867. Taught school in New Hampshire, Massachusetts and New Jersey from 1835 to 1840, and studied theology in his spare time. Joined the Universalist Church in 1840, and preached at Harvard, Massachusetts, and at Warner. Entered politics as a representative of Warner in 1849 and 1850. In 1851 he gave up preaching to open a general store in Warner as the partner of John S. Pillsbury, later governor of Minnesota. A Democrat, Harriman served as State Treasurer, 1853-54, clerk in the Pension Office, Washington, D. C., 1855-56, again as a state legislator, 1858-59, and as State Senator, 1859-61. He was a popular orator in national presidential campaigns from 1852 to 1864. In 1861 he was associated with James M. Campbell, editor of the *Weekly Union* (formerly and subsequently the *Union Democrat*) in Manchester, New Hampshire, and in 1863 he became assistant editor of the *Daily American*. Commissioned a Colonel in the 11th New Hampshire Volunteers, and served for some months during 1862 and 1863. Ran for Governor in 1863 as an Independent or War Democrat, capturing enough votes (4,372) to assure the selection of Republican Joseph A. Gilmore by the legislature. Rejoined the military in January 1864, and was taken prisoner at the Battle of the Wilderness, exchanged in September, and mustered out as a brevet Brigadier General in June 1865. Joined the Republican Party and was New Hampshire's Secretary of State between 1865 and 1867; defeated Democrat John G. Sinclair by 35,809 votes to 32,663 in 1867, and again in 1868 (39,778 to 37,260). As governor, Harriman urged attention to the development of agricultural, manufacturing and forestry resources as a means of building up New Hampshire's postwar industries. He personally drafted a revised school law abolishing the authority of county commissioners and establishing a department of instruction with one state school superintendent; he also signed an act providing for teachers' institutes; and oversaw the establishment of a $25,000 state education fund from sale of state lands. Harriman signed a number of acts designed to bolster New Hampshire's postwar economy, but he vetoed a bill to fix the allowable interest rate at six percent. In 1869 Harriman was appointed Naval Officer of the Port of Boston, Massachusetts, a position he held until 1877. As a representative of Concord, New Hampshire, he returned to the State Legislature in 1881. He published *History of Warner* in 1879. He also traveled to Europe and the Far East in 1882, and published *Travels and Observations in the Orient*, 1883. Harriman died on July 25, 1884, in Concord, and was buried in Pine Grove Cemetery in Warner. Bibliography: Amos Hadley, *Life of Walter Harriman* (Boston, 1888); James O. Lyford, *Life of Edward H. Rollins* (Boston, 1906); Otis F. R. Waite, *New Hampshire in the Great Rebellion* (Claremont, N. H., 1870); Leander W. Cogswell, *A History of the Eleventh New Hampshire Regiment* (Concord, N. H., 1891); Nathan F. Carter, *The Native Ministry of New Hampshire* (Concord, N. H., 1906); Joseph Fullonton, *The History of Raymond, New Hampshire* (Dover, N. H., 1875); John W. Moore, *Moore's Historical . . . Gatherings . . . Relative to Printers . . .* (Concord, N. H., 1886).

STEARNS, Onslow, 1869-1871

Born on August 30, 1810, in Billerica, Massachusetts, son of John Stearns, a farmer, and Mary (Lane) Stearns. Brother of Franklin, Mary, John Owen, Eliza Ann, Lorenzo and Bernard. Married Mary Abbot Holbrook on June 26, 1845; father of Charles Onslow, Mary Laurinda, Margaret Abbott, Sarah Holbrook, Grace, and of Frieda (d. young) and Thanlia, who died young. Received a common school education; awarded an honorary A.M. from Dartmouth College in 1857. An active member of the Unitarian Society of Concord, New Hampshire. Spent most of his business career in the construction and management of railroads, beginning in 1830 (in a joint venture with a brother in Virginia) as a contractor for construction of the Chesapeake and Ohio Canal; contracted for construction of various railroads in Pennsylvania, New Jersey and New York; returned to Massachusetts in 1837, and for the remainder of his life held executive positions with the Nashua and Lowell, the Northern, the Old Colony and Newport, and the Concord Railroads, serving as president of both the Northern and the Concord roads during the last years of his life. Initially a Whig, but had become a Republican by the time he was elected to the State Senate in 1862, where he served on committees dealing with railroads, elections and military affairs; President of the Senate, 1863-64, and a delegate to the Republican National Convention in 1864; lost Republican nomination for Governor at the State Convention to Walter Harriman by a vote of 349 to 318 in 1867, but won the nomination by acclamation in 1869, and defeated Democrat John Bedel in the general election (35,772 votes to 32,057); in 1870 narrowly won (with 34,847 votes) over Democrat Bedel (25,058), Prohibitionist candidate Rev. Lorenzo D. Barrows (1,135), and Labor Reform candidate Samuel Flint (7,369). While he served as governor, Stearns requested legislation to strengthen New Hampshire's agricultural, manufacturing and railroad interests. He reduced the state debt by nearly one third and taxes by nearly one half; discontinued annual exercises of the militia; attempted to put the state prison on a paying basis and to improve discipline; presided over the establishment of a Board of Agriculture; and saw the legislature ratify the Fifteenth Amendment by a vote of 187 to 131. Petitions requesting an amendment to allow women to vote were dismissed during his administration, and a Prohibitionist proposal for establishing a state police was rejected. Stearns entertained President Grant—and later President Hayes—when they visited New Hampshire. After the expiration of his second gubernatorial term, Stearns resumed his business interests, principally railroading, and returned to his home in Concord. Stearns died on December 29, 1878, and was buried in Blossom Hill Cemetery in Concord. Bibliography: James O. Lyford, *Life of Edward H. Rollins* (Boston, 1906); Avis Stearns Van Wagene, *Genealogy and Memoirs of Isaac Stearns and his Descendants* (Syracuse, N. Y., 1901); Mary Stearns Brooke, *Genealogies of the Stearns, Lane, Holbrook and Warren Families* (1898); *Messages and Addresses of Onslow Stearns* (Boston, 1872); James O. Lyford, ed., *History of Concord, New Hampshire*, 2 vols. (Concord, N. H., 1896); *Memorial of Onslow Stearns, Concord, N. H.* (n. p. n. d.) [sketch, funeral service, funeral address, memorial discourse]; "Hon. Onslow Stearns," *The Granite Monthly*, II (June 1879). There is a small collection of Stearns manuscripts at Dartmouth College, Hanover, New Hampshire.

WESTON, James Adams, 1871-1872, 1874-1875

Born on August 27, 1827, in Manchester, New Hampshire, son of Amos Weston, a farmer, town officer and member of the State Legislature, and Betsy (Wilson) Weston; youngest of five children. Married to Anna S. Gilmore of Concord, New Hampshire, on February 23, 1854; father of Grace Helen, James Henry, Edwin Bell, Anna Mabel and Charles Albert. Educated in a district school and studied engineering at the Manchester and Piscataquog Academies; received an honorary A.M. degree from Dartmouth College in 1871; was an active member and treasurer of the Franklin Street Congregational Church in Manchester. Joined the Concord Railroad as an assistant civil engineer in 1846; became chief engineer and resided in Concord, 1849-56; returned to Manchester, where he managed several other railroads and was engineer for the city waterworks. Entered politics as Democratic Mayor of Manchester, elected in 1861, 1867, 1869, 1870 and 1874; won nomination for Governor in 1871 and received 34,700 votes, but votes for Republican James Pike (33,892), Labor Reformer Lemuel Cooper (782) and Prohibitionist Albert G. Cummings (314) left the choice to the legislature, which selected Weston. During Weston's first term, the Democrats lacked control of the legislature, permitting him to accomplish little of significance. Weston lost the governorship in 1872 and 1873 to Ezekial Straw. In 1874 Weston again won a plurality, but returns for Republican Luther McCutchins (34,143) and Prohibitionist John Blackmer (2,100) necessitated another legislative verdict, and, as in 1871, the legislature chose Weston. Weston's second term differed from his first in that the Democrats enjoyed full control of the legislature for the first time in twenty years. Republican offices were filled with Democrats, voting districts were gerrymandered, and the state judiciary changed to give the Democrats control over the appointment of judges. The legislature sanctioned the merger of the Boston and Lowell and the Nashua and Lowell Railroads, two lines that later evolved into the important Boston and Maine system. The legislators did not, however, adopt a liquor licensing system that had been part of the Democratic platform. Weston retired from the governor's office to his banking business and other financial enterprises. While acting as president of the City National Bank and its successor, the Merchants National Bank, he served as director of the Manchester Horse Railway and vice president of the New Hampshire Fire Insurance Company. He was an active Mason. Weston died on May 8, 1895, in Manchester. Bibliography: Ezra S. Stearns, *Genealogical and Family History of the State of New Hampshire*, vol. 3 (New York, 1908); James O. Lyford, *Life of Edward H. Rollins* (Boston, 1906); John B. Clarke, *Manchester, a Brief Record of its Past and a Picture of its Present* (Manchester, N.H., 1875); George F. Willey, *Willey's Semi-Centennial Book of Manchester, 1846-1896* (Manchester, N. H., 1896); John M. Comstock, *Dartmouth Necrology: Obituary Record of the Graduates of Dartmouth College* (Hanover, 1895); "Hon. James A. Weston," *The Granite Monthly*, II (August, 1879).

STRAW, Ezekiel Albert, 1872-1874

Born on December 30, 1819, in Salisbury, New Hampshire, son of James B. Straw, a surveyor and overseer of a cotton mill, and Mehitable (Fiske) Straw. Brother of four boys and two girls. Married to Charlotte Smith Webster (d. March 15, 1852) on

April 6, 1842, in Amesbury, Massachusetts, and father of Albert, Charlotte Webster, Herman Foster and Ellen. Educated at public schools in Lowell, Massachusetts, where the family moved shortly after his birth, and at Phillips Andover Academy, which he left in 1838; received an honorary A.M. degree from Dartmouth College in 1860; was a founder of the First Unitarian Society in Manchester, New Hampshire, in 1842—he later became its clerk, treasurer and president. Entered business in 1838 at Manchester as an engineer with the Amoskeag Manufacturing Company, for which he surveyed city lots and constructed dams and canals. Sent to England in 1844 to obtain information and machinery for the Manchester Print Works, was appointed agent of land and water power departments in 1851, and in 1858 was placed in complete charge of Amoskeag's operations in Manchester; provided plans and specifications for the city's waterworks, and was made president of the facility in 1871. Entered politics as a Republican legislator from 1859 to 1864; member of the State Senate, 1864-66, and its President, 1865-66. Served on the governor's staff under Onslow Stearns in 1869, and in 1870 was appointed by President Grant to the executive board of the planning commission for the Centennial Exposition in Philadelphia; won the Republican nomination for Governor in 1872, and (with 38,752 votes) defeated Democrat James A. Weston (36,584), Labor Reformer Lemuel P. Cooper (446), and Prohibitionist John Blackmer (436); repeated victory in 1873 (34,023 votes), defeating Weston (32,016), Blackmer (1,098), and Labor Reformer Samuel K. Mason (687). Governor Straw worked to reduce the war debt which the state had taken over from the towns; recommended a system of manual and industrial training in the public schools; and suggested local option to resolve the issue surrounding the sale of intoxicating liquor. Straw's election in March 1872 had the effect of making certain the renomination of President Grant at the Republican Convention in June. Straw retired to his business interests in 1874, serving as director of the Langdon Mills and as president of the Amoskeag Axe Company; he was president of many other concerns, including the Manchester Gas Light Company, the New England Cotton Manufacturing Association, and the New Hampshire Fire Insurance Company. In 1876 Straw returned to politics as a delegate to the Republican National Convention. Straw died on October 23, 1882, in Manchester. Bibliography: Ezra S. Stearns, *Genealogical and Family History of the State of New Hampshire*, 4 vols. (New York, 1908); John B. Clarke, *Manchester, A Brief Record of Its Past and a Picture of its Present* (Manchester, 1875); John M. Comstock, *Dartmouth Necrology: Obituary Record of the Graduates of Dartmouth College* (Hanover, 1883); George O. Seilhamer, *History of the Republican Party*, 2 vols. (New York, n. d.); "Hon. Ezekial A. Straw," *The Granite Monthly*, I (October, 1877). A collection of Straw Papers are on deposit in the Manchester Historic Association.

WESTON, James Adams, 1871-1872, 1874-1875

CHENEY, Person Colby, 1875-1877

Born on February 25, 1828, in Holderness (now Ashland), New Hampshire, son of Moses Cheney, a paper manufacturer, and Abigail (Morrison) Cheney. Brother of Oren Burbank, Ester M., Sarah Burbank, Moses, Jr., Abigail Morrison, Charles Gilman, Ruth Elizabeth, Elias Hutchins, Marcia Ann and Harriet Olivia. Married on May 22, 1850 to S. Anna Moore; after the death of his first wife (January, 1858); married Mrs. Sarah (White) Keith (on June 29, 1858); father of Agnes Annie. Left his parents' Baptist faith to become a Unitarian. Attended academies at Peterborough and Hancock, New Hampshire, and at Parsonfield, Maine; received an honorary A.M. degree from Dartmouth College in 1876. Learned details of his father's paper manufacturing business, and in 1845 assumed management of the paper mill at Peterborough, where the family had moved in 1835; member of the firm of Cheney, Hadley and Going in 1853. In 1866 moved to Manchester, New Hampshire, where he engaged in the sale of paper supplies and managed a paper mill at Goffstown, New Hampshire. Also head of Cheney & Thorpe, and of P. C. Cheney Company. Appointed quartermaster of the 13th Regiment of New Hampshire Volunteers in September 1862, but became seriously ill and sent a substitute; received an honorable discharge in August 1863. Entered politics as a representative from Peterborough in 1853, and reelected in 1854; won election as Railroad Commissioner, 1864-67, and as Mayor of Manchester, 1871 and 1872. Republican candidate for Governor (39,293 votes) in 1875, and selected over Democratic candidate Hiram R. Roberts (39,121) and Prohibitionist Nathaniel White (773), by vote of the legislature; nominated by acclamation in 1876, and on (41,761) handily over Democrat Daniel Marcy (38,133) and Prohibitionist Asa S. Kendall (411). As governor, Cheney presided over a restoration of the old judiciary system and a redistribution of state offices to Republicans. He served during a period of business depression, but economical and improved administration of state government resulted in reduction of the public debt. The state building and exhibits at the 1876 Centennial Exposition in Philadelphia were officially opened by Cheney, who also gave an address on that occasion. When a constitutional convention met in December 1876, he urged a simplified amending process, a smaller Lower House and a larger Senate, abolition of the religious test for officeholding, and biennial elections. After his gubernatorial terms, Cheney returned to his extensive business and civic activities, principally in Manchester. Governor Moody Currier appointed him to the United States Senate to fill the unexpired term of Austin A. Pike, and he served in that capacity in 1886 and 1887. He was also a delegate to the Republican National Convention in 1888, and a member of the Republican National Committee until 1900. In 1892-93 he was an Envoy Extraordinary to Switzerland. Cheney died on June 19, 1901, while visiting his daughter's family in Dover, New Hampshire. He was buried in Pine Grove Cemetery in Manchester. Bibliography: Charles Henry Pope, *The Cheney Genealogy* (Boston, 1897); James O. Lyford, *Life of Edward H. Rollins* (Boston, 1906); John B. Clarke, *Manchester: A Brief Record of its Past and a Picture of its Present* (Manchester, N. H., 1875); Augustus D. Ayling, *Revised Register of the Soldiers and Sailors of New Hampshire in the War of the Rebellion* (Concord, N. H., 1895); George F. Willey, *Willey's Semi-Centennial Book of Manchester, 1846-96* (Manchester, N. H., 1896); Jacob Biley Moore, *New Hampshire at the Centennial* (Manchester, N. H., 1876); J. N. McClintock, "Hon. Person C. Cheney," *The Granite Monthly*, III (December, 1879).

PRESCOTT, Benjamin Franklin, 1877-1879

Born on February 26, 1833, on the Prescott farm in Epping, New Hampshire, the only child of Nathan Gove Prescott and Betsy Hills (Richards) Prescott. Married to Mary Little Noyes of Concord, New Hampshire, on June 10, 1869; father of one child, Benjamin F. Prescott, Jr. Attended Pembroke Academy, 1848-49, Phillips Exeter Academy, 1850-52, and Dartmouth College, 1853-56; read law with Henry A. and Abel M. Bellows of Concord, and was admitted to the bar in 1859. After a brief law practice, he became associate editor from 1861 to 1865 of the *Independent Democrat,* the leading anti-slavery paper in the state and a strong supporter of Abraham Lincoln. Entered politics as secretary of the Republican State Committee, 1859-74; appointed special agent of the United States Treasury Department, for New England, 1865-69; served as New Hampshire's Secretary of State, 1872-73 and 1875-76. In 1860, 1864, 1868, 1872, 1876 and 1880 Prescott was Secretary of the New Hampshire College of Electors of President and Vice-President of the United States. In 1877 the Republican State Convention selected Prescott over Natt Head as its gubernatorial candidate, and he was elected, polling 40,755 votes to Democrat Daniel Marcy's 36,721, and Prohibitionist Asa S. Kendall's 338. The following year he was reelected; Prescott received 38,372 votes, the Democrat Frank A. McKean 37,860, the Labor Reformer Samuel Flint 269, and Kendall 205. Of the thirteen amendments submitted by the State Constitutional Convention of 1876, eleven were ratified by the town meetings held in March 1877. These included changing the time of holding state elections to November instead of March; the substitution of biennial for annual elections; an increase in the membership of the State Senate from twelve to twenty-four; and the abolition of the religious test as a qualification for holding office. Prescott, desiring more efficient handling of lawsuits, recommended an increase in the number of judges and the abolition of the privilege of retrial for the defeated party. In 1878 a vagrancy law required that tramps be sent to the state prison for fifteen months. A new state prison was also erected on twenty-seven acres of land costing $230,000. Always a student of history, Prescott was made president of the Bennington (Vermont) Battle Monument Association in 1876. As governor, he sent three companies of militia to the celebration of the hundredth anniversary of the Battle of Bennington. He was present at the laying of the cornerstone for the monument in 1891. Prescott was responsible for collecting about two hundred and seventy portraits and busts of New Hampshire notables for the State House, Dartmouth College, Phillips Exeter Academy and the New Hampshire Historical Society. He was vice president of the New Hampshire Historical Society, and a fellow of the Royal Historical Society of London. He became a trustee of the New Hampshire College of Agriculture and the Mechanic Arts in 1874, and a trustee of Dartmouth College in 1878. He was also the author of two small volumes: *Portraits of Governors, Judges, Senators, and Other Public Men of New Hampshire* (Boston, 1874); and *Stars and Stripes: The Flag of the United States of America; When, Where and by Whom was it First Saluted?* (Concord, 1878). In 1880 Prescott was elected delegate-at-large to the Republican National Convention at Chicago, and chaired the New Hampshire delegation which nominated James A. Garfield for president. In 1887 he was appointed a member of the State Board of Railroad Commissioners. Prescott retired in 1893, and died at his home in Epping on February 21, 1895. Bibliography: James O. Lyford, *Life of Edward H. Rollins* (Boston, 1906); William Prescott, *The Prescott Memorial*

(Boston, 1870); *The New England Historical and Genealogical Register*, XLIX (1895); Henry Robinson, "The New Hampshire State Prison," *The Granite Monthly*, XXIII (1897); "Our Governor Elect," *The Granite Monthly*, I (1877-78); New Hampshire Historical Society *Proceedings*, II (1895). The Prescott Papers are on deposit in the New Hampshire Historical Society, Concord.

HEAD, Natt, 1879-1881

Born on May 20, 1828, in Hooksett, New Hampshire, son of John Head, a farmer, saw-mill operator and Lieutenant Colonel in the militia, and Anna (Brown) Head. Brother of Hannah Ann, Sally Brown, John A. and William F. Married to Abbie M. Sanford on September 19, 1863; father of Annie Sanford, Lewis Fisher (d. 1872), and Slice Perley (d.1879). Attended Pembroke Academy, then took over management of the family farm and lumber business. Joined by his brother William F. in 1852, and added brick-making to the business—the Head and Dowst Contracting and Building Company of Manchester, New Hampshire, specializing in the construction of railways and public buildings. Head became director of the Suncook Valley Railroad, the First National Bank in Manchester, and the New Hampshire Fire Insurance Company; he was also president of the China Savings Bank of Suncook and the New Hampshire State Agricultural Society. Head was not a member of any church, but was a prominent Freemason. He received an honorary A.M. degree from Dartmouth College in 1879, and was vice-president of the New Hampshire Historical Society. Always interested in military affairs, he was drum major in the 11th Regiment of militia in 1847, bugler in the Governor's Horse Guards, a member of the Amoskeag Veterans, and honorary member of the Ancient and Honorable Artillery of Boston and of the Lancers of that city. Entered politics as a member of the State Legislature from Hooksett, 1861 and 1862; from 1864 to 1870 was Adjutant General assigned the job of obtaining complete records of all those who served in the Civil War. His *Report of the Adjutant-General of the State of New Hampshire* (1865-70) contained the military record of every man in the service, brief histories of the regiments, and a military history of the state from 1623 to 1861, written by Chandler E. Potter (later published separately). Although elected to the State Senate in 1874, Head was disqualified because the ballot read Natt instead of Nathaniel. He was chosen Senator in 1876 and 1877, serving as President of the Senate in 1877. In 1878 the Republican State Convention selected him for Governor, relying on his appeal to farmers and veterans' groups. He won the election (38,075 votes) over his Democratic opponent, Frank A. McKean (31,138). The Greenback Party joined with the Labor Reformers to nominate Warren G. Brown as its candidate; and Brown polled 6,407 votes. Governor Head was the first governor elected for a two-year term. During his administration the new state prison was completed, and the famous murder case of Joseph B. Buzzell was tried, with the governor refusing to commute the death sentence. Legislation passed included a law prohibiting employment of children under ten in factories, and one requiring telegraph companies to keep offices in railroad stations to insure service to every community. Head returned to business life at the end of his period as governor, but soon retired due to ill health. Head died on November 12, 1883, in Hooksett. Bibliography: Otis F. R. Waite, *New Hampshire in the Great Rebellion* (Claremont, N. H., 1870); Ezra S. Stearns, *Genealogical and Family History of the State of New*

Hampshire, vol. 4 (New York, 1908); James O. Lyford, *Life of Edward H. Rollins* (Boston, 1906); "Gen. Natt Head," *The Granite Monthly*, II (1879); "William F. Head & Sons, Brick and Lumber Co., Hooksett, N. H., Letterbooks, 1865-1912," 5 vols., MS, New Hampshire Historical Society, Concord. These letterbooks contain letters of Natt Head concerning politics, the Masons, etc. Scattered letters by Head are among the manuscripts at Dartmouth College.

BELL, Charles Henry, 1881-1883

Born on November 18, 1823, in Chester, New Hampshire, son of Governor John and Persis (Thom) Bell. Brother of Mary Anne Persis, Eliza Thom, John, Susan Jane, Harrietta Adelia, Jane Gibson, Caroline (d. young), Christopher Sargeant and James Isaac. His uncle, Samuel Bell, was also a Governor of New Hampshire. Married to Sarah Almira Gilman on May 6, 1847; father of Helen and Mary Persis. Married a second time to Mrs. Mary Elizabeth (Gray) Gilman on June 3, 1867. Attended Pembroke Academy, and spent one year, 1837, at Phillips Exeter; later attended Dartmouth College, graduating in 1844. Studied law with Bell & Tuck of Exeter, then with his cousin, Samuel Dana Bell, who was subsequently chief justice of the New Hampshire Supreme Court. Charles Henry Bell was admitted to the bar in 1847, and practiced in Chester and in Great Falls from 1848 to 1854; from 1854 to 1868 he practiced in Exeter, his residence for the rest of his life; edited the *Exeter News Letter*, 1871-75. Solicitor of Rockingham County, 1856-66, 1878; member of the State Legislature, 1858-60, 1872-73, and its Speaker in 1860; State Senator in 1863 and 1864, and President of the Senate in 1864. Bell was considered for the Republican nomination for governor in 1879, but lost to Natt Head. He was then appointed to the United States Senate to fill out the term of Bainbridge Wadleigh, and served from March 13 to June 17, 1879, a gap left by the new election laws. In 1880 the Republican Party nominated Bell for Governor by acclamation, and he was elected (44,432 votes) over Democrat Frank Jones (40,813), Greenbacker Warren G. Brown (503), and Prohibitionist George D. Dodge (341). The chief business of the legislature in 1881 was to decide whether to elect a successor to United States Senator Edward H. Rollins, or to postpone the choice until the next legislature. The decision was left to the 1883 legislature, and Rollins was not reelected. Bell proposed changes in laws governing marriage and divorce; he also advocated prohibiting the manufacture of intoxicating liquor. A State Board of Health was established during his administration. Governor Bell, who had not been engaged in an active law practice since 1868, returned to his historical and literary pursuits after stepping down as governor. He was president of the State Constitutional Convention of 1889, and trustee of Robison Female Seminary and of Phillips Exeter Academy. He also received an LL.D. degree from Dartmouth in 1881, was president of the New Hampshire Historical Society from 1868 to 1887, and was a member of several other historical societies. His many historical writings include a *History of the Town of Exeter, Memoir on John Wheelwright*, and *Bench and Bar of New Hampshire*. Bell died in Exeter on November 11, 1893, and was buried in the Exeter Cemetery. Bibliography: Edmund F. Slafter, "Memoir of the Hon. Charles H. Bell, LL.D.," *New England Historical and Genealogical Register*, XLIX (1895); John Carroll Chase, *History of Chester, New Hampshire* (Derry, N. H., 1926); *Memorial Biographies of the New England Historic Genealogical Society*,

IX (1908); James O. Lyford, *Life of Edward H. Rollins* (Boston, 1906); Jeremiah Smith, "Biographical Notice of the Author," in Charles H. Bell's, *The Bench and Bar of New Hampshire* (Boston & New York, 1894); John Templeton, "Hon. Charles H. Bell," *The Granite Monthly*, IV (1881). The Bell Papers are principally in the New Hampshire State Library at Concord, with small collections in the New Hampshire Historical Society, Concord, and in the Dartmouth College Library, Hanover.

HALE, Samuel Whitney, 1883-1885

Born on April 2, 1823, in Fitchburg, Massachusetts, son of Samuel Hale, a farmer, and Saloma (Whitney) Hale. Brother of John Moses, Henry Augustus and Mary Elizabeth. Married to Emelia M. Hay of Dublin, New Hampshire, on June 13, 1850; father of William Samuel and Mary Louise. Attended the district school and academy of Fitchburg, then joined his brother John in trade in Dublin; moved to Keene in 1859, and began a business manufacturing chairs, and later shoe pegs, furniture and woolens. Owned two farms, director of two banks, and involved in railroad enterprises, especially in the building of the Manchester & Keene Railroad. He was active in organizing and building the Second Congregationalist Church in Keene, and was a Master Mason. Hale's first vote was cast for a Free Soil candidate, but he joined the Republican Party when it was organized. He was elected to the State Legislature in 1866 and 1867, and was chosen a member of the Governor's Council in 1869 and 1870. In 1880 he was selected as one of the delegates to the Republican National Convention at Chicago. On September 12, 1882, he was chosen as the Republican candidate for Governor after a bitter contest between his supporters and those of Moody Currier of Manchester, New Hampshire. Hale was eventually elected Governor, receiving 38,402 votes to defeat his Democratic opponent, Martin V. B. Edgerly (36,916), Greenbacker John F. Woodbury (444), and Prohibitionist Josiah M. Fletcher (357). During Hale's administration the legislature, after forty-three ballots, chose Austin F. Pike to succeed Edward H. Rollins as United States Senator; fifty-two men had been considered for the office. The controversy over railroad consolidation resulted in the passage of the Colby Bill, which removed restraints to consolidation; a second act established a new railroad commission to be chosen by the legislature. The governor vetoed the latter law, but approved a second version of the bill which satisfied his objections. He approved the Colby Bill after much consideration. After his term as governor, Hale returned to his home in Keene, formerly the home of Ex-Governor Samuel Dinsmoor. Hale died in Brooklyn, New York, at the home of his brother John Moses, on October 16, 1891. He was buried in Keene, New Hampshire. Bibliography: Walter A. Davis, comp., *The Old Records of the Town of Fitchburg, Massachusetts,* III (Fitchburg, 1900); W. DeLoss Love, Jr., *Memorial of Samuel Whitney Hale* (Hartford, Conn., 1895); James O. Lyford, *Life of Edward H. Rollins* (Boston, 1896); Leon B. Richardson, *William E. Chandler, Republican* (New York, 1940); Jacob H. Gallinger, "Samuel Whitney Hale," *The Granite Monthly*, VI (1882).

CURRIER, Moody, 1885-1887

Born on April 22, 1806, in Boscawen, New Hampshire, son of Moody M. Currier and Rhoda (Putney) Currier. Married three times: to Lucretia C. Dustin on December 8, 1836; to Mary W. Kidder on September 5, 1847; and to Hannah A. Slade on November 16, 1869; father of three children all of whom died before their father. As a boy Currier worked on a farm in Bow, New Hampshire. Largely self educated, attended Hopkinton Academy for a few months, and graduated from Dartmouth College in 1834; taught school in Concord, New Hampshire, and edited the *New Hampshire Literary Gazette* with Asa Fowler for a year; taught school and studied law in Hopkinton, New Hampshire, and Lowell, Massachusetts, settling in Manchester, New Hampshire, to practice law in 1841. In 1848 Currier gave up his law practice and became cashier of the Amoskeag Bank; he remained in the banking business for the rest of his life, while developing other interests in business and railroads in Manchester. He maintained a life-long interest in education and literature, receiving his LL.D. degrees from Bates in 1881 and Dartmouth in 1885. He also belonged to the Unitarian Church in Manchester. In politics Currier was first a Democrat, in 1842 becoming proprietor and editor of the Manchester *Democrat*, a newspaper with strong anti-slavery views. In 1852 he joined the Free Soil Party, and then became a Republican. Served as clerk of the New Hampshire State Senate in 1843 and 1844, a member of the Senate in 1856 and 1857, and its President in 1857; became a member of the Governor's Council in 1860 and 1861, and chairman of the War Committee. In 1876 he was one of the presidential electors casting New Hampshire's vote for Hayes and Wheeler. Currier lost the hotly-contested Republican nomination for governor in 1882 to Samuel W. Hale, but party discord was smoothed over by his nomination in 1884. He won the election (42,514 votes) over Democrat John M. Hill (39,637), Prohibitionist Larkin D. Mason (1,803), and Greenbacker George Carpenter (490). As governor, Currier advocated economy in government during a time of business depression. A law was passed in 1885 requiring fire insurance companies to pay losses to the full value named in the policy, causing fifty-eight companies to withdraw simultaneously from New Hampshire. Within a year new companies were formed, including five stock companies and sixteen general and twenty-one local mutual companies. The governor also appointed ex-Governor Person C. Cheney to the vacancy caused by the death of United States Senator Austin F. Pike. Currier died on August 23, 1898, at his home in Manchester. His widow published a volume of his *State Papers, Addresses and Poems* (Manchester, 1899) and established the Currier Gallery of Art in his memory. Bibliography: American Series of Popular Biographies, *Representative Citizens of the State of New Hampshire* (Boston, 1902); Manchester Historic Association, *Collections*, I (1897); Charles C. Coffin, *The History of Boscawen and Webster* (Concord, N. H., 1878); John W. Moore, *Moore's Historical, Biographical, and Miscellaneous Gatherings, Relative to Printers, Printing and Editing* (Concord, N.H., 1886); Leon B. Richardson, *William E. Chandler, Republican* (New York, 1940); James O. Lyford, *Life of Edward H. Rollins* (Boston, 1906).

SAWYER, Charles Henry, 1887-1889

Born on March 30, 1840, in Watertown, New York, son of Jonathan Sawyer, owner of the F. A. & J. Sawyer Flannel Mill in Dover, New Hampshire, and Martha (Perkins) Sawyer; brother of Mary Elizabeth, Francis Asbury, Roswell Douglas, Martha Frances, Alice May and Frederick Jonathan. Married to Susan Ellen Cowan on February 8, 1865; father of William Davis, Charles Francis, James Cowan, Edward and Elizabeth Coffin. Educated in the public schools of Dover and at Franklin Academy; entered his father's mill and eventually (in 1881) became president of the Sawyer Woolen Mills; was also a director of banks, railroads and civic enterprises in Dover. Belonged to the First Congregationalist Church, and was a prominent Freemason. Sawyer, a Republican, served on the City Council and Board of Aldermen in Dover, and was a representative to the State Legislature in 1869-71 and again in 1876-78. In 1881 he was appointed Aide-de-Camp to Governor Charles H. Bell with the rank of Colonel. He was delegate-at-large to the Republican National Convention at Chicago in 1884, and in 1886 was the Republican candidate for Governor, receiving a plurality of the popular vote (37,796) over Democrat Thomas Cogswell (36,554) and Prohibitionist Joseph Wentworth (2,137). The legislature then selected Sawyer as governor by a vote of 178 to 146. During Sawyer's term, he represented New Hampshire in state and national centennial celebrations. Among the events commemorated were the laying of the cornerstone of the Battle of Bennington Monument; the promulgation of the national constitution in Philadelphia; and the inauguration of President Washington in New York. The 1887 session of the legislature was primarily concerned with the state's railroads, since the State Supreme Court in March 1887 had declared long-term railroad leases invalid. The Hazen Bill, passed by the legislature, would have given the Boston & Maine Railroad eventual control over New Hampshire's railroads, but the bill was vetoed by Sawyer. The legislature also elected William E. Chandler to the United States Senate to fill the vacancy left by the death of Austin F. Pike. While Sawyer was Governor, the State Constitutional Convention of 1888 changed the time of the meeting of the legislature from June to January, removing an awkward gap in senatorial terms. In 1889 Sawyer visited Europe and was appointed by Governor Goodell to represent New Hampshire at the Paris Exposition. He eventually retired from business and lived quietly at Middlebrook Farm in Dover. Sawyer died on January 18, 1908, in Dover. Bibliography: Ezra S. Stearns, *Genealogical and Family History of the State of New Hampshire*, 4 vols. (New York, 1908); American Series of Popular Biographies, *Representative Citizens of the State of New Hampshire* (Boston, 1902); Leon B. Richardson, *William E. Chandler, Republican* (New York, 1940); Charles H. Bell, "Col. Charles H. Sawyer," *The Granite Monthly,* IX (1886); "Obituary," *The Granite Monthly,* XXXX (1908).

GOODELL, David Harvey, 1889-1891

Born on May 6, 1834, in Hillsborough, New Hampshire, the only child of Deacon Jesse Raymond Goodell, a farmer, and Olive Atwood (Wright) Goodell, both of whom were Baptists. Married to Hannah Jane Plumer (d.1911) on September 1, 1857; father of Dura Dana and Richard Carter; married a second time to Emma S.

McCoy. As a child moved with family to a farm in Antrim, New Hampshire, in 1841; attended academies in Hancock, New Hampton and Francestown, New Hampshire, graduating in 1852; later attended Brown University, but ill health caused him to leave in his sophomore year. Received honorary A.M. degrees from Brown and Dartmouth in 1889. Became agent of the Antrim Shovel Co.; invented and manufactured the "lightning apple parer," the nucleus of Goodell Co., which manufactured table cutlery, seed-sowers and fruit and vegetable parers. He lived on the family farm, studied scientific farming, and was president of the Oak Park Association and trustee of the New England Agricultural Society. A lifelong prohibitionist, he served as president of the New Hampshire State Temperance Union, and later of the New Hampshire Anti-Saloon League. In politics Goodell moved from the Democratic to the Republican Party in 1863; he was a representative to the legislature, 1876-79, a member of the State Board of Agriculture, 1876-83, and a member of the Governor's Council, 1883-85. In 1888 he received the Republican nomination for Governor, and was endorsed by the Prohibition Party. Nevertheless, the election was close, with Goodell polling 44,809 votes, Democrat Charles H. Amsden 44,217, and 1,597 votes scattered. The legislature then chose Goodell, 168 to 114. Governor Goodell tried to enforce the law prohibiting the sale of liquor, and recommended that manufacture as well as sale be prohibited. During his administration the Concord and the Boston and Maine Railroads divided their territory, and the legislature opposed the arrangements; the Board of Bank Commissioners was also made permanent, and a revision of the state's statutes was ordered. A special session of the legislature was called on December 2, 1889, to elect a clerk and to determine the membership from small towns, a problem left over from the constitutional changes of 1889. While Goodell was seriously ill from April 22 until July 1, 1890, David A. Taggart, president of the Senate, acted as governor. After the governorship Goodell continued his fight for temperance and returned to his business and agricultural interests. He died on January 22, 1915, in Antrim. Bibliography: Ezra S. Stearns, *Genealogical and Family History of the State of New Hampshire*, 4 vols. (New York, 1908); Leon B. Richardson, *William E. Chandler, Republican* (New York, 1940); *David Harvey Goodell, Born May 6, 1834, Died January 22, 1915* (n.p., n.d); "Argument of Ex-Governor David H. Goodell before the Judiciary Committee," *The Granite Monthly*, XIII (1890).

TUTTLE, Hiram Americus, 1891-1893

Born on October 16, 1837, in Barnstead, New Hampshire, son of George Tuttle and Judith Mason (Davis) Tuttle. Married to Mary C. French on March 17, 1859; father of Hattie French. His father, George Tuttle, a farmer, moved to Pittsfield, New Hampshire, in 1846 to work in the cotton mill, and Hiram attended the local public schools and Pittsfield Academy. He was employed by Lincoln & Shaw, clothiers of Concord, New Hampshire; he later acted as manager of a branch store in Pittsfield, and became its proprietor in 1858. Tuttle also had large interests in banking, lumbering and real estate. He was president of the Pittsfield Savings Bank, the Manchester Savings Bank, and the Suncook Valley Railroad; he also became one of the organizers of the Pittsfield Aqueduct Company, and a trustee of Pittsfield Academy. A member of the Episcopal Church, Tuttle in politics was a Republican, and, although the town was traditionally Democratic, he became Pittsfield's town clerk in 1860. He went to the State Legislature in 1873 and 1874, was a Colonel on Governor Cheney's staff, a member of the Governor's Council, 1878-81, and a delegate to the Republican National Convention in 1888. He lost the Republican nomination for Governor to David H. Goodell in 1888, but was the almost unanimous choice in 1890. The election was close: Tuttle 42,479, Democrat Charles H. Amsden 42,386, and Prohibitionist Josiah M. Fletcher 1,363. The legislature then selected Tuttle, who took office in January 1891. Governor Tuttle and his staff attended the World Columbian Exposition in Chicago in 1892, and were present at the dedication of the monument commemorating the Battle of Bennington. During Tuttle's administration the state college was moved from Hanover to Durham, with the governor officiating at the laying of the cornerstone of the new building. The state library building was erected in Concord, and troubles with the railroads continued. Austin Corbin offered the state $1 million in cash for its interest in the Concord Railroad, but the question was referred to the courts. Dartmouth College conferred an honorary A.M. degree on Tuttle in 1891. In 1894 he hoped to run for the United States Congress, but did not receive the nomination. Tuttle died on February 10, 1911, at his home in Pittsfield. Bibliography: Ezra S. Stearns, *Genealogical and Family History of the State of New Hampshire*, vol. II (New York, 1908); Leon Burr Richardson, *William E. Chandler, Republican* (New York, 1940); Everett B. Sackett, *New Hampshire's University* (Somersworth, 1974); "Gov. Hiram A. Tuttle," *The Granite Monthly*, XIII (1890); G. A. Cheney, "Pittsfield, Queen of the Suncook Valley," *The Granite Monthly*, XXXIX (1907); Hiram A. Tuttle to Charles Marseilles, March 31, 1894, in "Papers of Charles Marseilles," New Hampshire Historical Society.

SMITH, John Butler, 1893-1895

Born on April 12, 1838, in Saxton's River, Vermont, son of Ammi Smith and Lydia (Butler) Smith; brother of Eliza Ann, Frank Pierce, Cynthia Jane, Lydia Ellen and three who died in childhood. Married to Emma Lavender on November 1, 1883; father of Butler Lavender (who died in 1888), Archibald Lavender and Norman. Ammi Smith was a native of New Hampshire who operated a sawmill in Hillsborough, New Hampshire; manufactured woolen goods in Saxton's River from 1833 to 1847, and eventually returned to Hillsborough, where he retired. John B. Smith was educated in the public schools of Hillsborough and at Francestown Academy. After several business ventures in Manchester from 1863 to 1880, he settled in Hillsborough near his hosiery factory, incorporated as the Contoocook Mills Company in 1882. In addition, he owned real estate in New Hampshire and Boston, and was president of the Hillsborough Guaranty Savings Bank. He was a member of the Congregationalist Church and a Mason. A Republican in politics, he was an alternate delegate to the Republican National Convention at Chicago in 1884, and was a Presidential Elector that same year. He was a member of the Governor's Council, 1887-89, and in 1890 was chosen as chairman of the Republican State Committee. In 1892 he received the nomination for Governor by acclamation at the Republican State Convention. Partly as a result of his popularity with labor, the Republicans swept the state in New Hampshire, taking the two United States Congressional seats from the Democrats and giving the state's electoral votes to Harrison, although the Democrats carried the nation with Cleveland. Smith himself defeated the Democratic gubernatorial candidate, the Rev. Luther F. McKinney, 43,676 to 41,501, with a scattering of 1,803 votes going to minor candidates. Smith was the first governor for six years not chosen by the legislature. During his incumbency, forestry and labor commissions were appointed. The state assumed control over the insane, abolishing the county asylums after forty-one inmates died in a fire at the Dover Insane Asylum. Smith's period as governor was also marked by the unveiling in Washington, D.C. of statues of Gen. John Stark and Daniel Webster, presented by the state of New Hampshire. Smith retired from manufacturing in 1911, but resumed his financial interests. Smith died on August 10, 1914, at his home in Hillsborough after a year's illness. Bibliography: Ezra S. Stearns, *Genealogical and Family History of the State of New Hampshire*, vol. IV (New York, 1908); D. Hamilton Hurd, ed., *History of Hillsborough County, New Hampshire* (Philadelphia, 1885); New Hampshire Board of Health, *Preliminary Report . . . Relating to the Burning of the Strafford County Asylum for the Insane* (1893); "Hon. John Butler Smith," *The Granite Monthly*, XIV (1892); XLIII (1911); XLVI (1914).

BUSIEL, Charles Albert, 1895-1897

Born on November 24, 1842, in Meredith Village, New Hampshire, son of John W. Busiel and Julia (Tilton) Busiel. Brother of John T. and Frank E. Married to Eunice Elizabeth Preston on November 21, 1864; father of Frances Evelyn. His family moved to Laconia (then Meredith Bridge), New Hampshire, in 1846. Charles attended the public schools and Gilford Academy, then entered his father's hosiery mill. Later, in partnership with his two brothers, he established the firm of J. W. Busiel & Co., hosiery manufacturers. He was also connected with many other business enterprises, including banking, railroading and building interests. He published the Laconia *Independent Democrat,* belonged to the Congregationalist Church, and was a prominent Mason. In politics Busiel considered himself to be an independent. He was a Democrat until 1888, and was elected by that party to the State Legislature in 1878 and 1879; he also served as a delegate to the Democratic National Convention in Cincinnati in 1880. A strong proponent of a protective tariff, he supported Harrison and the Republican platform in 1888, and became the Republican Mayor of the new city of Laconia in 1892 and 1893. He won the Republican nomination for Governor in 1894 in a heated contest against veteran Republican George A. Ramsdell, and went on to victory in the general election. He polled 46,491 votes, against Democrat Henry O. Kent's 33,959, and Prohibitionist Daniel C. Knowles' 1,750. 856 votes were scattered among minor candidates. Governor Busiel served during a period of economic depression, and he placed a heavy emphasis on frugality in government, vetoing more than twenty bills to save nearly $1 million. He believed in the extension of branch railroads in electric trolley lines, and battled the powerful Boston and Maine Railroad, which nevertheless succeeded in leasing the Concord and Montreal Railroad in 1895. After his governorship, Busiel was a prominent candidate for election to the United States Senate, although he eventually lost to the incumbent, Jacob H. Gallinger. He was New Hampshire's selection for a cabinet-level post under President McKinley, but was not appointed. Busiel died suddenly in Laconia on August 29, 1901. Bibliography: Leon Burr Richardson, *William E. Chandler, Republican* (New York, 1940); George

O. Seilhamer, *History of the Republican Party*, vol. II (New York, n. d.); New Hampshire Historical Society, *Proceedings*, IV (1899-1905); Henry Robinson, "Charles Albert Busiel," *The Granite Monthly*, XVII (1894); E. W. Forrest, "Some 'Lake City' Men and Industries," *The Granite Monthly*, XXIX (1900); obituary, *The Granite Monthly*, XXXI (1901). There are approximately 120 Busiel letters in the William E. Chandler Papers, New Hampshire Historical Society.

RAMSDELL, George Allen, 1897-1899

Born on March 11, 1834, on his father's farm in Milford, New Hampshire, son of William Ramsdell and Maria A. (Moore) Ramsdell. Brother of William Humphrey, Hannah Peabody, Mary Maria, Charles Augustus, Maria Moore, Timothy Harrodon and Edward E. Married to Eliza D. Wilson on November 29, 1860; father of Harry W., Arthur D., Charles T. and Anne M. Attended Appleton Academy (McCollom Institute) in Mont Vernon, New Hampshire; entered Amherst College in 1853 and remained one year; read law with Bainbridge Wadleigh of Milford, and Daniel Clark and Isaac W. Smith of Manchester, New Hampshire; admitted to the bar in 1857, and set up a practice in Peterborough, New Hampshire. Clerk of the Supreme Court in Hillsborough County, 1864-87, residing in Nashua after 1866; engaged in private law practice after 1887, and was appointed auditor and referee in many cases. Ramsdell was a director of banks, railroads, manufacturing companies and educational institutions; he was also a strong temperance advocate, a member of the First Congregationalist Church in Nashua, and a Mason. Politically a staunch Republican, he was Treasurer of Hillsborough County, 1861-62; member of the State Legislature, 1869-72; member of the State Constitutional Convention in 1876; and member of the Executive Council, 1891-92. He declined appointment to the State Supreme Court in 1893, and lost the Republican nomination for Governor to Charles A. Busiel in 1894, but won it by acclamation in 1896. The Bryan presidential campaign was a disaster for the Democratic Party in the state, and established New Hampshire as a Republican stronghold for the next fifteen years. The Republican landslide gave Ramsdell 48,387 votes; Henry O. Kent, Democrat, 28,333; John C. Berry, Prohibitionist, 1,057; Gardner J. Greenleaf, People's Party, 286; George W. Barnard, Nationalist, 229; and Harry H. Acton, Socialist Labor, 483. Governor Ramsdell favored economy in government; he also recommended a licensing board for the practice of medicine and surgery, and a law changing the distribution of intestate estates and lowering the age of consent to sixteen. In 1898 he supplied a regiment from New Hampshire for the war with Spain. After his service as governor, he completed his *History of Milford* (Concord, N. H., 1901). Ramsdell died on November 16, 1900, at his home in Nashua, and was buried in Edgewood Cemetery. Bibliography: Ezra S. Stearns, *Genealogical and Family History of New Hampshire*, vol. I (New York, 1908); *Messages of Gov. George A. Ramsdell, 1897-1898, with Biographical Sketches and Occasional Papers* (Nashua, N. H., 1900); Leonard A. Jones and Conrad Reno, *Memoirs of the Judiciary and the Bar of New England for the Nineteenth Century*, vol. II (Boston, 1901); Charles H. Burns, "George Allen Ramsdell," in *Proceedings of the Bar Association of the State of New Hampshire*, I (Concord, 1900-1903); Obituary, "Last, Sad Rites," *Weekly Telegraph* [Nashua] (November 24, 1900.). There are approximately sixty Ramsdell letters in the William E. Chandler Papers, New Hampshire Historical Society.

ROLLINS, Frank West, 1899-1901

Born on February 24, 1860, in Concord, New Hampshire, son of United States Senator Edward H. Rollins and Ellen Elizabeth (West) Rollins. Brother of Edward Warren, Mary Helen and Montgomery. Married Katherine W. Pecker on December 6, 1882; father of Douglas. Attended the public schools of Concord and was tutored by Moses Woolson; entered the Massachusetts Institute of Technology and graduated in 1881; studied law at Harvard and in the office of John Y. Mugridge; admitted to the bar in August 1882. Received an honorary A.M. degree from Dartmouth College in 1893. Entered the banking firm established by his father in 1884, and was vice-president and manager of the Boston office of E.H. Rollins & Sons, although he maintained his home in Concord. He enlisted in the National Guard in 1880, and between 1890 and 1895 was Assistant Adjutant General with the rank of Lieutenant-Colonel. He was a member of the State Senate and its President, 1895-96. In 1896 he suggested that the New Hampshire Republican Party platform endorse the gold standard, but his proposal was voted down; he was selected to make the address for the New England delegation which went to Canton, Ohio, to visit William McKinley. In 1898 he won the Republican nomination for Governor, and polled 44,730 votes to easily defeat his opponents in the general election: Charles F. Stone, Democrat, 35,653; Augustus G. Stevens, Prohibitionist, 1,333; Gardner J. Greenleaf, People's Party, 104; Benjamin T. Whitehouse, Socialist Labor, 263; and Sumner F. Claflin, Socialist Democrat, 350. Governor Rollins was noted for establishing the state's "Old Home Week" festival, observed in 1899 by about one hundred communities and 10,000 people. He also saw the importance of good roads as an incentive to tourism. After the expiration of his gubernatorial term, he was president of the New Hampshire Old Home Week Association, the Society for the Protection of New Hampshire Forests, and the New Hampshire Good Roads League. Rollins was also an author, and, in addition to novels and short stories, wrote *The Tourists' Guide-Book to the State of New Hampshire* (Concord, 1902). He was a member of St. Paul's Episcopal Church in Concord, treasurer and trustee of St. Paul's School, trustee of the Massachusetts Institute of Technology, and trustee of other institutions and clubs. Rollins died in Boston on October 27, 1915, and was buried in Blossom Hill Cemetery, Concord, New Hampshire. Bibliography: James O. Lyford, *Life of Edward H. Rollins* (Boston, 1906); George O. Seilhamer, *History of the Republican Party* (New York, n. d.); Paul E. Bruns, *An Illustrated History of the Society for the Protection of New Hampshire Forests* (n. p., 1909); Charles R. Corning, "Governor Rollins," *The Granite Monthly*, XXVII (1899); "Hon. Frank West Rollins," *Ibid.*, XLVIII (1916). Also see "Frank West Rollins, Old Home Week Scrap Books," 4 vols., New Hampshire Historical Society.

JORDAN, Chester Bradley, 1901-1903

Born on October 15, 1839, in Colebrook, New Hampshire, son of Johnson Jordan, a farmer, and Minerva (Buel) Jordan, both of whom were Congregationalist. Brother of Julia, Mary Sessions, Benjamin Buel, Malvina and Violetta. Married to Ida Rose Nutter on July 19, 1879; father of Roxannah Minerva, Hugo, Gladstone and Chester Bradley. He farmed, attended district schools, and graduated from Kimball Union

Academy at Meriden, New Hampshire, in 1866, having served as superintendent of schools in Colebrook the previous year. He moved from Colebrook to Lancaster, New Hampshire, in 1868, when he was appointed clerk of the Coos County Court; he also read law in the offices of Judge William S. Ladd and of Ray, Drew & Heywood; admitted to practice in New Hampshire in 1875, and in the United States Circuit Court in 1881. He became a member of Ray, Drew and Jordan, later Drew, Jordan and Buckley. In 1870 he purchased the newspaper *Coos Republican*, and wrote many political and historical articles for this and other papers. Politically he was a Republican, casting his first vote for Lincoln. He was chairman of the town and county Republican committee in Lancaster; appointed to the staff of Governor Straw in 1872 with the rank of Colonel; served on a committee to investigate the normal school in 1876; elected to the State Legislature in 1880, and chosen as its Speaker; and served as a member and President of the State Senate from 1896. He declined the nomination for Governor in 1898, but accepted in 1900 and was easily elected, defeating his Democratic opponent, Frederick E. Potter, by a vote of 53,891 to 34,956. During Jordan's administration the old court was abolished, and a dual court was established with five judges on each bench. Jordan approved of the measure, and appointed the ten judges the day after the bill was passed. Also under Jordan, the state debt was reduced by $400,000, the State House, library, and prisons were all insured, the boundary between Massachusetts and New Hampshire was finally settled in 1901, and the state's eighth constitutional convention met in 1902. Jordan also represented the state at the Webster Centennial at Hanover, New Hampshire. Jordan received honorary A.B. and LL.D. degrees from Dartmouth College in 1881 and 1901, and a B.S. from New Hampshire College in 1901. He was a Mason, an honorary member of several military organizations, and a member of the New Hampshire Historical Society and the Webster Historical Society in Boston. Jordan died in Lancaster, New Hampshire, on August 24, 1914. Bibliography: Ezra S. Stearns, *Genealogical and Family History of the State of New Hampshire*, vol. III (New York, 1908); H. B. Brown, *Biographical Sketches of the New Hampshire Legislature for 1901-1902* (Concord, N.H., 1901); *Chester Bradley Jordan, the Man and Citizen* (Concord, 1916) (no author, 147 pp.); *History of Coos County* (Boston, 1880; repr. 1972); William T. Davis, ed., *The New England States,* vol. IV (Boston, 1897); Leon B. Richardson, *William E. Chandler, Republican* (New York, 1940); American Series of Popular Biographies, *Representative Citizens of the State of New Hampshire* (Boston, 1902).

BACHELDER, Nahum Josiah, 1903-1905

Born on September 3, 1854, in East Andover, New Hampshire, son of William Adams Bachelder, a farmer, and Adeline Elizabeth (Shaw) Bachelder; a Congregationalist. Brother of Lizzie Cornelia, Bertha Sarah and Mary Emery. Married to Mary Abbie Putney on June 30, 1887; father of Ruth and Henry Putney. Educated at Franklin Academy and the New Hampton Institute; after a brief period as a teacher, began a career marked by a steady devotion to agriculture. He joined the Highland Lake Grange in 1877, becoming master of the local grange and then secretary and master of the State Grange, 1891-1903; served as chairman of the Executive Committee of the National Grange, a lecturer 1899, master in 1905-11; he was also secretary of the New Hampshire Grange State Fair Association, 1886-

96. Bachelder was secretary of the State Board of Agriculture from 1887 to 1913, and retained that post while governor. He held the office of Commissioner of Immigration, established in 1889 to bring about the reoccupation of abandoned farms; this office merged with the Board of Agriculture in 1891. Published *New Hampshire Farms for Summer Homes*, 1902-13; was a member of the State Cattle Commission from 1891, and served as secretary of the New Hampshire Old Home Week Association. Accepted the Republican nomination for Governor in 1902, and received 42,115 votes to defeat Democrat Henry F. Hollis, 33,844; Prohibitionist John C. Berry, 1,621; Socialist Michael H. O'Neil, 1,057; and Independent Alonzo Elliot, 468. Governor Bachelder was especially enthusiastic about a program designed to make extensive improvements to the state agricultural college. During his administration the Laconia State School for the mentally retarded received a notably large appropriation; a state armory was built at Manchester; and the ban on sales of intoxicating liquor in the state was lifted after fifty years of prohibition. Bachelder also vetoed a bill proposing the construction of a state sanitorium for consumptives. He received an honorary M.A. degree in 1891 from Dartmouth College, and an honorary M.S. from New Hampshire College in 1903. Bachelder returned to his farm after his service as governor, but retained his membership in the University and Wonolancet Clubs of Concord, New Hampshire. He was a Mason, having been accepted by the Kearsarge Lodge, No. 81, in 1902. Bachelder died on April 22, 1934, in Manchester, New Hampshire, and was buried in Proctor Cemetery in Andover. Bibliography: Ezra S. Stearns, *Genealogical and Family History of the State of New Hampshire*, vol. III (New York, 1908); Ralph G. Chaffee, *History of Andover, New Hampshire, 1900-1965* (Orford, N. H., 1966); George H. Moses, *New Hampshire Men* (Concord, N. H., 1893); Gerald D. Foss, *Three Centuries of Freemasonry in New Hampshire* (Concord, N. H., 1972); H. H. Metcalf, "Hon. Nahum J. Bachelder," *The Granite Monthly*, XXXIII (July, 1902); "A New Honor for New Hampshire," *Ibid*, XXXVIII (January, 1906); *Union* [Manchester, N. H.] (April 23, 1934).

McLANE, John, 1905-1907

Born on February 27, 1852, in Lenoxtown, Scotland, son of Alexander McLane, a wood engraver, and Mary (Haye) McLane, who came to America in 1853. His parents settled in Manchester, New Hampshire, and later moved to Milford, New Hampshire, in 1869. Married to Ellen L. Tuck on March 10, 1880; father of Clinton Averill, Hazel Ellen, John Roy and Charles Malcolm. Attended public schools in Manchester; apprenticed to a cabinet maker, and entered business in 1876 as a manufacturer of post office furniture and equipment. His business eventually grew into the McLane Manufacturing Company, the largest supplier of post office equipment in North America. Held positions as director of the Milford Granite Company; director and president of the Souhegan National Bank; and director of the New Hampshire Fire Insurance Company. A Mason (grandmaster of the Grand Lodge of New Hampshire, 1898), McLane was also an Odd Fellow, a Patron of Husbandry, and a Congregationalist. Entered the legislature as a Republican in 1885, and appointed chairman of the Insurance Committee in the 1887 session; elected to the State Senate in 1891 and 1893, and became the first member to serve two terms as President of that body. Delegate to the Republican National Convention in 1900; won Republican nomination in 1904 gubernatorial race, and received 51,171 votes to defeat his opponents: Democrat Henry F. Hollis (35,437), Prohibitionist David Heald (857), and Socialist Sumner F. Claflin (943). Governor McLane welcomed the delegates to the Russo-Japanese Peace Conference, which President Roosevelt had elected to hold at Portsmouth, New Hampshire. McLane skillfully used the event to enhance New Hampshire's national and international prestige. He also witnessed the first large appropriations for the building of a vast system of roads and highways in the state. He went to Washington to appear before a Congressional committee in support of a bill proposing to create a national forest preserve, including New Hampshire's Presidential Range, and was present at the launching of the battleship *New Hampshire* at Camden, New Jersey, on June 30, 1906. After his gubernatorial term had expired, McLane returned to his business in Milford, and held active membership in various civic organizations, including the Boston Club, the Amoskeag Veterans and the New Hampshire Club. He received an honorary A.M. degree from Dartmouth College. McLane died on April 13, 1911, in Pinehurst, North Carolina, and was buried six days later in Milford Cemetery. Bibliography: Harlan C. Pearson, *The Brown Book of the New Hampshire Legislature of 1905* (Concord, N. H., 1905); State of New Hampshire, *Manual for the General Court, 1905* (Concord, 1905); George A. Ramsdell, *The History of Milford* (Concord, N. H., 1901); Gerald D. Foss, *Three Centuries of Freemasonry in New Hampshire* (Concord, N. H., 1972); George H. Moses, *New Hampshire Men* (Concord, N. H., 1893); Howard H. Brown, "The Battleship 'New Hampshire,' " *The Granite Monthly*, XL (1908); *Telegraph* [Nashua, N. H.] (April 19, 1911). There are scattered McLane Papers in collections of the New Hampshire Historical Society.

FLOYD, Charles Miller, 1907-1909

Born on June 5, 1861, in Derry, New Hampshire, son of Sewall Floyd, a farmer, and Sarah J. (Sleeper) Floyd. Brother of Edward, Laura, Linnae, William H., Joseph, John, Benjamin, Minnie, Ernest and James Edward. Married to Carrie E. Atwood on September 16, 1886; father of Marion Beatrice. Received a general education at Pinkerton Academy, and went to work on a farm at the age of fourteen; later worked in a shoe shop, and subsequently as a hardware clerk in Haverhill, Massachusetts in 1881. Successful in the retail clothing business with his brother in Manchester, New Hampshire, operating a business in 1888 which became the Manchester One Price Clothing Store and was later incorporated in 1914 as the Charles M. Floyd Company. He also held part ownership in the F. M. Hoyt Company, one of the largest individually controlled factories in New England, and eventually became heavily involved in other industries. He was a trustee of the Amoskeag Savings Bank, a director of the Manchester Building and Loan Association, and a director of the Manchester Board of Trade. He was a Mason and a member of the Congregationalist Church. Floyd won election as a Republican to the State Senate, 1899-1901, served on the Executive Council, 1905-07, and survived a bitter fight in the state convention to become the Republican gubernatorial nominee in 1906. Polling 40,581 votes in the November election, Floyd defeated Democrat Nathan C. Jameson (37,672), Prohibitionist Edmund B. Tetley (2,212), and Socialist William H. McFall (1,011), in an election ultimately decided on

January 2, 1907, by the State Legislature, where Floyd received 263 votes to 144 for Jameson. As governor, Floyd supported the good roads movement; several hundred miles of roads were built during his administration. He established the State Tax Commission; signed acts giving new rules and reforms for the state prison; and abolished the practice of free railroad passes for legislators. In 1908 Floyd attended a governors' conference called by President Roosevelt. Floyd was chairman of the New Hampshire delegation to the Republican National Convention in 1912, served as New Hampshire's Fuel Administrator during World War I, and was chairman of the State Tax Commission, 1921-23. Floyd died on February 3, 1923, in Manchester. Bibliography: Harlan C. Pearson, *The Brown Book of the New Hampshire Legislature of 1907* (Concord, N. H., 1907); Ezra S. Stearns, *Genealogical and Family History of the State of New Hampshire*, vol. I (New York, 1908); Henry H. Metcalf, *One Thousand New Hampshire Notables* (Concord, N. H., 1919); J. Duane Squires, *The Granite State of the United States*, vol. II (New York, 1956); Gerald D. Foss, *Three Centuries of Freemasonry in New Hampshire* (Concord, N. H., 1972); George F. Willey, *Willey's Book of Nutfield* (Derry Depot, N. H., 1895).

QUINBY, Henry Brewer, 1909-1911

Born on June 10, 1846, in Biddeford, Maine, son of Thomas Quinby and Jane E. (Brewer) Quinby. Brother of Lucretia Day, Fred and Thomas Freeman. Married to Octavia M. Cole on June 22, 1870; father of Henry Cole and Candace Ellen. Attended New Hampton Institute, Nichols Latin School in Lewiston, Maine, and graduated from Bowdoin College with a B.A. degree in 1869 and an M.A. in 1872. While a special agent with the Quartermaster Department of the Army, Quinby graduated with an M.D. degree in 1880 from the National Medical College in Washington, D. C.; he later received an honorary degree from Dartmouth College. Went into business for the Cole Manufacturing Company of Lakeport, New Hampshire, and served as an aide-de-camp on the staff of Gov. Ezekiel Straw with the rank of Colonel, 1872-73. Member of the Unitarian Church. A Republican, he served in the State Legislature, 1887-89; the Senate, 1889-91; and on the Executive Council, 1891-93. Became a delegate to the Republican National Convention of 1893, and chairman of the State Republican Convention of 1896. He was also a trustee of the New Hampshire State Hospital, president of the Laconia National Bank and of the City Savings Bank of Laconia, and Grand Master in 1901 of the Masonic Grand Lodge of New Hampshire. Quinby won the governorship in 1908 over Democrat Clarence E. Carr, 44,630 votes to 41,386, with Socialist Sumner F. Claflin polling 1,120 votes, and Prohibitionist Edmund B. Tetley receiving 897. During his tenure as governor, Quinby stressed economy; he also thoroughly reorganized the State National Guard; built a state sanatorium for consumptives at Glencliff; and opened a state normal school at Keene. His administration enlarged and remodeled the State House, and added new facilities to the state hospital, state prison, state industrial school, state college and the normal school at Plymouth. Quinby returned to his business at Lakeport at the end of his gubernatorial term. He was also a trustee of several civic institutions, including the New Hampshire Historical Society at Concord. Quinby died on February 8, 1924, in New York City while visiting his daughter. He was buried in Lakeport. Bibliography: Harlan C. Pearson, *The Brown Book of the New Hampshire Legislature of 1909* (Concord, N.

H., 1909); Henry H. Metcalf, *One Thousand New Hampshire Notables* (Concord, N. H., 1919); Henry C. Quinby, *Genealogical History of the Quinby (Quimby) Family*, 2 vols. (New York, 1915-1923); Gerald D. Foss, *Three Centuries of Freemasonry in New Hampshire* (Concord, N. H., 1972); Leon B. Richardson, *William E. Chandler, Republican* (New York, 1940); George H. Moses, *New Hampshire Men* (Concord, 1893); Richard Herndon, *Men of Progress* (Boston, 1898).

BASS, Robert Perkins, 1911-1913

Born on September 1, 1873, in Chicago, Illinois, son of Perkins Bass, a lawyer, and Clara (Foster) Bass. Brother of Gertrude and John Foster. Married to Edith Harland Bird on January 20, 1912; father of Perkins, Edith, Joanne, Robert, Jr. and Jeremy. Parents moved to Peterborough, New Hampshire, when Robert was nine, and established a farm and an estate; graduated from Harvard with a B.A. degree in 1896, attended postgraduate courses for a year, 1896-97, and spent the next year in Harvard Law School; later received honorary degrees from Dartmouth and the University of New Hampshire. Became a trustee of his father's estate, and engaged in farming and forestry using modern scientific principles; served on the New Hampshire Forestry Commission, 1906-10, and as its chairman; also president of the American Forestry Association. Entered politics as a member of the State Legislature, 1905-09, but was absent due to illness for much of the first term; won election to the State Senate in 1909, and sponsored legislation that resulted in the first direct primary law in the eastern states. Entered the first primary election in September 1910 as a Republican candidate for Governor, and defeated fellow Republican Bertram Ellis, 19,484 votes to 10,393. In the general election of November 1910, Bass, a leader of the Lincoln Clubs, advocated a progressive platform and defeated Democrat Clarence E. Carr by a count of 44,908 to 37,737. John C. Berry, the Prohibitionist candidate, won 410 votes, and Socialist Asa Warren drew 1,100. Bass was the only successful Republican gubernatorial candidate east of the Mississippi River in 1910. While governor, Bass supported passage of a Workmen's Compensation Act; endorsed the state's first effective child labor law; and urged the establishment of a Bureau of Labor and a Public Service Commission, the latter as a means of regulating the state's public utilities. He also called for a new corrupt practices act which would limit campaign contributions and expenses. A State Constitutional Convention met during 1912. Bass aspired to the United States Senate, but failed his two attempts in 1913 and 1926. He supported the Progressive Party and Theodore Roosevelt for as long as it existed in New Hampshire. He also served as Director of Marine Labor during World War I, and afterward as Chairman of the National Adjustment Commission. Bass returned to the State legislature in 1923, joined many groups and institutions, and was a member and Chairman of the Board of the Brookings Institution, Washington, D. C., from 1946 to 1949. Bass died on July 29, 1960, in Peterborough. Bibliography: Harlan C. Pearson, *The Brown Book of the New Hampshire Legislature of 1911* (Concord, N. H., 1911); George E. Mowry, *Theodore Roosevelt and the Progressive Movement* (New York, 1960); Thomas R. Agan, "The New Hampshire Progressive Movement," Unpublished Ph.D. Thesis, State University of New York, 1975; George A. Morison and Etta M. Smith, *History of Peterborough, New Hampshire*, vol. II (Rindge, N.

H., 1954); Harrison H. Metcalf, *One Thousand New Hampshire Notables* (Concord, N. H., 1919); Jewell Bellush, "Reform in New Hampshire: Robert Bass Wins the Primary," *New England Quarterly*, XXXV (1962); Hobart Pillsbury, *New Hampshire: A History*, vol. VI (New York, 1927). The principal collection of Bass Papers is on deposit in the Dartmouth College Library, Hanover, New Hampshire.

FELKER, Samuel Demeritt, 1913-1915

Born on April 16, 1859, in Rochester, New Hampshire, son of William H. Felker and Deborah (Demeritt) Felker; member of the Congregationalist Church. Married Mary J. Dudley on June 26, 1900. Prepared for college at New Hampton, New Hampshire; attended Dartmouth College, graduating in 1882; received both A.M. and LL.B. from Boston University Law School in 1887. Soon began a successful law practice in Rochester, and served as a member of the State Constitutional Convention of 1889; elected to the State Senate in 1890 (the first Democrat in the Upper House to capture the former Twelfth District), and served for the 1891-92 term; Mayor of Rochester from 1896-97; City Solicitor of Rochester between 1899 and 1913; served in the New Hampshire House of Representatives from 1909-11, where he became the Minority Leader. Ran for Governor in 1912 against Republican Franklin Worcester, and received 34,210 votes to Worcester's 32,176, but failed to receive a majority. When the election went to the State Legislature for a verdict, the Progressives threw their support to the Democrats, thus giving Felker a victory over Worcester by a vote of 222 to 196. As governor, Felker proposed a number of progressive measures for the state, and made a number of controversial changes in top administrative positions. In response to Republican criticism blaming the economic problems of the Wilson administration on the Democratic Party, Felker wrote a defense of his party and of his governorship in the Republican paper, the Boston *Herald.* In 1915 Felker lost his bid for reelection to his Republican friend, Rolland Spaulding. After taking office, Spaulding appointed Felker Judge of the Rochester Municipal Court, and Felker held this position until his retirement in 1930. Felker died on November 14, 1932, and was buried in Rochester. Bibliography: Harlan Pearson, *Biographical Sketches of the Governor, Councilors, Men of the Senate and House of Representatives of the New Hampshire Legislature for 1913;* Henry Metcalf, *One Thousand New Hampshire Notables* (Concord, N. H., 1919); George Moses, *New Hampshire Men* (Concord, N. H., 1893); *Granite Monthly*, vol. XLV (March-April, 1913); P. E. Estaver, *New Hampshire Profiles*, vol. X, no. 6 (June, 1961).

SPAULDING, Rolland Harty, 1915-1917

Born on March 15, 1873, in Townsend Harbor, Massachusetts, son of Jonas Spaulding, a manufacturer of fibre products, and Emmaline (Cummings) Spaulding; a Protestant. Brother of Leon C., Governor Huntley Spaulding and Marion Spaulding. Married to Vera Gowan on December 18, 1918; father of Virginia Pauline and Betty Louise. Graduated from Phillips Academy, Andover, Massachusetts, in 1893. That same year he entered the family leather-board business. First became known in politics in 1905 as an early proponent of the progressive movement in New Hampshire politics. In 1912 he was a delegate to the Republican National Convention, and in 1914 he was nominated for Governor by the Republican Party. Although Spaulding refused to campaign seriously, he defeated Democrat A. W. Noone by a vote of 46,413 to 33,674. Governor Spaulding endeavored to establish a uniform accounting system for the state, and to reduce the state tax. He was instrumental in the reform of municipal finances and in improving the business management of state institutions. He also sponsored a comprehensive plan for future state highway improvement, and reorganized the State Highway Department. Though urged to run for a second term, Spaulding chose to return to his rapidly expanding family business. Spaulding devoted the remainder of his life to his various business interests. At various times he was a director of the United Life and Accident Insurance Co., Concord, New Hampshire; the Atlas Leather Co., Casyville, Illinois; the Rochester Trust Co., Rochester, New Hampshire; the Spaulding Frost Co.; and the Kennebunk Manufacturing Co. He also became president of the Rochester Trust Co., and vice president of the First National Bank of Rochester. Spaulding died in Rochester on March 14, 1942. Bibliography: Harlan Pearson, *Biographical Sketches of the Governor, Councilors, Men of the Senate and House of Representatives of the New Hampshire Legislature for 1915;* Henry Metcalf; *One Thousand New Hampshire Notables* (Concord, N. H., 1919); "The Public Career of Rolland H. Spaulding," *Granite Monthly* (April-June, 1918). The Spaulding Letters are on deposit in the New Hampshire Historical Society in Concord.

KEYES, Henry Wilder, 1917-1919

Born on May 23, 1862, in Newbury, Vermont, son of Henry Keyes, a farmer, merchant and railroad builder, and Emma Frances (Pierce) Keyes; an Episcopalian. Married to Frances Parkinson, a popular fiction writer, on June 8, 1904; father of Henry Wilder, John Parkinson and Francis. Attended Harvard University and graduated with an A.B. in 1887. After graduation he took charge of his father's estate, "Pine Grove Farm," one of the finest stock farms in New England, and became instrumental in introducing the Holstein-Friesian breed of cattle to this country. Organized the Woodsville National Bank in 1897, and remained its president until his death. In 1891 he was elected selectman of Haverhill Township, a position he continued to hold even after becoming governor; that same year, he was elected to the New Hampshire House of Representatives, was reelected in 1893, and served a third term from 1915-17. Elected to the State Senate in 1902, where he served as chairman of the committees on railroads and forestry until 1905. From 1903-13 he was treasurer of the State Excise Commission, and served as chairman of that body from 1915 until his candidacy for Governor in 1916 against Democrat John Hutchins. Keyes won by a vote of 45,851 to 38,853, notwithstanding Wilson's Democratic victory in New Hampshire during the presidential election of that year. Keyes' tenure as governor covered the period of World War I. Under his guidance numerous war measures were adopted, along with some of the state's most progressive legislation. Limits were placed on the working hours of women and children; a "blue sky" act was passed to protect the public against stock fraud; a standardized system of weights and measures was adopted; the Boston & Maine Railroad reorganization plan was approved; and the state's Library Commission was created.

Keyes' distinguished record as a war governor led to his election to the United States Senate in 1918, the first time in nearly one hundred years that a governor of New Hampshire was elected to the Senate while still in office. Keyes was reelected twice to the Senate, serving from 1919 until his retirement in 1937. During his Washington years, he was a member of the Navy, Appropriations, Forestry, Agriculture and Immigration Committees, and was Chairman of the Standing Committee on Public Buildings and Grounds. He introduced the bill that established the new Supreme Court building, served on the commission that supervised that building's construction, and sponsored the bill that created the Bureau of Aeronautics in the Navy Department. Keyes died in North Haverhill, New Hampshire, on June 19, 1938. He was buried in Oxbow Cemetery, Newbury, Vermont. Bibliography: Harlan Pearson, *Biographical Sketches of the Governor, Councilors, Men of the Senate and House of Representatives of the New Hampshire Legislature for 1917;* Henry Metcalf, *One Thousand New Hampshire Notables* (Concord, N.H., 1919); George Moses, *New Hampshire Men, A Collection of Biographical Sketches* (Concord, N. H., 1893); Henry Metcalf, *New Hampshire Agriculture. Personal and Farm Sketches* (1897).

BARTLETT, John Henry, 1919-1921

Born on March 15, 1869, in Sunapee, New Hampshire, son of John Zeron Bartlett, a farmer and businessman, and Sophronia Almeda (Sargent) Bartlett; a Methodist. Brother of Mott L. Bartlett. Married to Agnes Page on June 4, 1900; father of Calvin Page; remarried in 1944 to Mildred C. Lawson in Washington, D. C. Attended Dartmouth College and graduated with an A.B. in 1894; studied law during 1897-98 in the office of Calvin Page, Portsmouth, New Hampshire. Served as principal of the high school there for the 1896-97 term. Admitted to the New Hampshire Bar in 1894, and formed a law partnership under the firm name of Page & Bartlett, Portsmouth. From 1899-1907 he was Postmaster of Portsmouth; during 1905-06 he served as Colonel on Governor McLane's staff, and was active in making local arrangements for the Russo-Japanese Peace Conference held in Portsmouth in 1905; in 1916 he was presiding officer at the Republican State Convention, and during 1917-18 he served as a member of the New Hampshire House of Representatives. Elected Governor by a vote of 39,898 to 34,579 over Democrat Nathaniel Martin in 1918. During Bartlett's term as governor, an executive budget system was established, and control of many state institutions was vested in the governor and council. He also achieved a revision of the state's employee liability law, and signed a bill authorizing cities to acquire and operate street railways. He declined to run for reelection. In 1921 Bartlett was appointed president of the United States Civil Service Commission by President Harding. The next year he became the first Assistant United States Postmaster-General, sponsoring the first transcontinental air mail service, and setting up a rigid code of regulations to protect the Post Office Department from looting of the mails. In 1929 he was appointed chairman of the United States section of the Joint International Commission for the United States and Canada, a post he held until his retirement in 1939. His New Deal sympathies caused him to switch his political allegiance, and in 1939 he made an unsuccessful bid for the United States Congress on the Democratic ticket. At various times Bartlett was president of the New Hampshire Society for the

Prevention of Cruelty to Children, New Hampshire Society for the Prevention of Cruelty to Animals, Portsmouth Trust and Guarantee Co., and Granite State Fire Insurance Co. He was author of *Spice for Speeches* (1926), *Folks is Folks* (1927), *The Legend of Ann Smith* (1931), and *The Bonus March and the New Deal* (1937). Bartlett died in Portsmouth on March 19, 1952. He was buried in Harmony Grove Cemetery. Bibliography: "The Administration of Governor Bartlett," *Granite Monthly*, LIII (January, 1921); *Granite Monthly*, LI (January, 1919); Henry Metcalf, *One Thousand New Hampshire Notables* (Concord, N.H., 1919); *Official New Hampshire, 1919-1920.*

BROWN, Albert Oscar, 1921-1923

Born on July 18, 1853, in Northwood, New Hampshire, son of Charles Osgood Brown and Sarah Elizabeth (Langmaid) Brown; member of the Congregationalist Church. Married to Susie Jane Clarke on December 20, 1888. Attended Dartmouth College and was graduated with an A.B. in 1878. After graduation taught for three years at Lawrence Academy, Groton, Massachusetts, then began law study under Judge Henry E. Burnham, and later attended Boston University Law School, where he was graduated cum laude in 1884. That same year he was admitted to the New Hampshire Bar, and began practice in Manchester, New Hampshire, becoming successively a member of Burnham & Brown, Burnham, Brown & Warren, and Burham, Brown, Jones & Warren. As an attorney he was involved in much of the state's most important litigation, serving as Special Counsel for New Hampshire in the railroad tax appeals case in the Supreme Court during 1910-11. He was president of the Amoskeag Savings Bank, Manchester, New Hampshire, from 1905-12, and at various other times served as that institution's secretary, treasurer and later, again, as its president, until his retirement in March 1937. During World War I he was a member of the New Hampshire Committee of 100 on Public Safety, and vice-chairman of the Manchester War Savings Committee. He was also chairman of the State Tax Commission during 1911-21, and president of the New Hampshire Constitutional Convention, 1918-21. Ran for Governor on the Republican ticket, and won by a vote of 93,273 to 62,174 over Democrat Charles E. Tilton. As governor, Brown achieved a large reduction in the state debt; a substantial reduction in taxes; and made many important advances in the development of state highways. He declined to run for reelection. In 1922 Brown became president of the New Hampshire Bankers Association, and in 1924 served as delegate-at-large to the Republican National Convention. From 1925-26 he was a member of the New Hampshire General Court. He was a trustee of Dartmouth College between 1911 and 1931, and at various times was president of the Board of Trustees of Coe's Northwood Academy, and director of the Manchester Traction, Light & Power Co., the Amoskeag National Bank, the John B. Vavick Co., and the New Hampshire Fire Insurance Co. Brown died in Manchester on March 28, 1937. Bibliography: *Brown Book of the New Hampshire Legislature* (1921); Henry Metcalf, *One Thousand New Hampshire Notables* (1919); *Granite Monthly*, LII (January, 1920); *Granite Monthly*, LIII (February, 1921).

BROWN, Fred Herbert, 1923-1925

Born on April 12, 1879, in Ossipee, New Hampshire, son of Dana J. Brown and Nellie (Allen) Brown. Married to Edna C. McHarg of Littleton, New Hampshire, on May 16, 1925. Educated at Dow Academy in Franconia, New Hampshire, and attended Dartmouth College, 1899-1900. Played professional baseball briefly as a catcher for the Boston Braves of the National League. Read law with James A. Edgerly at Somersworth, New Hampshire, and attended the Boston University School of Law, 1904-06; admitted to the bar in 1907 and practiced with Edgerly until 1908. Was a Mason and a Democrat. Entered public service as City Solicitor for Somersworth, 1910-14, and was a member of the State Constitutional Convention in 1912. Democratic presidential elector, 1912; Mayor of Somersworth, 1914-22; and U. S. District Attorney, 1914-22. Brown was persuaded to enter the Democratic primary election in September 1922, and won 7,954 votes to defeat John C. Hutchins (6,215) and Albert W. Noone (2,006); he also won the November general election, polling 70,160 votes against the 61,526 cast for his Republican opponent, Windsor H. Goodnow. Brown's victory represented the largest plurality given a Democratic gubernatorial candidate in New Hampshire since the election of Isaac Hill in 1837. Brown ran unopposed in the Democratic primary of 1924, but was defeated in the general election by John G. Winant. Governor Brown urged economy in state expenditures; approved a $400,000 addition to the plant of the state mental hospital; and supported a large-scale program of tax reform, including a tax on gasoline and abolition of the woman's poll tax. He also supported legislation in favor of a forty-eight hour work week. Most of his proposals, however, were defeated in the Senate, where Republicans had maintained a large majority. Perhaps Brown's most significant achievement was the liquidation of the state debt, which had increased during the war. After his service as governor, Brown returned to his law practice, although he became Public Service Commissioner of the state between 1925 and 1933. In 1932 he won election to the United States Senate, but lost an attempt to be reelected in 1938. President Roosevelt appointed him Comptroller General of the United States in 1939, and a member of the United States Tariff Commission, 1940-41. In 1941 he retired from all public activity and returned to his home in Somersworth. Brown died on February 3, 1955, in Somersworth. He was buried in Ossipee Cemetery. Bibliography: Henry H. Metcalf, *One Thousand New Hampshire Notables* (Concord, N. H., 1919); *The Brown Book of the New Hampshire Legislature of 1923* (Concord, N. H., 1923); Gerald D. Foss, *Three Centuries of Freemasonry in New Hampshire* (Concord, N. H., 1972); Bernard Bellush, *He Walked Alone: A Biography of John Gilbert Winant* (The Hague, 1968); George E. Farrand, "Fred H. Brown of Somersworth, Democrat," *The Granite Monthly*, LVI (1924).

WINANT, John Gilbert, 1925-1927, 1931-1935

Born on February 23, 1889, in New York City, son of Frederick Winant, a real estate broker, and Jeanette (Gilbert) Winant; an Episcopalian. Brother of Clinton D., Frederick, Jr. and Cornelius. Married to Constance Rivington Russell on December 20, 1919, and father of Constance, John Gilbert, Jr. and Rivington Russell.

Attended private elementary schools in New York City, St. Paul's School in Concord, New Hampshire, and Princeton University. Appointed an instructor in history at St. Paul's School in 1913, and taught until enlistment in the American Expeditionary Force in 1917. Returned to teaching; invested successfully in Texas oil business, from which he profited until the stock market crash of 1929. As a Republican he was elected to the House of Representatives in 1916, to the State Senate in 1920, and again to the Lower House in 1922. Won the Republican nomination for Governor in the 1924 primary, receiving 20,627 votes against the 18,092 cast for Frank Knox of Manchester, and went on to win the general election from Democrat Fred H. Brown, 88,650 votes to 75,691. Defeated in his bid for reelection in 1926. In the direct primary of September 1930, he won the Republican nomination over Arthur P. Morrill, and then defeated Democrat Albert W. Noone in the general election, 75,518 votes to 54,441, to become the first man ever to serve more than one two-year term as governor of New Hampshire. Winant won the nomination again in 1932, and defeated Democrat Henri Ledoux in the general election, 106,777 votes to 89,487. Governor Winant's administration achieved notable social reforms. He pushed through legislation to improve highways; reorganized the State Banking Commission; and instituted accurate accounting practices. In 1930 he worked for measures to provide relief services to mothers and dependent children; tightened regulations on banking and stock transactions; and created an executive budget. He supervised the passage of an emergency credit act, which allowed the state to guarantee debts of financially distressed political subdivisions, and a state minimum wage act for women and children. He also centralized the state's poor-relief activities, and became the first governor to fill his enrollment quota in the Civilian Conservation Corps and the first to cooperate with the National Planning Board. In January 1935, following his years as governor, Winant was appointed by President Roosevelt to be Assistant Director of the International Labor Organization in Geneva, but was soon recalled to head the newly-created Social Security Board. In 1937 he returned to his International Labor Organization post at Geneva. He was appointed in 1940 as Ambassador to the Court of St. James, replacing Joseph P. Kennedy. During the war years, Winant made a favorable impression on the British people through his personal efforts on their behalf. He was a planner of the 1943 meeting in Moscow which led to the summit conference at Teheran, and served on the European Advisory Commission which would eventually define Allied zones of postwar occupation in Germany. Winant was awarded honorary degrees by Dartmouth College, the University of New Hampshire and Princeton University, and even while abroad remained a member of the Society for the Protection of New Hampshire Forests, the New Hampshire Historical Society, the Wonolancet Club of Concord, the Odd Volumes Club of Boston, and the Century, Racquet and Tennis Clubs of New York; he also held positions in many other organizations of national and international significance. He resigned his London post in March 1946, and President Truman appointed him as the United States representative to the Economic and Social Council of the United Nations. He soon retired to his home in Concord, New Hampshire, to write his memoirs, completing one volume, *Letter from Grosvenor Square*. Winant committed suicide on November 3, 1947, and was buried at St. Paul's School in Concord. Bibliography: Bernard Bellush, *He Walked Alone* (New York, 1968); *The Brown Book of the New Hampshire Legislature for 1933* (Concord, N. H., 1933); *Manual for the General Court* (Concord, N. H., 1925); Bert R. Whittemore, "A Quiet Triumph: The Mission of John Gilbert Winant to

London, 1941," *Historical New Hampshire* (Spring, 1975). The major collection of Winant Papers are on deposit in the Franklin D. Roosevelt Library, Hyde Park, New York.

SPAULDING, Huntley Nowell, 1927-1929

Born on October 30, 1869, in Townsend Harbor, Massachusetts, son of Jonas Spaulding, a manufacturer of fibre board, and Emmaline (Cummings) Spaulding, both of whom were Congregationalists. Brother of Leon C., Rolland H., and Marion L. Married to Harriet Mason of Topeka, Kansas, on August 11, 1901; no children. Educated in Townsend Harbor schools and graduated from Phillips Andover Academy in 1889. Entered business as superintendent of the family's mill at Townsend Harbor, became manager and expanded into New Hampshire, New York and England, eventually becoming chairman of the board of the Spaulding Fibre Company, which produced electrical insulating material; moved his home to Rochester, New Hampshire. A staunch Republican, he was a delegate to Republican National Conventions from 1900; chaired the New Hampshire Food Production Committee during World War I; was appointed New Hampshire Federal Food Administrator by Herbert C. Hoover in 1917, and later chairman of the European Relief Council. He also urged entrance of the United States into the League of Nations. In 1920 Spaulding entered the direct primary election as a Republican candidate for the United States Senate, but lost to George H. Moses. He chaired the State Board of Education, 1921-26; won the Republican nomination for Governor over John G. Winant in the direct primary election of 1926; and on November 2, 1926, won the gubernatorial election with 77,394 votes to defeat Democrat Eaton D. Sargent, who received 52,236. As governor, Spaulding brought efficiency to state government; sponsored forward-looking legislation; and achieved a national reputation for gubernatorial skills and party leadership. In the disastrous flood of 1927, Spaulding floated a three million dollar bond issue to meet the emergency, and favored the issuing of bonds to provide the funds urgently needed by the institutions of the state to carry on essential services. The legislature respected his integrity and business acumen, and supported his fiscal recommendations. Spaulding was widely known for his philanthropy in the fields of health, welfare, youth services and education. He received several honorary degrees, including those of M.A., M.S., and LL.D., and in 1944 was awarded the Charles Holmes Pettee Memorial Medal by the University of New Hampshire for outstanding state and national service. According to his instructions, the Spaulding-Potter Charitable Trusts between 1955 and 1972 made grants of approximately $16.8 million to philanthropic endeavors. Spaulding died on November 14, 1955, in Rochester. Bibliography: Willis McDuffee, *The Story of a Mill Hand Who Became Food Administrator and Candidate for United States Senator* (Rochester, 1920); Merrill Symonds, *George Higgins Moses of New Hampshire: The Man and the Era* (Worcester, Mass., 1955); Edward J. Gallagher, *George H. Moses: A Profile* (Laconia, 1975); Joseph M. Lucier, *Brown Book of the New Hampshire Legislature of 1927* (Concord, 1927); *New Hampshire Sunday News* [Manchester] (August 28, 1949); *The Orange Tree and the Inch Worm: The Spaulding-Potter Charitable Trusts* (Concord, 1973).

TOBEY, Charles William, 1929-1931

Born on July 22, 1880, in Roxbury, Massachusetts, son of William H. Tobey, a farmer, and Ellen Hall (Parker) Tobey. Brother of Doris, Marion and Mildred. Educated in Boston public schools and at Roxbury Latin School. Married to Francelia M. Lovett on June 4, 1902 (d. 1947); father of Russell Benjamin, Louise, Francelia and Charles William; married to Loretta C. Radenhorst on May 26, 1948 (d. 1951); married a third time, to Mrs. Lillian Compton in 1952. Moved to Temple, New Hampshire, shortly after his first marriage, where he took up farming and soon began a business career in insurance, banking and manufacturing at Manchester, New Hampshire; became president of the F. M. Hoyt Shoe Company. Chosen a selectman of Temple, and served as a representative to the legislature, 1915-17, 1919-21 and 1923-25, and as its Speaker, 1919-20; chairman of the Liberty Loan campaign in New Hampshire, 1914-17; served in the State Senate, 1924-26, and as its President 1926-26; won the primary election as Republican candidate for Governor in 1928, and defeated his Democratic opponent, John D. Sargent, 108,431 votes to 79,798. During Tobey's term New Hampshire issued its first bonds for the exclusive purpose of highway development, and began the practice of plowing roads in winter. Tobey used the influence of his office to improve correctional institutions, especially those for wayward youths. In 1929 he received an honorary A.M. degree from Dartmouth College, and an honorary LL.D. degree from the University of New Hampshire. The Depression forced Tobey to leave the governorship in an effort to bolster his faltering business interests, and so he chose not to run for reelection. Tobey soon returned to political life, however, serving in the United States Congress from 1933 to 1939, and in the United States Senate from 1939 until his death. He was a member of the United States delegation to the International Monetary Conference at Bretton Woods, New Hampshire, in July 1944, and a United States advisor at the UNESCO Conference in Paris in November-December 1952. Tobey also served as president of the Baptist State Convention, and as a trustee of Colby Junior College. He was a Mason. Tobey died on July 24, 1953, in Bethesda Naval Hospital, and was buried at Temple in Miller Cemetery. Bibliography: Anne D. Lunt, ed., *A History of Temple, New Hampshire* (Dublin, N. H., 1976); James W. Tucker, "The Legislature of 1915," *The Granite Monthly*, XLVII (1915); H. Styles Bridges, "Charles W. Tobey," *The Granite Monthly*, LX (1928); Obituary, *New York Times* (July 25, 1953). The Tobey Papers are on deposit in the Dartmouth College Library.

WINANT, John Gilbert, 1925-1927, 1931-1935

BRIDGES, Henry Styles, 1935-1937

Born on September 9, 1898, in West Pembroke, Maine, son of Earl L. Bridges and Alina (Fisher) Bridges. Brother of Ronald and Doris. His father died when Bridges was nine years old, and he was raised by his mother, a school teacher. Married to Sally Clement of Concord, New Hampshire, on June 30, 1928; father of Henry

Styles, Jr., David Clement and John Fisher; married again in February 1944, to Doloris Thauwald. Educated in public schools, and graduated from University of Maine at Orono in 1918; later received honorary degrees from numerous institutions. Employed as an instructor at Sanderson Academy in Ashfield, Massachusetts, 1918-19; member of the extension staff of the University of New Hampshire, 1921-22; secretary of the New Hampshire Farm Bureau Federation, 1922-23; editor of *The Granite Monthly* magazine, 1924-26; director and secretary of the New Hampshire Investment Company, 1924-29. Continued his interests in the fields of banking and publishing. Served as a Lieutenant in the United States Army Reserves, 1925-37, and as a member of the New Hampshire Public Service Commission, 1930-34. In the gubernatorial primary of September 1934, Bridges defeated his Republican opponent, Charles E. Carroll, 33,952 votes to 18,526. He went on to defeat Democrat John L. Sullivan, 89,481 to 87,019, in the general election that November. As governor, Bridges worked to tighten the state's economy, demanding smaller appropriations where possible, advocating a thorough study of expenditures at all levels of government, and encouraging the legislature to continue fund relief for the needy as the state emerged from the Depression. He succeeded in getting a stronger program for aid to needy mothers and dependent children, and appointed the first woman judge in the state. He also recommended passage of a reasonable and fair unemployment insurance law. In 1936 Bridges won a seat in the United States Senate, and kept it until his death. He served as President Pro Tempore in 1953-55, and as chairman of the Appropriations Committee and head of the Republican Policy Committee. In 1940 his name was placed in nomination at the Republican National Convention, and although Senator Charles L. McNary of Oregon was eventually chosen, many New Englanders expected that Bridges would be the vice-presidential nominee. Bridges died on November 26, 1961, in East Concord, and was buried in Pine Grove Cemetery. His former home in East Concord now serves as the governor's mansion and bears the name Bridges House. Bibliography: United States Congress, *Memorial Services* (Washington, 1962); Bernard Bellush, *He Walked Alone: A Biography of John Gilbert Winant* (The Hague, 1968); Laurie Hillyer, "Who Is H. Styles Bridges?: The Inspiring Story of the Rise of a New England Farm Boy," *Yankee*, VI (July, 1940); *Concord Monitor* (April 26, 1977). The Bridges Papers are housed at New England College in Henniker, New Hampshire [James J. Kiepper, ed., *Styles Bridges: A Register of His Papers in the New England College Library* (New England College, 1972)].

MURPHY, Francis Parnell, 1937-1941

Born on August 16, 1877, in Winchester, New Hampshire, son of Patrick E. Murphy, farmer, tannery worker and Civil War veteran, and Ellen (Lambert) Murphy, both of whom were Irish immigrants and Roman Catholics. Fourth boy in a family of eight. Married to Mae B. Herrick on June 24, 1902; father of Madeleine Gertrude, Walter Wyman, Kathryn Herrick, Eleanor Mae and Francis Parnell Jr. Graduated from high school in Hudson, Massachusetts, and later received honorary degrees from St. Anselm's College, the University of New Hampshire, Dartmouth College and Boston College. Started work in a local shoe factory as nailer of packing cases, and promoted to successively higher positions in companies in Newport, Manchester and Nashua, New Hampshire; in 1922 he and two partners organized the J. F. McElwain Company, which by 1936 operated twelve shoe factories and was the largest employer of labor in the state. Served as Lieutenant in Company M of the New Hampshire National Guard, and in World War I was chairman of the Committee on Electric Power Supply; in 1925 was Major on Governor Winant's military staff. Always active in local politics, he was elected a member of the New Hampshire Legislature in 1931, and to the Governor's Executive Council in 1933. In 1936, when the Democrats swept the country in the presidential election and even carried New Hampshire by 3,800 votes, Republican Murphy defeated his Democratic gubernatorial opponent, Amos N. Blandin, by over 29,000 votes (118,178 to 89,011). In 1938 he was reelected, 107,841 to 80,847, over John L. Sullivan. Governor Murphy's terms coincided with the spread of New Deal social legislation. He strongly supported laws that strenthened labor, and he endeavored to make certain that the state remained fiscally sound. During his administration the real estate tax was replaced by a tobacco tax; the State House Annex was built to bring the spreading government agencies under one roof; and New Hampshire entered the recreation business with the Cannon Mountain Tramway and the state bathhouse at Hampton Beach. Also, the State Police was established, and a statewide probation system set up. Murphy was the first son of a Civil War veteran to become governor, the second governor to serve two successive two-year terms, and the first Roman Catholic governor of New Hampshire. After his gubernatorial service, Murphy continued his business interests in the shoe industry and banking. He established radio station WMUR in Manchester, and later WMUR-TV. Retaining his interest in politics, he switched from the Republican to the Democratic Party and ran against incumbent United States Senator Styles Bridges in 1942, losing by 15,000 votes. He maintained a life-long interest in sports, particularly baseball, and was active in social, religious and charitable organizations. He was made a Knight of Malta by Pope Pius XII in 1941. Murphy died on December 19, 1958, and was buried in St. Patrick's Cemetery, Newport, New Hampshire. Bibliography: *Brown Book of the New Hampshire Legislature: 1937* and *1939* (Concord, N. H. 1937, 1939); Samuel R. Guard and Graham Lloyd, *Francis Parnell Murphy, Governor of New Hampshire* (East Aurora, N. Y., 1940); Mildred W. Frost, "Francis Parnell Murphy—A Man and His State," *New Hampshire Profiles*, VII (December, 1958); New Hampshire State Republican Committee, *Our Next Governor* (n.p. 1936).

BLOOD, Robert Oscar, 1941-1945

Born on November 10, 1887, in Enfield, New Hampshire, son of William E. Blood, a farmer and railroad worker, and Lorinda (Colby) Blood. Married to Pauline Shepard in 1916; father of Robert, Jr., Horace and Emily. Attended Dartmouth College and its medical school, receiving an M.D. degree in 1913; set up practice in Wells River, Vermont, then in 1915 in Concord, New Hampshire. In 1917 he enlisted as a Lieutenant in the United States Medical Corps, and retired in 1919 as Lieutenant-Colonel, having served in France with the 26th (Yankee) Division and received the Distinguished Service Cross and the Croix de Guerre. He practiced as a surgeon (and was a Fellow of the American College of Surgeons) in Concord for fifty-six years; he was also active in real estate and the dairy business, holding principal offices in the state and national Ayrshire Breeders Associations. Active in veterans' affairs (helped to organize and was first commander of Concord Post, American Legion), religion (held offices in Concord's South Congregationalist Church), and humanitarian agencies (particularly the Y.M.C.A., in which he held local and state offices). Entered politics as a Republican legislator, 1935-1936, and State Senator, 1937-1940, serving as President of the Senate from 1939 to 1940. In the direct primary for Governor of September 1940, he defeated James C. Farmer by less than 800 votes (29,599 to 28,813). He went on to win the governorship against F. Clyde Keefe by a margin of 3,000 votes (112,386 to 109,093), although President Roosevelt carried New Hampshire for the Democrats by 15,000 votes. In 1942 Blood was reelected over William J. Neal by 7,000 votes (83,766 to 76,782). As governor during World War II, Blood set up the State Council of Defense, which included numerous subcommittees of volunteers, and spent much of his time travelling throughout the state to oversee and encourage its efforts. Through cooperation with the legislature, he was able to promote benefits for veterans; initiate the state employees' classification system; make the office of attorney-general a full time job; and put the state on a biennial budget. A frugal man, Blood reduced the state's debt and left office with a surplus of $6 million in the treasury, the highest it had ever been. Although Blood tried for a third gubernatorial term, he was defeated in the 1944 Republican primary by Charles M. Dale. In 1946 he sought election to the United States Congress, but lost in the primary to Norris Cotton. He retained his interest in politics, however, attending every Republican National Convention from 1944 to 1960. Blood died on August 3, 1975, in Concord. He was buried in the Blossom Hill Cemetery. Bibliography: *Brown Book of the New Hampshire Legislature: 1941 and 1943* (Concord, N. H., 1941, 1943); Leon W. Anderson, "Of Tobey, Blood, King," mimeographed (Concord, N.H., 1970 [copy in N.H. State Library]); Deak Morse, "Dr. Blood, Man of Many Talents," *New Hampshire Profiles*, XXI (May, 1972); *The Concord Monitor* (August 4, 6, 7, 1975). Many of Blood's papers are on deposit in the New Hampshire State Library, Concord.

DALE, Charles Milby, 1945-1949

Born on March 8, 1893, in Brown's Valley, Minnesota, son of Fred Vernon Dale, a farmer, and Maude (Paine) Dale. Married on September 27, 1919, to Marion Marvin in Portsmouth, New Hampshire; father of Thomas Marvin and Joan. Educated in primary schools in Minnesota and North Dakota; graduated from high school in Minot, North Dakota; received a B.A. degree from University of Minnesota, 1915, and an LL.B. degree from University of Minnesota Law School, 1917. In 1945 received honorary degrees from Dartmouth College and the University of New Hampshire. Member of St. John's Episcopal Church, Portsmouth. Began work in a law firm in Minnesota, but left to join the Coast Artillery Corps of the United States Army during World War I, and advanced to the rank of First Lieutenant. Stationed in Portsmouth, where he was married and opened a law practice in 1920. Entered politics as Portsmouth City Solicitor in 1921-22. In 1926, at the age of thirty-three, Dale was elected Mayor of Portsmouth, serving two years; he was again Mayor in 1943-44. In 1933 he was elected to the State Senate, and reelected in 1935, serving as President during his second term. In 1937 Dale won election to the Governor's Council, and he returned to the Senate for another term in 1939. In

1944 he ran for Governor, defeating Gov. Robert O. Blood, who was trying for an unprecedented third term, in the Republican primary (29,190 to 20,275). Dale went on to win the general election against Democrat James J. Powers of Manchester (115,799 to 102,232). Running for reelection in 1946, he barely defeated Sherman Adams in the Republican primary (22,923 to 22,766), but went on to a second term, winning over Democrat Clyde Keefe of Dover (103,204 to 60,247). As governor, Dale reduced the state debt to its lowest point in fifteen years, established the first retirement system for state employees, set up a board to consider reclassification of state employees and examine the adequacy of wage scales, and substantially increased the budget for direct advertising in order to attract both industry and recreation. Dale returned to banking and radio interests after his four years as governor. He served as president of the New Hampshire National Bank in Portsmouth, and became the owner of Radio Station WHEB there. He has also been a member of the American Legion, the Masons and the Elks. He is now living in a nursing home in Portsmouth. Bibliography: *Brown Book of the New Hampshire Legislature* (Concord, 1945, 1947); Gerald D. Foss, *Three Centuries of Freemasonry in New Hampshire* (Concord, 1972); Deborah Blossom, "Home of the Month (or Mr. and Mrs. Charles M. Dale, North Hampton," *New Hampshire Profiles*, IV (1955); John P. Zanes, "The Seacoast's Senior Statesman, Hon. Charles M. Dale," *New Hampshire Profiles*, XIV (1965).

ADAMS, Llewelyn Sherman, 1949-1953

Born on January 8, 1899, in East Dover, Vermont, son of Clyde H. Adams and Winnie Marion (Sherman) Adams. Married to Rachel Leona White on July 23, 1923; father of Marion, Jean, Sarah and Samuel. Educated in public schools of Providence, Rhode Island; graduated from Dartmouth College, 1920. Left college in 1918 to serve briefly with the United States Marine Corps. Entered the lumber business at Headville, Vermont, in 1921, and continued a combined lumber and paper business in Lincoln, New Hampshire, 1923-44, at the same time doing limited business in banking. Entered politics as a Republican State Legislator, 1941-44 (Speaker, 1943-44); served in the United States Congress, 1945-47; acted as a delegate to the Republican National Conventions in 1944 and 1952. Lost the party primary in 1946 to Charles M. Dale; won the Republican primary in 1948 over John R. McIntire (39,094 to 7,673), and defeated Herbert W. Hill in the general election (116,212 to 105,207). Ran again in 1950, defeating Eugene S. Daniell, Jr. in the primary (57,499 to 16,943), and winning over Democrat Robert P. Bingham in the general election (108,907 to 82,258). Governor Adams urged economy on both a public and a personal basis; he also urged appropriations for state aid to the aged, and requested legislation to make New Hampshire citizens eligible for Federal Old Age and Survivors Insurance. He served as Chairman of the Conference of New England Governors, 1951-52, and called a special session of the legislature in April 1950 to implement his plan for reorganizing the state's operations [see State of New Hampshire, *Reorganization Commission: Report on Reorganization of State Administrative Agencies* (Concord, 1950)]. Adams is a Mason, and served as Chief of Staff of the White House under President Eisenhower from 1953 to 1958, a position which he was allowed to resign following criticism involving potential conflicts of interest. He is currently engaged in writing and lecturing, and has published *Firsthand Report: The Story of the Eisenhower Administration* (New York, 1961). Adams lives in Lincoln, where he is president of the Loon Mountain Corporation, a resort area. Bibliography: Duane Lockard, *New England State Politics* (Princeton, 1959); Gerald D. Foss, *Three Centuries of Freemasonry in New Hampshire* (Concord, 1972); Paul E. Estaver, "The Man from Lincoln," *New Hampshire Profiles*, VII (1958); Beverly Smith, "Ike's Yankee Lieutenant," *Saturday Evening Post*, CCXXV (January 24, 1953); Deak Morse, " 'When I say Scat...' " *New Hampshire Profiles*, XXVI (1977). The Adams' Papers are on deposit in the Dartmouth College Library, Hanover, New Hampshire.

GREGG, Hugh, 1953-1955

Born on November 22, 1917, in Nashua, New Hampshire, son of Harry Alan Gregg and Margaret Prentiss (Richardson) Gregg. Brother of David Almus, Harry Alan and Gail. Married to Catherine M. Warner on July 24, 1940; father of Cyrus Warner and Judd Alan. Attended Phillips Exeter Academy, graduating in 1935; graduated from Yale University in 1939, and from Harvard Law School in 1942; admitted to the bar in New Hampshire, 1942, and in Massachusetts, 1948. Received LL.D. degrees from Dartmouth and the University of New Hampshire in 1953, and a D.C.L. degree from New England College in 1954. He served overseas during World War II, 1942-46, and during the Korean War, 1950-52, assigned in each instance as a special agent in the Army Counter Intelligence Corps. Entered law practice in Nashua, becoming a member of the firm of Sullivan and Gregg; was also treasurer and later president of the family millwork business, Gregg & Son, Inc. Also served as a director of the Indian Head National Bank in Nashua, and became involved in other enterprises. An active member of the American Legion, the Veterans of Foreign Wars, and other organizations. Elected alderman-at-large in Nashua in 1947, and Mayor in 1949; entered the Republican primary as a candidate for Governor in 1952, and received 50,741 votes to defeat former Governor Blood (13,100), who was seeking a third term, and Charles F. Stafford of Laconia (15,697), who was a member of the Governor's Council. In the general election Gregg won easily, receiving 167,791 votes while his Democratic opponent, William H. Craig of Manchester, polled 97,924. Governor Gregg was very active in promoting New Hampshire, and established "New Hampshire Whooper Week" to encourage citizen enthusiasm and to increase interest in the state's agriculture, recreation and industry. While Gregg was governor, the State Legislature authorized the attorney general to investigate subversive activities, and a special session was held to consider the manner in which the state had purchased land for highways. Gregg did not seek a second term as governor in 1956, but in 1958 he again entered the Republican primary, losing by a very narrow margin to Wesley Powell, 39,365 votes to 39,761. He made another attempt in 1960, but again lost to Powell. In 1966 Gregg again ran for Governor, losing in the general election to John W. King. Gregg lives with his family in Nashua. Bibliography: State of New Hampshire, *Manual for the General Court,* nos. 33, 36 (Concord, N. H., 1953, 1959); Stuart Alden MacKown, "Factionalism in the Republican Party of New Hampshire," Unpublished Ph.D. Thesis, University of Massachusetts, 1967; Duane Lockard, *New England State Politics* (Princeton, 1959); James Perkins, "Yankee on the Move," *New Hampshire Profiles,* VII (September, 1958); Hugh Gregg, "Why I Proclaimed New Hampshire Whooper Week," *New Hampshire Profiles,* II (April, 1953).

DWINELL, Lane, 1955-1959

Born on November 14, 1906, in Newport, Vermont, son of Dean N. and Ruth (Lane) Dwinell. Married to Elizabeth Cushman on April 16, 1932. Came to Lebanon, New Hampshire, in 1923, when his father entered the garment manufacturing firm of Carter and Churchill in that community. He graduated from Lebanon High School in 1924, from Dartmouth College in 1928, and received an M.C.S. degree from the Amos Tuck School of Business Administration in 1929. He later received honorary degrees from Dartmouth, Suffolk University, the University of New Hampshire and New England College. From 1929 to 1935, Dwinell was financial analyst for the General Motors Corp. in New York; he then returned to Lebanon as a partner in Carter & Churchill, and by 1949 was principal owner of that industry, a director of the National Bank of Lebanon, and involved in other financial and civic enterprises. He was a member of the Congregationalist Church. In politics Dwinell is an active Republican. He was a member of the New Hampshire Constitutional Convention in 1948; the State House of Representatives, 1949-52 (its Speaker, 1951-52); and President of the State Senate, 1953-54. He entered the Republican primary for Governor in 1954, and won with little opposition; in the general election he defeated his Democratic opponent, John Shaw, by a vote of 107,287 to 87,344. In 1956 he ran for a second term, and again won the Republican primary, although he received strong opposition from Wesley Powell. The final count was Dwinell, 38,734; Powell, 33,408; and Elmer E. Bussey, 769. In the general election, however, Dwinell was an easy winner by a vote of 141,578 to 117,117, again over Shaw. As governor, Dwinell continued New Hampshire's tradition of economy in government, but also maintained the state's roads and facilities. His administration witnessed the building of 300 miles of new highways, and the construction of 100 new schools to house 25,000 pupils. During his years as governor, the state accounting procedures were overhauled; state salaries were increased in 1957 by 16 percent; a constitutional convention met in 1956; and steps were taken toward improving mental health care within the state. Dwinell has remained active in the Republican Party, acting as a delegate to National Conventions in 1952, 1956, 1968 and 1972. From 1969 to 1971 he was Assistant Administrator in the federal Agency for International Development. He is presently living in Lebanon, New Hampshire. Bibliography: Stuart A. MacKown, "Factionalism in the Republican Party of New Hampshire," Ph.D. Thesis, U. of Mass., 1967; *Brown Book of the New Hampshire Legislature of 1955* and *1957* (Concord, 1955 and 1957); State of New Hampshire, *Manual for the General Court,* Nos. 34, 35 (Concord, 1955 and 1957); Robert S. Monahan, Our New Governor and First Lady," *New Hampshire Profiles*, III (1954); Edward Androvette, "Governor at Work," *New Hampshire Profiles*, VI (1957).

POWELL, Wesley, 1959-1963

Born on October 13, 1915, in Portsmouth, New Hampshire, son of Samuel Wesley and Mary (Gosse) Powell, both born in Newfoundland. Fourth child in a family of seven. Married to Beverly Swain on September 2, 1942; father of Samuel Wesley, Peter Wendell and Nancy. Attended the public schools of Portsmouth and the University of New Hampshire; received an LL.B. degree from Southern Methodist

College of Law in 1940. Powell then became assistant to United States Senator Styles Bridges, 1940-49, a position interrupted in 1943-45 by his service in World War II in the Bomber Command of the Army Air Corps, European Theater of Operations. He was wounded in action, hospitalized for fourteen months, and decorated for bravery. In 1950 he returned to New Hampshire and established a law practice in Manchester and in Hampton Falls. Entered politics in the Republican primary of 1950, challenging United States Senator Charles W. Tobey, and lost by only 1,310 votes; ran as an Independent in the general election and lost again. Entered the Republican gubernatorial primary in 1956, and lost to Lane Dwinell; tried again in 1958 and won by a narrow margin (39,761) over former governor Hugh Gregg (39,365). In the general election he defeated Democrat Bernard L. Boutin of Laconia, 106,790 to 99,955. Powell ran for a second term in 1960, again opposed by Gregg in the primary, and won narrowly, 49,119 to 48,108; in the general election he again defeated Boutin, 161,123 votes to 129,404. Governor Powell was pledged to oppose any broad base (sales or income) tax. He supported an "open up New Hampshire" plan of large-scale highway building; aid to industry; and the expansion of recreation and tourist facilities. New taxes were to be avoided by consolidating state agencies for economy and efficiency. In 1959 a controversial Department of Commerce and a Department of Mental Health were voted down by the legislature, but in 1961 three mergers were passed, comprising the Departments of Safety, Health and Welfare, and Resources and Economic Development. Powell entered the Republican primary in 1962 seeking a third term, but lost to John Pillsbury of Manchester, 42,005 votes to 55,784. He then endorsed Democrat John King, on condition that the reorganization of state agencies remain unchanged. Powell lives in Hampton Falls, and practices law there and in Portsmouth. He owns the *Hampton Union and Rockingham County Gazette*, a weekly newspaper, and is a member of regional, state and national bar groups. He also belongs to veterans' organizations, and attends the Congregationalist Church. Bibliography: *The Brown Book of the New Hampshire Legislature, 1959, 1961* (Concord, N. H., 1959, 1961); J. Duane Squires, *The Granite State of the United States*, vol. III (New York, 1950); State of New Hampshire, *Manual for the General Court* (Concord, N. H., 1951); Stuart A. MacKown, "Factionalism in the Republican Party of New Hampshire," Unpublished Ph.D. Thesis, University of Massachusetts, 1967; Duane Bradley, "The Governor and the Waterfall," *New Hampshire Profiles*, VIII (March, 1959); Paul E. Estaver, "Health, Welfare—and Politics," *New Hampshire Profiles*, XIV (March, 1965).

KING, John William, 1963-1969

Born on October 10, 1918, in Manchester, New Hampshire, son of Michael J. King and Anna (Lydon) King, both workers in textile mills, and the only brother of five sisters. Married to Anna McLaughlin of New York City on October 13, 1945. Graduated from St. Joseph's High School in Manchester; received an A.B. degree from Harvard in 1938, an M.A. degree in public law, 1941, and an LL.B. in 1943 from Columbia University; later received honorary degrees from various institutions. Admitted to the New York Bar in 1942, and practiced in New York law firms until 1948, when he returned to Manchester to establish his own practice; became senior partner of King, Nixon, Christy and Tessier. King has been an instructor in business law at St. Anselm's College, Manchester, since 1948, and was editor of the *New Hampshire Bar Journal*, 1958-1969. He has also served on the Ballot Law Commission and the Manchester Charter Revision Commission, and is a member of various legal associations and civic groups. He attends the Roman Catholic Church. Politically a Democrat, King was chairman in 1957 of the Manchester delegation in the State House of Representatives, and Minority Leader in 1959 and 1961. In 1962 he received the Democratic nomination for Governor and won, after getting the endorsement of Ex-Governor Wesley Powell. King polled 135,481 votes to defeat the Republican candidate, John Pillsbury, who received 94,569. He thus became the first Democratic governor in New Hampshire in the twentieth century. In 1964 King was elected to a second term, again defeating Pillsbury, 190,863 votes to 94,824. In 1966 he was returned for an unprecedented third term, winning over ex-Governor Hugh Gregg, 125,882 to 107,259. Although a Democrat, King worked well with the Republican-dominated legislature. To provide money for schools, the New Hampshire Sweepstakes was created, becoming the first legal lottery in the United States in the twentieth century. A statewide university system was instituted, which resulted in the expansion of the state colleges and the construction of technical schools. Other developments during King's administration included the establishment of commissions on the arts, human rights, and manpower problems; the purchase of the Robert Frost homestead; the granting of increased home rule to the cities; the modernization of the courts; and the establishment of the position of Coordinator of Federal Funds. King is now an Associate Justice on the Superior Court of New Hampshire. He lives on a farm in Goffstown, and his office is in Manchester, New Hampshire. Bibliography: *The Brown Book of the New Hampshire Legislature* (Concord, N. H., 1963, 1965, 1967); State of New Hampshire, *Manual for the General Court* (Concord, N. H., 1963, 1965, 1967); Stuart A. MacKown, "Factionalism in the Republican Party in New Hampshire," Unpublished Ph.D. Thesis, University of Massachusetts, 1967; Richard Schuster, "John W. King," *New Hampshire Profiles*, XII (January, 1963); Eugene Hebert, "Point of Honor," *Ibid.*, XIII (July, 1964); Paul E. Estaver, "Health, Welfare—and Politics," *Ibid.*, XIV (March, 1965).

PETERSON, Walter Rutherford, 1969-1973

Born on September 19, 1922, in Nashua, New Hampshire, son of Walter Rutherford Peterson and Helen (Reed) Peterson; an Episcopalian. Married Dorothy Donovan on November 24, 1949; father of Margaret Joanna and Andrew Reed. Attended New Hampton School and the University of New Hampshire, and graduated from Dartmouth College in 1947, having spent four years as a United States Naval Reserve officer in the South Pacific. Became a partner in The Petersons, Inc., realtors, Peterborough, New Hampshire, a director of the National Association of Real Estate Boards, and a director of the Peterborough Industrial Development Corporation. Peterson is a member of veterans' organizations, civic clubs, and the New Hampshire Council of World Affairs. In politics a Republican, Peterson was a member of the State Legislature, 1961-69. In the Republican primary of 1968 there were three principal contenders for governor, and Peterson won (29,262) by defeating former Governor Wesley Powell (26,498) and future Governor Meldrim

Thomson, Jr. (25,275). In the general election, he defeated Democrat Emile R. Bussiere of Manchester, 149,902 votes to 135,378. In 1970 Peterson won a second term by beating Thomson in the Republican primary, 43,667 to 41,392, and going on to win the general election in November over Democrat Roger J. Crowley, Jr., and Meldrim Thomson, Jr., representing the American Party. Peterson amassed 102,298 votes, against Crowley's 98,098 and Thomson's 22,033. As governor, Peterson pledged not to seek a sales or income tax, and was greatly concerned with state revenues. During his administration the combination of a newly-enacted business profits tax and the revenue from liquor sales was sufficient to provide a budget surplus. A Citizens Task Force of 300 persons was established to study state organization and make recommendations. Also, a special session of the legislature was called in 1972 to adjust allocation of funds; consider the problem of property taxes in cities and towns; and provide for pollution abatement. After his governorship Peterson returned to his real estate business in Peterborough, where he now lives with his family. Bibliography: *The Brown Book of the New Hampshire Legislature* (Concord, N. H., 1969, 1971); State of New Hampshire, *Manual for the General Court* (Concord, N. H., 1969, 1971); State of New Hampshire, *Journal of the House of Representatives, Sessions of 1971, 1972, 1973* (Concord, N. H., 1971, 1972, 1973).

THOMSON, Meldrim, 1973-

Born on March 8, 1912, in Pittsburgh, Pennsylvania, son of Meldrim Thomson, a testing engineer, and Beulah (Booth) Thomson. Married to Anne Gale Kelley on October 29, 1938; father of Peter, David, Thomas, Marion Gale, Janet and Robb. Graduated from Miami (Florida) High School in 1930, and attended the University of Miami for two years. Later attended Mercer University Law School in Macon, Georgia, and Washington and Jefferson College in Washington, Pennsylvania; graduated with an LL.B. degree from the University of Georgia Law School. Joined the Florida National Guard in 1931, and was honorably released in 1933. Served briefly as an instructor of political science at the University of Georgia; accepted by the Florida Bar in March 1936, but almost immediately joined the publishing company of Edward Thompson in Brooklyn, New York, remaining from 1936 to 1951, when he formed his own company, the Equity Publishing Company in New York. In 1954 he moved the company and his family home to Orford, New Hampshire, where he has lived since. A lifelong Republican, Thomson is also a member of the Baptist Church. Served six years as member and chairman of the school board of Stony Brook, New York, and elected to the Orford School Board from 1959 to 1962. Entered state politics as a candidate for the House of Representatives in 1964, but lost; won election to the State Constitutional Convention in 1964. Ran for Governor in 1968 and 1970, but lost both times in the primary election. In the 1972 primary Thomson received 43,611 votes, defeating Walter Peterson (41,252) and James Koromilas (3,975); in the 1972 general election he won 133,702 votes to beat Democrat Roger J. Crowley (126,107) and Independent Malcolm McLane (63,199). Thomson repeated his victory in 1974 by defeating David L. Nixon and Ralph W. Brewster in the primary, and then beating Democrat Richard W. Leonard in the general election, 115,933 votes to 110,591. In the September 1976 primary, Thomson won over Gerard Zeiller and Ralph Brewster; he earned a third term in the November general election by defeating Democrat Harry Spanos,

197,589 votes to 145,015. As governor Thomson has continued to oppose any broad base taxes (New Hampshire remains the only state in the Union with no general sales or personal income tax) and to advocate economy in administration. He has called for a reasoned balance between progress and environmental concerns, and supports offshore drilling for oil along the Atlantic coast and the establishment of oil refineries in New England. Thomson is a member of the bar of the Supreme Court of the United States. He currently resides in the executive mansion (Bridges House) in Concord, New Hampshire, and at his home, Mount Cube Farm, in Orford. Bibliography: Howard Gaines, "Meldrim Thomson, Jr.: An American Success Story," *New Hampshire Times*, VI (October 20-26, 1976) [Concord]; *The Brown Book of the New Hampshire Legislature, 1973* (Concord, 1973); State of New Hampshire, *Manual for the General Court, 1973, 1975* (Concord, 1973, 1975).

NEW JERSEY

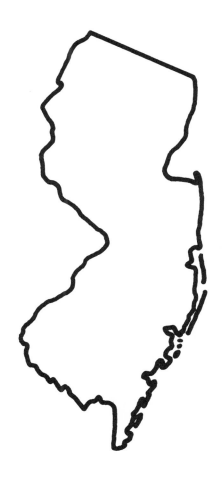

NEW JERSEY

LIVINGSTON, William, 1776-1790

Born on November 30, 1723 in Albany, New York, son of the first Philip Livingston, one of the patroons of New York, and Catherine (Van Brugh) Livingston, both of whom were brought up in the Dutch Reform Church. Brother of Philip and Peter Livingston. Married to Susanna French in 1745, and father of thirteen children, the most notable being Henry Brockholst and Susanna. Attended Yale University and graduated in 1741. Became a prominent lawyer and popular writer soon after; elected to the Provincial Legislature from Livingston Manor in New York; in 1760 moved to New Jersey. Appointed a delegate to the Continental Congress in 1774 and again in 1775. Appointed Brigadier-General of the New Jersey militia in 1776. When the new state's first constitution was ratified, he was unanimously elected Governor by the New Jersey Legislature, and was sworn into office on August 28, 1776. For the next fourteen years, until his death, he was reelected annually with only slight occasional opposition. As governor, Livingston vehemently supported the war against the British, being dubbed by one pro-British newspaper "the spurious governor." At one point during the war, Hessians ransacked his house. Raising money for the war effort and attacking Tories, Governor Livingston became the foremost revolutionary leader in New Jersey. In 1786 he became a member of a society promoting the emancipation of slaves, and later freed the only two slaves he owned. In 1787 he represented New Jersey at the Constitutional Convention, and played the role of a compromiser; he further proved his value to the young nation when he succeeded in gaining rapid ratification of the document in his state. In 1785, Congress appointed him Minister to Holland, but he declined in order to retain the governorship. He remained an active governor until his death. Livingston died on July 25, 1790 in Elizabethtown, New Jersey. Bibliography: Theodore Sedgwick, *A Memoir of the Life of William Livingston* (New York, 1833); E. B. Livingston, *The Livingstons of Livingston Manor* (1916); C. H. Levermore, "The Whigs of Colonial New York," *American Historical Review* (January, 1896); Richard McCormick, *New Jersey from Colony to State, 1609-1789* (Princeton, New Jersey, 1964). The Livingston Papers are on deposit in the Massachusetts Historical Society.

PATERSON, William, 1790-1793

Born on December 24, 1745 in County Antrim, Ireland, son of Richard, a merchant, and Mary Paterson; a Presbyterian. Brother of Thomas and Edward. Married to Cornelia Bell on February 9, 1779; after her death, remarried to Euphemia White in 1785; father of Cornelia, Fanny (who died young) and William Bell. Graduated from the College of New Jersey in 1763; studied law with Richard Stockton; Masters of Arts from the College of New Jersey in 1766; founded the "Well Meaning Society," 1765-1768 (later changed to the literary "Cliosophic Society"). Admitted to the New Jersey Bar in 1768; began practice in Bromley, New Jersey; returned to Princeton, New Jersey in 1776, where he practiced law and operated a general store until he moved to Somerset County. Elected in 1775 to the New Jersey Provincial Congress; reelected in 1776; a member of the State Constitutional Convention in 1776; served as State Attorney General, 1776-1783; member of the Legislative Council in 1776; member and officer of the Somerset County Minute Men Battalion and member of the Council of Safety in 1777; member of the New Jersey Senate from 1776 to 1777; New Jersey delegate to the United States Constitutional Convention in 1787; chosen United States Senator in the first Senate from 1789 to 1790; a Democrat. Elected Governor of New Jersey by the State Legislature to three consecutive one-year terms; Paterson took office on October 30, 1790. During his administration he began to revise and codify the New Jersey legal system and created a manufacturing center within the state. He resigned in 1793 and was appointed Associate Supreme Court Justice, serving until his death in 1806. Paterson died on September 9, 1806 in Albany, New York and was buried in the Van Rensselaer Manor House Vault, near Albany. Bibliography: Leonard B. Rosenberg, "William Paterson: New Jersey's Nation-Maker," *New Jersey History,* vol. I, no. 1 (Spring, 1967); G. S. Wood, *William Paterson of New Jersey* (Fairlawn, New Jersey, 1933); E. M. Norris, *The Story of Princeton* (Boston, 1917); A. V. Honeyman, "Early Career of Governor William Paterson," *Somerset County Historical Quarterly,* vol. I (1912).

HENDERSON, Thomas, 1793

Born on August 15, 1743 in Monmouth (now Freehold), New Jersey, son of John, a farmer, and Ann (Stevens) Henderson; a Presbyterian. Brother of six. Married to Mary Hendricks on September 23, 1767; after her death, remarried to Rachel Burrowes on January 2, 1778; father of seven daughters. Graduated from the College of New Jersey in 1761; studied medicine with Nathaniel Scudder; began practice in Freneau, New Jersey in 1764. In 1766 he became a member of the New Jersey Medical Society (the first society of its kind in the country). During the Revolution, he was made a member of the Freehold Committee of Observation and Inspection, December 10, 1774, and Lieutenant of the local militia in 1776. On February 15, 1776, he was commissioned a Major of Stewart's Minute Men, and later, Major of Militia. From June 14, he held the rank of Major in Heard's Battalion; later he was commissioned Lieutenant-Colonel in Heard's Brigade; and on January 12, 1777, he became Lieutenant-Colonel of Forman's Additional Continental Regiment. He served as Brigade-Major at Monmouth in June 1778, and reported on General Charles Lee's retreat to General George Washington. He was elected to the Continental Congress on November 17, 1779, but declined the office. He served from 1780 to 1784 in the New Jersey Assembly, and on the local Committee of Retaliation from July 1, 1780. Served as surrogate of Monmouth County, 1776; Judge of Common Pleas, 1783, and again in 1799; and Master of Chancery in 1790. He was elected to the New Jersey Council, 1793-1794, and served as vice president of the Council. Henderson became Governor of New Jersey on March 30, 1793 according to Section VIII of the 1776 Constitution of New Jersey. Governor-elect Richard Howell had taken charge of the New Jersey troops during the Whiskey Rebellion, and as vice president of the Council, Henderson became Governor, serving until June 3, 1793. Elected to the Fourth Congress, 1795-1797; served again on the New Jersey Council, 1812-1813. Afterwards, Henderson held no further political office. Governor Henderson died on December 15, 1824 and was buried in Old Tennent Cemetery, Freehold, New Jersey. Bibliography: Roy Glashan, *American Governors and Gubernatorial Elections, 1775-1975* (Stillwater, Minnesota, 1975); W. S. Stryker, *Official Register of the Officers and Men of New Jersey in the Revolutionary War* (Trenton, 1872); F. R. Symmes, *History of the Old Tennent Church* (Newark, 1904); James S. Norton, *New Jersey in 1793* (Salt Lake City, Utah, 1973).

HOWELL, Richard, 1793-1801

Born on October 25, 1754 in Newark, Delaware, son of Ebenezer, a farmer, and Sarah (Bond) Howell; originally Quakers, they later became Episcopalians. Twin brother of Lewis Howell. Married to Keziah Burr in November of 1778; father of nine children (one of whom was later to become the father of Mrs. Jefferson Davis). Attended school in Delaware; Howell did not attend college, but rather studied law under an attorney in 1774. While studying law he became involved in rebellious acts against the British, joining a band of patriots who burned a store of imported tea. In 1775 he was appointed an officer in a company of infantry, and was promoted to Captain in December; he served in the North at Ticonderoga and Quebec. He resigned his commission in 1778 and returned to New Jersey to practice law. Howell reportedly served as a special agent for General George Washington. In 1788 he was elected clerk of the New Jersey Supreme Court. After Governor William Paterson resigned in 1793, Richard Howell, at the age of thirty-eight, announced his candidacy, and outpolled two fellow Federalists by an undisclosed vote in a joint meeting of the legislature. Even though Howell became Governor of New Jersey on March 30, 1793, he did not assume office until June 3, so that he could take charge of the New Jersey troops during the Whiskey Rebellion. Throughout the early national period in New Jersey, the governor had little authority, save his judicial and military powers; therefore, Governor Howell's most noted accomplishment was his leadership of the New Jersey militia into Pennsylvania to help end the Whiskey Rebellion. He always thought of himself more as a soldier than a politician, and due to his apolitical nature he gained few enemies. He was reelected every year until 1801, unopposed in all years but 1799. In 1801 he retired from office in favor of his friend, Joseph Bloomfield. Howell returned to his law practice after leaving office. He died on May 5, 1803 at his residence near Trenton, New Jersey. Bibliography: L. Q. C. Elmer, *The Constitution and Government of the Province and State of New Jersey* (1872); Hamilton Schuyler, *A History of St. Michael's Church, Trenton* (1926); J. G. Leach, *Genealogy and Biography, Memorials of the Reading, Howell, Yerkes, Watts, Latham, and Elkins Families* (1898); Rudolph J. Pasler, *The New Jersey Federalists* (Rutherford, New Jersey, 1974). Papers of Howell are in the New Jersey State Historical Society in Newark.

BLOOMFIELD, Joseph, 1801-1802, 1803-1812

Born on October 18, 1753 in Woodbridge, New Jersey, son of Dr. Moses Bloomfield, a member of the legislature and Provincial Congress during the Revolution, and Sarah Ogden; both were Presbyterians. Married to Mary McIlvaine in 1779, who died in 1818; later remarried to Isabella (family name unknown); no children resulted from either marriage. Attended classical school at Deerfield, Cumberland County, and afterwards studied law with Cortlandt Skinner, the Attorney General of New Jersey; in 1775 he was admitted to the bar, practicing in Bridgeton, New Jersey. In 1776 he was commissioned a Captain in the Third New Jersey Regiment; later became Judge-Advocate of the Northern Army; promoted to Major of his regiment; led his troops at the battles of Brandywine and Monmouth before being wounded; resigned his commission in 1778. Elected Attorney General of the state, and reelected in 1788. During the Whiskey Rebellion, he commanded a brigade, and in 1792 was chosen a presidential elector. At the age of forty-seven, Bloomfield, a former Federalist, converted to Jeffersonianism, and supported Jefferson in the election of 1800. In 1801, Bloomfield, now a Jeffersonian Republican, was elected Governor, defeating Richard Stockton by a vote of thirty to twenty in a joint meeting of the legislature. He took office on October 31, 1801. Bloomfield's election reflected the Federalists' declining control of the Assembly, for that party's share of seats had declined from 68 percent to 38 percent in one year. Bloomfield, the first Republican Governor of New Jersey, served only one year, however, before falling victim to a Federalist comeback, which emptied the governor's chair when a tie vote could not be broken. While John Lambert was nominated Acting-Governor, another election was held, which ended with Bloomfield returning as Governor, after winning by a vote of thirty-three to seventeen over Richard Stockton. In 1804 Bloomfield again defeated Stockton (thirty-seven to sixteen). Thereafter, he was elected without opposition until 1812. In 1804 Governor Bloomfield had the distinction of signing the Gradual Emancipation Act of New Jersey. In 1812, anticipating war with the British, he reorganized the state militia. Later that same year, President Madison appointed Bloomfield Brigadier-General, whereupon he resigned from office. In 1816 Bloomfield was elected a member of Congress; he served in that office until March 4, 1821. Bloomfield died on October 3, 1823, as a result of excessive bleeding in the treatment of a bruise. He was buried in Burlington, New Jersey. Bibliography: L. Q. C. Elmer, "Reminiscences," *New Jersey Historical Society Collections*, vol. VII; William Nelson, "Notes," *New Jersey Historical Society Collections*, vol. IX; C. E. Prince, *New Jersey's Jeffersonian Republicans: The Genesis of an Early Party Machine, 1789-1817* (Williamsburg, Virginia, 1967); L. Q. C. Elmer, *The Constitution and Government of the Province and State of New Jersey* (1872).

LAMBERT, John, 1802-1803

Born in 1746 (exact date unknown), in the township of Amwell, New Jersey, son of Gershom, a land owner and farmer in New Jersey, and Sarah (Merriam) Lambert. Married to Susannah Barber in 1765; father of seven children; married a second time to Hannah Dennis, by whom he had six children, the oldest named Jerusha, and the next oldest named Merriam. He attended common school and it is not known whether he attended college. However, he was a self-educated man, owning the best library in Hunterdon County, which included the town of Trenton. He early assumed control of the family's estate, spending most of his life as a country squire. He was elected to the State Council (Senate), serving for many years before being elected vice president of that body in 1795. He held that position until 1800. In the gubernatorial election of 1802, Republican Joseph Bloomfield's reelection was stalled when his Federalist opponent equalled his vote count in the legislative ballot. While attempts were made to break the deadlock, the well-liked Republican John Lambert was nominated Acting Governor. He assumed office on October 28, 1802. As acting governor, Lambert wielded little authority save his judicial power. However, he guided and supported the fledgling Republican Party, working to increase its voting strength in the legislature. In the joint meeting of the legislature held in October of 1803, his fellow Republican, Joseph Bloomfield, was reelected. In 1805 Lambert was elected as a member of Congress from New Jersey, a post he retained until 1809. From 1809 to 1815 he served as an influential member of the United States Senate. After retiring from political office, Lambert returned to his estate. Lambert died on February 4, 1823 at Amwell, New Jersey. Bibliography: L. Q. C. Elmer, *The Constitution and Government of the Province and State of New Jersey* (1872); J. P. Snell, *History of Hunterdon and Somerset Counties, New Jersey* (1881); C. E. Prince, *New Jersey's Jeffersonian Republicans; The Genesis of an Early Party Machine, 1789-1817* (Williamsburg, Virginia, 1967); Duane Lockard, *The New Jersey Governor; A Study in Political Power* (1964).

BLOOMFIELD, Joseph, 1801-1802, 1803-1812

OGDEN, Aaron, 1812-1813

Born on December 13, 1756 in Elizabethtown, New Jersey, son of Robert Ogden, surrogate for Essex County, council member, and Speaker of the House for several years, and Phoebe (Hatfield) Ogden, both of whom were Presbyterians. Brother of Robert Ogden. Married to Elizabeth Chetwood in October of 1787; father of two daughters and five sons. Attended Princeton College and graduated in 1773, after which he served as an assistant in a well-known grammar school. In the winter of 1777 he joined the First New Jersey Regiment, serving until the end of the war at various ranks, including Captain, Brigade Major, Inspector, and aide-de-camp. In 1784 he was admitted to the bar and began a law practice in Elizabethtown; in 1799 reentered the army as Deputy Quarter-Master-General of the United States Army. In 1801 the Assembly of New Jersey chose Ogden as United States Senator; at the same time he became Clerk of Essex County. In 1812, as leader of the Peace Party in New Jersey, he was elected Governor by an undisclosed vote over minor candidates, due to the strong anti-war sentiment in New Jersey. His victory was particularly noteworthy, since he was a Federalist in a state dominated at the time by Republicans. He took the oath of office on October 29, 1812. Although he did not support the declaration of war against the British, he directed all state agencies to comply fully with all national laws affecting the militia. He even pushed a bill through the Assembly which raised $5,000 for military expenses. In 1813, after the war had begun, William Pennington defeated Ogden by an undisclosed vote, as the Federalist majority in the New Jersey Legislature had declined to 43 percent of the seats held. After leaving office Ogden entered the steamboat business, establishing a route from Elizabethtown to New York. However, this brought him into conflict with the Fultons and Livingstons, who had exclusive steamboating rights on the rivers of New York. After lengthy litigation, during which Ogden invested all of his resources in the steamboat venture, the federal courts ruled against him. Losing his fortune, he spent his remaining years employed in a Jersey City custom house. Ogden died April 19, 1839 in Jersey City. Bibliography: Aaron Ogden, *Autobiography of Aaron Ogden* (1893); W. O. Wheeler, *The Ogden Family in America* (1907); E. F. Hatfield, *History of Elizabeth, New Jersey* (1868); L. H. Stockton, *A History of the Steamboat Case* (1815); Rudolph J. Pasler, *The New Jersey Federalists* (Rutherford, New Jersey, 1974). The Aaron Ogden Papers are in the archives of the Morristown National History Park and the Rutgers Library.

PENNINGTON, William S., 1813-1815

Born in 1757 (exact date unknown) in Newark, New Jersey, son of Samuel, a farmer, and Mary (Sanford) Pennington. Married Phoebe Wheeler in 1786; father of William (later to become the fourteenth governor of New Jersey); after Phoebe's death, remarried to Elizabeth Peirson. Apprenticed as a farmer to his uncle until the Revolutionary War began. Although his uncle was a Loyalist, he joined the colonial forces, serving as a non-commissioned artillery officer until 1780, when he was commissioned a Lieutenant. During this period he was commended for bravery, having single-handedly continued loading and firing a piece of artillery while under fire. He was later wounded at the Battle of Yorktown, and retired with the rank of Captain. For a time thereafter, he worked as a hatter and businessman in Newark. From 1797 to 1799, he studied law with Elias Boudinot, and in 1802 was admitted to the bar. In 1803 he was appointed clerk of Essex County and in 1804 was elected an Associate Justice of the State Supreme Court. When in 1813 public opinion in New Jersey shifted to supporting the war effort against the British, the Republican Pennington was elected over his Federalist opponent, Aaron Ogden, as Republican control of the legislature had increased to 57 percent of all seats held. He took office on October 29, 1813. Although not taking a military role in the war, he warned the Assembly that the coastline was exposed and vulnerable to British vessels. As a result, he toured the coastal area and made recommendations for its defense. Later he used the office of Governor to attack the Hartford Convention as a "combination . . . hostile to the Constitution and Government of the Union." In 1814 Republicans still had control of the legislature, and Pennington was reelected by majority vote in a joint session of that body. In 1815 President Madison appointed him Judge of the Federal District Court for New Jersey, replacing Robert Morris, whereupon he resigned as governor. Pennington held the position of Federal Judge until his death. He died on September 18, 1826 in Newark, New Jersey. Bibliography: A. C. M. Pennington, *The Pennington Family* (1871); L. Q. C. Elmer, *The Constitution and Government of the Province and State of New Jersey* (1872); W. S. Pennington, "Revolutionary War Diary" (in the New Jersey State Historical Society at Newark, New Jersey); Duane Lockard, *The New Jersey Governor: A Study in Political Power* (1964). Papers of Pennington are in the New Jersey Historical Society.

DICKERSON, Mahlon, 1815-1817

Born on April 17, 1770 in Hanover, New Jersey, son of Jonathan, a property owner and iron mine operator, and Mary (Coe) Dickerson, both of whom were Episcopalians. Brother of Philemon, Silas and Aaron Dickerson. Unmarried. Attended Princeton, then known as the College of New Jersey; graduated in 1789. Studied law and was licensed as an attorney in 1793. He volunteered for service in the New Jersey militia during the Whiskey Rebellion, ending his service in Pennsylvania. In Philadelphia he continued to study law; in 1797 he was admitted to the Pennsylvania Bar. In 1799 he was chosen to serve in the Common Council of Philadelphia, and in 1802 President Jefferson appointed him a Commissioner of Bankruptcy. In 1805, still in Philadelphia, he became Adjutant-General, and he became Recorder of the city in 1808. During this period he was a zealous supporter of Jefferson. In 1810 his father died, leaving him vast property holdings in New Jersey, whereupon he returned to his native state; two years later he was elected to the State Assembly. In 1813 he was appointed Justice of the State Supreme Court. In 1814 he ran for Governor, but after an intra-party struggle, he withdrew. The next year, after William Pennington had resigned as governor, Dickerson was nominated by the Republicans to replace him. He won without opposition and took office on October 26, 1815. Although a Republican, Dickerson's philosophy of government was close to Alexander Hamilton's emphasis on the importance of commercial and industrial development. Known as "that ultra-protectionist," manufacturer Dickerson was an uncompromising advocate of a high protective tariff. New Jersey, under Dickerson's pressure, was instrumental in passing the nation's first real protective tariff on April 27, 1816. To aid business interests further, he advocated the construction of a canal connecting the Delaware River with the Raritan. Such a project was not undertaken during his administration, but his support initiated a movement which would succeed in the 1820s. In 1817 he resigned and was elected United States Senator, an office to which he was reelected six years later. In 1829 he was defeated for reelection to the Senate, but was later elected to fill a vacancy in that body. Altogether he spent sixteen years in the Senate. While in office he was noted for his support of high tariff measures and for a program which divided treasury surpluses among the states. In 1834 President Andrew Jackson appointed Dickerson Secretary of the Navy (a position he retained for four years). He then became a District Court Judge in New Jersey. He was also an investor in mining interests. Dickerson died on October 5, 1853 in Morris County, New Jersey. Bibliography: William Dunham, "Mahlon Dickerson: A Great But Almost Forgotten Jerseyan," *Proceedings of the New Jersey Historical Society,* vol. LXVII (October, 1950); J. C. Pumpelly, "Mahlon Dickerson," *Proceedings of the New Jersey Historical Society,* vol. XI (1890); C. E. Prince, *New Jersey's Jeffersonian Republicans; The Genesis of an Early Party Machine, 1789-1817* (Williamsburg, Virginia, 1967). Papers of Dickerson are in the New Jersey Historical Society.

WILLIAMSON, Isaac H., 1817-1829

Born on September 27, 1767 in Elizabethtown, New Jersey, the youngest son of General Matthias Williamson, a soldier and landowner, and Susannah (Halsted) Williamson; both were Presbyterians. Married to Anne Crossdale on August 6,

1808; father of two sons, the eldest named Benjamin. Received only a grammar school education, but later studied law with a brother; licensed in 1791 as an attorney, in 1796 as a counselor, and in 1804 as a sergeant-at-law. He was a successful lawyer, attaining a high rank in the bar, and was considered to be one of the best advisors in the state concerning intricate legal questions. Due to his legal acumen he became Deputy Attorney General of Morris County, and in 1815 was elected to the State Assembly. During this period Williamson befriended Aaron Ogden, who controlled the votes of a majority of eastern New Jersey assemblymen. In 1817, after Mahlon Dickerson resigned as Governor, the Republican Williamson, with the support of Ogden, was elected Governor by a majority vote in a joint meeting of the legislature. He was sworn into office on February 6, 1817. The period from 1817 to 1825 in New Jersey politics, and in the nation as a whole, was known as the "Era of Good Feelings." Governor Williamson benefitted from the stable political atmosphere, for he was reelected annually until 1829, never being opposed. His most important accomplishment during his tenure was the increase in the power and duties of the Chancery Court. His uninterrupted service as governor ended in 1829, when Andrew Jackson's supporters in the state organized to defeat him, electing G. D. Wall by a majority vote in the legislature. Williamson then returned to his lucrative law practice. In 1831 he was elected to the State Council (Senate) from Essex County; later he became Mayor of Elizabethtown, New Jersey. In 1844 he was chosen unanimously to be president of the State Constitutional Convention. Williamson died that same year on July 10, 1844 in Elizabethtown, New Jersey. Bibliography: L. Q. C. Elmer, *The Constitution and Government of the Province and State of New Jersey* (1872); O. S. Halsted. *Address Upon the Character of the Late Honorable Isaac H. Williamson* (1844); John Whitehead, *The Judicial and Civil History of New Jersey* (1897); Duane Lockard, *The New Jersey Governor: A Study in Political Power* (1964). Papers of Williamson are in the New Jersey Historical Society.

VROOM, Peter, 1829-1832, 1833-1836

Born on December 12, 1791 in Hillsborough Township, New Jersey, son of Colonel Peter D. Vroom, an old and respected land owner in Somerset County, and Elsie (Bogart) Vroom, both of whom were members of the Dutch Reformed Church. In 1818 married the daughter (name unknown) of Peter Dumont, having two children, John and Maria, before she died; remarried to the daughter of General G. D. Wall and had four sons, Peter, Garret, James and Governeur. Attended college at Somerville Academy; in 1806 entered Columbia College in New York and graduated in 1808. Studied law with George McDonald and in 1813 entered the bar; in 1816 he became a counselor and in 1828 a sergeant. In 1824 Vroom supported General Andrew Jackson for President. In 1826, 1827 and 1829, he was elected to the State Assembly. As evidence of the rising political power of the Jacksonian Democrats in New Jersey, Republican Governor Isaac Williamson was unseated in 1829 by the Jacksonian, G. D. Wall, by majority vote in a joint meeting of the legislature. Wall then yielded the office to Vroom, his fellow Democrat. He took office on November 6, 1829. His major accomplishment as governor was the enactment of a bill incorporating the Delaware and Raritan Canal Company in February, 1830. Industrialists and merchants had been advocating such a bill since 1816. The company, in which the state was a part owner, proved successful, as it connected the eastern commercial area with the nation's internal markets. Vroom was reelected in 1830 and 1831 before being defeated by Samuel Southard, the leader of the anti-Jacksonians in the state. He was returned to office in 1833, as the Jacksonians again controlled a majority of the votes in the joint meeting of the legislature. He repeated his success in 1834 and in 1835. In 1836 he retired from office and resumed his law practice in Somerville. In 1837 President Martin Van Buren appointed him Claims Commissioner to the Chickasaw Tribe in Mississippi. The next year he was elected to Congress as a Democrat, holding that position until 1841. After 1844, having resettled in New Jersey, he was a member of the State Constitutional Convention, and in 1846 aided in revising the statutes of the state. In 1853, in return for supporting President Franklin Pierce, he was appointed Minister to Prussia, and resided in Berlin until 1857. During the remaining years of his life he remained active in both state and national politics. Vroom died on November 18, 1873 in Trenton, New Jersey. Bibliography: Abraham Messler, *Sermons on the Death of the Honorable Peter D. Vroom* (1874); Abraham Messler, *Centennial History of Somerset County* (1878); L. Q. C. Elmer, *The Constitution and Government of the Province and State of New Jersey* (1872); Florence I. Holmes, "The Vroom Papers," *Proceedings of the New Jersey Historical Society*, vol. LXXVI (1958). Papers of Vroom are in the New Jersey Historical Society and the Rutgers University Library.

SOUTHARD, Samuel Lewis, 1832-1833

Born on June 9, 1787 in Baskingridge, New Jersey, son of Henry, a statesman and state legislator, and Sarah (Lewis) Southard; a Presbyterian. Brother of Isaac Southard. Married to Rebecca Harrow in June of 1812; father of one daughter, Virginia. Attended a private, classical academy in Baskingridge; attended Princeton University, graduating in 1804; became a successful teacher; tutored for the family of Congressman John Taliaferro in Virginia for five years (1804-1809); studied law and was admitted to the bar in 1809; returned to New Jersey in 1811 to practice law. Beginning his public career as a Federalist, Southard was elected to the State House of Representatives in 1814. From 1815 to 1820 he served on the New Jersey Supreme Court and from 1821 to 1823 served as United States Senator. Appointed Secretary of the Navy in 1823, he remained in that position until 1829, when he ran unsuccessfully for the United States Senate. He was chosen Attorney General of New Jersey in 1830 and remained in that office until 1832, when the legislature (by an undisclosed majority) elected him Governor as a Whig. During his brief time as governor, Southard presided over a state that was rapidly changing. Progress in canal and railroad building highlighted his term, as did pronounced opposition of the governor and his supporters to the South Carolina nullification movement. In 1833 Southard resigned the governorship after he was chosen United States Senator, a position he held until 1842. While in the Senate he participated actively in its proceedings but established no reputation as a Whig Party leader. After resigning from the Senate in 1842, he returned to private life. Active in community service during his long career, in 1822 Southard was named as a trustee of Princeton College and in 1832 received the LL.D. from the University of Pennsylvania in recognition of his contributions as a public servant. In great demand as a speaker, Southard travelled widely and lectured to college audiences. Southard died on June 26, 1842 in Fredericksburg, New Jersey. Bibliography: Roy Glashan, *American Governors and Gubernatorial Elections, 1775-1975* (Stillwater, Minnesota, 1975); Congressional Quarterly, Inc., *Guide to U. S. Elections* (Washington, D. C., 1975); John T. Cunningham, *New Jersey* (Garden City, New York, 1966); Works Progress Administration, *New Jersey: A Guide to Its Present and Past* (Newark, 1939); William Meyers, *The Story of New Jersey* (New York, 1945).

SEELEY, Elias P., 1833

Born in 1791 (exact date unknown) in Fairfield Township, New Jersey, a descendant of one of the earliest settlers of Cumberland County, New Jersey. Seeley's father held several elective county offices and was elected to the State Assembly and Council. The early life of Elias Seeley is relatively unknown, except that he received a common school education, studied law with Daniel Elmer, and was admitted to the bar in 1815. In 1829 he was elected to the State Council, and was re-elected four times thereafter, becoming vice-president of that body in 1832. Upon the resignation of Governor Southard, who had been elected United States Senator, Seeley was chosen Governor by majority vote in a joint session of the legislature. He was sworn into office on February 27, 1833. While governor, he delivered several opinions in Chancery Court, the most famous being the "Quaker Case." His opinion on the disputes among members of the sect was later formalized in a special law, stating that the "rights, estates, property, and privileges" of the Quakers should not be injured due to internal division within the religious community. After serving only eight months, the Whig coalition which had elected Southard and himself had weakened. In the legislative balloting in October of 1833, Peter Vroom, a Democrat, ousted Seeley by controlling a majority of the votes in a joint session of the legislature. After the loss, Seeley was frequently elected to the State Legislature. Seeley died in 1846 at the age of fifty-five (place unknown). Bibliography: L. Q. C. Elmer, *The Constitution and Government of the Province and State of New Jersey* (1872); Duane Lockard, *The New Jersey Governor: Study in Political Power* (1964); John Whitehead, *The Judicial and Civil History of New Jersey* (1897); Herbert Ershkowitz, "Samuel L. Southard: A Case Study of Whig Leadership in the Age of Jackson," *Proceedings of the New Jersey Historical Society*, vol. LXXXVIII (1970).

VROOM, Peter, 1829-1832, 1833-1836

DICKERSON, Philemon, 1836-1837

Born on June 26, 1788 in Succasunna, New Jersey, to Jonathan and Mary (Coe) Dickerson; an Episcopalian. Brother of Mahlon, Silas and Aaron Dickerson. Married to Sidney Stotesbury in 1812; father of two sons. Attended public school in Philadelphia; graduated from the University of Pennsylvania in 1808. Lawyer, 1813; counselor at law, 1817; sergeant-at-arms, 1834 (only sergeants-at-arms could practice before the State Supreme Court). Member, New Jersey Assembly, 1821-1822; member, United States House of Representatives, 1833-1836; Chancellor, New Jersey, 1836. A Democrat, Dickerson was elected by secret ballot of the State Legislature. He took office on November 3, 1836, following his brother, Mahlon Dickerson, who had been Governor of New Jersey from 1815 to 1817. His administration lasted less than one year; thus the accomplishments of his tenure were limited. New Jersey was at the time in the midst of political upheaval, with the Whigs attempting to wrest power from the Jacksonians. Dickerson's governorship was cut short when the Whigs gained control of the legislature and elected William Pennington in 1837. Dickerson left office on October 27, 1837. After leaving office Dickerson served as United States District Judge for New Jersey, 1841-1862. During this time he was instrumental in obtaining a charter for Paterson, New Jersey, his adopted home. He authored *The City of Paterson: Its Past, Present, and Future* in 1856. He died in Paterson on December 10, 1862. Bibliography: Joseph Folsom, ed., *Cyclopedia of New Jersey, Historical and Biographical*, 3 vols. (New York, 1921); Bennett Rich, *The Government and Administration of New Jersey* (New York, 1957); Irving Kull, *New Jersey: A History*, 5 vols. (New York, 1930); Leonard B. Irwin, *New Jersey: The State and Its Government* (New York, 1942).

PENNINGTON, William, Jr., 1837-1843

Born on May 4, 1796 in Newark, New Jersey, to William Sanford, a former governor of New Jersey, and Phoebe (Wheeler) Pennington; a Presbyterian. Married to Caroline Burnet (circa 1835). Educated in the common school of Newark; attended the College of New Jersey (Princeton). Attorney, 1817; counselor, 1820; sergeant-at-arms, 1834 (only sergeants-at-arms could practice before the State Supreme Court). Member, New Jersey State Assembly, 1829-1833. As a Whig, Pennington was elected Governor by secret session of the New Jersey Legislature, taking office on October 27, 1837. He also acted as Chancellor of New Jersey, the highest judicial official in the state. Pennington's tenure as chancellor was marked by just decisions; however, his administration as governor was marred by the eruption in 1839 of the so-called "Broad Seal War." This conflict arose over the congressional campaign of 1838, in which the results of five elections were contested. Pennington was prevented by law from making an in-depth study of the returns, and so confirmed the five Whig candidates. However, the congressmen from New Jersey were not accepted by the House of Representatives, and eventually the five Democratic nominees received seats in the House. Also, Pennington's term was marked by increased popular demand for a greater voice in government. This clamor was finally recognized in 1844, with the calling of a constitutional convention to consider the matter. After winning six consecutive annual elections, Pennington left office on October 27, 1843. He then returned to his law practice in Newark. Pennington was elected to the United States House of Representatives in 1858, serving as Speaker of the House from 1859 to 1861. He returned to Newark, where he died on February 16, 1862 and was buried in Mt. Pleasant Cemetery. Bibliography: Joseph Folsom, ed., *Cyclopedia of New Jersey, Historical and Biographical*, 3 vols. (New York, 1921); Bennett Rich, *The Government and Administration of New Jersey* (New York, 1957); Irving Kull, *New Jersey: A History*, 5 vols. (New York, 1930); Leonard B. Irwin, *New Jersey: The State and Its Government* (New York, 1942).

HAINES, Daniel, 1843-1845, 1848-1851

Born on January 6, 1801, to Elias and Mary (Ogden) Haines in New York City; a Presbyterian. Married to Ann Marie Austin on June 28, 1827; remarried to Mary Townsend on July 6, 1865. Attended private school in New York City; an academy in Elizabethtown, New Jersey; and graduated from the College of New Jersey (Princeton) in 1820. Attorney, 1828; counselor, 1826; sergeant-at-arms, 1837 (only sergeants-at-arms could practice before the State Supreme Court). Member, New Jersey Council, 1837-1839; member, New Jersey Senate, 1839-1840. As a Democrat, Haines was elected Governor by secret session of the State Legislature, taking office on October 27, 1843. Haines' first administration supported a constitutional convention for New Jersey, and in 1844 Haines proclaimed the new charter. He did not run for election under the new constitution in 1844, leaving office on January 21, 1845. However, in 1847 Haines defeated the Whig candidate, William Wright, 34,765 votes to 32,251. Haines' second term was uneventful, primarily because the legislature was dominated by Whigs. Under the new constitution Haines could not succeed himself and he left office on January 21, 1851. Haines was active as an attorney, both between his terms as governor and after his last administration. From 1844 to 1848 he took part with Daniel Webster in cases concerning the Goodyear patents for vulcanizing rubber. Also, in 1845 he was appointed as a commissioner to select the site for the state insane asylum. Associate Justice, New Jersey Supreme Court, 1852-1866; member, New Jersey Boundary Commission, 1870-1876; trustee, College of New Jersey (Princeton), 1845-1877; vice-president, National Prison Association of United States, 1872. Haines died in Hamburg, New Jersey on January 26, 1877. Bibliography: Joseph Folsom, ed., *Cyclopedia of New Jersey, Historical and Biographical*, 3 vols. (New York, 1921); Bennett Rich, *The Government and Administration of New Jersey* (New York, 1957); Irving Kull, *New Jersey: A History*, 5 vols. (New York, 1930); Leonard B. Erwin, *New Jersey: The State and Its Government* (New York, 1942).

STRATTON, Charles Creighton, 1845-1848

Born on March 6, 1796 in Swedesboro, New Jersey, to parents who had come to America during the colonial period; an Episcopalian. Educated in public school in Swedesboro; attended Rutgers College and graduated in 1814. Began farming, 1815. Member, New Jersey General Assembly, 1821-1839, 1841-1843; member, New Jersey Constitutional Convention, 1844. As a Whig, Stratton was elected Governor of New Jersey in 1844, defeating Democrat William Thompson, 37,949 votes to 36,591. He took office on January 21, 1845. Stratton had been a prominent member of the State Convention in 1844 which gave New Jersey a new constitution, and as the first governor to be elected under the provisions of the new charter, he was the first popularly-elected governor of the state. The main accomplishment of his term in office was the full-scale implementation of the state constitution. Since the constitution of New Jersey prohibited the governor from succeeding himself, he left office on January 17, 1848. Stratton then returned to his farm in Gloucester County near Swedesboro. He died on March 30, 1859 and was buried in the Episcopal Cemetery in Swedesboro. Bibliography: Joseph Folsom, ed., *Cyclo-*

pedia of New Jersey, Historical and Biographical, 3 vols. (New York, 1921); Bennett Rich, *The Government and Administration of New Jersey* (New York, 1957); Irving Kull, *New Jersey: A History,* 5 vols. (New York, 1930); Leonard B. Erwin, *New Jersey: The State and Its Government* (New York, 1942).

HAINES, Daniel, 1843-1845, 1848-1851

FORT, George Franklin, 1851-1854

Born in May 1809 in Pemberton, New Jersey; a Methodist. Graduated from the University of Pennsylvania, receiving a medical degree in 1830. Practiced medicine from 1830 to 1840. Member of the New Jersey Constitutional Convention, 1844; member, New Jersey Senate, 1846-1850. A Mason. Fort, a Democrat, was elected Governor in 1850 with 39,723 votes to Whig challenger Felix Runk's 34,054. Fort took office on January 21, 1851. He faced a hostile legislature dominated by the opposition Whigs throughout most of his administration. Nevertheless, the foundation for improvements in the state's road system was laid by surveys approved during Fort's years as governor. Fort was prevented by the state constitution from succeeding himself, and left office on January 17, 1854. He then returned to his medical practice in New Egypt, Monmouth (now Ocean) County, New Jersey. Fort served from 1855 to 1862 as Judge of the New Jersey Court of Errors and Appeals. He died on April 22, 1872. Bibliography: Joseph Folsom, ed., *Cyclopedia of New Jersey, Historical and Biographical,* 3 vols. (New York, 1921); Bennett Rich, *The Government and Administration of New Jersey* (New York, 1957); Irving Kull, *New Jersey: A History,* 5 vols. (New York, 1930); Leonard B. Erwin, *New Jersey: The State and Its Government* (New York, 1942).

PRICE, Rodman McCauley, 1854-1857

Born on November 5, 1816 in Sussex County, New Jersey, son of Francis, a wealthy landowner, and Anne (McCauley) Price; a Presbyterian. Married to Matilda Tranchard; father of one son, Rodman Price, Jr. Attended schools in New York City and Lawrenceville, New Jersey; studied law, but gave it up in 1840 when he was appointed purser in the United States Navy. Served on the *Fulton* and the *Missouri,* as well as on the *Cyane* when it formed part of the United States fleet that took Monterey, California during the Mexican War. Served as Prefect and Alcalde for Monterey from 1846 to 1848. Price left the Navy in 1850 and began his political career as a Democrat in New Jersey. He served in the U.S. House of Representatives from 1850 to 1854. In 1853 Price was chosen Governor of the state by an overwhelming majority over a field of minor candidates. As the youngest man ever to head the state government, Price was inaugurated on January 17, 1854, and proved to be an excellent administrator. He established the public school system, including common schools, a normal, a teachers' institute, and a model school. He also initiated a geological survey, which allowed scientists and businessmen to develop the mineral resources of the state. He reorganized the state militia to increase its efficiency. One of Price's greatest achievements as governor was the settlement of a dispute involving monopoly rights. In 1830 the Camden and Amboy Railroad Company secured a charter which gave it a monopoly of railroad construction in the state. By the 1850s many groups were complaining that the company charged excessive rates. Governor Price negotiated with both the company and the legislature, and these negotiations led to a new state law which continued to give the company exclusive railroad rights for a fixed time, but then opened New Jersey to all competition. Constitutionally prohibited from serving more than one three-year term, Price retired from the governorship on January 20, 1857 but continued to serve his state. Concerned about the sectional crisis, he was a member of a state commission which went to Washington, D. C. to attend a conference called in 1860 for the purpose of averting civil war. The conference produced no results, and Price retired to private life. Price died on June 7, 1894 at Weehawken, New Jersey. Bibliography: Roy Glashan, *American Governors and Gubernatorial Elections, 1775-1975* (Stillwater, Minnesota, 1975); Congressional Quarterly, Inc., *Guide to U.S. Elections* (Washington, D. C., 1975); John T. Cunningham, *New Jersey* (Garden City, New York, 1966); Works Progress Administration, *New Jersey: A Guide to Its Present and Past* (Newark, 1939); William Meyers, *The Story of New Jersey* (New York, 1945).

NEWELL, William Augustus, 1857-1860

Born on September 5, 1817 to James H. and Eliza D. (Hankinson) Newell; a Presbyterian. Married to Joanna Van Deursen (*c.* 1837); father of three children. Attended Rutgers College and graduated in 1836; studied medicine at the University of Pennsylvania and graduated in 1841; began medical practice. Served in the United States House of Representatives, 1847-1851. A Mason. Although originally a Whig, Newell was elected Governor in 1856 as a member of the Fusion Party, defeating Democrat Leonard Alexander, 50,903 votes to 48,246. He took office on January 20, 1857. As a member of the Fusion Party, Newell faced stiff opposition from a Democratic-dominated legislature during his administration. The primary accomplishment of his term in office was his success in making the new Republican Party a force in the state's politics. At the start of the Civil War, New Jersey's Republican Party was powerful enough to compete successfully with the Democratic Party, which contained many pro-slavery members. Newell could not succeed himself according to the state constitution, and he left office on January 17, 1860. Newell served as superintendent of New Jersey's Life Saving Service from 1860 to 1864; member of the United States House of Representatives from 1865 to 1867; Governor of the Washington Territory from 1880 to 1884; United States Indian Inspector in 1884; Resident Surgeon to Soldiers' and Sailors' Home, Washington from 1894 to 1898. He returned to New Jersey in 1898. Newell died on August 8, 1901 in Allentown. Bibliography: Joseph Folsom, ed., *Cyclopedia of New Jersey, Historical and Biographical* 3 vols. (New York, 1921); Bennett Rich, *The Government and Administration of New Jersey* (New York, 1957); Irving Kull, *New Jersey: A History*, 5 vols. (New York, 1930); Leonard B. Erwin, *New Jersey: The State and Its Government* (New York, 1942).

OLDEN, Charles Smith, 1860-1863

Born on November 19, 1799 in Stony Brook, near Princeton, New Jersey, son of Hart, a farmer and merchant, and Temperance (Smith) Olden; a Quaker. Married to Phoebe Ann Smith (*c.* 1832); father of an adopted daughter. Attended the local schools. Assisted his father in operating a general store in Princeton; worked for the firm of Matthew Newkirk in Philadelphia. Engaged in business in New Orleans, Louisiana from 1826 to 1832. Returned to Princeton and engaged in farming; became a director of the Trenton Banking Company in 1842. Elected to the New Jersey Senate in 1844, serving from 1845 to 1851. As the Republican gubernatorial candidate, Olden was elected Governor of New Jersey by popular vote on November 8, 1859, defeating the Democratic candidate, E. R. V. Wright, by a vote of 53,315 to 51,714; Olden was inaugurated on January 17, 1860. During his administration the United States became embroiled in the Civil War. The State Legislature appropriated money to the families of volunteers, as well as to volunteers themselves; authorized a loan of $2,000,000 and a state tax of $100,000; and authorized the purchase of arms, artillery, and munitions of war. Because the New Jersey Constitution of 1844 prohibited a governor from succeeding himself, Olden left office on January 20, 1863. He later served as a Judge of the New Jersey Court of Errors and Appeals; he also served as a member of the Court of Pardons from 1868 to 1873, when he resigned. Served as a Fish Commissioner from 1869 to 1875; served as head of the New Jersey electors in the presidential election of 1872. Served as treasurer of the College of New Jersey from 1845 to 1869 and as trustee from 1863 to 1875. Olden died in Princeton on April 7, 1876 and was buried in the Friend's Cemetery near Princeton, New Jersey. Bibliography: Joseph E. Folsom, ed., *Cyclopedia of New Jersey, Historical and Biographical*, 3 vols. (New York, 1921); Irving S. Kull, *New Jersey: A History*, 5 vols. (New York, 1930); Congressional Quarterly, Inc., *Guide to U.S. Elections* (Washington, D. C., 1975); Roy Glashan, *American Governors and Gubernatorial Elections, 1775-1975* (Stillwater, Minnesota, 1975).

PARKER, Joel, 1863-1866, 1872-1875

Born on November 24, 1816 near Freehold, New Jersey; son of Charles, the State Treasurer and State Librarian, and Sarah (Coward) Parker; a Protestant. Married to Maria M. Gummere in 1843; father of two sons and one daughter. Attended the local schools; graduated from the College of New Jersey in 1839; studied law under Henry Woodhull Green; admitted to the bar in 1842 and began practice in Freehold. Elected Democratic Assemblyman for Monmouth County in 1847; served as Monmouth County Prosecutor from 1852 to 1857. Reorganized the local militia, in which he attained the rank of Major General in 1861. As the Democratic gubernatorial candidate, Parker was elected Governor of New Jersey by popular vote on November 4, 1862, defeating the Republican candidate, Marcus L. Ward, by a vote of 61,307 to 46,710; he was inaugurated on January 20, 1863. Elected again on November 7, 1871, defeating his Republican opponent, Cornelius Walsh, by a vote of 82,362 to 76,383; inaugurated for a second time on January 16, 1872. During his administration, Parker continued New Jersey's contribution to the Union war effort. Legislation provided for the organization of a State Reform School for Juvenile Offenders; efforts were renewed to have the New York Quarantine established in New Jersey; and the U. S. War Department was restrained from using the roadway of the Raritan and Delaware Bay Railroad. Because the New Jersey Constitution of 1844 prohibited a governor from succeeding himself, Parker left office on January 16, 1866 and later on January 19, 1875. He was nominated for President by the New Jersey delegation to the Democratic National Conventions of 1868 and 1876. He served as Attorney General of New Jersey from January to April, 1875, when he resigned and returned to private practice. Parker was appointed to the New Jersey Supreme Court in 1880 and served until his death. He died on January 2, 1888 in Philadelphia. Bibliography: Joseph E. Folsom, ed., *Cyclopedia of New Jersey, Historical and Biographical*, 3 vols. (New York, 1921); Irving S. Kull, *New Jersey: A History*, 5 vols. (New York, 1930); Congressional Quarterly, Inc., *Guide to U. S. Elections* (Washington, D. C., 1975); Roy Glashan, *American Governors and Gubernatorial Elections, 1775-1975* (Stillwater, Minnesota, 1975).

WARD, Marcus Lawrence, 1866-1869

Born on November 9, 1812 in Newark, New Jersey, son of Marcus, a manufacturer, and Fanny (Brown) Ward; a Protestant. Married to Susan Morris on June 30, 1840; father of eight children, among whom was Marcus Lawrence Ward, Jr. Attended the local schools; entered business with his father, eventually becoming a partner in the firm of M. Ward & Son. Became a director of the National State Bank in Newark in 1846; served as chairman of the executive committee of the New Jersey Historical Society for many years; aided in the formation of the Newark Library Association and the New Jersey Art Union. Served as a delegate to the Republican National Convention at Chicago in 1860 and at Baltimore in 1864. During the Civil War, he established a pension bureau and founded a soldiers' hospital in Newark. Unsuccessful candidate for the New Jersey governorship, having been defeated by Joel Parker in the general election of November 4, 1862 by a vote of 61,307 to 46,710. Served as a Republican presidential elector in 1864. As the Republican gubernatorial candidate, Ward was elected Governor of New Jersey by popular vote on November 7, 1865, defeating the Democratic candidate, T. Runyon, by a vote of 67,525 to 64,736; he was inaugurated on January 16, 1866. During his administration, Ward was a strong supporter of many reform measures securing the passage of a public school law and an act eliminating partisanship in the control of the state prison. Because the New Jersey Constitution of 1844 prohibited a governor from succeeding himself, Ward left office on January 19, 1869, resuming his law practice. Ward served as chairman of the Republican National Committee in 1866, and was elected as a Republican to the United States House of Representatives, serving from March 4, 1873 to March 3, 1875. He was an unsuccessful candidate for reelection to the House; declined the office of Commissioner of Indian Affairs, and retired to private life. Ward died on April 25, 1884 in Newark, New Jersey and was buried in Mount Pleasant Cemetery. Bibliography: Joseph E. Folsom, ed., *Cyclopedia of New Jersey, Historical and Biographical*, 3 vols. (New York, 1921); Irving S. Kull, *New Jersey: A History*, 5 vols. (New York, 1930); Congressional Quarterly, Inc., *Guide to U. S. Elections* (Washington, D. C., 1975); Roy Glashan, *American Governors and Gubernatorial Elections, 1775-1975* (Stillwater, Minnesota, 1975).

RANDOLPH, Theodore Fitz, 1869-1872

Born on June 24, 1826 in New Brunswick, New Jersey, son of James Fitz, a New Jersey Congressman and founder of the New Brunswick *Fredonian*; a Presbyterian. Married to Fannie Coleman in 1852. Attended Rutgers Grammar School. Engaged in business in Vicksburg, Mississippi from 1846 to 1850; returned to Jersey City, New Jersey and entered his father's coal and iron business. Moved to Morristown, New Jersey in 1865 and engaged in property development; elected president of the Morris and Essex Railroad in 1867. Served as a member of the New Jersey House of Assembly in 1859 and the New Jersey Senate in 1862 and 1863; served as a delegate to the Democratic National Convention in 1864; was instrumental in creating the office of State Comptroller in 1865. As the Democratic gubernatorial candidate, Randolph was elected Governor of New Jersey by popular vote on November 3, 1868, defeating the Republican candidate, John I. Blair, by a vote of 83,619 to 79,072; he was inaugurated on January 19, 1869. During his administration, plans were made to establish one of the largest mental institutions in the world at that time in Morristown, New Jersey; laws against election bribery were adopted; a policy was formulated to make the state prison self-supporting; and the Camden and Amboy Railroad monopoly tax was repealed. Because the New Jersey Constitution of 1844 prohibited a governor from succeeding himself, Randolph left office on January 16, 1872. He served as a delegate to the Democratic National Convention in 1872. Randolph was elected as a Democrat to the United States Senate, serving from March 4, 1875 to March 3, 1881. He died on November 7, 1883 in Morristown, New Jersey and was buried in Woodlawn Cemetery. Bibliography: Joseph E. Folsom, ed., *Cyclopedia of New Jersey, Historical and Biographical*, 3 vols. (New York, 1921); Irving S. Kull, *New Jersey: A History*, 5 vols. (New York, 1930); Congressional Quarterly, Inc., *Guide to U. S. Elections* (Washington, D. C., 1975); Roy Glashan, *American Governors and Gubernatorial Elections, 1775-1975* (Stillwater, Minnesota, 1975).

PARKER, Joel, 1863-1866, 1872-1875

BEDLE, Joseph Dorsett, 1875-1878

Born on January 5, 1831 in Middletown Point (present Matawan), Monmouth County, New Jersey, son of Thomas I., a merchant, and Hannah (Dorsett) Bedle; a Protestant. Married to Althea F. Randolph; father of Bennington F., Joseph D., Thomas F., Randolph and Althea R. Bedle. Attended school in Middletown Point; read law with William L. Dayton in Trenton, New Jersey and Henry S. Little in Middletown Point; attended the law school in Ballston Spa, New York for one semester. Admitted to practice by the Supreme Court of New Jersey in June, 1853; engaged in law practice in Freehold, New Jersey from 1855 until March, 1865, when he was appointed as a Justice on the New Jersey Supreme Court. As the Democratic gubernatorial candidate, Bedle was elected Governor of New Jersey by popular vote on November 3, 1874, defeating the Republican candidate, G.

Halsey, by a vote of 97,283 to 84,050; he was inaugurated on January 19, 1875. During his administration legislation passed included the enactment of a general election law; the reduction of the salaries of state officials; the creation of a commission to establish the boundary between New York and New Jersey; the creation of the State Board of Health; the creation of district courts of one judge in cities of 15,000 or more inhabitants; and the establishment of orphanages. Because the New Jersey Constitution of 1844 prohibited a governor from succeeding himself, Bedle left office on January 15, 1878 and resumed his law practice in Jersey City, New Jersey. Bedle died on October 21, 1894. Bibliography: Joseph E. Folsom, ed., *Cyclopedia of New Jersey, Historical and Biographical*, 3 vols. (New York, 1921); Irving S. Kull, *New Jersey: A History*, 5 vols. (New York, 1930); Congressional Quarterly, Inc., *Guide to U. S. Elections* (Washington, D. C., 1975); Roy Glashan, *American Governors and Gubernatorial Elections, 1775-1975* (Stillwater, Minnesota, 1975).

McCLELLAN, George, 1878-1881

Born on December 3, 1826 in Philadelphia, Pennsylvania; son of George, a physician, and Elizabeth (Brinton) McClellan; a Presbyterian. Brother of John Hill Brinton and Arthur McClellan. Married to Ellen Mary Marcy on May 22, 1860; father of a daughter and son. Attended the University of Pennsylvania from 1840 to 1842; appointed as a cadet to the United States Military Academy at West Point in 1842, graduating second in the class of 1846; brevetted First Lieutenant on August 20, 1847 for gallant and meritorious conduct at the battles of Contreras and Churubusco, Mexico. Promoted to Brevet Captain on September 13, 1847 for gallant and meritorious conduct at the Battle of Chapultepec, Mexico; appointed First Lieutenant on July 1, 1853 and promoted to Captain of the First Cavalry on March 3, 1855; resigned on January 16, 1857. McClellan became chief engineer of the Illinois Central Railroad in 1857; vice-president in charge of operations in Illinois in 1858; and president of the Ohio and Mississippi Railroad in 1860. He was appointed Major General of the Ohio Volunteers on April 23, 1861, and Major General in the Regular Army on May 14, 1861; served as Commanding General of the United States Army from November 1, 1861 to March 11, 1862. McClellan resigned on November 8, 1864. An unsuccessful candidate for the presidency in 1864, McClellan spent time travelling abroad from 1864 to 1867. He declined the presidency of the University of California in 1868 and of Union College in 1869. He was appointed chief engineer of the New York City Department of Docks in 1870, serving until his resignation in 1872; declined appointment as New York City Comptroller in 1871. As the Democratic gubernatorial candidate, McClellan was elected Governor of New Jersey by popular vote on November 9, 1877, defeating the Republican candidate, W. Newell, by a vote of 97,837 to 85,094; he was inaugurated on January 15, 1878. During his administration, the governor was authorized to appoint a Special Tax Commission to investigate existing tax laws; a commission was authorized to prepare a system of general laws for the government of incorporated cities; provisions were made for the establishment of schools for industrial education; the summary investigation of county and municipal expenditures was authorized; and the state militia was reorganized. Because the New Jersey Constitution of 1844 prohibited a governor from succeeding himself, McClellan left office on January 18, 1881 and retired to private life, spending much time abroad. Author of *McClellan's*

Own Story (1887). McClellan died on October 29, 1885, with funeral services being held at the Madison Square Presbyterian Church in New York City; he was buried in Trenton, New Jersey. Bibliography: *The Life, Campaigns, and Public Services of General McClellan* (Philadelphia, 1864); H. J. Eckenrode and Bryan Conrad, *George B. McClellan, the Man Who Saved the Union* (Chapel Hill, North Carolina, 1941); Congressional Quarterly, Inc., *Guide to U. S. Elections* (Washington, D. C., 1975); Roy Glashan, *American Governors and Gubernatorial Elections, 1775-1975* (Stillwater, Minnesota, 1975).

LUDLOW, George C., 1881-1884

Born on April 6, 1830 in Milford, New Jersey; a Protestant. Attended the local schools; graduated from Rutgers in 1850; studied law; admitted to the bar in 1853 and began law practice in New Brunswick, New Jersey. Elected to the New Jersey Assembly in 1876, serving as president during one session. As the Democratic gubernatorial candidate, Ludlow was elected Governor of New Jersey by popular vote on November 2, 1880, defeating the Republican candidate, F. Potts, by a vote of 121,666 to 121,015. He was inaugurated on January 18, 1881. During his administration, the number of hours children could work was limited; the establishment of public libraries in muncipalities and towns was encouraged; milk dealers and their agents were licensed and regulated; women were made eligible as school trustees; the sale of petroleum and its products was regulated; and the Board of State Charities and Correction was created. Because the New Jersey Constitution of 1844 prohibited a governor from succeeding himself, Ludlow left office on January 15, 1884 and resumed his law practice. Ludlow died on December 18, 1900. Bibliography: Irving S. Kull, *New Jersey: A History*, 5 vols. (New York, 1930); Bennett M. Rich, *The Government and Administration of New Jersey* (New York, 1957); Congressional Quarterly, Inc., *Guide to U. S. Elections* (Washington, D. C., 1975); Roy Glashan, *American Governors and Gubernatorial Elections, 1775-1975* (Stillwater, Minnesota, 1975).

ABBETT, Leon, 1884-1887, 1890-1893

Born on October 8, 1836 in Philadelphia, Pennsylvania, son of Ezekiel and Sarah (Howell) Abbett; a Protestant. Married to Mary Briggs on October 8, 1862. Graduated from Central High School in 1853; studied law; admitted to the bar in 1858. Moved to Hoboken, New Jersey in 1862 and to Jersey City, New Jersey in 1866; formed law partnership with William J. A. Fuller in Hudson County, New Jersey. Appointed Corporation Attorney of Hoboken in 1863; elected to the New Jersey House of Assembly in 1864, 1866 and 1868, serving as chairman of the Democratic caucus during the first two terms and Speaker during the third term; served as a delegate to the Democratic National Convention in Baltimore in 1872 and in St. Louis in 1876, serving as chairman of the latter; elected to the New Jersey Senate in 1874, serving as its President in 1877. Unsuccessful candidate for the New Jersey Democratic gubernatorial nomination in 1877; appointed corporation counsel for Jersey City, Bayonne and Union; served as president of the Jersey City Board of

Education. As the Democratic gubernatorial candidate, Abbett was elected Governor of New Jersey by popular vote on November 6, 1883, defeating the Republican candidate, Judge Jonathan Dixon, by a vote of 103,856 to 97,047; he was inaugurated on January 15, 1884. Elected again on November 5, 1889, defeating the Republican candidate, General E. Burd Grubb, by a vote of 138,245 to 123,992; inaugurated for a second time on January 21, 1890. During his administration, the State Board of Agriculture was organized; a civil rights bill was enacted; railroads were prevented from leasing their road or franchises without the consent of the State Legislature; legislation was passed making it illegal to sue unincorporated companies; railroad and canal companies were allowed to pay their taxes quarterly; the real and personal estate of every manufacturing corporation was taxed the same as real and personal estates of individuals; the collection of more than one poll tax was made illegal; the "Australian ballot system" was introduced; and the state was redistricted for legislative representation. Because the New Jersey Constitution of 1844 prohibited a governor from succeeding himself, Abbett left office on January 18, 1887 and later on January 17, 1893. Unsuccessful candidate for the United States Senate in 1887 and 1892. Appointed an Associate Justice of the New Jersey Supreme Court in 1893, serving in that capacity until his death. Received LL.D. from the College of New Jersey in 1884. Abbett died on December 4, 1894 in Jersey City, New Jersey. Bibliography: Joseph E. Folsom, ed., *Cyclopedia of New Jersey, Historical and Biographical*, 3 vols (New York, 1921); Irving S. Kull, *New Jersey: A History*, 5 vols. (New York, 1930); Congressional Quarterly, Inc., *Guide to U.S. Elections* (Washington, D. C., 1975); Roy Glashan, *American Governors and Gubernatorial Elections, 1775-1975* (Stillwater, Minnesota, 1975).

GREEN, Robert Stockton, 1887-1890

Born on March 25, 1831 in Princeton, Mercer County, New Jersey, grandson of the Reverend Ashbel Green, president of the College of New Jersey; a Presbyterian. Married to Mary E. (c. 1858); father of Catherine, Belle and Robert S. Green. Attended the common schools; graduated from the College of New Jersey in Princeton in 1850; studied law and was admitted to the bar in 1853; moved to Elizabeth, New Jersey in 1856 and was appointed Prosecutor of the Borough Courts in 1857. Elected City Attorney of Elizabeth in 1858, serving in that capacity until 1868; served as a delegate to the Democratic National Conventions of 1860, 1880 and 1888; elected surrogate of Union County, New Jersey in 1862 and served in that capacity until 1867. Served as a member of the Elizabeth City Council from 1863 to 1873; appointed presiding judge of the Court of Common Pleas in 1868, serving in that capacity until 1873. Unsuccessful candidate for the United States House of Representatives in 1868; appointed one of the commissioners to suggest amendments to the State Constitution in 1873. Admitted to the New York Bar in 1874; elected as a Democrat to the United States House of Representatives, serving from March 4, 1885 to January 17, 1887, when he resigned to become Governor of New Jersey. As the Democratic gubernatorial candidate, Green was elected Governor of New Jersey by popular vote on November 2, 1886, defeating the Republican candidate, B. Howey, and the Prohibition candidate, C. Fisk, by a vote of 109,939 to 101,919 and 19,808, respectively; he was inaugurated on January 18, 1887. During his administration, a State Board of Agriculture, State Board of Health and

Bureau of Vital Statistics were established; women were given the right to vote at school district meetings; the publication of the public laws of each session of the State Legislature in the newspapers of several counties was required; the militia law was revised; with the exception of railroad and canal corporations, all corporations were authorized to increase their capital stock; the polls at all elections were required to be opened from 6:00 a.m. to 7:00 p.m; and the Local Option Act of 1888 was repealed. Because the New Jersey Constitution of 1844 prohibited a governor from succeeding himself, Green left office on January 21, 1890. Appointed Vice-Chancellor of New Jersey in 1890, and served in that capacity until 1895; served as judge of the Court of Errors and Appeals in 1894 and 1895. Robert S. Green died on May 7, 1895 in Elizabeth, New Jersey and was buried in Greenwood Cemetery, Brooklyn, New York. Bibliography: Joseph E. Folsom, ed., *Cyclopedia of New Jersey, Historical and Biographical*, 3 vols. (New York, 1921); Irving S. Kull, *New Jersey: A History*, 5 vols. (New York, 1930); Congressional Quarterly, Inc., *Guide to U. S. Elections* (Washington, D. C., 1975); Roy Glashan, *American Governors and Gubernatorial Elections, 1775-1975* (Stillwater, Minnesota, 1975).

ABBETT, Leon, 1884-1887, 1890-1893

WERTS, George Theodore, 1893-1896

Born on March 24, 1846 in Hackettstown, Warren County, New Jersey; married to Emma M. (*c.* 1877); father of Mary E. Werts; a Protestant. Graduated from Bordentown High School and the State Model School, Trenton. Admitted to the New Jersey Bar in November, 1867; settled in Morristown, New Jersey and began the practice of law; served as the Recorder in Morristown from 1883 to 1885; served as Mayor of Morristown from 1886 to 1892; served as a member of the New Jersey Senate for six years, where he led the fight against the local option and high license measures which had been approved by the Republican State Legislature. Author of the Werts Law, the new license law. Appointed to the New Jersey Supreme Court in 1892 to fill the vacancy caused by the death of Justice Knapp and served in this capacity until his inauguration as governor. As the Democratic gubernatorial candidate, Werts was elected Governor of New Jersey by popular vote on November 8, 1892, defeating the Republican candidate, John Kean, Jr., by a vote of 167,257 to 159,632; he was inaugurated on January 17, 1893. During his administration, the disagreements over representation in the State Senate were such that for a time two separate Senates were in operation, the Democratic Senate being recognized by the governor and the Republican Senate being recognized by the New Jersey House of Assembly. By a vote of eight to one, the Supreme Court held that the Republican Senate, under the leadership of Maurice A. Rogers, was the lawful Senate of New Jersey. Legislation passed during Werts' administration included bills authorizing and regulating the construction of street railways upon turnpikes; amending the election law by providing that the Common Pleas Court would sit before the spring elections to revise the registry of election; providing for the construction of a free public library in cities of the second class by issuing bonds up to the sum of $50,000; and fixing the rate of interest on tax arrears at seven percent.

Because the New Jersey Constitution of 1844 prohibited a governor from succeeding himself, Werts left office on January 21, 1896 and resumed his law practice. Werts died on January 17, 1910 in Jersey City, New Jersey. Bibliography: *New York Times*, (January 18, 1910); Joseph E. Folsom, ed., *Cyclopedia of New Jersey, Historical and Biographical*, 3 vols. (New York, 1921); Congressional Quarterly, Inc., *Guide to U. S. Elections* (Washington, D. C., 1975); Roy Glashan, *American Governors and Gubernatorial Elections, 1775-1975* (Stillwater, Minnesota, 1975).

GRIGGS, John William, 1896-1898

Born on July 10, 1849 near Newton, Sussex County, New Jersey; youngest son of Daniel, a farmer, and Emeline (Johnson) Griggs; a Protestant. Married to Carolyn Webster Brandt in 1874; after her death, remarried to Laura Elizabeth Price on April 15, 1893; father of five daughters and two sons, among whom were John L., Helen and Eliza Griggs. Attended Collegiate Institute in Newton, New Jersey; received an A. B. degree from Lafayette College in 1868; studied law with Robert Hamilton and Socrates Tuttle; admitted to the bar in 1871, forming a partnership with Tuttle. Elected to the New Jersey House of Assembly in 1876, serving as chairman of the Committee on the Revision of Laws; reelected in 1877, but was defeated in 1878; appointed counsel to the Board of Chosen Freeholders of Passaic County, New Jersey in 1878; served as City Counsel of Paterson, New Jersey from 1879 to 1882; elected to the New Jersey Senate in 1882 and 1885, serving as its President during the 1886 session; served as delegate-at-large to the Republican National Convention of 1888; declined appointment as judge to the New Jersey Supreme Court. As the Republican gubernatorial candidate, Griggs was elected Governor of New Jersey by popular vote on November 5, 1895, defeating the Democratic candidate, A. McGill, by a vote of 162,900 to 136,000; he was inaugurated on January 21, 1896. During his administration, constitutional amendments against gambling and permitting *ad interim* appointments to state offices were adopted; a measure giving women the right to vote on school issues was defeated; the damming of the Delaware River was authorized; and the governor was authorized to appoint one or more commissioners to revise and codify the General Statutes. Griggs resigned the New Jersey governorship on January 25, 1898, upon his appointment as Attorney General in the cabinet of President William McKinley. He served in that capacity until his resignation on March 30, 1901, when he resumed his private law practice. Griggs was appointed to the Permanent Court of Arbitration at The Hague, serving from 1901 to 1912; an unsuccessful candidate for the Republican nomination to the United States Senate in 1902; served as president of the Marconi Wireless Telegraph Company and director of the Radio Corporation of America, New York Telephone Company, Bethlehem Steel Corporation and the American Locomotive Company. Griggs died on November 28, 1927. Bibliography: Joseph E. Folsom, ed., *Cyclopedia of New Jersey, Historical and Biographical*, 3 vols. (New York, 1921); Irving S. Kull, *New Jersey: A History*, 5 vols. (New York, 1930); Congressional Quarterly, Inc., *Guide to U. S. Elections* (Washington, D. C., 1975); Roy Glashan, *American Governors and Gubernatorial Elections, 1775-1975* (Stillwater, Minnesota, 1975).

VOORHEES, Foster MacGowan, 1898, 1899-1902

Born on November 5, 1856 in Clinton, New Jersey, son of Nathaniel Whitaker and Naomi (Leigh) Voorhees. Unmarried. Attended private schools; graduated from Rutgers University, ranking second in the class of 1876; received an M.A. degree in 1897 from Rutgers. Taught languages in Rutgers Grammar School while studying law in the office of Magie and Cross in Elizabeth, New Jersey; admitted to the bar in 1880 and began law practice in Elizabeth; served as a member of the Elizabeth Board of Education from 1884 to 1887; served as a member of the New Jersey House of Assembly in 1888, 1889 and 1890; served as a member of the New Jersey Senate from 1894 to 1898, and held the position of President of the Senate in 1898. Voorhees assumed the New Jersey governorship on January 31, 1898, after the resignation of Governor John W. Griggs, and served until October 18, 1898, when he resigned to seek the governorship by election. As the Republican gubernatorial candidate, Voorhees was subsequently elected Governor of New Jersey by popular vote on November 8, 1898, defeating the Democratic gubernatorial candidate, Elvin W. Crane, by a vote of 164,051 to 158,552; he was inaugurated on January 17, 1899. During his administration an "anti-spring election" law, providing that city officers no longer be elected at special elections in the spring, but be placed on the same ballot as state and county officers, was enacted; a general system for improving the state's roads was devised; towns were permitted to issue bonds in the amount of $50,000 for school buildings; and the construction of an armory in Trenton was authorized. Because the New Jersey Constitution of 1844 prohibited a governor from succeeding himself, Voorhees left office on January 21, 1902 and returned to private practice. Voorhees died on June 4, 1927 in High Bridge, New Jersey. Bibliography: Irving S. Kull, *New Jersey: A History,* 5 vols. (New York, 1930); *New York Times,* (June 15, 1927); Congressional Quarterly, Inc., *Guide to U.S. Elections* (Washington, D. C., 1975); Roy Glashan, *American Governors and Gubernatorial Elections, 1775-1975* (Stillwater, Minnesota, 1975).

WATKINS, David Ogden, 1898-1899

Born on June 8, 1862 in Woodbury, New Jersey, son of William and Hannah Watkins; a Protestant. Brother of Joseph and William Watkins, Jr. Married to Mrs. Lidie M. Andrews of Woodbury. Studied law; admitted to the New Jersey Bar in 1893; served as Mayor of Woodbury from 1886 to 1890, and as a member of the City Council from 1892 to 1898, holding the office of president from 1895 to 1897; served as Solicitor of the City of Woodbury and counsel to the Board of Freeholders of Gloucester County, New Jersey; served as a member of the New Jersey House of Assembly from 1897 to 1899, holding the office of Speaker in 1898 and 1899. As Speaker of the New Jersey House of Assembly, Watkins a Republican, assumed the New Jersey governorship on October 18, 1898 upon the resignation of Acting Governor Foster M. Voorhees, who had been President of the New Jersey Senate. Watkins served until January 17, 1899, when Voorhees was inaugurated as governor after winning the election of November 8, 1898. Returning to the New Jersey House of Assembly, Watkins resumed his duties as Speaker. He served as United States Attorney for the District of New Jersey from 1900 to 1903, when he resigned. Watkins served as New Jersey Commissioner of Banking and Insurance from 1903 to

1909, and as a member of the Republican State Committee from 1904 to 1908. He served as president of both the Woodbury Trust Company and the Farmers and Mechanics National Bank. Watkins died on June 20, 1938 and was buried in Woodbury, New Jersey. Bibliography: Joseph E. Folsom, ed., *Cyclopedia of New Jersey, Historical and Biographical*, 3 vols. (New York, 1921); Irving S. Kull, *New Jersey: A History*, 5 vols. (New York, 1930); Congressional Quarterly, Inc., *Guide to U. S. Elections* (Washington, D.C., 1975); Roy Glashan, *American Governors and Gubernatorial Elections, 1775-1975* (Stillwater, Minnesota, 1975).

VORHEES, Foster MacGowan, 1898, 1899-1902

MURPHY, Franklin, 1902-1905

Born on January 1, 1846 in Jersey City, Hudson County, New Jersey; an Episcopalian. Married to Janet Colwell in 1868; father of Franklin and Helen Murphy. Attended Newark Academy until July, 1862, when he enlisted in the Thirteenth Regiment of New Jersey Volunteers. Took part in the battles of Antietam, Chancellorsville and Gettysburg, as well as in Sherman's "March to the Sea;" left the army as a First Lieutenant. Served as President of the Board of Aldermen of Newark, New Jersey from 1883 to 1886; elected to the New Jersey House of Assembly in 1885; served as Trustee of the Reform School for Boys in Jamesburg, New Jersey from 1886 to 1889; served as a member of the executive committee of the Republican National Committee; declined appointment as Ambassador to Russia by President William McKinley; appointed Commissioner to the International Exposition in Paris in 1901. As the Republican gubernatorial candidate, Murphy was elected Governor of New Jersey by popular vote on November 5, 1901, defeating the Democratic nominee, James M. Seymour, by a vote of 183,814 to 166,681; he was inaugurated on January 21, 1902. During his administration, the first state primary law was passed; child labor laws were improved; a tuberculosis sanitarium was established at Glen Gardner, New Jersey; the fee system in state and county offices was abolished; and banks were required to pay interest on deposits of state money which yielded the state more than 50,000 dollars per year. Because the New Jersey Constitution of 1844 prohibited a governor from succeeding himself, Murphy left office on January 17, 1905. He served as a delegate to five Republican national conventions and was chairman of the Republican State Committee of New Jersey for twenty years. He engaged in various business interests until his death. Murphy died on February 24, 1920 in Palm Beach, Florida and was buried in Mt. Pleasant Cemetery in Newark, New Jersey. Bibliography: *New York Times* (February 25, 1920); *New York Times* (February 26, 1920); Congressional Quarterly, Inc., *Guide to U. S. Elections* (Washington, D. C., 1975); Roy Glashan, *American Governors and Gubernatorial Elections, 1775-1975* (Stillwater, Minnesota, 1975).

STOKES, Edward Casper, 1905-1908

Born on December 22, 1860 in Philadelphia, Pennsylvania, son of Edward H., a bank president, and Matilda G. (Kemble) Stokes; a Protestant. Brother of Marian H., John W., and Alice W. Never married. Attended the public schools of Millville, New Jersey and Friends School, Providence, Rhode Island; received an A.B. degree from Brown University in 1883. Associated with the Millville National Bank from 1883 to 1888. Served as Superintendent of Millville Public Schools from 1889 to 1898. Elected to the New Jersey House of Assembly in 1891; served as a member of the New Jersey Senate from 1892 to 1901, holding the office of President in 1895; became first president of the First Mechanics National Bank of Trenton, New Jersey in 1899; served as vice-chairman of the New Jersey Republican Committee in 1900; served as clerk of the Court of Chancery from 1901 to 1905. As the Republican gubernatorial candidate, Stokes was elected Governor of New Jersey by popular vote on November 8, 1904, defeating the Democratic nominee, C. Black, by a vote of 231,363 to 179,719; he was inaugurated on January 17, 1905. During his administration, Stokes dispensed with much unnecessary formality. He initiated many helpful reforms, among which was a substantial increase in railroad taxation, an increase which had been successfully opposed for a number of years. Because the New Jersey Constitution of 1844 prohibited a governor from succeeding himself, Stokes left office on January 21, 1908 and returned to his banking interests. Defeated in his bids for the United States Senate in 1902 and 1928, and for Governor in 1913; served as chairman of the Republican State Convention in 1936; received an LL.D. from Temple University in 1909. Stokes died on November 4, 1942 in Trenton, New Jersey. Bibliography: *New York Times* (November 5, 1942); Walter E. Edge, "New Jersey During the Past Half Century," *Proceedings of the New Jersey Historical Society*, vol. LXVII, no. 3 (July, 1949); Congressional Quarterly, Inc., *Guide to U.S. Elections* (Washington, D.C., 1975); Roy Glashan, *American Governors and Gubernatorial Elections, 1775-1975* (Stillwater, Minnesota, 1975).

FORT, John Franklin, 1908-1911

Born on March 20, 1852 in Pemberton, New Jersey, son of Andrew Heisler and Hannah A. (Brown) Fort. Married to Charlotte E. Stainsby on April 22, 1876; father of Margretta, Franklin W., and Leslie R. Fort. Attended Pennington Seminary; studied law with Edward M. Paxson, Garitt S. Cannon and Ewan Merritt; received an LL.B. from Albany Law School in 1872; admitted to the bar in 1873. Served as a journal clerk of the New Jersey House of Assembly for one year; began law practice in Newark, New Jersey; appointed Judge of the First District Court of the City of Newark in 1878, serving in that capacity until his resignation in 1883. Fort also served as a delegate-at-large from New Jersey to the Republican National Conventions of 1884 and 1896; as chairman of the New Jersey Republican Conventions of 1889 and 1895; as a member of the New Jersey Constitutional Commission in 1894; as president of the East Orange National Bank; as founder and member of the Board of Trustees of the Newark Security Savings Bank; and as director of the City Trust Company of Newark and the Essex County Trust Company of East Orange,

New Jersey. He was appointed Judge of the Essex Court of Common Pleas in 1896 to fill the vacancy caused by the resignation of Andrew Kirkpatrick, and was subsequently appointed to a full term; was also appointed as a Justice of the New Jersey Supreme Court in May 1900 for a full term of seven years. As the Republican gubernatorial candidate, Fort was elected Governor of New Jersey by popular vote on November 5, 1907, defeating the Democratic candidate, Frank S. Katzenbach, by a vote of 194,313 to 186,300. Inaugurated on January 21, 1908, Fort was an advocate of reforms in corporation, public utility and liquor laws. He also recommended the abolition of useless state agencies. Because the New Jersey Constitution of 1844 prohibited a governor from succeeding himself, Fort left office on January 17, 1911 and returned to his banking interests. He served as a delegate to the Progressive Convention in 1912; as a special United States envoy to the Dominican Republic in 1914 and to Haiti in 1915; and as a member of the Federal Trade Commission until 1919, when he retired to private life. Fort died on November 16, 1920 in South Orange, New Jersey. Bibliography: *New York Times* (November 18, 1920); Walter E. Edge, "New Jersey During the Past Half Century," *Proceedings of the New Jersey Historical Society*, vol. LXVII, no. 3 (July, 1949); Congressional Quarterly, Inc., *Guide to U. S. Elections* (Washington, D. C., 1975); Roy Glashan, *American Governors and Gubernatorial Elections, 1775-1975* (Stillwater, Minnesota, 1975).

WILSON, (Thomas) Woodrow, 1911-1913

Born on December 28, 1856 in Staunton, Virginia, son of the Reverend Joseph Ruggles Wilson, a Presbyterian minister, and Jessie (Woodrow) Wilson. Brother of Marion, Annie Josephine and Joseph Ruggles Wilson. Married to Ellen Louise Axson on June 24, 1885; after her death, remarried to Edith (Bolling) Galt on December 18, 1915; father of Margaret Woodrow, Jessie Woodrow and Eleanor Randolph Wilson by his first marriage. Privately educated; attended Davidson College in Davidson, North Carolina from 1873 to 1874; graduated from Princeton in 1879; attended the University of Virginia Law School from 1879 to 1881. Established a law office in Atlanta, Georgia in 1882; began graduate study at Johns Hopkins University in 1883. Served as associate professor of history at Bryn Mawr College from 1885 to 1888; as professor of history and political economy at Wesleyan University, Middletown, Connecticut from 1888 to 1890; and as professor of jurisprudence and political economy at Princeton University from 1890 to 1902. Elected president of Princeton University on June 9, 1902, serving in that capacity until his resignation on October 20, 1910. As the Democratic gubernatorial candidate, Wilson was elected Governor of New Jersey by popular vote on November 8, 1910 defeating the Republican candidate, Vivian M. Lewis, by a vote of 233,682 to 184,626; he was inaugurated on January 17, 1911. During his administration, Wilson succeeded in getting a series of reforms approved in the State Legislature, including a primary election law, an employers' liability law, a corrupt practices act, and a public utilities act. In addition, a law was enacted which permitted cities to adopt the commission form of government, and various school reform laws were passed. Wilson left office on March 3, 1913, the day before his inauguration as President of the United States. He served two terms as president, from March 4, 1913 to March 3, 1921, and received the Nobel Peace Prize on December 10, 1920 for his work in founding the League of Nations. After leaving the presidency, he formed a law partnership with Bainbridge Colby. Author among other works, of *Congressional Government, A Study in American Politics* (1885), *The State: Elements of Historical and Practical Politics* (1889), *Division and Reunion, 1829-1889* (1893), *George Washington* (1896), *A History of the American People* (1902), and *Constitutional Government in the United States* (1908). Wilson died on February 3, 1924 and was buried in the National Cathedral, Washington, D. C. Bibliography: Henry A. Turner, "Woodrow Wilson and the New Jersey Legislature," *Proceedings of the New Jersey Historical Society*, vol. LXXIV, no. 1 (January, 1956); Ransom E. Noble, "Four Wilson Campaign Speeches," *Proceedings of the New Jersey Historical Society*, vol. LXXVII, nos. 2 & 3 (April and July, 1959); Congressional Quarterly, Inc., *Guide to U. S. Elections* (Washington, D. C., 1975); Roy Glashan, *American Governors and Gubernatorial Elections, 1775-1975* (Stillwater, Minnesota, 1975).

FIELDER, James Fairman, 1913, 1914-1917

Born on February 26, 1867 in Jersey City, Hudson County, New Jersey, son of George B., Register of Hudson County and a member of the Forty-third Congress, and Eleanor A. (Brinkerhoff) Fielder; an Episcopalian. Brother of George B. Fielder, Jr. Married to Mabel Crowell Miller on June 4, 1895; no children. Attended the public schools of Jersey City, and Selleck School in Norwalk, Connecticut; received an LL.B. degree from Columbia University Law School in 1887; admitted to the bar in 1888 and entered the law office of his uncle, William Brinkerhoff. Elected to the New Jersey House of Assembly in 1903 and 1904; elected to the New Jersey Senate in 1907 and 1910, serving as President of the Senate in 1913. By virtue of his position as President of the New Jersey Senate, Fielder assumed the New Jersey governorship on March 3, 1913 upon the resignation of President-elect Woodrow Wilson, and served in this capacity until October 28, 1913, when he resigned. As the Democratic gubernatorial candidate, Fielder was elected Governor of New Jersey by popular vote on November 4, 1913, defeating the Republican candidate, former New Jersey Governor Edward C. Stokes, by a vote of 173,148 to 140,298; inaugurated on January 20, 1914. During his administration the Pure Food Law was strengthened; a bank stock law and an inheritance tax law were passed; and legislation safeguarding the health of industrial employees was enacted. Because the New Jersey Constitution of 1844 prohibited a governor from succeeding himself, Fielder left office on January 16, 1917 and returned to his private law practice. He was appointed Vice-Chancellor of the New Jersey Court of Chancery in 1920. Fielder died on December 2, 1954 in Montclair, New Jersey. Bibliography: Joseph E. Folsom, ed., *Cyclopedia of New Jersey, Historical and Biographical*, 3 vols. (New York, 1921); *New York Times* (December 3, 1954); Congressional Quarterly, Inc., *Guide to U. S. Elections* (Washington, D. C., 1975); Roy Glashan, *American Governors and Gubernatorial Elections, 1775-1975* (Stillwater, Minnesota, 1975).

TAYLOR, Leon R., 1913-1914

Born on October 26, 1883 in Asbury Park, New Jersey, son of the Reverend Thomas R. Taylor, a Baptist minister. Attended Denison University in Ohio for three years; studied law and was admitted to the New Jersey Bar. Served as a member of the New Jersey House of Assembly for three terms; a Democrat. As Speaker of the New Jersey House of Assembly, Taylor assumed the New Jersey governorship on October 28, 1913 upon the resignation of James F. Fielder. He served until January 20, 1914, completing the gubernatorial term begun by Woodrow Wilson. He then returned to private law practice. From 1917 until 1919 he served as a Captain in the Red Cross, but ill health eventually forced him to retire. Subsequently, he moved to Colorado. Taylor died on April 1, 1924 in Denver, Colorado. Bibliography: Joseph E. Folsom, ed., *Cyclopedia of New Jersey, Historical and Biographical*, 3 vols. (New York, 1921); Irving S. Kull, *New Jersey: A History*, 5 vols. (New York, 1930); *New York Times* (April 3, 1924); Roy Glashan, *American Governors and Gubernatorial Elections, 1775-1975* (Stillwater, Minnesota, 1975).

FIELDER, James Fairman, 1913, 1914-1917

EDGE, Walter Evans, 1917-1919, 1944-1947

Born on November 20, 1873 in Philadelphia, Pennsylvania, son of William and Mary Elizabeth (Evans) Edge; an Episcopalian. Brother of Howard Hamilton Edge. Married Lady Lee Phillips on June 10, 1907; after her death, remarried to Camilla Loyal Ashe Sewall on December 9, 1922; father of Walter Evans Edge, Jr., by the first marriage, and Loyal Howard, Camilla Sewall and Mary Esther Edge by the second marriage. Moved to Pleasantville, New Jersey, where he attended the public schools. Began a business career as a "printer's devil" for the *Atlantic Review* in Atlantic City, New Jersey; worked with the Dorland Advertising Agency in Atlantic City and made it a world-wide concern; established daily hotel newspapers in Atlantic City and Jacksonville, Florida. Served as a Second Lieutenant in Company "F," Fourth New Jersey Volunteer Infantry during the Spanish-American War; after the war became a Captain with Company "L," Third Regiment of the New Jersey National Guard; commissioned Lieutenant-Colonel and made Chief of the Ordinance Department on the staff of Major-General C. Edward Murray of the New Jersey National Guard. Served as journal clerk of the New Jersey Senate from 1897 to 1899 and as secretary from 1901 to 1904; served as a Republican presidential elector in 1904; as a member of the New Jersey House of Assembly in 1910; and as a member of the New Jersey Senate from 1911 to 1916, holding the office of Senate President in 1915. As the Republican gubernatorial candidate, Edge was elected Governor of New Jersey by popular vote on November 7, 1916, defeating the Democratic candidate, H. Otto Wittpen, by a vote of 247,343 to 177,696; inaugurated on January 16, 1917. During his administration, all state departmental functions were coordinated; emergency war measures were enacted; a corrupt practices bill was passed; the Hudson River vehicular tunnel, the Delaware River

Bridge, and a state highway system were authorized and financed. Edge left office on May 16, 1919, having been elected to the United States Senate the previous year; he was reelected in 1924. Edge served as a member of the Senate from March 4, 1919 to November 21, 1929, when he resigned, having been appointed Ambassador to France; served until March 4, 1933. Edge was again elected Governor of New Jersey by popular vote on November 2, 1943, defeating his Democratic opponent, Vincent J. Murphy, by a vote of 634,363 to 506,604; inaugurated on January 18, 1944. During this administration, all public borrowing was stopped; a 25 million dollar post-war surplus fund was established; the State Civil Service was completely reorganized; a Department of Economic Development was established; legislation controlling strikes by public utilities was passed; and an anti-discrimination agency was established within the Department of Education. Because the New Jersey Constitution of 1844 prohibited a governor from succeeding himself, Edge left office on January 21, 1947 and resumed his newspaper and advertising interests. Edge died on October 29, 1956 in New York City; he was buried in Northbrook Cemetery in Downingtown, Pennsylvania. Bibliography: Irving S. Kull, *New Jersey: A History*, 5 vols. (New York, 1930); John F. Sly, "Walter Evans Edge, 1873-1956: A Tribute," *Proceedings of the New Jersey Historical Society*, vol. LXXIX, no. 1 (January, 1961); Congressional Quarterly, Inc., *Guide to U. S. Elections* (Washington, D. C., 1975); Roy Glashan, *American Governors and Gubernatorial Elections, 1775-1975* (Stillwater, Minnesota, 1975).

RUNYON, William Nelson, 1919-1920

Born on March 5, 1871 in Plainfield, New Jersey, son of Nelson and Wilhelmina Frances (Trow) Runyon; an Episcopalian. Married to Florence M. MacDonald on January 1, 1913; father of Jane Trow, William Nelson, Frederic Walter and Florence Felicia Runyon. Received an A.B. from Yale in 1892 and an LL.B. from New York Law School in 1894. Served as a member of the Common Council of Plainfield, New Jersey from 1897 to 1898; served as City Judge of Plainfield from 1899 to 1910; served as a member of the New Jersey House of Assembly from 1915 to 1917, and as a member of the New Jersey Senate from 1918 to 1922; a Republican. As President of the New Jersey Senate, Runyon assumed the New Jersey governorship on May 16, 1919, when Governor Walter E. Edge resigned to enter the United States Senate; served until January 13, 1920, when his term as president of the State Senate expired. He was an unsuccessful candidate in the New Jersey gubernatorial election of November 7, 1922, losing to George S. Silzer, 427,206 votes to 383,312. Runyon was appointed Judge of the United States District Court for the District of New Jersey on January 27, 1923, serving in that position until his death. Runyon died on November 9, 1931 and was buried in Hillside Cemetery, Plainfield, New Jersey. Bibliography: Irving S. Kull, *New Jersey: A History*, 5 vols. (New York, 1930); *New York Times* (November 10, 1931); Congressional Quarterly, Inc., *Guide to U. S. Elections* (Washington, D. C., 1975); Roy Glashan, *American Governors and Gubernatorial Elections, 1775-1975* (Stillwater, Minnesota, 1975).

CASE, Clarence E., 1920

Born on September 24, 1877 in Jersey City, Hudson County, New Jersey, son of Phillip and Amanda Case; a Protestant. Brother of Clifford Case. Married Anna Gist Rogers on January 29, 1913; after her death, remarried to Mrs. Ruth Weldon Griggs in 1925; father of Mrs. George S. Thompson, Philip and Clarence E. Case, Jr. Received an A.B. from Rutgers in 1900 and an LL.B. from New York Law School in 1902. Appointed clerk of the Judiciary Committee of the New Jersey Senate in 1908 and served in that position for two years; practiced law in Somerville, New Jersey; elected to the New Jersey Senate in 1918; a Republican. Case was named Governor of New Jersey by the State Legislature on January 13, 1920, upon the expiration of William N. Runyon's term as Senate President. Runyon had assumed the New Jersey governorship on May 16, 1919, when Governor Walter E. Edge resigned to become a member of the United States Senate. Case's term lasted until January 20, 1920, when Edward I. Edwards was inaugurated as Governor of New Jersey. Case was appointed chairman of the New Jersey Legislative Committee investigating irregularities in the Democratic administration of Hudson County, New Jersey; was appointed Justice of the New Jersey Supreme Court in 1929; and became Chief Justice on March 15, 1945. He served in the latter capacity until September 15, 1948, when he became Senior Associate Justice due to court reorganization. Retired from the bench in 1952; served as chairman of the New Jersey Law Enforcement Council in 1952. Case died on September 3, 1961 in Somerville, New Jersey. Bibliography: Irving S. Kull, *New Jersey: A History*, 5 vols. (New York, 1930); Bennett M. Rich, *The Government and Administration of New Jersey* (New York, 1957); *New York Times* (September 4, 1961); Roy Glashan, *American Governors and Gubernatorial Elections, 1775-1975* (Stillwater, Minnesota, 1975).

EDWARDS, Edward Irving, 1920-1923

Born on December 1, 1863 in Jersey City, New Jersey, son of William W. and Emma J. (Nation) Edwards; an Episcopalian. Brother of Georgette, William D., Jennie, Stephen S. and Emma Edwards. Married to Jule Blanche Smith on November 14, 1888; father of Edward Irving, Jr., and Elizabeth Jule Edwards. Attended the public schools of Jersey City; attended New York University from 1884 to 1886; studied law in the office of his brother, William D. Edwards. Engaged in banking and general contracting. Served as assistant to the president of the First National Bank of Jersey City in 1903, as cashier in 1911, as president in 1916, and as chairman of the board in 1925. Also served as vice-president of the Merchants' National Bank, and as a director of the National Paper and Type Company, the Raritan River Railroad Company, and the Standard Motor Construction Company. Elected Comptroller of New Jersey, serving from 1911 to 1917; elected to the New Jersey Senate, serving from November 5, 1918 to January 1, 1920. As the Democratic gubernatorial candidate, Edwards was elected Governor of New Jersey by popular vote on November 4, 1919, defeating his Republican opponent, Newton A. K. Bugbee, by a vote of 217,486 to 202,976; he was inaugurated on January 20, 1920. During his administration, the New Jersey Legislature ratified the Eighteenth Amendment to the United States Constitution; female employees required to submit to a medical examination were given the right to see a female doctor; workmen's compensation was extended to include 50 dollars each for medical and hospital services, with no time limits; and the Commissioner of Labor was directed to return to employers sums collected from them in cases where employees died leaving no dependents. Because the New Jersey Constitution of 1844 prohibited a governor from succeeding himself, Edwards left office on January 16, 1923. Elected as a Democrat to the United States Senate, Edwards served from March 4, 1923 to March 3, 1929. He was an unsuccessful candidate for reelection in 1928. Edwards died on January 26, 1931 in Jersey City, New Jersey, and was buried there in New York Bay Cemetery. Bibliography: Irving S. Kull, *New Jersey: A History*, 5 vols. (New York, 1930); Bennett M. Rich, *The Government and Administration of New Jersey* (New York, 1957); Congressional Quarterly, Inc., *Guide to U. S. Elections* (Washington, D.C., 1975); Roy Glashan, *American Governors and Gubernatorial Elections, 1775-1975* (Stillwater, Minnesota, 1975).

SILZER, George Sebastian, 1923-1926

Born on April 14, 1870 in New Brunswick, New Jersey, son of Theodore C. and Christina (Zimmerman) Silzer; an Episcopalian. Married to Henrietta T. Waite on April 18, 1898; father of Parker Waite Silzer. Attended the public schools of New Brunswick; studied law. Admitted to the New Jersey Bar in 1892; served as a member of the Board of Aldermen of New Brunswick, New Jersey from 1892 to 1898; served as chairman of the Middlesex County Democratic Committee for ten years. Twice elected to the New Jersey Senate, serving from 1907 to 1912; appointed Prosecutor of the Pleas of Middlesex County, serving from 1912 to 1914; appointed Circuit Judge by Governors Fielder and Edwards, serving from 1914 to 1922. As the Democratic gubernatorial candidate, Silzer was elected Governor of New Jersey by popular vote on November 7, 1922, defeating his Republican opponent, W. Runyon, by a vote of 427,206 to 383,312; he was inaugurated on January 16, 1923. During his administration, the payment of the soldier bonus was extended to 1924; night work for women in factories was prohibited; cities were authorized to adopt the city-manager form of government; a Uniform Arbitrations Act was adopted; and a commission was appointed to negotiate a conservation agreement for the Delaware River with New York and Pennsylvania. Because the New Jersey Constitution of 1844 prohibited a governor from succeeding himself, Silzer left office on January 19, 1926 and returned to his law practice in Newark. He was appointed chairman of the Port of New York Authority, serving from 1926 to 1928. He engaged in various banking and business interests, as well as in his law practice, until his death. Silzer died on October 16, 1940 in Metuchen, New Jersey. Bibliography: Irving S. Kull, *New Jersey: A History*, 5 vols. (New York, 1930); *New York Times* (October 17, 1940); Congressional Quarterly, Inc., *Guide to U. S. Elections* (Washington, D. C., 1975); Roy Glashan, *American Governors and Gubernatorial Elections, 1775-1975* (Stillwater, Minnesota, 1975).

MOORE, (Arthur) Harry, 1926-1929, 1932-1935, 1938-1941

Born on July 3, 1879 in Jersey City, New Jersey, son of Robert White and Martha (McComb) Moore; member of the Reformed Church. Married to Jennie Hastings Stevens on March 28, 1911. Attended public schools and received private tutoring; attended Cooper Union, New York City and received an LL.B. from the New Jersey Law School in 1924. Admitted to the New Jersey Bar in 1922. Served as secretary to Mayor Wittpenn of Jersey City from 1908 to 1911; served as City Tax Collector of Jersey City from 1911 to 1913; elected the first City Commissioner of Jersey City and served from 1913 to 1925. As the Democratic gubernatorial candidate, Moore was elected Governor of New Jersey by popular vote on November 3, 1925, defeating the Republican candidate, Arthur Whitney, by a vote of 471,549 to 433,121, and was inaugurated on January 19, 1926. He was again elected on November 3, 1931, defeating the Republican nominee, David Baird, Jr., by a vote of 735,504 to 505,451; he was inaugurated for a second time on January 19, 1932. During Moore's first administration, a commission of six was formed to revise the state's "Blue Laws;" a statute was enacted forbidding the issuance of an injunction by any state court against striking or strike picketing, providing that strike pickets maintained an interval of ten paces; and maximum compensation for injured workmen under the state compensation system was increased by statute to 20 dollars per week. During Moore's second administration, the Altman Act, empowering the Commissioner of Banking and Insurance to refuse payment to a state bank's depositors in whole or in part, when the condition of a bank should require delay, was passed; a narcotics law, giving the State Department of Health authority over the sale and use of narcotic drugs, was approved; a system of control over traffic in liquor was enacted; and a State Planning Board was created. Because the New Jersey Constitution of 1844 prohibited a governor from succeeding himself, Moore left office on January 15, 1929. He again resigned the governorship on January 3, 1935 to begin his term as a United States Senator. Moore served in that capacity from January 3, 1935 to January 17, 1938, when he resigned, having been elected Governor of New Jersey for a third time. As the Democratic gubernatorial candidate, Moore was elected Governor of New Jersey by popular vote on November 2, 1937, defeating the Republican candidate, Lester H. Clee, by a vote of 746,033 to 700,767, and was inaugurated on January 18, 1938. During this administration, the parimutuel system of betting at horse races was established; authority was granted to the state to enforce price-fixing contracts between producer and retailer of gasoline and liquor; and the sale of merchandise below dealer's cost was prohibited. Because the New Jersey Constitution of 1844 prohibited a governor from succeeding himself, Moore left office on January 21, 1941 and resumed his law practice in Jersey City, New Jersey. Moore died on November 18, 1952, and was buried in New York Bay Cemetery, Jersey City, New Jersey. Bibliography: Irving S. Kull, *New Jersey: A History*, 5 vols. (New York, 1930); Bennett M. Rich, *The Government and Administration of New Jersey* (New York, 1957); Congressional Quarterly, Inc., *Guide to U. S. Elections* (Washington, D. C., 1975); Roy Glashan, *American Governors and Gubernatorial Elections, 1775-1975* (Stillwater, Minnesota, 1975).

LARSON, Morgan Foster, 1929-1932

Born on June 15, 1882 in Perth Amboy, New Jersey; son of Peter, a blacksmith, and Regina (Knudson) Larson; a Presbyterian. Married Jennie Brogger in 1914; after her death, remarried to Adda Schmidt on November 20, 1930; father of Joan and Jorgan Foster Larson by his second marriage. Attended the public schools of Perth Amboy; received a B.S. degree in 1907 and a C.E. degree in 1910 from Cooper Union, New York City. Served as county engineer of Middlesex County, New Jersey from 1907 to 1910; organized the engineering firm of Larson and Fox in Perth Amboy in 1910, and continued as a partner until 1953. Served as city engineer for Perth Amboy from 1917 to 1923, and engineer for Middlesex County from 1923 to 1927. Elected to the New Jersey Senate in 1921, 1924 and 1927, serving as Majority Leader in 1925 and Senate President in 1926. As the Republican gubernatorial candidate, Larson was elected Governor of New Jersey by popular vote on November 6, 1928, defeating the Democratic candidate, William L. Dill, by a vote of 824,005 to 671,728; he was inaugurated on January 15, 1929. During Larson's administration, restrictions on building and loan associations were strengthened; the Jones Law, an act to regulate advertising on roadside billboards, was passed; the Holland Tunnel Commission was abolished and its powers transferred to the Port of New York Authority; issues of municipal bonds were limited to fifteen percent of the assessed taxable values; a centralized State Tax Department was created; provision was made for the organization of a State Purchasing Department and a central accounting department; the quarterly publication of state bank deposits was required; and the Delaware River Port Authority was created. Because the New Jersey Constitution of 1844 prohibited a governor from succeeding himself, Larson left office on January 19, 1932, resuming private practice as a consulting engineer. He was named New Jersey Commissioner of Conservation, serving from 1945 to 1948; he served as a consulting engineer with the Division of Water Policy and Supply of New Jersey from 1948 until his death. Larson died on March 21, 1961 in Perth Amboy, New Jersey. Bibliography: Bennett M. Rich, *The Government and Administration of New Jersey* (New York, 1957); *New York Times* (March 23, 1961); Congressional Quarterly, Inc., *Guide to U. S. Elections* (Washington, D. C., 1975); Roy Glashan, *American Governors and Gubernatorial Elections, 1775-1975* (Stillwater, Minnesota, 1975).

MOORE, (Arthur) Harry, 1926-1929, 1932-1935, 1938-1941

PRALL, Horace Griggs, 1935

Born on March 6, 1881 near Ringoes, Hunterdon County, New Jersey, son of Abraham J., a farmer, and Mary (Hill) Prall; a Presbyterian. Married to Inez Post on November 21, 1925; father of Horace Griggs, Jr., John Schofield, III and Thomas Peter Prall. Attended the State Model School at Trenton, New Jersey; received his B.A. from Harvard in 1906 and an LL.B. from New York University Law School in 1908. Admitted to the New York Bar in 1909 and practiced in New York until 1913. Admitted to the New Jersey Bar in 1915 and began practice at Lambertville, New Jersey in 1916. Served as a member of the New Jersey Assembly in 1926 and 1927; served as a member of the New Jersey Senate from 1928 to 1936, holding the position of president during the 1935-1936 session. Mason; Shriner; Odd Fellow. A Republican. Under New Jersey law, the President of the State Senate assumes the office of governor if a vacancy occurs. When A. H. Moore resigned as chief executive, C. R. Powell, President of the State Senate, assumed the office; however, when Prall succeeded Powell as Senate President, he also became Governor. He served from January 8, 1935 to January 15, 1935, when the newly-elected governor was inaugurated. Appointed Judge of the Court of Common Pleas in 1937 for a five-year term; vice president, Delaware Valley Protective Association. Prall died on April 23, 1951 in Trenton, New Jersey, Bibliography: Bennett M. Rich, *The Government and Administration of New Jersey* (New York, 1957); *New York Times* (April 24, 1951); Congressional Quarterly, Inc., *Guide to U.S. Elections* (Washington, D. C., 1975); Roy Glashan, *American Governors and Gubernatorial Elections, 1775-1975* (Stillwater, Minnesota, 1975).

HOFFMAN, Harold Giles, 1935-1938

Born on February 7, 1896 in South Amboy, New Jersey, son of Frank and Ada Crawford (Thom) Hoffman; a Methodist. Brother of Frank, Fletcher and Donald Hoffman. Married to Lillie Moss on September 20, 1919; father of Ada Moss, Lillie Moss and Hope Hoffman. Graduated from South Amboy High School in 1913. Enlisted as a private in Company "H," Third Regiment, New Jersey Infantry on July 25, 1917; promoted through the ranks to Captain, commanding Headquarters Company, One Hundred and Fourteenth Regiment Infantry, Twenty-ninth Division in 1918; discharged on June 4, 1919; became a Major in the United States Reserve in 1925. Served as secretary-treasurer of South Amboy from 1920 to 1925; as a member of the New Jersey House of Assembly in 1923 and 1924; as Mayor of South Amboy in 1925 and 1926; as president of the Middlesex County Bankers' Association in 1925 and 1926; and as a delegate to the New Jersey Republican Conventions of 1934, 1935, 1936 and 1937, and to the Republican National Convention of 1936. Twice elected to the United States House of Representatives, serving from March 4, 1927 to March 3, 1931; was not a candidate for renomination; appointed Motor Vehicle Commissioner of New Jersey, serving from 1931 to 1935. As the Republican gubernatorial candidate, Hoffman was elected Governor of New Jersey by popular vote on November 6, 1934, defeating the Democratic nominee, William L. Dill, by a vote of 686,440 to 674,096 and was inaugurated on January 15, 1935. Hoffman's administration was marked by continual strife between the governor and the legislature over methods to meet the cost of the state's contribution for relief of the poor. The passage of a two percent sales tax, in part intended to provide funds for state unemployment benefits, was later repealed. Also while Hoffman was governor, the New Jersey Compensation Commission and the Banking Advisory Board were created; the Highway Commission of four members was abolished and replaced by a single commissioner to be appointed by the governor; provisions were made for uniform policies to cover accident and health insurance; and anthracite coal entering the state by truck was required to bear a certificate of origin. Because the New Jersey Constitution of 1844 prohibited a governor from succeeding himself, Hoffman left office on January 18, 1938. Hoffman was appointed executive director of the New Jersey Unemployment Compensation Commission in 1938 and served in that capacity until June 15, 1942, when he was granted leave to reenter the United States Army. He served as a Major in the Transportation Corps, and was promoted to Lieutenant-Colonel on December 15, 1942. On June 24, 1946 Hoffman was discharged with the rank of Colonel and resumed his position as executive director of the New Jersey Unemployment Compensation Commission. Author of *Mile A Minute Men; Getting Away With Murder;* and *The Crime, The Case, The Challenge.* Hoffman died on June 4, 1954 in New York City, and was buried in Christ Church Cemetery, South Amboy, New Jersey. Bibliography: Bennett M. Rich, *The Government and Administration of New Jersey* (New York, 1957); Duane Lockard, *New Jersey Governor: A Study in Political Power* (New Brunswick, New Jersey, 1964); Congressional Quarterly, Inc., *Guide to U. S. Elections* (Washington, D. C., 1975); Roy Glashan, *American Governors and Gubernatorial Elections, 1775-1975* (Stillwater, Minnesota, 1975).

MOORE, (Arthur) Harry, 1926-1929, 1932-1935, 1938-1941

EDISON, Charles, 1941-1944

Born on August 30, 1890 in West Orange, New Jersey; son of Thomas Alva, the inventor, and Mina (Miller) Edison; a Presbyterian. Brother of Madeleine and Theodore M. Edison; half-brother of Marion Estell, Thomas Alva, Jr., and William Edison. Married to Carolyn Hawkins on March 27, 1918; no children. Received preparatory education at Carteret Academy, Orange, New Jersey and Hotchkiss School, Lakeville, Connecticut; received an E.E. degree from the Massachusetts Institute of Technology in 1913. Moved to Greenwich Village, where he helped finance the Thimble Theater and a literary magazine; directed the manufacture of war materials during World War I; entered Thomas A. Edison, Inc. in 1919, becoming its president in 1932. Appointed vice-chairman of the New Jersey Recovery Board in 1933; served as a member of the Regional Labor Board and the National Industrial Recovery Board; served as NRA Compliance Director and State Director of the National Emergency Council; served as a consultant and regional director of the Federal Housing Administration; appointed Assistant Secretary of the Navy in November, 1936 and Secretary of the Navy on December 30, 1939, serving until June 24, 1940. As the Democratic gubernatorial candidate, Edison was elected Governor of New Jersey by popular vote on November 5, 1940, defeating the Republican nominee, Robert C. Hendrickson, by a vote of 984,407 to 920,512, and was inaugurated on January 21, 1941. During his administration, New Jersey's military and industrial defenses were strengthened in order to achieve maximum cooperation between state and local officials in connection with the national defense program; appointed judges of the Courts of Errors and Appeals, and Advisory Masters in the Court of Chancery were prohibited from practicing law in any of the state courts; the governor was given the right to investigate state agencies; a five-member Mediation Board was created; discrimination on the basis of sex and marital status was prohibited; and appropriations were made for the operation of the New Jersey State Guard. Because the New Jersey Constitution of 1844 prohibited a governor from succeeding himself, Edison left office on January 18, 1944. Edison served as chairman of the Board of Trustees of Town Hall, Inc. from May 1944 to May 1947; as president of the National Municipal League from 1947 to 1950; as chairman of the Board of Thomas A. Edison, Inc. from 1950 to 1957 and of McGraw-Edison Company from 1957 to 1961. Afterwards, he retired to private life. Edison died in New York City on July 31, 1969; funeral services were held at the Madison Avenue Presbyterian Church, New York City. Bibliography: Bennett M. Rich, *The Government and Administration of New Jersey* (New York, 1957); *New York Times* (August 1, 1969); Congressional Quarterly, Inc., *Guide to U. S. Elections* (Washington, D. C., 1975); Roy Glashan, *American Governors and Gubernatorial Elections, 1775-1975* (Stillwater, Minnesota 1975).

EDGE, Walter Evans, 1917-1919, 1944-1947

DRISCOLL, Alfred Eastlack, 1947-1954

Born on October 25, 1902 in Pittsburgh, Pennsylvania, son of Alfred Robie and Mattie (Eastlack) Driscoll; a Presbyterian. Married to Antoinette Ware Tatum in May 1932; father of Patricia Ware, Alfred Tatum and Peter Eastlack Driscoll. Graduated from high school in Haddonfield, New Jersey; received an A.B. degree from Williams College, Williamstown, Massachusetts in 1925 and an LL.B. from Harvard University in 1928. Admitted to the New Jersey Bar in 1929 and entered the law firm of Starr, Summerhill and Lloyd; served as a member of the Haddonfield Board of Education from 1929 until 1937, when he became president of that body; elected to the Haddonfield Borough Commission, serving as director of revenues and finances; served as a member of the New Jersey Senate from 1938 to 1941, holding the position of Senate Majority Leader in 1940; accepted the position of State Alcoholic Beverage Control Commissioner on August 11, 1941. As the Republican gubernatorial candidate, Driscoll was elected Governor of New Jersey by popular vote on November 5, 1946, defeating the Democratic candidate, Lewis G. Hansen, by a vote of 807,378 to 585,960. He was reelected on November 8, 1949, defeating his Democratic opponent, Elmer H. Wene, by a vote of 885,882 to 810,022. Driscoll was inaugurated on January 21, 1947. A significant event during his administration was an extensive revision of the New Jersey Constitution. Under this new constitution, a Bill of Rights was established; collective bargaining was specified as a means of ending labor disputes; and more power was given to the governor by granting him the privilege of appointing many more officials. Also, the governor's term was extended to four years, and he was permitted to succeed himself for one term. Legislation passed during Driscoll's administration included: permission for the state government to seize and operate all public utilities in which service was interrupted or threatened by labor disputes; repeal of the intangible personal property tax and its replacement by a net worth tax; adoption of an "equal pay for equal work" law designed to eliminate salary discrimination against women; and reorganization of state agencies. Because the New Jersey Constitution of 1947 prohibits a governor from succeeding himself for more than one term, Driscoll left office on January 19, 1954 and returned to his business interests. He served as a member of the executive committee of the Warner-Lambert Company, Inc. from 1954 to 1971, and as its president from 1954 to 1967, and its chairman in 1967. He was vice-chairman of the President's Commission on Intergovernmental Relations during 1954 and 1955; president of the National Municipal League from 1963 to 1967; and chairman of the New Jersey Turnpike Authority and the New Jersey Tax Policy Commission from 1969 to 1975. Driscoll died on March 9, 1975. Bibliography: *The New York Times* (November 6, 1946); *The New York Times* (November 9, 1949); Congressional Quarterly, Inc., *Guide to U.S. Elections* (Washington, D.C., 1975); Roy Glashan, *American Governors and Gubernatorial Elections, 1775-1975* (Stillwater, Minnesota, 1975).

MEYNER, Robert Baumle, 1954-1962

Born on July 3, 1908 in Easton, Pennsylvania, son of Gustave Herman, a textile worker, and Mary Sophia (Baumle) Meyner; a Protestant. Married to Helen Day Stevenson on January 19, 1957. Graduated from Phillipsburg High School (New Jersey) in 1926. Received an A.B. from Lafayette College in 1930 and an LL.B. from Columbia School of Law in 1933; admitted to the New Jersey Bar in 1934 and served as a law clerk with the firm of Walscheid and Rosenkranz; established his own law office in Phillipsburg, New Jersey in 1936; admitted to practice before the United States Supreme Court in 1940. Defeated for election to the New Jersey Senate in 1941; served as counsel for Warren County, New Jersey in 1942; was an unsuccessful candidate for the United States House of Representatives in 1946; elected to the New Jersey Senate in 1947, serving as minority leader in 1950; permanent chairman of the Democratic State Convention in 1951; defeated for reelection in 1951; served as an alternate delegate-at-large to the Democratic National Convention in 1952. As the Democratic gubernatorial candidate, Meyner was elected Governor of New Jersey by popular vote on November 3, 1953, defeating the Republican candidate, Paul L. Troast, by a vote of 962,710 to 809,068. He was reelected on November 5, 1957, defeating his Republican opponent, Malcolm S. Forbes, by a vote of 1,101,130 to 897,321. Meyner was inaugurated on January 19, 1954. During his administration, Meyner made strenuous efforts to combat organized crime and official corruption; a new compensation schedule for state employees was adopted; the New Jersey Neuropsychiatric Institution was established; absentee voting by civilians was authorized; benefits under workmen's compensation were increased; bingo and raffles conducted for charitable purposes were legalized; the "secret caucus" system in the State Legislature was abolished; and the system of motor vehicle registration and fees was completely revised. Also, a comprehensive highway program was inaugurated; the Green Acres Land Acquisition Act and the Green Acres Bond Act were passed, enabling the state to take steps to acquire 60 million dollars worth of additional lands for recreation and conservation purposes; the General Assembly was reapportioned and a new congressional district was created; the Delaware River Basin Compact was ratified; and the establishment of county improvement authorities and private urban renewal corporations was authorized. Because the New Jersey Constitution of 1947 prohibits a governor from succeeding himself for more than one term, Meyner left office on January 16, 1962 and resumed his law practice with the firm of Meyner, Landis and Verdon of Newark, New Jersey. He was defeated in his attempt to return to the State House in 1969, when defeated by Republican William Cahill. Meyner served as director of the Prudential Insurance Company; Engelhard Minerals and Chemicals Corporation; Phillipsburg National Bank and Trust Company; 1st National State Bank of Newark; U.S. Savings Bank of Newark; and the Delaware and Bound Brook Railroad. Bibliography: Bennett M. Rich, *The Government and Administration of New Jersey* (New York, 1957); *Facts on File Yearbook, 1954* (New York, 1955); Congressional Quarterly, Inc., *Guide to U.S. Elections* (Washington, D.C., 1975); Roy Glashan, *American Governors and Gubernatorial Elections, 1775-1975* (Stillwater, Minnesota, 1975).

HUGHES, Richard Joseph, 1962-1970

Born on August 10, 1909 in Florence, New Jersey, son of Richard Paul and Veronica (Gallagher) Hughes; a Roman Catholic. Brother of Mrs. Edward Hulse, Mrs. Kathryn Cope and the Reverend Joseph Hughes. Married first to Miriam McGrory in 1934; after her death, remarried to Mrs. Elizabeth (Sullivan) Murphy on May 7, 1954; father of Richard P., Robert F., John and Mary Hughes by the first marriage, and Brian, Helen and Thomas More Hughes by the second marriage; step-father of William Michael, Patrick and Timothy Murphy. Graduated from Cathedral High School in Trenton, New Jersey in 1926; attended St. Charles College, Catonsville, Maryland from 1926 to 1928, and St. Joseph's College, Philadelphia, Pennsylvania in 1928; received an LL.B. degree from New Jersey Law School in 1931. Admitted to the New Jersey Bar in 1932 and established a law practice in Trenton, New Jersey. Elected statewide president of the Young Democrats; elected a member of the Democratic State Committee from Mercer County, New Jersey in 1937; unsuccessful candidate for the United States House of Representatives in 1938; appointed Assistant United States Attorney for the District of New Jersey in 1939, serving in that position until his resignation in 1945; formed a law partnership with Thorn Lord in 1945; appointed Judge of the Mercer County Court in 1948, serving in that capacity until 1952; appointed a Judge of the Superior Court of New Jersey in 1952 and served until 1959, when he resigned to resume his law practice. As the Democratic gubernatorial candidate, Hughes was elected Governor of New Jersey by popular vote on November 7, 1961, defeating the Republican candidate, James P. Mitchell, by a vote of 1,084,194 to 1,049,274. He was reelected on November 2, 1965, defeating his Republican opponent, Wayne Dumont, Jr., by a vote of 1,279,568 to 915,996. He was first inaugurated on January 16, 1962. During Hughes' administration, the state's civil rights law was amended to prohibit discrimination against the aged; the proposed amendment to the U.S. Constitution outlawing poll taxes as a requirement to vote was ratified; and a fiscal note indicating the cost of any legislative proposal affecting state revenues or expenditures was required. Also, residence requirements for voting were liberalized; a three percent sales tax was enacted; and the executive branch of the state government was reorganized and all levels of government were reapportioned. Because the New Jersey Constitution of 1947 prohibits a governor from succeeding himself for more than one term, Hughes left office on January 21, 1970 and resumed his law practice with the firm of Hughes, McElroy, Connell, Foley and Geiser in Newark, New Jersey. He was appointed Chief Justice of the New Jersey Supreme Court in 1973. Bibliography: *Facts on File Yearbook, 1962* (New York, 1963); *New York Times* (November 3, 1965); Congressional Quarterly, Inc., *Guide to U. S. Elections* (Washington, D. C., 1975); Roy Glashan, *American Governors and Gubernatorial Elections, 1775-1975* (Stillwater, Minnesota, 1975).

CAHILL, William Thomas, 1970-1974

Born on June 25, 1912 in Philadelphia, Pennsylvania, son of William P., an Irish immigrant, and Rose J. (Golden) Cahill; a Roman Catholic. Married to Elizabeth B. Myrtetus on February 1, 1941; father of Kathleen, Mary, William, Jr., Regina, John, Patricia, Eileen and Theresa Cahill. Graduated from Camden Catholic High School (New Jersey) in 1929; received a B.A. from St. Joseph's College, Philadelphia in 1933 and an LL.B. from Rutgers in 1937. Served as a special agent of the Federal Bureau of Investigation from October 1937 to May 1938. Admitted to the New Jersey Bar in 1939 and began law practice in Camden, New Jersey. Served as City Prosecutor of Camden during 1944 and 1945; served as First Assistant Prosecutor of Camden County from 1948 to 1951 and Special Deputy Attorney General of New Jersey in 1951; served as a member of the New Jersey House of Assembly from 1951 to 1953. He was not a candidate for reelection but chose to resume his law practice; was six times elected to the United States House of Representatives, serving from January 3, 1959 to January 19, 1970. As the Republican gubernatorial candidate, Cahill was elected Governor by popular vote on November 4, 1969, defeating the Democratic candidate, former Governor Robert B. Meyner, by a vote of 1,411,905 to 911,003. He was inaugurated on January 21, 1970. During his administration, the state sales tax was increased from 3 percent to 5 percent; the New Jersey Supreme Court struck down the existing system of financing the state's public schools; increased tax deductions for elderly citizens were approved; full legal rights were granted to eighteen year-olds; superior court trials for offenses not punishable by imprisonment were eliminated; a State Housing Authority was created; and the structure of the State Tax Commission was revised. Having been defeated in the Democratic primary for the gubernatorial nomination, Cahill left office on January 15, 1974 upon the inauguration of Brendan Byrne, and resumed his law practice. Bibliography: *New York Times* (February 6, 1972); *Facts on File Yearbook, 1973* (New York, 1974); Congressional Quarterly, Inc., *Guide to U. S. Elections* (Washington, D. C., 1975); Roy Glashan, *American Governors and Gubernatorial Elections, 1775-1975* (Stillwater, Minnesota, 1975).

BYRNE, Brendan Thomas, 1974-

Born on April 1, 1924 in West Orange, New Jersey, son of Francis A., a president of the Essex County Tax Board, and Genevieve Thecia (Brennan) Byrne; a Roman Catholic. Married to Jean Featherly on June 27, 1953; father of Brendan Thomas, Susan, Nancy, Timothy, Mary Anne, Barbara and William Byrne. Served in the U. S. Army Air Force from 1943 to 1945, during which time he was decorated with the Distinguished Flying Cross and the Air Medal with three oak leaf clusters. Received an A.B. from Princeton in 1949 and an LL.B. from Harvard Law School in 1951. Admitted to the New Jersey Bar in 1951 and practiced law in Newark, New Jersey from 1951 to 1955; appointed assistant counsel to Governor Robert B. Meyner in 1955 and executive secretary in 1956, serving in that capacity until 1958. Appointed Deputy Attorney in charge of the Essex County Prosecutor's Office during 1958 and 1959; appointed Essex County Prosecutor in 1959, serving in that capacity until 1968; served as president of the New Jersey Public Utilities Commission from 1968 to 1970. Appointed a Judge of the Superior Court of New Jersey, serving from 1970 to 1972; served as assignment judge of Morris, Essex and Warren counties from 1972 to 1974. As the Democratic gubernatorial candidate, Byrne was elected Governor of New Jersey by popular vote on November 6, 1973, defeating the Republican candidate, Charles W. Sandman, Jr., by a vote of 1,397,613 to 676,235, and was inaugurated on January 15, 1974. A major concern of Byrne's administration has been the personal income tax issue. In a 1973 decision of the New Jersey Supreme Court, the state was ordered to find a new way to finance public education. In the past this financing had been based on seventy percent of the local property taxes. Several attempts at passing a personal income tax failed, but when the State Supreme Court ordered the public schools closed on July 1, 1976 because the State Legislature had not provided an alternative to the local property taxes financing education, Byrne signed New Jersey's first law providing for a statewide income tax on July 8, 1976. Other legislation included required public financing of gubernatorial election campaigns, with private contributions limited to 600 dollars per person; legalization of casino gambling in Atlantic City; and an increased state sales tax. In the 1977 gubernatorial election, Byrne was reelected defeating Republican Raymond Bateman 1,168,468 votes to 870,034. Bibliography: *New York Times* (November 7, 1973); *Facts on File Yearbook, 1976* (New York, 1977); Congressional Quarterly, Inc., *Guide to U.S. Elections* (Washington, D.C., 1977); Roy Glashan, *American Governors and Gubernatorial Elections, 1775-1975* (Stillwater, Minnesota, 1975).

NEW MEXICO

NEW MEXICO

McDONALD, William C., 1912-1917

Born on July 25, 1858 in Jordanville, New York, son of John, a farmer, and Lydia Marshall Biggs McDonald. Brother of John, Lydia, Edward, David, Byron, Ira, William, Calhoun, Demmie, and Ann. Married to Francis McCourt Tarbell on August 31, 1891; father of Frances; stepfather of John, Genevieve, Paul and Margie. Attended public schools; attended Cazenovia Seminary, Cazenovia, New York; studied for the bar. Admitted to the Kansas Bar in 1880; moved to White Oak, New Mexico in 1880. Employed as a store clerk, 1880; worked as a mining and civil engineer, 1881-1890; appointed United States Deputy Mineral Surveyor for New Mexico, 1881; Assessor, Lincoln County, New Mexico in 1885-1887; manager, Carrizozo Cattle Ranch Company, 1890 (he eventually purchased the company); member, New Mexico Territory House of Representatives in 1891; chairman, Lincoln County Board of Commissioners from 1895 to 1897; member, New Mexico Cattle Sanitary Board from 1905 to 1911; chairman, Democratic Territorial Central Committee in 1910. After winning the Democratic gubernatorial nomination, McDonald was elected as the first governor of New Mexico on November 7, 1911, in the general election. He received 31,036 votes to Republican Holm O. Bursum's 28,019. He was sworn into office on January 6, 1912, and served for five years. Other than McDonald, all of New Mexico's governors prior to 1970 were limited to two consecutive two-year terms, and were prohibited by the New Mexico Constitution from seeking election to any state office for two years thereafter. Though McDonald was faced with the task of implementing the new state government, he was hampered by a Republican-controlled legislature. As a result, his administration was generally uneventful. On March 9, 1916, Columbus, New Mexico was raided by Mexican bandits. Within a week, Brigadier General John J. Pershing, in command of a punitive expedition of 6,000 men, crossed the Mexican border in pursuit. As a result of such raids, New Mexico was in a constant state of alarm for the remainder of McDonald's term. McDonald left office on January 1, 1917. After his years as governor, he retired to his ranch at Carrizozo, but he returned to politics when the United States entered World War I, serving as the state's Fuel Administrator until 1918. McDonald died on April 11, 1918, and was buried in Carrizozo. Bibliography: Marion Dargan, "New Mexico's Fight for Statehood, 1895-1912," *New Mexico Historical Review*, vol. XV, no. 1 (January, 1939), vol. XV, no. 2 (April, 1939), vol. XVI, no. 2 (April, 1940), vol. XVII, no. 4 (October, 1941), vol. XVIII, no. 1 (January, 1943), vol. XVIII, no. 2 (April, 1943); Charles F. Coan, *History of New Mexico*, 3 vols. (Chicago, 1925); Frederick C. Irion, *Selected and Annotated Bibliography on Politics in New Mexico* (Santa Fe, 1959); Warren A. Beck, *New Mexico: A History of Four Centuries* (Norman, 1962).

DE BACA, Ezequiel Cabeza, 1917

Born on November 1, 1864 in Las Vegas, New Mexico, son of Thomas Dolores Cabeza, a member of the New Mexico Territorial Legislature, and Estefanita (Delgado) de Baca; a Catholic. Married to Margarita C. de Baca on December 14, 1889; father of Adolfo, Margarita, Horacio, Celia, Hortencia, Alfonso, Natalia, Adelina and Alicia. Attended Las Vegas College, 1878-1882. Teacher in the district schools for two terms; mercantile and railway clerk; Deputy County Clerk, San Miguel County, New Mexico; Deputy Assessor, San Miguel County. One of the organizers and incorporators of Martinez Publishing Company, publisher of *La Voz Del Pueblo*, in 1904; business manager, *La Voz Del Pueblo*; president of the Board of Directors, New Mexico Asylum for the Insane, from 1912 to 1916. Delegate, Democratic National Convention, 1900; Lieutenant Governor of New Mexico from 1912 to 1917. After winning the Democratic gubernatorial primary, de Baca was elected Governor of New Mexico on November 7, 1916, receiving 32,732 votes to Republican Holm O. Bursum's 31,522. He was sworn into office on January 1, 1917. De Baca was already seriously ill when he was inaugurated, and six weeks later, on February 18, 1917, he died. De Baca was buried in Las Vegas, New Mexico. Bibliography: Coronado Cuarto Centennial Commission, *New Mexico* (Albuquerque, 1940); Frederick C. Irion, *Selected and Annotated Bibliography on Politics in New Mexico* (Santa Fe, 1959); Warren A. Beck, *New Mexico: A History of Four Centuries* (Norman, 1962); Roy Glashan, *American Governors and Gubernatorial Elections, 1775-1975* (Stillwater, Minnesota, 1975).

LINDSEY, Washington Ellsworth, 1917-1919

Born on December 20, 1862 near Armstrong, Ohio, son of Robert, a farmer, and Julia Anna Washington Lindsey; a Congregationalist. Brother of Alonzo, James, Eveline, William, David, John, and Mary. Married to Deane C. Haughton in October, 1891; father of Howard W., Helen M., and Michael R.; shortly before his death Lindsey married a Miss Becker of Albuquerque, New Mexico. Attended public schools; received a B.S. degree from Scio College in Ohio in 1884; received an LL.B. degree from the University of Michigan in 1891. Taught school for several years; practiced law in Chicago, Illinois from 1891 to 1900; moved to New Mexico in March, 1900; appointed United States Commissioner, 1900; County Clerk, Roosevelt County, New Mexico from 1903 to 1905; Assistant District Attorney from 1905 to 1909; Mayor, Portales, New Mexico from 1909 to 1910; member, New Mexico Constitutional Convention, 1910; President, Portales Board of Education, from 1912 to 1916. Elk; Woodman of the World; Knight of Pythias. On November 7, 1916, Lindsey was elected Lieutenant Governor on the Republican ticket. When Governor Ezequiel C. de Baca, a Democrat, died in office, Lindsey assumed the position of chief executive. He was sworn in as Governor on February 19, 1917. Described as "the most progressive of the progressives," during his term Lindsey pressed for the enactment of a corrupt practices law, introduction of the "Australian ballot," and adoption of the initiative and referendum. However, these proposals alienated the Spanish-American population and many Republican supporters. As governor when the United States entered World War I, Lindsey called the Legislature into special session to place the state on a wartime footing. Because of his progressive views, Lindsey failed to win renomination by the Republican Party, and he left office on January 1, 1919. Afterward he returned to his law practice in Portales. He was a New Mexico delegate to the Republican National Convention in 1924. Lindsey died on April 5, 1926, and was buried in Portales. Bibliography: Lansing E. Bloom, ed., "Washington E. Lindsey," *New Mexico Historical Review*, vol. 1, no. 4 (October, 1926); Ira C. Ihde, "Washington Ellsworth Lindsey, Third Governor of New Mexico," Unpublished Ph.D. Dissertation, University of New Mexico, 1950; Charles F. Coan, *History of New Mexico*, 3 vols. (Chicago, 1925); Warren A. Beck, *New Mexico: A History of Four Centuries* (Norman, 1962).

LARRAZOLO, Octaviano Ambrosio, 1919-1921

Born on December 7, 1859 near Alenda, Chihuahua, Mexico, son of Octaviano, a farmer, and Donaciana Corral Larrazolo; a Roman Catholic. Married to Rosalia Cobos in 1881; father of Juan B. and José M.; remarried to Maria Garcia on August 4, 1892, and father of Octaviano A., Heliodoro A., Maria, Pablo, Rafael and Caros. Emigrated to the United States in 1870. Attended St. Michaels College, Santa Fe, New Mexico, 1875-1876; studied for the bar. Taught school from 1878 to 1884; Clerk, United States District and Circuit Courts, Western District of Texas in 1885; Clerk, District Court, El Paso County, Texas from 1886 to 1888; admitted to the Texas Bar in 1888; District Attorney, Western District of Texas from 1890 to 1894. Moved to Las Vegas, New Mexico in January, 1895 and opened law practice; unsuccessful Democratic candidate for Congress, 1890, 1900, and 1908; joined the Republican Party in 1910. An Elk. After winning the Republican gubernatorial primary, Larrazolo was elected Governor on November 5, 1918 in the general election, receiving 23,752 votes to Democrat Felix Garcia's 22,433. He was sworn into office on January 1, 1919. As governor, Larrazolo stressed the need for improvement in bilingual instruction, free textbooks, and other measures that would aid the Spanish-American population of the state. In addition, the Girls' Welfare Home, the Child Welfare Board, and the State Health Board were created during his term. When New Mexico's coal miners struck in 1919, Larrazolo declared martial law, called out the militia, and ended the disturbance. He also called a special legislative session in 1920 to enact tax reforms. Because many Republicans opposed his programs, Larrazolo failed to be renominated in 1920, and he left office on January 1, 1921. Afterward he remained active in politics. He was an unsuccessful candidate for Justice of the New Mexico Supreme Court in 1924; however, he was elected to the New Mexico House of Representatives in 1927 and 1928. In 1928 he was elected to the United States Senate to fill an unexpired term, and served until 1929. He returned to his law practice in Albuquerque, New Mexico, after leaving office. Larrazolo died on April 7, 1930, and was buried in Albuquerque. Bibliography: Paul A. F. Walter, "Octaviano Ambrosio Larrazolo," *New Mexico Historical Review*, vol. VII, no. 2 (April, 1932); Alfred G. Cordova, "Octaviano Ambrosio Larrazolo, The Prophet of Transition in New Mexico; An Analysis of his Political Life," Unpublished Master's Thesis, University of New Mexico, 1950; Charles F. Coan, *History of New Mexico*, 3 vols. (Chicago, 1925); Warren A. Beck, *New Mexico: A History of Four Centuries* (Norman, 1962).

MECHEM, Merritt Cramer, 1921-1923

Born on October 10, 1870 in Ottawa, Kansas, son of Homer C., a lawyer, and Martha Shannon Davenport Mechem; a Baptist. Brother of Ralph, Nellie, and Edwin. Married to Eleanor Frances O'Heir on February 12, 1910. Educated in public schools; attended Baptist University in Ottawa, Kansas; attended the University of Kansas; studied for the bar. Admitted to the Arkansas Bar in 1895; moved to Tucumcari, New Mexico in 1903 for health reasons. District Attorney, Quay and Guadalupe counties, Arizona from 1905 to 1907; member, New Mexico Territorial Council, 1909; Associate Justice, New Mexico Territorial Supreme Court from 1909 to 1911; District Judge from 1911 to 1920. Mason; Elk; Son of the American Revolution; member, New Mexico Historical Society. After winning the Republican gubernatorial primary, Mechem was elected Governor on November 2, 1920 in the general election, receiving 54,426 votes to Democrat Richard H. Hanna's 50,755. He was sworn into office on January 1, 1921. As governor, Mechem was instrumental in persuading the New Mexico Legislature to ratify the Nineteenth Amendment to the United States Constitution. In so doing, New Mexico became the thirty-sixth state to approve the amendment, and this allowed President Woodrow Wilson to proclaim its adoption. In addition, Mechem did much to heal the wounds in the Republican Party resulting from the administration of Governor Octaviano A. Larrazolo. Mechem was also a champion of women's rights on the state level. He nominated a woman to serve on nearly all of the state's institutional boards. Declining to seek reelection, Mechem retired from politics at the end of his term. He left office on January 1, 1923. Afterward he resumed his law practice in Albuquerque, New Mexico. Mechem died on May 24, 1946, and was buried in Albuquerque. Bibliography: Paul A. F. Walter, "Merritt Cramer Mechem," *New Mexico Historical Review*, vol. XXI, no. 3 (July, 1946); John P. Seman, "The Administration of Governor Merritt Cramer Mechem (1921-1923)," Unpublished Master's Thesis, University of New Mexico, 1953; Charles F. Coan, *History of New Mexico*, 3 vols. (Chicago, 1925); Warren A. Beck, *New Mexico: A History of Four Centuries* (Norman, 1962).

HINKLE, James Fielding, 1923-1925

Born on October 20, 1864 near Boles, Missouri, son of Miles Parsons, a farmer, and Sarah Sappington Hinkle; a Methodist. Brother of Emmet. Married to Lillie E. Roberts on December 14, 1892; father of Rolla, Vera, Clarence and Lillian. Attended public schools and the University of Missouri. Moved to New Mexico and engaged in ranching, 1885-1911; entered the banking business in 1911; vice president, First National Bank, Roswell, New Mexico, 1915-1934; became president, First National Bank, Roswell, 1934; president, Pecos Valley Lumber Building and Loan Association. Elected to the New Mexico Territory House of Representatives, 1893, 1894, and 1895; elected to the New Mexico Territory Senate, 1901; Mayor, Roswell, 1905-1906; member of the New Mexico Senate, 1912-1917; member, New Mexico Board of Equalization for eleven years. Mason; Shriner; S.A.R.; Elk; member, Fin and Feather; Kiwanis. After winning the Democratic gubernatorial primary, Hinkle was elected Governor on November 7, 1922 in the general election, receiving 60,317 votes to Republican C. L. Hill's 49,363. He was sworn into office on January 1, 1923. Hinkle had campaigned on a platform which promised a $2,000 property-tax exemption for veterans of World War I. Though the exemption was enacted by the legislature, other liberal proposals by Hinkle caused a break with some state Democrats. In addition, Hinkle came under intense criticism when his opponents complained that the Spanish-American members of the Democratic Party had been discriminated against in the dispensing of political patronage. Thereby, as a result, Hinkle was not the party's nominee in the 1924 election. Hinkle left office on January 1, 1925. Afterward he returned to his ranching and banking interests. Hinkle died on March 26, 1951, and was buried in Roswell. Bibliography: Charles F. Coan, *History of New Mexico*, 3 vols. (Chicago, 1925); Frederick C. Irion, *Selected and Annotated Bibliography on Politics in New Mexico* (Santa Fe, 1959); Warren A. Beck, *New Mexico: A History of Four Centuries* (Norman, 1962); James Albert Hense, "The History of Roswell, New Mexico—1886-1908," Unpublished Master's Thesis, Eastern New Mexico University, 1955.

HANNETT, Arthur Thomas, 1925-1927

Born on February 17, 1884 near Lyons, New York, son of William, a farmer, and Mary Emily Hannett; an Episcopalian. Brother of Maggie, Ella, William, George and Mary. Married Louise Westfall on August 13, 1913; father of William. Attended the University of Buffalo, College of Law; received an LL.B. degree from Syracuse University in 1910; received an honorary LL.D. degree from Syracuse University in 1926. Established a private law practice in Gallup, New Mexico in 1911; delegate, Democratic National Convention, 1912, 1920, 1936, and 1940; City Attorney, Gallup, 1914-1916; Food Administrator, McKinley County, New Mexico, during World War I; Mayor, Gallup, 1918-1922; chairman, New Mexico Highway Commission, 1923-1925. Vice president, Central Credit Corporation, Albuquerque, New Mexico; director, Gallup Townsite Company; Special Assistant to the New Mexico Attorney General. Mason; Elk. After winning the Democratic gubernatorial primary, Hannett was elected Governor of New Mexico on November 4, 1924 in the general election, receiving 56,183 votes to Republican Manuel B. Otero's 55,984. He was sworn into office on January 1, 1925. Hannett, who had the backing of organized labor in the state, was elected after one of the most bitterly-contested elections in New Mexico history. Because of his ties with labor, the Republicans had portrayed him as a radical with Communist ties. This, combined with the closeness of the race and Republican victories in the legislature, hampered Hannett's extremely liberal programs. Nevertheless, he plunged ahead, and proposed a drastic revision of the state's election laws. The proposed reform became the center of the 1926 gubernatorial campaign. Hannett, the Democratic nominee, enthusiastically advocated adoption of the program, while the Republicans bitterly attacked the measure. In the end, Hannett lost the November, 1926 general election to Republican Richard C. Dillon by 3,771 votes, and left office on January 1, 1927. Afterward he returned to his investments and private law practice in Albuquerque. In addition, he was appointed to the Democratic National Committee in 1936. Bibliography: Robert Thompson and Charles Judah, *Arthur T.*

Hannett: Governor of New Mexico (Albuquerque, 1950); Frederick C. Irion, *Selected and Annotated Bibliography on Politics in New Mexico* (Santa Fe, 1959); Warren A. Beck, *New Mexico: A History of Four Centuries* (Norman, 1962); Roy Glashan, *American Governors and Gubernatorial Elections, 1775-1975* (Stillwater, Minnesota, 1975).

DILLON, Richard Charles, 1927-1931

Born on June 24, 1877 in St. Louis, Missouri, son of Richard, a railroad man, and Hattie (Patterson) Dillon. Married to Maurine Williams on November 9, 1904; father of Florence, Virginia, Betty Jo, Kenneth and Malcom. Dillon's family moved to New Mexico when he was a child. He was educated in the public schools in Springer, New Mexico. Employed as a laborer on the railroad in 1892; entered the mercantile and stock business in 1900; associated with G. W. Bond and Brothers, Encino, New Mexico, 1907-1927. Member, New Mexico Senate, 1925-1927. Mason; Elk. After winning the Republican gubernatorial primary, Dillon was elected Governor of New Mexico on November 2, 1926 in the general election, receiving 56,294 votes to Democrat incumbent Governor Arthur T. Hannett's 52,523. Dillon was sworn into office on January 1, 1927. Dillon had campaigned on the promise of a business-like administration, and espoused the theory "that government governs best which governs least." As a result, during his administration the daily affairs of government were left to subordinates; he was, however, capable of decisive action. In January, 1928, he called out the state militia, and declared a state of insurrection along the Colorado-New Mexico border in order to prevent members of the Industrial Workers of the World from entering the state. Also while Dillon was governor, President Herbert Hoover proclaimed Carlsbad Caverns a national monument. In the November 6, 1928 general election, Dillon was reelected to a second term, defeating Democrat Robert C. Dow, 65,967 votes to 52,550. Prohibited by the state constitution from seeking a third consecutive term, Dillon left office on January 1, 1931. Afterward, he returned to G. W. Bond and Brothers, and in 1936, became manager of R. C. Dillon and Company. Dillon died on January 5, 1966, and was buried in Encino. Bibliography: Charles B. Judah, *Governor Richard C. Dillon: A Study in New Mexico Politics* (Albuquerque, 1948); Frederick C. Irion, *Selected and Annotated Bibliography on Politics in New Mexico* (Santa Fe, 1959); Warren A. Beck, *New Mexico: A History of Four Centuries* (Norman, 1962); Roy Glashan, *American Governors and Gubernatorial Elections, 1775-1975* (Stillwater, Minnesota, 1975).

SELIGMAN, Arthur, 1931-1933

Born on June 14, 1871 in Santa Fe, New Mexico, son of Bernard, a businessman and politician, and Frances Nusbaum Seligman; Jewish. Brother of James L., Eva May, and Minnie. Married to Frankie E. Harris on July 4, 1896. Attended public schools; taught by private tutors; graduated from Swarthmore College Preparatory School in 1887; attended Pierce's Business College, Philadelphia, Pennsylvania, 1891. President, Seligman Brothers Company, 1903-1924; president, La Fonda Building

Corporation, 1912-1924; president, First National Bank of Santa Fe, 1924-1933. Member, Territorial Board of Equalization, 1906-1908; Mayor, Santa Fe, 1910-1912; chairman, Santa Fe County Commissioners, 1910-1920; chairman, Santa Fe County Road Board, 1914-1916; chairman, Santa Fe County Council of Defense, 1917-1918; delegate, Democratic National Convention, 1916, 1920, 1924, and 1932; member, Democratic National Committee, 1920-1933; chairman, New Mexico Educational Survey Commission, 1921-1923; trustee, University of New Mexico. Mason; Elk; Rotary Club; member, New Mexico Historical Society. After winning the Democratic gubernatorial primary, Seligman was elected Governor on November 4, 1930 in the general election, receiving 62,789 votes to Republican Clarence M. Botts' 55,026. He was sworn into office on January 1, 1931. As New Mexico's governor in the midst of the Great Depression. Seligman's program stressed fiscal reform. His goal was a balanced state budget, but, although he kept state expenditures to a minimum, Seligman could not achieve a balanced budget, and a tax increase was therefore necessary. Seligman also increased state funding for the New Mexico Historical Society,. and took great interest in the development of the state's scenic attractions. On November 8, 1932, he was reelected to a second term, defeating former Republican Governor Richard C. Dillon, 83,612 votes to 67,406. He died in office on September 25, 1933, and was buried in Santa Fe. Bibliography: Paul A. F. Walter, "Arthur Seligman," *New Mexico Historical Review,* vol. VIII, no. 4 (October, 1933); Charles F. Coan, *History of New Mexico,* 3 vols. (Chicago, 1925); Frederick C. Irion, *Selected and Annotated Bibliography on Politics in New Mexico* (Santa Fe, 1959); Warren A. Beck, *New Mexico: A History of Four Centuries* (Norman, 1962).

HOCKENHULL, Andrew W., 1933-1935

Born on January 16, 1877 near Bolivar, Missouri, son of Charles H., a farmer, and Maria Hockenhull; a Baptist. Brother of James, Charles and Gertrude. Married to Mamie Drake on November 20, 1901; father of Virginia, Helen and Gertrude. Educated in public schools; attended the University of New Mexico; received an LL.B. degree from the University of Texas in 1904. Practiced law in Bolivar from 1904 to 1908; moved to Quay County, New Mexico in 1908; moved to Clovis, New Mexico and opened a law office in 1909; City Attorney, Clovis; Assistant District Attorney until 1930; elected Lieutenant Governor of New Mexico in the November 4, 1930 general election, on the Democratic ticket. On September 25, 1933, Governor Arthur Seligman died in office and, as Lieutenant Governor, Hockenhull succeeded him as chief executive. He was sworn into office on that same day. Having assumed the office of governor at the height of the Great Depression, Hockenhull was faced by the state's severe economic problems. The effect on New Mexico's economy was so great that in January, 1935, the month Hockenhull left office, 135,670 persons, or about one-third of the state's population, were on relief. Though Hockenhull attempted to alleviate the problem, control of the relief administration was used by Democratic leaders as a political weapon, and dispensed along the lines of party patronage. Hockenhull completed the remainder of Seligman's term before leaving office on January 1, 1935. Afterward, he served as vice president of the Production Credit Corporation in Wichita, Kansas for a year and a half before he returned to Clovis, where he resumed his legal practice. In July, 1939, he was appointed Postmaster of Clovis. He was also an attorney for the Rural Electrification Administration and president of the Clovis National Bank. Bibliography: Frederick C. Irion, *Selected Annotated Bibliography on Politics in New Mexico* (Santa Fe, 1959); Warren A. Beck, *New Mexico: A History of Four Centuries* (Norman, 1962); Roy Glashan, *American Governors and Gubernatorial Elections, 1775-1975* (Stillwater, Minnesota, 1975); Frederick C. Irion, "Politics in New Mexico," Unpublished Manuscript, Department of Government, University of New Mexico, Albuquerque, 1959.

TINGLEY, Clyde, 1935-1939

Born on January 5, 1883 in London, Ohio, son of George, a farmer, and Bell T. Tingley, a Congregationalist. Married to Carrie Wooster on April 21, 1912. Educated in public schools. Served in the Ohio National Guard. Employed in railroad construction; worked as a locomotive fireman; machinist for Dayton Cash Register Company; superintendent of Graham Motor Company. District Maintenance Superintendent, New Mexico State Highway Department; Mayor, Albuquerque, New Mexico; delegate, Democratic National Convention, 1928, 1932, and 1936. After winning the Democratic gubernatorial primary, Tingley was elected Governor of New Mexico on November 6, 1934 in the general election, receiving 78,390 votes to Republican Jaffa Miller's 71,899. He was sworn into office on January 1, 1935. New Mexico's economy was virtually paralyzed by the effects of the Great Depression; in January, 1935, the same month that Tingley became chief executive, 135,670 people, or about one-third of the state's population, were on relief.To combat the economic stranglehold of the depression, during Tingley's term the legislature established the New Mexico Relief and Security Authority to help people on relief to find work on various federal projects. On November 3, 1936, Tingley was reelected to a second term, defeating Miller again, by a vote of 97,090 to 72,539. In May, 1937, a conference was held in Chihuahua City, Mexico between Mexican and New Mexican officials to discuss the reopening of the sixteenth-century highway between Mexico City, Mexico, and Santa Fe, New Mexico. Near the end of Tingley's administration, the state's economy was given a boost by the discovery and development of several oil wells in the southeastern portion of New Mexico. Prohibited by the state constitution from serving more than two consecutive terms, Tingley left office on January 1, 1939. Tingley died on December 24, 1960, and was buried in Albuquerque. Bibliography: Coronado Cuarto Centennial Commission, *New Mexico* (Albuquerque, 1940); Thomas C. Donelly, ed., *Rocky Mountain Politics* (Albuquerque, 1940); Warren A. Beck, *New Mexico: A History of Four Centuries* (Norman, 1962); Roy Glashan, *American Governors and Gubernatorial Elections, 1775-1975* (Stillwater, Minnesota, 1975).

MILES, John Esten, 1939-1943

Born on July 28, 1884 in Murfreesboro, Tennessee, son of Manuel and Frances (Howland) Miles. Married and father of seven children. Educated in public schools. Moved to Texas at age seventeen and became a farmer; three years later he moved to Oklahoma; after one year he moved to Endee, Quay County, New Mexico; acquired a homestead and became a rancher; engaged in mercantile business in Endee, 1918; served as Postmaster in Endee; publisher, *New Mexico Democrat*, Santa Fe, New Mexico, and Las Vegas *Independent*, Las Vegas, New Mexico, 1927-1928; owner of a farm near Santa Cruz, New Mexico; operated New Mexico Tax Service, 1928. Unsuccessful candidate for County Commissioner of Quay County, 1916; County Tax Assessor, Quay County, 1920-1924; Democratic County Chairman, Quay County, 1924; appointed Secretary of the New Mexico State Tax Commission, 1925; later he served as Chief of the Field Division, Internal Revenue Department, Albuquerque, New Mexico; became a member of the New Mexico State Democratic Central Committee, 1926; State Chairman, New Mexico Democratic Party, 1934-1938. After winning the Democratic gubernatorial primary, Miles was elected Governor of New Mexico on November 8, 1938, in the general election, receiving 82,344 votes to Republican Albert K. Mitchell's 75,017; he was sworn into office on January 1, 1939. On November 5, 1940, Miles was reelected, defeating Republican Maurice Miera, 103,035 votes to 82,306. During Miles' administration the Conchas Dam was completed, thus making possible the irrigation of 39,000 acres around Tucumcari, New Mexico. In addition, the Coronado Cuarto Centennial celebration of the expedition of Francisco Vasquez de Coronado to New Mexico was held. In 1939, the gross income from all classes of livestock and livestock products amounted to over $40,000,000, while industrial manufacturing accounted for only seven percent of non-agricultural hourly employment. However, with the change to a wartime economy during Miles' second term, industrial development began a period of tremendous growth in the state. New Mexico's Constitution, prior to 1970, limited governors to two consecutive two-year terms, and prohibited them from seeking election to any state office for two years after the expiration of their administration. As a result, Miles left office on January 1, 1943. The same day he left office, Miles was appointed Chairman of the New Mexico Public Service Commission. Bibliography: Coronado Cuarto Centennial Commission, *New Mexico* (Albuquerque, 1940); Frederick C. Irion, *Selected and Annotated Bibliography on Politics in New Mexico* (Santa Fe, 1959); Warren A. Beck, *New Mexico: A History of Four Centuries* (Norman, 1962); Roy Glashan, *American Governors and Gubernatorial Elections, 1775-1975* (Stillwater, Minnesota, 1975).

DEMPSEY, John Joseph, 1943-1947

Born on June 22, 1879 in White Haven, Pennsylvania, son of William, a railroad brakeman, and Mary; a Catholic. Brother of Edward and Mary E. Married to Katheryn McCarthy in 1905; father of William J., Muriel, and Mary E.; married a second time to Gladys Everett in September, 1931. Educated in the common schools. Became a water boy for a railroad contracting crew when he was thirteen; telegrapher; worked for the Brooklyn Union Elevator Company; vice president of the Brooklyn Rapid Transit Company until 1919; entered the petroleum business in Oklahoma in 1919; vice president, Continental Oil and Asphalt Company; moved to Santa Fe, New Mexico in 1920 and became an independent oil operator; became president of the U.S. Asphalt Company in 1928. Appointed New Mexico State Director for the National Recovery Administration, 1933; New Mexico State

Director of the Federal Housing Administration and National Emergency Council; member, U.S. House of Representatives, 1935-1941; did not seek reelection in 1940, but was an unsuccessful candidate for the U.S. Senate nomination; member, U.S. Maritime Commission, January, 1941 to July, 1941; U.S. Undersecretary of the Interior, 1941-1942. Member and president, University of New Mexico Board of Regents. As a Democrat, Dempsey was elected Governor of New Mexico on November 3, 1942, defeating Republican Joseph F. Tondre, 59,258 votes to 49,380. Dempsey took office on January 1, 1943. He was reelected to a second term on November 7, 1944, polling 76,443 votes to Republican Carroll G. Gunderson's 71,113. During his administration, the Los Alamos Atomic Energy Project was created near Santa Fe; also, the first atomic bomb tests were carried out at White Sands Proving Grounds near Alamogordo, New Mexico. The large federal expenditures connected with the atomic energy projects, and the vast amount of military funds spent during this period, greatly stimulated the growth of the state. New Mexico's Constitution, prior to 1970, limited governors to two consecutive two-year terms, and as a result, Dempsey left office on January 1, 1947. Dempsey was an unsuccessful candidate for nomination to the U.S. Senate in 1946; however, he was later elected to the U.S. House of Representatives, and served from 1951 until his death in 1958. Dempsey died in Washington, D.C. on March 11, 1958, and was buried in Rosario Cemetery in Santa Fe. Bibliography: American Guide Series, *New Mexico: A Guide to the Colorful State* (New York, 1953); **Warren A. Beck**, *New Mexico: A History of Four Centuries* (Norman, 1962); Congressional Quarterly, Inc., *Guide to U.S. Elections* (Washington, 1975); Roy Glashan, *American Governors and Gubernatorial Elections, 1775-1975* (Stillwater, Minnesota, 1975).

MABRY, Thomas Jewett, 1947-1951

Born on October 17, 1884 in Carlisle County, Kentucky, son of Jesse J. and Onie L. (Nance) Mabry; a Presbyterian. Married to Winifred White on June 20, 1907; she died on June 6, 1912; married a second time to Katherine Burns on June 10, 1915; father of Scott H., Katherine L. and Thomas J., Jr. Attended the University of Oklahoma, 1904-1906; attended the University of New Mexico, 1908-1909; studied law. Admitted to the New Mexico Bar in 1915. Moved to New Mexico in 1907; founder and publisher of Clovis, New Mexico, *Journal*, 1909-1915; began law practice in Albuquerque, New Mexico, 1915. Member, New Mexico Constitutional Convention, 1910; member, New Mexico Senate, 1912-1917; member, Albuquerque City Commission, 1926-1927; District Attorney, Albuquerque, 1932-1936; District Judge, Albuquerque, 1937-1939; Chief Justice, New Mexico Supreme Court, 1939-1946. Mason; Shriner; Elk. After winning the Democratic gubernatorial primary, Mabry was elected Governor on November 5, 1946 in the general election, receiving 70,055 votes to Republican Edward L. Safford's 62,575. He was sworn into office on January 1, 1947. During Mabry's administration a New Mexico Fair Employment Practice Commission was established to prevent unfair employment practices in the state, and a Commission on Alcoholism was created to study the care, treatment, and rehabilitation of alcoholics. In addition, the New Mexico Department of Civil Air Patrol was organized. Mabry was reelected to a second term on November 2, 1948, defeating Republican M. Lujan, 103,969 votes to 86,023. Prohibited by the state constitution from holding office for more than two consecutive terms, Mabry left office on January 1, 1951. He died on December 24, 1962, and was buried in Albuquerque. Bibliography: Frederick C. Irion, *Selected and Annotated Bibliography on Politics in New Mexico* (Santa Fe, 1959); Warren A. Beck, *New Mexico: A History of Four Centuries* (Norman, 1962); Roy Glashan, *American Governors and Gubernatorial Elections, 1775-1975* (Stillwater, Minnesota, 1975); Frederick C. Irion, "Politics in New Mexico," Unpublished Manuscript, Department of Government, University of New Mexico, Albuquerque, 1959.

MECHEM, Edwin Leard, 1951-1955, 1957-1959, 1961-1962

Born on July 2, 1912 in Alamogordo, New Mexico, son of Edwin, a lawyer and judge, and Eunice Leard Mechem; a Methodist. Brother of Davenport and Jesse. Married to Dorothy Ellen on December 30, 1932; father of Martha, John, Jesse and Walter. Attended New Mexico Agricultural and Mechanical College, 1930-1931 and 1935; received an LL.B. degree from the University of Arkansas in 1939. Admitted to the New Mexico Bar in 1939. Employed as a Land Surveyor, United States Reclamation Service, Las Cruces, New Mexico, 1932-1935; private legal practice, Las Cruces, 1939-1950, 1955-1956; agent, Federal Bureau of Investigation, 1942-1945; member, New Mexico House of Delegates, 1947-1948; member, Committee on Government Security, 1956-1957; member, New Mexico Commission on Reorganization of the Executive Branch; member, New Mexico State Police Commission. Member, American Law Institute. After winning the Republican gubernatorial primary, Mechem was elected Governor on November 7, 1950 in the general election, receiving 96,846 votes to Democrat John E. Miles' 83,359. He was sworn into office on January 1, 1951. Mechem's election ended twenty years of Democratic control of the governor's office, and was a reflection of voter dissatisfaction with local and state Democratic policies. However, Mechem did not carry the remainder of the Republican ticket with him, and with the Democrats maintaining control of the legislature and gaining other elective offices, his efforts to enact Republican-oriented programs were greatly hindered. Nevertheless, he remained popular with the voters and won reelection in the November 4, 1952 general election by defeating Democrat Everett Grantham, 129,116 votes to 111,034. New Mexico's constitution, prior to 1970, limited governors to two consecutive two-year terms, and prohibited them from seeking election to any state office for two years after the expiration of those terms. As a result, Mechem left office on January 1, 1955, and returned to his law practice. On November 6, 1956, Mechem was again elected Governor, receiving 131,488 votes to incumbent Democratic Governor John F. Simms' 120,263; however, he was defeated in a bid for reelection in November, 1958 and left office on January 1, 1959. Mechem was again elected Governor on November 8, 1960, by defeating incumbent Democratic Governor John Burroughs, 153,765 votes to 151,777. On November 30, 1962, he resigned the governorship, and that same day was appointed to the U.S. Senate to fill the vacancy left by the death of Senator Dennis Chavez. He served in the Senate until 1964, when he was defeated in the general election. Afterward, Mechem returned to his law practice in Las Cruces. Bibliography: Frederick C. Irion, *Selected and Annotated Bibliography on Politics in New Mexico* (Santa Fe, 1959); Warren A. Beck, *New Mexico: A History of Four Centuries* (Norman, 1962); Frederick C. Irion, "Politics in New Mexico," Unpublished Manuscript, Department of Government, University of New Mexico, Albuquerque, 1959; Thomas A. Donnelly, "The 1950 Gubernatorial Campaign in New Mexico as Interpreted Through the State Press," Unpublished Master's Thesis, University of New Mexico, 1952.

SIMMS, John Field, 1955-1957

Born on December 18, 1916 in Albuquerque, New Mexico, son of John Field, a lawyer, and Anna Schluter Simms; an Episcopalian. Brother of Albert Gallatin and Frances Anne. Married to Ruth Reynolds on November 25, 1950; father of John Field, III, Ruth Camille, Charlotte, Joshua R., and Thomas H. Educated in public schools; attended New Mexico Military Institute, 1933; received a B.A. degree from the University of New Mexico in 1937; received an LL.B. degree from Yale University in 1940. Entered the U.S. Army Air Corps as a private in 1942 and was discharged as a Lieutenant Colonel in 1945. Became a partner in Simms and Modrall Legal Firm in 1940; partner in Simms, Modrall, Seymour, and Simms Legal Firm in 1945; invested in ranching; Director, Trinchera Ranch Incorporated; elected to the New Mexico Legislature in 1947 and 1949; Speaker of the New Mexico House of Representatives; member, New Mexico Commission for Promotion of Uniform State Laws, 1950-1954; president, New Mexico Share Corporation. American Legion; Veterans of Foreign Wars. After winning the Democratic gubernatorial primary, Simms was elected Governor on November 2, 1954 in the general election, receiving 110,583 votes to Republican Alvin Stockton's 83,373. He was sworn into office on January 1, 1955. During his administration, Simms served as Chairman of the Interstate Oil Compact Commission between 1955 and 1956. The economy of New Mexico was undergoing a shift from agriculture to manufacturing during Simms' term, and in 1956 earnings from agriculture constituted 2.7 percent of earnings within the state, while manufacturing wages and salaries amounted to 11.2 percent. However, while Simms was in office, the federal government remained the largest source of personal income, as the wages paid to civilian and military employees totaled 21.6 percent of individual incomes within New Mexico. Though Simms was the Democratic candidate for Governor in 1956, he lost the general election to Republican Edwin L. Mechem and left office on January 1, 1957. After leaving office, Simms completed a short course on oil and gas laws at Southern Methodist University in 1957, and then returned to his private legal practice in Albuquerque, concentrating on oil and gas leases. He also maintained his ranching interests. Bibliography: Frederick C. Irion, *Selected and Annotated Bibliography on Politics in New Mexico* (Santa Fe, 1959); Warren A. Beck, *New Mexico: A History of Four Centuries* (Norman, 1962); Frederick C. Irion, "Politics in New Mexico," Unpublished Manuscript, Department of Government, University of New Mexico, Albuquerque, 1959.

MECHEM, Edwin Leard, 1951-1955, 1957-1959, 1961-1962

BURROUGHS, John, 1959-1961

Born on April 7, 1907 in Robert Lee, Texas, son of James, a farmer, and Amertius (Ashley) Burroughs. Married to Jean Mitchell in 1935; father of Jan, Nan, Karen and Belinda. Received a B.S. degree from Texas Technological College, 1929; did graduate work at Colorado State University. Vocational agricultural teacher, 1929-1933; petroleum salesman, Texas Company, 1934-1935; assistant to the general manager, Consumers Cotton Oil Company, Dallas, Texas, 1936-1942; owner, Cotton Oil Mill and Peanut Mill, San Antonio, Texas, and Portales, New Mexico, 1943-1946; president, Portales Valley Mills Incorporated, New Mexico; president, American Net Corporation, Lewisville, Texas; president, Cisco Peanut Company, Texas; president, Plains Broadcast Company, with stations in Portales and Farmington, New Mexico, and Texas. Member, New Mexico House of Representatives, 1957. Rotarian; New Mexico Broadcasters Association. After winning the Democratic gubernatorial primary, Burroughs was elected Governor of New Mexico on November 4, 1958 in the general election, receiving 103,481 votes to incumbent Republican Governor Edwin L. Mechem's 101,567. He took office on January 1, 1959. During his administration, Burroughs emphasized a business-like approach to both state government and industrial development. In an attempt to avoid an increase in taxes, Burroughs urged a vigorous campaign to collect all funds due the state under current New Mexico law. This was an important concern to state authorities, inasmuch as the census of 1960 indicated a 39.6 percent growth in population within the last ten years, and the expanding number of citizens demanded increased spending by the government to provide essential services. On November 8, 1960, Burroughs was defeated in a reelection bid by E. Mechem, when he polled 151,777 votes to the victor's 153,765. Burroughs left office on January 1, 1961, and returned to his investments and his home in Portales. Bibliography: Warren A. Beck, *New Mexico: A History of Four Centuries* (Norman, 1962); Congressional Quarterly, Inc., *Guide to U.S. Elections* (Washington, 1975); Roy Glashan, *American Governors and Gubernatorial Elections, 1775-1975* (Stillwater, Minnesota, 1975); New Mexico State Library Extension Service, "Biography of John Burroughs, Governor of New Mexico," (Santa Fe, New Mexico).

MECHEM, Edwin Leard, 1951-1955, 1957-1959, 1961-1962

BOLACK, Thomas Felix, 1962-1963

Born on May 18, 1918 in Cowley County, Kansas, son of Ralph W., a rancher, and Christol Hazel (Sheets) Bolack; Methodist. Married to Alice Schwerdtfeger on March 14, 1946; father of Tommy, Terry and Terry Ellen. Educated in public schools and correspondence courses. Engrossing clerk, Kansas Legislature, 1939-1940; agent, Kansas Corporation Commission, 1940-1941; superintendent, Hospah Oil Field, Prewitt, New Mexico, 1942; moved to San Juan County, New Mexico in 1943 and became an independent oil and gas producer; president, Bolack Oil and Gas Company, 1950-1953; vice president, Mesa Shopping Center, Farmington,

New Mexico, 1952; chairman of the Executive Committee, Petro Atlas Corporation, 1953; became owner, Albuquerque "Dukes" Baseball Club, 1957; Director, First State Bank, Cuba, New Mexico; director, Hidden Solendor Uranium Company; organizer and director, Western American Life Insurance Company. Mayor, Farmington, 1952-1953; member, New Mexico House of Representatives, 1956-1958; unsuccessful Republican congressional candidate, 1957; became adviser, United States Small Business Administration, 1957; member, United States Assay Commission, 1958-1959; Lieutenant Governor of New Mexico, 1960-1962. Oil Man of the Year, *Oil Reporter*, 1950; Elk; Lion. A Republican. On November 30, 1962, New Mexico Governor Edwin L. Mechem resigned and, as Lieutenant Governor, Bolack assumed the governor's office. After becoming Governor, Bolack appointed Mechem to the U.S. Senate, filling the vacancy left by the death of U.S. Senator Dennis Chavez. Bolack completed the remainder of Mechem's term, and left office on January 1, 1963. Afterward, Bolack returned to his home in Farmington and to his investments. Bibliography: Warren A. Beck, *New Mexico: A History of Four Centuries* (Norman, 1962); United States Government, *Biographical Directory of the Congress of the United States, 1774-1971* (Washington, 1971); Congressional Quarterly, Inc., *Guide to U.S. Elections* (Washington, 1975); Roy Glashan, *American Governors and Gubernatorial Elections, 1775-1975* (Stillwater, Minnesota, 1975).

CAMPBELL, John M., 1963-1967

Born on September 10, 1916 in Hutchinson, Kansas, son of John M., a salesman, and Blanche E. (Chain) Campbell; a Catholic. Married to Ruthanne DeBus on November 17, 1945; father of Patricia Ann, Michael Bruce, Kathleen Marie and John Terence. Received an A.B. degree, magna cum laude, Washburn College, 1938; LL.B., 1940; honorary doctorate, College of Santa Fe, 1965; honorary doctorate, New Mexico State University; honorary doctorate, New Mexico Mining and Technological Institute, 1966. Admitted to the New Mexico Bar, 1944. Entered the U.S. Marine Corps as a private in 1942; discharged as a First Lieutenant in 1945; Captain, U.S. Marine Corps Reserve. Began law practice in Albuquerque, New Mexico, 1940; Federal Bureau of Investigation Agent, 1941-1942; Executive Secretary, New Mexico Oil and Gas Association, 1946-1947; partner, Campbell and Russell Law Firm, Roswell, New Mexico, 1953-1963. Member, New Mexico House of Representatives, 1956-1962; Speaker, New Mexico House of Representatives, 1961-1962; chairman, Legislative Council, 1962. After winning the Democratic gubernatorial primary, Campbell was elected Governor of New Mexico on November 6, 1962 in the general election, receiving 130,933 votes to Republican Edwin L. Mechem's 116,184. Campbell was sworn into office on January 1, 1963. During his administration, the legislature enacted a Highway Beautification Act and ratified the Twenty-fifth Amendment to the United States Constitution. In addition, the State Senate was reapportioned, providing a more equitable representation. During Campbell's years as governor, the Democrats dominated New Mexico politics. In the November 3, 1964 general election the state voted for Lyndon Johnson and elected two Democrats to the U.S. House of Representatives and one to the U.S. Senate. In addition, Campbell was reelected to a second term in 1964, defeating Republican Merle H. Tucker, 191,497 votes to 126,640. Prohibited by New

Mexico's constitution from seeking a third consecutive term, Campbell left office on January 1, 1967. Afterward, he served as a member of the Atomic Safety and Licensing Board of the Atomic Energy Commission, 1967-1971; was elected President of the Federation of Rocky Mountain States, 1969; and was appointed a member of the National Atomic Energy Space Applications Board, 1973. In addition, he was director of the Institute for Sociological Research and Development, University of New Mexico, 1969-1972, and became a partner in Campbell and Bingaman Law Firm, 1973. Bibliography: State of New Mexico, *Laws of the State of New Mexico* (Portales, 1966); Roy Glashan, *American Governors and Gubernatorial Elections, 1775-1975* (Stillwater, Minnesota, 1975); Congressional Quarterly, Inc., *Guide to U.S. Elections* (Washington, 1975).

CARGO, David F., 1967-1971

Born on January 13, 1929 in Dowagiac, Michigan, son of Francis Clair and Mary E. (Harton) Cargo; a Catholic. Married to Ida Jo Anaya on September 22, 1960; father of Veronica Ann, David Joseph, Patrick Michael, and Maria Elena Christina. Received an A.B. degree from the University of Michigan, 1951; received a Master's degree in Public Administration from the University of Michigan, 1953; received an LL.B. degree from the University of Michigan, 1957. Admitted to the Michigan Bar, 1957; admitted to the New Mexico Bar, 1957. Served in the United States Army, 1953-1955. Began private law practice in Albuquerque, New Mexico, 1957; Assistant District Attorney, Albuquerque, 1958-1959; member, New Mexico House of Representatives, 1962. Izaak Walton League; American Legion; Veteran of Foreign Wars. After winning the Republican gubernatorial primary, Cargo was elected Governor of New Mexico on November 8, 1966 in the general election, receiving 134,625 votes to Democrat T. E. Lusk's 125,587. Cargo was sworn into office on January 1, 1967. During his administration, a Department of Motor Transportation was created, a Department of Military Affairs was established, and a State Department of Corrections was organized. In addition, a New Mexico Commission on Aging was created to maintain a statewide program of social services for the aged. While Cargo was governor, New Mexico's constitution was amended to provide four-year terms for the executive officers of the state beginning in 1970, with the restriction that after serving one term, they would be ineligible to hold any state office until another full term had intervened. One exception was the Lieutenant Governor, who would be eligible to hold the office of Governor. On November 6, 1968, Cargo was reelected to a second term, defeating Democrat Fabian Chevez, Jr., 160,140 votes to 157,230. Prohibited by the state constitution from seeking a third consecutive term, Cargo left office on January 1, 1971. Afterward, he returned to his private law practice in Albuquerque. Bibliography: State of New Mexico, *Laws of the State of New Mexico* (Albuquerque, 1968); State of New Mexico, *Laws of the State of New Mexico* (Albuquerque, 1970); Roy Glashan, *American Governors and Gubernatorial Elections, 1775-1975* (Stillwater, Minnesota, 1975); Congressional Quarterly, Inc., *Guide to U.S. Elections* (Washington, 1975).

KING, Bruce, 1971-1975

Born on April 6, 1924, near Stanley, New Mexico, son of William, a rancher, and Molly (Schooler) King. Married to Alice Marie Martin on June 1, 1947; father of Bill and Gary. Attended the University of New Mexico, 1943-1944. Served in the Field Artillery, United States Army, 1944-1946. Rancher and farmer near Stanley; co-owner, King's Butane Company. County Commissioner, Santa Fe County, New Mexico, 1955-1958; chairman, Santa Fe County Board of Commissioners, 1957-1958; member, New Mexico House of Representatives, 1959-1968; Speaker, New Mexico House of Representatives, 1963-1968; member, National Advisory Committee, Democratic Party, 1966; chairman, New Mexico Democratic Party, 1966; president, New Mexico Constitutional Convention, 1969; member, Governor's Task Force on Education, 1968; and member and vice president, New Mexico Soil and Water Conservation Commission. Member, National Conference of State Legislators; Western Conference of the Council of State Governors; New Mexico Farm and Livestock Bureau; New Mexico Cattle Growers; American Cattle Growers; American Legion; Elks. After winning the Democratic gubernatorial primary, King was elected Governor of New Mexico on November 3, 1970 in the general election, receiving 148,835 votes to Republican Pete V. Domenici's 134,640. He was sworn into office on January 1, 1971, and became the first chief executive of New Mexico elected to a four-year term under the provisions of a constitutional amendment adopted in 1970. While governor, King served as chairman of the Four Corners Regional Commission, 1972; chairman of the National Oil and Gas Compact Commission, 1973; vice chairman of the Western Governors' Conference, 1975; and chairman of the Western Governors' Conference, 1974. Also during his administration, the legislature ratified the Equal Rights Amendment to the United States Constitution, created a Children's Court Division of the District Courts, organized a Department of Corrections, and established a State Capitol Improvement Fund. Prohibited by the state constitution from seeking a second consecutive term, King left office on January 1, 1975. Afterward, he returned to his ranching and cattle investments. Bibliography: State of New Mexico, *Laws of the State of New Mexico* (Albuquerque, 1971); State of New Mexico, *Laws of the State of New Mexico* (Portales, 1973); Roy Glashan, *American Governors and Gubernatorial Elections, 1775-1975* (Stillwater, Minnesota, 1975); Congressional Quarterly, Inc., *Guide to U.S. Elections* (Washington, 1975).

APODACA, Jerry, 1975-

Born on October 3, 1934 in Las Cruces, New Mexico, son of Raymond, a businessman, and Elisa; a Catholic. Brother of Raymond, Juliette Altamirano, Rudy, and Priscilla Provencio. Married to Clara Melendres on August 18, 1956; father of Cindy, Carolyn, Jerry, Jeff, and Judy. Received a B.S. degree from the University of New Mexico, 1957. Served in the U.S. Marine Corps Reserve. Taught and coached, Valley High School, Albuquerque, New Mexico, 1957-1960; owner, Jerry Apodaca Insurance Agency, Las Cruces; owner, Jerry Apodaca Realty, Las Cruces; president, Family Shoe Center of New Mexico. Member, New Mexico

Senate, 1966-1974; chairman, Legislative School Study Committee, 1969-1970; chairman, New Mexico Democratic Party, 1969-1970. Director, Dona Ana County March of Dimes, 1962; member, Board of Directors, Las Cruces Boys Club; Las Cruces Jaycees; member, Chamber of Commerce, Las Cruces. After winning the Democratic gubernatorial primary, Apodaca was elected Governor of New Mexico on November 5, 1974 in the general election, receiving 164,172 votes to Republican Joseph R. Skeen's 160,430. He was sworn into office on January 1, 1975. During his administration Apodaca established periodic "open office hours," during which citizens of the state could talk with the governor. In addition, he created a cabinet system of state government organized into twelve functional units designed to produce a more effective executive office. While governor, Apodaca served as chairman of the Western Governors' Regional Energy Policy Office. Also during his term, the legislature established a statewide kindergarten program, created an Indian Education Division of the State Department of Education, and organized a Human Rights Commission. Apodaca's current term will expire on January 1, 1979.
Bibliography: Roy Glashan, *American Governors and Gubernatorial Elections, 1775-1975* (Stillwater, Minnesota, 1975); State of New Mexico, *Laws of the State of New Mexico* (Portales, 1975); Governor's Office, "Governor Jerry Apodaca" (Santa Fe, New Mexico).

NEW YORK

NEW YORK

CLINTON, George, 1789-1795, 1801-1804

Born on July 26, 1739 in Little, Britain, Ulster County, New York, (later part of Orange County); the youngest child of Elizabeth Denniston and Charles Clinton. His parents, of Scot and English ancestry, were both born in Ireland, and came to America in 1729. His father was a surveyor, land speculator, Justice of the Peace, and, from 1769 to his death in 1773, the first Judge of the Ulster Court of Common Pleas. Clinton's brothers Alexander and Charles were physicians; his sister Catherine died in 1762; and his brother James, three years his senior, was a Revolutionary War general and the father of DeWittClinton. Clinton never attended college, but studied law with William Smith, Jr. in New York City. His legal practice expanded in Ulster County during the mid-1760s with his increased involvement in surveying and politics. He married Cornelia Tappen on October 28, 1769; they had six children, one son and five daughters. Clinton was elected to the New York Assembly in 1768, reelected in 1769, and served until that body's dissolution in 1775. An increasingly outspoken critic of the royal government, Clinton was a delegate to the Second Continental Congress in 1775. In the same year he was named Brigadier General in the militia by the colony's Provincial Congress. On July 30, 1777, Clinton took the oath of office as New York State's first elected Governor; Clinton received 1,828 votes, defeating Philip Schuyler (1,199), John Morin Scott (368), and John Jay (367). Clinton's margins of victory increased in the next three elections. Unopposed in 1780, he received 3,624 votes. In 1783 he got 3,584 to 643 for Schuyler and 520 for Paine. Clinton was again unopposed in 1786, and even Alexander Hamilton, whose political beliefs were far removed from those of Clinton, conceded that he had been an effective war governor. Clinton recognized the need for a more viable central government, but was a critic of the Federal Constitution of 1787. After this document was ratified, Hamilton was determined to oust Clinton from the governorship and thus obtain leadership more sympathetic to the national government. In 1789 Robert Yates (5,962 votes), a former Clintonian, opposed the governor in a close race (6,391 votes going to Clinton). John Jay would have won the governorship in 1792, had not the ballots of three counties been voided on technical grounds by a partisan legislature. The final tally gave Clinton 8,440 votes to Jay's 8,332. Clinton was increasingly criticized for having remained in power for so long, and for developing a patronage-supported political machine. He declined to stand for reelection in 1795, citing problems of age and health. An unsuccessful effort was made to turn these issues against Clinton when he won the governorship for a seventh term in 1801. As governor of New York, Clinton helped to promote the establishment of the University of New York. His vigorous opposition to Hamilton contributed to the emergence of political parties. He was particularly forceful in his support of France against Great Britain in the 1790s; his daughter Cornelia married the French agent Edmond Genet, in 1794. Deeply conscious of popular suspicion of executive authority during the Revolutionary era, Clinton strove to protect civil liberties, emphasizing the superiority of civil authority over the military, and upholding the role of civil courts. Still, he was considered among the best governors in aiding the war effort and in developing viable state financing. Clinton was forceful in opposing civil disorder (Shays' Rebellion) and he opposed New Hampshire's claims to Vermont. He served as Vice President during Jefferson's second term and Madison's first administration. Clinton died in Washington, D. C. on April 20, 1812. Bibliography: E. Wilder Spaulding, *His Excellency George Clinton* (New York, 1938); Alfred F. Young, *The Democratic Republicans of New York* (Chapel Hill, 1967); Linda Grand DePauw, *The Eleventh Pillar* (Ithaca, 1966); L. K. Caldwell, "George Clinton: Democratic Administrator," *New York History* (April, 1951). Most of Clinton's manuscripts were destroyed in the Albany fire of 1911; the State Library at Albany, the New York Historical Society and the New York Public Library have a few of his letters. Also see *Public Papers of George Clinton, First Governor of New York, 1777-1795, 1801-1804,* 10 vols. (New York, 1899-1914).

JAY, John, 1795-1801

Born on December 12, 1745 in New York City, New York, the son of Peter, a West Indian merchant, and Hannah (McVickar) Jay; an Episcopalian. One of eight children; married to Sarah Livingston on April 28, 1774, and the father of Peter Augustus, William and five daughters. Educated at a boarding school in New Rochelle, New York; graduated from Kings College (now Columbia University) in New York City in 1764; studied law. Admitted to the bar in 1768. Commissioned a Colonel in the New York Militia. Private law practice. Served on the New York Committee of Correspondence; member, Continental Congress, 1774-1777 and 1778-1779; served as a delegate to the New York Provincial Congress, 1776; drafted the New York Constitution, 1777; Chief Justice of New York, 1777-1778; President of the Continental Congress, 1778-1779. Appointed United States Minister Plenipotentiary to Spain in 1779; appointed one of the ministers to negotiate the peace treaty between the United States and Great Britain in 1781; signed the Peace of Paris ending the American Revolution; appointed one of the ministers to negotiate treaties with European powers in 1783; appointed United States Secretary of Foreign Affairs under the Articles of Confederation in 1784; appointed as the first Chief Justice of the United States in 1789 and served until 1795; unsuccessful candidate for Governor of New York in 1792; United States Envoy Extraordinary and Minister Plenipotentiary to Great Britain, 1794-1795. As a Federalist, Jay was elected Governor of New York on April 27, 1795, defeating the Democratic-Republican candidate, R. Yates, 13,481 to 11,892. He took office on July 1, 1795. Jay was reelected to a second term on April 23, 1798, polling 16,012 votes to Democratic-Republican Richard Livingston's 13,632. During his administration, the New York Legislature convened in Stadt Huis in Albany, New York; the state's public records were moved to Albany; and the Cherry Valley Turnpike was incorporated. In addition, while he was governor the state legislature provided for the gradual emancipation of slaves within New York. Jay declined to seek renomination, and left office on July 1, 1801. He also declined reappointment as Chief Justice of the United States, and retired to his farm in Bedford, New York. He served as president of the Westchester Bible Society in 1818, and as president of the American Bible Society in 1821. Jay died on May 17, 1829, and was buried in the family cemetery in Rye, New York. Bibliography: D. S. Alexander, *A Political History of the State of New York*, 4 vols. (New York, 1906-1923); Alexander C. Flick, ed., *History of the State of New York*, 10 vols. (New York, 1933-1937); Donald L. Smith, *John Jay: Founder of the State and Nation* (New York, 1968); Roy Glashan,

American Governors and Gubernatorial Elections, 1775-1975 (Stillwater, Minnesota, 1975).

CLINTON, George, 1789-1795, 1801-1804

LEWIS, Morgan, 1804-1807

Born on October 16, 1754 in New York City, New York, the second son of Francis and Elizabeth (Annesley) Lewis. Married to Gertrude Livingston on May 11, 1779. He was educated at home, and in Elizabethtown, New Jersey; graduated from the college of New Jersey—now Princeton—in Princeton, New Jersey in 1773; he was studying law at the beginning of the American Revolution. Served as a volunteer with the American forces in the summer of 1775; elected Captain of a company of New York Militia; served as Deputy Quartermaster General for the Department of New York from 1776 until the end of the Revolution; served as Chief-of-Staff for General Horatio Gates. At the close of the conflict, Lewis resumed his legal studies, and was admitted to the bar. Began a private law practice in New York City in 1783. Member, New York Assembly, 1789-1790 and 1792; Attorney General of New York, 1791-1792; Justice of the New York Supreme Court, 1792-1801; Chief Justice of the New York Supreme Court, 1801. As a Democratic-Republican, Lewis was elected Governor of New York on April 23, 1804, receiving 30,829 votes to the Independent Democratic-Republican candidate, Aaron Burr's 22,139. Lewis took office on July 1, 1804. During his administration, he did much to advance the cause of education and strengthen the state militia. Also while Lewis was governor, the United States Military Academy at West Point, New York was formally opened. Lewis was defeated in his bid for a second term in the April 27, 1807 election, polling only 30,989 votes as the Quid or Anti-Caucus Democratic-Republican candidate while Daniel D. Tompkins, the Democratic-Republican nominee, received 35,074. Lewis left office on July 1, 1807. Afterwards, he served in the New York Senate in 1810, and on the Council of Appointment. During the War of 1812, Lewis was appointed a Quartermaster General in the United States Army in 1812; promoted to Major General in 1813, and served on the Niagara frontier; later he commanded the region around New York City in 1814. Lewis was a founder of New York University, and was Grand Master of the Freemasons of the United States in 1821. He was president of the New York Historical Society from 1832 to 1836, and president-general of the Society of the Cincinnati from 1839 to 1844. Lewis died in New York City on April 7, 1844. Bibliography: D. S. Alexander, *A Political History of the State of New York,* 4 vols. (New York, 1906-1923); Alexander C. Flick, ed., *History of the State of New York,* 10 vols. (New York, 1933-1937); David M. Ellis, et al., *A History of New York State* (Ithaca, 1967); Roy Glashan, *American Governors and Gubernatorial Elections, 1775-1975* (Stillwater, Minnesota, 1975).

TOMPKINS, Daniel D., 1807-1817

Born on June 21, 1774 in Fox Meadows (Scarsdale), New York, son of Jonathan G. Tompkins, a farmer and politician, and Sarah Hyatt Tompkins; one of nine children (the seventh son); a Presbyterian. Married Hannah Minthorne on February 20, 1798; father of Arietta, Griffin, Hannah Ellsworth, Sarah Ann, Minthorne, Daniel Hyatt, Susan McLaren and Ray. Attended local schools and graduated from Columbia College in 1795. Studied law and began law practice in New York City in 1797. Elected delegate to the State Constitutional Convention in 1801; served in the State Assembly, 1803-1804. Elected to the House of Representatives in 1804 as a Jeffersonian Republican, but resigned before taking a seat when appointed to the State Supreme Court; served until elected Governor in 1807 by 4,000 votes out of 66,000, receiving 35,074 to Morgan Lewis' 30,989. Reelected in 1810 over Federalist candidate Jonas Platt by a margin of 6,600, receiving 43,094 votes to Platt's 36,484; reelected in 1813 over Stephen Van Rensselaer by 3,600 votes, receiving 43,324 to Van Rensselaer's 39,718. In 1815, Tompkins defeated Federalist Rufus King, 45,412 votes to 38,647. As governor, Tompkins supported the national administration in the Embargo and the War of 1812. He also sponsored liberal reform measures in education, prison codes, the treatment of blacks and the militia system. He also assumed command of the Third Military District in 1814. In 1817, with his approval, the State Legislature abolished slavery in New York, effective July 4, 1827. Although not accused of personal dishonesty, discrepancies in his accounts plagued him for years after the war. While governor, he declined nomination as Secretary of State under James Madison. In 1816 he ran successfully on the ticket with James Monroe and served as Vice President for both Monroe terms. While Vice President he ran unsuccessfully for Governor in 1820, losing to DeWitt Clinton by about 1,500 votes out of the more than 90,000 cast, receiving 45,990 to Clinton's 47,447. Tompkins died on June 11, 1825 and was buried in St. Mark's Churchyard, New York City. Bibliography: Ray W. Irwin, *Daniel D. Tompkins: Governor of New York and Vice President of the United States* (New York, 1968); John S. Jenkins, *Lives of the Governors of the State of New York* (Syracuse, 1852); Hugh Hastings, ed., *Public Papers of Daniel D. Tompkins, 1807-1817*, 3 vols. (New York and Albany, 1898-1902); Charles Z. Lincoln, ed., *State of New York: Messages from the Governors, Comprising Executive Communications to the Legislature, and Other Papers . . . 1683-1906*, 11 vols. (Albany, 1909). Papers of Tompkins are in the Library of Congress, New York Historical Society and New York State Library.

TAYLER, John, 1817

Born on July 4, 1742 in New York City, New York. Moved to Albany, New York, when he was seventeen. During the American Revolution, Tayler was sent on a mission into Canada by General Philip Schuyler. He was also a businessman. Member, Provincial Congress, 1776 and 1777; member, Council of Safety, 1777; member of the Assembly from Albany during the first, second, fourth, ninth and tenth sessions, 1777-1787; Canal Commissioner of New York, 1792; appointed Recorder of Albany in 1793; became First Judge of Albany County, New York in 1797; member, New York Senate, 1802 and 1804-1813; Capitol Commissioner of New York, 1804; Lieutenant Governor of New York, 1811 and 1813-1817; member, Board of Regents of the University of New York; vice chancellor of the University of New York; chancellor of the University of New York. He was a Democratic-Republican. On February 24, 1817, Governor of New York Daniel D. Tompkins resigned from office after being elected Vice President of the United States, and as Lieutenant Governor, Tayler succeeded to the office. He was the first lieutenant governor to assume the governor's office, and during his administration he did not take the oath of office, but instead served under the Lieutenant Governor's Oath. Tayler completed the remainder of Tompkins' term, and then left office on July 1, 1817. Tayler died in Albany on March 19, 1829. Bibliography: DeAlva S. Alexander, *A Political History of the State of New York*, 4 vols. (New York, 1906-1923); Alexander C. Flick, ed., *History of the State of New York*, 10 vols. (New York, 1933-1937); David M. Ellis, *et al., A History of New York State* (New York, 1967); Roy Glashan, *American Governors and Gubernatorial Elections, 1775-1975* (Stillwater, Minnesota, 1975).

CLINTON, De Witt, 1817-1823, 1825-1828

Born on March 2, 1769 in Little Britain, New York, son of James Clinton, a military man who served with distinction during the Revolutionary War, and Mary De Witt Clinton. His father, James, was of English ancestry and his mother of Dutch background; one of seven children; a Presbyterian. On February 10, 1796, married Maria Franklin, by whom he had ten children; she died in 1818. On April 21, 1819, remarried to Catharine Jones. Educated at Kingston Academy and Columbia College, from which he graduated at the head of his class in 1786. Studied law and was admitted to the bar in 1790, but did not become a practicing lawyer. Became private secretary to his uncle, Governor George Clinton. This began his public and political career. An anti-Federalist, he was elected to the New York Assembly in 1797 and to the State Senate in 1798. On the resignation of John Armstrong from the United States Senate in 1802, Clinton was appointed as his successor. He resigned in 1803 to become Mayor of New York City, a post he held intermittently until 1815. While mayor, he also served as State Senator (1806-1813). In 1812 he was defeated for the presidency by James Madison. When Governor Daniel Tompkins resigned in February 1817 to become Vice President of the United States, a state convention of Republicans, later supported by others, nominated Clinton for the position. He was opposed by Peter B. Porter but won decisively, 43,310 votes to 1,479. He was reelected in 1820 over Vice President Tompkins by a narrow margin of 1,457 votes out of 93,437, receiving 47,447 votes to Tompkins' 45,990. Clinton retired from the governor's office in 1823, but a popular outcry over his removal as Canal Commissioner in 1824 led to his reelection that year as a People's Party candidate. He defeated Samuel Young by a vote of 103,452 to 87,093. In the gubernatorial election of 1826, Clinton again won, receiving 99,785 votes to William B. Rochester's 95,135. Clinton had a distinguished career as governor. His greatest achievement was the development of the Erie Canal. This 362-mile waterway, coupled with the 71-mile Champlain Canal, elevated New York City into leadership among the cities along the Atlantic seaboard. He also made impressive contributions in the realm of public education; he was a powerful advocate of free public schools. He was a positive force in the movements for religious freedom, scientific agriculture and cultural expansion, and supported art and literary societies, as well as both history and natural history programs. Clinton died suddenly on February 11, 1828 at his home in Albany during his fourth term as governor. His remains were placed in a cemetery vault in Albany and transferred to Greenwood Cemetery in Brooklyn, New York in 1844. Bibliography: Dorothie Bobbé, *De Witt Clinton* (New York, 1933); William W. Campbell, *Life and Writings of De Witt Clinton* (New York, 1849); C.

Z. Lincoln, ed., *State of New York, Messages from the Governors* (Albany, 1909); Edward Fitzpatrick, *Educational Views and Influence of De Witt Clinton* (New York, 1911); Cuyler Staats, *Tribute to the Memory of De Witt Clinton* (Albany, 1828); David Hosack, *Memoir of De Witt Clinton* (New York, 1829). The bulk of Clinton's manuscript correspondence is in the Columbia University Library and the New York Public Library; his diary is in the New York Historical Society.

YATES, Joseph C., 1823-1825

Born on November 9, 1768 in Schenectady, New York, son of Christopher and Jane Bradt Yates; brother of Henry, John B., Andrew and "several sisters"; Presbyterian. Married three times: to Ann Ellice, to Maria Kane (by whom he had one daughter) and to Ann Elizabeth Delancy (by whom he had two daughters). Educated in local schools and studied law; later practiced in Schenectady. In 1798 became first Mayor of the city. Elected to the State Senate as a Jeffersonian Republican in 1805 and appointed Justice of the State Supreme Court in 1808. Running virtually unopposed, Yates was elected Governor in 1822, receiving 120,493 votes to Independent Solomon Southwick's 2,910. Yates assumed office on January 1, 1823, under a new constitution calling for extensive changes in administrative structure; thus there were many new positions to fill. As a result, his two-year term was marked by numerous disputes, climaxed by his opposition to the placing of the election of electors in the hands of the people (unless done on a nationwide basis). His popularity quickly dissipated and he retired from politics at the end of his term. He lived in Schenectady for the remainder of his life, seldom participating in politics, although he supported Andrew Jackson and Martin Van Buren. Yates died on March 19, 1837 and was buried in Schenectady. Bibliography: John S. Jenkins, *Lives of the Governors of the State of New York* (Syracuse, 1852); Dixon Ryan Fox, *The Decline of Aristocracy in the Politics of New York* (New York, 1919); Charles Z. Lincoln, ed., *State of New York, Messages from the Governors, Comprising Executive Communications to the Legislature, and Other Papers . . . 1683-1906*, 11 vols. (Albany, 1909).

CLINTON, De Witt, 1817-1823, 1825-1828

PITCHER, Nathaniel, 1828

Born on a farm in Litchfield County, Connecticut on November 30, 1777, son of Nathaniel Pitcher, a farmer and militia captain in the Revolution, who moved his family to Kingsbury, Washington County, New York after the war. Nathaniel Pitcher, Jr.'s mother, whose name is not recorded, died soon after her son's birth. Before his death in 1802, the elder Pitcher married Margaret Stevenson, by whom three sons were born: Zina, Sidney and Charles. Nathaniel's education was limited to country schools. He joined the militia and the Masonic Order early in his life; served as Kingsbury Town Supervisor, 1804-1810; and spent one year in the State Assembly (1806). During this period, he married Anna B. Merritt; father of Montgomery, who became a physician, and Matthew, who became an army officer. Pitcher continued in various local offices and returned to the State Assembly, 1815-1817. Elected to Congress as a Republican in 1818, he served three undistinguished terms. As a delegate to the State Constitutional Convention in 1821, he usually sided with the moderates under Martin Van Buren. Nominated by the Van Buren "bucktail" faction of Republicans, he was narrowly elected Lieutenant Governor in 1826 on a separate line from that of DeWitt Clinton, who won the governorship. Pitcher became Governor on Clinton's death on February 11, 1828 and served the remaining months of his term, partly as a "lame duck"; since the party's gubernatorial nomination went to Van Buren in September. Pitcher's Masonic membership may have hurt his prospects, although his first message to the legislature had called for a special prosecutor to find the murderer of William Morgan, the renegade Mason, in that *cause célèbre*. Pitcher returned to Congress for the 1833-1835 term, but did not seek reelection. He died of heart disease on May 25, 1836, and was buried in Wright Cemetery, Sandy Hill. Bibliography: Stephen Fiama, "Who?: A Biography of Nathaniel Pitcher," Unpublished Manuscript on deposit in the New York State Library, Albany; Jabez D. Hammond, *History of Political Parties in the State of New York,* 2 vols. (Cooperstown, 1842); "Obituary," *Herald* [Sandy Hill] (May 31, 1836). Some letters of Pitcher are in the New York Public Library and New York State Library.

VAN BUREN, Martin, 1829

Born on December 5, 1782 in Kinderhook, New York, son of Abraham, a farmer and tavern keeper, and Maria (Hoes Van Alen) Van Buren, both of Dutch descent; brother of Derike, Hannah, Lawrence and Abraham. Married to Hannah Hoes on February 21, 1807; father of Abraham, John, and Martin. Van Buren was a member of the Dutch Reformed Church. Self-educated and trained in law; licensed to practice in 1803. Became active in local and state politics as a Jeffersonian Republican. Served as Surrogate of Columbia County, 1808-1813. Elected State Senator in 1812 and served until 1820. Became key leader of the "Albany Regency." Served as Attorney General of New York, 1815-1819. Served as United States Senator, 1821-1828. When Governor De Witt Clinton died in 1828, Van Buren ran for Governor against Smith Thompson, a member of the United States Supreme Court, and won by more than a 30,000 vote margin; Van Buren received 136,794 votes to Smith Thompson's 106,444 and Solomon Southwick's 33,345. Served as governor only from January 1, 1829 to March 5, 1829. His sole purpose in running was to secure the chief executive's office for his party. He resigned the governorship to become Secretary of State in Andrew Jackson's cabinet. Because of his brief tenure as governor, Van Buren made little impact upon state government. He did effect an important reform in banking with the establishment of the Safety Fund. Even as governor, Van Buren was preoccupied with national politics. From the time of his entry into the United States Senate, he became a national political figure and power broker in presidential politics. His was a leading voice in major national issues, from internal improvements to foreign policy. While he favored Republican William Crawford in the presidential campaign of 1824, he later became a Jackson supporter. He was elected Vice President under Jackson in 1832. In 1836, he was elected President. He lost the presidency in 1840 to Ohio's William Henry Harrison by an electoral vote of 234 to 60 in the celebrated "Log Cabin" campaign of that year. After leaving the presidency, Van Buren returned to Kinderhook. While president, he had purchased a 200-acre farm there with a thirty-room red brick mansion which he refurbished and named "Lindenwald." He remained intensely active in state and national politics until his death. Van Buren suffered from asthma and died on July 24, 1862; he was buried in Kinderhook. Bibliography: George Bancroft, *Martin Van Buren to the End of His Public Career* ((New York, 1889); Denis T. Lynch, *An Epoch and a Man; Martin Van Buren and His Times* (New York, 1929); Holmes M. Alexander, *The American Talleyrand; The Career and Contemporaries of Martin Van Buren, Eighth President* (New York, 1935); Robert V. Remini, *Martin Van Buren and the Making of the Democratic Party* (New York, 1959); C. Z. Lincoln, ed., *State of New York, Messages from the Governors* (Albany, 1909). Some Van Buren papers are in the New York State Library and in the Library of Congress.

THROOP, Enos Thompson, 1829-1833

Born on August 21, 1784 in Johnstown, New York, son of George Bliss, a teacher and minor office holder, and Abiah (Thompson) Throop; brother of George B., Mehitable and Mary Ann. Married Evelina J. Vredenburgh on July 14, 1814; father of three children, each of whom died in infancy. Throop had little formal schooling but studied law and began practicing in Poplar Ridge; he soon moved to Auburn. Appointed county clerk in 1811 and served until his election to the United States House of Representatives in 1814 as a Jeffersonian Republican; Throop was not reelected for a second term and resumed his law practice. In 1823 he was appointed Circuit Judge and in 1828 was elected Lieutenant Governor on the ticket with Martin Van Buren. Shortly after Van Buren resigned to become Secretary of State in the Andrew Jackson cabinet, Throop became Acting Governor. In 1830 he was elected Governor over the Antimasonic candidate, Francis Granger, by a margin of 8,500 votes out of a quarter million cast. He refused to run for reelection in 1832. While governor he opposed both further canal building and increases in the state debt; the first state insane asylum was also established. Constant political bickering discouraged him and he decided to leave politics at the end of his term. In 1833 Throop was appointed naval officer of the Port of New York, serving until 1838, when President Van Buren appointed him *chargé d'affaires* to the Kingdom of the Two Sicilies. He returned to the United States in 1842 and lived near Auburn; four years later he moved to his farm near Kalamazoo, Michigan. Throop returned to New York twenty years later; he died in Auburn on November 1, 1874 and was buried in St. Peter's Churchyard. Bibliography: John S. Jenkins, *Lives of the Governors of the State of New York* (Syracuse, 1852); Charles Z. Lincoln, ed., *State of New York: Messages from the Governors, Comprising Executive Communications to the Legislature, and Other Papers . . . 1683-1906*, 11 vols. (Albany, 1909); L. M. Sears, "The Neapolitan Mission of Enos Throop, 1838-1842," *New York State Historical Society Quarterly* (1928). Throop Papers are in the New York State Library and New York Historical Society.

MARCY, William Learned, 1833-1839

Born on December 12, 1786 in Southbridge, Massachusetts, son of Jedediah Marcy, II, a farmer, and Ruth (Learned) Marcy; brother of Jedediah, III. Married Dolly Newell on September 27, 1812; father of William G. and Samuel N. Remarried to Cornelia Knower in 1825; father of Cornelia and Edmund. Educated at Leicester Academy; graduated from

Brown University in 1808; taught school in Newport, Rhode Island; studied law and began practicing in Troy, New York in 1811. Served in War of 1812 as First Lieutenant in the State Militia, participating in two minor battles; remained in the militia until 1821, when he was appointed Adjutant General. Entering politics as a Jeffersonian Republican, he served as Recorder and Vice Mayor of Troy from 1816 to 1818 and 1821 to 1823. Also served as editor of the Troy *Northern Budget*. As a member of the "Albany Regency," he was State Comptroller, 1823-1829, and Justice of the State Supreme Court, 1829-1831. Elected to the United States Senate in 1830, he served from March 4, 1831 until the end of 1832, when he was elected Governor over Francis Granger by a margin of 10,000 votes out of over 300,000, receiving 166,410 votes to Granger's 156,672. While replying to Henry Clay in the Senate, Marcy made the famous statement "to the victor belong the spoils of the enemy." Reelected Governor in 1834 when he defeated Whig William H. Seward by a vote of 181,905 to 168,800, and in 1836 when he received 166,122 votes to Whig Jesse Buel's 136,648 and Equal Rights candidate Edwin Smith's 3,496. He was defeated for a fourth term in 1838 by William H. Seward by approximately 10,000 votes out of the nearly 400,000 cast, receiving 182,461 votes to Seward's 192,882. While governor, he supported "hard money" policies and the Independent Treasury, as well as most other measures of the Jackson and Van Buren administrations. The first State Geological Survey was conducted (and the highest mountain named for him) and a boundary dispute with New Jersey was settled. Following his defeat, in 1838, Marcy served as Mexican Claims Commissioner, 1839-1842; practiced law; and in 1845 was appointed Secretary of War in the Polk cabinet, serving until 1849. He again returned to law practice, until President Franklin Pierce appointed him Secretary of State, in which position he remained for the term, 1853-1857. At the end of the Pierce administration, Marcy returned to New York. He was resting at Ballston Spa when he died on July 4, 1857; he was buried in Rural Cemetery, Albany. Bibliography: Ivor Debenham Spencer, *The Victor and the Spoils: A Life of William L. Marcy* (Providence, 1949); Samuel Flagg Bemis, ed., *The American Secretaries of State and Their Diplomacy*, 10 vols. (New York, 1927-1929); John S. Jenkins, *Lives of the Governors of the State of New York* (Syracuse, 1852); Charles Z. Lincoln, ed., *State of New York: Messages from the Governors, Comprising Executive Communications to the Legislature, and Other Papers. . . 1683-1906*, 11 vols. (Albany, 1909). Papers of Marcy are in the Library of Congress, New York State Library, New York Public Library, and the New York Historical Society.

SEWARD, William Henry, 1839-1843

Born on May 16, 1801 in Florida, New York, son of Samuel S. and Mary (Jennings) Seward, who were of English stock with a mixture of Welsh and Irish; brother of Benjamin Jennings, Edwin Polydore, George Washington and Louisa Cornelia (Canfield); an Episcopalian. His father, a Jeffersonian Republican, was a doctor, postmaster, county judge, and land speculator. Married to Frances Miller on October 20, 1824 and father of Augustus Henry, Frederick William, Cornelia, William Henry, Jr. and Fanny. Attended Union College (Schenectady) and graduated in 1820. Studied law and was admitted to the bar in 1822. Began practicing in Auburn, New York in 1823. Became active in local and state politics as a Jeffersonian Republican, but later switched to the Whigs. Was elected to the State Senate in 1830 and served two terms. With the support of Thurlow Weed, he ran for the governorship in 1834 against William L. Marcy, but was defeated, receiving 168,800 votes to Marcy's 181,905. He ran for Governor again in 1838, receiving 192,882 votes to Democrat William Marcy's 182,461 in the general election, and won the governorship. Seward was reelected in 1840, receiving 222,011 votes to William Bouck's 216,808 and Gerrit Smith's 2,662. He served as governor for four years. As governor, he developed a reputation as a social reformer, progressive leader and humanitarian. Seward was a strong supporter of internal improvements. He sought reforms in the school system of New York City so as to provide special assistance for the children of Catholics and recent immigrants; he also called for the abolition of capital punishment and urged prison reform. Seward was a strong spokesman for both women's rights and a more humane treatment of Indians and blacks. He was one of the earliest active political opponents of slavery. His governorship, however, was stronger in promises than in results; few of his noble pronouncements were translated into public policy. However, he did push New York State in a liberal direction during the critical ante-bellum period. After two terms, he declined to be a candidate for a third, due to the poor state of his personal finances. With his election to the United States Senate in 1848, Seward entered upon the national scene. He was a prominent contender for the presidential nomination in 1856 and 1860, but failed to win the Republican Party's support. He served as Secretary of State under Presidents Abraham Lincoln and Andrew Johnson, and was one of the nation's leading political figures during the Civil War era. Seward returned to Auburn in the autumn of 1871 in poor health; he died on October 10, 1872 and was buried there. Bibliography: Glyndon G. Van Deusen, *William Henry Seward* (New York, 1967); Frederic Bancroft, *The Life of William Seward*, 2 vols. (New York, 1900); William H. Seward, *Autobiography, From 1801 to 1834*, ed. F. W. Seward (New York, 1877-1891); J. W. Pratt, "Governor Seward and the New York City School Controversy, 1840-42," *New York History*, vol. XLII, no. 4 (October, 1961). Papers of Seward are in the Rhees Library at the University of Rochester.

BOUCK, William C., 1843-1845

Born on January 7, 1786 in Schoharie Valley, New York, son of Christian, a wealthy farmer, and Margaret (Borst) Bouck, of German ancestry. Bouck had little formal education. Married Catherine Lawyer in 1807; father of eleven children. Elected Town Clerk in 1807 and Town Supervisor in each of the next two years as a Jeffersonian Republican. Appointed Sheriff in 1812, but was removed by Federalists in the next year. Elected to the State Assembly in 1813, serving until 1820 when he was elected to the State Senate for one term. Appointed Colonel in the State Militia in 1819. Appointed supervisor of the Erie Canal in 1821, he remained in that position until 1840. Identified with the Hunker faction of the Democratic Party, Bouck ran for Governor in 1840 and lost to William H. Seward, receiving 216,808 votes to Seward's 222,011. Elected in 1842 by a 22,000 vote margin over Whig Luther Bradish, with 208,072 votes to Bradish's 186,060. Bouck's one term as governor was stormy because of the split in the Democratic Party. He aroused much opposition by his appointments and lost popularity when he called out the militia to settle an anti-rent dispute in Columbia County. Because the radical faction of the Democratic Party often joined with Whigs in the legislature, Governor Bouck was not able to accomplish many of his plans. He was not renominated, the party choosing Silas Wright instead. In 1846 Bouck was a delegate to the State Constitutional Convention; while attending the convention he was appointed Federal Assistant Treasurer in New York City, but was removed by the incoming Whig administration in 1849. Bouck retired to his Schoharie farm where he died on

April 19, 1859; he was buried nearby. Bibliography: John S. Jenkins, *Lives of the Governors of the State of New York* (Syracuse, 1852); Ronald E. Shaw, *Erie Water West: A History of the Erie Canal, 1792-1854* (Lexington, 1966); George W. Roach, "The Presidential Campaign of 1844," *New York History*, vol. XIX (1938); Charles Z. Lincoln, ed., *State of New York: Messages from the Governors, Comprising Executive Communications to the Legislature, and Other Papers . . . 1683-1906*, 11 vols. (Albany, 1909). Papers of Bouck are in the New York Historical Society.

WRIGHT, Silas, 1845-1847

Born on May 24, 1795 in Amherst, Massachusetts, the fifth son of Silas, a farmer, and Eleanor (Goodale) Wright; a Presbyterian. Married to Clarissa Moody on September 11, 1833; they had no children. Wright grew up in Weybridge, Vermont, where he attended district schools; entered Addison County Grammar School when he was fourteen; graduated from Middlebury College, Middlebury, Vermont in 1815; studied law with Roger Skinner in Sandy Hill, New York. Admitted to the New York Bar in 1819. Appointed Brigadier General of the New York Militia in 1827. Began private law practice in Canton, New York. Surrogate of St. Lawrence County, New York, 1821-1824; member, New York Senate, 1824-1827; chairman, Committee on Canals; member, United States House of Representatives, 1827-1829; resigned from Congress; appointed Comptroller of the State of New York in 1829 and served until 1833. Member, United States Senate, 1833-1844; declined an appointment by President John Tyler to the United States Supreme Court in 1844; resigned from the United States Senate after being elected Governor of New York. Delegate to the Democratic National Convention of 1832. As a Democrat, Wright was elected Governor of New York on November 4, 1844, receiving 241,087 votes to Whig Millard Fillmore's 231,060. He was sworn into office on January 1, 1845. During his administration, Wright, though he sympathized with the tenants' grievances and urged them to seek redress under the law, ordered the New York militia to crush the 1845 anti-rent disturbances and prosecuted those responsible for the violence. However, the following year, he advocated a tax on income from rents and short-term leases. While Wright was governor, the consolidation of small schools was implemented; the Hudson River Railroad Company was organized; and the University of Buffalo was founded. In 1845, the New York Constitution was amended to remove any property qualification for public office holders within the state. A Constitutional Convention met in Albany, New York, from June 1, 1846 until October 9, 1846, to frame a new constitution, which was actually ratified in November 1846. Wright was defeated in his bid for reelection on November 2, 1846; polling 192,361 votes to Whig John Young's 197,627, Wright left office on January 1, 1847. Afterwards, he retired to private life. Wright died in Canton on August 27, 1847 and was buried in Old Canton Cemetery. Bibliography: D. S. Alexander, *A Political History of the State of New York*, 4 vols. (New York, 1906-1923); Alexander C. Flick, ed., *History of the State of New York*, 10 vols. (New York, 1933-1937); Roy Glashan, *American Governors and Gubernatorial Elections, 1775-1975* (Stillwater, Minnesota, 1975). Silas Wright Collection, St. Lawrence University, Canton, New York.

YOUNG, John, 1847-1849

Born on June 12, 1802 in Chelsea, Vermont, the only child of Thomas, a farmer, and Mary (Gale) Young; Episcopalian. Married to Ellen Harris in 1833; father of four children. Moved with his parents to Freeport (now Conesus) in Livingston County, New York in 1806. Attended the district school; studied law. Admitted to the New York Bar in 1829, and started a private law practice in Geneseo, New York. As a Jackson Democrat, he was an unsuccessful candidate for Livingston County Clerk in 1828; elected to the New York State Assembly as an Anti-Mason candidate; member, New York State Assembly, 1833 and 1844-1845; elected as a Whig to the United States House of Representatives; member, United States House of Representatives, 1836-1837 and 1841-1843. As a Whig, Young was elected Governor of New York on November 2, 1846, receiving 197,627 votes to Democratic incumbent Governor Silas Wright's 192,361. He was sworn into office on January 1, 1847. Almost immediately after taking office, Young pardoned the anti-rent rioters who had been sent to jail. During his administration, the Oneida Utopian community was established, and a women's rights convention was held in Seneca Falls, New York. New York's 1846 Constitution stripped the governor of much of his appointive power; even so, Young appointed those he was permitted to, without consulting local leaders. This, together with his opposition to the Mexican War, did not make him a popular governor. While in office, Young remained a staunch Whig and was a delegate to the Whig National Convention held in Philadelphia, Pennsylvania in 1848. Young left office on January 1, 1849. Because of his loyalty to the Whig Party, he was appointed Assistant Treasurer of the United States at New York City in June 1849. He held the post until his death. Young died on April 23, 1852 in New York City and was buried in Temple Hill Cemetery in Geneseo. Bibliography: D. S. Alexander, *A Political History of the State of New York*, 4 vols. (New York, 1906-1923); Alexander C. Flick, ed., *History of the State of New York*, 10 vols. (New York, 1933-1937); Roy Glashan, *American Governors and Gubernatorial Elections, 1775-1975* (Stillwater, Minnesota, 1975). Papers of Young are in the New York State Library, Albany, New York.

FISH, Hamilton, 1849-1851

Born on August 3, 1808 in New York City, New York, son of Nicholas, an officer in the American Army during the Revolutionary War, and Elizabeth (Stuyvesant) Fish; an Episcopalian. Married to Julia Kean on December 15, 1836; father of Nicholas, Hamilton, Stuyvesant, and five daughters. Received a primary education in the private school of M. Bancel; graduated with honors from Columbia College, New York City, in 1827; studied law in the office of Peter A. Jay. Admitted to the New York Bar in 1830; began a private law practice in New York City. Commissioner of Deeds for the City and County of New York, 1832-1834; unsuccessful Whig candidate for the New York Legislature, 1834; member, United States House of Representatives, 1843-1845; unsuccessful candidate for Lieutenant Governor of New York, 1846; Lieutenant Governor of New York, 1848-1849. Trustee, Columbia College; president-general, Society of the Cincinnati; president, Union League Club; president, New York Historical Society. As a Whig, Fish was elected Governor of New York on November 7, 1848, receiving 218,280 votes to Free Soil candidate John Dix's 123,360 and Democrat Reuben Walworth's 114,457. He was sworn into office on January 1, 1849. During his administration, the legislature enacted a free school system for the state, and the University of Rochester was opened. In addition, New York's canal system was extended, and the Hudson River railroad was opened as far as Poughkeepsie, New York. While he was governor, Fish was outspoken in his opposition to the extension of slavery into the region acquired from Mexico by the Treaty of Guadalupe Hidalgo. He was selected by President John Tyler to be United States Secretary of the Treasury; however, Tyler died in 1850 before appointing Fish to the position. Fish was not nominated for reelection, but was instead selected by the New York Legislature to serve in the United States Senate. As a result, he left the governor's office on January 1, 1851. Fish served in the United States Senate from 1851 to 1857. Afterwards, he spent two years traveling in Europe. He was appointed by President Abraham Lincoln to the Board of Commissioners for the Relief and Exchange of Union Prisoners captured by the South during the Civil War. In March, 1869, he was appointed by President Ulysses S. Grant to be United States Secretary of State, a post he held until March, 1877. During this time, he was a member of the Joint High Commission which negotiated the Treaty of Washington between the United States and Great Britain that was signed in 1871. After his service as Secretary of State, Fish returned to his private law practice and real estate holdings in New York City. Fish died in Garrison, New York on September 7, 1893 and was buried in St. Phillip's Cemetery. Bibliography: D. S. Alexander, *A Political History of the State of New York*, 4 vols. (New York, 1906-1923); A. Elwood Corning, *Hamilton Fish* (New York, 1918); Alexander C. Flick, ed., *History of the State of New York*, 10 vols. (New York, 1933-1937); Roy Glashan, *American Governors and Gubernatorial Elections, 1775-1975* (Stillwater, Minnesota, 1975).

HUNT, Washington, 1851-1853

Born on August 5, 1811 in Windham, New York, son of Sanford and Fanny (Rose) Hunt; an Episcopalian. Married Mary Hosmer Walbridge in 1834. He had only a common school education, but determined to follow a profession; he began to study law at an early age and in 1834 was admitted to the bar. In 1836 he became the first Judge of Niagara County. A member of the Whig Party, he was elected to Congress in 1842 and served until 1849, when he was elected State Comptroller. In 1850 Hunt received the Democrat nomination for the governorship of New York, and was elected over Horatio Seymour by only 262 votes, receiving 238,421 votes to Seymour's 238,159. As governor, Hunt emphasized the need for economy and efficiency in state government, and recommended the improvement of roads and the expansion of the canal system to compete with the railroads. Hunt was not always tactful in his methods, and as a consequence he became a party to a legislative squabble regarding the Erie Canal. He was influential in publicizing the problems of the large number of immigrants arriving in New York. In 1852, Horatio Seymour defeated him for reelection, with Hunt receiving 227,931 votes to Seymour's 250,837. Hunt returned to his farm in Lockport, New York. In 1856, Hunt was chosen temporary chairman of the final Whig National Convention. When the Whig Party was dissolved, he became a Democrat, strongly opposing the Republican Party. In 1860, he declined an offer to run as the Democratic nominee for Vice President. Hunt died on February 2, 1867 and was buried in Glenwood Cemetery in Lockport, New York. Bibliography: *New York Times* (February 3, 1867); D. S. Alexander, *A Political History of the State of New York*, 4 vols. (New York, 1906-1923); Ray B. Smith, ed., *History of the State of New York: Political and Governmental*, 4 vols. (Syracuse, 1922).

SEYMOUR, Horatio, 1853-1855, 1863-1865

Born on May 31, 1810 in Pompey Hill, New York, son of Henry and Mary (Forman) Seymour; a Protestant. His father was a political lieutenant of Martin Van Buren, a canal commissioner and president of the Farmers' Loan and Trust Company of New York. Married Mary Bleeker on May 31, 1835; they had no children. Attended the Utica Academy, Oxford Academy and then Geneva Academy; entered Captain Partridge's Military Academy in Middletown, Connecticut. After graduating from the latter in two years, he studied law and was admitted to the bar in 1832. In 1833, Seymour became military secretary to Governor Marcy for six years. In 1841, was elected to the Assembly; in 1842, elected Mayor of Utica; in 1844, elected again to the Assembly and became that body's Speaker in 1845. In 1850, Seymour received the Democratic nomination for Governor, but was defeated by Washington Hunt by 262 votes, receiving 238,159 votes to Hunt's 238,421. In 1852 he again ran, this time defeating Hunt by 22,906 votes, receiving 250,837 votes to Hunt's 227,931. During his first term as governor, Seymour took particular care to improve the administration of the penal system. Also, he vetoed a bill prohibiting the sale of liquor; however, it was largely because of this that he was defeated in his bid for reelection in 1854 by the temperance candidate, Myron Clark, by 309 votes. Clark received 234,716 votes in the election, while Seymour polled 234,407. In 1856, Seymour went to Cincinnati as a delegate to the Democratic National Convention; soon afterwards he left politics for a few years and returned to his farm, where he displayed a great interest in agriculture. When the Civil War began, he donated funds for the purpose of enlisting soldiers for the Union cause. In 1862 Seymour was again elected Governor by a majority of 10,752 votes, receiving 265,789 votes to Republican Frederick Schaffer's 255,037. During the draft riots of July, 1863, Seymour proclaimed New York City in a state of insurrection. He urged the mobs to disperse, insisted upon obedience to the law in his public addresses, and thereby helped to end the riots. Although Seymour supported the Union cause, he opposed Lincoln's policies on emancipation, conscription and military arrest. In 1864, he was defeated for reelection by Republican Reuben Fenton by 8,293 votes, receiving 361,264 votes to Fenton's 369,557. After the Civil War ended, Seymour continued to oppose the Republican Party and was elected chairman of the Democratic National Convention which met in July, 1868. The convention nominated Seymour for President, but he lost the subsequent election to General Ulysses S. Grant. Seymour died on February 12, 1886. Bibliography: *New York Times* (September 19, 1872); *New York Times* (February 13, 1886); D. S. Alexander, *A Political History of the State of New York*, 4 vols. (New York, 1906-1923); Ray B. Smith, ed., *History of the State of New York: Political and Governmental*, 4 vols. (Syracuse, 1922).

CLARK, Myron, 1855-1857

Born on October 23, 1806 in Naples (Ontario County), New York, son of Major Joseph and Mary (Sutton) Clark. Married Zilpha Watkins; the father of four daughters and one son. Had a common school education; served as a Lieutenant Colonel in the state militia when he finished his schooling. He began his public career as Sheriff of Ontario County in 1837; was elected to the State Senate in 1851 and reelected in 1853. In the Senate, he became a strong proponent of temperance and aided in securing the passage of a prohibitory liquor law in 1854, only to have it vetoed by Governor Seymour. In 1854 he was nominated for

Governor of New York by the Whig, Free Democracy, Anti-Nebraska and Temperance parties; Clark was elected Governor over Democrat Horatio Seymour by 309 votes, the smallest majority ever given to a governor of New York, receiving 234,716 votes to Seymour's 234,407. As governor, Clark succeeded in obtaining the passage of a bill prohibiting intoxicants, but the law was partially enforced for only eight months until it was declared unconstitutional by the Court of Appeals. In 1856, Clark engaged in a controversy with the legislature; he refused to call an extra session of the legislature to pass appropriation bills which had earlier been delayed for the purpose of forcing such a session. During his term, Clark approved the law authorizing the construction of the Albany Bridge. He was not nominated at the end of his term because the leaders of his party were convinced that he could not be elected again. In 1862, President Lincoln appointed Clark as the first Collector of the Internal Revenue of the Port of New York. After serving in that office he retired to Canandaigua. In 1874 he emerged as a third-party Prohibitionist candidate, but was not successful. Myron Clark died on August 23, 1892 in Canandaigua, New York. Bibliography: *New York Times* (August 24, 1892); Ray B. Smith, ed., *History of the State of New York: Political and Governmental*, 4 vols. (Syracuse, 1922); D. S. Alexander, *A Political History of the State of New York*, 4 vols. (New York, 1906-1923).

KING, John Alsop, 1857-1859

Born on January 3, 1788 in New York City, the eldest son of Rufus and Mary (Alsop) King; an Episcopalian. Brother of Charles, James G., and Edward. His father was United States Minister to England. Married Mary Ray on January 3, 1810; they had seven children. Attended school in Harrow, England, and upon his return to New York studied law and was admitted to the bar. During the War of 1812, he was a Lieutenant of Cavalry in New York. After the war, he engaged in farming in Jamaica, New York. He was a member of the State Assembly in 1819-1821 and of the State Senate in 1823-1825; resigned his seat to accompany his father to the Court of St. James in London as Secretary of Legation. When his father returned to the United States due to poor health, he remained in England as *chargé d'affaires* until the new minister arrived. He returned to the legislature in 1839; in 1849, King was sent to Congress as a Whig Representative. King opposed all compromise measures regarding slavery, in particular the Fugitive-Slave Bill, and urged the admission of California as a free state. In 1855, he presided at a convention in Syracuse, New York, where the state's Republican Party was formed. He was a delegate to the first Republican National Convention in 1856 held in Philadelphia. In 1856, King was nominated for Governor of New York in the Republican State Convention and was elected, receiving 266,328 votes to Democrat Amasa J. Parker's 197,172. King's term of office was largely uneventful; he advocated the improvement of the state's educational system and the expansion of the Erie Canal. Also, King founded the New York Agricultural Society. When his governorship ended, he declined renomination and retired at the age of seventy-one. King's retirement was interrupted only once, when he was appointed a member of the New York delegation to the Peace Conference of 1861 at Washington. King died on July 7, 1867 at his home in Jamaica, New York. Bibliography: *New York Tribune* (July 8, 1867); Ray B. Smith, ed., *History of the State of New York: Political and Governmental*, 4 vols. (Syracuse, 1922); D. S. Alexander, *A Political History of the State of New York*, 4 vols. (New York, 1906-1923).

MORGAN, Edwin Denison, 1859-1863

Born on February 8, 1811 in Washington, Massachusetts, son of Jasper Avery, a farmer, and Catherine (Copp) Morgan; a Presbyterian. Married to Eliza Matilda Waterman in 1833; father of five children. Morgan moved with his parents to Windsor County, Connecticut in 1822. Educated in public schools; attended Bacon Academy, Colchester, Connecticut. During the Civil War, he served as a Major General of Volunteers, United States Army from 1861 to 1863, and was a commander of the Department of New York. Became a clerk in his uncle's grocery store in Hartford, Connecticut, and later became a partner; moved to New York City, New York in 1836 and became a partner in the wholesale grocery firm of Morgan and Earl. In 1837 the partnership was dissolved and Morgan began a grocery business, E. D. Morgan and Company, which eventually became involved in banking and brokerage investments as well. Elected to the Hartford City Council in 1832; elected as a member of the New York City Board of Assistant Aldermen in 1849; president, New York City Board of Assistant Aldermen; member, New York Senate, 1850-1855; New York State Commission of Immigration, 1855-1858. Vice president, Republican National Convention, 1856; chairman, Republican National Convention, 1856, 1860, 1864, 1872 and 1876; delegate, Republican National Convention, 1860. As a Republican, Morgan was elected Governor of New York on November 2, 1858, receiving 257,868 votes to Democrat Amasa J. Parker's 230,329 and American Party candidate Lorenzo Burrows' 61,137. He was sworn into office on January 1, 1859. During his administration, he improved the state's credit and strengthened the canal system. A popular chief executive, Morgan was reelected on November 6, 1860, polling 358,002 votes to Stephen H. Douglas Democratic candidate, William Kelly's 294,803. In 1861, Vassar College in Poughkeepsie, New York was chartered. While Morgan was governor, the Civil War broke out. The New York Legislature appropriated 3 million dollars to sustain the Union, and Morgan called for 25,000 troops. By the end of his administration, New York had sent 120 regiments to serve in the United States Army. Declining to be nominated for reelection, Morgan left office on January 1, 1863. Afterwards, he was commissioned by the New York Legislature to place the harbor of New York City in a state of defense. He also served as Major General of Volunteers in the United States Army. Morgan was a member of the United States Senate from 1863 to 1869. He was an unsuccessful candidate for election to the United States Senate in 1875, and was defeated in the 1876 New York gubernatorial election by Democrat Lucius Robinson. In 1881, he declined an offer by President Chester A. Arthur to be United States Secretary of the Treasury. Morgan died in New York City on February 14, 1883 and was buried in Cedar Hill Cemetery in Hartford. Bibliography: D.S. Alexander, *A Political History of the State of New York,* 4 vols. (New York, 1906-1923); Alexander C. Flick, ed., *History of the State of New York,* 10 vols. (New York, 1933-1937); New York State Historical Association, *New York: A Guide to the Empire State* (New York, 1940); Roy Glashan, *American Governors and Gubernatorial Elections, 1775-1975* (Stillwater, Minnesota, 1975).

SEYMOUR, Horatio, 1853-1855, 1863-1865

FENTON, Reuben Eaton, 1865-1869

Born on July 4, 1819 in Carroll, New York, the youngest son of George W., a business-man, and Elsie (Owen) Fenton. Married to Jane Frew in 1838; after her death he remarried to Elizabeth Scudder on June 14, 1844; father of Josephine, Jeanette and Reuben E. Received a preparatory education; was forced to curtail his academic studies when he was seventeen because of the failure of his father's business; studied law. Worked in logging camps; engaged in mercantile pursuits. One of the founders of the Republican Party; chairman, New York Republican Convention, 1855. Supervisor of the township of Carroll, 1846-1852; member, United States House of Representatives, 1853-1855; unsuccessful candidate for reelection in 1855; member, United States House of Representatives, 1857-1864; resigned from Congress after being elected Governor. As the Union Party candidate, Fenton was elected Governor of New York on November 8, 1864, receiving 369,557 votes to Democrat Horatio Seymour's 361,264. He was sworn into office on January 1, 1865. During his administration, he vetoed several special charters and insisted that incorporated firms comply with the general laws. He also urged that liberal provisions be made for disabled veterans, widows and orphans of soldiers. While he was governor, an agency was established to care for sick and wounded soldiers; Cornell University, Ithaca, New York, was chartered; public schools were made free of charge; and the New York Constitution was amended to prohibit voters from being denied the franchise because of service in the military. Also a Constitutional Convention was convened, and a new constitution was prepared; however, it was rejected by the voters. Fenton was reelected to a second term on November 6, 1866, receiving 366,315 votes to Democrat John T. Hoffman's 352,526. Fenton left office on January 1, 1869, after being elected to the United States Senate. He was a member of the Senate from 1869 until 1875. Fenton served as chairman of the United States Commission to the International Monetary Conference held in Paris, France in 1878. Afterwards, he engaged in banking. Fenton died on August 25, 1885 in Jamestown, New York and was buried in Lakeview Cemetery. Bibliography: D. S. Alexander, *A Political History of the State of New York*, 4 vols. (New York, 1906-1923); Homer Stebbins, *A Political History of the State of New York, 1865-1869* (New York, 1913); Alexander C. Flick, ed., *History of the State of New York,* 10 vols. (New York, 1933-1937); Roy Glashan, *American Governors and Gubernatorial Elections, 1775-1975* (Stillwater, Minnesota, 1975).

HOFFMAN, John Thompson, 1869-1873

Born on January 10, 1828 in Sing Sing (later Ossining), New York, son of Adrian Kissam, a physician, and Jane Ann (Thompson) Hoffman. Married to Ella Starkweather in 1854. Graduated with honors from Union College, Schenectady, New York in 1846. Studied law with Aaron Ward and Albert Lockwood; admitted to the New York Bar in 1849. Formed a law partnership with Samuel M. Woodruff and William M. Leonard. Became a member of the New York State Democratic Central Committee in 1848; member of the Young Men's Tammany Hall General Committee in 1854; member of the Tammany Society in 1859; elected to the Central Committee of the Tammany Society; Grand Sachem of the Tammany Society, 1866-1868. Elected Recorder of New York City, New York in 1860 and 1863; elected Mayor of New York City in 1865 and 1867; unsuccessful candidate in the 1866 New York gubernatorial election; resigned as Mayor of New York City in 1868.

As a Democrat, Hoffman was elected Governor of New York on November 3, 1868, receiving 439,301 votes to Republican John A. Griswold's 411,355; he was sworn into office on January 1, 1869. Hoffman's candidacy for governor had been supported by Tammany Hall and "Boss Tweed"—William M. Tweed—but no charge was ever proved that Hoffman profited from Tammany graft. However, because of his intimate contact with the members of Tammany Hall, he probably knew of the existence of many irregularities. Hoffman was reelected to a second term on November 8, 1870, polling 399,552 votes to Republican Stewart L. Woodford's 366,436. During his administration, the cornerstone for the new State Capitol was laid, and Syracuse University was opened. While Hoffman was governor, public indignation toward the "Tweed Ring" grew, and the extent of its graft became known. Though Hoffman began to show signs of breaking with the "Tweed Ring," he was already a ruined man politically. Hoffman left office on January 1, 1873 and returned to his private law practice. As his health began to fail, he traveled abroad to seek help. Hoffman died on March 24, 1888 in Wiesbaden, Germany. Bibliography: Samuel J. Tilden, *The New York City "Ring"* (New York, 1873); D. S. Alexander, *A Political History of the State of New York*, 4 vols. (New York, 1906-1923); Alexander C. Flick, ed., *History of the State of New York*, 10 vols. (New York, 1933-1937); Roy Glashan, *American Governors and Gubernatorial Elections, 1775-1975* (Stillwater, Minnesota, 1975).

DIX, John Adams, 1873-1875

Born on July 24, 1798 in Boscawen, New Hampshire, son of Timothy, a merchant, and Abigail (Wilkins) Dix; one of nine children; an Episcopalian. Married to Catharine Morgan in 1826; father of Morgan. Received an elementary education in the classics, English literature and public speaking; attended Phillips Exeter Academy for one year; attended the College of Montreal in Canada for fifteen months, but withdrew at the beginning of the War of 1812; privately tutored in Boston, Massachusetts, but left to join the United States Army. Was appointed a Cadet during the War of 1812; promoted to Second Lieutenant in March, 1814; served as an Adjutant with the Twenty-first Infantry stationed in New Hampshire; transferred to the Third Artillery in 1819. He was appointed aide-de-camp to Major General Jacob Brown; and attained the rank of Captain. Studied law under the direction of William Wirt; admitted to the District of Columbia Bar in 1824. Dix resigned his military commission in July, 1828. Began private law practice in Cooperstown, New York in 1828. Moved to Albany, New York, in 1830; appointed Adjutant General of New York in 1830. Secretary, Democratic National Convention, 1832; Regent, University of the State of New York; Secretary of State of New York, 1833-1839. Published the *Northern Light*, 1841-1843; member, New York House of Representatives, 1842; member, United States Senate, 1845-1849; unsuccessful Free Soil candidate for Governor of New York, 1848; Assistant Treasurer of the United States in New York City, 1853; Secretary of the Treasury of the United States, 1861. Postmaster of New York City, New York, 1860-1861; Major General, United States Army, 1861-1865; president, Mississippi and Missouri Railway Company; president, Union Pacific Railroad Company; president, Erie Railroad Company. United States Minister to France, 1866-1869. Author: *A Winter in Madeira; and a Summer in Spain and Florence* (1850); *Speeches and Occasional Addresses*, 2 vols. (1864); translation of *Dies Irae* (1863); translation of *Stabat Mater* (1863). Though he was a Democrat, Dix was nominated by the Republican Party in the 1872 New York gubernatorial election. On November 5, 1872, he was elected Governor of New York, receiving

445,801 votes to the Liberal Republican candidate Francis Kernan's 392,350. He was sworn into office on January 1, 1873. During his administration, the International Bridge across the Niagara River was completed; the first Chautauqua Assembly met at Lake Chautauqua, New York; and a compulsory education law was passed. Also while he was governor, New York and the rest of the United States was struck by the economic Panic of 1873. Dix was nominated by the Republicans for reelection; however, in the November 3, 1874 gubernatorial election, he was defeated by Democrat Samuel J. Tilden, 416,391 votes to 366,074. Dix left office on January 1, 1875 and retired to New York City. He died on April 21, 1879 in New York City, and was buried in Trinity Cemetery. Bibliography: D. S. Alexander, *A Political History of the State of New York*, 4 vols. (New York, 1906-1923); Alexander C. Flick, ed., *History of the State of New York*, 10 vols. (New York, 1933-1937); New York State Historical Association, *New York: A Guide to the Empire State* (New York, 1940); Roy Glashan, *American Governors and Gubernatorial Elections, 1775-1975* (Stillwater, Minnesota, 1975).

TILDEN, Samuel Jones, 1875-1877

Born on February 9, 1814 in New Lebanon, New York, son of Eliam, a storekeeper and postmaster, and Polly Younglove (Jones) Tilden; brother of John, Mary B., Moses Y., George F., Henry A., and Henrietta. Tilden never married. Because of uncertain health, he spent little time in the local village school; was privately tutored at home; attended an academy in Williamstown, Massachusetts. Moved to New York City, New York in 1832, to continue his preparatory studies; entered Yale University, New Haven, Connecticut in June, 1834, but withdrew after one term; attended the University of the City of New York intermittently; graduated from the Law School of the University of the City of New York in 1841. Admitted to the New York Bar in 1841. As a political writer, Tilden often used the pseudonyms "Jacksonis Amicus" and "Crino." Was a clerk in the law office of John W. Edmonds in New York City; set up a private law practice. Tilden established and published the *New York Morning News* in 1844. He specialized in the refinancing and reorganization of railroads, acquired an interest in mining, and eventually accumulated assets valued at approximately 6 million. Became Corporation Counsel of New York City in 1843. Leader of the "Barnburners" faction of the Democratic Party, 1845. Member, New York Legislature, 1846 and 1872; member, New York Constitutional Convention, 1846 and 1867. Opposed the election of Abraham Lincoln; took little part in Civil War activities; chairman, New York State Democratic Committee, 1866-1874; leader in the elimination of the "Tweed Ring" of New York City; actively participated in presidential elections of 1868 and 1872. Founder of the Bar Association of the City of New York. As a Democrat, Tilden was elected Governor of New York on November 3, 1874, defeating Republican incumbent Governor John A. Dix, 416,391 votes to 366,074; he was sworn into office on January 1, 1875. Elected as a proponent of reform, Tilden substantially reduced state taxes and expenditures by the elimination of fraud and the encouragement of economy in his administration. Also while he was governor, Tilden exposed the fraudulent activities of the "Canal Ring" which controlled the funds spent on the repair and expansion of New York's canal system. In 1875, Tilden received an honorary LL.D. degree from Yale University. In June, 1876, the Democratic National Convention met in St. Louis, Missouri, and on the second ballot nominated Tilden for the presidency of the United States. In the 1876 presidential election, Tilden appeared to have won more electoral votes than Republican Rutherford B.

Hayes; however, the results in several states were disputed, and an Electoral Commission, created by the United States Congress, awarded these electoral votes to Hayes. To avoid any possible civil disturbance, Tilden accepted the decision. Tilden left office on January 1, 1877. Afterwards, he traveled to England, and eventually purchased "Greystone," an estate near Yonkers, New York. He founded the Tilden Trust to establish a free library for New York City. Tilden died at "Greystone" on August 4, 1886. Bibliography: John Bigelow, *The Life of Samuel J. Tilden*, 2 vols. (New York, 1895); D. S. Alexander, *A Political History of the State of New York*, 4 vols. (New York, 1906-1923); Alexander C. Flick, ed., *History of the State of New York*, 10 vols. (New York, 1933-1937); Papers of Tilden in the New York Public Library, New York City.

ROBINSON, Lucius, 1877-1880

Born on November 4, 1810 in Windham in Greene County, New York, the son of Captain Eli Palmer Robinson, of Puritan stock. Married to Eunice Osborn in 1833; father of Nellie, D. C., and Qurelia; after his first wife died in 1861, Robinson married a second time to Mrs. James D. Burt in 1864, who died in 1872. Received a common school education; attended Delaware Academy in Delhi, New York; studied law in Delhi. Admitted to the New York Bar in 1832. Began private law practice in Catskill, New York; appointed District Attorney of Greene County, 1837; Master of Chancery, New York City, New York, 1843-1847. Though he had been a Democrat, Robinson switched to the Republican Party when it was formed. Elected to the New York Assembly, 1859; elected Comptroller of the State of New York, 1861 and 1863; in 1865, he was nominated by the Democrats for Comptroller, but was defeated; member, New York Constitutional Commission, 1875-1876; as a Democrat, he was again elected Comptroller of New York in 1875. Robinson, the Democratic candidate, was elected Governor of New York on November 7, 1876, receiving 519,831 votes to Republican Edwin D. Morgan's 489,371. He was sworn into office on January 1, 1877. In 1874, the New York Constitution had been amended to provide for three year gubernatorial terms, and Robinson was the first governor to be elected under the new provision. Also during his administration, the first State Reformatory for Adults was established in Elmira, New York, and the new Capitol at Albany, New York was opened. Though he was renominated for governor by the Democrats, Robinson was defeated in the November 4, 1879 election. He polled only 375,790 votes to Republican Alonzo B. Cornell's 418,567 and the Tammany Democrat candidate John Kelly's 77,566. As a result, Robinson left office on January 1, 1880. Robinson died on March 23, 1891. His New York residence was at Elmira in Chemung County. Bibliography: D. S. Alexander, *A Political History of the State of New York*, 4 vols. (New York, 1906-1923); Alexander C. Flick, ed., *History of the State of New York,* 10 vols. (New York, 1933-1937); Congressional Quarterly, *Guide to U. S. Elections* (Washington, D. C., 1975); Roy Glashan, *American Governors and Gubernatorial Elections, 1775-1975* (Stillwater, Minnesota, 1975).

CORNELL, Alonzo B., 1880-1883

Born on January 22, 1832 in Ithaca, New York, son of Ezra, founder of Cornell University and one of the organizers of the Western Union Telegraph Company, and Mary Ann (Wood) Cornell; his father was born of Quaker stock; one of nine children. Married to Ellen Augusta Covert on November 9, 1852; after she died in 1893, married a second time to Esther Elizabeth Covert, his first wife's younger sister, in 1894. Educated at Ithaca Academy. Telegraph operator, manager, and later superintendent of the Western Union Telegraph Company. Employed in a bank in Ithaca, 1852-1856; owner of a line of steamboats on Cayuga Lake. Unsuccessful Republican candidate for Lieutenant Governor of New York, 1868; chairman, New York Republican State Central Committee, 1870-1878; elected to the New York Assembly, 1872; Speaker, New York Assembly. Vice president, Western Union Telegraph Company; acting president, Western Union Telegraph Company, 1875; Naval Officer of Customs for the Port of New York, 1876-1878. As a Republican, Cornell was elected Governor of New York on November 4, 1879, receiving 418,567 votes to Democrat Lucius Robinson's 375,790 and Tammany Democrat candidate John Kelly's 77,566. He was sworn into office on January 1, 1880. During his administration, a State Board of Health was created; a State Railway Commission was organized; and a Women's Reformatory in Hudson, New York was established. Also while he was governor, News York's usury laws were amended, and the Corporation State Tax Law was enacted. Cornell's term was marked by his use of the veto to eliminate scandalous legislation. Though Cornell was a candidate for renomination, he was not supported by other Republican Party leaders, and Charles J. Folger was the 1882 Republican gubernatorial nominee. Cornell left office on January 1, 1883. Afterwards, he retired from political life and returned to his financial interests. Cornell died on October 15, 1904. Bibliography: D. S. Alexander, *A Political History of the State of New York*, 4 vols. (New York, 1906-1923); Alexander C. Flick, ed., *History of the State of New York*, 10 vols. (New York, 1933-1937); New York State Historical Association, *New York: A Guide to the Empire State* (New York, 1940); Roy Glashan, *American Governors and Gubernatorial Elections, 1775-1975* (Stillwater, Minnesota, 1975).

CLEVELAND, Steven Grover, 1883-1885

Born on March 18, 1837 in Caldwell, New Jersey, son of the Reverend Richard Falley and Anne (Neal) Cleveland; brother of Anna, Mary, William Neal, Richard Cecil, Margaret Louise, Lewis Frederick, Susan and Rose; a Presbyterian. Married to Frances Folsom on June 2, 1886; father of Ruth, Richard Folsom, and Francis. Cleveland moved with his family to Fayetteville, New York in 1840. Attended village schools; studied law in a Buffalo, New York legal firm. Moved to Clinton, New York in 1850; clerked in a grocery store; became an assistant teacher at the New York Institution for the Blind in 1853; clerk and copyist for a Buffalo law firm; admitted to the New York Bar in 1859; established a private law practice. Editor: *American Shorthorn Herb Book* (1861). Elected Ward Supervisor in Buffalo, 1862; appointed Assistant District Attorney, Erie County, New York, 1863-1865; unsuccessful candidate for District Attorney, 1865; elected Sheriff of Erie County, 1871-1873; elected Mayor of Buffalo, 1882. As a Democrat, Cleveland was elected Governor of New York on November 7, 1882, receiving 535,318 votes to Republican Charles J. Folger's 341,464; he was sworn into office on January 1, 1883. As governor,

Cleveland refused to treat politics as a game of spoils, patronage, and party regularity; during his administration, he worked for the passage of municipal reform legislation for New York City. His proposals were eventually approved by the State Legislature in March, 1884. Also while he was governor, the New York Civil Service Commission was created, and the New York and West Shore Railroad was opened. In July, 1884, the Democratic National Convention met in Chicago, Illinois and nominated Cleveland for the presidency on the second ballot. Cleveland defeated Republican James G. Blaine, polling 219 electoral votes to Blaine's 182, after a campaign filled with charges of scandal and immorality. After being elected President of the United States, Cleveland resigned as governor of New York on January 6, 1885. Cleveland served as president from 1885 until 1889, when he left office after being defeated in a bid for election to a second term. Afterwards, he returned to his private law practice. Cleveland was again elected President of the United States in 1892, and served from 1893 until 1897. He became a Trustee of Princeton University, Princeton, New Jersey in 1901; he was the author of several books: *Principles and Purposes of Our Form of Government* (1892), *Self Made Man in America* (1897), *Independence of the Executive* (1900), and *Presidential Problems* (1900). In 1905, he assisted in the reorganization of the Equitable Life Assurance Society. Cleveland died in Princeton on July 24, 1908 and was buried there. Bibliography: D. S. Alexander, *A Political History of the State of New York*, 4 vols. (New York, 1906-1923); Robert McElroy, *Grover Cleveland: The Man and the Statesman*, 2 vols. (New York, 1923); Alexander C. Flick, ed., *History of the State of New York*, 10 vols. (New York, 1933-1937); Allan Nevins, *Grover Cleveland: A Study in Courage* (New York, 1947).

HILL, David B., 1885-1892

Born on August 29, 1843 in Havana, New York, son of Caleb, a carpenter, and Eunice (Durfey) Hill. Never married. Educated in the common schools; began studying law in Havana and continued it in the office of Erastus P. Hart in Elmira, New York. Admitted to the bar in 1864 and was named City Attorney in 1865. Was a delegate to Democratic State Conventions from 1868 to 1881 and presided over two of these, 1877 and 1881. Became a member of the New York Assembly in 1871 and in 1872 was chosen Speaker. Was an Alderman of Elmira from 1880 to 1881 and Mayor in 1882. He resigned following his election to the lieutenant governorship of New York in 1882. In 1885, Hill took over the governorship when Grover Cleveland resigned to become President. He was elected in his own right in 1885 over Republican Ira Davenport, receiving 530,300 votes to Davenport's 519,826. In 1888 he was reelected over Republican Warner Miller, receiving 650,467 votes to Miller's 631,293. Hill's governorship was marked by superior administrative efficiency. He guarded the credit of the state; advocated home rules for cities and other subordinate municipalities; and opposed the multiplication of special laws for particular purposes. He championed reform of the codes of civil and criminal procedure, and strongly favored the substitution of electrocution for hanging, in cases of capital punishment. He supported the abolition of contract labor in relation to state prisons; the institution of Labor Day and Saturday half-holidays; legislation against child labor; and the establishment of a state forestry preserve. His veto of the State Census Bill of 1885, on the grounds that it should have provided only for an enumeration of the inhabitants of the state, caused considerable furor in both Democratic and Republican circles. During his entire career he was a party man and a machine politician; long before he left the executive chair at Albany, he had come to be recognized as the leader of the Democratic Party in the state. Hill had a genius for organization and detail, and his greatest skill as a politician was shown in opposing upstate New York with New York City and "Tammany Hall" interests. He retired from the governorship at the end of his second term on January 1, 1892. In 1891 Hill was elected to the United States Senate, where he later opposed many of President Grover Cleveland's policies. He sought the Democratic presidential nomination in 1892, but the convention nominated Cleveland. In 1894 he again ran for the office of governor, but lost to Republican Levi Morton, receiving 517,710 votes to Morton's 673,818. At the expiration of his term as Senator in 1897, Hill resumed the practice of law in Albany, New York and enjoyed a lucrative practice until the time of his death. A charter member of the New York State Bar Association, he was its president from 1885 to 1887, and was recognized as a man of high legal ability. David B. Hill died on October 20, 1910 at his home near Albany, New York. Bibliography: *New York Times* (October 21, 1910); D. S. Alexander, *A Political History of the State of New York*, 4 vols. (New York, 1906-1923); Ray B. Smith, ed., *History of the State of New York: Political and Governmental*, 4 vols. (Syracuse, 1922).

FLOWER, Roswell Petibone, 1892-1895

Born on August 7, 1835 in Theresa in Jefferson County, New York, the son of Nathan Monroe, a wool carder, cloth manufacturer and farmer, and Mary Ann (Boyle) Flower; a Presbyterian. Married to Sarah M. Woodruff in 1859. Educated in the public schools; graduated from high school in 1851. Jeweler in Watertown, New York; Assistant Postmaster of Watertown, 1854-1860; moved to New York City, New York in 1869, and engaged in banking; administrator of the large estate of Henry Keep, president of the New York Central Railroad and one of his wife's relatives; admitted to the New York Stock Exchange in 1873; engaged in the brokerage business; connected with the Brooklyn Rapid Transit System and Federal Steel. Member of the United States House of Representatives, 1889-1891. As a Democrat, Flower was elected Governor of New York on November 3, 1891, defeating Republican Jacob Sloat Fassett, 582,893 votes to 534,956. Flower took office on January 1, 1892. During his administration, the World's Columbian Exposition opened in New York City; a new banking code was enacted by the New York Legislature; and a convention was called to meet in Albany, New York in June, 1893, for the purpose of revising and amending the State Constitution. The new instrument of government provided for two-year gubernatorial terms instead of three, and placed the speaker of the Assembly in the line of succession to the Governor's office after the President of the State Senate. Flower was not renominated by the Democrats in 1894, and he left office on January 1, 1895. Afterwards, he returned to his business interests. Flower died on May 12, 1899 and was buried in Brookside Cemetery in Watertown. Bibliography: D. S. Alexander, *A Political History of the State of New York*, 4 vols. (New York, 1906-1923); Alexander C. Flick, ed., *History of the State of New York*, 10 vols. (New York, 1933-1937); David M. Ellis, et al., *A History of New York State* (Ithaca, 1967); Roy Glashan, *American Governors and Gubernatorial Elections, 1775-1975* (Stillwater, Minnesota, 1975).

MORTON, Levi Parsons, 1895-1897

Born in Shoreham, Vermont on May 16, 1824, the youngest of three children born to Daniel Oliver, a Congregationalist minister, and Lucretia (Parsons) Morton. Brother of Daniel, Jr., and Lucretia. In 1856 married Lucy Young Kimball; after her death in 1871, remarried to Anna Livingston Reade Street (d. 1918) in 1873, by whom he had six children. Ended his formal schooling at age fourteen and began work as a retail clerk. From managing a branch store in Hanover, New Hampshire for six years, he moved to Boston in 1849 as partner in a drygoods firm; he then moved to New York City in 1854 to start an investment banking firm. Bankrupted by the outbreak of war in 1861, he later voluntarily paid his debts in full. Morton, Bliss, and Co. prospered. In 1878, on his second try, he won election to Congress as a Republican from New York City's 11th District. After reelection, and the chairmanship of the Finance Committee during the Garfield presidential campaign, he accepted the president's offer to become Minister to France, serving from June, 1881 to March, 1885. He served as Vice President under Benjamin Harrison, 1889-1893, but was not renominated. As Republican candidate for Governor in 1894, he defeated David B. Hill, 673,818 votes to 517,710, with 84,173 votes scattered among four other candidates. Morton supported civil service reform and the creation of a consolidated New York City. His policies and appointments as governor strained, but never broke, a working relationship with the party organization led by Senator Thomas C. Platt. Morton was briefly his state party's candidate for the presidency in 1896; he declined to run for renomination as governor in that year. Returning to investment banking, he organized the Morton Trust Co., in 1899 and headed it until its merger into the new Guaranty Trust Co. in 1909. He died on his ninety-sixth birthday, May 16, 1920, at his estate, "Ellerslie," in Rhinecliff. He was buried in Rhinecliff Cemetery. Bibliography: Robert McElroy, *Levi Parsons Morton* (New York, 1930); Charles Z. Lincoln, ed., *Messages From the Governors* (Albany, N.Y., 1909); "Obituary," *New York Times* (May 20, 1920). Papers of Morton are in the Manuscript Division, New York Public Library; a smaller collection of gubernatorial papers is in the Syracuse University Library.

BLACK, Frank Swett, 1897-1899

Born on March 8, 1853 near Limington in York County, Maine, one of eleven children of Jacob, a farmer, and Charlotte (Swett) Black. Married Lois B. Hamlin in 1875; father of Arthur. After a rural school education, he taught school while preparing for college at Limerick and Lebanon academies. He worked his way through Dartmouth, graduating in 1875. He became editor of the Johnstown, New York *Journal*, until he was let go for supporting Republican James G. Blaine for President in 1876. He then moved to Troy, New York to continue his news writing and reading law. Admitted to the bar in 1879, he had his own practice the following year. By 1894, he had won election to Congress on the strength of his performance as a Republican orator, election law reformer, and Rensselaer County chairman. As a delegate to the Republican National Convention in 1896, he supported McKinley's nomination, and throughout this period was close to Louis F. Payn and Senator Thomas C. Platt. Nominated for the governorship in 1896, he defeated the Democrat, Wilbur F. Porter, 787,516 votes to 574,514, the largest plurality to that date. During his term Black pressed for completion of the State Capitol, and advocated biennial sessions of the State Legislature, civil service and election law reforms, and forest preservation. He actively supported the Spanish-American War. His appointment of Payn to the Canal Commission antagonized reformers, and proved embarrassing when heavy cost overruns and waste in the new Erie Canal improvements were reported in August, 1898. Senator Platt was then persuaded to shift his gubernatorial support to Theodore Roosevelt, and Black was rejected for renomination by the Republican State Convention. Black resumed a successful law practice in New York City until his death there of heart disease on March 22, 1913. Bibliography: "Obituary," *Albany Journal* and *New York Times* (March 13, 1913); Rutherford Haynes, *Troy and Rensselaer County* (New York, 1925); Charles E. Fitch, ed., *Official New York From Cleveland to Hughes* (New York, 1911); Charles Z. Lincoln, ed., *Messages From the Governors* (Albany, 1909).

ROOSEVELT, Theodore, 1899-1901

Born in New York City on October 27, 1858, the son of Theodore, Sr., and Martha (Bulloch) Roosevelt. His sister Anna was older; Elliott and Corinne were younger. All were raised as Presbyterians in a family of moderate inherited wealth. Married on his twenty-second birthday (October 27, 1880) to Alice Hathaway Lee, by whom he had one daughter, Alice (Longworth), at whose birth the mother died, February 14, 1884. In December, 1886 in London, remarried to Edith Kermit Carow, by whom Theodore, Jr., Kermit, Archibald, Ethyl and Quentin were born. After preparatory school he entered Harvard in 1876, and upon graduation in 1880, read law and studied for one year at Columbia University Law School. He spent two years (1884-1886) in North Dakota, ranching, hunting and writing; he then returned to run unsuccessfully for Mayor of New York City in 1886. His political career began as a Republican State Assemblyman from New York City's Twenty-first District in 1882 for three annual terms before he moved westward. Appointed by President Harrison a member of the United States Civil Service Commission in 1889, he resigned in mid-1895 to become president of the Board of Police Commissioners, New York City. Two years later he was appointed Assistant Secretary of the Navy (1897-1898). In 1898 he helped organize the First Volunteer Cavalry Regiment with Leonard Wood, and as its Lieutenant Colonel he gained fame leading these "Rough Riders" in Cuba. He returned to find that friends had obtained the backing of New York's Republican leader, Senator Thomas C. Platt, for Roosevelt's gubernatorial nomination. He was elected Governor in 1898 with 661,707 votes to 643,921 for Augustus Van Wyck, a Democrat. Roosevelt's term as governor was marked by the first state tax on public utility earnings; new restrictions on insurance companies and banks; stronger sweatshop labor regulation; factory inspection; minimum wage and hour laws; an end to local-option racial segregation in public schools and improved forestry and park programs. He made extensive use of independent experts in preparing legislation, predating Robert La Follette's "Wisconsin Idea." Roosevelt's growing interest in reform troubled Platt, however, and he finally persuaded a reluctant Roosevelt to be McKinley's vice-presidential running mate in 1900. Roosevelt succeeded to the presidency on September 14, 1901 after McKinley's assassination. Elected in his own right in 1904, he became a candidate again in 1912 on the Progressive Party ticket and ran second to Wilson. He returned to the Republican fold in 1916, supporting Hughes and later, America's intervention in World War I. Roosevelt died on January 6, 1919 from an embolism. He was buried near the family home at Sagamore Hill, Oyster Bay, New York. Bibliography: G. Wallace Chessman, *Governor Theodore Roosevelt* (Cambridge, Mass., 1965); William H. Harbaugh, *Power and Responsibility: The Life and Times of Theodore*

Roosevelt (New York, 1961); Elting E. Morison and John M. Blum, eds., *The Letters of Theodore Roosevelt*, 8 vols. (Cambridge, Mass., 1951-1954); Theodore Roosevelt, *An Autobiography* (New York, 1913); Howard L. Hurwitz, *Theodore Roosevelt and Labor in New York State, 1880-1900* (New York, 1943). The major collections of Roosevelt Papers are in the Harvard College Library and the Library of Congress.

ODELL, Benjamin Baker, 1901-1905

Born on January 14, 1854 in Newburgh, New York, the eldest son of Benjamin Barker, a businessman and politician, and Ophelia (Bookstaver) Odell. Married to Estelle Crist in 1877; she drowned in the Hudson River in 1888. He married a second time in 1891, to Linda (Crist) Traphagen, the widowed sister of his first wife; father of two sons and one daughter. Educated in the public schools; attended Newburgh Academy; attended Bethany College in Bethany, West Virginia; attended Columbia College in New York City, New York, but left before graduating. Worked in his father's ice-delivery company in Newburgh; engaged in commercial businesses; president, Orange County Traction Company; president, Central Hudson Steamboat Company. Member, United States House of Representatives, 1895-1899. Represented the Seventeenth District of New York on the Republican State Committee for ten years; chairman of the Executive Committee of the New York Republican State Committee. President, Newburgh Chamber of Commerce. As a Republican, Odell was elected Governor of New York on November 6, 1900, defeating Democrat John B. Stanchfield, 804,859 votes to 693,733. Odell took office on January 1, 1901. He was elected to a second term on November 4, 1902, polling 665,150 votes to Democrat Bird S. Coler's 655,398. During his administration, Odell urged strict economy of government, and administered a policy of indirect taxation to such a point that direct taxation practically ceased. However, while he was governor, he continued to serve as chairman of the New York Republican Party, which resulted in much criticism by his opponents. Also during his years as governor, the first dental school in the United States was opened at Rochester, New York; and the citizens of the state authorized the use of 101 million dollars for the improvement of the Erie Canal. Odell left office on January 1, 1905. Afterwards, he returned to his business interests, remaining active in Republican Party affairs; however, in 1910, he announced his retirement from politics. Odell died in Newburgh on May 9, 1926, and was buried in Woodlawn Cemetery in New Windsor, New York. Bibliography: D. S. Alexander, *A Political History of the State of New York*, 4 vols. (New York, 1906-1923); Alexander C. Flick, ed., *History of the State of New York*, 10 vols. (New York, 1933-1937); David M. Ellis, et al., *A History of New York State* (Ithaca, 1967); Roy Glashan, *American Governors and Gubernatorial Elections, 1775-1975* (Stillwater, Minnesota, 1975).

HIGGINS, Francis Wayland, 1905-1907

Born on August 18, 1856 in Rushford in Allegany County, New York, the son of Orrin Thrall, a businessman, and Lucia Cornelia (Hapgood) Higgins. His mother died while he was still a child. Married to Catherine Corrinne Noble in June, 1878. Attended Rushford Academy; graduated from Riverview Military Academy in Poughkeepsie, New York in 1873; took courses in a commercial college. Sales agent for an oil company in Denver,

Colorado and Chicago, Illinois; at the age of nineteen, he became a partner in the mercantile firm of Wood, Thayler and Company in Stanton, Michigan. Entered into a partnership with his father in Olean, New York in 1879; purchased extensive tracts of timber land in the West; maintained the family grocery business. Member, New York Senate, 1894-1902; Lieutenant Governor of New York, 1903-1905. As a Republican, Higgins was elected Governor of New York on November 8, 1904, defeating Democrat D. Cady Herrick, 813,264 votes to 732,704. Higgins took office on January 1, 1905. During his administration, he urged rigid economy in public expenditures, and resisted wasteful spending of governmental funds. As governor, Higgins advocated tax reforms, a revamping of the state's election laws, and the revision of New York's insurance legislation. He declined to seek reelection and left office on January 1, 1907. Higgins had a long history of a heart condition, and he died soon after leaving office on February 15, 1907. Bibliography: D. S. Alexander, *A Political History of the State of New York*, 4 vols. (New York, 1906-1923); Alexander C. Flick, ed., *History of the State of New York*, 10 vols. (New York, 1933-1937); David M. Ellis, et al., *A History of New York State* (Ithaca, 1967); Roy Glashan, *American Governors and Gubernatorial Elections, 1775-1975* (Stillwater, Minnesota, 1975).

HUGHES, Charles Evans, 1907-1910

Born on April 11, 1862 in Glens Falls, New York, the only child of David Charles, a Baptist minister, and Mary Catherine (Connelly) Hughes. Married to Antoinette Carter on December 5, 1888; father of Charles, Jr., Helen, Catherine and Elizabeth. Started college at the age of fourteen at Madison University; two years later transferred to Brown University, from which he graduated in 1880. Taught school in Delhi, New York, for one year; in 1882 he entered Columbia Law School and graduated in 1884. Began his law practice in New York City and later became a professor of law at Cornell University. In 1905, he led an inquiry into the malpractices of the New York City utilities industry and the New York life insurance scandals. In 1906 he ran as a Republican candidate for Governor of New York against Democrat William Randolph Hearst, and won, receiving 912,345 votes to Hearst's 854,448. He remained in the governorship for almost two terms, winning again in 1908 defeating Democrat Lewis S. Chanler by a vote of 1,014,362 to 901,327. As governor, Hughes' administration was notable for its progressive labor and welfare legislation and administrative reforms. In 1908, he strongly opposed race-track gambling as conflicting with a direct prohibition against gambling in any form contained in the State Constitution; this attack succeeded in crippling all forms of race-track gambling. Hughes persuaded the legislature to create two new regulatory commissions, one for utilities serving the metropolis, and the other for the rest of the state. Both were equipped with rate-fixing powers and freedom from arbitrary judicial interference. Hughes also gained important advances in labor laws, including a Workmen's Compensation Act, which created the first significant social insurance plan in the nation. A little-noticed reform of the Hughes period was the Moreland Act, which authorized and directed the governor to carry on executive investigations, not only in the state field, but also with regard to city and county officials. In 1910, Hughes left office when he accepted President Taft's offer of a seat on the Supreme Court. In 1916 Hughes was nominated for the presidency, but was narrowly defeated by Woodrow Wilson. Hughes became Secretary of State from 1921 to 1925 under Presidents Harding and Coolidge. After heading a committee to reorganize the New York state government, Hughes became a Judge of the Permanent Court of International Justice until 1930, when President Hoover appointed him Chief Justice of the United States Supreme

Court. In 1941 Hughes retired from the court. He continued to devote time to such organizations as the Legal Aid Society and the World Council of Christians and Jews, but most of his time was spent with his family. Hughes died on August 27, 1948, and was buried beside his wife in Woodlawn Cemetery in New York. Bibliography: Dexter Perkins, *Charles Evans Hughes and American Democratic Statesmanship* (Boston, 1956); Merlo J. Pusey, *Charles Evans Hughes* (New York, 1951); *The New York Times* (August 28, 1948); Robert F. Wessler, *Charles Evans Hughes: Politics and Reform in New York, 1905-1910* (Ithaca, 1967).

WHITE, Horace, 1910-1911

Born on October 7, 1865 in Buffalo, New York, son of Horace Keep and Marion (Strong) White; brother of Andrew and Ernest; Episcopalian. Married Jane Lines Denison on March 14, 1903. Graduated from Cornell in 1887 and from Columbia University Law School in 1889; studied law in the office of Frank Hiscock and then entered law practice in partnership with Jerome L. Cheney. In 1896 he was elected to the State Senate, representing Onondaga County. The Civil Service Law, the Tenement House Law, and similar legislation were either revised or put on the books during his period in the legislature. He served six terms in the Senate until 1908; in 1909 he was elected Lieutenant Governor. Upon the resignation of Governor Hughes to accept an appointment as Justice of the Supreme Court, White became Governor in October, 1910 for three months until the inauguration of John Alden Dix. After serving as governor, White resumed the practice of law in Syracuse. At the time of his death, he was president of the Post-Standard Company and publisher of the Syracuse *Post-Standard*. He was also a member of the Board of Trustees of Cornell University, as he had been for several decades. Horace White died on November 28, 1943, and was buried in Oakview Cemetery in Syracuse, New York. Bibliography: D. S. Alexander, *A Political History of the State of New York*, 4 vols. (New York, 1906-1923); Ray B. Smith, ed., *History of the State of New York: Political and Governmental*, 4 vols. (Syracuse, 1922); *New York Times* (November 29, 1943).

DIX, John Alden, 1911-1913

Born on December 25, 1860 in Glens Falls, New York, the son of James Lawton and Laura (Stevens) Dix; an Episcopalian. Married to Gertrude Alden on April 24, 1889. Graduated from the Glens Falls Academy in 1879; received an A. B. degree from Cornell University in Ithaca, New York in 1883; was awarded an LL. B. degree from Hamilton College in 1912. Member of the black marble firm of Reynolds and Dix, 1882-1887; member of Thomson and Dix Lumber Company in Thomson, New York, 1887-1897; president, Iroquois Paper Company; treasurer, American Wood Board Company; vice president, Blandy Paper Company; vice president, First National Bank of Albany, New York; manager, Moose River Lumber Company; director, Albany Trust Company; director, Glens Falls Trust Company; director, National Bank of Schuylerville, New York; director, Adirondack Trust Company. Delegate, Democratic National Convention, 1904; received seventeen votes for the New York Democratic gubernatorial nomination in 1906; Democratic nominee for Lieutenant Governor of New York, 1908; chairman, Washington County, New York, Democratic Committee, 1908; chairman, New York Democratic State

Committee, 1910. Trustee, Cornell University. A Mason. As a Democrat, Dix was elected Governor of New York on November 8, 1910, defeating Republican Henry L. Stimson, 689,700 votes to 622,299. Dix took office on January 1, 1911. During his administration, a disastrous fire swept the State Capitol in Albany, and the New York Legislature adopted legislation providing for direct primary election of political candidates. Dix left office on January 1, 1913. Afterward he returned to his business investments, dividing his time between his homes in Thomson and Albany. Later Dix moved to Santa Barbara, California. Dix died on April 9, 1928. Bibliography: New York State Historical Association, *New York: A Guide to the Empire State* (New York, 1940); David M. Ellis, et al., *A History of New York State* (Ithaca, 1967); Congressional Quarterly, Inc., *Guide to U. S. Elections* (Washington, 1975); Roy Glashan, *American Governors and Gubernatorial Elections, 1775-1975* (Stillwater, Minnesota, 1975).

SULZER, William, 1913

Born on March 18, 1863 in Elizabeth, New Jersey, the son of Thomas, a farmer, and Lydia (Jelleme) Sulzer; one of seven children; one brother was Charles A.; a Presbyterian. Married to Clara Rodelheim on January 7, 1908; they had no children. Educated in the public schools; attended Columbia College in New York City, New York; studied law. Admitted to the bar in 1884. Private law practice in New York City. Member, New York Assembly, 1889-1894; Speaker of the New York Assembly, 1893; Minority Leader of the New York Assembly, 1894; member United States House of Representatives, 1895-1912; resigned after being elected Governor of New York. Delegate, Democratic National Conventions, 1892-1912. A Mason. As a Democrat, Sulzer was elected Governor of New York on November 5, 1912, polling 649,559 votes to Republican Job E. Hedges' 444,105 and the Independent League and National Progressive candidate, Oscar S. Straus' 393,183. Sulzer took office on January 1, 1913. As governor, he refused to go along with "Tammany Hall" on many of their patronage demands, and ordered an investigation which revealed vast corruption, inefficiency and maladministration in state government. However, "Tammany Hall" dominated the State Legislature, and twice it refused to approve Sulzer's bill replacing party nominating conventions with primary elections. Resentful legislators seeking to discredit him uncovered diverted campaign contributions. Impeachment proceedings began, and on October 17, 1913, Sulzer was removed from office. Afterwards, he returned to his law practice, and became involved in some Alaskan gold mining investments. Sulzer remained active in politics, and in November, 1913 he was elected as an Independent to the New York Assembly. He was also an unsuccessful gubernatorial candidate on the American Party ticket in 1914, and declined the American Party's nomination for President in 1916. Sulzer died in New York City on November 6, 1941, and was buried in Evergreen Cemetery in Hillside, New Jersey. Bibliography: D. S. Alexander, *A Political History of the State of New York*, 4 vols. (New York, 1906-1923); David M. Ellis, et al., *A History of New York State* (Ithaca, 1967); Roy Glashan, *American Governors and Gubernatorial Elections, 1775-1975* (Stillwater, Minnesota, 1975). Papers of Sulzer are in the Cornell University Library, Ithaca, New York; "William Sulzer Scrapbook," containing correspondence of Sulzer and related printed items, in the National Library of Scotland, Edinburgh, Scotland.

GLYNN, Martin Henry, 1913-1915

Born on September 27, 1871 in Kinderhook, Columbia County, New York, the son of Martin and Anne (Scanlon) Glynn, both of Irish descent; a Catholic. Married to Mary C. E. Magrane on January 2, 1901. Educated in the public schools of Kinderhook; graduated from St. John's College of Fordham University in New York City, New York in 1894; he was the honor man of his class; studied law. Admitted to the bar in 1897. Worked as a reporter for the *Times-Union* in Albany, New York; became managing editor of the *Times-Union* in 1895; later he became editor and publisher of the *Times-Union*. Established a private law practice in Albany in 1897; remained involved in the newspaper business. Member, United States House of Representatives, 1899-1901; unsuccessful candidate for reelection; Comptroller of New York State, 1906-1908; Lieutenant Governor of New York, 1913. Vice president, National Commission of the Louisiana Purchase Exposition, 1901-1905. A Democrat. When New York Governor William Sulzer was impeached and removed, Glynn, as Lieutenant Governor, succeeded to the office on October 17, 1913. During his administration, he secured the passage of a Workmen's Compensation Law, reduced state taxes, and established a system of land-banks to finance farm operations. Also while he was governor, the system of party conventions was abolished and statewide primary elections introduced. Glynn completed the remainder of Sulzer's term, and then sought to be elected governor in his own right; however, he was defeated in the November 3, 1914 election, polling 541,269 votes to Republican Charles S. Whitman's 686,701 and the American Party candidate, former Governor Sulzer's 126,270. Glynn left office on January 1, 1915. Afterwards, he remained active in politics, and served as temporary chairman of the 1916 Democratic National Convention. Glynn was appointed a member of the Federal Industrial Commission in 1919, and while traveling abroad in 1921, he attempted to help restore peace between the English and Irish in Ireland. Glynn died on December 14, 1924 in Albany, and was buried in St. Agnes Cemetery. Bibliography: Alexander C. Flick, ed., *History of the State of New York*, 10 vols. (New York, 1933-1937); New York State Historical Association, *New York: A Guide to the Empire State* (New York, 1940); David M. Ellis, et al., *A History of New York State* (Ithaca, 1967); Roy Glashan, *American Governors and Gubernatorial Elections, 1775-1975* (Stillwater, Minnesota, 1975).

WHITMAN, Charles Seymour, 1915-1919

Born on August 28, 1868 in Hanover, Connecticut, the son of the Reverend John Seymour and Lillie (Arne) Whitman; a Presbyterian. Married to Olive Hitchcock on December 22, 1908, who died on May 29, 1926; the father of Charles S. and Olive. Received an A.B. degree from Amherst College in Amherst, Massachusetts in 1890; received an LL.B. degree from New York University in New York City, New York in 1894. Private law practice. Assistant Corporation Counsel of New York, 1901-1903. Awarded an honorary M.A. degree from Williams College in 1904. Member and later president, Board of City Magistrates of New York, 1904-1907; appointed a Judge of the Court of General Sessions of New York, 1907; District Attorney, New York County, New York, 1910-1914. Awarded honorary LL.D. degrees from New York University in 1913, Amherst College in 1913, Williams College in 1914, and Hamilton College in 1918. Mason; Society of the Cincinnati; Society of Colonial Wars; Sons of the American Revolution; Nicholas Society. As a Republican, Whitman was elected Governor of New York on November 3, 1914, polling

686,701 votes to the Democratic and Independence League candidate, incumbent Governor Martin H. Glynn's 541,269 and the American Party candidate, former Governor William Sulzer's 126,270. Whitman took office on January 1, 1915. He was reelected to a second term on November 7, 1916 as the Republican and National Progressive candidate, receiving 850,020 votes to Democrat Samuel Seabury's 686,862. During his administration, physical and military training in public schools were made compulsory; the Catskill Aqueduct, originally the Ashokan Aqueduct, was completed; the State Constabulary was created; and the New York State Barge Canal was opened. Also while Whitman was governor, the United States entered World War I. He was responsible for mobilizing the state's resources for the war effort, and eventually 518,868 men from New York served in the military. Whitman left office on January 1, 1919, after losing the 1918 gubernatorial election to Alfred E. Smith. Afterwards, he returned to his law practice in New York City. He was Commander of the Port Authority of New York, and president of the American Bar Association from 1926 to 1927. Whitman died on March 29, 1947. Bibliography: New York State Historical Association, *New York: A Guide to the Empire State* (New York, 1940); David M. Ellis, et al., *A History of New York State* (New York, 1967); Congressional Quarterly, Inc., *Guide to U.S. Elections* (Washington, D.C., 1975); Roy Glashan, *American Governors and Gubernatorial Elections, 1775-1975* (Stillwater, Minnesota, 1975).

SMITH, Alfred E., 1919-1921, 1923-1929

Born on December 30, 1873 in New York City, son of Alfred Emanuel Smith, a truckman (the driver of a horse-drawn wagon), and Catherine (Mulvihill) Smith, both of whom were Roman Catholic; brother of Mary Smith. Married to Catherine Dunn on May 6, 1900; father of Alfred E., Emily, Arthur, Walter and Catherine. Left St. James' Parochial School in the eighth grade to help support his widowed mother and sister. Became an investigator for the City Commissioner of Jurors in 1895; in 1903 was elected to the New York State Assembly, running as a Democrat. Elected Sheriff of New York County in 1915, and in that year became a delegate to the State Constitutional Convention. In 1918, Smith defeated Republican Charles S. Whitman for Governor, receiving 987,438 votes to Whitman's 975,200. He was sworn into office on January 1, 1919. As governor, Smith and his administration amended the Workmen's Compensation Law, correcting a defect alleged to have deprived workers of adequate compensation. A measure was adopted authorizing the construction of a vehicular tunnel between New York and New Jersey. Smith also supported women's suffrage, and urged the extension of labor laws to protect women in industry. When William Hearst charged him with being a friend of the "milk trust barons" and with being responsible for the deaths of many children, Smith publicly denounced him in what was considered the worst political backlashing in history. In 1920, he was defeated in his campaign for reelection for the governorship by Republican Nathan Miller, receiving 1,248,456 votes to Miller's 1,306,508. From 1920 to 1922, Smith served as chairman of the United States Trucking Corporation. In 1922, he again ran against Miller, this time defeating him by 1,401,464 votes to 1,012,034. He assumed office in 1923. In 1924, Smith defeated Republican Theodore Roosevelt, Jr. by a vote of 1,617,634 to 1,501,952. In 1926, he defeated Republican Ogden Mills by a vote of 1,517,410 to 1,256,652. During his second period as governor, Smith was partially successful in his fight for state development of water power for sale to communities and private companies. He advocated an executive budget, bond issues for state buildings, the short ballot and a four-year term of office for the governorship. In 1928, he was the Democratic candidate for President, but was defeated by Herbert Hoover. After his defeat, Smith became chairman of the board of the New York Trust Company (later the Lawyers Trust Company) and engaged in the ambitious project of erecting the Empire State Building. Throughout the period from 1933 to 1940, Smith was a major opponent of his fellow Democrat, Franklin D. Roosevelt. He mounted a challenge to Roosevelt's leadership of the Democratic Party in 1935, when he joined the Liberty League. In the following year, he attempted to defeat Roosevelt for the Democratic nomination for President, but failed. Smith died on the morning of October 4, 1944, and was buried in Calvary Cemetery, Long Island City, New York. Bibliography: Richard O'Conner, *The First Hurrah* (New York, 1970); Matthew and Hannah Josepson, *Al Smith: Hero of the Cities* (Boston, 1969); Norman Hapgood and Henry Moscowitz, *Up From the City Streets* (New York, 1928); *New York Times* (October 5, 1944). Papers of Smith are in the State Library, Albany, New York.

MILLER, Nathan L., 1921-1923

Born on October 10, 1868 in Solon, New York, son of Samuel and Almera (Russell) Miller; a Roman Catholic. Married Elizabeth Davern on November 23, 1896; father of Mildred, Marian, Louise, Elizabeth, Eleanor and Constance. Attended the Groton Union School and the Cortland Normal School (N. Y.); graduated in 1887 and taught public school for three years. In 1890, began the study of law at Cortland. Admitted to the New York Bar in 1893 and practiced independently until 1899. From 1894 to 1900, was School Commissioner of the First District of Cortland County; became corporation counsel for the City of Cortland from 1901 to 1902, and State Comptroller in 1902. He resigned in 1903 to accept an appointment as Justice of the New York Supreme Court, a post he held until 1913. When he was named Associate Judge of the Court of Appeals, he resigned from the bench in 1915 in order to resume private practice. In 1920 he became the Republican candidate for Governor and defeated Democrat Alfred Smith for the position, receiving 1,306,508 votes to Smith's 1,248,456. He was sworn into office in January of 1921. During his tenure of office, Miller enforced economy by eliminating unnecessary jobs and discharging superfluous employees (2,000 positions for state employees were abolished). Miller's administration reorganized the Public Service, Tax, and Industrial Commissions and a Motion Picture Censor Commission was established. Miller also reformed the management of charitable and penal institutions; encouraged the use of water power for the production of electricity; and created a State Department of Purchase and Supply. In 1922 Miller was nominated for reelection, but this time he was defeated by Alfred Smith by almost 400,000 votes. After his loss to Smith, he joined the law firm of Steele and Otis, which became Miller and Otis. As a lawyer, he was known for his promotion of welfare work among the employees of the great companies for which he was general counsel. He was general counsel, director and member of the finance committee of the United States Steel Corp.; trustee of the Mutual Life Insurance Co. of New York City; and director of the Delaware and Hudson Railroad Corp. Nathan L. Miller died on June 26, 1953 and was buried in Cortland, New York. Bibliography: *New York Times* (June 27, 1953); Warren Moscow, *Politics in the Empire State* (New York, 1948); D. S. Alexander, *A Political History of the State of New York*, 4 vols. (New York, 1906-1923).

SMITH, Alfred E., 1919-1921, 1923-1929

ROOSEVELT, Franklin Delano, 1929-1933

Born on January 30, 1882 near Hyde Park, New York, the son of James and Sara (Delano) Roosevelt; half-brother of James; an Episcopalian. Married to Anna Eleanor Roosevelt, a distant cousin, on March 17, 1905; father of Anna E., James, Franklin, Jr., Elliot and John Aspinall. Educated by private tutors until he was fourteen; graduated from Groton School in 1900; graduated from Harvard University in Cambridge, Massachusetts in 1904; attended the Columbia Law School in New York City, New York until 1907. Admitted to the bar in 1907. Began the practice of law in New York City with the firm of Carter, Ledyard, and Milburn. Member, New York Senate, 1911-1913; Assistant Secretary of the United States Navy, 1913-1920; unsuccessful Democratic vice presidential nominee in 1920. Joined the law firm of Emmet, Marvin, and Roosevelt in 1920; vice president, Fidelity and Deposit Company of Maryland, 1920-1928; became a member of the legal firm of Roosevelt and O'Connor in 1924. President, Woodrow Wilson Foundation; president, the Boy Scouts Foundation; president, the Seamans' Institute; chairman, Taconic Park Commission; trustee of Vassar College. Author: *Government, Not Politics* (1932); *Looking Forward* (1933); *On Our Way* (1934). As a Democrat, Roosevelt was elected Governor of New York on November 6, 1928, defeating Republican Albert Ottinger, 2,130,238 votes to 2,104,630. Roosevelt took office on January 1, 1929. He was elected to a second term on November 4, 1930, polling 1,770,342 votes to Republican Charles H. Tuttle's 1,045,231 and the Law Preservation candidate, Robert P. Carroll's 191,666. During his administration, a 450 million dollar power system was formed connecting the major cities in northwestern New York; the new Port of Albany, New York was dedicated; and the Winter Olympic Games at Lake Placid, New York got underway. Governor at the beginning of the Great Depression, Roosevelt's term saw the passage of the Old Age Security Act, and the establishment of the New York Temporary Emergency Relief Administration. In November 1932, Roosevelt was elected President of the United States, and he left the governor's office on January 1, 1933. He was elected to the presidency for four terms, and served from 1933 until his death in office. Roosevelt died in Warm Springs, Georgia on April 12, 1945, and was buried in the family plot in Hyde Park, New York. Bibliography: New York State Historical Association, *New York: A Guide to the Empire State* (New York, 1940); Bernard Bellush, *Franklin D. Roosevelt as Governor of New York* (New York, 1967); Roy Glashan, *American Governors and Gubernatorial Elections, 1775-1975* (Stillwater, Minnesota, 1975); James MacGregor Burns, *Roosevelt: The Lion and The Fox* (New York, 1956).

LEHMAN, Herbert Henry, 1933-1942

Born on March 28, 1878 in New York City, New York, son of Mayer and Babette (Newgass) Lehman; Jewish. Married to Edith Altschul on April 28, 1910; father of Peter G., John R. and Hilda Jane. Attended Sachs Collegiate Institute, New York City; received a B. A. degree from Williams College, Williamstown, Massachusetts in 1899. Employed by

J. Spencer Turner Company, a textile manufacturer; became vice president and treasurer of J. Spencer Turner Company, 1906; became a partner in Lehman Brothers, investment bankers, New York City, 1908. Commissioned Captain, Officers' Reserve Corps, United States Army, August, 1917; attained the rank of Colonel on the General Staff, April, 1919; served as Assistant Director of Purchase, Storage, and Traffic, United States War Department; awarded the Distinguished Service Medal. In 1921 he received an M. A. degree from Williams College; he was awarded an LL. D. degree from Williams College in 1929. He also received numerous honorary degrees. Chairman, Finance Committee, Democratic National Committee, 1928; delegate to all Democratic National Conventions from 1928 to 1956. Lieutenant Governor of New York, 1929-1932. Trustee, Henry Street Settlement, New York Foundation; director, Welfare Council, New York City; director, Surprise Lake Camp, National Association for the Advancement of Colored People. As a Democrat, Lehman was elected Governor of New York on November 8, 1932, receiving 2,659,597 votes to Republican William J. Donovan's 1,812,002. He was sworn into office on January 1, 1933. Lehman, as the Democratic and American Labor Party candidate, was reelected to a second term on November 6, 1934, polling 2,201,727 votes to Republican Robert Moses' 1,393,744. As the Democratic and American Labor candidate, he was elected to a third term on November 3, 1936, receiving 2,970,595 votes to Republican William F. Bleakley's 2,450,105. On November 8, 1938, Lehman, the Democratic and American Labor candidate, was elected to a fourth term, defeating the Republican and Independent Progressive nominee, Thomas E. Dewey, 2,391,331 votes to 2,326,892. During his administration, the New York Legislature ratified the Twenty-first Amendment to the United States Constitution; a State Racing Commission was organized; an Unemployment Insurance Law was enacted; an Old Age Pension Bill was passed; women were given the duty of serving on juries; and an Unemployment Insurance System was established. Also while he was governor, the New York World's Fair was held; New York's Eighth Constitutional Convention met; and the governor's term was extended to four years. Lehman resigned the governorship of New York on December 3, 1942. Afterwards, he was Director of Foreign Relief and Rehabilitation Operations in the United States State Department in 1943, and Director General of the United Nations Relief and Rehabilitation Administration from 1943 to 1946. Lehman was an unsuccessful candidate for the United States Senate in 1946. He served as a member of the Public Advisory Board of the Economic Cooperation Administration in 1948, and as a member of the United States Senate from 1949 to 1957. He was not a candidate for renomination to the United States Senate in 1956. His home was in New York City. Lehman died on December 5, 1963. Bibliography: New York State Historical Association, *New York: A Guide to the Empire State* (New York, 1940); David M. Ellis, et al., *A History of New York State* (Ithaca, 1967); Congressional Quarterly, Inc., *Guide to U. S. Elections* (Washington, D. C., 1975); Roy Glashan, *American Governors and Gubernatorial Elections, 1775-1975* (Stillwater, Minnesota, 1975).

POLETTI, Charles, 1942-1943

Born on July 2, 1903 in Barre, Vermont, son of Dino, a stonecutter, and Carolina (Gervasini) Poletti, both of whom were Presbyterian. Married to Jean Knox Ellis on June 2, 1934; father of Carla Knox, Charles Ellis and Joanna Shattuck. Married a second time to Elizabeth Munn Vanderloo on September 1, 1975. Graduated in 1924 from Harvard University with a B. A. Won the Eleanora Duse Scholarship and went to the University of

Rome from 1924 to 1925; studied at the University of Madrid in 1928; returned to Harvard Law School and received an LL. B. (1928). He immediately found employment with the legal firm of Davis, Polk, Wardell, Gardiner and Reed, and was admitted to the New York State Bar in 1930. In 1930, was appointed legal counsel to the St. Lawrence Power Development Commission; from 1933 to 1937 was a counsel to Governor Lehman; appointed as a Justice of the State Supreme Court in 1937. In 1938 he resigned to run as the Democratic candidate for Lieutenant Governor, won, and occupied the office until 1942, when he was defeated by Thomas W. Wallace by 20,000 votes. Upon Governor Herbert Lehman's resignation on December 3, 1942 before his assuming his new post as United States Director of Foreign Relief, Poletti became Governor of New York, and held the job for twenty-nine days, until Thomas Dewey's inauguration on January 1, 1943. During Poletti's tenure as governor, he won much praise. To meet a growing food scarcity, he issued orders that all available acres, and all state farms, increase production to make state institutions "more nearly self-sufficient as to food supplies." In his last day in office, he presented a program of social legislation, which called for the creation of a "Beveridge Commission" to recommend social security for the post-war years. Among the agenda items were: state health insurance; extension of benefits for unemployment insurance; funds for construction of low-rent housing projects; ten million dollars for financing child relief in war-caused emergencies; prohibition by law of any discriminatory advertising for hiring; development of the St. Lawrence water power resources under state ownership; and the lowering of the voting age in New York State to eighteen. After Thomas Dewey's inauguration as governor, Poletti became Special Assistant to the Secretary of War. From 1943 to 1946, he served with the United States Army in Italy; afterwards he resumed his law practice in New York City. Bibliography: Warren Moscow, *Politics in the Empire State* (New York, 1948); *New York Times* (April 18, 1943); *Time* (June 25, 1943); *New Republican* (August 4, 1941).

DEWEY, Thomas Edmund, 1943-1955

Born on March 24, 1902 in Owosso, Michigan, son of George Martin, Postmaster of Owosso and publisher of the *Owosso Times*, and Annie (Thomas) Dewey; an Episcopalian. Married to Frances E. Hutt on June 16, 1928; father of Thomas E. and John Martin. Received an A. B. degree from the University of Michigan at Ann Arbor in 1923; received an LL. B. degree from Columbia University, New York City, New York in 1925; numerous honorary degrees. Began his legal practice with Larking, Rathbone, and Perry Legal Firm, 1925-1927. Admitted to the New York Bar in 1926. Associated with McNamara and Seymour Legal Firm, 1927-1931. Chief Assistant to the United States Attorney for the Southern District of New York, 1931-1933; United States Attorney for the Southern District of New York, 1933; counsel to the Association of the Bar in New York in the removal of Municipal Justice Harold L. Kunstier, 1934. Private law practice, 1934-1935. Special Prosecutor, Investigation of Organized Crime in New York, 1935-1937; elected District Attorney, New York County, New York, 1937; unsuccessful Republican gubernatorial candidate, 1938. Columbia University Medal for Excellence, 1936; Cardinal Newman Distinguished Service Award, University of Illinois at Urbana, 1939; trustee, Roosevelt Hospital, New York City, New York; American College of Trial Lawyers; Council of Foreign Relations. A Mason. Author: *The Case Against the New Deal* (1940); *Journey to the Far Pacific* (1952); *Thomas E. Dewey on the Two Party System* (1966). As a Republican, Dewey was elected Governor of New York on November 3. 1942, receiving

2,825,633 votes to Democrat John J. Bennet, Jr.'s 1,501,039, and American Labor Party candidate, Dean Alfange's 403,626. He was sworn into office on January 1, 1943. During his administration, he urged a large-scale highway construction program; secured passage of legislation eliminating discrimination in employment; improved New York's unemployment and disability benefits; and established an effective Labor Mediation Board. Dewey was the Republican nominee for President of the United States in 1944, but was defeated by Democrat Franklin D. Roosevelt, 432 electoral votes to 88. He was reelected to a second term as governor of New York on November 5, 1946, polling 2,825,633 votes to the Democrat and American Labor candidate, James M. Mead's 2,138,482. Again in 1948 Dewey was the Republican candidate for President of the United States; again he was defeated, receiving 189 electoral votes to Democrat Harry S. Truman's 303. Dewey was elected to a third term as Governor of New York on November 7, 1950, polling 2,819,523 votes to the Democratic and Liberal Party candidate, Walter A. Lynch's 2,246,855. At the end of his third term, Dewey returned to his lucrative private law practice with the legal firm of Dewey, Ballantine, Bushby, Palmer, and Wood in New York City. He left office on January 1, 1955. He remained a close adviser to Republican presidential administrations, and in 1968, he declined an offer by President Richard M. Nixon to be nominated as Chief Justice of the United States Supreme Court. Dewey died on March 16, 1971. Bibliography: Fred McGhee, ed., *Facts on File Five-Year Index, 1946-1950* (New York, 1958); Fred McGhee, ed., *Facts on File Five-Year Index, 1951-1955* (New York, 1957); Congressional Quarterly, Inc., *Guide to U. S. Elections* (Washington, D. C., 1975); Roy Glashan, *American Governors and Gubernatorial Elections, 1775-1975* (Stillwater, Minnesota, 1975).

HARRIMAN, William Averell, 1955-1959

Born on November 15, 1891 in New York City, New York, son of Edward Henry, a financier, and Mary W. (Averell) Harriman. Married to Kitty Lanier Lawrence on September 21, 1915; this marriage ended in divorce. Married a second time to Mrs. Marie Norton Whitney on February 21, 1930. Father of Mary and Kathleen by his first wife. Attended Groton School; graduated from Yale University, New Haven, Connecticut in 1913. During his college vacations, he worked as a clerk and section hand in the railroad yard in Omaha, Nebraska; became vice president in charge of purchase and supplies for the Union Pacific Railroad in 1915; owner of a shipyard in Chester, Pennsylvania; chairman of the board, Merchant Shipping Corporation; chairman of the board, W. A. Harriman and Company, 1920-1930; became a partner in Brown Brothers, Harriman, and Company in 1931; chairman of the Executive Committee, Illinois Central Railroad, 1931-1942; chairman of the board, Union Pacific Railway in 1932. Became a member of the Business Advisory Council, United States Department of Commerce in 1933; appointed Special Assistant Administrator, National Recovery Administration in 1934; chairman, Business Advisory Council, Department of Commerce, 1937-1940; chief of Raw Materials Branch, Office of Production Management in 1941; appointed Defense Expediter and liaison between the British and American governments in March, 1941; United States Ambassador to the Soviet Union, 1943-1946; United States Ambassador to Great Britain, 1946. Director, Illinois Central Railroad, 1946. Interim appointment as United States Secretary of Commerce, 1946-1947; United States Secretary of Commerce, 1947-1948; United States Representative in Europe under the Economic Cooperative Act of 1948; United States Ambassador Extraordinary and Plenipotentiary, 1948-1950; Special Assistant to the President, 1950-1951; American Representative, North Atlantic Treaty Organization committee to study Western defense plans, 1951; director, Mutual Security Agency, 1951-1953. As a Democrat, Harriman was elected Governor of New York on November 2, 1954, receiving 2,560,738 votes to Republican Irving M. Ives' 2,549,613. He was sworn into office on January 1, 1955. During his administration, a Two Track Racing Bill was passed; bingo was legalized; and the state's Jobless Pay Plan was ruled legal by the courts. Harriman was defeated for reelection in the November, 1958 general election by Republican Nelson A. Rockefeller. As a result, Harriman left office on January 1, 1959. Afterwards, he was appointed United States Ambassador-at-Large in 1961 and 1965; United States Assistant Secretary of State for Far Eastern Affairs, 1961-1963; and American Representative, Vietnam Peace Talks, 1968-1969. He was a member of the Democratic Party Policy Council. Bibliography: Lester A. Sobel, ed., *Facts on File Five-Year Index, 1956-1960* (New York, 1961); Robert Sobel, ed., *Biographical Directory of the Executive Branch, 1774-1971* (Westport, Connecticut, 1971); Congressional Quarterly, Inc., *Guide to U. S. Elections* (Washington, D. C., 1975); Roy Glashan, *American Governors and Gubernatorial Elections, 1775-1975* (Stillwater, Minnesota, 1975).

ROCKEFELLER, Nelson Aldrich, 1959-1973

Born on July 8, 1907 in Bar Harbor, Maine, son of John Davison Rockefeller, Jr., a philanthropist and an heir to the fortune of John D. Rockefeller, Sr., and Abby Greene (Aldrich) Rockefeller; brother of John, Laurence, Winthrop, David and Abby; a Baptist. Married to Mary Todhunter Clark on June 23, 1930; the marriage ended in divorce in 1962. Married a second time to Margaretta Fitler Murphy in May 1963. Father of Rodman, Ann, Steven, Michael and Mary by his first wife; father of Nelson Aldrich and Mark Fitler by his second wife. Graduated from Lincoln School, Teachers College, New York City, New York in 1926; received a B. A. degree from Dartmouth College, Hanover, New Hampshire in 1930; Phi Beta Kappa; numerous honorary degrees. Director, Rockefeller Center Incorporated, 1931-1958; director, Creole Petroleum Corporation, 1935-1940; president, Rockefeller Center Incorporated, 1938-1945 and 1948-1951; chairman of the board, Rockefeller Center Incorporated, 1945-1953 and 1956-1958. Coordinator, Office of Inter-American Affairs, 1940-1944; Assistant Secretary of State of the United States for American Republic Affairs, 1944-1945; chairman, International Development Advisory Board, 1950-1951; United States Under Secretary of Health, Education, and Welfare, 1953-1954; chairman, President's Advisory Committee on Government Organization, 1953-1958; Special Assistant to the President, 1954-1955. Treasurer, president, and chairman of the Museum of Modern Art; founder, Museum of Primitive Art; awarded the Order of Merit of Chile, 1945; awarded National Order of the Southern Cross by Brazil, 1946; awarded the Order of the Aztec Eagle by Mexico, 1949. Author: *The Future of Federalism* (1962); *Unity, Freedom, and Peace* (1968); and *Our Environment Can be Saved* (1970). As a Republican, Rockefeller was elected Governor of New York on November 4, 1958, receiving 3,126,929 votes to incumbent Democratic Governor Averell Harriman's 2,553,895. He was sworn into office on January 1, 1959. Rockefeller was reelected governor three times: in 1962 he defeated Democratic Liberal candidate Robert M. Morgenthau, 3,081,587 votes to 2,552,418; in 1966, he polled 2,690,626 votes to Democrat Frank O'Connor's 2,298,363, Conservative Paul L. Adams' 510,023, and Liberal Franklin

Roosevelt, Jr.'s 507,234; in 1970, as the Republican and Civil Service Independents' candidate, Rockefeller received 3,151,432 votes to Democratic and Liberal candidate, Arthur J. Goldberg's 2,421,426 and Conservative Paul L. Adams' 422,514. During his administration, the State Legislature ratified the Twenty-fourth and Twenty-fifth Amendments to the United States Constitution, and federal courts ordered the reapportionment of the state. While he was governor, he served as a member of the President's Advisory Commission on Intergovernmental Relations from 1965 to 1969, and as a member of the President's Foreign Intelligence Advisory Board from 1969 to 1974. Rockefeller resigned as governor of New York on December 18, 1973. On August 20, 1975, he was nominated by President Gerald R. Ford to be Vice President of the United States, and after Senate confirmation, he was inaugurated on December 19, 1975. He served as Vice President of the United States until January 20, 1977. After leaving office, Nelson Rockefeller engaged in various foundation work. Bibliography: Facts on File, Inc., *Facts on File Five-Year Index, 1961-1965* (New York, 1966); Dorothy Kattleman, *Facts on File Five-Year Index, 1966-1970* (New York, 1971); Congressional Quarterly, Inc., *Guide to U. S. Elections* (Washington, D. C., 1975); Roy Glashan, *American Governors and Gubernatorial Elections, 1775-1975* (Stillwater, Minnesota, 1975).

WILSON, Charles Malcolm, 1973-1975

Born on February 26, 1914 in New York City, New York, son of Charles H., a patent attorney, and Agnes (Egan) Wilson; one of four children; a Catholic. Married to Katharine McCloskey on September 6, 1941; father of Kathy and Anne. Attended elementary and secondary parochial schools; graduated from Fordham Preparatory School in 1929; received a B. A. degree from Fordham University in New York City in 1933; received an LL. B. degree from Fordham University in 1936; numerous honorary degrees. Admitted to the bar in 1936. Commissioned an Ensign in the United States Naval Reserve in 1943; served on an ammunition ship in the Atlantic during World War II; discharged in 1945. Worked on his uncle's dairy farm in upstate New York; became an associate attorney with the legal firm of Kent, Hazzard and Jagger in White Plains, New York in 1936; in 1946, he became a partner of the firm and the name was changed to Kent, Hazzard, Wilson, Freman, and Greer. Member, New York Assembly, 1938-1958; Lieutenant Governor of New York, 1959-1973. Member, National Conference of Christians and Jews; Ancient Order of Hibernians; Knights of Columbus; Society of the Friendly Sons of St. Patrick. A Republican. On December 18, 1973, New York Governor Nelson A. Rockefeller resigned, and as lieutenant governor, Wilson succeeded to the office. During his administration, the 2.5 percent state income tax surcharge was repealed, and legislative committees were established to study election reform and rent control. One of the major problems confronting Wilson was the energy crisis, and in February 1974, he instituted a voluntary gasoline rationing plan; however he shortly afterwards implemented compulsory gasoline rationing. He strongly opposed petroleum price gouging, and released gas reserves to energy-short areas. Also while he was governor, Wilson signed a bill in 1974 postponing the state primary election from June to September. Wilson sought to be elected governor in his own right, but was defeated in the November 5, 1974 election. As the Republican and Conservative candidate, he polled 2,219,667 votes to the Democratic and Liberal candidate, Hugh L. Carey's 3,028,503. Wilson left office on January 1, 1975. Afterwards, he returned to his law practice in White Plains. Wilson also served as a director of the Carrier Corporation, a trustee of the Manhattan Savings Bank, and a director of Shearson Hayden Stone. Bibliography: *New York Times* (December 15, 1973); Congressional Quarterly, Inc., *Guide to U. S. Elections* (Washington, D.C., 1975); Roy Glashan, *American Governors and Gubernatorial Elections, 1775-1975* (Stillwater, Minnesota, 1975).

CAREY, Hugh L., 1975-

Born on April 11, 1919 in Brooklyn, New York, son of Dennis J. and Margaret (Collins) Carey; a Catholic. Married to Helen Owen on February 27, 1947, who died in March, 1974; father of Alexandria, Christopher, Susan, Peter, Hugh L., Michael, Donald, Marianne, Nancy, Helen, Bryan, Paul, Kevin and Thomas. Served in the United States Army during World War II; rose to the rank of Major; Lieutenant Colonel, New York National Guard; awarded the Bronze Star; awarded the Croix de Guerre with Silver Star by France. Admitted to the New York Bar in 1951. Private law practice in Brooklyn; past director of several industrial firms. Member, United States House of Representatives, 1960-1975. Member, Board of Governors, National Democratic Club; member, Board of Visitors, United States Merchant Marine Academy; delegate, Interparliamentary Union Conference, Brussels, Belgium, 1961. Was awarded an LL. D. degree from St. John's College in 1967; numerous honorary degrees. Delegate, Democrat Mid-Term Conference, 1974. Named Knight of the Holy Sepulchre of Jerusalem by Pope Pius XII; Veterans of Foreign Wars; American Legion; Catholic War Veterans; director, Emerald Association; Boy Scouts Finance Committee. The Democratic and Liberal candidate, Carey was elected Governor of New York on November 5, 1974, receiving 3,028,503 votes to the Republican and Conservative Party candidate, Malcolm Wilson's 2,219,667. He was sworn into office on January 1, 1975. During his administration, the state's Food Stamp Plan was invalidated; offshore oil leasing by the United States was upheld; and the oil tariff was ruled illegal. In 1976 the Democratic National Convention met in New York City, New York. While Carey was governor, New York City faced a financial crisis, as expenditures outdistanced revenue; in response, the Municipal Assistance Corporation was created. Hugh Carey's present term will expire in 1979. Bibliography: Congressional Quarterly, Inc., *Guide to U. S. Elections* (Washington, D.C. 1975); Roy Glashan, *American Governors and Gubernatorial Elections, 1775-1975* (Stillwater, Minnesota, 1975); Charles Monaghan, ed., *Facts on File Yearbook, 1975* (New York, 1976); Charles Monaghan, ed., *Facts on File Yearbook, 1976* (New York, 1977).

NORTH CAROLINA

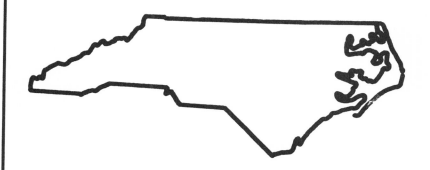

NORTH CAROLINA

MARTIN, Alexander, 1789-1792

Born in 1740 in Hunterdon County, New Jersey, son of Hugh Martin, a Presbyterian minister. Brother of James, Thomas, Samuel, Robert, Martha Martin Rogers and Jane Martin Henderson. Never married. Attended Newark College; graduated from College of New Jersey (now Princeton University) with an A.B. in 1756, an A.M. in 1759 and an honorary LL.D. in 1793. Settled in North Carolina about 1761. Began career as a merchant, and later acquired a large plantation. Studied law; admitted to the Guilford County Bar in 1772; active in local politics as Justice of Peace, Royal Attorney, and judge; elected a member of the Colonial Assembly in 1774. Appointed Lieutenant Colonel of the Second North Carolina Regiment of the Continental Army in 1775 and promoted to Colonel in 1776; fought at Brandywine and Germantown, resigning his commission in 1777 after his acquittal in a court martial. Elected to the General Assembly and served in the State Senate, 1778-1782, 1785, 1787-1788. Chairman of the Senate's Board of War in 1780 and its Speaker from 1780 to 1782. Acting Governor in 1781-1782 and then elected by the General Assembly as Governor, serving annual terms from 1782 to 1784. The General Assembly chose Martin, a moderate Federalist, as a delegate to the Constitutional Convention of 1787. In 1788 he was defeated in an attempt to be elected to the state convention voting on the federal constitution after North Carolina's second state convention finally ratified the Constitution in 1789. Martin was elected the state's first Governor under the new federal constitution by a majority vote of the General Assembly; he served three terms, from 1789 to 1792. Martin's politics were moderate and conciliatory. A Federalist, he worked assiduously to gain public support for central government, but was also concerned about federal encroachment on state sovereignty in areas such as the assignment of circuit courts and the question of whether the national government would assume the states'debts. He was a strong advocate of education; was instrumental in securing funds in 1791 for the founding of North Carolina University; served on the University Board of Trustees 1790-1807; board president in 1792 and 1793. Constitutionally forbidden from seeking another term as governor, Martin was elected after five ballots of the General Assembly to the United States Senate, where he served from 1793 to 1799. Though a Federalist, he supported economic restraint; opposed secret sessions; and voted against the Jay Treaty; later, however, he supported the Alien and Sedition Acts. After the General Assembly denied him a second term in the Senate, he retired in 1799 to his plantation "Danbury" and was politically inactive until 1804, when he returned to the State Senate, becoming its Speaker in 1805. A man of learning, Martin was the author of some minor patriotic verse. He died on November 10, 1807, and was buried on his estate.
Bibliography: John Hill Wheeler, *Historical Sketches of North Carolina: From 1584 to 1851* (Philadelphia, 1851); Walter Clark, ed., *The State Records of North Carolina* (Goldsboro, 1895-1906); Robert M. Douglas, "Alexander Martin," in Samuel A. Ashe,

Biographical History of North Carolina (Greensboro, 1906); Richard Walser, "Alexander Martin, Poet," *Early American Literature*, vol. VI, no. 1 (Spring, 1971). Papers from his first administration and letterbooks from both administrations are located at the State Archives in Raleigh. The Southern Historical Collection at the University of North Carolina in Chapel Hill holds other documents and letters.

SPAIGHT, Richard Dobbs, 1792-1795

Born on March 25, 1758 in New Bern, North Carolina, son of Richard Spaight, Secretary of the Crown in the Province, and Margaret (Dobbs) Spaight, sister of Royal Governor; member of the Church of England, Episcopalian. Married to Mary Leech on September 24, 1788; father of Richard, Jr. (Governor of North Carolina, 1835-1836), Charles and Margaret. Orphaned in early youth, he was sent in 1767 to attend school in Ireland, later graduating from the University of Glasgow. Returned to America about 1778 and joined the North Carolina militia as Aide-de-Camp to General Caswell, with whom he served until 1781. First elected to the House in North Carolina in 1779, though he was denied his seat after a challenge. Member of the House from 1781 to 1783 as representative from New Bern. Elected by the General Assembly as delegate to the Continental Congress, serving from 1782-1785. Elected to the House as representative from Craven County, 1785-1787; he was Speaker of the House in 1785. Elected in 1787 by the General Assembly as delegate to the Constitutional Convention. Nominated for Governor in 1787 but defeated in the General Assembly. Served in 1788 as a member of the state convention at Hillsborough which voted on the federal constitution; it was not ratified, though Spaight supported it. In 1789 he was nominated for the United States Senate as an anti-Federalist, but was defeated. Resigned as Colonel of Artillery in the North Carolina State Regiment, 1789. Remained politically inactive from 1789 to 1792 due to poor health. Served again in the House in 1792 and elected Governor by majority vote of the General Assembly after four days of balloting; inaugurated on December 14, 1792, the first native North Carolinian to serve as governor. Subsequently reelected by the General Assembly to one-year terms in 1793 and 1794. In 1793 Governor Spaight issued a proclamation of neutrality in international disputes and ordered the seizure of coastal privateers, an action for which he received the thanks of George Washington. When Indian troubles arose in the western part of the state, Spaight sent a patrol, but withdrew it in 1795 when the Indians proved friendly. During his tenure the sites for both the state capitol at Raleigh and the state university at Chapel Hill were chosen. A member of the University Board of Trustees from 1789 to 1803, and its President from 1792 to 1795, Spaight presided over the university's opening in 1795. In 1795, having served the constitutional limit of three terms, Spaight retired to New Bern. In 1798 he was elected to the U.S. House of Representatives to fill the unexpired term of Nathan Bryan. He became a supporter of Jefferson's Republican Party, and was reelected to the House in 1799, serving until 1801. After the expiration of this term, Spaight declined to run again, though he did serve in the North Carolina State Senate from 1801 to 1802. On September 5, 1802, Spaight was mortally wounded in a duel with John Stanly, the Federalist who succeeded him in Congress. He died the following day and was buried in New Bern. Bibliography: John H. Wheeler, *Sketch of the Life of Richard Dobbs Spaight* (Baltimore, 1880); Stephen B. Weeks, "Richard Dobbs Spaight, Senior," in Samuel A. Ashe, ed., *Biographical History of North Carolina* (Greensboro, 1906); Alexander B. Andrews, "Richard Dobbs Spaight," *North Carolina Historical Review*, vol. 1, no. 2

(April, 1924). A letter-book dealing with his administration as governor is located in the State Department of Archives and History in Raleigh. The Southern Historical Collection at the University of North Carolina in Chapel Hill holds other relevant letters and papers.

ASHE, Samuel, 1795-1798

Born in 1725 near Beaufort, North Carolina, son of John Baptista Ashe, Speaker of the Colonial Assembly, and Elizabeth (Swann) Ashe; an Episcopalian. Brother of John and Mary (Ashe) Moore. Married to Mary Porter before 1748; father of John Baptista, Samuel and Cincinnatus; widowed; remarried to Elizabeth Merrick; father of Thomas. Orphaned in 1734 and sent north for his education. Studied law. Appointed Assistant Attorney for the Crown in the Wilmington District. An ardent republican, he participated in North Carolina's first revolutionary convention which met at the Johnston County Court House in 1775. Served three terms in the Provincial Congress, 1775-1778. Appointed to the Council of Safety as representative of Wilmington, becoming the Council's president in 1776. Served as Paymaster of the North Carolina State Regiment in 1776 and as Captain of a troop of light horse in 1779. Member of the Halifax Congress of 1776, which framed the state's first constitution. Served in the first General Assembly under the state constitution as senator from New Hanover and elected Speaker of the Senate. Elected by the General Assembly and commissioned by Governor Caswell in 1777 as presiding judge of the first State Superior Court, serving until 1795. As a judge, he sided with the Assembly in opposing the restoration of confiscated property to former Tories but asserted the prerogative of judicial review over legislative acts, and refused to obey an *a certiorari* writ from the federal court. In 1795, at the age of seventy, he was elected Governor by majority vote of the General Assembly. In 1796 Ashe intervened in the Tennessee land grant scandal, opposing Secretary of State Glasgow who had been accused of attempting to burn the state records. Ashe supported laws governing court and grand jury procedures. Though a staunch Republican, he took a strong Federalist stand in 1798 by rallying public support and by appointing General Davie in charge of the state militia to counter the French threat. He also served on the University of North Carolina Board of Trustees as its President from 1795 to 1798. In 1798 Ashe retired as governor after serving the constitutional limit of three successive one-year terms. He remained active in support of the Republican cause, and became a member of the Electoral College in 1804. He died on his "Rocky Point" plantation on February 3, 1813. Bibliography: John Hill Wheeler, *Historical Sketches of North Carolina: From 1584 to 1851* (Philadelphia, 1851); Walter Clark, ed., *The State Records of North Carolina* (Goldsboro, 1895-1906); S.A. Ashe, "Samuel Ashe," in S. A. Ashe, ed., *Biographical History of North Carolina* (Greensboro, 1917). A letter-book dating from Ashe's administration as governor is in the State Department of Archives and History in Raleigh. The Southern Historical Collection at the University of North Carolina in Chapel Hill holds other letters, documents and papers.

DAVIE, William Richardson, 1798-1799

Born on June 22, 1756 in Cumberland County, England; son of Archibald and Mary (Richardson) Davie; both of whom were Presbyterian. Brother of Mary and Joseph. Married to Sarah Jones on April 11, 1782; father of Allen, Hyder Ali, Sarah, Mary Haynes, Rebecca and Frederick William. Emigrated to the Waxhaw Settlements, South Carolina, about 1763; raised there by his uncle, William Richardson, a Presbyterian pastor. Educated at Queen's Museum College, Charlotte until 1774; graduated from the College of New Jersey (now Princeton University) in 1776; led a volunteer company of students to join Washington's army. Studied law in Salisbury, North Carolina, about 1777, until joining the Halifax District militia. In 1779 received his first commission as Lieutenant of Dragoons in the District of Salisbury, later becoming Captain and then Major. Won distinction in the Battle of Stono; wounded and retired to his home to complete legal studies; licensed in law, 1780; appointed by North Carolina's governor to serve courts on the Holstein River. Authorized by the legislature to raise a troop of cavalry, which he financed himself. Brilliant military service at Camden and in western North Carolina; in 1780 participated in the defense of Charlotte, forcing Cornwallis to retreat. Appointed Commissary General in 1781 by the State Board of War. Settled in Halifax in 1782, riding the court circuits as a lawyer; became a noted orator, and rose to distinction in the state bar. Elected to the House of Commons, serving as representative of Northampton County, 1784-1785, and as representative of Halifax, 1785-1787, 1789, 1791-1796, 1798. Elected by the General Assembly as a delegate to the Federal Constitutional Convention of 1787, where he was an advocate of compromise. An ardent though unsuccessful supporter of ratification of the federal constitution at the 1788 North Carolina State Convention in Hillsborough; served the following year in the convention in Fayetteville that did pass it. Sponsored the charter of the University of North Carolina in the General Assembly, and served on the Board of Trustees, 1789-1807, and as Board President, 1798. In 1794 appointed as Major General in the state militia; during the French threat in 1797, was given command of state defenses by Governor Ashe. Appointed Brigadier General of the United States Army by President Adams in 1798. On December 4, 1798, Davie was elected Governor by majority vote of the General Assembly. He supervised the drawing of the state's western border; endeavored to settle the boundary dispute with South Carolina; and prosecuted those involved in the Tennessee land grant scandal. In 1799 Davie endorsed an address by the North Carolina General Assembly to President Adams, which supported a strong stand against France; he also took steps to strengthen the state's defenses in the event of war. Davie resigned as governor on September 10, 1799, after being appointed by President Adams as a peace commissioner to France; he then negotiated the treaty which was signed on September 30, 1800. In 1802 he helped to frame a treaty with the Tuscarora Indians. Deploring the decline of Federalism, Davie ran for the U.S. Congress in 1803 as representative from Halifax, and was defeated when his opponent, William Alston, accused Davie of harboring aristocratic tendencies. In 1806 Davie retired to his estate "Tivoli" on the Catawba River in South Carolina, where he pursued his studies in literature and scientific planting. Known as the founder of the University of North Carolina, Davie received its first honorary LL.D. in 1811. He supported the Federalist position in the War of 1812, and was appointed a Major General in the United States Army in 1813. He was also a member of the South Carolina Agricultural Society, and in 1819 was appointed to the Board of Public Works. Davie died on November 18, 1820, and was buried in the Old Waxhaw Churchyard. Bibliography: Fordyce M. Hubbard,

"Life of William Richardson Davie," in Jared Spards, ed., *Library of American Biography* (Boston, 1848); Walter Clark, "William R. Davie," in W.J. Peele, ed., *Lives of Distinguished North Carolinians* (Raleigh, 1898); Samuel A. Ashe, "William Richardson Davie," *Biographical History of North Carolina* (Greensboro, 1907); Joseph Hamilton, "William Richardson Davie: A Memoir, Followed by His Letters with Notes," *James Sprunt Hill Historical Monograph, No. 7* (Chapel Hill, 1907); Henry Wagstaff, "William Richardson Davie and Federalism," *Publications of the North Carolina Historical Commission,* (December, 1920, December, 1921); Blackwell P. Robinson, *William R. Davie* (Chapel Hill, 1957). A letter-book covering Davie's period as governor is located in the State Department of Archives and History in Raleigh. The Southern Historical Collection at the University of North Carolina in Chapel Hill holds other relevant letters and papers.

WILLIAMS, Benjamin, 1799-1802, 1807-1808

Born in Johnston County, North Carolina, on January 1, 1751, son of John Williams and Ferebee (Pugh) Williams; Protestant. Brother of John Williams. Married to Elizabeth Jones on August 10, 1781; father of Benjamin. Attended public schools, later becoming a farmer. Served as a member of the state's first revolutionary convention at the Johnston County Courthouse in 1774, and elected to the Provincial Council which met in defiance of the Royal Governor; served two terms, 1774-1775. Elected to the Committee of Safety for the District of New Bern in 1775. In September 1775, the Provincial Congress appointed Williams a Lieutenant in the Second North Carolina Regiment; promoted to Captain in 1776; resigned in 1779. Elected to the House of Commons as representative of Craven County, serving from 1779-1780. Volunteered to lead a regiment of state troops during the British invasion of 1780-1781; promoted to Colonel for gallantry at the Battle of Guilford Courthouse. Represented Johnston County in the State Senate, 1781, 1784-1787, and in the House of Commons, 1785, 1789. Represented Craven County in the State Senate, 1788, 1789. In 1788 Williams was a member of the state convention at Hillsborough which ratified the Federal Constitution. Elected as a Republican to the U.S. House of Representatives, and served from 1793 to 1795. Elected to his first term as Governor after two ballots of the General Assembly on November 23, 1799. Subsequently reelected by a "large majority" in 1800 and in 1801, serving the constitutional limit of three terms in six successive years. As governor, Williams granted a pardon to John Stanly, who had killed former Governor Spaight in a duel. In 1802 he recommended "adequate and suitable means" of public education; he was also a member of the University of North Carolina Board of Trustees from 1789-1802, and served as Board President during his years as governor. In 1802 he advocated inland navigation systems to free North Carolina from dependence on the markets of bordering states. Nominated but defeated for Governor in 1805, he was reelected to the State Senate from Moore County in 1807. He was eventually reelected Governor after three ballots of the General Assembly on December 1, 1807, and retired after a single term. Williams was also reelected to the State Senate from Moore County in 1809; in his last years he remained active as a planter and a banker. Williams died on July 20, 1814, and was buried in Moore County. Bibliography: Marshall D. Haywood, "Benjamin Williams," in S.A. Ashe, *Biographical History of North Carolina* (Greensboro, 1906); W.J. Adams, *Governor Benjamin Williams* (Carthage, 1920); Blackwell P. Robinson, *A*

History of Moore County, North Carolina: 1747-1847 (Southern Pines, 1956). A letterbook for Williams' administration as governor is located in the State Department of Archives and History in Raleigh. The Southern Historical Collection at the University of North Carolina in Chapel Hill holds other pertinent papers and letters.

TURNER, James, 1802-1805

Born in Southampton County, Virginia, on December 20, 1766, son of Thomas Turner; Protestant. Married to Marian Anderson in 1793; father of Thomas, Daniel, Rebecca and Mary; remarried to Ann Cochran after 1802; remarried to Elizabeth Johnston on July 21, 1810; father of Sally and Ann. Moved to Warren County, North Carolina in 1770. Educated in the common schools; later engaged in farming. Served as a private under General Greene in the North Carolina Volunteers in 1780. First elected to the House of Commons as representative of Warren County in 1798; reelected for the sessions of 1799-1800. Served in the State Senate, 1801-1802. After the death of Governor-elect John Baptista Ashe, the General Assembly chose Turner as Governor; he was sworn in on December 6, 1802. Governor Turner argued in favor of a system of public schools for North Carolina, to be financed by state revenue. During his term of office, he also served as president of the University of North Carolina Board of Trustees, and attempted to settle the state's border dispute with Georgia. A Democratic-Republican, Turner was reelected by the General Assembly for three successive one-year terms, the maximum number permitted by the state constitution. His last term ended on December 5, 1805. While still governor, Turner was elected to the U.S. Senate by joint ballot of the General Assembly on November 22, 1805; reelected in 1811, and served until 1816, when he resigned due to poor health. During his years in the Senate, Turner was a staunch defender of the administration's war efforts in the War of 1812. Turner died on January 15, 1824, and was buried on his plantation "Bloomsbury" in Warren County. Bibliography: John Hill Wheeler, *Historical Sketches of North Carolina: From 1584 to 1851* (Philadelphia, 1851); Marshall D. Haywood, "James Turner," in Samuel Ashe, *Biographical History of North Carolina,* III (Greensboro, 1905); Manly W. Wellman, *The County of Warren, North Carolina* (Chapel Hill, 1959). Papers and letterbooks concerning the Turner administration are located at the State Archives in Raleigh. The Southern Historical Collection at the University of North Carolina in Chapel Hill holds other useful papers and letters.

ALEXANDER, Nathaniel, 1805-1807

Born in Mecklenburg County, North Carolina, on March 5, 1756, son of Moses Alexander, a sheriff, and Sarah (Taylor) Alexander; a Presbyterian. Brother of William, Mark, Wallace, Jane Alexander Trotter and Sarah Alexander Henderson. Married to Margaret Polk, the daughter of Colonel Thomas Polk. Educated at the College of New Jersey (now Princeton University), graduating with an M.D. in 1776. Commissioned Surgeon in the North Carolina Continental Line in 1778, and served until the end of hostilities in 1782. Practiced medicine in the High Hills of the Santee, South Carolina. Returned to Charlotte, and was elected to the House of Commons in 1797 as representative of Mecklenburg County; served in the State Senate, 1801-1802. Member of the U.S. House of Representatives, 1803-1805. On November 25, 1805, Alexander was elected Governor of North Carolina by majority vote of the General Assembly, and sworn in on December 10. He was reelected, serving until December 1, 1807. Although a Democratic-Republican, Alexander was elected with Federalist support. During his tenure as governor, the number of North Carolina's district courts was increased, and the district lines were redrawn. In 1807 Alexander took measures to settle the border dispute with Georgia, and throughout his administration he was a strong advocate of internal improvements and popular education. He also served as President of the University of North Carolina Board of Trustees from 1805 to 1807. Alexander declined to run for reelection to a third term as governor. Alexander died in Salisbury, North Carolina, on March 8, 1808, and was buried in the cemetery of the First Presbyterian Church in Charlotte. Bibliography: Walter Clark, ed., *The State Records of North Carolina* (Goldsboro, 1895-1906); Marshall D. Haywood, "Nathaniel Alexander," in Samuel Ashe, ed., *Biographical History of North Carolina*, vol. I (Greensboro, 1905). Papers and letter-books concerning Alexander's administration are located in the State Archives in Raleigh. The Southern Historical Collection at the University of North Carolina also holds important letters and papers.

WILLIAMS, Benjamin, 1799-1802, 1807-1808

STONE, David, 1808-1810

Born in Bertie County, North Carolina, on February 17, 1770, son of Zedekiah Stone, planter and State Senator, and Elizabeth Hobson (Williamson) Stone; Protestant. Brother of Elizabeth Charlton Stone. Married to Hannah Turner on March 13, 1793; father of one son and four daughters; remarried to Sarah Dashiell in June 1817. Attended Windsor Academy, and graduated with honors from the College of New Jersey (now Princeton University) in 1788. Studied law under William R. Davie in Halifax, North Carolina, and was licensed to practice law in 1790. Served in the Fayetteville convention that ratified the Federal Constitution in 1789. Member of the House of Commons as representative of Bertie County, 1790-1795. Elected to the State Superior Court, 1795-1798. Sat as a Democratic-Republican in the United States House of Representatives, serving from 1799 to 1801; voted for Jefferson when the 1800 presidential election went to the House for a decision. Defeated for reelection to the House. The North Carolina General Assembly elected Stone to the United States Senate, where he served from 1801 to 1807; he resigned his seat on February 17, 1807, to accept a State Superior Court judgeship, 1807-1808. On November 28, 1808, Stone was elected Governor by majority vote of the General Assembly; he was subsequently reelected for two terms, serving until December 5, 1810. Governor Stone sought to protect property owners from the land claims of the Granville heirs, and these claims were subsequently disallowed. He urged development of the state's agriculture through the introduction of new crops and the use of techniques which would produce larger yields. He also encouraged the growth of new industries as a means of decreasing the state's dependence on foreign markets, and advocated improvements in transportation. In 1810 he spoke in favor of an extensive educational system for all, regardless of sex or social standing. Having served the constitutional limit of three terms as governor, Stone was reelected to the House of Commons as representative of Bertie County, 1811-1812. In 1813 he returned to the United States Senate, replacing Jesse Franklin. Stone's failure to support the administration's war measures led to a vote of censure by the North Carolina General Assembly in December 1813; after a vigorous and eloquent defense of his actions, Stone resigned his Senate seat in December 1814. He then retired to his plantation in Wake County. Stone died on October 7, 1818, and was buried in Wake County. Bibliography: John Hill Wheeler, *Historical Sketches of North Carolina: From 1584 to 1851* (Philadelphia, 1851); Marshall D. Haywood, "David Stone," in Samuel Ashe, *Biographical History of North Carolina* (Greensboro, 1906); John Tyler, *Bertie County's Colonial and State Governors of North Carolina* (n.p., n.d.). Papers and letter-books pertaining to Stone's governorship are located at the State Archives in Raleigh. The Southern Historical Collection at the University of North Carolina in Chapel Hill also holds relevant documents and letters.

SMITH, Benjamin, 1810-1811

Born on January 10, 1756, in Brunswick County, North Carolina, son of Colonel Thomas Smith, a planter. Brother of James, George, William and several sisters. An Episcopalian. Married to Sarah Dry on November 20, 1777. On his mother's side a descendant of the Second Landgrave of South Carolina, Smith was born into wealth and high social standing. Admitted in 1774 to the Middle Temple of the Inns of Court. A Colonel in the Continental Army, he served as aide-de-camp to General Washington during the retreat from Long Island in 1776. Fought at Moultrie in 1779, and in the defense of South Carolina in 1780. Elected to the Continental Congress of 1784, though no record exists of his attendance there. A Federalist with Jeffersonian sympathies, he served in North Carolina's constitutional conventions, at Hillsborough in 1788, and at Fayetteville in 1789. Elected to the State Senate as representative of Brunswick County, serving 1784, 1792-1800, 1806-1810; acted as Speaker of the Senate, 1795-1799. Member of the House of Commons as representative of Brunswick County in 1789-1792 and 1804-1805, and as representative of Burke County in 1801. Defeated for the United States Senate in 1789 by Benjamin Hawkins. Named in 1789 to the first Board of Trustees of the University of North Carolina; donated 20,000 acres of western land to support its endowment. Appointed Brigadier General in the state militia in 1794, and promoted to Major General in 1797 during the French crisis. Defeated for the United States Congress in 1804 by Samuel Ashe. Built the defenses in Wilmington harbor, a project which resulted in his financial ruin. In 1807 appointed Adjutant General for the state. Increasingly Republican in his sympathies, Smith was elected Governor on December 1, 1810 by majority vote of the General Assembly, and served a single one-year term. As governor, Smith urged the establishment of a penitentiary system; reform of the criminal code; and encouraged domestic industry and public support for education. He also served as president of the University Board of Trustees in 1810 and 1811, and remained a member until 1824. After trailing William Hawkins on the first ballot for Governor in 1811, Smith withdrew, declaring that he did not seek reelection. He returned to the State Senate in 1816. Smith's later years were troubled by the harassment of his creditors and by a number of political feuds, several of which ended in duels. Smith died on January 27, 1826, at his home in Smithville (now Southport). He was buried in the Episcopal Churchyard in Wilmington. Bibliography: Samuel Ashe,

"Benjamin Smith," in Samuel Ashe, ed., *Biographical History of North Carolina*, vol. II (Greensboro, 1905); Collier Cobb, "Governor Benjamin Smith." *North Carolina Booklet*, vol. XI, no. 3 (January, 1912); James Sprunt, *Chronicles of the Cape Fear River* (Raleigh, 1916); Earley Bridges, *The Masonic Governors of North Carolina* (Greensboro, 1937); Donald R. Lennon, Political Views and Public Activities of Benjamin Smith of Brunswick County," M.A. thesis, East Carolina College, 1961. Papers and letterbooks of Smith's administration are located at the State Archives in Raleigh.

HAWKINS, William, 1811-1814

Born on October 10, 1777, in Pleasant Hill, North Carolina, son of Colonel Philemon Hawkins, Jr., a member of the General Assembly, and Lucy (Davis) Hawkins; Protestant. Brother of Eleanor Howard (Hawkins) Haywood, Ann (Hawkins) Little, John Davis, Delia (Hawkins) Haywood, Sarah (Hawkins) Polk, Joseph, Benjamin Franklin, Philemon, Frank, George Washington, Lucy Davis Ruffin Hawkins Henry and Mildred Brehon. Married to Ann Swepson Boyd on December 24, 1804; father of Emily, Matilda, Lucy, William, Celestia, Henrietta and Mary Jane. Studied law in Granville County under Judge Williams. Served in 1797 as Assistant Indian Agent at Fort Hawkins, Georgia, under his uncle, Benjamin Hawkins. Further law studies in Philadelphia in 1797; returned to North Carolina in 1801 and practiced law. In 1801 Governor Turner asked Hawkins to settle a dispute with the Tuscarora Indians. Member of the House of Commons as representative of Warren County, 1804-1805, and as representative of Granville County, 1809-1811; served as Speaker of the House, 1810-1811. On December 9, 1811, elected Democratic-Republican Governor of North Carolina by majority vote of the General Assembly, and served the constitutional limit of three terms, ending on December 7, 1814. Hawkins' term coincided with the War of 1812; at President Madison's request, he raised 7,000 volunteers to meet the state's troop quota. He also personally inspected the state's coastal defenses when a British fleet arrived at New Bern, and urged internal unity to meet the threat. In his comments to the state General Assembly, Hawkins advocated improvements in North Carolina's agriculture, industry, roads, inland navigation and educational system. From 1803 to 1819, he served on the University of North Carolina Board of Trustees, and as Board president during his gubernatorial tenure. Hawkins returned to his plantation after his years as governor were over, but he was reelected to the House of Commons from Granville County in 1817. Hawkins died on May 17, 1819, while travelling to Fort Hawkins and was buried in Sparta, Georgia. Bibliography: Brant and Fuller, *Eminent and Representative Men of the Carolinas,* II (Madison, 1892); Marshall D. Haywood, "William Hawkins," in Samuel Ashe, *Biographical History of North Carolina,* V (Greensboro, 1906). Governor's papers and letterbooks of Hawkins' administration are in the State Archives in Raleigh. The Southern Historical Collection at Chapel Hill also holds papers and letters of interest.

MILLER, William, 1814-1817

Born about 1770, a native of Warren County, North Carolina, son of Thomas Miller, a planter; Protestant. Brother of Allen, John and two other brothers. Orphaned in 1792, and inherited a large plantation. Attended the University of North Carolina in 1802, but did not graduate. Engaged in legal practice in 1805. On August 21, 1810, selected State Attorney General. Elected to the House of Commons as representative of Warren County, serving 1810-1814, and as Speaker of the House, 1812-1814. Chosen as Governor on November 29, 1814, by majority vote of the General Assembly. As governor, Miller applauded the nation's war effort. In his addresses to the legislature, he endorsed state support of education as a safeguard of democratic rule and as a means of preventing the development of an aristocracy of wealth and learning. In response to his address, the General Assembly established a joint committee on education. Senator Archibald D. Murphy's reports of 1816 and 1817 were the first results of this committee, and his suggestions laid the groundwork for an extensive educational system. Miller served as president of the University of North Carolina Board of Trustees from 1814 to 1817, and remained a member until his death. He was also the first governor to occupy the governor's mansion. Reelected in 1815 and 1816, Miller served the constitutional limit of three one-year terms, leaving office on December 6, 1817. He was returned to the State Senate in 1821-1822, but was defeated in a bid for reelection due to his defense of the state's western interests. In 1825 President John Quincy Adams appointed Miller *Chargé d'Affaires* to Guatemala. Miller died in Guatemala shortly after his arrival there, probably in early 1826. Bibliography: Marshall D. Haywood, "William Miller," in Samuel Ashe, *Biographical History of North Carolina*, IV (Greensboro, 1906); Manly Wade Wellman, *The County of Warren, North Carolina* (Chapel Hill, 1959). The Governor's papers and letterbooks of the Miller administration are located at the State Archives in Raleigh. The Southern Historical Collection in Chapel Hill holds other pertinent papers and letters.

BRANCH, John, 1817-1820

Born in Halifax County, North Carolina, on November 4, 1782, son of Colonel John Branch, a planter and a member of the General Assembly, and Rebecca (Bradford) Branch. An Episcopalian. Brother of James, Martha Branch Whitaker, Joseph and William; step-brother of Washington Branch, and Elizabeth Ann Branch Alston Burge. Married to Elizabeth Foort on April 6, 1803; father of Martha, Rebecca, Margaret, James, Sarah, Mary Eliza, John, William and Susan; remarried to Mrs. Mary Eliza Jordan Bond on November 9, 1853. Graduated from the University of North Carolina with an A.B. in 1801, and studied law under John Haywood of Halifax; never practiced. Lived on his Enfield estate, superintending his plantation. Represented Halifax County in the State Senate, 1811, 1813-1817; Speaker of the Senate, 1815-1817. In 1814 lost in his bid for a United States Senate seat. On December 3, 1817, elected Governor by the General Assembly, defeating Duncan Cameron by a vote of 118 to 60. Served three terms, ending on December 7, 1820. As governor, Branch advocated internal improvements, and appealed for a less severe penal code, which would reduce the number of capital offenses and abolish imprisonment for debt. In 1818 his call for reform and expansion of the State's Superior Court led to the formation of the State Supreme

Court. He cautioned against imposters in the medical profession, and urged state regulation of physicians in 1820. Branch also presided over the local chapter of the American Colonization Society, which raised funds for the resettlement of emancipated slaves in Africa. In 1820 he resisted a public outcry, and refused to grant clemency to a white man sentenced to die for murdering a slave. A strong advocate of public education, Branch served on the University of North Carolina Board of Trustees from 1817 to 1844, and as Board President from 1817 to 1820. After serving the constitutional limit of three one-year terms as governor, Branch was reelected to the North Carolina State Senate in 1822. He was later appointed to the U.S. Senate by the legislature, and served from 1823 to 1829, allying himself with the Jacksonians. Though elected to a second Senate term, Branch resigned in 1829 to accept President Jackson's offer of the office of the Secretary of the Navy, thus becoming the first North Carolinian to be appointed to the federal cabinet. He resigned in 1831 as a result of a social feud involving the wives of Cabinet members, the so-called Eaton affair. Branch then declined the territorial governorship of Florida, and returned to Halifax County. He was elected to the House of Representatives, 1831-1833, and served in the State Senate in 1834. As a delegate to the State Constitutional Convention of 1835, he urged repeal of the religious test for officer holders, and opposed the disenfranchisement of free land-holding blacks. Although a Democrat, he opposed Van Buren in 1836. In 1838, in the second popular election for governor, Branch ran as the Democratic candidate, and was defeated by the Whig incumbent, Edward B. Dudley, by a vote of 33,993 to 29,950. In 1843 President Tyler appointed Branch governor of the Florida Territory, where he served from 1844 to 1845, the last man to hold that office before statehood. Branch died in Halifax County on January 4, 1863, and was buried in the family cemetery in Enfield.
Bibliography: Marshall D. Haywood, "John Branch," in Samuel Ashe, ed., *Biographical History of North Carolina,* VII (Greensboro, 1908); R.D.W. Connor, "John Branch, North Carolinians in the Navy Department," *The North Carolina Review, Raleigh News and Observer* (April 6, 1913); Marshall D. Haywood, "John Branch: 1782-1863," *The North Carolina Booklet, vol. 15, no. 2 (October, 1915);* W.C. Allen, *History of Halifax County* (Boston, 1918); William S. Hoffmann, "John Branch and the Origins of the Whig Party in North Carolina," *North Carolina Historical Review,* vol. XXXV, no. 3 (July, 1958). Governor's papers and letterbooks of the Branch administration are located at the State Archives in Raleigh. The Southern Historical Collection in Chapel Hill also holds relevant papers and letters.

FRANKLIN, Jesse, 1820-1821

Born in Orange County, Virginia on March 24, 1760, son of Bernard Franklin, a farmer, and Mary (Cleveland) Franklin, the daughter of Colonel Benjamin Cleveland; a Presbyterian. Brother of Benjamin, Abna, Shadrach, Polly Franklin Naul, Meshack, Abednego and Betsy. Married to Meeky Perkins before 1790; father of three sons and five daughters. Left the common schools before he was twelve, and was largely self-educated. Volunteered for the militia about 1777. Moved with his family to Surry County, North Carolina, about 1778. Fought in the Revolutionary Army, distinguishing himself at King's Mountain and at Guilford Courthouse; promoted to Major. Active in partisan warfare, he was captured by the Tories and hanged by his own bridle, escaping when it broke. Moved to Wilkes County and served as Justice of the Peace, 1785. Elected to the North Carolina

House of Commons, 1784-1785, 1787, 1790-1793, serving in the Council of State 1789. Returned in 1793 to Surry County, and elected to the House of Commons, 1793-1795. Elected as a Democratic-Republican to the United States House of Representatives, 1795-1797. Returned to the House of Commons, 1797-1798. The General Assembly elected Franklin to the United States Senate, and he served from 1799 to 1805, acting as President Pro Tempore in 1804. Served in the State Senate from Surry, 1805-1806. Reelected to a second term in the United States Senate, 1806-1813; declined reelection. Elected by the legislature to the Council of State, 1816-1817. Supervised public sale of the Cherokee lands, and in 1816 received a presidential appointment to negotiate a treaty with the Chickasaw Indians. Elected Governor of North Carolina by majority vote of the General Assembly on December 5, 1820, and inaugurated two days later. Governor Franklin advocated reform of the state courts and a less severe penal code, opposing espcially the procedure of cropping the ears of perjurers. He urged reorganization of the state militia and, though an advocate of strict economy, spoke in favor of internal improvements. He also sought to settle the state's persistent border disputes. Franklin was a firm supporter of public education, serving as president of the University of North Carolina Board of Trustees, which he had first joined in 1805. After a single one-year term, Franklin declined reelection in 1821 due to failing health. Franklin died in Surry County in September 1823; in 1906 he was reburied on the Guilford battle ground. Bibliography: E.W. Caruthers, *Interesting Revolutionary Incidents: Sketches of Character, Chiefly in the Old North State* (Philadelphia, 1854); Jasper Atkinson, "A Sketch of the Career of the Hon. Jesse Franklin," *North Carolina University Magazine*, n.s., vol. XVII, no. 2 (December, 1899); Marshall D. Haywood, "Jesse Franklin," in Samuel Ashe, ed., *Biographical History of North Carolina*, IV (Greensboro, 1906); J.T. Alderman, "Governor Jesse Franklin," *The North Carolina Booklet*, vol. VI, no. 3 (January, 1907); W.R. Edmonds, "Sketch of Jesse Franklin," *University of North Carolina Magazine*, n.s., vol. XXVIII, no. 4 (March, 1911). Governor's papers and letterbooks of Franklin's administration are located at the State Archives in Raleigh. The Southern Historical Collection at Chapel Hill holds other papers and letters.

HOLMES, Gabriel, 1821-1824

Born near Clinton, North Carolina in 1769. Son of Gabriel Holmes, a planter, and Mary (Caison) Holmes; Protestant. Brother of Hardy, Ann, Dorothy, Owen, Penelope, Lewis and one other sister. Married to Mary Smith Hunter before 1795; father of Maria, Hardy, Jane Smith, Theophilus Hunter, Mary and Julia. Educated at Zion Parnassus Academy: later attended Harvard College, but did not graduate. Returned to North Carolina and studied law under John Louis Taylor. Admitted to the bar in 1790, and practiced law in Clinton. Elected to the North Carolina House of Commons as representative of Sampson County, serving 1793-1795; member of the State Senate, 1797, 1801-1802, 1812-1813. Also served on the University of North Carolina Board of Trustees, 1801-1804, 1817-1829. Elected to the Council of State, 1810, 1814-1816. In 1821 Holmes was elected Governor after at least eight ballots of the General Assembly; the final count was Holmes, 106; James Mebane, 65; Hutchins Burton, 13. Holmes was inaugurated on December 7, 1821. In his addresses to the General Assembly, Holmes asked for a school tax, to be used to finance a state fund for education; this fund would provide educational opportunities for the poor; advocated internal improvements, but suggested that state monies be spent more efficiently, directing the Assembly's attention to the need for roads and navigation. He was a Democratic-Republican, and, like Thomas Jefferson, he placed great emphasis on the agrarian segment of American society. As president of the University Board of Trustees from 1821 to 1824, he called for agricultural courses at the university, and for the creation of a model farm to encourage scientific farming. He believed that emphasis on education be on the useful arts, and not on the overcrowded "learned professions." In 1824 he announced the impending visit of General Lafayette, and called for public celebration worthy of the occasion. Holmes was reelected in 1822 and 1823, serving the constitutional limit of three one-year terms. He was later elected to the United States House of Representatives in 1825, and served in that body until his death. Holmes died on September 26, 1829, and was buried on his estate in Sampson County. Bibliography: Marshall D. Haywood, "Gabriel Holmes," in Samuel Ashe, ed., *Biographical History of North Carolina*, III (Greensboro, 1905); C.L. Coon, *The Beginnings of Public Education in North Carolina* (Raleigh, 1908). Papers and letterbooks of Holmes' administration are in the State Archives in Raleigh. The Southern Historical Collection in Chapel Hill also holds relevant papers and letters.

BURTON, Hutchins Gordon, 1824-1827

Born in Virginia about 1774, son of John Burton and Mary (Gordon) Burton; Protestant. Married to Sarah Wales Jones, daughter of Willie Jones, after 1813; father of several children. Orphaned at age three and raised by his uncle, Colonel Robert Burton, of Granville County, North Carolina. Attended the University of North Carolina, 1795-1798; studied and practiced law, rising to prominence in the state bar. Elected to the House of Commons from Mecklenburg County in 1809, resigning in 1810 to become State Attorney General; he held this post until 1816. Returned in 1817 to the House of Commons as representative of the town of Halifax. In 1819 elected to the United States House of Representatives, resigning on March 23, 1824. A Federalist, Burton was elected governor on December 2, 1824, after six ballots of the General Assembly; he received 100 votes to defeat Montford Stokes (47), Alfred Moore (27), and E. Avery (16). In speeches to the General Assembly, Burton emphasized the need to fulfill the state constitution's provisions concerning education. He asserted that education should hold priority over internal improvements, and that primary schools were of more importance to the people's welfare than institutions of higher learning. While governor, he presided over the Literary Fund, and served as president of the University Board of Trustees. He also called for reform of North Carolina's penal code, and asked for a more systematic development of the state's roads and waterways. In 1825 he welcomed and escorted General Lafayette during his tour of the state. Reelected without opposition in 1825 and again in 1826, Burton served the constitutional limit of three successive one-year terms. In 1827 President John Quincy Adams nominated him for Governor of the Territory of Arkansas, but he was not confirmed by the Senate. He then retired to Halifax and practiced law. Burton died on April 21, 1836, while on a visit to Lincoln County. He was buried in the cemetery of the Unity Church at Beatty's Ford. Bibliography: Marshall D. Haywood, "Hutchins Burton," in Samuel Ashe, ed., *Biographical History of North Carolina*, IV (Greensboro, 1906); C.L. Coon, *The Beginnings of Public Education in North Carolina* (Raleigh, 1908). Governor's papers and letterbooks of the Burton administration are located at the State Archives in Raleigh. The Hutchins Burton Papers are part of the Southern Historical Collection in Chapel Hill.

IREDELL, James, 1827-1828

Born on November 2, 1788 in Edenton, Chowan County, North Carolina, son of James Iredell, Associate Justice of the United States Supreme Court, and Hannah (Johnston) Iredell; a Protestant. Brother of Annie. Married to Francis Johnston Treadwell; father of James, Campbell, Cadwallader, Penelope Eden and five other daughters. Orphaned in youth, and raised by his uncle, former Governor Samuel Johnston. Educated at Edenton Academy; graduated from Princeton College with an A.M. in 1806. Studied law; admitted to the bar in 1809, and practiced in Edenton. As Captain, led a company of volunteers in the defense of Norfolk, Virginia, in 1812. Elected to the University of North Carolina Board of Trustees in 1813, serving as a member until his death. Member of the House of Commons as representative of Edenton, 1813, 1816-1820; as Speaker of the House, 1816-1818. Appointed in 1819 to the State Superior Court, resigning at the end of a month. Returned to the House of Commons as a member from Edenton, 1820, 1823-1828; as Speaker Pro Tempore in 1826-1827; and as Speaker in 1827-1828. On December 5, 1827, elected Governor by the General Assembly; after J. Stanly and W. Polk withdrew, Iredell defeated Richard Dobbs Spaight, Jr., on the third ballot by a vote of 104 to 82. Iredell spoke ardently against the Tariff of 1828, calling it a violation of the spirit of the federal compact. He also called for internal improvements, and especially for the development of a coastal port; the drainage of swamps; and the building of railways. After a single term as governor, Iredell resigned on December 1, 1828, following his election to the United States Senate. He served as a Democrat from 1828 to 1831, but did not seek reelection. Iredell moved to Raleigh in 1830 and practiced law. He was later appointed to the commission to revise state laws in 1836 and 1837, and served as reporter of the State Supreme Court, 1840-1852. He also published law and equity digests, and wrote several works on North Carolina political and judicial history, including *Treatise on the Law of Executors and Administrators*. Iredell died while visiting Edenton on April 13, 1853. He was interred in the Johnston family cemetery on the Hayes plantation. Bibliography: John Hill Wheeler, *Historical Sketches of North Carolina: From 1584 to 1851* (Philadelphia, 1851); Griffith J. McRee, *Life and Correspondence of James Iredell* [Senior] (New York, 1858); C.L. Coon, *The Beginnings of Public Education in North Carolina* (Raleigh, 1908); Fred A. Olds, "James Iredell, Junior," *The Orphan's Friend and Masonic Journal*, vol. XLIX, no. 9 (July 11, 1924). Papers and letterbooks concerning Iredell's gubernatorial administration are located at the State Archives in Raleigh. The Southern Historical Collection at Chapel Hill also holds papers and letters.

OWEN, John, 1828-1830

Born in August 1787 in Bladen County, North Carolina, son of Colonel Thomas Owen, a judge and State Senator, and Eleanor (Porterfield) Owen; Protestant. Brother of Mary Owen Stedman and James. Married to Lucy Brown; father of Lucy. Attended the University of North Carolina in 1804 but did not graduate. Elected to the House of Commons as representative of Bladen County, serving 1812-1814; also a member of the Senate, 1819-1820. Served on the Council of State from 1824-1827, returning to the Senate, 1827-1828. On December 8, 1828, Owen was chosen Governor after several ballots of the General Assembly, defeating Richard Dobbs Spaight, Jr., by a vote of 96 to 92. He was reelected to a second term on December 9, 1829. Governor Owen called for internal improvements and increased spending for education, the latter to be financed by the taxation of wealthy property holders. He also sought to promote the growth of primary schools and of the university, serving on the University of North Carolina Board of Trustees, from 1820 to 1824, and as Board President during his term as governor. Politically, Owen was a National Republican with Federalist sympathies. Owen's term expired on December 18, 1830, and although he was nominated for a third term as governor, he withdrew, citing personal reasons. In 1830 he was defeated for the United States Senate, losing to Willie Mangum by one vote in the General Assembly. Owen was a leading member of the 1835 State Constitutional Convention, where he opposed the disenfranchisement of free land-holding Negroes and the religious test for officeholders. On November 12, 1839, he presided over the first Whig Party Convention in the state. Three weeks later, he served as President of the National Whig Convention meeting in Harrisburg, Pennsylvania. After the nomination of William Henry Harrison in 1840, Owen was offered the vice-presidency, but declined. He then retired to his plantation, where he experimented with scientific farming. Owen died in Chatham County on October 9, 1841, and was buried in St. Bartholomew's Churchyard in Pittsboro. Bibliography: John Hill Wheeler, *Historical Sketches of North Carolina: From 1584 to 1851* (Philadelphia, 1851); C.L. Coon, *The Beginnings of Public Education in North Carolina* (Raleigh, 1908); Marshall D. Haywood, "John Owen," in Samuel Ashe, ed., *Biographical History of North Carolina*, VIII (Greensboro, 1917). Papers and letterbooks of Owen's administration are located at the State Archives in Raleigh. The Southern Historical Collection in Chapel Hill also holds papers and letters.

STOKES, Montford, 1830-1832

Born in Lunenburg County, Virginia on March 12, 1762, son of David Stokes, a soldier and judge, and Sarah (Montfort) Stokes; Protestant. Youngest of eleven children. Married to Mary Erwin on September 1, 1790; father of Adelaide; widowed in 1791, and remarried Rachel Montgomery on January 6, 1796; father of Hugh, Thomas Jefferson, David, Montfort Sidney, Henry Irvin, Anne Neville, Rachel Adelaide, Rebecca Camelia, Sarah and Kate. Enlisted in the United States Merchant Marine at age thirteen, later joining the Continental Navy under Commodore Stephen Decatur. After the War of 1812, travelled extensively as Captain of a merchant ship, eventually settling in Halifax, North Carolina, where he became a planter. Moved to Salisbury about 1786, and studied law in the office of his brother, John Stokes. Served as Assistant Clerk of the State Senate, 1786-1790, and as Clerk of the Superior Court of Rowan, 1790. Appointed Captain of Cavalry, 1790-1792. From 1799 to 1816 served as Clerk of the State Senate. In 1800 chosen as a Presidential Elector, a post he held quadrennially until 1832. Appointed Major General in the state militia in 1804, resigning in 1816. Elected to the United States Senate in 1804, but declined the office. Moved to Wilkes County about 1810, settling on family lands; elected Justice of the Peace in 1811. Resigned his Senate clerkship on November 30, 1816, after his election to the United States Senate to fill the seat left vacant by the resignation of James Turner; served until 1823, when he was defeated for reelection by John Branch. President in 1823 of a convention held in Raleigh which urged constitutional reform to give greater representation to the western counties. Represented Wilkes County in the State Senate, 1826-1827, and in the House of Commons, 1829-1831. From 1830 to 1832 served as President of the Board of Visitors of the United States Military Academy at West Point. On December 17, 1830, Stokes was elected Governor after nine ballots of the General Assembly; Cadwallader Jones having withdrawn, Stokes defeated Richard Dobbs

Spaight, Jr., by a vote of 111 to 75. He was reelected to a second term on December 12, 1831, defeating Spaight by a vote of 98 to 93. As governor, Stokes supported internal improvements, particularly the construction of canals along the coast. While he took steps to tighten the state's security in 1830 and 1831, he took a moderate stance in the face of public fears over a possible general slave insurrection. An ardent Jacksonian, he opposed the doctrine of nullification, and urged North Carolina's House of Commons to pass resolutions in support of the President. He was a member of the University of North Carolina Board of Trustees from 1804 to 1836, and its president *ex officio* during his term as governor. On November 19, 1832, Stokes resigned as governor, having been appointed by President Jackson to be Chairman of the Federal Indian Commission; he then supervised the resettlement in the west of the southeastern Indians. Stokes later moved to Fort Gibson, Arkansas Territory (now Oklahoma), and in 1836 was appointed sub agent for the Cherokees, Senecas and Shawnees; in 1837 he became agent for the Cherokees. Denied reappointment in 1841 by President Tyler, he was nevertheless made sub-agent in 1842 for the Senecas, Shawnees and Quapaws. Stokes worked to maintain the peace and to negotiate treaties; in his reports he showed a strong sympathy for the plight of the Indian. Stokes died on November 4, 1842. He was buried near Fort Gibson. Bibliography: John Meserve, "Governor Montford Stokes," *Chronicles of Oklahoma*, vol. XIII, no. 3 (September, 1935); William Foster, "The Career of Montford Stokes in North Carolina," *North Carolina Historical Review*, vol. XVI, no. 3 (July, 1939); William Foster, "The Life of Montford Stokes," unpublished M.A. thesis, University of North Carolina, 1939); Grant Foreman, "The Life of Montford Stokes in the Indian Territory," *North Carolina Historical Review*, vol. XVI, no. 4 (October, 1939); Johnson Hayes, *The Land of Wilkes* (Wilkesboro, 1962). Governor's papers and letterbooks of Stokes' administration are located at the State Archives in Raleigh. The Southern Historical Collection in Chapel Hill holds other relevant papers and letters.

SWAIN, David Lowry, 1832-1835

Born on January 4, 1801 in Buncombe County, North Carolina, son of George Swain, a legislator, hatter and farmer, and Caroline (Lane) Lowry Swain. His mother was a Methodist and his father a Presbyterian; Swain himself was a devout Christian, loosely affiliated with the Presbyterian Church. Brother of Caroline Swain Hall, Cynthia Swain Coleman, Althia Swain Siler, Mathilda Swain Siler and George, Jr.; half-brother of Charles Lowry, James Lowry, Mary Lowry and Patience Lowry Ervin. Married to Eleanor H. White on January 12, 1823; father of Anna, David Lowry, Eleanor and Richard Caswell. Educated at New Academy near Asheville; attended the University of North Carolina for four months in 1821, and then left for Raleigh to study law under Chief Justice Taylor; admitted to the bar in June 1823. Member of the House of Commons as representative of Buncombe County, 1824-1830. After one year as a solicitor in the Edenton District, served as Judge on the State Superior Court, 1830-1832. Swain then resigned, having been elected Governor by the General Assembly on December 1, 1832; after Thomas Polk and John Branch withdrew on earlier ballots, Swain won a majority on the third ballot, receiving 99 votes to defeat Richard Dobbs Spaight (85) and John Bryan (4). He was inaugurated on December 6, the youngest governor and the first Whig chief executive in the state's history. Swain contended that the state's weak economy and poor means of communication had hindered the development of an extensive educational system. He enthusiastically supported internal improvements, and called for state financing and control of major projects. He also advocated the building of railroads. The legislature, however, curtailed most of his plans in 1833. Swain supervised the collecting of the state's records, and laid the cornerstone for the state capitol building. Although he was unopposed for reelection in 1833, in 1834 the Democrats mounted a strong challenge; after three ballots of the General Assembly, Swain narrowly defeated House Speaker William Moseley by a vote of 97 to 89. A dedicated Whig, Swain was the first North Carolina governor to play an active role in party politics. In 1834 his appeal for a more equitable tax policy was resisted by the legislature, but he did manage to appoint a commission to revise and publish the state's penal laws; he also called for a state constitutional convention to consider more equitable representation for the western counties. Swain was Chairman Pro Tempore of the State Constitutional Convention which met in 1835, and political leader of the reform faction. He was a firm opponent of the religious test for officeholders, and of the disenfranchisement of free land-holding blacks. His last official act as governor was to issue a proclamation ratifying the new state constitution. After serving the constitutional limit of three one-year terms, Swain was chosen president of the University of North Carolina by the Board of Trustees; he held this office from 1835 to 1868. He worked to ensure the financial stability of the university, and to increase its enrollment and faculty. In 1841 he received an LL.D. from the College of New Jersey, and another from Yale. An energetic teacher and scholar, he founded the North Carolina Historical Society and the *University of North Carolina Magazine*. He supervised the collection of the state's colonial and state records in 1854, and was the author of several scholarly tracts on state history. Though a Whig Unionist, he was appointed in 1861 to a commission sent to Montgomery, Alabama to represent the state's interests in the Confederate government. Swain declined Governor Vance's offer in 1863 to serve in the Confederate Senate, and when Raleigh's fall was imminent in 1865, he went as a peace commissioner to negotiate the surrender with General Sherman. For the next three years, Swain was a close adviser of President Johnson on reconstruction policies. (In 1865 Johnson appointed him to the Board of Visitors of the Military Academy at West Point.) Though Swain had worked diligently to keep the University of North Carolina open during the war, by 1868 it had fallen into economic ruin; the State Legislature eventually appointed new trustees, who requested the resignation of the president and faculty. Swain died in Chapel Hill on August 27, 1868, as a result of injuries suffered in a buggy accident; he was later reinterred in Oakwood Cemetery, Raleigh. Bibliography: Fisk Brewer, *Memoir of Hon. David Lowry Swain, LL.D.* (Boston, 1870); Zebulon Vance, *Life and Character of Hon. David L. Swain* (Durham, 1878); Kemp Battle, "David Lowry Swain," *North Carolina Journal of Education*, vol. III, no. 2 (September, 1899); Samuel Ashe, "David Lowry Swain," in Samuel Ashe, ed., *Biographical History of North Carolina*, I (Greensboro, 1905); R.D.W. Connor, *Ante-Bellum Builders of North Carolina* (Raleigh, 1914); Carolyn Andrews Daniel,"David Lowry Swain:1801-1835," unpublished doctoral dissertation University of North Carolina, 1954; Carolyn Andrews Wallace, "David Lowry Swain, the First Whig Governor of North Carolina," *James Sprunt Studies in History and Political Science* (Vol. 39). The David L. Swain Papers are located at the Southern Historical Collection in Chapel Hill. The State Archives in Raleigh holds other governor's papers.

SPAIGHT, Richard Dobbs, Jr., 1835-1836

Born in New Bern, North Carolina in 1796, son of Richard Dobbs Spaight, former Governor of North Carolina, and Mary (Leach) Spaight. Brother of Charles B. and Margaret Spaight Donnell; an Anglican. Never married. Orphaned in 1802, when his father was killed in a duel. Educated at the New Bern Academy; later attended the University of North Carolina, graduating with an A.B. in 1815. Studied law and admitted to the bar in 1818. Elected to the House of Commons as representative of Craven County in 1819; served in the State Senate, 1820-1822. In 1823 Spaight was elected to the United States House of Representatives, but was defeated for reelection by John Bryan, a Whig. He returned to the State Senate, from 1825 to 1835. Defeated for Governor in 1827 by James Iredell, Jr., in 1828 by John Owen, in 1830 and 1831 by Montford Stokes, and in 1832 by David Swain. In 1835 Spaight served in the State Constitutional Convention, where he opposed the religious test for officeholders. He was elected Governor on November 23, 1835, the last governor to be elected by the General Assembly; he defeated William B. Meares by a vote of 103 to 86. As governor, Spaight reported to the General Assembly on the assets of the Literary Fund, and deferred to the legislature on the ways in which the state's funds should be appropriated. A representative of eastern interests, he did not endorse internal improvements, and justified his position by noting that competition among the various projects caused inefficiencies. Politically, Spaight was leader of the Old Republican faction. He was also a classics scholar, serving on the University of North Carolina's Board of Trustees from 1821 to 1850, and as president *ex officio* of that body during his term as governor. In 1836 Spaight ran against Whig Edward B. Dudley in the state's first popular election for Governor, as mandated by the 1835 Constitution. Neither man campaigned, with each relying on political and newspaper endorsements. Spaight was defeated by a vote of 33,993 to 29,950, and then retired to New Bern, where he practiced law and farmed. Spaight died on November 2, 1850; he was buried in the family cemetery on the Clermont plantation near New Bern. Bibliography: Marshall D. Haywood, "Richard Dobbs Spaight, Junior," in Samuel Ashe, ed., *Biographical History of North Carolina*, IV (Greensboro, 1906); C.L. Coon, *The Beginnings of Public Education in North Carolina* (Raleigh, 1908); Marshall D. Haywood, "Grand Masters Spaight, Jenkins, and Clark," *The North Carolina Booklet*, vol. XXI, nos. 1-4 (July-October, 1921, April, 1922). Governor Spaight's papers and letterbooks are located at the State Archives in Raleigh. The Southern Historical Collection in Chapel Hill also holds some relevant letters and papers.

DUDLEY, Edward Bishop, 1836-1841

Born on December 15, 1789 near Jacksonville in Onslow County, North Carolina, son of Christopher Dudley, politician and planter, and Margaret (Snead) Dudley; Episcopalian. Brother of Robert, Christopher, Polly, John and Anne Elizabeth Dudley Hill. Married to Eliza E. Haywood on November 20, 1815; father of Christopher, William Henry, Robert Edward, Eliza Anne, Jane and Margaret. Educated at Onslow Academy. Engaged in business. Commissioned Major in the Onslow Regiment of the militia in 1809. Elected to the House of Commons as representative from Onslow County in 1811 and 1813, and to the State Senate in 1814. In 1814-1815 Dudley commanded the garrison at Wilmington, having been promoted to Colonel. From 1816 to 1817 he represented the town of

Wilmington in the House of Commons. The General Assembly promoted him to Brigadier General in 1817, a post he held until 1819. Dudley was appointed to the State Board for Internal Improvements in 1824. At first an ardent Jacksonian, he served as a Presidential Elector in 1824 and 1828. In 1829 he was elected as a National Republican to fill the seat in the United States House of Representatives left vacant by the death of Gabriel Holmes; he served from 1829 to 1831, but declined reelection. Increasingly disillusioned with Jacksonian policies, he eventually became an active Whig. Dudley returned to the State House of Commons as a member from Wilmington, 1834-1835. A supporter of western interests, constitutional reform and state aid for railroads, Dudley received the endorsement of Whig county conventions in 1836, and won that party's nomination for Governor. Under the provisions of the 1835 Constitution, Dudley became, on December 31, 1836, the first popularly-elected governor in the state's history, defeating the Democratic incumbent, Richard Dobbs Spaight, Jr., by a vote of 33,993 to 29,950. In 1836 Dudley asked the legislature to appropriate North Carolina's share of the federal surplus for the development of the state's resources, and for the establishment of free common schools. While governor, he was instrumental in organizing the Wilmington and Raleigh Railroad Company in 1836, serving as its first president. His administration became deeply involved in the tactical problem of removing the Cherokees from North Carolina to the western territories, a problem which led to a bitter jurisdictional dispute with Tennessee. In the 1838 gubernatorial election, Dudley, a reluctant candidate, withstood the token candidacy of the Democrat John Branch, and defeated him by a vote of 38,166 to 21,130. In his 1838 message to the General Assembly, he advocated linking the state with a system of turnpikes and railways built at state expense, but the legislature balked. He also called for state-wide schools supported by teacher scholarships, and this time the General Assembly responded with the North Carolina School Law of 1839, which allowed county referenda on the question. Similarly, Dudley advocated the building of a penitentiary, an insane asylum, and an orphan home. He was constitutionally restricted from seeking a third term. After his years as governor had ended, Dudley became involved with the financing, construction and expansion of the Wilmington & Raleigh Railroad Company; the Weldon line was at the time the longest in the world. He served as company president until 1846, risking his personal fortune to secure its capital. In 1847 he was chosen president of the Wilmington & Manchester Railroad. His health declining, Dudley was baptized in 1854 at St. James Episcopal Church in Wilmington. He died on October 30, 1855, and was buried in Oak Dale Cemetery in Wilmington. Bibliography: Robert Cowen, *An Oration Commemorative of the Life and Character of the Late Edward Dudley* (n.p., 1855); John Wheeler, *Reminiscences and Memoirs of North Carolina and North Carolinians* (Washington, 1883-1884); C.L. Coon, *The Beginnings of Public Education in North Carolina* (Raleigh, 1908); James Sprunt, *Chronicles of the Cape Fear River, 1660-1916* (Raleigh, 1916); Luther Byrd, "The Life and Public Service of Edward Bishop Dudley, 1789-1855, unpublished M.A. Thesis, University of North Carolina, 1949; Herbert Pegg, *The Whig Party in North Carolina* (Chapel Hill, n.d.). Papers concerning Dudley's years as governor are located at the State Archives in Raleigh. The Southern Historical Collection in Chapel Hill also holds pertinent letters and papers.

MOREHEAD, John Motley, 1841-1845

Born on July 4, 1796 in Pittsylvania County, Virginia, son of John Morehead, a planter, and Obedience (Motley) Morehead; a Presbyterian. Brother of James Turner, Samuel, Abraham Forrest, Prudence Morehead Reynolds, Mary Morehead Scales, Elizabeth Morehead Woodson, Anne Morehead Hobson and Delilah Morehead Holderby. Married to Ann Eliza Lindsay on September 6, 1821; father of Letitia, Mary Corrina, Ann Eliza, Mary Louise, Emma Victoria, John Lindsay, James Turner and Eugene. His family settled in Rockingham County in 1798. Educated in the classics by Thomas Settle, and attended Dr. David Caldwell's academy near Greensboro. Entered the University of North Carolina, graduating with an A.B. in 1817 and an A.M. in 1837. Studied law under Archibald D. Murphey; admitted to the bar in 1819 and practiced in Wentworth. Served in the House of Commons as representative of Rockingham County, 1821-1822. Moved to Greensboro and again elected to the House of Commons, where he represented Guilford County, 1826-1828. Joined the University of North Carolina Board of Trustees in 1828, a post he held until his death. Served in the State Constitutional Convention of 1835 where he sided with the western forces urging reform. A Jackson Democrat prior to 1835, Morehead joined the Whig Party. In 1840 he received the Whig nomination for Governor, and in the popular election defeated Democrat R. M. Saunders by 44,484 votes to 35,903. Morehead was inaugurated on January 1, 1841. The 1840 election was the first in the state's history in which the candidates canvassed the state. Governor Morehead called for agricultural and industrial development, and for the expansion of North Carolina's common school system. In 1842 he urged extension of the railroad lines, construction of turnpikes, and improvement of canals, all to be linked in a unified transportation network. Morehead's schemes, however, were resisted by the Democratic General Assembly. In 1842, with the Whig Party disorganized, he narrowly won reelection, defeating the Democrat Louis D. Henry by a vote of 37,943 to 34,411. In 1845 Morehead appealed for improved facilities for the deaf, dumb and blind, an appeal which led to the founding of a state home. Though constitutionally barred from serving a third term, Morehead remained politically active. In 1848 he presided over the National Whig Convention which met in Philadelphia. As president of the North Carolina Railroad, he sought expansion of a rail system that would ultimately cross the entire state. Morehead was elected to the House of Commons from Guilford County in 1858-1859, and served in the State Senate in 1860-1861, where he argued for state aid to railroads. In 1861 he represented the state at the Peace Conference in Washington; at first a Unionist, he attempted to find a compromise that would avert war, but returned home an advocate of the secession. He served in the Provisional Congress of the Confederate government in 1861 and 1862. Morehead died on August 27, 1866, in Rockbridge Alum Springs, Virginia. He was buried in the cemetery of the First Presbyterian Church in Greensboro. Bibliography: *In Memoriam: Hon. John M. Morehead* (Raleigh, 1868); John Wheeler, *Reminiscences and Memoirs of North Carolina and North Carolinians* (Washington, 1883-1884); C. Alphonso Smith, "John Motley Morehead," in Samuel Ashe, ed., *Biographical History of North Carolina*, II (Greensboro, 1905); R.D.W. Connor, *Ante-Bellum Builders of North Carolina* (Raleigh, 1914); John Motley Morehead, III, *The Morehead Family of North Carolina and Virginia* (New York, 1921); Burton Konkle, *John Motley Morehead and the Development of North Carolina: 1796-1866* (Philadelphia, 1922). Governor Morehead's papers and letterbooks are located at the State Archives in Raleigh. The Southern Historical Collection in Chapel Hill holds other papers of interest.

GRAHAM, William Alexander, 1845-1849

Born on September 5, 1804, near Vesuvius Furnace in Lincoln County, North Carolina, son of General Joseph Graham, a legislator and iron founder, and Isabella (Davidson) Graham; a Presbyterian. Brother of Polly, John Davidson, Sophia Graham Witherspoon, James, Joseph, George Franklin, Robert Montrose, Alfred, Violet Wilson Graham Alexander, Mary Graham Morrison and Isabella. Married to Susannah Sarah Washington on June 8, 1836; father of Joseph, John Washington, William Alexander, James Augustus, Robert Davidson, George Washington, Augustus Washington, Susan Washington, Alfred Octavius and Eugene. Attended Pleasant Retreat Academy in Lincolnton, Dr. Muchat's Classical Academy in Statesville, and the Hillsboro Academy. Graduated from the University of North Carolina with honors in 1824. Studied law under Chief Justice Thomas Ruffin in Hillsboro; admitted to the bar in 1827, and established a law practice in Hillsboro. Elected three times to the House of Commons as representative of the town of Hillsboro, 1833-1835, and as representative of Orange County, 1836-1840, serving as Speaker of the House, 1838-1840. On November 24, 1840, elected to the United States Senate as a Whig, filling the seat left vacant by the resignation of Robert Strange; served until March 31, 1843, when he retired after the Democrats had taken a majority in the State General Assembly. Received the Whig nomination for Governor in 1844, and defeated the Democratic nominee, Michael Hoke, by a vote of 42,586 to 39,433; inaugurated on January 1, 1845. As governor, Graham supported internal improvements and a common school system. He sought to secure the financial stability of the troubled railroads, and under legislative mandate, supervised the collection of documents pertaining to state history. In 1846 Graham was reelected, defeating the Democrat James B. Shepard by a vote of 43,486 to 35,627. In 1848 Graham called for the legislature to found a state hospital, and he eventually saw his plans for rail construction lead to the chartering of the North Carolina Railroad. Graham was constitutionally forbidden from seeking a third term. In 1849 Graham declined President Taylor's offer of an official role during diplomatic missions to Spain and Russia. He served as Secretary of the Navy under President Fillmore, 1850-1852, and was instrumental in dispatching expeditions to the Amazon and to Japan; he also reorganized the coastal survey and navy personnel. In June 1852, Graham resigned as Secretary, and ran for Vice President on a Whig ticket headed by General Winfield Scott. Defeated for national office, he returned to North Carolina, serving in the State Senate, 1854-1855. Graham, a staunch Unionist, urged moderation as the nation moved towards civil war, and he received support as a possible presidential nominee of the Constitutional Union Party in 1860. With the outbreak of war, however, he embraced the Confederate cause, serving as President Pro Tempore in North Carolina's Secessionist Convention of 1861-1862. In 1862 he was reelected to the State Senate, resigning in 1863. Elected to the Confederate Congress, he at first declined, but when reelected he served from 1864 to 1865, and advocated a negotiated peace. He returned to the State Senate in 1865. On April 11, 1865, when Sherman's Army appeared before Raleigh, Graham was appointed a Peace Commissioner to negotiate surrender. On December 4, he resigned from the State Senate, having been elected to the United States Senate; since he had not received a presidential pardon for his activities during the war, he never presented his credentials. He was a delegate to the Philadelphia Union Convention in 1866, and the next year became one of the original trustees of the Peabody Fund. In 1875 he was elected to North Carolina's Constitutional Convention. At the time of his death, he was serving as an arbitrator at a conference to resolve the Maryland and Virginia border dispute. Graham died suddenly in Saratoga Springs, New York, on August 11,

1875. He was buried in the Presbyterian Church Cemetery in Hillsboro. Bibliography: Montford McGehee, "Life and Character of Hon. William A. Graham," in W.J. Peele, ed., *Lives of Distinguished North Carolinians* (Raleigh, 1898); Frank Nash, "William Alexander Graham," *Bulletin of the North Carolina Historical Commission* (Raleigh, 1910); Walter Clark, "William Alexander Graham," *The North Carolina Booklet*, vol. XVI, no. 1 (July, 1916); J.G. de Roulac Hamilton, *The Papers of William Alexander Graham* (Raleigh, 1957); Max Williams, "The Education of William A. Graham," *North Carolina Historical Review*, vol. XL, no. 1 (Winter, 1963); M. Williams, "William A. Graham, North Carolina Whig Party Leader, 1804-1849," Doctoral Dissertation, University of North Carolina, 1965; Max Williams, "William A. Graham and the Election of 1844: A Study in North Carolina Politics," *North Carolina Historical Review*, vol. XLV, no. 1 (Winter, 1968). The State Archives in Raleigh and the Southern Historical Collection in Chapel Hill hold relevant papers and documents.

MANLY, Charles, 1849-1850

Born in Chatham County, North Carolina on May 13, 1795, son of Captain Basil Manly, a planter, and Elizabeth (Maultsby) Manly. Though his father was Roman Catholic and his mother a Baptist, Manly became an Episcopalian. Brother of Basil, Matthias Evans, Maurice Ford, Louisa Sophia Manly Thompson Powell, and Julia Ann. Married to Charity Hare Haywood on October 7, 1817; father of Ann Eliza, John Haywood, Langdon Cheves, Charles, William Henry, Cora, Edward, Julia, Helen, Sophia Louisa, Basil Charles and Ida. Studied at the Pittsboro Academy under William Bingham. Entered the University of North Carolina in 1811, receiving an A.B. in 1814 and later an A.M. Worked as a tutor and studied law; admitted to the bar in 1816. Appointed in 1828 to the University of North Carolina Board of Trustees, a post he held until 1868; served on the commission to sell the Cherokee lands to support the university's endowment. Clerk in 1823 to the commission settling claims under the Treaty of Ghent. After moving to Washington, D.C., Manly returned to North Carolina in about 1824. Appointed Clerk of the House of Commons, a post he held from 1831 to 1841 and from 1844 to 1847. Defeated in 1844 for the State Senate from Wake County. Abandoning the National Republicans, Manly became a supporter of Henry Clay and an active Whig, serving on the party's central and campaign committees. In 1840 he was a Presidential Elector, and on August 3, 1848, he was nominated for Governor and went on to defeat the Democrat David S. Reid by a vote of 42,536 to 41,682. Manly strongly supported popular education and internal improvements, especially railways and canals. He urged a geological survey of the state, and called for redistribution of the assets of the Literary Fund to counties on the basis of white population, not according to federal census statistics. A personal friend of Dorothea Dix, he spoke eloquently for more humane treatment of the insane, and secured an asylum bill from the legislature. In 1850 he defended national unity and warned against secessionist sentiments; nevertheless, he also defended states' rights, particularly on the slave issue. Renominated by the Whigs in 1850, he ran once more against David Reid, but was defeated by a vote of 45,080 to 42,337. His term as governor expired on December 31, 1850. With the Whig party in decline, Manly retired from politics. Though a late convert to secession, he actively supported the Confederate cause. Manly died on May 1, 1871, and was buried in the city cemetery in Raleigh. Bibliography: James Cleveland, *Biographical Sketch of Charles Manly* (Raleigh, 1853); John Wheeler, *Reminiscences and Memoirs of North Carolina and Eminent North Carolinians* (Washington, 1883-1884);

Marshall D. Haywood, "Charles Manly," in Samuel Ashe, ed., *Biographical History of North Carolina*, VI (Greensboro, 1908); Louise Manly, *The Manly Family* (Greenville, 1930). Governor's papers and letterbooks dealing with the Manly administration are located in the State Archives in Raleigh. The Southern Historical Collection in Chapel Hill holds other pertinent letters and documents.

REID, David Settle, 1851-1854

Born on April 19, 1813 near Reidsville, Rockingham County, North Carolina, son of Reuben Settle Reid, a constable and farmer, and Elizabeth (Settle) Reid; Protestant. Brother of Hugh Kearns, Frances Reid Adams, Rhoda Reid Scott, Henrietta Reid Price, Anne Reid Reid, and Reuben. Married to Henrietta Settle after 1848; father of David Settle, Thomas Settle, and Reuben David. Attended county schools and an academy in Middletown, Connecticut. Studied law and admitted to the bar in 1833; the following year began a law practice in Wentworth. Elected to the State Senate from Rockingham County, serving 1835-1841. Elected to the United States House of Representatives, serving in the 28th and 29th Congresses, 1843-1847; did not seek a third term. Without his consent, the Democrats nominated him for Governor in 1848; he campaigned vigorously, but was narrowly defeated by Whig candidate, Charles Manly, 42,536 votes to 41,682. He asked not to be a candidate again, but the Democrats nominated him a second time in 1850; in the popular election he defeated Governor Manly, 45,080 votes to 41,337. The issue in both elections was free suffrage, with Reid asserting his opposition to a landholding qualification for voting in State Senate elections. Reid was inaugurated on January 1, 1851. In his address to the General Assembly, Reid defended slavery and warned against federal interference. He worked to have a free suffrage bill passed, but the legislature was initially reluctant. Tentative approval for such a bill was granted in 1850 and 1854, but the act did not secure final legislative approval until 1856. In the 1852 gubernatorial election, Reid defeated the Whig candidate, John Kerr, by a vote of 48,567 to 43,003. His 1852 address to the General Assembly called for the strengthening of the common school system as North Carolina's first priority. He also endorsed financial aid to the county schools on the basis of the federal census, not on white population only, and cited the need for increased taxation to support education. On December 5, 1854, Reid resigned as governor, having been elected by the General Assembly to the United States Senate; he served in that capacity from 1854 to 1859, defending the policies of the Buchanan administration. He was defeated for reelection, but in 1861 served at the Peace Conference in Washington. Reid was an active member of the State Secession Convention in 1861 and 1862, and eventually retired to Reidsville, where he practiced law. In 1875 Reid helped to organize North Carolina's Constitutional Convention of that year, and acted as a convention delegate. Reid died on June 19, 1891, and was buried in the Greenview Cemetery in Reidsville. Bibliography: John Wheeler, *Reminiscences and Memoirs of North Carolina and Eminent North Carolinians* (Washington, 1883-1884); M.C.S. Noble, *A History of the Public Schools of North Carolina* (Chapel Hill, 1930); Paul Reid, "Gubernatorial Campaigns and Administrations of David S. Reid, 1848-1854" *Bulletin of Western Carolina College*, vol. XXX, no. 3 (July, 1953). Relevant papers and letters are located at the State Archives in Raleigh, the Southern Historical Collection in Chapel Hill, Duke University, and Reid's home in Reidsville.

WINSLOW, Warren, 1854-1855

Born on January 1, 1810 in Fayetteville, North Carolina, son of John Winslow, a magistrate, and Caroline Martha Winslow; an Episcopalian. Brother of Edward Lee and Lucy Ann Winslow Ochiltree. Educated at Fayetteville Academy, and graduated from the University of North Carolina with an A.B. in 1827. Studied law and admitted to the bar; practiced in Fayetteville. From 1853 to 1854 Winslow was Magistrate of Police in Fayetteville. Elected to the State Senate, 1854-1855, serving as Speaker. When Governor David Reid resigned to take a seat in the United States Senate, Winslow, as Speaker of the Senate, became Governor. A dispute arose between former Governor Graham and former Chief Justice Ruffin whether Winslow should hold the offices of Governor and Senate Speaker; by a single vote of the State Senate, Winslow was permitted the joint office. Governor Winslow, a Democrat, reported on the progress of the state's agricultural and geological survey. He was not a candidate for Governor in the 1854 election, and served only from December 6, 1854, to January 1, 1855. Following his term of office, Winslow was sent by President Pierce to Spain in 1855 on a special mission concerning the Black Warrior Affair. Winslow was also elected to the United States House of Representatives, serving from 1855 until North Carolina seceded in 1861. In 1860, after Governor Ellis fell ill, Winslow was appointed one of three members of a board to supervise the state's naval and military affairs. He eventually negotiated the surrender of the federal garrison at Fayetteville. In 1861 Winslow was a member of North Carolina's Secession Convention, but resigned in 1862. Winslow died on August 16, 1862, in Fayetteville, and was buried in the Cross Creek Cemetery. Bibliography: John Wheeler, *Reminiscences and Memoirs of North Carolina and Eminent North Carolinians* (Washington, 1883-1884); John A. Oates, *The Story of Fayetteville and the Upper Cape Fear* (Charlotte, 1950). The State Archives in Raleigh, and the Carolina and Southern Historical Collections in Chapel Hill hold relevant papers.

BRAGG, Thomas, 1855-1859

Born on November 9, 1810, son of Thomas Bragg, a carpenter and contractor, and Margaret (Crossland) Bragg; an Episcopalian. Brother of John, Alexander, Braxton, Dunbar, William, and Mary Bragg Cuthbert. Married to Isabella Cuthbert on October 4, 1837; father of three sons and four daughters. Educated at the Warrenton Academy and at Captain Partridge's Military Academy in Middletown, Connecticut. Studied law with Supreme Court Justice Hall in Warrenton; admitted to the bar and established a practice in Jackson, Northampton County; elected County Attorney. A Democrat, Bragg served in the House of Commons as a representative of Northampton County from 1842 to 1843, but was defeated for reelection. Rose to distinction in the state bar, winning several landmark cases. In 1844, 1848 and 1852 Bragg was a delegate to Democratic National Conventions, and canvassed the state as a Presidential Elector. Bragg received the Democratic nomination for Governor in 1854, and defeated the Whig candidate, General Alfred Dockery, by a vote of 48,705 to 46,644; he was inaugurated on January 1, 1855. In his message to the legislature, Bragg warned that a common school system might weaken North Carolina's private schools. He supported internal improvements, a geological survey of the state, and expansion of the state's railways. In 1856 he held informal meetings with other southern governors to consider the national policy which might develop in the event of Fremont's election. Bragg took a conservative stand, warning against federal encroachments, but urging caution on the part of the southern states. In the 1856 gubernatorial election, he defeated John A. Gilmer of the American "Know-Nothing" Party by a vote of 57,598 to 44,970. In 1858 he commented on the substantial improvements which had been made in North Carolina's common school system. Constitutionally limited to two terms, Bragg was elected to the United States Senate by the legislature on November 23, 1858. On March 8, 1861, just prior to the outbreak of war, Bragg resigned from the Senate; he was officially expelled on July 11. From 1861 to 1862, Bragg served as Attorney General of the Confederacy. He later returned to Raleigh to resume the practice of law, and after the war he took an active role in the reorganization of North Carolina's government. He also represented the state in the impeachment trial of Governor Holden. Bragg died in Raleigh on January 19, 1872, and was buried in Oakwood Cemetery. Bibliography: John Wheeler, *Reminiscences and Memoirs of North Carolina and Eminent North Carolinians* (Washington, 1883-1884); Pulaski Cowper, "A Sketch of the Life of Governor Thomas Bragg," *North Carolina University Magazine*, n.s., vol. X, no. 3 (1891); M.C.S. Noble, *A History of the Public Schools of North Carolina* (Chapel Hill, 1930). The State Archives in Raleigh hold letterbooks and governor's papers dealing with the Bragg administration. The Southern Historical Collection in Chapel Hill also holds some papers, including Bragg's diary.

ELLIS, John Willis, 1859-1861

Born on November 23, 1820 in the Jersey Settlement in Rowan (now Davidson) County, son of Anderson Willis, a wealthy planter, and Judith (Bailey) Ellis; an Episcopalian. Brother of Elizabeth Ellis Pearson and Mary Ellis Douglass. Married to Mary White on August 25, 1844; widowed, remarried to Mary McKinley Daves on August 11, 1858; father of Mary Daves and Jean Graham. Attended Robert Allison's school in Beatties' Ford, and enrolled at Randolph-Macon College, graduating with an A.B. in 1841. Attended Judge Richmond M. Pearson's law school in Mocksville. Admitted to the bar in 1842, and established a law practice in Salisbury, riding the court circuit. In 1843 Ellis was a delegate to the Democratic State Convention. The following year he was elected to the House of Commons from Rowan County, serving from 1844 to 1849. A Major in the Rowan Company of the state militia, he was unsuccessful in raising a company of volunteers for the Mexican War. He was appointed Judge of the State Superior Court in December 1848, a post he held until 1858. The candidate of the slave-holding gentry, Ellis defeated William Holden in 1858 for the Democratic nomination for Governor. In the general election the Whig Party did not nominate a candidate, but Duncan K. McRae ran as an Independent Democrat; Ellis defeated him by a vote of 56,429 to 40,046. Governor Ellis supported internal improvements, especially those which would result in a more efficient operation of the railways. An advocate of moderation during the sectional crisis, he hosted President Buchanan on a state tour. Nevertheless, after the John Brown raid, Ellis called for the reforming of the state militia and the raising of troops. In the 1860 gubernatorial election, the reorganized Whig Party held an Opposition State Convention, and nominated John Pool for Governor. The campaign was fought over national politics, and over Ellis' opposition to ad valorem taxation of slaves. Ellis defeated Pool by a vote of 59,463 to 53,123. In his 1860 message to the General Assembly, he called for a break from the policies of the national Republican Party, and urged that a conference of southern states be followed by a state convention; a popular referendum narrowly defeated the latter proposition in 1861. By now a secessionist, he at first opposed military action, ordering the return to federal control of two forts seized by local citizens. After the firing on Fort Sumter, however, he called for 30,000 volunteers. He also convened an extra session of the legislature, which led to the formation of the Secession Convention. Ellis died on July 7, 1861, in Red Sulphur Springs, Virginia (now West Virginia). He was buried in the old English Cemetery in Salisbury, North Carolina. Bibliography: Jethro Rumple, *A History of Rowan County* (Salisbury, 1881); John Wheeler, *Reminiscences and Memoirs of North Carolina and Eminent North Carolinians* (Washington, 1883-1884); Marshall Haywood, "John Willis Ellis," in Samuel Ashe, ed., *Biographical History of North Carolina*, VII (Greensboro, 1908); James Boykin, *North Carolina in 1861* (New York, 1961); Noble Tolbert, ed., *The Papers of John Willis Ellis* (Raleigh, 1964). The State Archives in Raleigh holds relevant letterbooks and papers.

CLARK, Henry Toole, 1861-1862

Born on February 7, 1808 in Walnut Creek near Tarboro, North Carolina, son of James W. Clark, a legislator and planter, and Arabella (Toole) Clark; an Episcopalian. Brother of Maria Clark Waddell and Laura Clark Cotten. Married to Mrs. Mary Weeks Parker Hargrove in February 1850; father of Laura, Haywood, Henry Irwin, Maria and Arabella. Educated at George Phillips' School in Tarboro and the Louisburg Academy. Graduated from the University of North Carolina with an A.B. in 1826, and an A.M. in 1832. Studied law under William H. Haywood, Jr.; admitted to the bar, but never practiced. Won election in 1840 as Court Clerk and in 1850 as a member of the State Senate from Edgecombe County, serving from 1850 to 1861; Speaker of the Senate, 1858-1861. After Governor John Ellis fell ill, Clark, as Senate Speaker, became effective chief executive; when Ellis died on July 7, 1861, Clark became Governor. Nominally a Democrat, Clark organized North Carolina into military districts, and supervised the raising and supplying of state troops during the first year of the Civil War. He ordered the seizure of the federal arsenal at Fayetteville, and sent emissaries to purchase arms in Europe. Clark had to mediate between the demands of the Confederate government and the pressing military needs of the state, as federal troops occupied the coastal and eastern areas of North Carolina. In 1862, when his Senate term expired, Clark survived a challenge to his governorship. A more effective administrator than a political leader, he called for unity and an end to partisan activity. When his term expired in September 1862, he declined to seek reelection. He then retired to his plantation, narrowly escaping Union troops who plundered his home and property. From 1866 to 1867, he served in the State Senate. Clark died on April 14, 1874, and was buried in the Calvary Episcopal Cemetery in Tarboro. Bibliography: John Wheeler, *Reminiscences and Memoirs of North Carolina and North Carolinians* (Washington, 1883-1884); J. Kelly and J.L. Bridgers, Jr., *History of Edgecombe County, North Carolina* (Raleigh, 1920); Garry Mercer, "The Administration of Governor Henry Toole Clark, 1861-1862," unpublished M.A. thesis, East Carolina College, 1965. Governor's papers concerning the Clark administration are located at the State Archives in Raleigh. The Southern Historical Collection in Chapel Hill also holds pertinent letters and papers.

VANCE, Zebulon, 1862-1865, 1877-1879

Born on May 13, 1830 in Buncombe County, North Carolina, son of David Vance, a farmer and merchant, and Mira Margaret (Baird) Vance. Brother of Laura Vance Neilson, Robert B., James N., Ann E., Sarah P., Hannah M., and David L. Married to Harriet Espy on August 3, 1853; father of David, Charles, Zebulon and Thomas. After his wife's death in 1878, Vance joined the Presbyterian Church. Married Mrs. Florence Steele Martin in 1880. Educated at local schools, and in 1843 attended Washington College in east Tennessee. Studied law at the University of North Carolina, 1851-1852; awarded an honorary LL.D. in 1890. Licensed to practice law, and sworn in as Asheville's County Solicitor in 1852. Elected as a Whig to the House of Commons from Buncombe County, 1854-1855. In 1855 became co-editor of the Asheville *Spectator*. Defeated in 1856 for the State Legislature, running as a "Know-Nothing." Defeated by Thomas Clingman for the United States Congress in 1857; after Clingman resigned, Vance, the nominee of the American Party, was elected to the United States House of Representatives, serving 1858-1861. Although reelected to a third term, he did not serve, North Carolina having seceded. First a Unionist, Vance organized a Confederate troop company when war began, and served as its Captain. Promoted to Colonel in the North Carolina Regiment, he fought at New Bern and in the Seven Days' Battle. In the 1862 gubernatorial election, Vance was nominated by the Conservative Party; his opponent, W.J. Johnson, accused Vance of Unionist sympathies, but Vance won by a vote of 54,423 to 20,488, and was inaugurated on September 8, 1862. Governor Vance appropriated funds for procuring arms and outfitting troops, and started a blockade-running operation. He also clashed with the Confederate government, chiefly over the issue of conscription. Vance refused to allow the drafting of state officials, insisting that the army defer to legally proper writs of *habeas corpus*. In 1863 he granted a pardon to North Carolina deserters. Vance was opposed in 1864 by William Holden, who ran as a peace candidate; Vance won by a vote of 58,070 to 14,491. As the war's end neared, Vance resisted appeals that the state negotiate a separate surrender, though he met with Sherman in April 1865. Vance fled Raleigh and was arrested on May 13 by presidential order; a short time later, Holden became Provisional Governor on May 29. Released from the Old Capitol Prison in Washington on July 6, 1865, Vance formed a law partnership in Raleigh. In 1867 he received a pardon, and he served at the Democratic National Convention in 1868. He was elected to the United States Senate in 1870, but did not take his seat, since his political disabilities still remained. Later cleared by Congress, he ran as a Democrat for the Senate, but was defeated. In 1876 he ran again for Governor against the Republican Thomas Settle; both men were powerful orators, with Vance winning by a vote of 118,258 to 104,330. Vance urged improvement of the public educational system; the establishment of normal schools for both races; and the hiring of women teachers. He revived interest in railroad construction, and tried to restore the state's finances after post-war mismanagement. Vance served only two years of his term, having been elected to the United States Senate on January 21, 1878; twice reelected, he served from 1879 to 1893, and was a leading spokesman for southern interests. Vance was a popular lecturer on the Chautauqua circuit, noted especially for his speech "The Scattered Nation," dealing with Jewish history. Vance died in Washington on April 14, 1894; after funeral services in the Senate chamber, he was buried in Riverside Cemetery, Asheville. Bibliography: *Memorial Addresses on the Life and Character of Zebulon Baird Vance* (Washington, 1895); Clement Dowd, *Life of Zebulon B. Vance* (Charlotte, 1897); Richard H. Battle, "Zebulon Baird Vance," in Samuel Ashe, ed., *Biographical History of North Carolina*, VI (Greensboro, 1907); Frontis W. Johnston,

"Zebulon Baird Vance: A Personality Sketch," *North Carolina Historical Review*, vol. XXX, no. 2 (April, 1953); Richard Yates, *The Confederacy and Zeb Vance* (Tuscaloosa, 1958); Frontis W. Johnston, ed., *The Papers of Zebulon Baird Vance*, vol. I (Raleigh, 1963); Glenn Tucker, *Zeb Vance: Champion of Personal Freedom* (New York, 1965). Papers and letterbooks concerning Vance's years as governor are located at the State Archives in Raleigh. The Zebulon Baird Vance Papers are held by the Southern Historical Collection in Chapel Hill.

HOLDEN, William Woods, 1865, 1868-1870

Born on November 24, 1818 near Hillsborough in Orange County, North Carolina, son of Holden, a miller, and Priscilla Woods; Protestant. Born out of wedlock, he was taken at the age of six from his mother's home and raised with his father's ten legitimate children. Married to Anne Young in 1841; father of one son and two daughters; remarried to Louisa Virginia Harrison in 1854. Educated at an old field school; at about age ten, left home and became a printer's devil under Dennis Heartt of the Hillsborough *Recorder*. Worked for newspapers in Milton, North Carolina, and Danville, Virginia, later returning to Hillsborough. Moved in 1837 to Raleigh, where he worked as a printer and writer for the *Star*. Studied law and was licensed to practice in 1841. In 1843 he was offered the editorship of the North Carolina *Standard*, on condition that he become a Democrat; he accepted these terms and turned the newspaper into the most powerful journal in the state, advocating "free suffrage" and an extreme secessionist position. Member of the House of Commons from Wake County, 1846-1847. Lost the Democratic nomination for governor to John Ellis in 1858, and was defeated by Governors Reid and Bragg for a United States Senate seat. A delegate to the Charleston and Baltimore Democratic conventions, he supported Stephen A. Douglas, though he eventually campaigned for John C. Breckenridge. He was elected to the 1861 Secession Convention from Wake County as a Union man; however, he eventually endorsed separation from the Union. As the war progressed, Holden became increasingly disillusioned, but when he advocated peace and opposed the Confederate administration, his newspaper presses were wrecked. In 1864 he ran for governor as a peace candidate against Zebulon Vance, whom he had formerly supported, and called for the state to secede from the Confederacy and to negotiate a separate peace. Holden lost by a vote of 58,070 to 14,491. He then formed a secret political party, "Heroes of America," or the "Red Strings," to promote the peace movement. On May 29, 1865, President Johnson appointed Holden Provisional Governor of North Carolina. In October 1865 Holden, following the directives of the President, convened a state convention to return North Carolina to the Union, the convention was to repeal secession; abolish slavery, and set new elections to replace the provisional government. The 1865 election was marked by bitter factionalism, and Holden was defeated for governor by Jonathon Worth by a count of 31,643 to 25,704. In 1866 Holden was nominated as Minister to San Salvador, but the United States Senate failed to confirm him. Though originally an opponent of black suffrage and testimony, he became an active supporter of the Fourteenth Amendment in his *Standard* editorials, and advocated radical reconstruction policies. In 1867 he helped to organize the state's Republican Party, allying himself with the carpetbaggers. Under the new state constitution, Holden was elected Governor in 1868, defeating Thomas Ashe by a vote of 92,235 to 73,594. The military authorities removed Governor Worth, and appointed Holden Provisional Governor until his term began. His administration was marked by corruption and mismanagement, though Holden himself did not personally profit. At his urging the 1870 legislature passed anti-Ku Klux Klan acts that gave the governor the power to declare a county in insurrection, and which included the discretionary power to suspend habeas corpus and to institute military law. Holden declared Alamance and Caswell Counties to be in insurrection. An irregular army under Colonel Kirk arrested political opponents, prominent citizens and editors, at least one of whom did not reside in the affected counties. Ignoring the edicts of the state's courts, Holden finally submitted to the writ of a federal court and released the prisoners. The Democrats then swept the election of 1870, and the State House of Representatives issued eight counts of impeachment for high crimes and misdemeanors against Holden; he was immediately removed from office. On March 23, 1871, he was convicted on six counts, and replaced in office by Lieutenant Governor Caldwell. Holden was forbidden from holding state office again. Holden later moved to Washington and became editor from 1871 to 1872 of the *Daily Chronicle*. He declined appointment in 1872 to be Minister to Peru, and in 1873 was appointed Postmaster of Raleigh, a post he held until 1881. He remained an active Republican until 1883, when he quit the party in protest against black suffrage, the tariff and sectionalism. As in politics, Holden's religious views were diverse; at different times he joined the Baptists and Methodists, among others. Holden died on March 1, 1892, and was buried in Oakwood Cemetery in Raleigh. Bibliography: *Trial of William W. Holden . . . on Impeachment . . . for High Crimes and Misdemeanors* (Raleigh, 1871); Thomas Pittman, "William Woods Holden," in Samuel Ashe, ed., *Biographical History of North Carolina*, III (Greensboro, 1905); W.K. Boyd, ed., *Memoirs of W.W. Holden* (Durham, 1911); Edgar Folk, *W.W. Holden, Political Journalist* (Nashville, 1934); Cortez Ewing, "Two Reconstruction Impeachments," *North Carolina Historical Review*, vol. XV, no. 3 (July, 1938); Edgar Folk, "W.W. Holden and the Election of 1858," *North Carolina Historical Review*, vol. XXI, no. 4 (October, 1944); Horace Raper, "William Woods Holden: A Political Biography," unpublished dissertation, University of North Carolina, 1951; Horace Raper, "William W. Holden and the Peace Movement in North Carolina," *North Carolina Historical Review*, vol. XXXI, no. 4 (October, 1954). Holden's papers are located at the State Archives in Raleigh, the North Carolina and Southern Historical Collections in Chapel Hill, and Duke University.

WORTH, Jonathon, 1865-1868

Born on November 18, 1802, son of David Worth, a doctor and a farmer, and Eunice (Gardner) Worth. Both his parents were Quakers, though Worth never joined a church. Brother of Steven, Rachel, John Milton, Thomas Clarkson, Joseph Addison, Barzillai Gardner, Miriam Worth Coffin, Louisa Worth Clark, Rugh Worth Porter and one other sister. Married to Martitia Daniel on October 20, 1824; father of David, Louisa, Elvira Evelina, Sarah Corinna, Adelaide Ann, Mary Martitia, Roxana and Lucy Jane. Educated at the Greensboro Academy in 1823, and then studied law under Judge Archibald D. Murphey; licensed to practice in 1824. Moved to Asheville. Overcoming a habitual shyness, Worth was elected to the House of Commons from Randolph County, serving from 1830 to 1832; known as an opponent of nullification. Established a lucrative legal practice, and acquired large financial holdings. Elected to the State Senate, 1840-1841; a Clay Whig, he was defeated for the United States Congress in 1841 by Abraham Rencher. Defeated for Congress again in 1845 by Alfred Dockery. Clerk and Master in Equity for Randolph County; elected to the State Senate, 1858-1862. Resigned on December 3, 1862, having been elected State Treasurer, a post he held until 1865. A staunch Unionist, Worth strongly opposed the referendum in 1861 on the convening of a secession convention. He opposed the Confederate administration, but declined to participate in the peace movements of 1863-1864. Worth was appointed Provisional Treasurer in 1865 by Governor Holden, and later that year ran for Governor as a Conservative against Holden, defeating him by a vote of 31,643 to 25,704. Worth was inaugurated on December 15, 1865. As governor, Worth supported the reconstruction policies of President Johnson. In the 1866 election, he defeated Alfred Dockery, nominated by the supporters of Holden, by a vote of 34,250 to 10,759. That same year he led the legislature in opposing the ratification of the Fourteenth Amendment, on the grounds that it placed disabilities on former Confederates. Worth defended civil authority against usurpations by military rule; supported black testimony; and interceded on the state's behalf with the northern Generals Sickles and Canby. He urged whites to register and to refrain from voting as a means of preventing the adoption of a state constitution that would grant black suffrage. Worth declined to run for Governor in 1868; William Holden was elected under the 1868 constitution. Worth denied the constitutionality of the election, and had to be removed from office by military decree. Worth died at his home "Sharon" in Raleigh on September 6, 1869, and was buried in Oakwood Cemetery. Bibliography: Seaton Gales, *Hon. Jonathon Worth* (n.p., n.d.); John Wheeler, *Reminiscences and Memoirs of North Carolina and Eminent North Carolinians* (Washington, 1883-1884); J.G. deRoulhac Hamilton, "Jonathon Worth," in Samuel Ashe, ed., *Biographical History of North Carolina*, III (Greensboro, 1905); J.G. deRoulhac Hamilton, ed., *The Correspondence of Jonathon Worth* (Raleigh, 1909); Henry McFadyen, "The Administration of Governor Jonathon Worth, 1865 to 1868," unpublished M.A. thesis, University of North Carolina, 1942; Richard L. Zuber, *Jonathon Worth: A Biography of a Southern Unionist* (Chapel Hill, 1965). Worth's papers are located at the State Archives in Raleigh and in the Southern Historical Collection in Chapel Hill.

HOLDEN, William Woods, 1865, 1868-1870

CALDWELL, Tod Robinson, 1870-1874

Born on February 19, 1818 in Morganton, North Carolina, son of John Caldwell, a merchant; Protestant. Married to Minerva Ruffin Cain in February 1841; father of John. Studied under William Bingham in Hillsborough, and attended the University of North Carolina, graduating with an A.B. in 1840. Studied law with David Lowry Swain; admitted to the bar in 1840, and established a large legal practice. Served as County Solicitor. Entered politics as a Whig, serving in the House of Commons from Burke County, 1842-1845, 1848-1849, 1858-1859, and in the State Senate, 1850-1851. In 1848 Caldwell served as Presidential Elector, supporting Taylor and Fillmore. He was Secretary Pro Tempore of the Constitutional Convention of 1866. In 1867 he was elected Lieutenant Governor on the ticket headed by William Holden. Caldwell was the first lieutenant governor of North Carolina, an office which had been established by the new state constitution; he also served as President of the Senate, 1868-1870. When Holden was impeached, Caldwell succeeded him as Governor on December 15, 1870. As governor, Caldwell refused to authorize the election of a new state constitutional convention as the General Assembly had requested; the legislature over-ruled him, but a subsequent referendum was defeated by popular vote. In 1872 Caldwell defeated Judge Settle for the Republican nomination for Governor, and in the general election he later beat the Conservative candidate, Augustus S. Merrimon, by a vote of 98,132 to 96,234. Although there were charges of fraud, the General Assembly, with a Conservative majority, investigated the election and reaffirmed the results. Caldwell sought to revive the state's finances, and appointed a commission to review the settlement of the state debt. He also attempted to reopen the public schools closed by the war, and called for increased emphasis on the lower rather than the higher levels of education. His policies were in general conciliatory. Caldwell died in Hillsboro on July 11, 1874, while still in office; he was buried in Morganton. Bibliography: *News and Observer* [Raleigh] (July 14,1874); John H. Wheeler, *Reminiscences and Memoirs of North Carolina and Eminent North Carolinians* (Washington, 1883-1884). Papers dealing with Caldwell's years as governor are located at the State Archives in Raleigh. The North Carolina Collection holds other documents, and the Caldwell Papers are in the Southern Historical Collection in Chapel Hill.

BROGDEN, Curtis Hooks, 1874-1877

Born on November 6, 1816 near Goldsboro, Wayne County, North Carolina, son of Pierce Brogden, a farmer, and Amy (Beard) Brogden; Protestant. Never married. Attended local schools; largely self-educated. Joined the state militia at age eighteen; elected Captain, subsequently rising through the ranks to Major General. Elected as a Jackson Democrat to the House of Commons from Wayne County, serving 1838-1851. In 1838 elected County Justice of the Peace, a post he held for twenty years. Admitted to the bar in 1845, but never practiced; from 1854 to 1856 acted as Chairman of the County Clerks. Elected to the State Senate, 1852-1857. Chosen State Comptroller by the General Assembly, serving 1857-1867. Represented Wayne County in 1867 at a state constitutional convention convened by General Canby; supported Republican policies, particularly black suffrage. In 1868 presided over the Electoral College as a supporter of Ulysses S. Grant. Returned to the State Senate from 1868 to 1872. Elected Lieutenant Governor in 1872 on a ticket headed by Tod R. Caldwell; also served as President of the State Senate. After the death of Governor Caldwell, Brogden succeeded to the governorship on July 14, 1874. Governor Brogden's policies continued the conciliatory pattern established by his immediate predecessor. In 1875 he was instrumental in reopening the University of North Carolina, and affirming the right of every citizen to an education. He also called for the founding of a state Negro college; supported railway expansion and the building of the state penitentiary; and sought to eliminate inequities in the state penal code. While still governor, Brogden was elected in 1876 to the United States House of Representatives, and was a member from 1877 to 1879. He then retired to his farm, though he once again served in North Carolina's lower house in 1887. Brogden died on January 5, 1901, in Goldsboro, and was buried in Willow Dale Cemetery. Bibliography: *News and Observer* [Raleigh] (July 14, 1874); John Wheeler, *Reminiscences and Memoirs of North Carolina and Eminent North Carolinians* (Washington, 1883-1884); George Wills, "Curtis Hooks Brogden," in Samuel Ashe, ed., *Biographical History of North Carolina*, III (Greensboro, 1907). Relevant papers are located at the State Archives in Raleigh and in the Southern Historical Collection at Chapel Hill.

VANCE, Zebulon, 1862-1865, 1877-1879

JARVIS, Thomas Jordan, 1879-1885

Born on January 18, 1836 in Jarvisburg, Currituck County, North Carolina, son of Bannister Hardy Jarvis, a Methodist minister and farmer, and Elizabeth (Daley) Jarvis. Brother of George, Ann, Margaret and Elizabeth. Married to Mary Woodson on December 23, 1874. Educated at local common schools. Attended Randolph-Macon College, 1855-1860, receiving an A.B. in 1860 and an M.A. in 1861. Awarded LL.D. in 1883 by the University of North Carolina. Opened a school in Pasquotank County. At the outbreak of the Civil War, Jarvis enlisted and was commissioned a Lieutenant in the Eighth North Carolina Regiment. Captured and exchanged in 1862, and promoted to Captain in 1863. At the battle of Drewry's Bluff in 1864, Jarvis sustained a wound which permanently disabled him. Became a delegate to the State Constitutional Convention of 1865, and opened a small general store. Canvassed the state in 1868 as a Democratic Presidential Elector. Elected to the State House of Representatives, 1868-1872; Speaker of the House, 1870-1872. An opponent of Republican reconstruction policies. Moved to Greenville. Led the Democratic forces in the 1875 State Constitutional Convention, and the following year won the nomination for Lieutenant Governor on a ticket headed by Zebulon Vance. Served two years as lieutenant governor and as President of the State Senate. When Vance resigned as governor to enter the United States Senate, Jarvis succeeded him on February 5, 1879. Governor Jarvis supported increased expenditures for agriculture, education and care of the insane. He urged the legislature to settle the state debt, which had been inflated by Republican corruption, and oversaw the state's sale of the Western North Carolina Railroad. In June 1880, Jarvis defeated Daniel G. Fowle for the Democratic nomination for Governor; in the general election he went on to win over the Republican candidate, Ralph Buxton, by a vote of 121,827 to 115,590. Jarvis's 1881 address to the legislature called for racial harmony and increased immigration to the state. He supported prohibition, but the proposal was defeated in a state-wide referendum. Jarvis was constitutionally barred from running again when his term expired in 1885. In 1885 President Cleveland appointed Jarvis Ambassador to Brazil, a post he held until 1889. He then returned to Greenville and practiced law. In 1892 Jarvis became permanent chairman of the state Democratic Party, and after the death of Zebulon Vance, he filled Vance's seat in the United States Senate. Jarvis served in 1894 and 1895, but failed to win the nomination for another term. In 1896 he was a delegate to the Democratic National Convention, and a supporter of William Jennings Bryan. Jarvis was also a founder of the East Carolina Training School, now East Carolina University. Jarvis died on June 17, 1915, in Greenville; he was buried in Cherry Hill Cemetery. Bibliography: John Wheeler, *Reminiscences and Memoirs of North Carolina and Eminent North Carolinians* (Washington, 1883-1884); Samuel Ashe, ed., "Thomas Jordan Jarvis," *Biographical History of North Carolina*, I (Greensboro, 1905); *News and Observer* [Raleigh] (June 18, 1915); Thomas Davis, ed., "Thomas Jordan Jarvis, 1836-1915," *Proceedings of the North Carolina Bar Association* (Wilmington, 1916); Henry Connor, "Thomas Jordan Jarvis and the Rebuilding of North Carolina," *Proceedings of the State Literary and Historical Associaton of North Carolina* (Raleigh, 1916); W. B. Yearns, ed., *The Papers of Thomas Jordan Jarvis* (Raleigh, 1969); Elgiva D. Watson, "The Election Campaign of Governor Jarvis, 1880: A Study of Issues," *North Carolina Historical Review*, vol.

XLVIII, no. 3 (July, 1971). Pertinent papers are located at the State Archives in Raleigh and in the North Carolina and Southern Historical collections in Chapel Hill.

ROBINSON, James Lowry, 1883

Born on September 17, 1838 in Franklin, Macon County, North Carolina, son of James Robinson, a merchant, and Matilda (Lowry) Robinson; Protestant. Brother of Mary Jane, Charles Lane, David Olin, and Jesse Siler. Married to Alice Lowry Siler in 1884; father of Walter, Annie, Mary Swain, Julius Siler, James, Jr., Kate Isabel, Charles, William Coleman and Paul Patton. Educated in county common schools and at a village academy; attended Emory and Henry College for one year. Volunteered in 1861 for the North Carolina Troops, and became Quarter-master Sergeant; elected Captain in 1862. Wounded at the Battle of Seven Pines; fought in the Maryland campaign; served until 1863. Operated a general store. Elected to the State House of Representatives from Macon County, serving 1868-1875, 1885; also spent two terms as House Speaker, 1872-1875. Member of the State Senate from Macon County, 1876-1877, 1879-1880; President Pro Tempore 1876-1877; and President, 1879-1880. Elected Lieutenant Governor on the Democratic ticket headed by Thomas Jarvis in 1881, and also served as President of the State Senate in 1881 and 1883. When Governor Jarvis left the state temporarily to attend an exposition, Robinson was sworn in as Governor. Robinson served four weeks, from September 1 to September 28, 1883, until Jarvis's return. As governor, Robinson extended pardons to a dying Cherokee in a state prison, and to a murderer whom he believed had acted in self-defense. Robinson later became Director of the Western North Carolina Railroad, and was instrumental in its extension across the mountains to the western counties. Elected to the State House of Representatives from Macon County in 1885, Robinson ran as a Democrat that same year for the United States House of Representatives, but was defeated by Thomas Johnston in an election marred by charges of fraud. Robinson, increasingly troubled by financial difficulties, soon moved to Wisconsin where he became an Indian agent. Robinson died in 1887. Bibliography: John H. Wheeler, *Reminiscences and Memoirs of North Carolina and Eminent North Carolinians* (Washington, 1883-1884); Samuel A. Ashe, ed., *Biographical History of North Carolina* (Greensboro, 1905-1917); James L. Robinson, *Robinson Family Memoirs* (n.p., 1962); W. Buck Yearns, ed., *The Papers of Thomas Jordan Jarvis* (Raleigh, 1969). The Thomas Jarvis letterbooks in the State Archives in Raleigh include papers concerning Robinson's term. The Southern Historical Collection in Chapel Hill also holds letters written by Robinson's son containing useful biographical data.

SCALES, Alfred Moore, 1885-1889

Born on November 26, 1827 in Ingleside in Rockingham County, son of Robert H. Scales, a planter and doctor, and Jane W. (Bethell) Scales. Brother of Robert, Nathaniel, Wallace, James P., Dick, Junius Irving, Emma, Sarah Scales Galloway and Anne Scales Montgomery. A Presbyterian. Educated at the Caldwell Institute; entered the University of North Carolina in 1845, and attended one year but did not graduate. Taught at a free school and later at the Caldwell Institute. Studied law under Judge Settle and Judge Battle; licensed to practice in the county court, and appointed County Solicitor in 1852. Elected to the General Assembly from Rockingham County in 1852 and in 1856-1857. Ran as a Democrat for the United States Congress twice against the Whig R.C. Puryear. Scales was defeated in 1854, but won in 1856, and served in the House of Representatives from 1857 to 1859; defeated for reelection. Served in 1858 as Clerk and Master of the Court of Equity. In the 1860 popular referendum on the secession issue, Scales, a proponent of compromise, ran as an advocate of a state convention, and was narrowly defeated. The same year he was a Presidential Elector on the Breckenridge-Lane ticket. When war broke out, Scales volunteered as a private in a Confederate company, and was elected Captain. Promoted in 1861 to Colonel in the North Carolina Volunteers; fought at Williamsburg, Richmond and Fredericksburg, and severely wounded at Chancellorsville. In 1863 appointed a Brigadier General shortly before Gettysburg, where he was again severely wounded. Fought in the Virginia campaigns. After the war practiced law; declined to run for governor in 1872. Elected again to the U.S. Congress, 1875-1884, serving as Chairman of the Committee on Indian Affairs. Scales resigned from Congress on December 30, 1884, having been elected Governor; he defeated Tyre York in the general election by a vote of 143,249 to 122,914. During Scale's gubernatorial term, railroad expansion increased at a rapid pace. He called for an extended school term and better teachers, and suggested that the federal surplus be used to supplement the state's educational funds. In 1881 he called for convict labor to improve the state's roads. Constitutionally limited to a single term, Scales retired to Greensboro. He later organized the Piedmont Bank, and served as Moderator of the State Synod of the Presbyterian Church. Scales died on February 9, 1892, in Greensboro. He was buried in Green Hill Cemetery. Bibliography: John H. Wheeler, *Reminiscences and Memoirs of North Carolina and Eminent North Carolinians* (Washington, 1883-1884); *News and Observer* [Raleigh] (February 10, 1892); R.D.W. Connor, *Address on Alfred Moore Scales* (Raleigh, 1907); W.C. Smith, "Alfred Moore Scales," in Bettie D. Caldwell, ed., *Founders and Builders of Greensboro, 1808-1908* (Greensboro, 1925). Papers concerning Scales' administration are located at the State Archives in Raleigh. The Southern Historical and North Carolina collections in Chapel Hill hold other letters, papers and documents.

FOWLE, Daniel Gould, 1889-1891

Born on March 3, 1831 in Washington, North Carolina, son of Samuel R. Fowle, a merchant, and Martha (Marsh) Fowle; a Presbyterian. Brother of James, Sarah Fowle Telfair, Martha Fowle Wiswall, Mary Fowle Perry, Margaret Fowle Satterthwaite, and Anna Fowle Welborn. Married to Ellen Brant Pearson on April 15, 1856; father of Margaret and Martha; remarried to Mary E. Haywood on January 30, 1867; father of Helen, Mary and Dan. Educated at William Bingham's Academy, and graduated from Princeton College in 1851, receiving an A.M. in 1854, and an LL.D. in 1890. Studied law under Judge Richmond Pearson, and admitted to the bar in 1853. Settled in Raleigh in 1854. In 1861 volunteered for the Raleigh Rifles, and elected Lieutenant; appointed Major in the commissary of the state military department. Resigned and joined a state regiment as Lieutenant Colonel; captured at Roanoke Island and paroled. Elected to the House of Commons from Wake County in 1862, and appointed Adjutant General of North Carolina with the rank of Major General. Resigned in 1863, and returned to the House of Commons, 1864-1865. On August 3, 1865, appointed Judge of the Superior Court by

Provisional Governor Holden. Resigned in 1867 rather than enforce orders from General Sickles, the governor of the military. Defeated by Thomas Ashe the same year in an attempt to win the Conservative gubernatorial nomination. Served in 1868 as chairman of State Democratic Committee. Defeated for State Senate, 1870. In 1876 was Democrat elector on Tilden ticket. Lost the nomination for Governor to Thomas Jarvis in 1880, and later campaigned vigorously for Jarvis. In 1884 defeated by W.R. Cox for the United States Congress. Fowle defeated C.M. Stedman and S.B. Alexander in 1888 for the Democratic gubernatorial nomination, and in the general election he received 148,406 votes to beat the Republican Oliver H. Dockery (134,026), and the Prohibitionist William Walker (3,124). Fowle was inaugurated on January 17, 1889. Governor Fowle supported railroad construction, but sought to curb abuses of power by the railway interests through the creation of a railroad commission. He strongly supported the public school system and the university, and advocated county land taxes as a means of financing longer school terms. Fowle died on April 7, 1891, while still in office; he was buried in Oakwood Cemetery, Raleigh. Bibliography: John H. Wheeler, *Reminiscences and Memoirs of North Carolina and Eminent North Carolinians* (Washington, 1883-1884); *News and Observer* [Raleigh] (January 18, 1889 and April 10, 1891); *Cyclopedia of Eminent and Representative Men of the Carolinas of the Nineteenth Century* (Madison, 1892). Papers pertaining to Fowle's years as governor are in the State Archives in Raleigh. The North Carolina and Southern Historical Collections at Chapel Hill also hold papers, letters and documents.

HOLT, Thomas Michael, 1891-1893

Born on July 15, 1831 in Orange (now Alamance) County, North Carolina, son of Edwin M. Holt, a farmer and manufacturer, and Emily (Farish) Holt; a Presbyterian. Brother of Alfred, James Henry, Alexander, Frances Ann Holt Williamson, William, Lynn Banks, Mary Elizabeth Holt Williamson, Emily Virginia Holt White and Lawrence. Married to Louisa Moore in October 1855; father of Charles, Cora, Daisy, Ella and Thomas. Educated at the Caldwell Institute, and entered the University of North Carolina in 1849, but left after a year; awarded an LL.D. by the university in 1895. Spent 1850-1851 in a dry goods store in Philadelphia, learning the mercantile business. Returned to North Carolina and joined his father's company, Alamance Cotton Mills, in Haw River. In 1862 Holt purchased the firm, now known as Granite Mills, and rapidly expanded its operations. Chosen President in 1872 of the State Fair and of the State Agricultural Society. Director of the North Carolina Railroad, becoming its president in 1874. Having served as a Magistrate and County Commissioner, Holt was elected and served in the State Senate from Alamance County in 1876-1877, and sat in the State House of Representatives, 1883, 1885 and 1887; he was House Speaker in 1885. He became Lieutenant Governor in 1889, and presided as President of the State Senate from 1889 to 1891. When Governor Fowle died, Holt became Governor on April 8, 1891. As governor, Holt actively supported the state's common school system and higher education, having helped to found North Carolina State College in Raleigh and two state colleges in Greensboro. He argued for the mutual dependence of industrial and agricultural development; was instrumental in establishing a State Department of Agriculture; urged increased expenditures for state hospitals and for a state school for the deaf; and sought to protect state property while resolving the state debt. Nevertheless, Holt failed to receive the Democratic nomination for Governor in 1892, losing to Elias Carr. Holt served on the Boards of Trustees of both the University of North Carolina and Davidson College. His last years were marked by ill health. Holt died on April 11, 1896, and was buried in Graham. Bibliography: John Wheeler, *Reminiscences and Memoirs of North Carolina and Eminent North Carolinians* (Washington, 1883-1884); C.B. Denson, *An Address in Memory of Thomas M. Holt* (Raleigh, 1899); William D. McCorkle, "Thomas Michael Holt," Samuel Ashe, ed., *Biographical History of North Carolina* (Greensboro, 1908); Archibald Henderson, ed., *North Carolina: The Old North State and the New* (Chicago, 1941). Governor's papers and letterbooks from the Holt administration are located at the State Archives in Raleigh. The Southern Historical and North Carolina collections in Chapel Hill hold other relevant letters, documents and papers.

CARR, Elias, 1893-1897

Born on February 25, 1839 in Bracebridge Farm near Old Sparta, Edgecombe County, North Carolina, son of Jonas Johnston Carr, a planter, and Elizabeth Jane (Hilliard) Carr; an Episcopalian. Married to Eleanor Kearney in 1859; father of William Kearney, John Buxton, Mary Elizabeth, Elias, Eleanor Kearney and Annie Bruce. Educated at the Oaks School under William Bingham, and spent two years at the University of Virginia. Served in a cavalry regiment during the war. After the Civil War, Carr, a wealthy planter, engaged in agricultural pursuits, and served as a County Commissioner, member of the Board of Trustees at North Carolina State College, and Commissioner with the Geological Survey. By the 1880s he had become actively involved with the agrarian movement, serving as a state delegate to the 1886 National Farmers' Congress in St. Paul, and as president of the State Farmers' Convention in 1887. He became active in the Farmers' Alliance in 1890, and in 1891 was chosen as its president. Carr rejected radical political action, however, and supported conservative policies. He opposed a third party, believing that it would end in a return to black rule. In 1891 he served as a commissioner at the World's Fair, and the next year, with Thomas M. Holt failing to win renomination as the Democratic gubernatorial candidate, Carr's name was entered as a compromise between the radicals and their opponents. Dissidents in the Farmers' Alliance responded by forming a state Populist Party which nominated Dr. Wyatt P. Exum; the Republican nominee was David M. Furches. Carr won the election with a vote of 135,519 against 94,684 for Furches, and 47,840 for Exum. He was inaugurated on January 18, 1893. Governor Carr supported an efficient common school system, with a special emphasis on rural schools; increased state aid to the universities; endorsed improvements to the state's road system; supported increased taxes on intangibles and realty, and personally inspected the state's various institutions, taking particular interest in the prisons and convict farms. In 1895 he authorized the long-term leasing of the North Carolina Railroad to the Southern Railway, an action which was strongly opposed by the Farmers' Alliance and by Carr's successor, Daniel L. Russell. After his gubernatorial term had expired, Carr retired to Bracebridge Farm and resumed his interests in scientific agriculture. Carr died in Bracebridge on July 22, 1900. He was buried in Edgecombe County. Bibliography: *News and Observer* [Raleigh] (July 24, 1900); Marshall D. Haywood, "Elias Carr," in Samuel Ashe, ed., *Biographical History of North Carolina*, VIII (Greensboro, 1917); J. Kelly Turner and J.L. Bridgers, Jr., *History of Edgecombe County, North Carolina* (Raleigh, 1920); Archibald Henderson, ed., *North Carolina: The Old State and the New*, III (Chicago, 1941).

Governor's papers from the Carr administration are located at the State Archives in Raleigh. The Elias Carr Papers can be found at East Carolina University; the North Carolina and Southern Historical collections in Chapel Hill hold other useful papers.

RUSSELL, Daniel Lindsay, 1897-1901

Born on August 7, 1845 in Brunswick County, North Carolina, son of Daniel L. Russell, a planter, and Caroline (Sanders) Lindsay; a Protestant. Married to Sarah Amanda Sanders in 1869. Attended William Bingham School in Hillsboro. Entered the University of North Carolina in 1860; when the Civil War began, enlisted in a county regiment and elected Captain. Court martialed in 1863 following an altercation with another officer, and relieved of his command. Election to the State House of Commons in 1864-1865 prevented his conscription into the Confederate Army. Studied law after the war, and admitted to the bar in 1866; established a law practice in Wilmington. Joined the Republican Party, serving in the House of Commons from Brunswick County, 1864-1866; became a member of the ruling "ring" of the party. Elected Judge of the Superior Court in Wilmington; ruled in 1873 blacks could not be barred from public places. Retired in 1874; declined President Grant's offer of the territorial governorship of Colorado. In 1876-1877 returned to the State House of Representatives. Served as a delegate to the Republican National Convention in 1876, and was a Presidential Elector on the Hayes ticket. Elected as a Greenbacker to the United States House of Representatives, serving 1879-1881; did not run for a second term. Russell defeated Alfred Dockery for the Republican nomination for Governor in 1896. In the general election Russell won again, receiving 153,787 votes to defeat Democrat Cyrus Watson (145,266), and Populist William Guthrie (31,143). Opposing black rule, Russell did not court the black vote; he was also an advocate of free silver. In his first year as governor, Russell, a political progressive, attempted to terminate the long-term lease of the North Carolina Railroad to the Southern Railway, but lost his battle in the federal court. Russell supported anti-monopoly legislation, higher corporate taxes, and increased aid for education. He also sought to free politics from the race issue; however, after Democratic gains in 1898 and the end of Republican-Populist fusion rule, Russell was severely attacked on racial grounds, and eventually began to fear for his personal safety. Although he appointed few blacks to state offices, Russell did place black officers in charge of a black regiment in 1898. Russell did not support black disenfranchisement, nor did he politically oppose it; instead, he urged blacks to rely on the judgements of federal courts. By the end of his administration Russell was allied with the business interests of his party; he considered appointing himself Chief Justice in 1900, but declined in the midst of a political controversy. After the expiration of his gubernatorial term, Russell retired to his plantation near Wilmington and resumed the practice of law. In 1904 he successfully argued the South Dakota Bond Case before the United States Supreme Court, a decision which compelled North Carolina to pay its reconstruction bonds. Russell died on his Belleville plantation on May 14, 1908, and was buried in the family cemetery in Hickory Hill, Onslow County. Bibliography: *News and Observer* [Raleigh] (October 30, 1896); Philip Weaver, "The Gubernatorial Election of 1896 in North Carolina," unpublished M.A. thesis, University of North Carolina, 1937; Rosalie Fitzhugh McNeill, "The First Fifteen Months of Governor Daniel Lindsay Russell's Administration," unpublished M.A. thesis, University of North Carolina, 1939; Robert Durden, *Reconstruction Bonds and*

Twentieth-Century Politics (Durham, 1962); Louis Goodman and Alice Sawyer Cooper, "Daniel Lindsay Russell: Governor of North Carolina, A Family and Friend's Memoir," unpublished typescript (1964); Jeffrey Crow, "Maverick Republican in the Old North State: The Governorship of Daniel L. Russell, 1897-1901," unpublished Ph.D. dissertation, North Carolina College at Durham, 1974; Jeffrey Crow, " 'Populism to Progressivism' in North Carolina: Governor Daniel Russell and His War on the Southern Railway Company," *The Historian*, vol. 37, no. 4 (August, 1975). Governor's papers and letterbooks are located at the State Archives in Raleigh. The North Carolina Collection holds other documents, including a "Scrapbook"; the Southern Historical Collection also holds letters and papers, including the Goodman-Cooper "Memoir."

AYCOCK, Charles Brantley, 1901-1905

Born on November 1, 1859 near Fremont in Wayne County, North Carolina, son of Benjamin Aycock, a farmer and legislator, and Serena (Hooks) Aycock; a Baptist. Brother of Piety Melvina, Francis Marion, James Robert, Jesse Thomas, William Butler, John Wilkinson, Benjamin Franklin, Catherine and Bardin H. Married to Varina D. Woodard on May 20, 1881, and father of Ernest, Charles Brantley and Alice; after his wife's death in 1889, remarried her sister, Cora L. Woodard, on January 7, 1891; father of William Benjamin, Mary Lily, Connor Woodard, John Lee, Louise Rountree, Frank Daniels and Brantley. Educated at the Wilson Collegiate Institute, 1872-1875, and the Kinston Collegiate Institute in 1876. Taught school in Fremont. Graduated from the University of North Carolina with a Ph.B. in 1880; awarded an LL.D. by the University of Maine in 1905 and by the University of North Carolina in 1907. Read law, and licensed to practice in 1881; opened a law office in Goldsboro. Appointed County Superintendent of Schools from 1880 to 1882. Administrator and proponent of popular education, serving as Director of a Negro normal school. Became co-founder of the Goldsboro *Daily Argus* in 1885. In 1888 and 1892 was a Presidential Elector on the Democratic ticket. Failed to secure the Democratic nomination for the United States Congress in 1890, but in 1893 appointed United States District Attorney, a post he held until 1898. A powerful orator, Aycock canvassed the state in 1898 on behalf of Democratic candidates, advocating white supremacy and gaining the support of militant Red Shirts. In 1899 he led the campaign for "grandfather clause" suffrage amendments as a means of disenfranchising black voters. Aycock received the Democratic nomination for Governor in 1900, and in the general election defeated the Republican Spencer B. Adams by a vote of 186,650 to 126,296. He was inaugurated on January 15, 1901. Although Aycock opposed racial equality, he advocated protection of the black man's educational and judicial rights, threatening to resign in 1901 when the legislature considered appropriating school funds according to the respective tax contributions of each race. He insisted that white and black schools should stay open for equal terms. Aycock was known as the "Educational Governor" and spoke eloquently on the importance of "universal education." In 1901 he devised a compromise for more equitable tax assessment of railroad property; he also supported increased corporate taxes. Aycock sought to make the state penitentiary self-supporting; advocated liquor regulation; and urged passage of a child labor law. In 1904 he was invited to Maine to campaign for education. In his final address before the North Carolina State Legislature he called for curbing the economic power of the railways. Though constitutionally limited to a single term, he helped to determine the Democratic platform in 1905. Aycock resumed his law practice in Goldsboro after his years as governor, and moved to Raleigh in 1909. As a lawyer, he was a noted courtroom defender of civil liberties. He also served as chairman of the Democratic State Convention in 1906, supported Bryan in 1908, and joined North Carolina's prohibition campaign. In 1911 Aycock agreed to run for the United States Senate in the state's first popular election for the office. Aycock died on April 4, 1912, while speaking before the Alabama Educational Association in Birmingham; he was buried in Oakwood Cemetery in Raleigh. Bibliography: F.A. Daniels, "Governor C.B. Aycock," *North Carolina University Magazine*, n.s., vol. XVIII, no. 4 (April, 1901); Samuel Ashe, ed., *Biographical History of North Carolina*, I (Greensboro, 1905); R.D.W. Connor and Clarence Poe, *The Life and Speeches of Charles B. Aycock* (New York, 1912); Joseph Daniels, "Charles Brantley Aycock—The Historical Address," *North Carolina Historical Review*, vol. I, no. 3 (July, 1924); Rupert B. Vance, "Aycock of North Carolina," *Southwest Review*, vol. XVIII (Spring, 1933); Frank P. Graham, "Charles Brantley Aycock of North Carolina, The South's Greatest Educational Governor," typescript (Raleigh, 1951); Robert B. House, "Aycock and Universal Education," *North Carolina Historical Review*, vol. XXXVII, no. 2 (April, 1960); Oliver H. Orr, *Charles Brantley Aycock* (Chapel Hill, 1961). Governor's papers and the Charles Brantley Aycock Papers are located at the State Archives in Raleigh. The North Carolina and Southern Historical collections in Chapel Hill hold other documents and papers.

GLENN, Robert Broadnax, 1905-1909

Born on August 11, 1854 in Yadkin County, North Carolina, son of Chalmers L. Glenn, a planter and lawyer, and Annie (Dodge) Glenn; a Presbyterian. Brother of James D. and Edward T.B. Married to Nina Deaderick on January 8, 1878; father of Louise, Chalmers and Rebecca. In 1862 Glenn's father was killed in the Civil War, and the young boy was raised by a relative, Dr. Edward Broadnax. Educated at common schools in Rockingham County, and entered Davidson College in 1870; formed a friendship with Woodrow Wilson; attended pre-law course at the University of Virginia in 1874; enrolled in Judge Richmond Pearson's law school in Richmond Hill. Admitted to the bar in 1877, and established a law practice in Wentworth, later moving to Danbury. Elected to the North Carolina House of Representatives from Stokes County in 1880. Became an elector for Grover Cleveland in 1884 and 1892. Moved to Winston-Salem in 1885, and started a law partnership. In 1886 appointed to an unexpired term as District Solicitor, but defeated for reelection. Served as Captain in the Forsyth Rifles of the National Guard, 1890-1893; promoted to Major. In 1892 appointed United States Attorney for the Western District by President Cleveland. Elected to the North Carolina State Senate in 1898. Became an active spokesman for white supremacy during the Democratic Party's resurgence in the 1898 elections, and in 1900 served as Governor Aycock's chief assistant in support of the constitutional amendments designed to disenfranchise Negro voters. Received the gubernatorial nomination at the Democratic State Convention in 1904, defeating Charles M. Stedman, Wilfred Turner and Theodore Davidson. In the general election Glenn defeated the Republican candidate, C.J. Harris, by a vote of 128,761 to 79,505; he was inaugurated on January 11, 1905. As governor, Glenn strongly supported more stringent temperance legislation and a more restrictive divorce law. He continued the emphasis placed on public education by his predecessors, endorsing a minimum school term and compulsory attendance. He also made financial arrangements to facilitate the repayment of the state's reconstruction bonds, which had been ordered by the Supreme Court. In 1905 he sought increased funding for state hospitals and care of the insane, and in the following year he acted firmly to halt an outbreak of lynching. He called for a department of immigration to support development of state land, and led the state campaign for prohibition in 1908. Finally, he supported a bill in the legislature to reduce railway rates, a bill which was resisted by the railroads; a compromise was eventually reached after federal intervention. Glenn retired from elective politics at the end of his gubernatorial term, and moved to Winston-Salem. He later served as counsel to Southern Railways and to Western Union, and became known as a defender of prohibition. In 1920 he served as a member of President Wilson's International Boundary Commission. Glenn died on May 16, 1920, in Winnipeg, Canada. He was buried in Winston-Salem. Bibliography: *News and Observer* [Raleigh] (January 2, 1905, May 17, 1920); *Prominent People of North Carolina* (Asheville, 1906); A.B. Andrews, *Proceedings of the 22nd Annual Session of the North Carolina Bar Association* (1920); Margaret L. Chapman, "The Administration of Governor Robert B. Glenn," unpublished M.A. thesis, University of North Carolina, 1956. Governor's papers and letterbooks are located at the State Archives in Raleigh. The North Carolina Collection in Chapel Hill holds speeches and documents; the Southern Historical Collection holds other letters and papers.

KITCHIN, William Walton, 1909-1913

Born on October 9, 1866 near Scotland Neck, North Carolina, son of William Hodges Kitchin, a lawyer and United States Congressman, and Maria Figus (Arrington) Kitchin; a Baptist. Brother of Claude and Thurmond D. Married to Musette Satterfield on December 22, 1892; father of Sue, Anne, Elizabeth, Clement, William and Musette. Attended Vine Hill Academy. Graduated from Wake Forest College with an A.B. in 1884. Edited the Scotland Neck *Democrat* in 1885, and taught school on and off. Studied law in Scotland Neck and at the University of North Carolina; awarded an honorary LL.D. in 1912. Admitted to the bar in 1887, and established a law practice in Roxboro a year later. Served as Chairman of the County Democratic Executive Committee in 1890; defeated for the State Senate in 1892. In 1896, despite an overwhelming Republican and Populist trend in the state, Kitchin's considerable oratorical skills won him election to the United States House of Representatives over Thomas Settle; he served 1897-1909. Having supported William Jennings Bryan in the Democratic State Conventions of 1902 and 1906, Kitchin sought the nomination for Governor in 1908 on an anti-trust platform. Although he was opposed by party leaders, he defeated Locke Craig and Ashley Horne for the nomination after sixty-one ballots. In the general election Kitchin received 145,102 votes to defeat the Republican J. Elwood Cox, who polled 107,760. Kitchin resigned from Congress in early January, and was inaugurated as Governor on January 12, 1909. As governor, Kitchin recommended direct primaries as a means of bringing the common man into the political process. He greatly increased public expenditures for education, health care for the retarded, and sponsored a systematic program for developing roads and railways and draining swamplands. Kitchin balanced the budget through the assessment of property at real value; advocated child labor laws; urged improved sanitation in factories; was a strong proponent of prohibition. A progressive, he sponsored anti-trust legislation and more stringent regulation of business, despite criticism that his policies were socialistic. While still governor, Kitchin sought nomination to the United States Senate in the state's first popular election for that office, opposing former Governor Charles Aycock, Chief Justice Walter Clark, and the incumbent Senator F.M.

Simmons. Kitchin was defeated decisively by Simmons. With the return of "machine" politics and the resurgence of the state's business interests, Kitchin retired from politics, and resumed his law practice in Raleigh. After suffering a stroke in 1919, he returned to Scotland Neck where he died on November 9, 1924. He was buried in the Baptist Cemetery. Bibliography: Thomas Hufham, "Wake Forest's First Gift to the Governor's Chair," *The Wake Forest Student*, vol. 24, no. 4 (January, 1909); Carey Hunter, "Governor Kitchin: the Man and the Principles that Guide Him," *Carolina Democrat* (n.p., n.d.); *News and Observer* [Raleigh] (November 10, 1924); H.M. London, ed., *Proceedings of the Twenty-seventh Annual Session of the North Carolina Bar Association* (Raleigh, 1925); Archibald Henderson, ed., *North Carolina: The Old North State and the New*, vol. III (Chicago, 1941); Christopher Crittenden, William Powell, Robert Woody, eds., *100 Years, 100 Men: 1871-1971* (Raleigh, 1971). Governor's papers and letterbooks from the Kitchin administration are located at the State Archives in Raleigh. The North Carolina Collection holds some documents and speeches, and the Southern Historical Collection contains the William Walton Kitchin Papers.

CRAIG, Locke, 1913-1917

Born on August 16, 1860 in Bertie County, North Carolina, son of Andrew Murdock Craig, a Baptist minister, and Rebecca (Gilliam) Craig; a Baptist. One of two sons. Married to Annie Burgin on November 18, 1891; father of Carlyle, George, Arthur and Locke. Attended local common schools and enrolled in the University of North Carolina, graduating with an A.B. in 1880; awarded an LL.D in 1915. Taught at the university and in Chapel Hill. Admitted to the bar in 1882, returning to Asheville the next year to practice law. Served as County Attorney and City Corporation Counsel. In 1892 and again in 1896, campaigned as a Democratic presidential elector in support of Bryan. Elected to the State House of Representatives, 1899 and 1901, where he supported the suffrage amendments disenfranchising Negro voters. Defeated in 1903 by L.S. Overman for a United States Senate seat. Practiced law in Asheville, 1903-1912. Defeated by W.W. Kitchin for the Democratic gubernatorial nomination in 1908; won unanimous nomination in 1912. In the popular election he received 149,975 votes to win easily over the Republican Thomas Settle (43,625) and the Progressive Iredell Meares (49,930). Craig was inaugurated on January 15, 1913. Governor Craig made a "Pledge to Progress," and instituted a program to develop the state's road system which included the establishment of a Highway Commission. He expanded the state park system, purchasing Mt. Mitchell. He also revised intrastate freight rates to make North Carolina more competitive; advocated increased regulation of the fishing industry; enacted conservation measures; and worked to have Cuba withdraw its claim for payment of the state's reconstruction bonds. Constitutionally forbidden from succeeding himself, Craig retired to Asheville in 1917, where he resumed the practice of law. He died on June 9, 1924, and was buried in Riverside Cemetery, Asheville. Bibliography: *News and Observer* [Raleigh] (January 15, 1893, June 10, 1924); John Kerr, "Locke Craig," in Samuel Ashe, ed., *Biographical History of North Carolina*, VI (Greensboro, 1907); May F. Jones, ed., *Public Letters and Papers of Locke Craig* (Raleigh, 1916); Artus M. Moser, "The Career of Ex-Governor Locke Craig," *The Carolina Magazine*, n.s., vol. 39, no. 5 (February, 1922); May F. Jones, ed., *Memoirs and Speeches of Locke Craig* (Asheville, 1923); H.M. London, *Proceedings of the 27th Annual Session of the North Carolina Bar Association* (1925); *Locke Craig* (Raleigh, 1944). Governor's papers and letterbooks are located at the State Archives in Raleigh.

The Southern Historical and North Carolina collections in Chapel Hill contain speeches, papers and documents, while Duke University holds the Locke Craig Papers.

BICKETT, Thomas Walter, 1917-1921

Born on February 28, 1869 in Monroe, North Carolina, son of Thomas Winchester Bickett, a doctor, and Mary A. (Covington) Bickett; one of four children; an Episcopalian. Married to Fannie Yarborough on November 19, 1898; father of William Yarborough. Educated in public schools and studied at Wake Forest College, graduating with an A.B. in 1890. Taught school in Marion and Winston-Salem. Entered the law school of the University of North Carolina in 1892, and admitted to the bar in 1893. Practiced law in Danbury; moved to Louisburg in 1895, where he became a leading lawyer and community leader. Served in the State House of Representatives from Franklin County, 1907-1908. Sponsored the Bickett Bill, which made state care of the insane a legal requirement. Bickett's speech nominating Ashley Horne for governor at the 1907 Democratic Convention won him wide recognition. Twice elected State Attorney General, serving 1909-1917; represented the state in five cases before the United States Supreme Court and won them all, including that involving a border dispute with Tennessee. Received the Democratic gubernatorial nomination in 1916 after defeating Elijah L. Daughtridge in North Carolina's first state-wide primary. In the general election, he defeated the Republican Frank A. Linney by a vote of 167,761 to 120,157; Bickett was inaugurated on January 11, 1917. Governor Bickett supported reform in a number of areas. He worked to enable tenant farmers to become land owners, and called for a more extensive agricultural education, including subjects like home economics. In 1917 he endorsed acts to establish a six-month school term; to raise the compulsory school age to fourteen; and to increase salaries for teachers. He continued the state's roadbuilding program, and called for increased expenditure on public health, to be administered through the new Department of Public Welfare. He also urged a more stringent child labor law; worked for a more humane prison system; and established juvenile courts and a parole grading scheme. In 1919 Bickett urged passage of the state income tax system. Bickett's reforms were limited by demands of the First World War; he campaigned actively for Liberty Bonds, and at the end of the war spoke in favor of the League of Nations. Constitutionally limited to a single term, Bickett returned to the practice of law in Raleigh after his years as governor. Bickett died on December 27, 1921, and was buried in Louisburg. Bibliography: *News and Observer* [Raleigh] (January 11-12, 1917, December 29, 1921); "Bickett's Contribution to the Spirit of Social Service" *North Carolina Community Progress*, vol. III (April 5, 1922); James Manning, "Thomas Walter Bickett," in H.M. London, ed., *Proceedings of the 24th Annual Session of the North Carolina Bar Association* (Raleigh, 1922); "Governor Bickett's Service," *The Southern Workman*, vol. LI (February, 1922); R.B. House, ed., *Public Letters and Papers of Thomas Walter Bickett*; Lou Rogers, "Governor Thomas Walter Bickett," *We the People of North Carolina*, vol. IV, no. 7; Sandra Sue Horton, "The Political Career of Thomas Walter Bickett," unpublished M.A. thesis, University of North Carolina, 1965; Christopher Crittenden, William Powell, Robert Woody, eds., *100 Years, 100 Men: 1871-1971* (Raleigh, 1971). Governor's papers and private papers relating to Bickett are held by the State Archives in Raleigh. The North Carolina and Southern Historical collections in Chapel Hill also hold relevant letters and documents.

MORRISON, Cameron, 1921-1925

Born on October 5, 1869 near Rockingham, Richmond County, North Carolina, son of Daniel M. Morrison, a farmer and contractor, and Martha (Cameron) Morrison; one of four children; a Presbyterian. Married to Lottie May Tomlinson on December 6, 1905; father of Angelia; remarried to Mrs. Sarah Virginia Ecker Watts on April 2, 1924. Attended local common schools and N.C. McCaskill's Academy. Unable to afford college, Morrison farmed, clerked in a store, and served as Register of Deeds. In 1890 served as delegate to the Republican State Convention, but shortly thereafter joined the Democrats. Studied law under Judge Robert B. Dick in Greensboro, and was licensed to practice in 1892; opened an office in Rockingham. Spoke before the Democratic State Convention in 1892, and campaigned actively in opposition to the Republicans and Negro rule. Defeated in 1896 for the State Senate. Made Chairman of the Richmond County Democratic Executive Committee in 1898, and became a leader of the Red Shirts, a militant movement advocating white supremacy. Supported suffrage amendments designed to disenfranchise black voters. Served as Mayor of Rockingham; elected to represent Richmond County in the State Senate in 1901. Declined appointment to the Superior Court, 1913. In 1916 was a Presidential Elector. Established a law practice in Charlotte. In the 1920 gubernatorial primary, Morrison opposed Lieutenant Governor O. Max Gardner and Congressman Robert N. Page; Morrison received a narrow plurality over Gardner, while Page was eliminated. Morrison then defeated Gardner in the primary runoff by 9,000 votes. In the general election Morrison went on to win over Republican John J. Parker by a vote of 308,151 to 230,175; he was inaugurated on January 12, 1921. As governor, Morrison introduced a bond issue, financed by automobile and gasoline taxes, which would be used in the construction of a highway system of hard-surfaced roads, linking the state's principal towns and cities. He strengthened the state's banking laws; increased educational expenditures through a bond issue for the state's institutions of higher learning; and established a loan fund for county schools. During the 1921 mill strikes and the 1922 railway strikes, Morrison ordered state troops to restore order; he also forcibly suppressed lynching during his term as governor. In 1923 a training school for delinquent Negro boys was established in Richmond County. His call for a port commission to regulate and operate shipping traffic, however, was defeated in a referendum in 1924. Constitutionally limited to a single term, Morrison returned to Charlotte, where he resumed his law practice after his gubernatorial service. In December 1930, he was appointed to the United States Senate seat left vacant by the death of Lee S. Overman, but was defeated by Robert R. Reynolds in the general election to fill the unexpired term; Morrison retired from the Senate on December 4, 1932. He was later elected to the United States House of Representatives in 1942, and served in the 78th Congress, from 1943 to 1945. Morrison also ran for the United States Senate in 1944, and lost to Clyde R. Hoey. He then returned to his law practice. Morrison died on August 20, 1953, in Quebec, Canada. He was buried in Elmwood Cemetery, Charlotte. Bibliography: "Cameron Morrison" in R.D.W. Connor, William Boyd, and J.G. deRoulhac Hamilton, eds., *History of North Carolina*, V (Chicago and New York, 1919); D.L. Corbitt, ed., *Public Papers and Letters of Cameron Morrison* (Raleigh, 1927); W.J. Cash, "Paladin of the Drys," *American Mercury*, vol. 24 (October, 1931); *News* [Charlotte] (November 18-22, 1947); Frank P. Graham, *Cameron Morrison: An Address* (Charlotte, 1956); Nathaniel F. Magruder, "The Administration of Governor Cameron Morrison of North Carolina, 1921-1925," unpublished dissertation, University of North Carolina, 1968; Christopher Crittenden, William Powell and Robert Woody, eds., *100 Years, 100 Men: 1871-1971*

(Raleigh, 1971). Governor's papers and letterbooks concerning the Morrison administration are located at the State Archives in Raleigh. The North Carolina Collection holds the Cameron Morrison Clipping Collection, as well as relevant addresses and documents.

McLEAN, Angus Wilton, 1925-1929

Born on April 20, 1870 near Floral College, Robeson County, North Carolina, son of Archibald Alexander McLean, a planter, and Carolina Amanda (Purcell) McLean; a Presbyterian. Brother of Harriet Purcell McLean Armfield, Mary Jane, Sallie Amanda, Alexander Torrey, Hector and Mattie Williams McLean Sutpen. Married to Margaret Jones French on April 14, 1904; father of Angus Wilton, Margaret French and Hector. Attended local schools, the McMillan Military School (graduating in 1884), and the Laurinburg Academy. Enrolled at the University of North Carolina, and received a Bachelor of Laws in 1892; awarded an LL.D. in 1926. Admitted to the bar in 1892, and established a law practice in Lumberton. Became Chairman in 1892 of the Robeson County Democratic Executive Committee. Founded and served as president of the Bank of Lumberton, 1897-1914. Established the Lumberton Cotton Mills, and served as an officer in several other textile companies; organized the Virginia and Carolina Southern Railroad. Was also active in local real estate development. Became a delegate in 1904 to the Democratic National Convention. In 1912 and 1916 served as State Chairman of Woodrow Wilson's campaign, and from 1916 to 1924 was a member of the National Democratic Executive Committee. President of the State Bar Association in 1917. Served on the War Finance Corporation, 1918-1922, and as its director, 1920-1921; also served as Assistant Secretary of the Treasury, 1920-1921. After a well-planned campaign, McLean defeated Josiah W. Bailey in the Democratic gubernatorial primary of 1924. McLean also won the general election, beating the Republican candidate, Isaac M. Meekins, by a vote of 294,441 to 185,627; he was inaugurated on January 4, 1925. Governor McLean sought to introduce sound fiscal management and efficiency into the administration of state government, and to achieve this goal he devised an executive budget system to supervise expenditures. A Department of Revenue was created to oversee state income and spending, reestablishing the state's credit. The 1925 legislature passed thirty measures proposed by McLean to restore government operations to a cash basis. He also urged industrial diversification and utilization of the state's natural resources, creating a Department of Conservation and Development for that purpose. A strong believer in educational opportunity, McLean endeavored to improve the school system available to rural children. Finally, in 1927, he pressed for the passage of a bill that led to the establishment of the Great Smoky Mountains National Park. McLean returned to his law practice after his term as governor, and opened an office in Washington, D.C.; he also continued to pursue his business interests. He declined to run for the United States Senate in 1930, but remained active, lecturing widely and writing several tracts on economics and on the history of the Scots. He served on the boards of trustees of the University of North Carolina and the Union Theological Seminary. McLean died on June 21, 1935, in Washington, D.C., and was buried in Lumberton. Bibliography: B. Hume Bardin, "A Son of Carolina and a National Figure," *Carolina Magazine*, n.s., vol. 39, no. 9 (June, 1922); David L. Corbitt, *Public Papers and Letters of Angus Wilton McLean* (Raleigh, 1931); R.L. Varser, "Angus Wilton, McLean," in H.M. London, ed., *Proceedings of the Thirty-seventh Annual Session of the North Carolina Bar Association* (Raleigh, 1935); *News and*

Observer [Raleigh] (June 22, 1935); A.W. McLean and others, *Lumber River Scots and their Descendants* (Richmond, 1942); Mary Evelyn Underwood, "Angus Wilton McLean, Governor of North Carolina: 1925-1929," unpublished Ph.D. dissertation, University of North Carolina, 1962; Christopher Crittenden, William Powell, Robert Woody, eds., *100 Years, 100 Men: 1871-1971* (Raleigh, 1971). Governor's papers and letterbooks from the McLean administration are located at the State Archives in Raleigh. In Chapel Hill, the North Carolina Collection holds speeches and articles, and the Southern Historical Collection holds the Angus Wilton McLean Papers, 1910-1933, in ten volumes.

GARDNER, Oliver Max, 1929-1933

Born on March 22, 1882 in Shelby, North Carolina, son of Dr. Oliver Perry Gardner, a physician and farmer, and Margaret (Young) Gardner; a Baptist. The youngest of twelve children; orphaned in early youth and raised by his half-sister, Hessie G. McMurry. Married to Fay Lamar Webb on November 6, 1907; father of Margaret Love, James Webb, Ralph Webb and O. Max, Jr. Volunteered as a teamster in the Second Illinois Regiment in 1898. Educated at Shelby High School, and won a scholarship to North Carolina State College in 1900, graduating with a B.S. in 1903. Taught chemistry at the college until 1905, when he entered the University of North Carolina Law School; awarded an honorary LL.D. in 1939. Established a law practice in Shelby, 1907-1928. In 1908 organized North Carolina's Young Men's Democratic Clubs. Founded the Cleveland Cloth Mill. Elected to the State Senate from Cleveland County in 1911, and reelected in 1915, serving as President Pro Tempore in 1915. Elected Lieutenant Governor on a ticket headed by Thomas W. Bickett in 1917, also serving as President of the State Senate. In 1920 Gardner was defeated in the Democratic gubernatorial primary by Cameron Morrison, the only election defeat of his career. He was appointed to the State Board of Agriculture in 1921, and served in that capacity for eighteen years. In 1924 he was chairman of the state delegation to the Democratic National Convention. Gardner was unopposed for the Democratic gubernatorial nomination in 1928, and in the general election he defeated Republican Herbert F. Seawell by a vote of 362,009 to 289,415; he was inaugurated on January 11, 1929. As governor, Gardner's programs were designed to help the state recover from the Great Depression. During his term the state budget was reduced by ten million dollars; governmental functions were centralized; and the State Tax Commission was created. The state also assumed the counties' financial burdens for transportation and education. Gardner's "live at home" program encouraged farmers to grow subsistence produce in place of cash crops. Other developments during Gardner's years in office include the passage of a workmen's compensation bill, the abolition of chain gangs, and the introduction of a secret ballot law. The achievement of which Gardner was most proud was the consolidation of the University of North Carolina, North Carolina State College, and North Carolina College for Women into a unified system. After his term expired, Gardner moved to Washington, D.C., and established a law practice. He endowed scholarships to Boiling Springs Junior College in North Carolina, which renamed itself Gardner-Webb in his honor. In 1944 President Roosevelt appointed him chairman of the Advisory Board of the Office of War Mobilization and Reconversion. He served in 1946 as Undersecretary of the Treasury in the Truman administration, and was appointed United States Ambassador to Great Britain. He suffered a stroke while preparing to embark, and did not live to assume the post. Gardner died on February 6, 1947 in New York. He was buried in Shelby. Bibliography: *News and Observer* [Raleigh] (January 12, 1929); David L. Corbitt, ed., *Public Papers and Letters of Oliver Max Gardner* (Raleigh, 1937); *New York Times* (February 7, 1947); Charles Burrus, "Oliver Max Gardner," *Proceedings: 49th Annual Session of the North Carolina Bar Association* (1947); Edwin Gill, *An Address: Oliver Max Gardner—The Man* (Raleigh, 1933); Joseph Morrison, *Governor O. Max Gardner: A Power in North Carolina and New Deal Washington* (Chapel Hill, 1971); Christopher Crittenden, William Powell, Robert Woody, eds., *100 Years, 100 Men: 1871-1971* (Raleigh, 1971). Governor's papers and letterbooks from the Gardner administration are located at the State Archives in Raleigh. The Oliver Max Gardner Papers are held by the Southern Historical Collection in Chapel Hill; the North Carolina Collection holds speeches and documents. Gardner-Webb College owns the Gardner Scrapbooks.

EHRINGHAUS, John Christoph Blucher, 1933-1937

Born on February 5, 1882 in Elizabeth City, North Carolina, son of Erskine Ehringhaus, a bookkeeper, and Catherine Colville (Matthews) Ehringhaus; eldest of three children; an Episcopalian. Married to Matilda Bradford Haughton on January 4, 1912; father of John Christoph Blucher, Jr., Haughton and Matilda. Attended Elizabeth City public schools, and graduated from Atlantic Christian Collegiate Institute in 1898. Entered the University of North Carolina, receiving a B.A. in 1901, an LL.B. in 1903, and an honorary LL.D. in 1934. Taught English at the University of North Carolina, 1902-1903. Admitted to the bar in 1903; opened a law practice. Elected to State House of Representatives from Pasquotank County as a Democrat, 1905, 1907-1908. Sponsored bills creating East Carolina Teachers College and a state-wide high school system. Served three terms from 1910 to 1922 as Solicitor of the First Judicial District. Resumed law practice in Elizabeth City. Ehringhaus's support for Alfred E. Smith's presidential try in 1928 gained him a state-wide political reputation. In the 1932 Democratic gubernatorial primary, Ehringhaus defeated Richard Fountain and Allen Maxwell, but failed to secure a majority; in the runoff he defeated Maxwell by 14,000 votes. Ehringhaus went on to win the general election, defeating Republican Clifton C. Frazier by a vote of 497,657 to 212,561; he was inaugurated on January 5, 1933. Despite the Great Depression, Ehringhaus sought to balance North Carolina's budget; aided by a sales tax, he reduced the state deficit and left office with a state surplus of over five million dollars. His years as governor were marked by an exceptional concern for education, and included the assumption by the state of control of public schools; the establishment of an eight-month academic term for all schools of all races; the creation in 1935 of a rental system for school books as a step towards a free text program; and the institution of a transportation system for rural schools. In other areas, Ehringhaus conducted a rural electrification survey, joined the prison and highway systems by putting prisoners to work; reformed the parole system; and modernized prisons. In 1935 he established a commission to study unemployment compensation, and to make state laws comply with federal statutes. He also sought to procure federal support for tobacco, potato and peanut farmers, and abolished tolls on all state roads and bridges. Constitutionally limited to a single term, Ehringhaus retired to Raleigh and resumed the practice of law. He later served as Special Assistant to the United States District Attorney. He died on July 31, 1949 in Raleigh, and was buried in Elizabeth City. Bibliography: *News and Observer* [Raleigh] (January 1-6, 1933, August 1, 1949);

Archibald Henderson, ed., *North Carolina—The Old North State and the New*, vol. IV (Chicago, 1941); David L. Corbitt, ed., *Addresses, Letters and Papers of John Christoph Blucher Ehringhaus* (Raleigh, 1950); Lennox McLendon, "Ehringhaus—the Courageous Leader," in *Presentation of Portrait of John Christoph Blucher Ehringhaus* (Raleigh, 1960); Christopher Crittenden, William Powell, Robert Woody, eds., *100 Years, 100 Men: 1871-1971* (Raleigh, 1971). Governor's papers and private papers are located at State Archives in Raleigh. The Southern Historical and North Carolina collections in Chapel Hill hold other pertinent papers and documents.

HOEY, Clyde Roark, 1937-1941

Born on December 11, 1877, son of Captain Samuel Alberta Hoey, a planter, and Mary Charlotte (Roark) Hoey; a Methodist. Brother of William R., S. Ernest, Nellie Hoey Warren and Eula Hoey Shannonhouse. Married to Bess Gardner, sister of O. Max Gardner, on March 22, 1900; father of Clyde Roark, Jr., Charles and Isabel. Educated in local public schools; at age twelve quit school and became a printer's devil with the Shelby *Aurora*. Joined the Charlotte *Observer* as a printer. At age sixteen purchased the debt-ridden Shelby *Review*, and began his own newspaper, the Cleveland *Star*; ardently supported Democratic causes. Though below the legal voting age, he ran for the State House of Representatives from Cleveland County and was elected, serving from 1899-1900, 1901, and in the State Senate in 1903. Studied law during a summer at the Law School of the University of North Carolina, and admitted to the bar in 1899. Established a law practice in Shelby. Chairman of the Cleveland County Democratic Executive Committee, 1903-1909, and Assistant United States District Attorney, 1913-1919. After the resignation of Edwin Y. Webb, Hoey ran for the United States House of Representatives, and defeated John Motley Morehead; served 1919-1921 but declined renomination. Resumed his law practice until 1936. In the 1936 Democratic gubernatorial primary, Hoey defeated Dr. Ralph McDonald, Lieutenant Governor A.H. Graham and John McRae, but failed to win a majority. The runoff was contested over the issue of McDonald's opposition to the sales tax; with Graham's support, Hoey defeated McDonald. In the general election Hoey went on to win over the Republican Gilliam Grissom by a vote of 542,139 to 270,843. He was inaugurated on January 7, 1937. On Hoey's recommendation, the state began providing free textbooks in the elementary schools. He increased school expenditures by thirty percent; raised teachers' salaries; and started graduate programs in Negro colleges. Other developments during Hoey's administration include the improvement of the state highway system; the start of a state building program; the launching of a tourist promotion program; the establishment of the State Board of Alcohol Beverage Control; and the creation of the State Bureau of Investigation. Hoey also supported passage of stringent child labor laws; instituted a modern probate system; and maintained a balanced budget. Constitutionally limited to a single term, Hoey resumed the practice of law in 1941. Between 1941 and 1944, he served as State Democratic National Committeeman. In 1944 he defeated Cameron Morrison for the Democratic nomination to the United States Senate, and in the general election he beat the Republican candidate, A.I. Feree; he was reelected in 1950 over Halsey Leavitt. Hoey died on May 12, 1954, in his Senate office in Washington; he was buried in Sunset Cemetery in Shelby. Bibliography: *News and Observer* [Raleigh] (January 9, 1941, May 13, 1954); Archibald Henderson, ed., *North Carolina—The Old North State and the New*, vol. V (Chicago, 1941); David L. Corbitt, ed., *Addresses, Letters and Papers of Clyde Roark Hoey* (Raleigh, 1944); James and Ann C. Free, "You Know He's a Senator," *Collier's*, vol. 129, no. 5 (February 2, 1952); *Clyde Roark Hoey: Memorial Addresses Delivered in Congress* (Washington, 1954); Christopher Crittenden, William Powell, Robert Woody, eds., *100 Years, 100 Men: 1871-1971*, (Raleigh, 1971). Governor's papers from the Hoey administration are located at the State Archives in Raleigh. Duke University holds the Clyde Roark Hoey Papers, and the North Carolina and Southern Historical collections in Chapel Hill also hold papers and documents.

BROUGHTON, Joseph Melville, 1941-1945

Born on November 17, 1888 in Raleigh, North Carolina, son of J.M. Broughton, a realtor, and Sallie (Harris) Broughton; a Baptist. Brother of Florence Broughton Vinson, Minnie Broughton Dowell, James and Ernest H. Married to Alice Harper Willson on December 14, 1916; father of Alice Willson, Joseph Melville, Jr., Robert Bain and Woodson Harris. Attended Raleigh public schools and graduated from Hugh Morson Academy in 1906. Attended Wake Forest College, receiving an A.B. in 1910. Studied law at Wake Forest, and continued his legal education at Harvard Law School; received an LL.B. in 1913; awarded honorary LL.D. degrees by Davidson College, Wake Forest College and the University of North Carolina. After college served as principal of Bunn High School for two years, 1910-1912, and later worked as a staff reporter for the Winston-Salem *Journal*. In 1914 Broughton moved to Raleigh and began a law firm, developing a large and lucrative practice. He also served as a member of the Raleigh School Board and as City Attorney. Elected to the State Senate from Wake County, serving 1927 and 1929. Sponsored bills on a secret ballot, extended school terms and workmen's compensation. Served as president of the Wake County Bar in 1932, and of the North Carolina Bar Association in 1935. Became an at-large Presidential Elector in 1936. Served on the Boards of Trustees of Wake Forest College, Shaw University and the University of North Carolina. In the 1940 Democratic gubernatorial primary, Broughton led a field of seven candidates; the second place candidate, Lieutenant Governor Wilkins P. Horton, withdrew, leaving Broughton with the nomination. In the general election Broughton defeated the Republican candidate, Robert H. McNeill, by a vote of 608,744 to 195,402, the largest margin in state history. He was inaugurated on January 9, 1941. Despite the exigencies of being a war governor, Broughton proceeded with a plan for domestic reform. A nine-month school term was established, and a twelfth grade was added to North Carolina's schools. In addition, salaries for white and black teachers were equalized; the state began giving aid to public libraries; institutional boards were consolidated; and a broad medical care and hospital plan—the Good Health Program—was instituted. In 1941 Broughton hosted the National Governors' Conference in Asheville. Other developments during Broughton's term include the repeal by the legislature of the sales tax on food for home consumption, and the establishment of the Teachers' and State Employees' Retirement System. In the 1944 Democratic National Convention, Broughton was nominated for vice-president, and finished sixth of sixteen candidates after the first ballot. Broughton was constitutionally limited to a single gubernatorial term, but on November 2, 1948, he was elected to fill the United States Senate seat left vacant by the death of Josiah W. Bailey; in the same election he defeated William B. Umstead for a full term. Broughton served from December 31, 1948 until his death. Broughton died in Washington on March 6, 1949, and was buried in Montlawn Memorial Park in Raleigh.

Bibliography: *News and Observer* [Raleigh] (January 9-10, 1941, March 7, 1949); "A Second Aycock," *The Uplift*, vol. XXXIII, no. 4 (January 27, 1945); David Leroy Corbitt, ed., *Public Addresses, Letters, and Papers of Joseph Melville Broughton* (Raleigh, 1950); Christopher Crittenden, William Powell, Robert Woody, eds., *100 Years, 100 Men: 1871-1971* (Raleigh, 1971). Governor's papers and letterbooks from the Broughton administration are located at the State Archives in Raleigh. The North Carolina and Southern Historical collections in Chapel Hill hold other pertinent papers and letters.

CHERRY, Robert Gregg, 1945-1949

Born on October 17, 1891 in Catawba Junction, York County, South Carolina, son of Chancellor Lafayette Cherry, a farmer, and Harriet (Davis) Cherry; a Methodist. Married to Mildred Stafford on June 28, 1921. Orphaned in early youth, and raised by his mother's relatives in Gastonia, North Carolina. Attended local public schools and graduated from Gastonia High School in 1908; enrolled at Trinity College (now Duke University), receiving his A.B. in 1912; obtained his law degree and admitted to the bar in 1914. Attended Democratic and Republican Conventions as an observer in 1912. Returned to Gastonia and established a law practice. Elected in 1917 as Captain of a group of Gaston County men who formed themselves into an artillery company; saw action in France. Later served as a Major in the State National Guard. While still in Europe, Cherry was nominated in 1919 as Mayor of Gastonia, and was elected after his return; reelected in 1921. Elected to the State House of Representatives from Gaston County, serving in the assemblies of 1931, 1933, 1935, 1937 and 1939; also chosen Speaker of the House in 1937, and earned the nickname the "Iron Major." From 1937 to 1940 Cherry was chairman of the State Democratic Executive Committee; he represented Gaston County in the State Senate in 1941 and 1943. In the 1944 Democratic gubernatorial primary, Cherry defeated Ralph McDonald and Olla Ray Boyd, and in the general election he received 528,995 votes against the 230,998 cast for Frank C. Patton, the Republican candidate. He was inaugurated on January 4, 1945. Governor Cherry was confronted by numerous problems caused by post-war shortages. A fiscal conservative, he increased the state's reserve funds, and advocated using the state surplus for public construction projects. He raised the salaries of state employees and teachers; supervised the conversion of facilities at Camp Butner into a center for the mentally ill; established a Good Health Association; expanded state-wide clinics and hospitals; and instituted a major program in 1946 to improve rural roads. From 1945 to 1948, state expenditures for education increased by $22,000,000. At the 1947 Southern Governors' Conference, Cherry refused to participate in the Dixiecrat movement, and declined to join in the issuing of a "Southern Statement." He supported Truman in the 1948 election. After his term expired, Cherry resumed his law practice in Gastonia. He served on the boards of trustees of the University of North Carolina and Duke University. Cherry died on June 25, 1957, and was buried in Gastonia.
Bibliography: Archibald Henderson, ed., *North Carolina: The Old North State and the New*, vol. IV (Chicago, 1941); *North Carolina Manual, 1947* (Raleigh, 1947); *News and Observer* [Raleigh] (January 2, 1949, June 26, 1957); David L. Corbitt, ed., *Public Addresses and Papers of Robert Gregg Cherry* (Raleigh, 1951); Christopher Crittenden, William Powell, Robert Woody, eds., *100 Years, 100 Men: 1871-1971* (Raleigh, 1971). The State Archives in Raleigh hold both the governor's papers and private papers. The North Carolina and Southern Historical collections contain other letters and documents.

SCOTT, William Kerr, 1949-1953

Born on April 17, 1896 near Haw River, Almance County, North Carolina, son of Robert W. Scott, a prosperous farmer and legislator popularly known as "Farmer Bob," and Elizabeth (Hughes) Scott; a Presbyterian. Brother of Fannie Scott Hudson, Robert W. Jr., James E., Margaret Scott Smith, Albert, Samuel, Henry, Elizabeth Scott Carrington, Ralph H., Agnes Scott Haeseler and Anderson. Married to Mary Elizabeth White on July 2, 1919; father of Osborne, Robert (Governor of North Carolina, 1969-1973), and Mary Kerr. Attended Alamance County public schools, and graduated from Hawfield High School in 1913. Enrolled at North Carolina State College, receiving a B.S. in 1917; awarded a Doctor of Agriculture degree by North Carolina State College, and honorary LL.D. by Elon College and by the University of North Carolina. After his graduation from college, Scott was appointed as an Emergency Food Production Agent, but resigned to enlist in the army; served in the field artillery, 1918. After the war, began farming in Alamance County; served as Farm Agent, 1920-1930, and as Master of the State Grange, 1930-1933. President Roosevelt appointed him Regional Director of the Farm Debt Adjustment Program, 1934-1936. Scott was elected State Commissioner of Agriculture in 1936, and was twice reelected, serving 1937-1948. In 1947 he was a member of a federal commission studying hoof and mouth disease in Mexico, and from 1946 to 1948 he served on the National Advisory Committee of Agricultural Research and Marketing. After resigning as Commissioner of Agriculture in February 1948, Scott sought the Democratic gubernatorial nomination. In the first primary ballot, he finished a close second to Charles M. Johnson-other candidates included R. Hayne Albright, Oscar Barker, Olla R. Boyd and W.F. Stanly. Scott decisively defeated Johnson in the runoff by almost 35,000 votes. Scott also won the general election, receiving 570,995 votes to beat the Republican George M. Pritchard (206,166) and the Progressive Mary Price (3,364). "The Squire of Haw River," as Scott was popularly known, was inaugurated on January 6, 1949. As governor, Scott advocated a "Go-Forward Program," which would use the state surplus to promote education and public service projects, including construction of schools and hospitals, and expanded care for the handicapped and the aged. He also proposed a system of paved farm-to-market roads. Scott's plans were strongly opposed and blocked by conservatives in the General Assembly, and the governor responded by launching a radio appeal directly to the people. The General Assembly then called a special election in 1949, in which bond issues on a farm-to-market road system and on school expansion were overwhelmingly approved. As a result of the bond issue for road construction, paved road mileage in the state more than doubled during Scott's term as governor. Scott also campaigned for better telephone and electric services for rural counties. He appointed the first black to the State Board of Education, and oversaw the construction of modern deep water port facilities at Morehead City and Wilmington. In 1949 Scott appointed Frank P. Graham to the United States Senate to fill the seat left vacant by the death of J. Melville Broughton. Constitutionally forbidden from succeeding himself, Scott returned to his Hawfields farm at the end of his term of office. After the death of Willis Smith, Scott was elected on November 2, 1954 to fill Smith's unexpired term in the United States Senate; at the same time, he was elected to a full term to begin on January 3, 1955. Scott died on April 16, 1958, in Burlington, North Carolina, and was buried in Hawfields Presbyterian Church Cemetery near Mebane. Bibliography: *News and Observer* [*Raleigh*] (April 18, 1948 and January 7, 1949); *North Carolina Manual, 1951* (Raleigh, 1951); David L. Corbitt, ed., *Public Addresses, Letters, Papers of William Kerr Scott* (Raleigh, 1957); *William Kerr Scott: Memorial Addresses*

Delivered in Congress (Washington, 1958); Terry Sanford, "Address . . . for the Presentation of Portrait of Governor William Kerr Scott," unpublished typescript in the North Carolina Collection (Raleigh, 1959); John W. Coon, "Kerr Scott: The 'Go Forward' Governor: His Origins, His Program, and the North Carolina General Assembly," unpublished M.A. thesis, University of North Carolina, 1968; Herbert Turner, *The Scott Family of Hawfields* (n.p., 1971); Christopher Crittenden, William Powell, Robert Woody, eds., *100 Years, 100 Men: 1871-1971* (Raleigh, 1971). Governor's papers and the William Kerr Scott Papers are located at the State Archives in Raleigh. The North Carolina and Southern Historical collections in Chapel Hill also hold relevant documents and papers.

UMSTEAD, William Bradley, 1953-1954

Born on May 13, 1895 near Mangum Township, Durham County, North Carolina, son of John W. Umstead, a farmer and legislator, and Lulie Lunsford Umstead, a teacher; a Methodist. Brother of Lucille Umstead Long and John W., and half-brother of Henry V. Umstead and Maggie Umstead Rose. Married to Merle Davis on September 5, 1929; father of Merle Bradley. Attended Mangum School and Durham High School; entered the University of North Carolina, graduating with an A.B. in 1916; awarded an honorary LL.D. in 1954. Taught school in Kinston. Enlisted in the army in 1917, and commissioned as a Second Lieutenant; saw action in France; resigned in 1919. Studied law at Trinity College (now Duke University) under Dean S.F. Mordecai, 1919-1921, and admitted to the bar in 1920. Opened a law practice in Durham in 1921. Elected Prosecuting Attorney of the Durham County Recorder's Court, serving until 1926. Acted as Solicitor of the Tenth Judicial District, 1927-1933. Elected as a Democrat to the United States House of Representatives in 1932, serving from 1933 to 1939; did not seek renomination. In 1944 Umstead managed R. Gregg Cherry's gubernatorial campaign, and served as chairman of the State Democratic Executive Committee. On December 18, 1946, appointed to the United States Senate seat left vacant by the death of Josiah W. Bailey; he sat in the Senate from 1947 to 1948, but was defeated for nomination to a full term by J. Melville Broughton. In the 1952 Democratic gubernatorial primary, Umstead defeated Hubert F. Olive by 30,000 votes, and in the general election he went on to win over the Republican candidate, H.F. Seawell, Jr., by a vote of 796,306 to 383,329. Umstead was inaugurated on January 8, 1953. Two days after assuming office, Umstead suffered a heart attack. He remained determined, however, to complete his term, and endeavored to reorganize the Board of Paroles, calling for equitable and uniform policies. He also urged new and more diversified industry for the state, and presided over the Department of Conservation and Development. During his term both North Carolina Senators died, and Umstead appointed Alton A. Lennon and Sam J. Ervin, Jr., to their respective seats. Though he criticized the 1954 Supreme Court decision to desegregate schools as an invasion of state sovereignty, Umstead urged moderation. He attended a meeting of southern governors, but refused to commit the state to a plan of action; he then appointed a bi-racial Governor's Special Advisory Committee on Education to study the situation and to make recommendations. Umstead also worked on government reorganization and convened hearings on the 1955 budget. On November 4, 1954, he was hospitalized with pneumonia, aggravated by his chronic heart condition. Umstead died on November 7, 1954, in Durham, and was buried in Mount Tabor Church Cemetery in Mangum Township, Durham County. Bibliography: Robert Sykes, "The Honorable William B. Umstead," *The*

Orphan's Friend and Masonic Journal, vol. LXII, no. 16 (August 15, 1938); *News and Observer* [Raleigh] (January 9, 1953, November 8, 1954); *History of North Carolina: Family and Personal History*, vol. IV (New York, 1956); David L. Corbitt, ed., *Public Addresses, Letters and Papers of William Bradley Umstead* (Raleigh, 1957); *Presentation of Portrait of William B. Umstead*.... (Raleigh, 1957); Edwin Gill, "The Dedication of the William B. Umstead Building," *We the People*, vol. XX, no. 1 (May, 1962); Ed Rankin, "The Death of a Governor," *We the People*, vol. XXVIII, no. 11 (November, 1970). Governor's papers from the Umstead administration are located at the State Archives in Raleigh. The North Carolina and Southern Historical collections in Chapel Hill hold other papers and documents.

HODGES, Luther Hartwell, 1954-1961

Born on March 9, 1898, near Cascade, Pittsylvania County, Virginia, son of John James Hodges, a tenant farmer and grocer, and Lovicia (Gammon) Hodges; eighth of nine children; a Methodist. Married to Martha Elizabeth Blakeney on June 24, 1922; father of Betsy, Nancy and Luther Hartswell, Jr. Married to Louise B. Finlayson, February 1970. Family moved to North Carolina in 1901. Attended public schools of Spray and Leaksville, graduating from high school in 1915. Entered the University of North Carolina, receiving a B.A. in 1919; awarded an honorary LL.D. in 1946. Served in the Student Army Training Corps, 1918, and enlisted in the United States Army; commissioned a Second Lieutenant. Returned to Leaksville as secretary to the manager of Marshall Field Mills, rising through the ranks from Personnel Manager, 1920, to National and International Production Manager, 1938. Member of the State Vocational Education Board, 1929-1933, and the State Highway Commission, 1933-1937. Resided, New York, 1940-1947; became Vice President of Marshall Field in 1943, retiring in 1950. Active in Rotary affairs, 1923-1945, as chairman of its International Convention in 1948, and as its consultant and advisor to the United Nations. Served as Special Consultant to the Secretary of Agriculture, 1945. Director, Textile Division, Office of Price Administration, 1944. Served in West Germany as Chief of the Industry Division of the Economic Cooperation Division in 1950, and as consultant to the Department of State at the International Management Conference in 1951. In his first political campaign, Hodges ran for Lieutenant Governor in the Democratic primary of 1952; he defeated Roy Rowe, Marshall D. Kurfees and Ben J. McDonald; though Hodges failed to win a majority, Rowe, the next largest vote-getter, did not call for a runoff. In the general election Hodges defeated Republican Warren H. Pritchett by a vote of 783,792 to 374,530. He was also President of the State Senate in 1953. After the death of Governor William B. Umstead on November 7, 1954, Hodges succeeded to the governorship. Governor Hodges was known as the businessman's governor. His "Operation Bootstrap" launched a broad program of industrial development. He also reformed the Highway Commission by appointing nonpolitical members on a state-wide basis, rather than through local patronage. In the face of the desegregation challenge, Hodges urged law and order, and worked to keep the schools open. He actively supported the Pearsall Plan policy of selective integration which allowed local options on school openings, and which provided tuition grants to students not wishing to attend integrated schools. This plan was endorsed by a state-wide referendum on September 8, 1956. In the 1956 Democratic gubernatorial primary, Hodges overwhelmingly defeated three token candidates Tom Sawyer, Harry P. Stokely and C.E. Earle, Jr; he went on in the general election to defeat Republican Kyle Hayes by a vote of 760,480 to 375,379. After his election to a full term, Hodges travelled widely to attract industry to the state. In 1956 the Research Triangle, a laboratory center between Duke University in Durham, the University of North Carolina in Chapel Hill, and North Carolina State College in Raleigh, was incorporated. Hodges also appointed B. Everett Jordan to the U.S. Senate in 1958, and in 1959 urged passage of the first state minimum wage legislation in the South. He called out the National Guard during the 1959 Henderson textile mill strikes after his efforts at negotiation failed, and the same year toured Russia. Hodges was appointed Secretary of Commerce by President Kennedy, and served from 1961 to 1965. He was particularly instrumental in the passage of the Grade Expansion Act of 1962. After leaving the Cabinet, Hodges served as chairman of the Board of the Research Triangle Foundation, from 1965 to 1972. He was also elected chairman of Financial Consultant International, and served as president of International Rotary, 1967-1968. Hodges eventually retired to Chapel Hill, where he died on October 6, 1974. He was buried in Overlook Cemetery in Eden, North Carolina. Bibliography: *News and Observer* [Raleigh] (November 8, 1954); James W. Patton, ed., *Messages, Addresses and Public Papers of Luther Hartwell Hodges* (Raleigh, n.d.); Dan Oberdorfer and Walter Pincus, "Businessmen in Politics: Luther Hodges," in Lester Tanzer, ed., *The Kennedy Circle* (Wash., D.C., 1961); Luther H. Hodges, *Businessman in the Statehouse* (Chapel Hill, 1962); "When a Businessman Gets into Politics," *Business Week*, no. 1262 (September 13, 1962); Luther H. Hodges, *The Business Conscience* (Englewood Cliffs, 1963); A.G. Ivey, *Luther H. Hodges: Practical Idealist* (Minneapolis, 1968); Christopher Crittenden, William Powell, Robert Woody, eds., *100 Years, 100 Men: 1871-1971* (Raleigh, 1971). Governor's papers dealing with the Hodges administration are located in the State Archives in Raleigh. The North Carolina Collection holds papers and a clippings file; the Southern Historical Collection holds the Luther H. Hodges Papers.

SANFORD, Terry, 1961-1965

Born on August 20, 1917 in Laurinburg, North Carolina, son of Cecil L. Sanford, a merchant and realtor, and Elizabeth Martin Sanford, a teacher; a Methodist. Brother of Cecil L. Jr., Betsy Sanford Rose and Helen Sanford Wilhelm. Married to Margaret Rose Knight on July 4, 1942; father of Terry, Jr., and Betsy. Graduated from Laurinburg High School and attended Presbyterian Junior College, transferring to the University of North Carolina; received A.B. in 1941; an honorary LL.D. in 1961. Served 1941-1942 as a special agent for the Federal Bureau of Investigation, resigning to join the army; served as a Second Lieutenant in the paratroopers, 1942-1946, in Italy, France and Belgium; awarded a bronze star and purple heart. Entered the law school of the University of North Carolina, receiving his LL.B.-J.D. in 1946; admitted to the bar. Served as Assistant Director of the Institute of Government from 1946 to 1948. Established a law practice in Fayetteville, where he became a civic leader. In his first state-wide campaign in 1949, Sanford defeated two opponents to become president of the Young Democratic Clubs. In 1950 Governor Scott appointed him to the State Ports Authority. Elected to the 1953 State General Assembly as Senator from Cumberland County. Successfully managed the campaign of W. Kerr Scott for the Senate in 1954. In the 1960 Democratic gubernatorial primary, Sanford defeated I. Beverly Lake, Malcolm B. Seawell and John D. Larkins, Jr, but failed to secure a majority. In the second primary election, Sanford, a racial moderate, withstood criticism of his progressive programs, and defeated the segregationist Lake by over 75,000 votes. Shortly thereafter, Sanford led the "Dirty Dozen" at the Democratic National Convention, a minority of the North Carolina delegation who endorsed John F. Kennedy; Sanford later delivered a seconding speech. In the general election for Governor, Sanford defeated Republican Gavin by a vote of 735,248 to 613,975; his victory helped Kennedy to carry the state by a narrow margin. Sanford was inaugurated on January 5, 1961. Governor Sanford encouraged increased spending on schools through a "Quality Education Program" financed by higher taxes, including a sales tax on food. The program affected a number of areas, and resulted in higher teacher salaries, the hiring of more teachers, the expansion of libraries, and the reform of curriculum. As did former Governor Aycock, Sanford travelled extensively to promote quality education. His 1963 Higher Education Act established a comprehensive system of community colleges to promote literacy and vocational training; opened new senior colleges in Wilmington, Charlotte and Asheville; and raised North Carolina State and the Women's College to the rank of universities. The Governor's School for gifted children, the North Carolina School of the Arts, the Advancement School for under-achievers, the research-oriented Learning Institute, the Center for Mental Retardation, and Operation Second Chance for drop-outs were all established while Sanford was governor. His term also marked the state's greatest period of industrial development, as $1.2 billion was invested in new plants, and 120,489 new jobs were created. International trade fairs were held in Charlotte, and to promote agriculture emphasis was placed on the importance of building a food processing industry in the state. In 1963 Sanford established an anti-poverty program, the North Carolina Fund, which was intended to help the state's poor to become self-supporting and to eradicate illiteracy. Sanford was the leading spokesman for the "New South." He called for an end to discrimination, and in 1963 appointed a bi-racial Good Neighbor Council to promote employment and educational opportunities without regard to race. After serving the constitutional limit of a single term, Sanford resumed the practice of law. He launched a two-year study of state government, culminating in his *Storm over the States;* he also formed the Southern Growth Policy Board. Sanford was for a time a member of the Advisory Board of Higher Education of the Department of Health, Education, and Welfare, and in December, 1969, was appointed President of Duke University. In 1972 he became a late entry in the presidential race, but his decisive defeat by George Wallace in the North Carolina Democratic primary crippled his campaign. Sanford presided as chairman of the Democratic Charter Commission in 1974, and on May 19, 1975, he announced his candidacy for President, becoming the first candidate to call for full employment as the basis of the nation's economic policy. Though he raised sufficient money to qualify for federal matching funds, Sanford fared poorly in the early primaries, and withdrew in late January 1976, after being hospitalized with chest pains. He then resumed his position at Duke. Bibliography: Sam Regan, *The New Day* (Zebulon, 1964); Terry Sanford, *Needed: A Comprehensive Policy for Public Education* (Cambridge, 1964); Memory Mitchell, ed., *Messages, Addresses, and Public Papers of Terry Sanford* (Raleigh, 1966); Terry Sanford, *But What About the People*(New York, 1966); Terry Sanford, *Storm Over the States* (New York, 1967); Christopher Crittenden, William Powell, Robert Woody, eds., *100 Years, 100 Men: 1871-1971* (Raleigh, 1971); Roger M. Williams, "Terry Sanford: Can He Save the South," *World* (July 18, 1972); Wayne King, "Sanford Pins Victory Hope on his Non-Political Stance," *New York Times* (December 29, 1975). Governor's papers concerning Sanford's administration are located at the State Archives in Raleigh. The North Carolina and Southern Historical collections in Chapel Hill contain papers and documents, including a clippings file and campaign papers.

MOORE, Dan Killian, 1965-1969

Born on April 2, 1906, in Asheville, North Carolina, son of Fred Moore, a superior court judge, and Lela (Enloe) Moore; a Methodist. Brother of Edith Moore Hall, Margaret Moore Council, Fred, Jr. and William Enloe. Married to Jeanelle Coulter on May 4, 1933; father of Edith and Dan, Jr. When Moore was two, his father died; he was then raised by his mother. Attended Sylvia public schools and enrolled at the University of North Carolina, receiving a B.S. in Commerce in 1928; attended the University of North Carolina Law School, 1927-1928. Established a law practice, and served as Town Attorney for Sylvia, 1931-1933. Became Attorney for Jackson County and legal representative to the County Board of Education. Elected to the State House of Representatives from Jackson County, serving in 1941. Member of the armed forces from 1943 to 1945; stationed in Europe with a medical unit and in the Judge Advocate General's office. Elected Solicitor of the Thirtieth District in 1945, and in 1948 appointed by Governor Cherry to replace Felix Alley as Judge of the Superior Court; elected Judge in 1950, serving until 1958. Moved to Canton, and became legal counsel to Champion Papers. Member of the State Board of Water Resources, 1959-1964. In the 1964 Democratic gubernatorial primary, Moore opposed L. Richardson Preyer and I. Beverly Lake; Moore finished second to Preyer by 24,000 votes in the first primary, but defeated Preyer by a vote of 480,431 to 293,863 in the runoff. In the general election, Moore defeated Republican Robert Gavin by a vote of 790,343 to 606,165; he was inaugurated on January 8, 1965. At his inauguration ceremony, Moore made a commitment to "total development"; he expanded state services and travelled to promote industrial investment. A $300 million road bond issue was passed during his administration, and when the University of North Carolina was threatened with loss of accreditation because of the Speaker Ban Law passed by the General Assembly, Moore appointed a special commission to study the issue. At Moore's urging an extra session of the General Assembly was convened in November 1965, returning university control from the State Legislature to the Board of Trustees. In 1966 he convened another special General Assembly session to apportion State Senate and Congressional districts as ordered by federal courts. Moore also appointed a Law and Order Committee intended initially to limit the activities of the Ku Klux Klan. In 1967 he called for a broad program of court reform; increased expenditures on education and public health; and statutory authority for the Good Neighbor Council. In the 1968 Democratic National Convention, Moore was the state's favorite son candidate. After serving the constitutional limit of a single term, Moore joined a Raleigh law firm. He was appointed by his successor, Governor Robert Scott, to be an Associate Justice of the State Supreme Court on November 20, 1969, replacing William H. Bobbitt; Moore was elected to a full term on November 11, 1970. Bibliography: Archibald Henderson, ed., *The Old North State and the New,* vol. III (Chicago, 1941); *News and Observer* [Raleigh] (July 5, 1964); Doug Reed, "Governor Moore: Exclusive Interview," *Citizen-Times* [Asheville] (October 24, 1965); "The Dan Moore Years Begin," *We the People,* vol. XXII, no. 8 (January, 1965) James R. Spence, *The Moore-Preyer-Lake Primaries of 1964:The Making of a Governor* (Winston-Salem, 1968); *Dan K. Moore: Proceedings of a Ceremony for the Presentation of the Portrait . . .* (Raleigh, 1969); Ed Rankin, "People, Places, Events," *We the People of North Carolina,* vol. XXVIII, no. 1 (January, 1970); Memory F. Mitchell, *Messages, Addresses, and Public Papers of Daniel Killian Moore* (Raleigh, 1971). Governor's papers pertaining to Moore's administration are located in the State Archives in Raleigh. The North Carolina Collection in Chapel Hill holds other documents, including a clippings file.

SCOTT, Robert Walter, 1969-1973

Born on January 13, 1929 near Haw River, Alamance County, North Carolina, son of William Kerr Scott, farmer and Governor of North Carolina, and Mary Elizabeth (White) Scott; a Presbyterian. Brother of Osborne and Mary Kerr. Married to Jessie Rae Osborne on September 1, 1951; father of Susan, Margaret, Mary, W. Kerr and Jan. Attended public schools and studied at Duke University, 1947-1949, transferring to North Carolina State University, where he received a B.S. in Animal Husbandry in 1952. Member of the U.S. Army Counter Intelligence Corps, 1953-1955. Active in the National Grange, serving as Master of the North Carolina Grange, 1959-1961. Elected to local Democratic Party posts and served on the Solicitorial Democratic Executive Committee. Member of the Conservation and Development Board, Kerr Reservoir Development Commission, and North Carolina Seashore Commission. Elected Lieutenant Governor on a ticket headed by Dan K. Moore, serving 1965-1969; also acted as President of the State Senate, 1965-1967. In the 1968 Democratic gubernatorial primary, Scott defeated J. Melville Broughton, Jr., son of a former governor, and Dr. Reginald Hawkins, the first black to run for the governor's office in North Carolina; though Scott failed to secure a majority, Broughton declined a runoff. In the general election Scott defeated Republican James C. Gardner by a vote of 821,233 to 737,075; he was inaugurated on January 3, 1969. As governor, Scott vastly expanded road building by increasing gasoline taxes; in addition, he persuaded the legislature to pass tobacco and soft drink taxes, raising $97 million by this means, most of which was spent on public education. Scott's administration was also marked by the establishment of kindergartens; the development of vocational programs in high schools; the provision of free transportation for handicapped people; and the expansion of the community college and technical school system. In 1969 the budget for the State Bureau of Investigation was doubled, and drug abuse and organized crime units were added. In the early 1970s Scott sent state forces to control demonstrations at state campuses; he also oversaw a study of the penal system after a visit to Central Prison in 1970. Though he urged conservation and anti-pollution laws, Scott pushed for industrial development. In 1971 he began a policy of governmental reorganization, reducing the number of state agencies to twenty-four by 1975. Despite the failure of his proposal for a Department of Local Affairs, he increased home rule authority by sharing tax revenues with local government. In 1972 a new University of North Carolina system, including sixteen campuses, was created, with a single Board of Governors to set uniform policy and to submit a unified budget for higher education. Constitutionally limited to a single term, Scott left office in 1973 to become Executive Vice President of the North Carolina Agribusiness Council, serving 1973-1975; he also travelled to Eastern Europe on a trade mission. Scott now operates a dairy farm in Haw River, and serves as consultant to the Alamance County Technical Institute. In 1975 he chartered the Governmental Relations and Assistance Corporation. Bibliography: Herbert Turner, *The Scott Family of Hawfields* (n.p., 1971); "How the Governor Rates His Administration," *Daily News* [Greensboro] (December 17, 1972) Interview, *Journal and Sentinel* [Winston-Salem] (December 24, 1972); Nancy Roberts, *The Governor* (Charlotte, 1972); *The Portrait of Robert Walter Scott* (Raleigh, 1973); Russell Clay, ed., *The Long View: The Administration of Governor Robert Walter Scott* (Raleigh, n.d.); Memory F. Mitchell, ed., *Address, and Public Papers of Robert Walter Scott* (Raleigh, 1974). Governor's papers from the Scott administration are located at the State Archives in Raleigh. The North Carolina and Southern Historical Collections in Chapel Hill hold other papers and documents.

HOLSHOUSER, James Eubert, 1973-1977

Born on October 8, 1934 in Boone, North Carolina, son of James Eubert Holshouser, a lawyer and judge, and Virginia (Dayvault) Holshouser; a Presbyterian. Brother of Laura Mast Holshouser. Married to Patricia Hollingsworth on June 17, 1961; father of Virginia Walker. Attended local schools and Appalachian High School, graduating in 1952. Enrolled in Davidson College, receiving a B.S. in 1956. Entered the University of North Carolina Law School, LL.B., 1960; LL.D., 1974. Returned to Boone and began a law practice. Elected to the State House of Representatives from Watauga County as a Republican, serving 1963, 1965-1966, 1969 and 1971; served as House Minority Leader and as Chairman of the Republican State Executive Committee, 1966-1972. Led Richard M. Nixon's campaign in the state in 1968. National winner of the Freedom Guard Award from the United States Jaycees, 1971. In 1972 sought the Republican gubernatorial nomination; in the first primary Holshouser received 83,867 votes to 84,906 for James C. Gardner, but two minor candidates, Thomas Chappel and Leroy Gileson, received enough votes to necessitate a runoff. In the second primary Holshouser defeated Gardner by a vote of 69,916 to 68,134. Holshouser went on to win in the general election, polling 767,470 votes against 729,104 for Hargrove "Skipper" Bowles of the Democratic Party, and 8,211 for Artis F. Pettyjohn of the American Party. Richard M. Nixon's margin of over 600,000 in the state contributed greatly to Holshouser's victory. The first Republican governor since 1896, Holshouser was inaugurated on January 5, 1973. Governor Holshouser called for sound business management of the state's finances, and an Efficient Study Commission was set up to promote economy and improved services. A seven-year highway program was instituted, including a formula system for secondary roads. Holshouser supported area health education centers and a rural health program. In September 1973, he led a state delegation to Europe and the Soviet Union in an attempt to increase the state's foreign trade. He urged higher teacher salaries, increased school construction, and expanded kindergartens. Also during Holshouser's administration, a control land management program was begun, and the state parks system was improved. Holshouser called for increased industrialization of non-urban areas but in many ways his plans were limited by sizable Democratic majorities in the General Assembly. Holshouser was Southern Chairman of President Ford's campaign, and considered a possible vice presidential choice. After Ford's defeat by Ronald Reagan in the 1976 state presidential primary, however, Holshouser was denied a seat in the state delegation to the Republican National Convention by party conservatives. Constitutionally limited to a single term, he then resumed the practice of law, opening offices in Boone and Southern Pines. Bibliography: John Cheney, Jr., ed., *North Carolina Manual, 1973* (Raleigh, 1973); *News and Observer* [Raleigh] (September 9, 1973); "North Carolina Interview: Governor James E. Holshouser, Jr.," *We the People of North Carolina,* vol. XXI, no. 1; Ferry Guilloony, "The Man and his Office," *News and Observer* [Raleigh] (May 11, 1975). Governor's papers from the Holshouser administration are located at the State Archives in Raleigh. The North Carolina Collection holds other relevant papers and documents, including a clippings file.

HUNT, James Baxter, 1977-

Born on May 16, 1937 in Greensboro, North Carolina, son of James B. Hunt, a farmer and soil conservationist, and Elsie (Brame) Hunt, a teacher; a Presbyterian. Brother of Robert Brame Hunt. Married to Carolyn Joyce Leonard on August 20, 1958; father of Rebecca, Baxter, Rachel and Elizabeth. Graduated from Rock Ridge High School. Attended North Carolina State University, receiving a B.S. in agricultural education in 1959, an M.S. in agricultural economics in 1962; received a J.D. from the University of North Carolina Law School in 1964. President of the North Carolina Grange Youth and Future Farmers of America. Served in 1960 as chairman of Young Voters for Terry Sanford. National College Director for the Democratic National Committee, 1962-1963. In 1964 went to Nepal for two years under the sponsorship of the Ford Foundation as an economic advisor to the government. Established a law practice in Wilson. Elected president of the State Young Democratic Clubs, 1968. Served as a delegate to the 1968 Democratic National Convention. Appointed Assistant State Party Chairman in 1969. In the May 6, 1972 Democratic primary for Lieutenant Governor, Hunt defeated Roy Sowers, Margaret Harper, Allen Barbee and Reginald Grazier. Reversing a Republican trend in the state, Hunt was elected Lieutenant Governor in the November election, defeating John Walker, the Republican candidate, by over 200,000 votes. Hunt sought the 1976 Democratic nomination for Governor, and in the August primary he received 52.3% of the vote, defeating Edward M. O'Herron, Jr., George M. Wood, Thomas E. Strickland and Jetter Braker. In the general election Hunt won over Republican David T. Flaherty by a vote of 1,075,145 to 561,122; H.F. Seawell of the American Party received 13,785 votes. Hunt was inaugurated on January 8, 1977. In his inaugural address Hunt called for a "new beginning," seeking "to eliminate the last vestiges of discrimination." He called for renewed emphasis on the teaching of reading in the public schools, and advocated a new utilities regulation structure that would reflect consumer interests. He also appointed a black and a woman to high level posts. Bibliography: *Daily News* [Greensboro] (November 19, 1972); *News and Observer* [Raleigh] (January 9, 1977). The State Archives in Raleigh is the repository for Governors' papers, and those of Governor Hunt will eventually be deposited there. The North Carolina Collection in Chapel Hill also holds documents, including a clippings file.

NORTH DAKOTA

NORTH DAKOTA

MILLER, John, 1889-1891

Born on October 29, 1843, in Dryden, New York, to Archibald and Isabel (McKellar) Miller; an Episcopalian. Married to Addie S. Tucker on February 22, 1882; father of one daughter. Attended public school and academy in Dryden. Merchant; real estate broker; farmer. Mason. Miller emigrated to the Dakota Territory in 1880 as superintendent of the Dwight Farm and Land Company. Although he did not become involved in politics until 1888, he received the Republican Party's nomination for Governor, winning that office over William Roach with 25,365 votes. His opponent had 12,733 votes. Miller took office on December 12, 1889, and his most important contribution while governor was the establishment of an efficient state administration. He was also the leader in the fight to ban the Louisiana Lottery from North Dakota. Primarily because of his efforts, the lottery did not gain a foothold in the state. In 1890 Miller declined re-nomination for Governor and returned to private life. In 1896 he moved to Duluth, Minnesota, and founded the John Miller Company. Miller was president of this wheat brokerage. He died on October 26, 1908. Bibliography: Erling N. Rolfsrud, *Lanterns over the Prairies*, 2 vols. (Brainerd, Minn., 1949-1950); Lewis Crawford, *History of North Dakota*, 3 vols. (Chicago, 1931); Theodore Saloutos and John D. Hicks, *Agricultural Discontent in the Middle West, 1900-1939* (Madison, Wisconsin, 1951); Congressional Quarterly, Inc., *Guide to United States Elections* (Washington, 1975).

BURKE, Andrew H., 1891-1893

Born on May 15, 1850 in New York City; orphaned at an early age. Married to Caroline Cleveland in 1880; father of Amy and Ada Burke. Under the supervision of the New York Children's Aid Society, Burke was taken to Indiana at the age of nine. Entered the Seventy-fifth Indiana Volunteer Infantry as a drummer boy at the age of twelve. Attended Asbury University (now De Pauw University, Greencastle, Indiana) after the Civil War. Worked as a business manager of the *Evansville Courier* [Indiana]; was employed by a commercial agency in Cleveland, Ohio and by a lumber firm in New York Mills, Minnesota. Moved to Casselton, Dakota Territory, where he became the cashier of the First National Bank of Casselton. Three times elected as Treasurer of Cass County, Dakota Territory. As the Republican gubernatorial candidate, Burke was elected Governor of North Dakota by popular vote on November 4, 1890, defeating the Democratic candidate, W. Roach, and the Farmers' Alliance and Prohibition candidate, W. Muir, by a vote of

19,053 to 12,604 and 4,821, respectively. He was inaugurated on January 5, 1891. During his administration, the issuance of state bonds in the amount of 150,000 dollars was authorized to pay North Dakota's share of the indebtedness of the Territory of Dakota; a general election law was enacted; and the governor was empowered to appoint a commission to compile the state laws. Having been defeated for reelection, Burke left office on January 2, 1893, upon the inauguration of Eli C.D. Shortridge. He moved to Duluth, Minnesota, where he unsuccessfully engaged in the grain business. He was appointed an inspector of the United States Land Office, residing in Washington, D.C., Colorado and New Mexico. Burke died on November 17, 1918 in Rosewell, New Mexico and was interred in South Park. Bibliography: Clement A. Lounsberry, *Early History of North Dakota* (New York, 1919); *Rosewell Daily Record* [New Mexico] (November 18, 1918) Congressional Quarterly, Inc., *Guide to United States Elections* (Washington, 1975); Roy Glashan, *American Governors and Gubernatorial Elections, 1775-1975* (Stillwater, Minnesota, 1975).

SHORTRIDGE, Eli C.D., 1893-1895

Born on March 29, 1830 in Cabell County, Virginia (now West Virginia). Married to Virginia Brandy in 1860; after her death, remarried to Anna Burton in 1882; father of Mrs. D.A. Stewart, Charles G. and Lila V. Shortridge by his first marriage, and Juliette and France Shortridge by his second marriage. Moved with his parents to Monroe County, Missouri in 1833; attended the district schools and an academy in Paris, Missouri. Shortridge was an effective organizer of the Granger movement in Missouri before his move to Larimore, Grand Forks County, North Dakota. As the Populist gubernatorial candidate, Shortridge was elected Governor of North Dakota by popular vote on November 8, 1892, defeating the Republican candidate, incumbent Governor Andrew H. Burke, by a vote of 18,995 to 17,236. He was inaugurated on January 2, 1893. During his administration, the issuance of 50,000 dollars of bonds was authorized to construct the south wing of the Capitol; a commission to revise and codify the state laws was created; an executive mansion was purchased; and a general drainage law was enacted. Shortridge left office on January 7, 1895, upon the inauguration of Roger Allin. Afterwards, he moved to Devil's Lake, North Dakota, where he was appointed clerk of the United States Land Office. Shortridge died on February 4, 1908. Bibliography: Clement A. Lounsberry, *Early History of North Dakota* (New York, 1919); Elwyn B. Robinson, *History of North Dakota* (Lincoln, Nebraska, 1966); Congressional Quarterly, Inc., *Guide to United States Elections* (Washington, 1975); Roy Glashan, *American Governors and Gubernatorial Elections, 1775-1975* (Stillwater, Minnesota, 1975).

ALLIN, Roger, 1895-1897

Born on December 18, 1848 in Devonshire, England, son of Mr. and Mrs. Roger Allin. After the death of his father, his mother married William Bond and moved the family to Oshawa, Ontario, Canada in 1851. Received a common school education in Oshawa. Moved to Michigan in 1880 and to North Dakota in 1881 where he filed a homestead in Pembina County. Married to Isabella McKenzie on March 22, 1882; after her death, remarried to Anna McKenzie; father of Isabella. Served as Justice of the Peace of Fertile, North Dakota, 1882; elected member of the Territorial Council, 1886; reelected in 1888. Allin served as a member of the North Dakota Constitutional Convention in 1889. Elected State Senator, 1889-1891. Lieutenant Governor of North Dakota, 1891-1893. A Republican. Roger Allin received the Republican nomination for Governor of North Dakota in 1894. In the general election held on November 6, 1894, Allin defeated F. Kinter, a Democrat, and E. Wallace, a Populist, by a vote of 23,723 to 8,188 and 9,354, respectively. He was inaugurated on January 7, 1895. Allin took office after the Panic of 1893 when prices had dropped and farmers were unable to pay their taxes, and was faced with the difficult task of cutting the state budget because the legislature had appropriated more money than taxes had been collected. He vetoed appropriation for the funding of higher education for the State University and normal school at Valley City and Marville. Public protest of Allin's actions contributed to his losing the Republican nomination in 1896. During his term, a geological survey of the state was authorized; a historical commission was created; a protection of dairy products law was passed. Governor Allin left office at the end of his term on January 4, 1897. He returned to his farming interests in Walsh County, North Dakota, and never held political office again. For one year, from 1898-1899, he served on the board of directors of the North Dakota Agricultural College. Governor Allin died on January 1, 1936 in Park River, North Dakota. Bibliography: Roy Glashan, *American Governors and Gubernatorial Elections, 1775-1975* (Stillwater, Minnesota, 1975); Congressional Quarterly, Inc., *Guide to United States Elections* (Washington, 1975); Clement A. Lounsberry, *Early History of North Dakota* (New York, 1919); *Fargo Forum* [Morning Edition] (January 2, 1936).

BRIGGS, Frank A., 1897-1898

Born on September 16, 1858 to Thomas R. and Sarah (De Voll) Briggs in Minneapolis, Minnesota; a Methodist. Married to Nannie Rachel Meek on April 12, 1877; father of two daughters. Attended public school in Howard Lake, Minnesota. Newspaperman; real estate broker; editor, Howard Lake *Advocate,* 1879; reporter and editor, St. Paul *Pioneer Press,* 1880-1883. Postmaster, Mandan, North Dakota, 1883-1886; Treasurer, Morton County, North Dakota, 1886-1894; State Auditor, North Dakota, 1894-1896. Mason, Knights Templar. Briggs was elected Governor on the Republican Party ticket, collecting 25,918 votes and defeating Populist R.B. Richardson, who had 20,690 votes. His term in office began on January 8, 1897 and was marked by attempts to streamline the state's executive office; however, Briggs died on August 8, 1898, in Bismarck, North Dakota, during the second year of his term. He was succeeded by Lieutenant Governor Joseph M. Devine. Bibliography: Erling N. Rolfsrud, *Lanterns over the Prairies,* 2 vols. (Brainerd, Minn., 1949-1950); Lewis Crawford, *History of North Dakota,* 3 vols. (Chicago, 1931); Theodore Saloutos and John D. Hicks, *Agricultural Discontent in the Middle West, 1900-1939* (Madison, Wisconsin, 1951); Congressional Quarterly, Inc., *Guide to United States Elections* (Washington, 1975).

DEVINE, Joseph M., 1898-1899

Born in Wheeling, West Virginia on March 15, 1861, son of Hugh Calhoun and Jane (McMurray) Devine; a Presbyterian. Married to Ida Frances Holloway in 1891; remarried to Mary Bernadine Hanscom on July 18, 1900; father of Douglas, and three daughters. Attended public school in Wheeling and graduated from the University of West Virginia at Morgantown. Moved to Dakota Territory in 1884 and filed a homestead in LaMoure County, soon owning a large amount of land in the county. Served as superintendent of schools in La Moure County, 1886-1896. Elected president of the North Dakota Education Association, 1889; educational lecturer for the state from 1891-1896. Devine was elected Lieutenant Governor of North Dakota in 1896 and served until the death of Governor Frank A. Briggs, when he assumed the duties of Governor under North Dakota law. A Republican. Governor Devine took the oath of office on August 9, 1898 and served until the completion of Governor Briggs' term, which ended on January 2, 1899. During his short term Devine worked for public education in the state. Reelected Lieutenant Governor, 1898-1900; served as State Superintendent of Public Instruction, 1900, and as a member of the State Normal Board and superintendent of the State Training School. Served as Immigration Commissioner for the state from 1923 to 1933, when the office was abolished. Governor Devine died on August 31, 1938 at the training school in Mandan, North Dakota. Bibliography: Roy Glashan, *American Governors and Gubernatorial Elections, 1775-1975* (Stillwater, Minnesota, 1975); Congressional Quarterly, Inc., *Guide to U.S. Elections* (Washington, D.C., 1975); *Bismarck Tribune* (August 31, 1938); Clement A. Lounsberry, *Early History of North Dakota* (New York, 1919).

FANCHER, Frederick Bartlett, 1899-1901

Born on April 2, 1852 in Kenyonville, Orleans County, New York, son of Tillotson and Julia Ann (Kenyon) Fancher; a Protestant. Married to Florence S. Van Voorhies on October 1, 1874. Attended public schools in New York and Michigan and the State Normal School in Ypsilanti, Michigan, 1865. Worked as a fire insurance underwriter for the Continental Insurance Company, Chicago, Illinois, 1871. Moved to Jamestown, North Dakota in 1881, where he engaged in farming and real estate, and also managed several thousand acres of land for eastern companies. Organized the Alliance Insurance Company with insurance business over a five state area. Served as a member of the State Constitutional Convention in 1889 from Stutsman County; elected president of the Constitutional Convention. Elected State Insurance Commissioner of North Dakota, 1894-1898; served on the board of trustees of the State Hospital for the Insane. A Republican. Frederick Bartlett Fancher received the Republican nomination for Governor of North Dakota in 1898. At the general election held on November 8, 1898, Fancher defeated David Holmes, a Democratic and Populist candidate, by the vote of 28,308 to 19,496. Governor Fancher took the oath of office on January 2, 1899. During his administration a twine and cordage plant in the State Penitentiary was established; construction of railroads in the state was increased; and a Board of Pardons was established. Fancher was nominated for Governor again in 1900 on the Republican ticket; however, he withdrew due to health reasons. His term of office expired on January 7, 1901. Afterwards, he moved to Sacramento, California where he established a wholesale and retail grocery business, 1901-1925. Upon retirement, he moved to Los Angeles where he resided until his death. Governor Fancher died on January 10, 1944 in Los Angeles. Bibliography: Roy Glashan, *American Governors and Gubernatorial Elections, 1775-1975* (Stillwater, Minnesota, 1975); Congressional Quarterly, Inc., *Guide to U.S. Elections* (Washington, D.C., 1975); *Bismarck Tribune* (January 14, 1944); Clement A. Lounsberry, *Early History of North Dakota* (New York, 1919).

WHITE, Frank, 1901-1905

Born on December 12, 1856 in Stillman Valley, Illinois, son of Joshua, an Illinois State Senator, and Lucy Ann (Brown) White; a Congregationalist. Married to Elsie Hadley on September 19, 1894; father of one son. Attended Methodist Academy, Mt. Morris, Illinois, 1874-1875, where he taught one term; graduated from the University of Illinois, 1880 as a civil engineer; employed by the Chicago, Milwaukee and St. Paul Railroad, 1880-1882. Moved to Valley City, North Dakota where he bought a farm in 1882. Served in the North Dakota House of Representatives, 1891-1893; elected to the State Senate in 1893 and served until 1898 when he resigned. Volunteered as a Major in the 1st North Dakota, United States Volunteer Infantry and served until September, with duty in the Philippines. Served as Colonel, 41st. Division, United States Army during World War I, 1917-1919. Elected Governor of North Dakota on November 6, 1900, defeating M.A. Wipperman, a Democrat and Populist, by a vote of 34,052 to 22,275. A Republican. Governor White was inaugurated on January 7, 1901. Reelected on November 4, 1902, White defeated J. Cranan, a Democrat, 31,621 votes to 17,566 votes. During his administration an institution for the feeble minded was established in Grafton, North Dakota; construction was completed on the north wing of the state capitol building; and the legislature created the Eighth Judicial District. Governor White left office on January 2, 1905. White returned to his insurance business in Valley City. He was appointed to the State Board of Regents in 1915; was appointed Treasurer of the United States in 1921 and served in that office until 1928; became president of the Middlewest Trust Company. Governor White made his home in Chevy Chase, Maryland until his death on March 23, 1940. Bibliography: Roy Glashan, *American Governors and Gubernatorial Elections, 1775-1975* (Stillwater, Minnesota, 1975); Congressional Quarterly, Inc., *Guide to U.S. Elections* (Washington, D.C., 1975); Clement A. Lounsberry, *Early History of North Dakota* (New York, 1919); *New York Times* (March 24, 1940).

SARLES, Elmore Yocum, 1905-1907

Born on January 15, 1859 in Wonewoc, Juneau County, Wisconsin, son of Jesse D., a Methodist minister, and Margaret (Thompson) Sarles. Brother of O.C. Sarles. Married to Anna York on January 10, 1886; father of Earle Redmon, Doris York,

Duane York and Eleanor. Attended Galesville University (Wisconsin) for one year. Worked in a bank in Prescott, Wisconsin and later in Sparta, Wisconsin; secretary-treasurer, Wonewoc Manufacturing Company, 1878-1879; worked for a lumber company in 1880. With his brother, O.C., established a bank in Hillsboro, North Dakota, 1881; began the First National Bank of Hillsboro, 1885, serving as cashier and later as president; manager of the O.C. Sarles and Company Lumber Company, 1882, the name later being changed to Valley Lumber Company due to the acquisition of other banking and lumber concerns in Shelly, Minnesota, Northwood, Grandin, and Caledonia, North Dakota. Mayor of Hillsboro for two years; treasurer of the school board for twenty years. On November 8, 1904, Elmore Y. Sarles was elected Governor of North Dakota, defeating M.F. Hegge, a Democrat, by a vote of 47,828 to 16,744. A Republican. Governor Sarles took the oath of office on January 2, 1905. During his term, a pure food and drug act was passed by the legislature; state banks were put under the control of a State Banking Board; regulation of the sale of dairy products was established; an irrigation code was passed; and the office of Inspector of Weights and Measures was established. Governor Sarles was defeated for reelection in 1906 and left office on January 9, 1907. Sarles returned to his banking, farming, and real estate interests in Hillsboro. Governor Sarles died on February 14, 1929 in Hillsboro, North Dakota. Bibliography: Roy Glashan, *American Governors and Gubernatorial Elections, 1775-1975* (Stillwater, Minnesota, 1975); Congressional Quarterly, Inc., *Guide to U.S. Elections* (Washington, D.C., 1975); Clement A. Lounsberry, *Early History of North Dakota* (New York, 1919); Elwyn B. Robinson, *History of North Dakota* (Lincoln, Nebraska, 1966).

BURKE, John, 1907-1913

Born on February 25, 1859, in Sigourney, Iowa, son of John and Mary (Ryan) Burke; a Unitarian. Married to Mary E. Kane on August 22, 1891; father of three children, Thomas, Elizabeth and Marian Burke. Attended public school in Sigourney, Iowa; University of Iowa, 1882-1886. Attorney and partner, Burke and Burke, Attorneys-at-Law, 1886-1888. Member, House of Representatives, North Dakota, 1891-1893; member, Senate, North Dakota, 1893-1895; Judge, County Court, Rolette County, North Dakota, 1896-1906. Mason; Elks. In 1906 Burke became the first Democratic Governor of North Dakota, defeating Republican Elmore Y. Sarles, the incumbent, with 34,424 votes. Sarles has 29,309 votes. His administration began on January 9, 1907 and was marked by the passage of laws authorizing the insurance of bonds and warrants to secure seed grain for needy farmers. Other legislation approved the establishment of a State Tuberculosis Sanitarium; a State Capitol in Bismarck; and a library for the State Legislature. Provision was also made for nonpartisan judicial appointments. Governor Burke was reelected in 1908, defeating Republican C.A. Johnson by a vote of 49,398 to 46,849; he won a third term in 1910, defeating Johnson again, this time by a vote of 47,005 to 44,555. Burke left office on January 8, 1913. He died on May 14, 1937. Bibliography: Clement A. Lounsberry, *North Dakota History and People: Outlines of American History,* 3 vols. (Chicago, 1917); Robert L. Morlan, *The Nonpartisan League* (Minneapolis, 1955); Theodore Saloutos and John D. Hicks, *Agricultural Discontent in the Middle West, 1900-1939* (Madison, Wisconsin, 1951); Roy

Glashan, *American Governors and Gubernatorial Elections, 1775-1975* (Stillwater, Minnesota, 1975).

HANNA, Louis Benjamin, 1913-1917

Born on August 9, 1861, in New Brighton, Pennsylvania, son of Jason and Margaret A. (Lewis) Hanna; a Congregationalist. Married to Lottie L. Thatcher on November 18, 1884; father of three children, Jean E., Dorothy L. and Robert L. Hanna. Attended public school in Cleveland, Ohio, and New York City. Farmer; banker; merchant; businessman; president and founder, First National Bank of Page, 1900-1926; president, Fargo Street Railway Company, 1900-1912; owner, Carrington and Casey farm. Member, North Dakota House of Representatives, 1895-1901; member, North Dakota Senate, 1905-1909; member, United States House of Representatives, 1909-1911. Mason; Elks; Woodmen; Moose; Loyal Legion. Hanna, who was the cousin of Marcus Hanna of Ohio, was nominated by the Republican Party in 1912 for the governorship. He defeated the Democrat F.O. Hellstrom by winning 39,811 votes, against the 31,544 votes of his opponent. During his administration, which began on January 8, 1913, laws were passed to prevent procreation by confirmed criminals, the insane and mental defectives; to regulate practices in district courts and the Supreme Court; to establish inheritance taxes; and to provide for teacher's insurance and retirement funds. Governor Hanna was reelected in 1914 over his Democratic opponent, F.O. Hellstrom, by a count of 44,279 votes to 34,746. Hanna left office on January 3, 1917. He died on April 23, 1948. Bibliography: Clement A. Lounsberry, *North Dakota History and People: Outlines of American History*, 3 vols. (Chicago, 1917); Robert L. Morlan, *The Nonpartisan League* (Minneapolis, 1955); Theodore Saloutos and John D. Hicks, *Agricultural Discontent in the Middle West, 1900-1939* (Madison, Wisconsin, 1951); Roy Glashan, *American Governors and Gubernatorial Elections, 1775-1975* (Stillwater, Minnesota, 1975).

FRAZIER, Lynn Joseph, 1917-1921

Born in Steele County, Minnesota, on December 21, 1874, son of Thomas and Lois (Nile) Frazier; a Congregationalist. Married to Lottie J. Stafford on November 26, 1903; father of five children, Unie Mae, Versie Fae, Vernon, Willis and Lucille Frazier; widowed in 1935; remarried to Cathrine (Behrens) Paulson on September 7, 1937. Attended public school in Pembine County, North Dakota; Mayville State Normal School, 1891-1895; University of North Dakota, 1898-1901. Farmer. Member, Nonpartisan League, 1915. Frazier was nominated for Governor in 1916 by the Nonpartisan League, and after winning the primary in June of that year, he became the Republican candidate. He collected 87,665 votes to defeat D.H. McArthur, the Democratic nominee, who collected 20,351 votes. His first administration began on January 3, 1917, and was marked by the adoption of laws providing for the initiative and the referendum. Other legislation passed during Frazier's first term gave the vote to women; guaranteed bank deposits; reformed the state's land registration code; created a new grain grading scale; and relieved the tax burden on farmers by increasing taxes on commercial enterprises. In 1918 a special meeting of the legislature passed laws allowing counties to issue bonds in order to loan money to farmers to purchase seed grain. Frazier was easily reelected in 1918 over Democrat S.J. Doyle, 54,517 votes to 36,733. He continued to support progressive measures during his second term in office. With his urging the legislature established a State Industrial Commission to regulate corporations, and founded a State Bank, in which all state, county, township, municipal and school district funds had to be deposited. Two million dollars in state funds were appropriated for this purpose. Finally, the state-owned North Dakota Mill and Elevator Association was created, and state income and inheritance taxes were levied. Frazier was elected to a third term in 1920 over J.F.T. O'Connor, 117,018 to 107,332 votes. However, opposition to Frazier's progressive measures, particularly the state bank, resulted in a recall election in October 1921. In this election Frazier was defeated by Independent Republican Ragnvald Nestos, who collected 111,434 votes to Frazier's 107,332. After leaving the governor's office on November 23, 1921, Frazier ran for the United States Senate and won in 1922. He was reelected in 1928 and 1934. After retiring from politics, Frazier returned to farming. He died on January 11, 1947. Bibliography: Clement A. Lounsberry, *North Dakota History and People: Outlines of American History,* 3 vols. (Chicago, 1917); Robert L. Morlan, *The Nonpartisan League* (Minneapolis, 1955); Theodore Saloutos and John D. Hicks, *Agricultural Discontent in the Middle West, 1900-1939* (Madison, Wisconsin, 1951); Roy Glashan, *American Governors and Gubernatorial Elections, 1775-1975* (Stillwater, Minnesota, 1975).

NESTOS, Ragnvald Anderson, 1921-1925

Born on April 12, 1877 in Voss, Norway, son of Andres R. and Herborg (Saue) Nestos; a Lutheran. Brother of Dr. P.A. Nestos, Mrs. Jalmer Thorson, and seven others. Never married. Came to the United States at the age of sixteen and lived with his aunt and uncle in Buxton, North Dakota. Attended county school, and graduated from the Mayville Normal School, Mayville, North Dakota, 1900. Graduated Ph.B., University of Wisconsin, 1902; LL.B., University of North Dakota, 1904. Became a member of the law firm of Johnson and Nestos in Monit, North Dakota, 1904, and later became a partner in Nestos and Herigstad. Elected to the North Dakota House of Representatives, 1911-1912,; served as State's Attorney for Ward County, North Dakota, 1913-1916; unsuccessful candidate for the United States Senate, 1916. A Republican. On October 28, 1921 in a special recall election Ragnvald Anderson Nestos, of the Republican and Independent Voters Association, defeated Republican and Non-Partisan League candidate Lynn J. Frazier, by a vote of 111,434 to 107,332. Reelected on November 7, 1922 defeating William Lemke, a Non-Partisan League candidate by a vote of 110,321 to 81,048. During his administration changes were made in the State Banking Administration; North Dakota was admitted to the national registration area for birth and deaths; and a State Health Officer was appointed. However Nestos was left with the task of administering programs of the Non-Partisan League and was unable to pass any constructive acts during his term. He was defeated for renomination in 1924. Governor Nestos left office at the end of his term on January 5, 1925. He returned to his law practice in

Minot. He was a delegate to the Republican National Convention, 1932; was active in the Y.M.C.A.; served on the Board of Directors for the Boys Scouts of America; served on the National Board of Education of the Norwegian Lutheran Church; and served on the National Advisory Committee on illiteracy for five years. Governor Nestos died on July 15, 1942 in Minot, North Dakota. Bibliography: Clement A. Lounsberry, *Early History of North Dakota* (New York, 1919); *Minot Daily News* (July 15, 1942); Congressional Quarterly, Inc., *Guide to U.S. Elections* (Washington, D.C., 1975); Roy Glashan, *American Governors and Gubernatorial Elections, 1775-1975* (Stillwater, Minnesota, 1975).

SORLIE, Arthur Gustav, 1925-1928

Born in Albert Lea, Minnesota, on April 26, 1874, son of Iver Sorlie, a farmer, and his wife Mary Sorlie; a Lutheran. Married to Jennie Odegard on September 1, 1900; father of Arthur, Gladys and Ruth; after his wife's death in 1917, remarried to Grace Hilleboe on March 24, 1919; father of Alton, Evelyn and Charlotte. Attended the Albert Lea Lutheran Academy for three years, and in 1894 moved to Buxton, North Dakota. Worked as a bank clerk and general store manager, before becoming a traveling shoe salesman for four years. From 1903 until 1907, Sorlie operated a cracker factory. He organized several businesses, his interests ranging from feed stores to gas stations and car dealerships. He also served as vice-president of the Douglas State Bank, and served two terms on the Grand Forks City Council. In 1924 Sorlie received the gubernatorial nomination of the Non-Partisan League, and defeated the incumbent, Ragnvald Nestos, in the Republican primary. He went on to defeat Democrat Halvor L. Halvorson, 101,170 to 86,414 in the general election. He was reelected in 1926, defeating Democrat D.M. Holmes 131,003 to 24,287. Governor Sorlie sought to apply his business acumen to solve the problems of state government. He clashed with the legislature over the management of the state-owned mill and elevator, with the legislature calling for an investigation of his management in 1928. He continually sought to help the farmers of the state in their drive for fair prices for goods. Sorlie caused an uproar in 1925, by appointing Gerald P. Nye to fill the vacancy in the United States Senate left by the death of E.F. Ladd. Sorlie chose not to seek reelection in 1928, preferring to return to private life. In August of 1928, shortly before the expiration of his term, he fell ill. Sorlie died on August 28, 1928, and was succeeded by Walter Maddock. Bibliography: Theodore Saloutos and John D. Hicks, *Agricultural Discontent in the Middle West, 1900-1939* (Madison, Wisconsin, 1951); Roy Glashan, *American Governors and Gubernatorial Elections, 1775-1975* (Stillwater, Minnesota, 1975); Elwyn B. Robinson, *History of North Dakota* (Lincoln, Nebraska, 1966); Robert L. Morlan, *The Non-Partisan League* (Minneapolis, 1955).

MADDOCK, Walter Jeremiah, 1928-1929

Born in Grand Forks, North Dakota, on September 13, 1880, son of Patrick Maddock, a farmer, and Ellen Maddock; a Roman Catholic. Married to Marguerite Tierney on October 30, 1906; father of Wallace, Miles, Dore, Raymond, Bernard and Marguerite. He attended Northwestern Business College in Grand Forks, after which he farmed at Northwood, Berthold and Plaza, where he settled. Maddock was one of the organizers of the Non-Partisan League in North Dakota. In 1914 he was elected to the North Dakota House of Representatives. He was reelected to that office until 1924, when he was elected Lieutenant-Governor. After the death of Governor Arthur G. Sorlie in August of 1928, Maddock succeeded to the governor's office. He served the remainder of Sorlie's term and was a strong advocate of the Non-Partisan League's state-owned enterprises. He ran for reelection in 1928 after switching to the Democratic Party, but was defeated by Republican George F. Shafer, 131,193 votes to 100,205. Maddock returned to farming and helped to organize several farmers' cooperatives. In 1933 he was appointed senior administrative officer of the regional Agricultural Adjustment Administration. He was named to head the North Dakota office of the Farm Security Administration in 1937, and served in that capacity until 1950, when he retired. Maddock died in Bismarck, North Dakota, on January 25, 1951. Bibliography: Theodore Saloutos and John D. Hicks, *Agricultural Discontent in the Middle West, 1900-1939* (Madison, Wisconsin, 1951); Roy Glashan, *American Governors and Gubernatorial Elections, 1775-1975* (Stillwater, Minnesota, 1975); Elwyn B. Robinson, *History of North Dakota* (Lincoln, Nebraska, 1966); Robert L. Morlan, *The Non-Partisan League* (Minneapolis, 1955).

SHAFER, George F., 1929-1933

Born in Mandan, North Dakota, on November 23, 1888, son of Charles E. and Eva Shafer. Married to Frances Kellogg on September 1, 1915; father of George, Richard, Charles and Virginia. Attended the University of North Dakota from 1908 until 1912. Admitted to the bar in 1912, and began his law practice in Schafer, North Dakota. Was State Attorney for McKenzie County from 1915 until 1919; was Assistant Attorney General of North Dakota, 1921-1922; was elected Attorney General of North Dakota in 1922, and served in that position until 1929. Running as an independent Republican in 1928, Shafer defeated incumbent Governor Walter Maddock by 131,193 votes to 100,205, and became Governor. He was reelected in 1930, defeating Democrat Pierce Blewett, 133,264 to 41,988. Shafer was familiar with many of the problems of state government due to his experience as Attorney General. The most serious problems which faced the state during his administration were the often severe droughts which afflicted the state, and the low prices which the state's farmers were forced to accept for their agricultural produce. Shafer did what he could to alleviate these conditions. The state-owned mill and elevator, for example, showed their best profits in years under Shafer's guidance. He gave the state a conservative administration of government with a strong emphasis on economy. In 1932 he challenged Gerald P. Nye for the Republican nomination for the United State Senate and was defeated. Shafer died of a heart attack in Bismarck, North Dakota on August 13, 1948. Bibliography: Roy Glashan, *American Governors and Gubernatorial Elections, 1775-1975* (Stillwater, Minnesota, 1975); Elwyn B. Robinson, *History of North Dakota* (Lincoln, Nebraska, 1966); Theodore Saloutos and John D. Hicks, *Agricultural Discontent in the Middle West, 1900-1939* (Madison, Wisconsin, 1951); Robert L. Morlan, *The Non-Partisan League* (Minneapolis, 1955).

LANGER, William, 1933-1934, 1937-1939

Born in Everest, Dakota Territory, on September 30, 1886, son of Frank Langer, a farmer, and Mary Langer. Married to Lydia Cady on February 26, 1918; father of Emma, Lydia, Mary and Cornelia. Studied law at the University of North Dakota and received his LL.B. in 1906; attended Columbia University, receiving his A.B. in 1910. In 1911 he began to practice law in Mandan, North Dakota, and served as State's Attorney for Morton County from 1914-1916. With the support of the Non-Partisan League, Langer was elected Attorney General of the state in 1916, serving two terms. In 1920 he made an unsuccessful bid for the governor's office. After this defeat, he held no elective office until 1932, when with the support of the Non-Partisan League, he won the Republican nomination and defeated Democrat Herbert Depuy, 134,231 votes to 110,263. Governor Langer acted energetically to help the state's farmers combat the depression, at times declaring embargoes on wheat and moratoriums on foreclosures. He was removed from office in July of 1934 after being accused of soliciting funds from state and federal employees. He later cleared himself of the charges, and ran again in 1936 as an Independent. In that year, Langer defeated the incumbent governor, Walter Welford, and Democrat John Moses, by polling 98,750 votes, compared to the 95,697 and the 80,726 respectively tallied by his opponents. He continued to defend the interests of farmers in his second term. In 1938 Langer ran as an Independent for the United States Senate, but lost to Gerald Nye. In 1940 Langer won the Republican nomination for the United States Senate and went on to win in the general election. He was reelected to his post in 1946, 1952 and 1958. Senator Langer was noted for his many dissenting views. William Langer died of a heart ailment in Washington, D.C., on November 8, 1959. Bibliography: John M. Holzworth, *The Fighting Governor*; Elwyn B. Robinson, *History of North Dakota* (Lincoln, Nebraska, 1966); Robert L. Morlan, *The Non-Partisan League* (Minneapolis, 1955); Roy Glashan, *American Governors and Gubernatorial Elections, 1775-1975* (Stillwater, Minnesota, 1975). Papers of William Langer are on deposit in the Orin G. Libby Collection in the University of North Dakota Library.

OLSON, Ole H., 1934-1935

Born on September 19, 1872, in Mondoir, Buffalo County, Wisconsin, son of Hans, a farmer, and Inga Olson; a Lutheran. Brother of Olaus, Robert Albert, Anton and Ida. Married to Julia Ramberget on December 17, 1912; father of Clifford, Raymond, Rolf, Mrs. William Martin, Mrs. Larrel Nelson, Mrs. Jack McDowell, Mrs. Duane Birkeland, Venoie, Orin E. and one other. Graduated from Concordia College, Moorhead, Minnesota. Olson moved to North Dakota in 1892 and homesteaded in Eddy County, North Dakota, in 1895. Elected in 1916 to the North Dakota House of Representatives and served until 1918, when he was elected to the North Dakota Senate, where he held a seat until 1930; served as President Pro Tempore of the Senate in 1929. Lieutenant Governor of North Dakota, 1932-1934. A Republican. Ole H. Olson became Governor of North Dakota on July 19, 1934, upon the removal of Governor William Langer. Olson's brief term was one of the most turbulent periods in the political history of North Dakota, as demonstrators marched through the state capitol and the National Guard was called to duty. Governor Olson left office on January 7, 1935. Ole Olson was active in the Farmer's Union and as a member of the Farmers' Union Livestock Commission; he was also President of the Greenfield Mutual Fire and Lightning Insurance Company, New Rockford, North Dakota. He did not seek public office after serving as governor, and returned to his farming and business interests. Olson died on January 29, 1954, in New Rockford, North Dakota. Bibliography: Roy Glashan, *American Governors and Gubernatorial Elections, 1775-1975* (Stillwater, Minnesota, 1975); Congressional Quarterly Inc., *Guide to United States Elections* (Washington, D.C., 1975); North Dakota State Library "Vertical File," Olson, Ole H.

MOODIE, Thomas Henry, 1935

Born on May 26, 1878, in Winona, Minnesota, son of Scottish parents. Married to Julia Edith McMurray in 1908. Received a limited education, leaving school at the age of sixteen. Moved with his mother to Wadena, Minnesota, and began working for the Wadena *Pioneer* in the printing department; worked as a reporter; also worked for a short time as a brakeman on the Northern Pacific Railroad. Returned to the newspaper business as a printer and later was cub reporter for the Bismarck *Tribune*. Became a journeyman printer, reporter and editor of numerous newspapers throughout North Dakota; owner of a weekly newspaper in Wahpeton, North Dakota; Editor of the Bismarck *Tribune,* 1923-1924; owner of a weekly newspaper in Mohall, North Dakota, 1924-1930; editorial writer, Minneapolis *Tribune*, Minneapolis, Minnesota, 1930-1932; Editor of the Williston, North Dakota, *Herald*; appointed by President Franklin D. Roosevelt to a committee dealing with federal grants for public buildings, 1933. A Democrat. Thomas H. Moodie received the Democratic nomination for governor of North Dakota, and in the general election of November 6, 1934, he defeated Republican Lydia Langer, 145,333 votes to 127,954. He took office on January 7, 1935. Even before Moodie took office there was some mention of impeachment, although no charges were brought forward at that time. His opponents eventually learned that Governor Moodie had voted in a municipal election in Minneapolis in 1932. In order to be eligible for the governorship of North Dakota, an individual had to have been a citizen of the state for five consecutive years before the election; consequently, the State Supreme Court determined that Governor Moodie was ineligible to serve. He was taken out of office on February 16, 1936. After his brief term as governor, Moodie acted as administrator for the North Dakota Federal Housing Administration. He also worked as deputy administrator for the State War Finance Committee in Montana. Governor Moodie finished his years as financial editor and confidential agent for the publisher of the Spokane *Chronicle*. Governor Moodie died on March 3, 1948, in Spokane, Washington. He was cremated. Bibliography: Roy Glashan, *American Governors and Gubernatorial Elections, 1775-1975* (Stillwater, Minnesota, 1975); Congressional Quarterly Inc., *Guide to United States Elections* (Washington, D.C., 1975); North Dakota State Library, "Verticle File," Moodie, Thomas H.

WELFORD, Walter, 1935-1937

Born in England on May 21, 1869, son of Thomas and Jane Welford; an Episcopalian. Married to Edith Bachmann on June 27, 1900. Brought to the United States in 1879 and attended public school in North Dakota. Township clerk in Pembina, North Dakota from 1900 until 1920; elected to the North Dakota House of Representatives in 1906 and served in that post for two terms, being reelected in 1908; elected in 1916 and reelected in 1918 to the North Dakota State Senate. Welford entered state politics in the era of progressive reform, and continued in the State Senate in the early years of the Non-Partisan League, of which he was a supporter. In 1934 Welford was elected Lieutenant Governor of North Dakota. When Governor Thomas Moodie was removed from office on February 2, 1935, Welford succeeded to the office of the chief executive. During Welford's tenure as governor, the state suffered severely from the Great Depression. A sales tax was passed to provide funds for support of the unemployed and to maintain the public schools. In 1936 agricultural production was drastically lower than in the previous year, partly because of a severe drought in the state that summer. Welford discussed the situation with President Roosevelt, and succeeded in getting federal assistance for drought-stricken farmers. In the campaign of 1936 Welford contended with former Governor William Langer for the Republican nomination, and won by a small majority. In the general election however, Langer, running as an Independent, defeated Welford in a close three-way election. Welford died on June 28, 1952. Bibliography: Roy L. Miller, "The Gubernatorial Controversy in North Dakota," *American Political Science Review,* XXIX (June, 1935); Elwyn B. Robinson, *History of North Dakota* (Lincoln, Nebraska, 1966); Roy Glashan, *American Governors and Gubernatorial Elections, 1775-1975* (Stillwater, Minnesota, 1975); John Holzworth, *The Fighting Governor.*

LANGER, William, 1933-1934, 1937-1939

MOSES, John, 1939-1945

Born in Strand, Norway, on June 12, 1885, the son of Henrik and Isabelle Moses; a Lutheran. Married to Ethel Joslyn on June 29, 1918; father of John, James, Mary and Robert. Attended high school and junior college in Norway, coming to the United States in 1905. From 1906 until 1911, worked for the Great Northern Railway. In 1912 he entered the University of North Dakota, receiving his A.B. in 1914 and his J.D. in 1915. Admitted to the North Dakota Bar in 1915, and in 1917 moved to Hazen to practice law. A Democrat. Served as State's Attorney for Mercer County from 1919 until 1923, and again from 1927 until 1933. In 1934 he ran for the office of Attorney General of North Dakota and lost. In 1936 he came in third behind William Langer and Walter Welford in the gubernatorial race. However, he ran again in 1938 and succeeded, defeating Republican John Hagan, 138,270 votes to 125,246. He was reelected in 1940, beating Republican Jack Patterson 173,278 to 101,287, and in 1942, defeating Republican Oscar Hagen,

101,390 to 74,577. Governor Moses sought to reduce the influence of former Governor Langer. He worked to expose and correct irregularities in the state government; to cut governmental expenditures; and to balance the state's budget. He also sought to help his state by encouraging war-time industries to locate in North Dakota. In 1944 he ran for the United States Senate and won, defeating Gerald P. Nye for the post. John Moses died on March 3, 1945, shortly after he took his seat in the United States Senate. Bibliography: Elwyn B. Robinson, *History of North Dakota* (Lincoln, Nebraska, 1966); Roy Glashan, *American Governors and Gubernatorial Elections, 1775-1975* (Stillwater, Minnesota, 1975); Adam Schweitzer, "The Political Campaign of John Moses," *North Dakota History,* XXXII (January, 1965). Papers of John Moses are on deposit in the Orin L. Libby Collection in the University of North Dakota Library.

AANDAHL, Fred George, 1945-1951

Born in Litchville, North Dakota, on April 9, 1897, son of Sam Aandahl, who became State Railroad Commissioner in 1916, and Mamie Aandahl; a Lutheran. Married to Luella Brekke on June 28, 1926; father of Mamie, Margaret and Marilyn. Attended the University of North Dakota and graduated in 1921. He began farming in Litchville and in 1922 became Superintendent of Litchville High School, where he remained until 1927. He returned to farming in 1927 and served in the State Senate of North Dakota during the sessions of 1931, 1939 and 1941, where he was concerned primarily with school and tax legislation. Aandahl was elected Governor in 1944 with the support of the conservative Republican Organizing Committee, defeating Democrat William Depuy and Independent Republican Alvin Strutz, 107,863 votes to 59,961 and 38,997, respectively. He was reelected in 1946, defeating Democrat Quentin Burdick, 116,672 to 52,719, and won his third term in 1948, defeating Democrat Howard Henry, 131,764 to 80,655. As governor, Aandahl was concerned about the natural resources of the state and fought for the rights of the state to control its own conservation programs. He was a chairman of the North Dakota Water Conservation Commission and served on a voluntary committee which sought to coordinate the activities of federal and state land and water resources programs in the Missouri Basin. Aandahl was elected to the United States House of Representatives in 1950, where he served one term. In the 1952 Republican primary, he opposed William Langer for Langer's seat in the United States Senate and lost. Aandahl's experience and interest in natural resources led to his appointment by President Eisenhower in 1953 to the post of Assistant Secretary of the Interior for Water and Power Development. He held that position until 1960. Aandahl died on April 7, 1966. Bibliography: Roy Glashan, *American Governors and Gubernatorial Elections, 1775-1975* (Stillwater, Minnesota, 1975); Elwyn B. Robinson, *History of North Dakota* (Lincoln, Nebraska, 1966); Fred McGhee, ed., *Facts on File Five Year Index 1946-1950* (New York, 1958); Congressional Quarterly Inc., *Guide to United States Elections* (Washington, D.C., 1975). Papers of Fred George Aandahl are on deposit in the Orin G. Libby Collection at the University of North Dakota.

BRUNSDALE, Clarence Norman, 1951-1957

Born in Sherbrooke, North Dakota, on July 9, 1891, son of Knute, farmer and banker, and Anna Brunsdale; a Lutheran. Married to Carrie Lajord on August 30, 1924; father of Margaret and Helen. Attended Luther College in Decorah, Iowa, receiving his B.A. in 1913. He managed the Brunsdale farms from 1914 until 1939, in addition to teaching business in Portland in 1913 and 1914. He was director and vice president of the Goose River Bank in Mayville, North Dakota, from 1918 until 1950, in addition to being director of the First and Farmers' Bank in Portland, North Dakota. He served as the State Senator from the Eighth District in 1927-1935 and 1940-1951. He was President Pro Tempore of the State Senate in 1943; Majority Floor Leader in 1945, 1947 and 1949; and Chairman of the Republican Organizing Committee in 1946. He also served as a National Republican Committeeman from North Dakota between 1948 and 1952. In 1950 he was elected Governor, defeating Democrat Clyde Byerly, 121,822 to 61,950. He was reelected twice, in 1952 beating Democrat Ole Johnson, 199,944 to 53,990, and in 1954 defeating Democrat Cornelius Bymers, 124,253 to 69,248. Governor Brunsdale brought about efficient management of North Dakota's state-owned enterprises. He sought to attract new industries to the state, and worked with the federal government and other governors on the problem of effective water development in his region. Brunsdale also guided the state through the problems caused by the growth of the oil industry in North Dakota. In 1959 Brunsdale was appointed to fill the seat in the United States Senate which had been left vacant by the death of Senator William Langer, and served in that capacity from November of 1959 until August of 1960. He returned to farming until his retirement in 1968. Bibliography: Roy Glashan, *American Governors and Gubernatorial Elections, 1775-1975* (Stillwater, Minnesota, 1975); Elwyn B. Robinson, *History of North Dakota* (Lincoln, Nebraska, 1966); Fred McGhee, ed., *Facts on File Five-Year Index, 1951-1955* (New York, 1957); Congressional Quarterly Inc., *Guide to United States Elections* (Washington, D.C., 1975).

DAVIS, John Edward, 1957-1961

Born on April 18, 1913 in Minneapolis, Minnesota, son of James Davis, a banker and rancher, and Helen Davis; a Lutheran. Married to Pauline Huntley on June 4, 1938; father of John, Richard and Kathleen. Attended the University of North Dakota and graduated in 1935. Became vice president of the First National Bank of McClusky, North Dakota, in 1935, and managed the family ranch interests. Entered the United States Army in 1941; served in Europe and was released as a Lieutenant Colonel in 1945. Returned to McClusky, where he resumed his banking activities and where in 1946 he was elected Mayor, a position he held until 1952. In that year he was elected Republican State Senator, and was reelected in 1954. In 1956 he was elected Governor, defeating Democrat Wallace E. Warner, 147,566 to 104,869. He was reelected in 1958, defeating Democrat John Lord, 111,836 to 98,763. During his period as governor, Davis promoted the development of industry in the state, supporting the work of the North Dakota Economic Development Corporation. He also encouraged legislation for new and better highways and better health and welfare laws. In 1960 Davis ran for the United States Senate seat left vacant by the death of William Langer, but was defeated by Democrat Quentin Burdick in a close election. In 1961 Davis was the Chairman of the North Dakota Republican National Committee, and in 1969 became Director of Civil Defense in the Office of the Secretary of the Army. He became Director of the Defense Civil Preparedness Agency of the Department of Defense in 1972. Bibliography: Roy Glashan, *American Governors and Gubernatorial Elections, 1775-1975* (Stillwater, Minnesota, 1975); Elwyn B. Robinson, *History of North Dakota* (Lincoln, Nebraska, 1966); Lester A. Sobel, ed., *Facts on File Five Year Index 1956-1960* (New York, 1961); Congressional Quarterly Inc., *Guide to United States Elections* (Washington, D.C., 1975).

GUY, William Lewis, 1961-1973

Born in Devil's Lake, North Dakota, on September 30, 1919, the son of William and Mable Guy; a Presbyterian. Married to Jean Mason on January 30, 1943; father of William, James, Deborah, Holly and Nancy. Attended North Dakota State University, where he received his B.S. degree in 1941; from 1942 to 1945 he served in the United States Navy. In 1946 he received his M.A. from the University of Minnesota. Guy became Assistant County Agent for Cass County, North Dakota, in 1947. He was the proprietor of the Guy-Bean Farm Store in West Fargo, North Dakota, from 1947-1950. From 1952 until 1958, Guy was an instructor of agricultural economics at North Dakota State University. He served in the North Dakota House of Representatives from 1959 until 1961, where he was also Assistant Minority Leader. In 1960 Guy, a Democrat, broke a sixteen-year period of Republican rule in the state by being elected Governor, defeating Republican C.P. Dahl, 136,148 to 122,486. Guy served in the office of governor until 1973, and was reelected in 1962, when he defeated Republican Mark Andrews, 115,258 votes to 113,251. In 1964, Guy won a four-year term by defeating Republican Don Halerow, 146,414 votes to 116,247; in 1968, Guy was reelected, defeating Republican Robert P. McCarney, 135,955 votes to 108,382. As governor, he disagreed with the legislature often on the subject of taxation, calling a special session in 1965, for example, to renew the state's sales tax law. He tightened the state's control over the state mill and elevator. In 1967 he was sent to observe the South Vietnamese elections at the invitation of President Johnson, and in 1968 he served on the "Humphrey For President" Committee. He was chairman of the National Governors' Conference in 1967 and 1968, and chairman of the Council of State Governments in 1967. He declined to seek reelection in 1972. After leaving office Guy became an instructor in political science at Concordia College. In 1975 he became Staff Director of the Western Governors' Regional Energy Policy Office in Denver. Bibliography: Roy Glashan, *American Governors and Gubernatorial Elections, 1775-1975* (Stillwater, Minnesota, 1975); Elwyn B. Robinson, *History of North Dakota* (Lincoln, Nebraska, 1966); Facts on File, *Facts on File Five Year Index 1961-1965* (New York, 1966); Congressional Quarterly, Inc., *Guide to United States Elections* (Washington, D.C., 1975). Papers of Guy are on deposit in the Orin G. Libby Collection at the University of North Dakota.

LINK, Arthur A., 1973-

Born on May 24, 1914 in Alexander, North Dakota, son of homesteader parents; a Lutheran. Married to the former Grace Johnson; father of five sons and one daughter. Raised on a farm in McKenzie County. Educated in the public schools, later attending the North Dakota Agricultural College. In 1946 he was elected to the North Dakota House of Representatives, and was reelected consistently, serving in that capacity until 1970. He was Minority Floor Leader in the House for fourteen years, and Speaker of the House in the 1965 session. In 1970 Link was elected to the United States House of Representatives. He served one term there, and in 1972 ran for Governor. He defeated Republican Richard Larsen, 143,899 votes to 138,032. In 1976, Link was reelected, defeating Republican Richard Elkin by a vote of 125,261 to 112,302. During his administration the state's agricultural community prospered. Farmers were planting more and receiving high prices for their goods. The energy crisis significantly affected North Dakota, when the state's great mineral wealth became the subject of controversy between those who wished to exploit that wealth and those who were more concerned with environmental considerations. The legislature under Link passed laws which reformed income and property taxes, and there was also turmoil in the legislature about reapportionment of legislative districts. Link vetoed the reapportionment bill passed by the legislature, and the voters of the state also repudiated the legislature's solution in a referendum. Eventually apportionment by single-seat districts became the law.
Bibliography: Roy Glashan, *American Governors and Gubernatorial Elections, 1775-1975* (Stillwater, Minnesota, 1975); Henry H. Schulte, Jr., ed., *Facts on File Yearbook 1973* (New York, 1974); Henry H. Schulte, Jr., ed., *Facts on File Yearbook 1974* (New York, 1975); Congressional Quarterly Inc., *Guide to United States Elections* (Washington, D.C., 1975).

OHIO

OHIO

Born on June 19, 1761, in Carlisle, England; one of four children of Henry and Mary (Parker) Tiffin, both Episcopalians; himself a Methodist. Married Mary Worthington in 1789, who died childless; remarried to Mary Porter on April 16, 1809; father of Mary Porter, Diathea Madison, Eleanor Worthington, Rebecca Turner and Edward Porter. Studied medicine in England; emigrated with his family to Virginia, where he attended Jefferson Medical College in Pennsylvania from 1784 to 1786; practiced in Charles Town. Ordained in 1792 as a lay preacher in the Methodist Episcopal Church and served in that capacity throughout his life. Migrated to Chillicothe, Ohio, in 1798. Appointed Prothonotary of the Territorial Court of Common Pleas in 1798. Served as Speaker of the Territorial Legislature in 1799 and 1801. As leader of the "Chillicothe Junto," opposed Territorial Governor St. Clair, pushed for immediate statehood, and thwarted efforts of the Federalists. He served as President of Ohio's Constitutional Convention, and was nominated for Governor by the Democratic-Republican Convention in 1802 and again in 1805. He received 4,564 or 100 % of the votes cast on January 11, 1803, and 4,783 or 100 % of the votes cast on October 8, 1805. Tiffin's first concern as governor was to appoint his fellow Democratic-Republicans to state offices. In reaction to Governor St. Clair's autocratic rule, the first Ohio Constitution severely limited the authority of the governor, but Tiffin as head of his party and the "Junto" wielded a great deal of power. He was a strong advocate of free navigation of the Mississippi River, and an opponent of slavery. He is best remembered for preventing the Burr Conspiracy. Tiffin resigned as governor to become a United States Senator on March 4, 1807. When his wife died in July 1808 Tiffin resigned and returned to private life on his farm. In 1809 Tiffin was elected to the state's General Assembly and again became Speaker until 1811. He was appointed Commissioner of the newly created land office in 1812, and when the British invaded Washington, D.C., he was able to save his land books from being destroyed. Late in 1814, he exchanged offices with Josiah Meigs, Surveyor General for the Northwest, in order to reside at his home. He continued in this position until a few weeks prior to his death. He died on August 9, 1829, and was buried in Grandview Cemetery at Chillicothe. Bibliography: Colonel William Edward Gilmore, *Life of Edward Tiffin, First Governor of Ohio* (Chillicothe, Ohio, 1897); C.G. Conegys, *Reminiscence of Edward Tiffin* (1869); Randolph C. Downes, *Frontier Ohio: 1788-1803* (Columbus, 1935); "Ohio and the English Common Law," *Mississippi Valley Historical Review* (December, 1929); Tiffin MSS in Ohio State Library, Cleveland.

KIRKER, Thomas, 1807-1808

Born in Tyrone County, Ireland, in 1760, son of a poor farmer who emigrated with his large family to Lancaster, Pennsylvania; a Presbyterian. Married to Sarah Smith in 1790; father of five sons and a daughter who later married Ralph M. Voorheese. Moved first to Kentucky, then to Manchester, Ohio, around 1793. Settled permanently on a farm in Liberty Township, Adams County, in 1795. From 1808 until his death, he was a ruling elder in the Presbyterian church at West Union; developed a reputation as a local arbitrator; appointed by Governor St. Clair as Justice of the Peace and member of the first Court of Quarter Sessions in 1797. Served as delegate from Adams County to the first constitutional convention. Elected to State House in 1803. Elected to State Senate in the fall of 1803 and served in eleven consecutive general assemblies from 1804-1815. When Edward Tiffin resigned the governorship in March 1807, Kirker became Governor. Kirker expected to serve as governor for only nine months. However, Return J. Meigs, Jr., who had won the election of October 1807, was disqualified and Kirker's friends successfully kept him in the governorship until December 1808. As governor, Kirker called for the militia to protect the settlers from Indians in the western part of the state. He sent Thomas Worthington and Duncan McArthur to investigate, and when they and an Indian chief assured him that there was no danger, he recalled the militia. At the same time, the suit of M'Faddan vs. Rutherford established the state judiciary's power to turn aside unconstitutional laws of the legislature, an act which became the major issue in the campaign of 1808. Kirker and Thomas Worthington opposed a strong court and supported the preemption powers of the legislature. Samuel Huntington, also a Democratic-Republican, supported the courts. When the results were in, Huntington had 7,293 votes, Worthington had 5,601, and Kirker had 3,397. After this defeat, Kirker was reelected to the State House of Representatives in 1816. He served as an Associate Judge of the Court of Common Pleas in Adams County from January to October 1821, when he was elected to the State Senate. In 1824 he served as a Presidential Elector, voting for Henry Clay. He retired to his farm in 1825 and remained there until his death on February 20, 1837. He was buried in the family plot on his farm. Bibliography: S. Winfred Smith, "Thomas Kirker, 1807-1808," *The Governors of Ohio* (Columbus, 1969); W.J. Utter, "Judicial Review in Early Ohio," *Mississippi Valley Historical Review* (June, 1927); Anna McAllister, *In Winter We Flourished* (New York); Harry R. Stevens, *The Early Jackson Party in Ohio* (Durham, North Carolina, 1957).

HUNTINGTON, Samuel, 1808-1810

Born on October 4, 1765, in Coventry, Connecticut, son of Joseph Huntington, a distinguished minister, and Hannah (Devotion) Huntington; adopted by his uncle, Samuel Huntington, a signer of the Declaration of Independence and Governor of Connecticut. Married to Hannah Huntington, a distant cousin, on December 20, 1791; father of Julius C. and Robert. Attended Dartmouth College for three years, attended and graduated from Yale in 1785. Studied law and admitted to the Connecticut Bar in 1793. Moved to Cleveland, Ohio, in 1801. Appointed Lieutenant Colonel of the Trumbull County militia in 1801. Elected one of the supervisors of roads and appointed Justice of the Peace and Gains Priority on the Court of Quarter Sessions in 1802. Supported statehood and elected as delegate to the 1802 Ohio Constitutional Convention. In 1803 he was elected to the first General Assembly and was chosen Speaker, but resigned when the General Assembly selected him as Judge of the State Supreme Court. In 1804 he became Chief Justice and upheld the doctrine of judicial review of acts of legislation. Chosen to represent the conservative wing of the Democratic-Republican Party in the gubernatorial election of 1808, he polled 7,293 votes to Thomas Worthington's 5,601 and Thomas Kirker's 3,397. Although all three men were Democratic-Republicans, Kirker and Worthington both opposed judicial review, and thereby split the liberal vote; Huntington meanwhile, enjoyed the support of the Federalists. During Huntington's term as governor, the two other judges who had supported judicial review were impeached and saved from removal by a single vote. Huntington failed to forestall a law terminating the terms of judges holding seven-year terms. When war with Great Britain approached, the state capitol was moved to Zanesville, and there was much agitation over its permanent location. During Huntington's administration, Ohio's "blue laws" were passed. Governor Huntington chose to run for the United States Senate instead of seeking reelection, but was defeated by Thomas Worthington. At the close of his gubernatorial term, he retired to private life on his estate near Painesville, which he had purchased in 1807. Here he, with two others, founded the village of Fairport and built the first warehouse in Lake Coventry. He was a member of the Ohio House of Representatives in 1811-1812. In 1813 Governor William Henry Harrison appointed him District Paymaster in the regular army. He died on June 8, 1817, of injuries received while supervising repairs on the road from his estate to the Fairport harbor. Bibliography: *Western Reserve Historical Society Tracts*, no. 95 (1915); *The Huntington Family in America* (1915); W. T. Utter, "Judicial Review in Early Ohio," *Mississippi Valley Historical Review* (June, 1927); J. H. Kennedy, *A History of the City of Cleveland* (1896).

MEIGS, Return J., 1810-1814

Born November 17, 1764, in Middletown, Connecticut, son of Return Jonathan, a Revolutionary War hero and surveyor for the Ohio Company of Associates, and Joanna (Winborn) Meigs. Brother of John. Married to Sophia Wright in 1788; father of Mary (Meigs) Jackson. Attended Yale College and graduated in 1785. Studied law and was admitted to the Connecticut Bar. Moved to Marietta, Ohio, where he practiced law, kept a store, and engaged in farming. Appointed Court Clerk in 1788, made first Postmaster of Marietta in 1794, and in 1798 appointed a Judge of the Territorial Court. Elected to the Territorial Legislature in 1799, and in 1803 appointed Chief Justice of the newly-organized State Supreme Court, but resigned in that same year to accept an appointment as Commandant of the United States troops in the St. Charles District of Louisiana. He attained the rank of Brevet Colonel and retained his command until 1806. In 1805 he was chosen as Judge of the Supreme Court of Louisiana. In 1807 he was appointed Judge of the United States District Court for the Territory of Michigan, but resigned when asked to run for Governor of Ohio by an informal legislative caucus of Democratic-Republicans. He defeated Nathaniel Massie, also a Democratic-Republican, 5,550 votes to 4,757, but the legislature declared him ineligible to serve because of his absence from the state. The same legislature appointed him to the United States Senate to complete the term of John Smith, who had resigned. He was reelected to the Senate, but resigned on May 1, 1810, in order to run again for Governor. In the election of October 9, 1810, he defeated Thomas Worthington, also a Democratic-Republican, by a vote of 9,924 to 7,731. His cautious policies attracted the support of conservatives and Federalists, with whose backing he was reelected in 1812. He received 11,859 votes to the 7,903 of his Democratic-Republican opponent, Thomas Scott. During Meigs' first term, the capital was permanently located at Columbus. The legislature selected a commission to plan a State House and, at Meigs' insistence, a state penitentiary. Meigs recruited 1,200 state militia during the War of 1812, in time for Hull's rendezvous at Dayton. In recognition of his war service, President Madison appointed him Postmaster General in 1814. He resigned as governor of Ohio shortly before the term expired. He then served as Postmaster General until 1823, when forced to retire because of ill health. He died on March 29, 1825, in Marietta, Ohio, and was buried in Mound Cemetery. Bibliography: The Meigs' Papers are on deposit in the Library of Congress and in the Ohio State Library at Columbus; H.B. Meigs, *Record of the Descendants of Vincent Meigs* (1901); *American State Papers: Post Office Department* (1834).

LOOKER, Othneil, 1814

Born on October 4, 1757, on Long Island, New York (or possibly Hanover, Morris County, New Jersey), son of John Looker, who died in 1759, and his wife, a school teacher; a Baptist. Married to Pamela Clark in 1779; father of nine children, including James Harvy Looker and Rachel Looker, who became the wife of Judge Joseph Kitchell. There is no record of his having been educated by anyone other than his mother. In 1776 he enlisted in the New Jersey militia and served as a private throughout the Revolutionary War. After the war, he learned the weaving trade, but chose to teach school instead for the next thirty years. He moved his family to Vermont in 1788, then to New York State. He was elected as representative to New York's Assembly in 1803 and 1804. He received a grant of land in 1804 for his war service, and moved his family to Hamilton County, Ohio. He was elected to the Ohio House of Representatives in 1804 and served until his election to the State Senate in 1810. He served in the Senate 1810-1812, and 1813-1817. He was Speaker of the Senate in the 1813-1814 session, and therefore, became Governor when Return J. Meigs, Jr. resigned to become Postmaster General on March 25, 1814. The position of Governor during this period in Ohio was not a powerful one, and Looker's nine-month administration was uneventful, except for his call in August 1814 for five hundred volunteers to join in an expedition under General Duncan McArthur against the Indians on lower Lake Michigan. He became a Democratic-Republican candidate for governor for the following term, but lacked the prestige of his opponent, Thomas Worthington, and was defeated. Looker carried only five counties and polled only 6,171 votes to the 15,879 cast for Worthington. In 1816 he served as a Presidential Elector from Ohio, voting for James Monroe and Daniel D. Tompkins. He remained in the State Senate until 1817 and then became an Associate Judge of the Court of Common Pleas in Hamilton County. He later retired to his farm until his wife's death, when he went to live first with his oldest son in Cincinnati, and then with his daughter in Palestine, Illinois, where he made his last public address on July 4, 1845. He died on July 23, 1845, and was buried in the Kitchell family plot. Bibliography: S. Winfred Smith, "Othneil Looker," *The Governors of Ohio* (Columbus, 1969); Harry R. Stevens, *The Early Jackson Party in Ohio* (Durham, North Carolina, 1957); William Cooper Howells, *Recollections of Life in Ohio, 1813-1840* (Cincinnati, 1895); Harlan Hatcher, *The Western Reserve* (Indianapolis, n.d.).

WORTHINGTON, Thomas, 1814-1818

Born near present Charles Town, West Virginia, on July 16, 1773, son of Robert, a prominent planter, and Margaret (Matthews); raised by his older brothers and William Drake, after being orphaned at the age of seven; a devout Methodist. Married to Eleanor Van Swearingen on December 13, 1796; father of ten children including Sarah Worthington King Peter. Completed only his preparatory studies. At the age of eighteen went to sea on a Scotch merchantman for two years. Studied surveying, and with Duncan McArthur purchased Virginia military land warrants. In 1798 brought his family and that of his brother-in-law Edward Tiffin, Ohio's first governor, to Chillicothe, Ohio. As a leader of the "Chillicothe Junto," he quickly attained prominence in Ohio politics. Member of the Territorial House of Representatives from 1799-1803; appointed Register of Public Lands at Chillicothe in 1800; member of Ohio's Constitutional Convention in 1802, representative to the General Assembly 1803, 1807-1808. Elected United States Senator, serving from 1803 to 1807; re-elected in 1810, he resigned in December 1814 to become Governor. Worthington, under the very informal caucus method of selecting candidates, ran for governor as a Democratic-Republican a total of four times. In 1808 he ran against two other Democratic-Republicans, Samuel Huntington, who was elected with 7,293 votes, and Thomas Kirker, who totalled 3,397. Worthington received 5,601. In 1810 he was defeated by Return Jonathan Meigs, Jr., also a Democratic-Republican, by 9,924 votes to 7,731. In 1814 he defeated Democratic-Republican Othneil Looker by a count of 6,171 for Looker against the 15,879 cast for Worthington. He was re-elected in 1816 with 22,931 votes against the 6,295 of his Democratic-Republican opponent, James Dunlap. The State Constitution prohibited him from seeking another term. As governor, Worthington encouraged a strong militia; advocated county poor farms; proposed state regulation of banks; favored a public elementary school system; urged penal reforms; encouraged home manufacturing and secured funding for the state library; and was instrumental in establishing a branch of the Bank of the United States at Chillicothe, a decision which adversely affected his later political career. After retiring from the governorship, he devoted himself to his numerous business enterprises, including farming, stock raising, milling and river shipping. Between 1821 and 1825, he served three terms in the State House of Representatives; he also served as Canal Commissioner from 1818 until his death. He died while on a business trip to New York City on June 20, 1827. He was buried on his estate, "Adena," but was later moved to Grandview Cemetery, Chillicothe. Bibliography: The Worthington Papers are on deposit in the State Library, Columbus, Ohio, and in the Library of Congress; also see Duncan McArthur Papers, Library of Congress; Alfred B. Sears, "Thomas Worthington, Pioneer Business Man in the Old Northwest," *Ohio State Archeological and Historical Quarterly* (1949); Sarah W. K. Peter, *Private Memoirs of Thomas Worthington* (1882); "Thomas Worthington," *Ohio Archeological and Historical Publications,* vol. XII (1903).

BROWN, Ethan Allen, 1818-1822

Born on July 4, 1776, in Darien, Connecticut, son of Roger Brown, prosperous land owner and Revolutionary patriot; youngest of seven children; never married. Studied classics under an Irish tutor; in 1797 entered the law office of Alexander Hamilton, and admitted to the New York Bar in 1802. The following year, he purchased a large tract of land in Rising Sun, Indiana, and in 1804 established a law practice in Cincinnati. Appointed in 1810 as a Judge of the Ohio Supreme Court. Chosen as the Democratic-Republican candidate by party caucus and elected Governor in 1818, defeating James Dunlap, 30,194 to 8,075. Sworn into office on December 14, 1818. As governor, Brown was almost immediately confronted with the depression of 1819. In the eyes of many westerners, the severe economic distress was caused by the United States Bank. This view appeared to be borne out when the bank announced that it would no longer accept state bank notes. The resulting scarcity of specie—gold and silver—spelled financial ruin for many Ohioans. With Brown's approval, the Ohio Legislature authorized an annual tax of $50,000 on each of the Bank's two branches in the state. Brown also realized the need for making markets more accessible, and repeatedly advocated transportation improvements, especially canals. He prodded the legislature into creating a seven member commission to oversee exploratory surveys. In the election of 1820, Brown opposed another Democratic-Republican, Jeremiah Morrow, with William Henry Harrison running as a minor candidate. The results were Brown, 34,836 and Morrow, 9,426, with another 4,598 votes scattered between Harrison and other contenders. Midway through the term the legislature chose Brown to succeed the deceased William Trimble in the United States Senate. In the Senate, Brown became Chairman of the Committee on Roads and Canals. His term expired in 1825, with Harrison capturing the seat that year. For the next five years, Brown served as a Commissioner of Ohio's canal fund. In 1830, in gratitude for Brown's support, Andrew Jackson appointed him *chargé d'affaires* to Brazil. He returned from Brazil in 1834, and in July 1835, was appointed Commissioner of the General Land Office in Washington. He retired to Rising Sun in October 1836, but returned to politics from 1841 to 1843, when he served in the Indiana House of Representatives. He died on February 24, 1852, while acting as vice president of the Democratic State Convention, and was buried in the family plot at Rising Sun. Bibliography: William A. Taylor, *Ohio in Congress* (1900); Harry R. Stevens, *The Early Jackson Party in Ohio* (Durham, North Carolina, 1957); Register of the Debates in Congress, 18 Cong., 2 Sess. (Feb. 24, 1825); Thomas E. Powell, *The Democratic Party of the State of Ohio* (1913).

TRIMBLE, Allen, 1822, 1826-1830

Born on November 24, 1783, in Augusta County, Virginia, son of James Trimble, soldier and land owner; a Methodist Episcopalian. Brother of William A Trimble. Father of four sons and a daughter, Eliza. Educated in Lexington, Kentucky, schools, forced to discontinue education at age seventeen because of ill health. Moved to Highland County, Ohio, in 1804, and engaged in farming and surveying. In 1808 he became County Clerk of Courts and Recorder of Deeds. During the War of 1812, served as commander, with the rank of Colonel. Served in Ohio House of Representatives, 1816-1817. Served in Ohio Senate, 1818-1826. Served as Speaker for seven assemblies and became Acting Governor when Governor Brown resigned on January 4, 1822. Was defeated for Governor on October 8, 1822. In the election Jeremiah Morrow, a Democratic-Republican, received 26,059 votes, Trimble, a Clay Republican, received 22,889 votes and William Irwin, another Democratic-Republican, received 11,060 votes. In 1824 he was appointed to the first Canal Fund Commission. Trimble was again defeated by Morrow in 1824, 37,108 votes to 39,526. The Clay Republican caucus nominated him once again in 1826. This time he received 71,475 votes and J. W. Campbell, a Democratic-Republican, received 4,765. Tappen, another Democratic-Republican, received 4,192. As governor, Trimble consistently supported progressive legislation for education, especially higher education. When the state's population was swelled by an influx of blacks, he strongly favored a policy of colonizing freed slaves, but his plan had little success. He was reelected over J.W. Campbell, 53,971 votes to 51,591 in 1828, and was ineligible for a third consecutive term. Trimble returned to agricultural pursuits after 1830. He was especially interested in the improvement of domestic breeds of cattle and horses and was a stockholder in the Ohio Company for Importing English and first president of the State Board of Agriculture from 1846 to 1848. He served as a delegate to the National Republican Convention in 1831, was a losing candidate for the State Legislature in 1832, and was a candidate for governor on the American Party ticket in 1855, but ran a poor third. He died in Hillsboro on February 3, 1870. Bibliography: R. C. Downes, *Frontier Ohio, Ohio Historical Collection*, vol. III (Columbus, Ohio); Harry R. Stevens, *The Early Jackson Party in Ohio* (Durham, N. C., 1957); Joseph P. Smith, *History of the Republican Party in Ohio*, 2 vols. (Chicago, 1898); Edward Miller, "The History of Educational Legislation in Ohio," *Ohio State Archeological and Historical Society Quarterly*, vols. XXVII and XXXIV (Columbus, 1919).

MORROW, Jeremiah, 1822-1826

Born on October 6, 1771, near Gettysburg, Pennsylvania, son of John Morrow (changed from Murray), a farmer, and Mary (Lockart) Morrow; a Presbyterian. Married to Mary Parkhill on February 19, 1799; father of six children. Attended public schools in Pennsylvania. Moved to Ohio in 1794, settling in Deerfield Township, Warren County, and engaged in surveying, farming and school teaching. Elected to the second Territorial Legislature in October 1800, where he belonged to the "Chillicothe Junto." Served as delegate to the Constitutional Convention in 1802 and was a member of the first State Senate in 1803. Served in United States House of Representatives from 1803 to 1813 and the United States Senate from 1813 to 1819. Declined reelection in 1819 and returned to his farm. In 1820 and 1822 appointed Canal Commissioner. Chosen by the Democratic-Republican caucus in 1822 to run against Allen Trimble, a Clay Republican, and William W. Irwin, another Democratic-Republican. The vote total was Morrow 26,059, Trimble 22,889 and Irwin 11,060. Governor Morrow oversaw the state's recovery from the depression of 1819. One factor in this recovery was the Federal Land Act of 1820, which Morrow had drafted while in the Senate. Other internal improvements carried out under his administration included the completion of the Erie Canal; the extension of the

National Road into Ohio; and the beginning of construction on the Ohio and Erie and Miami Canals. In 1824 Morrow ran for a second term against Allen Trimble, winning in a close election by 39,526 votes to 37,108. During his second term, Morrow supported two very important laws. The first provided for a state-supported common school system, and the second established a method for the evaluation and taxation of property, a method which is substantially the basis for the state's present system. Morrow declined renomination. He served in the State Senate in the 1827-1828 session, and in the House in 1829-1830 and 1835-1836. In 1841 he was elected to the United States House of Representatives. In 1843, after the completion of his term, he refused reelection. Morrow was one of the founders of the Whig Party in Ohio. He presided at the Whig conventions of 1827 and 1836 and held the offices of Township Trustee, School Director and Supervisor of Canals in his later years. He died at Twenty-mile Stand, near Lebanon, Warren County, Ohio, on March 22, 1852, and was buried in Union Cemetery on the Montgomery Pike. Bibliography: Manuscripts of Jeremiah Morrow are in the Ohio State Library and in the Ohio State Archives and Historical Society Library in Columbus, Ohio; W. A. Taylor, *Ohio Statesmen and Hundred Year Book, 1832*; W. H. Smith, "Governor Jeremiah Morrow: Or a Familiar Talk about Monarchists and Jacobins," *Magazine of Western History* (October 1889); Josiah Morrow, "A Biography of Jeremiah Morrow," *"Old Northwest" Genealogical Quarterly* (January, April, July 1906).

TRIMBLE, Allen, 1822, 1826-1830

McARTHUR, Duncan, 1830-1832

Born in Dutchess County, New York, on January 14, 1772, son of John McArthur, laborer, and Margaret (Campbell) McArthur, both of whom were Presbyterians. Married to Nancy McDonald in February 1796; father of Effie and two other children. Had very little formal education, but could read and write by the age of twelve. Worked at various jobs and as a trans-Allegheny pack train driver until 1790, when he enrolled for service against the Indians. Joined Nathaniel Massie's surveying party into the Scioto Valley. Observed Indian movements as a ranger in the area for two years. In March 1795, rejoined Massie and learned surveying. Began purchasing land and locating land warrants, and by 1804 was considered one of the wealthiest land holders in the Scioto Valley. Elected to Ohio House of Representatives in 1805. The next year, he was elected to the State Senate for the first of eight consecutive terms, serving as Speaker for the 1809-1810 session. In 1806 he was elected a Colonel of the militia. Became a Major-General in February 1808. During the War of 1812, he was elected Colonel of one of the three militia regiments serving under General Hull. He was elected to Congress in 1812, but did not qualify, and entered active service in the Regular Army as a Brigadier General under General Harrison. After the latter's resignation, McArthur assumed command of the army in the Northwest. At the end of the War of 1812, he served as a member of several commissions appointed to make treaties with the Indians. He was frequently a member of the State Legislature, sitting in the Lower House for three sessions,

1815-1816, 1817-1818 (when he was Speaker) and 1826-1827, and in the Upper House for three sessions, 1821-1822, 1822-1823 and 1829-1830. In 1822 he was elected to Congress. He was nominated for Governor in 1830 by the National Republican caucus, and defeated Robert Lucas, a Democratic-Republican, by 49,668 votes to 49,186. McArthur's administration was not marked by events of great significance, but progress was made in revising and recodifying the legal system and in amending tax legislation to extend its coverage. McArthur decided to run for Congress instead of reelection as governor in 1832, but was defeated by William Allan, his future son-in-law, by one vote. After his retirement from politics, McArthur pursued his agricultural and business interests. He died in Chillicothe on April 29, 1839. Bibliography: The McArthur Papers are on deposit in the Library of Congress; some letters are in the Ohio State Library; John McDonald, *Biographical Sketches of General Nathaniel Massie, General Duncan McArthur* (Columbus, 1838); L. S. Evans, *A Standard History of Ross County, Ohio* (1917); W. A. Taylor, *Ohio Statesmen and Hundred Year Book* (Columbus, 1892); F. P. Weisenburger, *Ohio Politics During the Jacksonian Period* (1929).

LUCAS, Robert, 1832-1836

Born on April 1, 1781, in Shepherdstown, Virginia (now West Virginia), son of William Lucas, a wealthy Revolutionary soldier, and Susannah (Barnes) Lucas; a Methodist. Married to Elizabeth Brown on April 4, 1810; remarried to Friendly Ashley Summer on March 7, 1816; father of six children. Educated by private tutors, who instructed him especially in mathematics and surveying. Moved with his parents to Scioto. Became Surveyor for Scioto County, Justice of the Peace, member of the State Legislature in 1808 and 1809, and an officer in the militia, in which he reached the rank of Major-General. Served as a detached officer under General Hull in the War of 1812. Elected to the State Senate in 1814. Moved to Piketon, Pike County, and opened a general store in 1816. Lucas continued to represent his district in the State Senate until 1822, and again from 1824 to 1830. In the session of 1831-1832, he served in the Lower House. In 1830 Lucas was unanimously nominated for Governor by the Democratic-Republicans at their joint nominating convention in Ohio. He was narrowly defeated, polling 49,186 votes against the 49,668 cast for Duncan McArthur, a National Republican. He was again nominated by his party in 1832, and this time was successful in the general election, defeating Dorius Lyman, the joint candidate of the National Republicans and Anti-Masons, by a vote of 71,251 to 63,185. In 1832 Lucas was elected temporary and then permanent Chairman of the first Democratic National Convention. In 1834 he was reelected Governor over the Whig James Findley, 70,738 votes to 65,414. As governor, Lucas supported free public schools and recognized the need to revise the militia laws. During his second term, he took a vigorous part in the "Toledo War." Lucas marched out the militia to protect an eight-mile area of that part of Toledo which both Ohio and Michigan claimed. The acting governor of Michigan met Lucas with his own militia, and only the intervention of President Jackson managed to avert open war. After the expiration of his term, Lucas was defeated for the United States Senate by William Allen. In 1838 President Van Buren appointed Lucas Governor and Superintendent of Indian Affairs in the Territory of Iowa. He was replaced in

1841, after a stormy tenure. He returned to Ohio in 1843 to run for Congress, but was defeated and returned to Iowa where, except for service in that state's constitutional convention, he devoted his time to private affairs and to work in the Methodist church. He died on February 7, 1853, and was buried in Iowa City, Iowa. Bibliography: A collection of letters and papers of Lucas is on deposit in the Library of the State Historical Society of Iowa; "The Robert Lucas Journal of the War of 1812," *Iowa Journal of History and Politics* (July 1906); "Documents Relating to Governor Lucas," *Iowa Historical Record* (April 1900); J. C. Parish, *Robert Lucas* (1907); M.W. Evans, *A History of Scioto County* (1903); B.F. Shambowigh, ed., *Executive Journal of Iowa, 1838-41* (1906).

VANCE, Joseph, 1836-1838

Born in Catfish, near Washington, Pennsylvania, on March 21, 1786, son of Joseph C. Vance, soldier and farmer. Married to Mary Lemen in 1807. Had very little formal education. At fifteen purchased a team of oxen with money saved as a wood cutter at the May's Lick salt works, and peddled salt in the wilderness settlements. In 1809, after his father's death, he took over the family farm near Urbana. Appointed Secretary of the Board of County Commissioners the same year. He organized and was elected Captain of an independent rifle company in 1810, and during the War of 1812 his company joined the state militia, with Vance rising successively from Captain to Brigadier General. Served as Champaign County's representative in the State Legislature for the sessions of 1813-14, 1815-16 and 1819-20. In 1820 he was a delegate to the state's constitutional convention. Laid out the city of Findley and engaged in mercantile pursuits between sessions of the legislature. Elected to Congress, in 1820, serving from 1821 to 1835; defeated for reelection in 1834. Nominated in 1836 by the Whigs as their gubernatorial candidate, he defeated E. Baldwin by a vote of 92,204 to 86,158, and became the first Whig to govern Ohio. Governor Vance maintained that federal surplus funds should be used for the schools, and that the canals already under construction should be completed. He also favored the recharter of the United States Bank, and urged the abolition of capital punishment. Vance lost his popularity with the antislavery forces when he sanctioned the extradition of John B. Mahan, who was wanted in Kentucky for helping two fugitive slaves to escape. This action contributed to his defeat for reelection in 1838, when he lost to the Democratic candidate, Wilson Shannon, 107,884 to 102,146. Vance refused to be a candidate for Governor in 1840, but was elected to the State Senate for the 1839-1841 session. In 1842 he defeated Samuel Mason for the United States Congress, and served two terms from 1843 to 1847. After his time in Congress, he retired to his farm, although he was a delegate to the Whig National Convention in 1848 and to the Ohio Constitutional Convention in 1850-51. He died at his home near Urbana on August 24, 1852, and was buried in Oakdale Cemetery. Bibliography: Samuel P. Hildeeth, *Contributions to the Early History of the Northwest* (Cincinnati, 1864); Charles C. Huntington and C. P. McClelland, *History of Ohio Canals, Their Construction, Cost, Use, and Partial Abandonment* (Columbus, 1905); Harold E. Davis, "Economic Basis of Ohio Politics, 1820-1840," *Ohio State Archeological and Historical Society Quarterly*, vol. XLVII (1938); C. C. Huntington, "History of Banking and Currency in Ohio Before the Civil War," *Ohio State Archeological and Historical Society Quarterly*, vol. XXIV (1915).

SHANNON, Wilson, 1838-1840, 1842-1844

Born on February 24, 1802, in Mount Olivet, Belmont County, Ohio Territory, son of George Shannon, a farmer, and Jane (Milligan) Shannon, both of whom were Catholic. Brother of George Shannon, James Shannon and six others. Married to Elizabeth Ellis; upon her death, remarried to Sarah Osbun; father of eight children. Attended Ohio University, Franklin College and Transylvania University. Studied law under David Jennings and Charles Hammond and was admitted to the Ohio Bar in 1830. Formed a partnership with Judge Kennon and practiced law in St. Clairsville. In 1832 he was the Democratic candidate for Congress, but was defeated. The following year he was elected to the first of two consecutive terms as Prosecuting Attorney for Belmont County and served from 1833 through 1837. He was nominated for Governor by the Democratic convention in 1838, and defeated the Whig candidate, Joseph Vance, by a vote of 107,884 to 102,146. The first native governor of Ohio, Shannon pushed through legislation providing a limited program of internal improvements evenly distributed over the state, combined with extensive reform of the state's banking system. The most important of these laws was the Bank Commissioner Act of February 25, 1839. Although renominated by acclamation at the Democratic State Convention in January 1840, Shannon received only 129,312 votes, compared with the 145,442 of Thomas Corwin, his Whig opponent in the October general election. Two years later the situation was reversed, when Corwin received 117,902 votes to Shannon's 119,774. During his second term, Shannon returned to his policy of limited internal improvements and control of the banks, a policy which infuriated liberal Democrats. His support of Lewis Cass for president further divided the party. Rather than seek another term, Shannon resigned as governor to accept an appointment by President Tyler as Minister to Mexico. Because of Shannon's tactless communication with the Mexican government, President Tyler recalled him in March 1845. He returned to practice law in Cincinnati; led an expedition of "Forty-Niners" to California; served as an Ohio Congressman from 1853-55; and became Governor of the Kansas Territory on August 10, 1855. He served there under extremely difficult conditions until August 18, 1856, when he sent a letter of resignation to the President; three days later he received notice of his removal. Although he was frequently a delegate to State and National Democratic conventions, he never again sought office. He practiced law in Lecompton and then in Topeka, Kansas. He died on August 30, 1877, and was buried in Topeka. Bibliography: J. H. Smith, *The War with Mexico* (1919); G. L. Rines, *The United States and Mexico* (1913); "Biography of Governor Wilson Shannon," *Transactions of the Kansas State Historical Society*, vol. III (1886); "Hon. Wilson Shannon," *The U.S. Magazine and Democratic Review* (August, 1849); A. T. McKelney, *Centennial History of Belmont County, Ohio* (1903).

CORWIN, Thomas, 1840-1842

Born on July 29, 1794, in Bourbon County, Kentucky, son of Mathias Corwin, farmer and long-time Ohio legislator, and Patience (Halleck) Corwin; a Baptist. Brother of Moses Blades Corwin and others. Married to Sarah Ross in 1822; father of five children. Primarily self-educated; studied law and was admitted to the Ohio Bar in

1816. Served as Warren County Prosecuting Attorney from 1818 to 1828. Elected to the State Legislature for sessions of 1821-22, 1822-23 and 1829-30. Served as Ohio Congressman from 1830 to 1840. Nominated for Governor by the Whigs in 1840. During the race against Democrat Wilson Shannon, he gained the reputation of being the most famous stump speaker of his time; he won the election by a vote of 145,442 to 129,312. As governor, Corwin wished to stabilize the state after the Panic of 1837 by establishing a state bank and by rechartering the safest of existing banks, but with joint liability of all for the debts of any bank that defaulted; Corwin also hoped to impose restrictions on circulation and profits. Since the Democrats still controlled the State Senate, however, none of these proposals became law. He was defeated in 1842 by Wilson Shannon, 119,774 votes to 117,902, and refused renomination in 1844. But the Whig controlled legislature sent him to the United States Senate, and on February 11, 1847, Corwin delivered a powerful speech denouncing the war with Mexico. As a result of this oration, some groups turned to him as a presidential possibility, while others considered him a traitor and petitioned the Ohio Legislature to recall him. Nevertheless, he was given a vote of confidence by his State Legislature, and continued in the United States Senate until 1850, when President Fillmore appointed him Secretary of the Treasury. He retired to his practice in Lebanon in 1853, but he was elected to Congress again in 1858 as a Republican and reelected in 1860. He sponsored the "Corwin Amendment," which would have made it unconstitutional to interfere with slavery where it existed. Lincoln appointed him as Minister to Mexico, a position that he held from 1861 to 1864. Corwin successfully maintained Mexico's friendship with the North during the Civil War, and at the conclusion of his service, he returned to Washington and opened a law office. He died in Washington, D.C. on December 18, 1865, and was buried in Lebanon Cemetery, Lebanon, Ohio. Bibliography: The Corwin Papers are on deposit in the Library of Congress; E. T. Corwin, *Corwin Genealogy in the U. S.* (1872); Addison Perle Russell, *Thomas Corwin, A Sketch* (1882); L. Belle Hamlin ed., "Selections from the William Greene Papers," *Historical and Philosophical Society of Ohio Quarterly,* vol. XIII (1918); Isaac Strain, ed., "Speeches of Thomas Corwin with a Sketch of His Life (1859)," *Ohio Historical and Philosophical Society Quarterly Publication,* vol. IX (1914).

SHANNON, Wilson, 1838-1840, 1842-1844

BARTLEY, Thomas Welles, 1844

Born on February 11, 1812, in Jefferson County, Ohio; son of Mordecai Bartley, a farmer, merchant and politician, and Elizabeth (Welles) Bartley; member, Protestant Episcopal Church. Married to Susan Sherman and two others; father of a number of children. Attended Jefferson College and graduated in 1831. Studied law in Mansfield, Ohio, and Washington, D. C., and admitted to the Ohio Bar. Served two terms as Prosecuting Attorney for Richland County. Elected to the Ohio House of Representatives in 1839, and served until 1841. Elected to the State Senate for two consecutive terms, 1841-45. In 1843 he was elected Speaker and became Governor when Governor Shannon resigned to become Minister to Mexico on April 15, 1844. The legislature had adjourned a month before Bartley became Governor, and his official functions consisted primarily of delivering an annual message to the State Assembly on the same day that his father was inducted into office. A strong Van Buren man and a leader of the anti-bank Democrats, the younger Bartley had lost the nomination for Governor to David Tod by a single vote at the Democratic State Convention, and thus narrowly missed running against his father, who was the Whig candidate in the campaign of 1844. From 1845 to 1849 Bartley served as United States District Attorney for the Northern District of Ohio. Elected one of the first judges under the new constitution, he served on the bench from February 1852 to February 1859. He was Chief Justice for three years. After his retirement from the bench, he practiced law in Mansfield and Cincinnati, Ohio, and in Washington, D. C. He died on June 20, 1885, and was buried in Washington, D. C. Bibliography: Charles B. Galbreath, *History of Ohio*, 5 volumes, (New York, 1925); Carrington T. Marshall, ed., *A History of the Courts and Lawyers of Ohio*, 4 vols. (New York, 1934); Francis R. Aumann, "The Cause of Judicial Review in Ohio," *American Political Science Review*, vol. XXV (1931); Francis R. Aumann, "The Development of the Judicial System of Ohio," *Ohio State Archeological and Historical Quarterly*, vol. XLI (1932); Edgar A. Holt, "Party Politics in Ohio, 1840-1850," *Ohio State Archeological and Historical Society Quarterly*, vol. XXXVII (1928) and vol. XXXVIII (1929).

BARTLEY, Mordecai, 1844-1846

Born on December 16, 1783, in Fayette County, Pennsylvania, son of Elijah Bartley, a farmer, and Rachel (Pearshall); a member of the Protestant Episcopal Church. Married to Elizabeth Welles in 1804; father of Thomas Welles Bartley. Attended district school. Moved to Jefferson County, Ohio, at the age of twenty-six and began farming. Raised a company of volunteers, of which he was Captain, at the outset of the War of 1812, and subsequently served as Adjutant of a regiment under General William Henry Harrison. After the war, moved to Mansfield, Ohio, and continued farming and opened a mercantile house. Elected to Ohio State Senate in 1817. Appointed Register of the Land Office. Served in Congress from 1823 to 1831. Nominated for Governor by the Whig Convention in 1844, and polled 146,333 votes to Democrat David Tod's 145,062. He thus succeeded his son as governor. Governor Bartley signed into law the Kelley Bank Act, which remained the basic banking act of the state for the next two decades, and the Kelley Revenue Act, which equalized taxation and placed several classes of formerly exempt property on the tax rolls. When war broke out with Mexico in 1846, President Polk requested Bartley to raise troops. Bartley opposed the war, and his friends and associates urged him against taking steps to fill Ohio's quota, but Bartley complied, believing that he was constitutionally bound to respect the requests of the national government. Bartley also sought repeal of Ohio's "black laws," which placed restrictions on free blacks in the state, and became involved in a controversy with the governor of Virginia over the enforcement of the fugitive slave laws. He declined to accept renomination and retired to private life upon completion of his term. He continued his farming and business interests until his death on October 10, 1870. Bibliography: *Register of Debates in Congress, 1824-33*; John S.C. Abbott, *History of the State of Ohio* (1875); Edgar A. Holt, "Party Politics in Ohio, 1840-1850," *Ohio State Archeological and Historical Society Quarterly*, vol. XXXVII (1928) and vol. XXXVIII (1929); C. C. Huntington, "History of Banking and Currency in Ohio Before the Civil War," *Ohio State Archeological and Historical Society Quarterly*, vol. XXIV (1915).

BEBB, William, 1846-1849

Born on December 2, 1802, in Paddy's Run (now Sharralon), Butler County, Ohio, son of Edward Bebb, a Welsh immigrant farmer, and Margaret (Roberts Owens) Bebb; a Congregationalist. One of three children. Married to Sarah Shuck in 1824; father of Michael Bebb. Attended district schools and became a teacher at the age of twenty. In 1828 organized the Sycamore Grove School, a leading school for boys. Studied law under John Woods while conducting school. Passed the state bar examination in 1831. Abandoned teaching and entered the law firm of John M. Millikin. Gained some recognition as a Whig, when he campaigned for Harrison in 1840. Delegate to Whig National Convention in 1844. Nominated for Governor by the Whigs in 1846. His campaign slogan was "William Bebb and a Home Currency against David Tod and Pat Metal." The Whigs won the contest, with Bebb receiving 118,869 votes to 116,484 for David Tod, the Democratic candidate, and 10,797 for Samuel Lewis, the Liberty Party candidate. Soon after Bebb's inauguration, the Whigs in the General Assembly passed a resolution condemning both the war with Mexico and President Polk. Although Bebb agreed with these sentiments, he continued to raise troops as requested by the national government. During his administration, Bebb succeeded in maintaining the currency and revenue laws; continued the support of schools and colleges; reduced the state debt; curbed monopolies; improved conditions in the penitentiary; and hastened the completion of the new State House. The one campaign promise that he was not able to keep was the repeal of the state's "black laws." He declined to be a candidate for reelection and his term expired in December 1848, but his administration continued until January 22, 1849 because of a delay in organizing the two houses of the Assembly and in confirming his successor. After his retirement from public life, he returned to the practice of law and purchased 5,000 acres near Rockford, Illinois. In 1860 he moved to Knoxville, Tennessee to supervise a colony of Welshmen, but the threat of war and his support of Lincoln caused him to abandon Tennessee and the project. Lincoln made him an examiner in the Pension Office in Washington, and later Bebb declined an appointment as Consul at Tangier, Morocco. He returned to spend his last years in Rockford, and died there on October 23, 1873. Bibliography: E. L. Bogart, *Internal Improvements and State Debt in Ohio* (1924); George H. Porter, "Ohio Politics During the Civil War Period," *Studies in History, Economics and Public Law*, vol. XL (New York, 1911); Carrington T. Marshall, ed., *A History of the Courts and Lawyers of Ohio* (New York, 1934); Albert H. Ross, *Ohio Government, State and Local* (St. Louis, 1953).

FORD, Seabury, 1849-1850

Born in Cheshire, New Haven County, Connecticut on October 15, 1801; the fifth of seven children of John Ford, a large land holder, and Esther (Cook) Ford; a Congregationalist. Married to Harriet Cook in 1828. Attended Burton Academy and Yale University, graduating in 1825. Admitted to the Ohio Bar in 1827. Practiced law in Burton. Rose to rank of Major General in the state militia. Elected to the State House of Representatives in 1835 and served in either the House or the Senate through 1847. He was once Speaker of the House and once Speaker of the Senate. In 1838 he was narrowly defeated for a seat in the United States Congress. Campaigned vigorously for Henry Clay in 1844. In January 1848, Ford was the Whig nominee for Governor to oppose the Democrat John B. Weller. The vote was 148,756 for Ford, 148,445 for Weller, with 742 votes scattered among minor candidates. The election was the closest in the history of Ohio, and the only one which had to be decided by the legislature. The Whigs and Democrats were evenly divided at the time, and the Free Soilers held the balance of power. So divided was the legislature that Ford was not declared the winner until six weeks after his scheduled inauguration. With so badly divided a legislature, Ford could accomplish little. Nevertheless the "black laws," which discriminated against blacks, were repealed. The question of a constitutional convention was also submitted to and approved by the voters. The convention met on May 6, 1850, and the constitution they adopted is still the basic law of Ohio. Ford was faced with a cholera epidemic in Columbus in 1849, but he remained at the capital and managed to avert a serious crisis at the penitentiary. When the epidemic spread there, Ford pardoned the deserving and promised additional pardons to those who would aid in nursing the sick until the epidemic ended. Ford, who was not a candidate for reelection, was the last Whig governor of Ohio. When his term ended on December 12, 1850, he returned to his home in Burton. He soon suffered a paralytic stroke, from which he never fully recovered. He died in Burton on May 5, 1855. Bibliography: James K. Mercer, *Ohio Legislative History*, 6 vols. (Columbus, 1914-1926); George H. Porter, "Ohio Politics During the Civil War Period," *Studies in History, Economics, and Public Law*, vol. XL (New York, 1911); Clara B. Hicks, "The History of Penal Institutions in Ohio," *Ohio State Archeological and Historical Society Quarterly*, XXXIII (1924); Edgar A. Holt, "Party Politics in Ohio, 1840-1850," *Ohio State Archeological and Historical Society Quarterly*, vol. XXXVII (1928) and vol. XXXVIII (1929).

WOOD, Reuben, 1850-1853

Born in Middletown, Rutland County, Vermont, in 1792, son of the Reverend Nathaniel Wood, a Christian minister. Married to Mary Rice in 1816; father of two daughters. Studied at home until the age of fifteen, then studied classics and law in Canada. Was conscripted into the Canadian Army during the War of 1812, and served until his escape across Lake Ontario. Served for a short time in the American Army until the end of the war. Returned to Vermont to teach school and complete his legal studies under James Clark of Middletown. Moved to Cleveland, Ohio, in 1818. First elected to the State Senate in 1825 and served continuously through 1830. In 1830 the General Assembly elected him President Judge of the

Court of Common Pleas for the Third Judicial Circuit. In 1832 elected Judge of the state's Supreme Court, and served from February 1832 to February 1847. Nominated for Governor in 1850 by the Democratic State Convention. In the October election Wood received 133,093 votes to 121,105 for the Whig candidate William Johnston, and 13,747 for the Free Soil candidate, E. Smith. Wood became Governor in the closing days of the 1850 Constitutional Convention, which produced a new constitution that was adopted by popular vote on June 17, 1851. Since it provided for elections in odd numbered years, Wood had to run for governor again even before he had been in office a full year. In October, he was reelected for a second term over Samuel F. Vinton, the Whig candidate. The Free Soil candidate, Samuel Lewis, polled only 16,914 votes, compared with 119,596 for Vinton and 145,604 for Wood. Wood strongly opposed the Fugitive Slave Law, but would not countenance acts of violence in circumventing it. He favored the hard money platform of his party, and believed that banks should be taxed at the same rate as individuals. Among the more important laws passed on his recommendation were those reorganizing the courts. In 1853 he resigned to become the American Consul in Valparaiso, Chile. After his return from Chile in 1855, he practiced law in Cleveland, and soon retired to his farm near Rockport, Cuyahoga County. He died at the farm on October 1, 1864. He was buried there, but later was moved to Woodlawn Cemetery in Cleveland. Bibliography: Simeon D. Fess, *Ohio: A Reference Library on the History of a Great State* (Chicago, 1937); Charles C. Huntington, *A History of Banking and Currency in Ohio Before the Civil War* (Columbus, 1915); Carrington T. Marshall, ed., *A History of the Courts and Lawyers of Ohio*, 4 vols. (New York, 1934); George H. Porter, "Ohio Politics During the Civil War Period," *Studies in History, Economics, and Public Law*, vol. XL (1911). The Wood Papers are on deposit in the Ohio Archeological and Historical Society Library.

MEDILL, William, 1853-1856

Born in February 1802 at Whitely Creek Hundred, New Castle County, Delaware, son of William Medill, a farmer, and Isabella Medill; Catholic; never married. Studied at Newark Academy (later Delaware College and now the University of Delaware), and was graduated in 1825. Read law in the office of Judge Black of New Castle and admitted to the Delaware Bar in the summer of 1830. Moved to Lancaster, Ohio, that winter and admitted to Ohio Bar in 1832. Served in State Legislature from 1835 through 1838. Elected to United States Congress in 1838 and served until election defeat in 1842. Appointed Second Assistant Postmaster General in 1845. Resigned after a few months to serve as Commissioner of Indian Affairs for the duration of Polk's administration. Elected President of the State Constitutional Convention in 1850. Elected first Lieutenant Governor of Ohio in October 1851. On July 13, 1853, Governor Wood resigned and Medill became Governor. In October 1853, Medill was chosen as Democratic candidate for Governor and received 147,663 votes in the general election. N. Barnes, the Whig candidate, received 85,851, and S. Lewis, running as a Free Democrat, polled 50,346. Although there was a substantial majority of Democrats in both houses, no laws of great importance were enacted during Governor Medill's term. He did, however, believe that the state should withdraw from its many economic activities, and contended that the state should sell all of its canal, turnpike and railroad stock. No immediate steps were taken, but successive administrations used his arguments as a basis for action. In the city elections in Cincinnati in 1855, riots broke out, and Medill personally threatened to call out the state militia as a means of restoring order. The newly-formed State Republican Party nominated Salmon P. Chase in 1855, and Chase defeated Medill, receiving 146,770 votes to Medill's 131,019. Former Governor Allen Trimble, running on the American ticket, received 24,276 votes. After his defeat, Medill was selected by President Buchanan to be Comptroller of the Federal Treasury. This appointment was Medill's last before his retirement, although he did preside over Ohio's Democratic Convention in 1863. Medill died in Lancaster on September 2, 1865. Bibliography: Simeon D. Fess, *Ohio: A Reference Library on the History of a Great State* (Chicago, 1937); Carrington T. Marshall, ed., *A History of the Courts and Lawyers of Ohio*, 4 vols. (New York, 1934); James K. Mercer, *Ohio Legislative History*, 6 vols. (Columbus, 1914-1926); H.J. Webster "History of the Democratic Party Organization," *Ohio State Archeological and Historical Society Quarterly*, vol. XXIV (1915).

CHASE, Salmon Portland, 1856-1860

Born on January 13, 1808, in Cornish Township, Sullivan County, New Hampshire, son of Ithamar Chase, politican and tavern keeper, and Janette (Ralston) Chase; the eighth of eleven children. Married to Katherine Jane Garniss on March 4, 1834; re-married to Eliza Ann Smith on September 26, 1839; father of six daughters, four of whom died in infancy, and Katherine Chase Sprague and Janette Chase Hoyt. Educated at Worthington Church School and Cincinnati College by his uncle, Philander Chase, Episcopal Bishop of Ohio, and graduated from Dartmouth College in 1826. Read law under William Wirt in Washington, D. C., and admitted to the bar on December 14, 1829. Moved to Ohio in 1830 and became a lecturer and essayist; also wrote *Statutes of Ohio*. Became leader of the antislavery faction in the Whig, the Liberty, the Free Soil and finally the Republican Party. Elected to the United States Senate on February 22, 1849, and served until nominated for Governor by the newly-formed Ohio Republican Party at its convention in July 1855. In a bitter campaign Chase received 146,770 votes to Democratic Governor Medill's 131,019 and former Governor Allen Trimble's 24,276. Chase was reelected in 1857, after defeating the Democratic candidate H. Payne, 160,568 votes to 159,065. Chase was interested in national politics, but was forced to run for reelection when his state treasurer was accused of misconduct. As governor, Chase reformed the state militia; advocated the establishment of a geological survey; created a Bureau of Statistics and a Railroad Commission; and improved the status of women with regard to property holding and opportunities for education. During his first administration the Ohio Legislature passed liberty laws, strong anti-slavery laws, and a law exempting chartered banks from taxation, but most of these were overturned during his second term by the less sympathetic Democratic majority in the legislature. In 1856 and again in 1860, Chase was an avowed aspirant for the presidency, but was rejected by his party both times. In 1860 he was again chosen United States Senator, although he soon resigned to become Lincoln's Secretary of the Treasury. He held this office from March 1861 until July 1864. While treasurer, Chase devised a national banking system. He was again an unsuccessful candidate for nomination by his party in 1864, and in the summer of 1864 Lincoln finally accepted Chase's often-offered resignation. In October of that year, Lincoln appointed him Chief Justice of the Supreme Court. He presided at the treason trial of Confederate President Jefferson Davis and at the impeachment trial of President Andrew Johnson. He died in New York City on May 7, 1873, and was buried in Oak Hill Cemetery, Washington, D. C.; he was later reinterred in Spring Grove Cemetery, Cincinnati, Ohio. Bibliography: Chase's letters and manuscripts along with miscellaneous material are on deposit in the Library of the Pennsylvania Historical Society and in the Chase Collection of the Library of Congress; also see Robert B. Warden, *Account of the Private Life and Public Service of Salmon Portland Chase* (1874); J. W. Schucker, "Life and Public Services of Salmon Portland Chase," *Annual Report, American Historical Association* (1902); A. B. Holt, *Salmon P. Chase* (1899); Charles Warren, *The Supreme Court in U. S. History* (1922); Richard H. Luthrin, "Salmon P. Chase's Political Career Before the Civil War," *Mississippi Valley Historical Review*, vol. XXIV (1942-43).

DENNISON, William, 1860-1862

Born in Cincinnati on November 23, 1815, son of William Dennison, successful businessman, and Mary Dennison. Married to the eldest daughter of William Neil; father of seven children. Attended Miami University and graduated at the age of nineteen. Studied law under Nathaniel G. Pendleton and was admitted to the Ohio Bar in 1840. Moved to Columbus and elected to the State Senate in 1848. Served one term, then returned to private practice. His interests during this period were in the areas of finance and transportation, leading to his selection as president of the Exchange Bank of Columbus and president of Columbus and Xenia Railroad. In February of 1856 he became one of the first prominent Whigs to join the Republican Party. In June 1856, he acted as Chairman of the Ohio delegation to the nominating convention held by the Republicans in Philadelphia, and in 1859 the Ohio Republican State Convention nominated him for the governorship by acclamation. His gubernatorial campaign that year attracted greater attention than it might ordinarily have, due to the periodic presence in the state of Abraham Lincoln and Stephen A. Douglas. Dennison defeated his Democratic opponent, Judge Rufus P. Raney, by a vote of 184,557 to 171,226. Dennison was hampered from the beginning of his term by a lack of public confidence. When he had been in office for less than a year, the Civil War broke out, and Dennison quickly raised more than Ohio's quota of troops for the Union Army. Regarding the Ohio River as an unsafe line of defense, he dispatched McClellan with state troops to aid the loyal citizens of western Virginia in driving out the Confederates. He practically assumed control of the railways, telegraph lines and express companies at the beginning of the war. Against the advice of his attorney general, Dennison used money provided by the federal government to pay for state military expenditures without giving his treasury a chance to reappropriate the funds. As a war governor, Dennison proved effective, but was not renominated by his party in 1861 because of his unpopularity in the state. Despite being dropped by his own party, Dennison was frequently called on for advice by the next governor. In 1864 he served as Chairman of the Republican National Convention, and toward the end of the war was appointed Postmaster General by Lincoln. He held office until his dissatisfaction with President Johnson caused him to resign in 1866 and return to his business interests. He died in Columbus on June 15, 1882, after a lengthy illness. Bibliography: Whitelaw Reid, *Ohio in the War* (1868); Carrington T. Marshall, ed., *History of the Courts and Lawyers of Ohio,* 4 vols. (New York, 1934); James K. Mercer, *Ohio Legislative History,* 6 vols. (Columbus, 1914-1926); C.H. Moore, "Ohio in National Politics, 1865-1896," *Ohio State Archeological Historical Society Quarterly,* vol. XXXVII (1928).

TOD, David, 1862-1864

Born on February 21, 1805, near Youngstown in Trumbull, now Mahoning County, Ohio, son of George Tod, jurist, and Sarah (Isaacs) Tod. Married to Maria Smith on June 4, 1832; father of seven children. Attended neighborhood schools and later Burton Academy. Read law in the office of Powell Stone of Warren and was admitted to the bar in 1827. Appointed Postmaster of Warren in 1832 and elected to the Ohio State Senate in 1838. Tod, a Democrat, lost the gubernatorial race to Mordecai Bartley in 1844 and William Bebb in 1846. In March 1847, President Polk appointed Tod Minister to Brazil, where he served until 1857. Returning to Youngstown, he concentrated on his growing coal, iron and railroad interests. When he was nominated for Congress in 1858, he was unable to campaign effectively because of his business activities, and suffered a decisive defeat. Served as delegate, then Chairman, of the Democratic National Convention in 1860. After the outbreak of the Civil War, Tod turned his back on his party, made public appeals for political unity, and wholeheartedly supported Lincoln and the war. He was thus the logical Union Party choice for Governor. In a listless campaign, Tod overwhelmingly defeated Democrat Hugh J. Jewett, the final count giving Tod 206,997 votes to Jewett's 151,774. As governor, Tod dealt with draft evasion and resisters, the activities of the Peace Democrats, and the defense of Cincinnati against threatened Confederate raids. Tod established various agencies in the North to meet problems encountered by soldiers' transportation, pay, sickness and disability. He incurred some criticism for his involvement in the selection of officers to be promoted. Tod very much wanted to serve a second term, but his choice of appointees, mostly Democrats with whom he was familiar, and his lack of enthusiastic support for the Emancipation Proclamation disappointed the Union League, and he did not receive the nomination. He supported the Union ticket, though deeply offended by the party's refusal to endorse him. After Tod retired from office, Lincoln offered him the position of Secretary of the Treasury when Chase resigned. Tod refused, however, because of his failing health and his many business interests. He was chosen as one of the Republican Presidential Electors in 1868, but did not live to serve. He died of apoplexy on November 13, 1868. Bibliography: Tod's letters and papers are on deposit in the Archives of the Department of State, in the Ohio Archeological and Historical Society Library, Columbus, Ohio; in the Western Reserve Historical Society Library, Cleveland; and in the Library of Congress; also see G. B. Wright, *Honorable David Tod* (1900)—also in Ohio Archeological and Historical Society, *Publications,* vol. VIII (1900); J.G. Butler, *History of Youngstown* (1921); E.A. Holt, *Party Politics in Ohio, 1840-1850* (1931)—also in *Ohio State Archeological and Historical Quarterly* (July, 1929); G.H. Porter, *Ohio Politics During the Civil War* (1911); L. F. Hill, *Diplomatic Relations between the U.S. and Brazil (1932).*

BROUGH, John, 1864-1865

Born on September 17, 1811, in Marietta, son of John Brough, a tavern keeper, and Jane (Garnet) Brough; no religious affiliation. Oldest of five children, including Charles Brough. Married to Achsa Pruden in 1832, who bore him a son and a daughter, and to Caroline A. Nelson in 1843, who bore him two sons and two daughters. When orphaned at eleven, apprenticed himself to a printer and continued to work as printer and reporter while attending the Marietta schools and Ohio University. Owned a series of newspapers. Served as clerk of the Ohio Senate from 1835-1837; elected to the General Assembly in 1838, and served as chairman of the Committee on Banking and Currency. From 1839 to 1845 elected State Auditor by the legislature. When the Whigs assumed control in 1844, Brough returned to journalism. He purchased the Cincinnati *Advertiser* and changed its name to the *Enquirer*. He also practiced law. From 1848 to 1863, he was president of a number of railroad lines. At the outbreak of the Civil War, he refused to follow his Democratic Party in opposition to the war, and in June 1863 Brough spoke so movingly in support of the Union that within a week the Republican and Union parties nominated him for Governor. The fierce campaign brought out a record poll; Clement G. Vallandigham's vote of 187,728 surpassed that of all his Democratic predecessors, but Brough, who received 288,826 votes, amassed a majority that remained unequalled for forty years. As governor, he pledged his support to the Union and promised to prosecute the war successfully. He secured approval for a levy of two mills on the dollar for public support of soldiers' families, and authorization for city and county administrations to levy an additional charge on one and a half mills. He helped to furnish troops for the army; sent the state's National Guard into federal service; and brought into effect a fair system of officer promotion. He also made many enemies both within and outside the army, and as a result his renomination became doubtful. In the end, he decided not to seek reelection because of failing health. On August 29, 1865, four months before the expiration of his term, he died in Cleveland. His ashes rest in Woodland Cemetery in Cleveland. Bibliography: "John Brough," *Ohio State Archeological and Historical Society Quarterly,* vols. XIII and XVII; Whitelaw Reid, *Ohio in the War* (1868); E.O. Randall and O.F. Ryan, *History of Ohio,* 5 vols. (1912); George H. Porter "Ohio Politics During the Civil War Period," *Studies in History, Economics, and Public Law,* vol. XL (New York, 1911).

ANDERSON, Charles, 1865-1866

Born on June 1, 1814, within the boundaries of the present city of Louisville, Kentucky, son of Colonel Richard Clough Anderson, and Eliza (Marshall) Anderson, both of whom were Christians. Brother of Richard Anderson and Robert Anderson. Married to Eliza J. Brown; father of a son and two daughters. Attended Miami University and graduated in 1833. Read law in the office of Pitle and Anderson in Louisville and was admitted to the bar in 1835. Moved to Dayton, Ohio, and opened a law office; also farmed and served a term as Prosecuting Attorney of Montgomery County. Elected to the Ohio Senate in 1844 and established himself as a champion of black rights. Travelled to Europe after the expiration of his term. Moved to

Cincinnati in 1848 and entered into a successful partnership with Rufus King. In 1855 moved back to Dayton. Moved to Texas for his health in 1859 and managed farm property which he owned there. In 1860 Anderson addressed a large gathering in San Antonio and called for the "perpetuity of the National Union." At the outbreak of the Civil War, he attempted to leave the country via Mexico, but was arrested; he later escaped and returned to Dayton. After Lincoln sent him on a special mission to England, Anderson returned to the United States and was appointed a Colonel and Commander of the 93rd Ohio Volunteer Infantry. He was severely wounded in battle and resigned his commission in the belief that he would not live. He recovered, however, and was elected Lieutenant Governor in 1863 as a Republican on the Union ticket with John Brough. When Governor Brough died on August 29, 1865, Anderson assumed the office of Governor. During the period that Anderson served from August 1865 to January 8, 1866, routine matters, especially concerning the war, occupied most of his attention. He did not choose to seek election on his own, and at the completion of his term, returned to his law practice in Dayton. In 1870 he moved to a large estate on the Cumberland River in Lyon County, Kentucky. He died on September 2, 1895, in Kuttawa, a village which he had founded. Bibliography: Carrington T. Marshall, ed., *A History of the Courts and Lawyers of Ohio*, 4 vols. (New York, 1934); James K. Mercer, *Ohio Legislative History*, 6 vols. (Columbus, 1914-1926); George H. Porter, "Ohio Politics During the Civil War Period," *Studies in History, Economics and Public Law*, vol. XL (New York, 1911); Joseph P. Smith, *History of the Republican Party in Ohio*, 2 vols. (Chicago, 1898).

COX, Jacob Dolson, 1866-1868

Born on October 27, 1828, in Montreal, Canada, son of Jacob Dolson Cox, a contractor, and Thedia Redelia (Kenyon) Cox, both of whom were Presbyterians. Married to Helen Finney on Thanksgiving Day, 1849; father of eight children, including Kenyon Cox. Studied privately; apprenticed to a law firm in 1842, then apprenticed in the office of a banker and broker. Attended Oberlin College and received a degree in theology in 1851. Moved to Warren, Ohio, and served as principal of the high school there; Superintendent of Schools in Warren while reading for the bar. Began a law practice in 1853. Elected to the Ohio Senate in 1859 as a Republican. Formed the "Radical Triumvirate" with James Monroe and James A. Garfield. In the spring of 1860, Cox was appointed Brigadier General of the Ohio militia. He saw a great deal of fighting during the Civil War, and rose to the rank of Major-General; for a time he commanded the 23rd Army Corps. In 1865 143 soldier-delegates nominated the candidates running for the last time on the Union Party ticket, and Cox was nominated for Governor. Cox received 223,642 votes to the 193,797 of his Democratic rival, George Mayan. Governor Cox proposed creating a large Negro reserve in an area encompassing parts of South Carolina, Georgia, Alabama and Florida. He also sponsored a centralized Board of Charities, and attempted to bridge the gap between Ohio's Radical Republicans and President Johnson. The radicals and conservatives within the state Republican ranks were badly divided on critical postwar issues, producing much inaction. By the time of the 1867 State Convention, the radical faction was in control, but Cox refused to try for renomination. After his term as governor, Cox moved to Cincinnati and practiced law until March 1869, when President Grant appointed him Secretary of the Interior. After eighteen months he resigned as a protest against the spoils system of the Grant administration. Cox joined the Liberal Republican faction, and was elected to Congress in 1876, his last political office. From 1873 to 1878, Cox served as president of the Toledo and Wabash Railroad Company. In 1881 he became Dean of the Cincinnati Law School, and from 1885 to 1889 he was also President of the University of Cincinnati. In 1897 he retired to write his *Military Reminiscences of the Civil War.* Cox died while on vacation in Magnolia, Massachusetts, on August 4, 1900, shortly after completing his memoirs. Bibliography: Jacob D. Cox Manuscript Collection in Oberlin College Library; Jacob D. Cox, *Military Reminiscences of the Civil War* (New York, 1900); Felice A. Bonadio, *North of Reconstruction, Ohio Politics, 1865-1870* (New York, 1970); James R. Erving, *Public Service of Jacob D. Cox* (Washington, 1893); Eric L. McKitrick, *Andrew Johnson and Reconstruction* (Chicago, 1960); C. Vann Woodward, "Seeds of Failure in Radical Race Policy," in Harold Hyman, ed., *New Frontiers of the American Reconstruction* (Urbana, 1966).

HAYES, Rutherford Birchard, 1868-1872, 1876-1877

Born on October 4, 1822, in Delaware, Ohio, posthumous son of Rutherford Hayes, a farmer, and Sophia (Birchard) Hayes; Episcopalian. Married to Lucy Webb on December 30, 1852; father of eight children. Attended preparatory schools and graduated from Kenyon College in 1842. Read law in the offices of Spencer and Matthews, then attended Harvard Law School. Admitted to the Ohio Bar on March 10, 1845, and began to practice in Lower Sandusky (later Fremont), Ohio. Journeyed to Texas in 1848, a trip which broadened his knowledge of frontier life and slavery. In 1850 he opened his own law practice in Cincinnati, and joined the Episcopal Church and civic and cultural organizations. From 1857 to 1859, served as City Solicitor. Although Hayes had hoped to see the war averted, he entered the Union Army as a Major in the 23rd Regiment, Ohio Volunteer Infantry, on June 27, 1861. He served in various capacities, was wounded several times, and was brevetted Major General of Volunteers on March 13, 1865. He resigned in June, 1865 to serve in Congress. He resigned from Congress in June, 1867, after accepting the Republican nomination for Governor. In a spirited campaign, he defeated the Democrat, Allen Thomas, by a vote of 243,605 to 240,622. Two years later, he defeated another Democrat, George Pendleton, 236,082 to 228,576. As governor, Hayes established the Soldiers' and Sailors' Orphans' Home in Xenia; enlarged the powers of the state Board of Charities; founded the Agricultural and Mechanical College; secured minority representation on election boards. He carried out a program of systematic reductions in the state debt, and encouraged the expansion of knowledge of the state's history and geography. After his second term as governor, Hayes attempted to retire from politics, but was persuaded to run for Congress. Although he was unsuccessful in his congressional campaign, the Republicans again nominated him for Governor on June 2, 1875. His opponent this time was the incumbent William Allen, a Democrat and National Independent (Greenback Party). In the election, Hayes received 297,817 votes to Allen's 292,273. Hayes thus became Ohio's first governor to be elected to a third term. Hayes served only fourteen months of his third term, resigning on March 2, 1877, to run for the presidency of the United

States. Hayes accepted his party's nomination with the clear understanding that he would serve only one term. At the end of March 1881, he returned to his home, "Spiegel Grove," and devoted his time to public speaking, promotion of education, and other worthy causes. He died on January 17, 1893, after an illness of only three days. Originally interred in Oakwood Cemetery, his remains were reinterred in Spiegel Grove State Park, Fremont, Ohio, in 1915. Bibliography: The Hayes Papers, with other material on his life, are on deposit in the Memorial Library in Fremont, Ohio; Charles R. Williams, *Life of Rutherford Birchard Hayes*, 2 vols. (1914); H. J. Eckenrode, *Rutherford B. Hayes, Statesman of Reunion* (1930); C. R. Williams, ed., *Diary and Letters of Rutherford Birchard Hayes*, 5 vols. (1922-1926); James Ford Rhodes, "Rutherford B. Hayes," *Historical Essays* (1909).

NOYES, Edward F., 1872-1874

Born in Haverhill, Massachusetts on October 3, 1832. Orphaned at the age of three; raised by his grandfather and a guardian in New Hampshire. Married to Margaret; father of one son. Apprenticed to the printer of the *Morning Star*, a religious newspaper. Remained there for four and a half years, until leaving to enter an academy in Kingston, New Hampshire. Attended and graduated from Dartmouth College in 1857. After leaving Dartmouth he visited a classmate in Cincinnati, and was so impressed with the city that he remained and read law with M. E. Craven. He graduated from Cincinnati Law School in 1858, and established a law practice. At the outset of the Civil War, Noyes helped to raise the 39th Ohio Infantry Regiment, and on July 27, 1861 was commissioned a Major in this regiment. During the war he was engaged in many battles and skirmishes; he lost his left leg and reached the rank of Brigadier General in command of Camp Dennison, Ohio. On April 22, 1865, he resigned to become City Solicitor of Cincinnati. Before his term as solicitor expired, Noyes was elected in October 1866 to the position of Probate Judge of Hamilton County. The Republican State Convention chose him as its gubernatorial candidate in 1871. He polled 238,273 votes to the 218,105 of his Democratic opponent, Colonel George W. McCook. Governor Noyes sponsored new inspection laws for coal mines; investigated Ohio's pardon system; made recommendations for fish conservation measures; and supervised the division of the state into twenty congressional districts. Election laws were also amended to restrict election of judges, and acts were passed to more clearly define the powers and duties of county officers. In 1873 Noyes was again the Republican gubernatorial nominee, but an economic depression, the scandals of Grant's administration, and the aggressive campaign of William Allen, his Democratic rival, combined to defeat Noyes. The final results were 214,654 votes for Allen, as against 213,837 for Noyes. Shortly after this defeat, Noyes made an unsuccessful bid for the Senate. In 1876 he began and helped to manage Rutherford B. Hayes' successful attempt to win the Republican presidential nomination. In 1877 Hayes appointed Noyes Minister to France, an appointment which Noyes filled with distinction for four years, until he returned to Cincinnati to practice law. Noyes died suddenly on September 4, 1890, while serving on the bench of the Superior Court of Cincinnati, a position to which he had been elected a year earlier. Bibliography: Joseph B. Foraker, *Notes of a Busy Life* (Cincinnati, 1917); Carrington T. Marshall, ed., *A History of the Courts and Lawyers of Ohio*, 4 vols. (New York, 1934); Joseph P. Smith, *History of the Repub-

lican Party in Ohio, 2 vols. (Chicago, 1898); C. H. Moore, "Ohio in National Politics 1865-1896," *Ohio State Archeological and Historical Society Quarterly*, vol. XXXVII (1928).

ALLEN, William, 1874-1876

Born on December 18, 1803 in Edenton, North Carolina, son of Nathaniel Allen, Revolutionary soldier and land owner, and Sarah (Colburn) Allen. Half-brother to Joseph Hewes Allen and Mary Granbery Allen Thurman. Orphaned as a small child and reared by his half-sister, who had married Pleasant Thurman, a Methodist Episcopal minister. Married to Effie (McArthur) Coons in 1842 and the father of one daughter. Educated by his half-sister and apprenticed to a saddler. In the winter of 1819, Allen walked from Lynchburg, Virginia, to his half-sister's new home in Chillicothe, Ohio. Studied at Chillicothe Academy for two years and studied law in the office of Rufus King. Admitted to the bar in 1895 and began practice as a partner in King's firm. In 1832 Allen defeated his future father-in-law for a seat in the U.S. House of Representatives. He was defeated for reelection, but in 1837 was chosen by the Democratic State Legislature for a place in the United States Senate. He served until 1848, when he was suggested as a compromise presidential candidate. During the Civil War, Allen was a Peace Democrat and a bitter critic of the Lincoln administration. In 1873, when the Republicans were quarrelling among themselves, Allen's nephew, Senator Allen G. Thurman, nominated him for Governor. After a vigorous campaign Allen defeated the incumbent Republican, Edward F. Noyes, by 214,654 votes to 213,837. As governor, Allen was extremely conscientious. He stressed the need for economy, lower taxes and law enforcement. In 1874, at his suggestion, more than $400,000 was cut from the state's expenditures, and in 1875 the tax levy was reduced, saving the citizens of Ohio more than a million dollars. He called out the state militia twice to establish order during strikes. Allen believed that the rights of property should be protected by law, but that the law must also be respected. He became a fervent supporter of the Greenback crusade, and in a hard fought campaign, was defeated for a second gubernatorial term in 1875. Rutherford B. Hayes, a former Republican governor and a sound money advocate, polled 297,817 votes to Allen's 292,273. After his defeat, Allen retired to private life, and died in his home, "Fruit Hill," in Chillicothe on July 11, 1879. Bibliography: Reginald C. McGraw, *William Allen, A Study in Western Democracy* (1925); the manuscripts and papers of William Allen are on deposit in the Library of Congress; G.H. Porter, "Ohio Politics During the Civil War Period," *Columbia University Studies*, vol. 40 (New York, 1911); E. D. Ross, *The Liberal Republican Movement* (New York, 1919); L. S. Evans, *A Standard History of Ross County, Ohio* (Chicago, 1917).

HAYES, Rutherford Birchard, 1868-1872, 1876-1877

YOUNG, Thomas Lowry, 1877-1878

Born on December 14, 1832, in Killyleagh, County Down, Ireland, emigrated to the United States with his Catholic parents at the age of twelve; no further information available about his parents. Married three times, and survived by eight children. Educated in the public schools of New York City. Studied law after the Civil War, and was admitted to the Ohio Bar in April 1865. In 1848, near the end of the Mexican War, he enlisted in the United States Army as a musician. During the ten years in which he served, he was promoted from Private to First Sergeant. He left the army in 1858, and a year later settled in Cincinnati to become an Instructor and Assistant Superintendent of the Youth House of Refuge Reform School. After his offer to organize volunteer forces was refused by General Winfield Scott three weeks before the bombardment of Fort Sumter, Young became Captain of the Burton Cadets, Missouri Volunteers, and is said to have been General John C. Fremont's bodyguard between September and December of 1861. From then until August of 1862, he was an editor of a Democratic Party paper in Sidney, Ohio. He was soon commissioned Major of the 18th Regiment, Ohio Volunteer Infantry, and was actively involved in the war effort until the fall of 1864, when he was honorably discharged for a disability with the rank of Brigadier-General. His admission to the Ohio Bar in April 1865, was followed by his appointment as Assistant City Auditor of Cincinnati; in the fall of that year he was also elected to the State House of Representatives for one term. He was chosen Recorder of Hamilton County in 1867, and in the following year, President Andrew Johnson appointed him as Supervisor of the Internal Revenue Service for the Southern District of Ohio. He resigned that post at the end of one year. In 1871 he was the only Republican elected to the State Senate from Hamilton County. After the expiration of his Senate term, he returned to private law practice until the Republicans nominated him to run for Lieutenant Governor on a gubernatorial ticket headed by Rutherford B. Hayes. When Hayes moved from the governor's office to the presidency, Young became Governor of Ohio for slightly less than a year. Most of his duties as governor were routine, except for his need to forestall the rioting which in other states had followed in the wake of the railroad strikes of summer, 1877. He did not choose to seek a full term as governor, and retired. With the exception of serving in Congress from 1879 to 1883, Young continued in the legal profession until his death in Cincinnati on July 20, 1888. He was buried in Spring Grove Cemetery. Bibliography: W.A. Taylor, *Ohio in Congress, 1803 to 1901* (Columbus, 1900); J. P. Smith, *History of the Republican Party in Ohio*, 2 vols. (Chicago, 1898); E. O. Randall and C. T. Grene, eds., *Bench and Bar of Ohio*, 2 vols. (Chicago, 1897).

BISHOP, Richard Moore, 1878-1880

Born on March 4, 1812 in Fleming County, Kentucky; father of three sons; member of the Christian Church. Received the limited schooling available on the frontier. At the age of seventeen began his business career as clerk in a country store. Became a partner at the end of four years. In business with his brother from 1838 to 1841, shipping pork down river from Fleming County. This partnership continued until Richard Bishop moved to Cincinnati and established the wholesale grocery firm of Bishop, Wells and Company. This business later became the very successful firm of R. M. Bishop and Company. In 1857 Bishop was elected to the City Council of Cincinnati, and thereafter became presiding officer of that body. He was elected Mayor in 1859 and served until 1861. At the end of his term, both parties offered him the mayoral nomination, but he declined and returned to private life. Although Bishop had become a Baptist at the age of sixteen, he later joined the Church of the Disciples or the Christian Church, and became president of the General Christian Missionary Convention. In 1873 he served as a delegate to the Ohio Constitutional Convention. Four years later the Democratic convention nominated him for Governor. He opposed the Republican candidate, Judge William H. West, and the National or Greenback Labor candidate, S. Johnson. The results were Bishop 271,625, West 249,105, and Johnson 16,912; 17,325 votes were scattered among minor candidates. Bishop's political position was in the main conservative, and this attracted many Republican votes in the gubernatorial race. He campaigned against the Resumption Act of 1875 which let the federal government resume specie payment on legal tender notes, and he favored the remonetization of silver. Under his leadership the General Assembly passed joint resolutions condemning the Resumption Act and approved the Bland-Allison Act, which provided for the coinage of silver. Under Bishop the codification of state laws continued; bribery became a serious crime; and blackmail was defined as a crime. The state's penal and welfare institutions were also reorganized and put into the hands of the Democrats. However, the leaders of the Democratic Party in the state became disturbed by the influence one of the governor's sons was exercising in the making of political appointments, and Bishop was denied the Democratic gubernatorial nomination in 1879. At the end of his term, Bishop returned to his business and educational activities. He died in Jacksonville, Florida on March 2, 1893. Bibliography: Brand Whitlock, *Forty Years of It* (1914); Carl Wittke, ed., *The History of the State of Ohio*, 6 vols. (Columbus, 1941-42); Clara B. Hicks, "The History of Penal Institutions in Ohio," *Ohio State Archeological and Historical Society Quarterly*, vol. XXXIII (1924); H. J. Webster, "History of the Democratic Party Organization," *Ohio State Archeological and Historical Society Quarterly,* vol. XXIV (1915).

FOSTER, Charles, 1880-1884

Born on April 12, 1828 in Rome (now Fostoria), Seneca County, Ohio, son of Charles W. Foster, a dry goods merchant, and Laura (Crocker) Foster. Married to Ann M. Olmsted; father of two daughters. Attended Norwalk Academy until age fourteen, when he began working in his father's store. Became partner and manager at nineteen. Throughout life he was primarily a businessman, expanding his enterprises until they included banking and the gas and oil industry; he amassed a fortune, much of which was lost during the financial depression of the 1890s. Elected to Congress from a normally Democratic district in 1870, and served until defeated for reelection in 1878 in a gerrymandered district. In 1876 he was spokesman for his friend, Rutherford B. Hayes, in assuring southerners that Hayes' election would lead to the withdrawal of federal troops from the South. He was nominated by the Republicans for Governor in 1879 as a sound money candidate, and ran against the Democrat, Thomas Ewing. Foster introduced the preelection poll into his campaign, and sent party workers into doubtful areas; he also made the first large use of money in Ohio elections. He received 335,261 votes to Ewing's 319,132. Two years later he defeated the Democrat J. Bookwalter by a margin of 312,735 to 288,426. As governor, Foster applied ideas of business efficiency to government. He appointed bipartisan boards to manage public institutions, and advocated mine inspections, forest protection and a revision of the tax system. His support of the Pond Law for the taxation of saloons was very unpopular. In 1883 he endorsed the idea of submitting amendments to the voters in order to enable them to indicate whether they preferred prohibition or a license system. The proposed amendments were rejected and the entire Republican ticket was defeated that year, discrediting for a time Foster's leadership. Although he had been mentioned for several political positions, Foster returned to his business interests after his two terms as governor had expired. In February 1891, however, President Harrison named him Secretary of the Treasury. At the expiration of Harrison's term, Foster resumed his private life in Fostoria as a businessman. He died in Springfield, Ohio on January 9, 1904 and was buried in Fountain Cemetery, Fostoria, Ohio. Bibliography: F. C. Pierce, *Foster Genealogy* (1899); C. R. Williams, *The Life of Rutherford Birchard Hayes* (1914); C.R. Williams, ed., *Diary and Letters of Rutherford B. Hayes,* 5 vols. (Columbus, 1922-26); John Sherman, *Recollections of Forty Years* (1895); A. J. Boughman, *History of Seneca County Ohio* (1911); W.S. Kerr, *John Sherman, His Life and Public Service* (1907).

HOADLY, George, 1884-1886

Born in New Haven, Connecticut on July 31, 1826, son of George Hoadly, graduate of Yale and one-time mayor of New Haven, and Mary Ann (Woolset) Hoadly. Married to Mary Burnet Perry on August 13, 1857, and father of two sons and a daughter. Attended public schools in Cleveland; attended Western Reserve College, studied law for a year at Harvard, and completed his preparations for the bar in the office of Salmon P. Chase and his partner in Cincinnati. Admitted to the bar in August 1847. Began a judicial career in 1851 as Judge of the Superior Court of Cincinnati. In 1855 he became City Solicitor. Reelected Judge of the Superior Court in 1859 and 1864, but resigned in 1866. In 1864 Hoadly became a professor in the Cincinnati Law School, and he continued this appointment until 1887. Before his association with Chase, Hoadly had been a Democrat. Although Chase's influence encouraged Hoadly to join the Republicans, that party's reconstruction policy offended him, and he at first moved over to a Liberal Republican position. While the Republican tariff policy caused Hoadly to rejoin the Democratic Party after 1872, he did not espouse Greenback principles. He served as counsel for Tilden in the dispute after the presidential election of 1876, and in 1880 was chosen temporary chairman of the Democratic National Convention. Hoadly was nominated for Governor by the Democratic convention in 1883. Although he was ill during the campaign, the passage by the state's Republican-dominated legislature of a law taxing all places selling liquor assured his victory. He received 359,693 votes to Joseph B. Foraker's 347,164. Hoadly's term as governor was marked by many unpleasant developments. The election of Henry B. Payne to the United States Senate quickly gave rise to rumors of corruption. When labor riots broke out, Hoadly was slow to call out the militia, convincing many voters that he was indecisive. In 1884 Hoadly was nominated for president by the Democratic National

Convention, but was not chosen. He was renominated for governor of Ohio in 1885; however, the scandals touching his previous administration, along with Joseph Foraker's claim that the state had lost revenue when the Democrat-controlled State Supreme Court declared a liquor tax unconstitutional, put the incumbent governor at a disadvantage. Hoadly received only 341,830 votes to Foraker's 359,281. Hoadly renounced politics after his defeat, and in 1887 moved to New York, where he established the successful firm of Hoadly, Lauterbach and Johnson. Although never a man of well-defined religious views, he leaned toward Unitarianism in his later years. He died of acute bronchitis on August 26, 1902 at Watkins, New York. Bibliography: C. T. Greve, *Centennial History of Cincinnati* (1904); F. B. Troubridge, *The Hoadly Genealogy* (1894); Henry Howe, *Historical Collections of Ohio* (1908 edition); B. W. Dwight, *The History of the Descendants of John Dwight*, 2 vols. (1874); J. B. Foraker, *Notes of a Busy Life*, 2 vols. (Cincinnati, 1916).

FORAKER, Joseph Benson, 1886-1890

Born near Rainsboro, Highland County, Ohio on July 5, 1846, son of Thomas S. Foraker, land owner, and Margaret (Reece) Foraker; Methodist Episcopal Church. Brother of Buck, Creighton M. and Charles Foraker; married Julia Bundy on October 4, 1870; father of Arthur, Benson and three others. Attended district schools. In 1861 accepted a clerical position in the office of his uncle; auditor for Highland County. Enlisted July 14, 1862, as a private in Company A, Eighty-ninth Regiment, Ohio Volunteer Infantry; served with distinction until the close of the war, and retired with the rank of First Lieutenant and Brevet Captain. Attended Salem Academy, Ohio Wesleyan University, and graduated from Cornell in Ithaca, New York on July 1, 1869. Admitted to the Ohio Bar on October 14, 1869 and established a practice in Cincinnati. Foraker served as Judge of the Superior Court of Cincinnati from 1879 until his resignation in 1882. In 1883 he was an unsuccessful Republican candidate for Governor against the Democrat George Hoadly. Two years later, in 1885, Foraker was again nominated and again ran against Hoadly. This time Foraker won, receiving 359,281 votes to Hoadly's 341,830. In 1887 Foraker was reelected governor, defeating the Democrat T. Powell and the Prohibition candidate, M. Sharp. Foraker polled 356,534 votes, while Powell and Sharp, respectively received 333,205 and 29,700 votes. As governor, Foraker induced the legislature to pass a tax on liquor which satisfied previous constitutional objections. He secured the establishment of statutes providing for the appointment of a bipartisan Board of Elections and for the registration of voters in large cities; he also improved the system of taxation by appointing tax assessors. Foraker was nominated for governor a fourth time in 1889, but lost the election to his Democratic rival James Campbell, 368,551 votes to 379,423. Foraker was a delegate to the Republican National Convention in 1884, 1888, 1892, 1896 and 1900, and served as Chairman of Ohio's delegation in 1884 and 1888. He chaired the Republican State Convention in 1886, 1890, 1896 and 1900. On January 14, 1896, he was elected to the United States Senate, serving until March 3, 1909. He had been a candidate for reelection, but was defeated when it became known that he had been employed by the Standard Oil Company during his first term as Senator. In 1914 Foraker made an unsuccessful bid to return to the Senate; however, he was defeated in the primaries by Warren G. Harding. He then returned to Cincinnati, where he continued his law practice and wrote his memoirs. Foraker died in Cincinnati on May 10, 1917, and was buried in Spring Grove Cemetery. Bibliography: Joseph B. Foraker, *Notes of a Busy Life*, 2 vols. (Cincinnati, 1916); *Memorial to Joseph Benson Foraker* (1917); Julia Bundy Foraker, *I Would Live It Again* (New York, 1932); *Sketch of Joseph Benson Foraker* (1883); E.O. Randall and Daniel J. Ryan, *History of Ohio*, 5 vols. (New York, 1912).

CAMPBELL, James Edwin, 1890-1892

Born on July 7, 1843, in Middletown, Ohio, son of Andrew Campbell, a surgeon, and Laura (Reynolds) Campbell, both of whom were Presbyterian. Married to Libby Owens in 1870; father of four children. Attended public schools and studied privately with the pastor of Middletown Presbyterian Church. Studied law at Miami University and taught school. Served as a private in the Union Army and then as a Master's Mate in the United States Navy until illness resulted in his honorable discharge in September 1864. Admitted to the Ohio Bar in 1865, and in 1867 began the practice of law in Hamilton, Ohio. Acted as Internal Revenue Collector. Elected Prosecuting Attorney of Butler County in 1875 and 1877. Campbell switched from the Republican to the Democratic Party in 1872. He served in the United States Congress from 1882 to 1889, but did not seek reelection in 1888. After receiving the nomination for Governor from the Democrats at their State Convention in 1889, he urged an intensive campaign against Joseph Foraker, the Republican incumbent. Campbell won the election by a margin of 379,423 votes to 368,551. Campbell's campaign slogan had been "Home Rule for the Cities of Ohio," and during his term as governor he attempted to make the slogan a reality with varying degrees of success. Campbell insisted that the governor ought to be divested of the power to appoint election boards, clerks, and various other governing bodies, a power which could permit him virtual control over most cities. The legislature acted on his advice in most cases, but not in the case of Cincinnati's Board of Public Affairs. Campbell, greatly chagrined, appointed the board, but soon had reason to suspect some of the members' integrity. Using this case as an example, he called a special meeting of the legislature, which returned the appointive power to the mayor. During Campbell's administration, Ohio enacted various laws beneficial to labor, and introduced the Australian ballot system. Campbell also secured a tax levy to support Ohio State University. Although he was renominated for Governor in 1891, he had alienated many of his party's officials, including the former president of the Cincinnati Board of Public Affairs, who was also the chairman of the Democratic committee of Hamilton County. After a gentlemanly and hard-fought campaign, Campbell received 365,228 votes, compared with the 386,739 of his Republican opponent, William McKinley. The Prohibition Party candidate, Richard Seitz, captured 23,472 votes. Campbell was again nominated for Governor in 1895 and reluctantly accepted. Though he put up the hardest fight of his career, he was soundly defeated by Republican Asa S. Bushnell. Bushnell received 427,141 votes to Campbell's 334,519, while Jacob Coxey, the Prohibition candidate, polled 52,675. Campbell then resumed his law practice, returning to politics only from 1907 to 1910, when he was a member of the convention to revise and codify the statutes of Ohio. He died in Columbus on December 18, 1924, and was interred in Greenlawn Cemetery. Bibliography: Joseph B. Foraker, *Notes of a Busy Life* (Cincinnati,

1916); Brand Whitlock, *Forty Years of It* (New York, 1914); H. J. Webster, "History of the Democratic Party Organization," *Ohio State Archeological and Historical Society Quarterly,* vol. XXIV (1915); C.H. Moore, "Ohio in National Politics, 1865-1896," *Ohio State Archeological and Historical Society Quarterly,* vol. XXXVII (1928).

McKINLEY, William, 1892-1896

Born on January 29, 1843 in Niles, Ohio, son of William McKinley, an iron manufacturer, and Nancy (Allison) McKinley; a Methodist. Brother of David, James, Anna, Mary, Sarah Elizabeth, Helen and Abner. Married to Ida Saxton on January 24, 1871; father of Ida and Katie, both of whom died young. Attended public schools, Poland Seminary and, for a year, Allegheny College in Meadville, Pennsylvania. Enlisted in Company E, 23rd Ohio Volunteer Infantry on June 11, 1861. Mustered out on July 26, 1865, with the rank of Brevet Major. Studied law at Poland Seminary and at Albany Law School while a school teacher. Admitted to the bar in 1867 and set up practice in Canton. Campaigned for his old commander, Rutherford B. Hayes, who was running for governor. Elected Prosecuting Attorney of Stark County in 1869 and served until 1871. Served in the U. S. Congress from 1876 to 1890, with the exception of May 24, 1884, to March 3, 1885, when he was unseated in a contested election by Jonathan H. Welles. Defeated for Congress in 1890 and returned to private life, but was nominated for Governor in 1891. Served as an Ohio delegate at the Republican National Convention in 1884, 1888 and 1892. With the strong support of the Sherman-Hanna faction, he easily won the gubernatorial race. He received 386,739 votes against the 365,228 cast for the incumbent Democratic governor, James E. Campbell, and the 23,472 received by the Prohibition candidate. He was reelected two years later over the Democrat L. Neal by a margin of 433,342 votes to 352,347. Governor McKinley developed a new and more comprehensive tax system, which levied excise taxes on corporations and reduced the state debt. He insisted that legislation should be passed to require safety devices on railroads. He also promoted the enactment of a law which set up a State Board of Arbitration for labor disputes. In 1895 he organized private groups to aid unemployed coal miners in the Hocking Valley. In 1894, however, he responded to a coal miners' strike by calling out the National Guard to prevent the destruction of private property. Soon after his reelection, McKinley became the leading contender for the Republican presidential nomination. Mark Hanna managed his campaign and was successful in making McKinley the nominee at the 1896 convention. In the fall, McKinley defeated William Jennings Bryan by well over half a million votes. During his first term he led the U. S. into war with Spain and launched America on a more determined imperialist policy. He was reelected, but six months later an assassin shot him at the Buffalo Exposition. He died of complications resulting from the wound on September 14, 1901, and was buried in Canton, Ohio. Bibliography: William McKinley Papers in the Library of Congress; H. Wayne Morgan, *William McKinley and His America* (Syracuse, New York, 1963); Margaret Leech, *In the Days of McKinley* (New York, 1959); Paul W. Glad, *McKinley, Bryan and the People* (Philadelphia, 1964); Murat Halstead, *The Illustrious Life of William McKinley* (1901); Charles S. Alcott, *The Life of William McKinley,* 2 vols. (Boston, 1916).

BUSHNELL, Asa S., 1896-1900

Born on September 16, 1834, in Rome, New York, son of Daniel Bushnell, a school teacher, and Harriet (Smith) Bushnell; a member of the Protestant Episcopal Church. Married to Ellen Ludlow in 1857; father of two daughters and a son. Received a limited education in Cincinnati; left home at age seventeen and went to work in Springfield as a clerk and bookkeeper. At the outbreak of the Civil War, joined Company E of the 162nd Ohio Volunteer Infantry as Captain. After the war, he returned and began a business career. By 1867 became a partner in the business he later incorporated as the Warder, Bushnell and Glessner Company; Bushnell became its president in 1886. Served on the Springfield City Council and selected as its president in 1882. Managed Joseph Foraker's successful gubernatorial campaign in 1885, and remained active in Republican politics. As a result of factional strife, the Republican State Convention nominated Bushnell for Governor in 1895. He was a member of the Foraker faction of the party which had seized control of the party in that year. In the general election, Bushnell defeated the former Democratic governor, James Campbell, by 427,141 votes to 334,519. Two years later, he defeated H. Chapman, his Democratic rival, by a margin of 429,915 to 401,750. Bushnell's administration was noted for its efficient handling of state business. He improved the state's financial management and introduced the merit system into its civil service. Favoring war with Spain, Bushnell made advance preparations so that Ohio could become the first state to field troops when war was declared. He also recommended legislation to levy excise taxes on public utility companies and certain other corporations. Other legislative developments during Bushnell's tenure in office included the passage of the Valentine Act and social legislation which regulated the working hours of women and minors; the substitution of electrocution for hanging as a means of capital punishment in the state; and the establishment of a Board of Medical Registration and Qualification. When a vacancy occurred in the United States Senate, Bushnell delayed filling it. Loyal to Foraker, he did not want to appoint Mark Hanna, but under pressure from President McKinley and Boss Cox, he finally made the appointment. Although reelected in 1897, Bushnell became involved in a bitter and fruitless effort to prevent the election of Hanna to the United States Senate. This struggle left him so bitter that he refused to consider running for a third term. After the expiration of his second gubernatorial term, Bushnell resumed his business activities. He sold his mower company to International Harvester, and became president of the First National Bank of Springfield and of the Springfield Gas Company. At the time of his death, he was engaged in promoting an electric interurban railway. He was stricken with apoplexy at the inauguration of Governor Herrick, and died in Columbus on January 15, 1904. Bibliography: G. F. Wright, *Representative Citizens of Ohio* (1918); B. F. Pierce, ed., *A Standard History of Springfield and Clark County, Ohio* (1922); George W. Knight, "Sketch and Genealogy," *Old Northwest Genealogical Quarterly* (July, 1904); H.D. Croly *Marcus Alonzo Hanna* (1912); J.B. Foraker, *Notes of a Busy Life* (Cincinnati, 1916).

NASH, George Kilbon, 1900-1904

Born on August 14, 1842 in York Township, Medina County, Ohio; no other information available about his family except that he was preceded in death by his wife and only child, a daughter. Studied at Western Reserve Academy and attended Oberlin College for two years. Entered the Union Army as a private in 1864. Read law in Columbus and was admitted to the bar in 1867. Appointed Chief Clerk in the office of the Secretary of State in 1869. During the 1870's he was elected twice as Prosecuting Attorney of Franklin County and from June 1880 to 1884, he served as Attorney General in the administration of Governor Charles Foster. At the end of Foster's term, he appointed Nash to the Supreme Court Commission, a body which helped the court to clear its docket. Chosen for Governor by Mark Hanna in 1895, Nash lost the nomination to Asa Bushnell and the Foraker faction. Nash was, however, named Chairman of the Republican State Executive Committee in 1897, and at the Republican State Convention in 1899, supported by Hanna and Boss Cox of Cincinnati, he was chosen as the Republican nominee for Governor. In the election Nash received 417,199 votes; John R. McLean the Democratic candidate, received 368,176; and Samuel M. Jones, an Independent, received 106,721 votes. Two years later Nash defeated James Kilborne by a margin of 436,092 votes to 368,525. Nash had a reputation as a strong governor, and during his administration the power of the governor was considerably enhanced. In 1903 a constitutional amendment conferred a limited veto power on the governor, and the affairs of many municipal governments were brought under the control of the governor and his appointees. Under Nash's direction a uniform auditing system for state offices and institutions was established, and vigorous investigations of several state schools and hospitals were conducted. During his administration laws were passed requiring corporations to pay a fee of one-tenth of one percent upon their capital investments; the public utility tax was raised to one percent of gross receipts; and out-of-state insurance companies were taxed two and a half percent of their gross Ohio receipts. At the same time, the direct property tax was reduced from 28 to 13½ cents per hundred dollars of valuation. Nash chose to retire after his two terms as governor. He died on October 28, 1904, and was buried in Columbus, Franklin County. Bibliography: Joseph Benson Foraker, *Notes of a Busy Life*, 2 vols. (Cincinnati, 1916); Francis R. Aumann, "Ohio Government in the Twentieth Century: From Nash to White (1900-1931)," *Ohio in the Twentieth Century* (Columbus, 1943); Herbert Croly, *Marcus Alonzo Hanna* (New York, 1912); Tom L. Johnson, *My Story* (New York, 1913); Carrington T. Marshall, *A History of the Courts and Lawyers of Ohio*, 4 vols. (New York, 1934).

HERRICK, Myron, 1904-1906

Born on October 9, 1854, in Huntington, Lorain County, Ohio, son of Timothy R. Herrick, a farmer, and Mary (Hulbert) Herrick; a member of the Episcopal Church. Married to Carolyn M. Parmely on June 30, 1880; father of Parmely Webb. Attended public schools in Huntington and Wellington and, after teaching school and writing for a newspaper to earn enough money, attended Oberlin Academy for a year and a half and Ohio Wesleyan University for two years. Read law in the offices of G. E. and J. F. Herrick in Cleveland, and was admitted to the Ohio Bar in 1878. Opened a law office and began several profitable business ventures; gained the sponsorship of Mark Hanna, which enabled him to become secretary and treasurer, and by 1894 president and chairman of the board of the Society for Savings. He was also director of several railroads and trust companies; elected president of the American Bankers Association, 1901; elected to City Council of Cleveland in 1885 and served two terms. In 1888 he won control of a Republican district convention in opposition to Mark Hanna, but selected Hanna as the district's first delegate. He was also Colonel on McKinley's gubernatorial staff and a leading member of the Republican State and National Committees. He played an influential role in the nomination and election of McKinley for President in 1896. In June 1903, he received the nomination for Governor of Ohio. He was elected over the Democratic candidate, Tom L. Johnson, by a vote of 475,560 to 361,748. Herrick's administration as governor was characterized by a conservative conduct of public affairs, with close attention paid to sound fiscal policy. He vetoed several measures he thought inimical to the best interests of the state. The Republicans in Ohio had split into several factions, led respectively by Senator Hanna, George B. Cox of Cincinnati and Senator Joseph B. Foraker. It was very difficult for Herrick to take any action without incurring opposition from one or more of these groups. During his term, he was also forced to deal with the volatile gambling and liquor questions. He was presented with a bill allowing betting at race tracks, but vetoed the bill, gaining the church vote but alienating the leaders of Cleveland. When the Brannasck Bill, a local liquor option bill, was near its passage, he forced certain changes in it which alienated the pro-liquor leaders as well as some church people. Because of this, although he received his party's nomination in 1905, he received only 430,617 votes in the election, while John Pattison, his Democratic opponent, polled 473,264. After his defeat, Herrick returned to his business affairs. He received at least three offers of appointment from two presidents before accepting President Taft's appointment as Ambassador to France. He served until December 1914, and with special distinction during the first months of World War I. He was also an unsuccessful candidate for the United States Senate in 1916. President Harding again appointed him Ambassador to France in 1921, and he served until his death on March 31, 1929, which resulted in part from exhaustion after attending Marshal Foch's funeral. His body was returned to Cleveland for burial. Bibliography: Myron T. Herrick, *Rural Credits* (1914); T. Bentley Mott, *Myron T. Herrick, Friend of France* (1929); James K. Mercer, *Representative Men of Ohio* (1908); E. L. Bogart, *Financial History of Ohio* (Champaign-Urbana, 1912); Thomas Beer, *Hanna* (1929); C.H. Moore, "Ohio in National Politics, 1865-1896," *Ohio State Archeological and Historical Society Quarterly,* vol. XXXVII (1928); Jedediah and L.C. Herrick, *Herrick Genealogy* (1885).

PATTISON, John M., 1906

Born on June 13, 1847 near Owensville, Clermont County, Ohio, son of William Pattison, merchant, and Mary (Duckwall) Pattison; Methodist. Married to Alethia Williams on December 10, 1879 and much later in life to Anna Williams; father of Alethia, Ernestine and John. Attended public schools and worked as clerk in his father's store until joining the 153rd Ohio Volunteer Infantry in 1864 as a private. After the war, entered Ohio Wesleyan University and graduated in 1869. Became an agent for the Union Central Life Insurance Company in Bloomington, Illinois. Returned to Cincinnati, read law in the office of Alfred Yaple, and was admitted to the bar in 1872. Served as attorney for the Cincinnati and Marietta Railroad until his election to the State Legislature in 1873, representing Hamilton County. Declined renomination and entered the firm of Yaple, Moss and Pattison. In 1881 elected vice president of Union Central Life and became its president in 1891. Elected to the State Senate in 1890 and the U.S. Congress in 1891. Renominated but defeated. Nominated by the Democratic Party for Governor in 1905. He received 473,264 votes to defeat the Republican incumbent, Myron Herrick, who polled 430,617. Pattison, though ill during the entire session of the General Assembly bly, saw legislation passed which raised the sales tax from $350 to $1,000, and a law approved authorizing local option in residential areas. He was a Christian and an ardent temperance man. He also endorsed legislation designed to invest idle county funds and to establish salaries for county officials. A two-cent railroad fare was passed, and the office of commissioner of railroads and telegraphs was superseded by a Railroad Commission of three men. The campaign had been an arduous one for Pattison, who was the only Democrat elected to state office that year. He appeared frail and worn when delivering his inaugural address, and continued to decline. In April he was moved to Christ Hospital and was later taken to his home in Milford, Clermont County. He died there on June 18, 1906. Bibliography: T. E. Powell, *The Democratic Party in Ohio*, 2 vols. (1913); Hoyt Landow Warner, *Progressivism in Ohio, 1897-1917* (Columbus, 1964); James M. Cox, *Journey Through My Years* (New York, 1946); Brand Whitlock, *Forty Years of It* (New York, 1914).

HARRIS, Andrew L., 1906-1909

Born on November 17, 1835, in Butler County, Ohio, son of Benjamin Harris, farmer and school teacher, and Nancy (Lintner) Harris. Married to Caroline Conger in October 1865; father of one son. Attended county schools and Miami University. After graduation in 1860, read law in the firm of Thompson and Eaton. Enlisted in the Union Army in April 1861 as a private. Attained the rank of Colonel. Fought in eighteen battles; seriously wounded and elevated to Colonel and Regimental Commander. He was mustered out on January 15, 1865, and on March 13, 1866, was breveted Brigadier General for "gallant and meritorious" service. Admitted to bar in April 1865. Elected to State Senate in 1866. Formed a law partnership with Robert Miller in Easton in 1866. In 1875 and 1878, elected Probate Judge of Preble County. After a short-lived retirement, he was elected to the State Legislature in 1885 and 1887; served as Lieutenant Governor under William McKinley in 1892-1896; was appointed by President McKinley to the Federal Industrial Commission on Trusts and Industrial Combinations; and was chairman of the Subcommittee on Agriculture from 1898 to 1902. Harris was elected Lieutenant Governor as a Republican in 1905. On June 18, 1906, Democratic Governor Pattison died in office and Harris became Governor. Because of a constitutional amendment adopted in 1905 which provided that subsequent elections be held in even numbered years, the Pattison-Harris administration was to run for three years, from 1906 to 1909. Under Harris, the Ohio State Legislature was especially active. The lawmakers passed a pure food and drug law; adopted conservation measures; established a Bureau of Vital Statistics; and barred corporations from contributing money to political candidates or causes. In January 1909, Harris called the General Assembly into extraordinary session to elect a United States Senator, appropriate money, and consider other routine matters. He also supported the passage of the Rose Law, which enabled well over half the counties in the state to go dry. Because of this act, he incurred the displeasure of the liquor forces, and although he was nominated by acclamation at the Republican convention, he was defeated by the Democrat, Judson Harmon. Harmon received 552,569 votes, while Harris polled 533,917. At the expiration of his term, Harris retired to his farm in Easton. He died there of heart trouble on September 13, 1915. Bibliography: Joseph B. Foraker, *Notes of a Busy Life* (Cincinnati, 1916); Hoyt L. Warner, *Progressivism in Ohio, 1897-1917* (Columbus, 1964); Robert S. Maxwell, ed., "A Document on the Progressive Campaign of 1912," *Mississippi Valley Historical Review,* volume XXXVI (June, 1949); James K. Mercer, ed., *Ohio Legislative History*, 6 vols. (Columbus, 1914-1926); Francis R. Aumann, *Ohio Government in the Twentieth Century, 1900-1938* (Columbus, 1942).

HARMON, Judson, 1909-1913

Born on February 3, 1846, in Newton, Hamilton County, Ohio, son of Franklin Harmon, a teacher and Baptist preacher, and Julia (Bronson) Harmon; eldest of eight children; a Baptist. Married to Olivia Scobey in June 1870; father of three daughters. Entered Denison University at the age of sixteen and graduated four years later. Spent one summer vacation as a private in the Home Guard. Taught school in Columbia, then moved to Cincinnati and read law in the office of George Hoadly. In 1896 received his law degree from Cincinnati Law School and was admitted to the bar. Elected Judge of Court of Common Pleas in Cincinnati in 1876, but was ousted by the Ohio Senate. In 1878 he was elected to the local Superior Court and served until resigning in 1887. Although originally a Republican, Harmon joined the Democratic Party after the Civil War. In June 1895, President Cleveland appointed him Attorney General. He returned to his law practice in 1897, and was then appointed Special Investigator. In 1908, despite the opposition of Tom L. Johnson, Harmon received the Democratic nomination for Governor. His Republican opponent, A. L. Harris, received 533,197 votes to Harmon's 552,569. Two years later Harmon was reelected, winning 477,077 votes to defeat the Republican, Warren G. Harding, who polled 376,700 votes, and the Socialist, Felix Clifford, who received 60,637. Governor Harmon's administration was marked by Ohio's ratification of the federal income tax amendment; the adoption of a law which created a single board for the state's penal, benevolent and reformatory institutions; and the passage of a new corrupt practices act to insure against the traffic in votes. Harmon also signed a model workmen's compensation act, another act which provided for the direct popular election of United States Senators, and a statute creating a Public Utility Commission. In 1912 Harmon was Ohio's favorite son candidate for President. He had strong support, but when he declared his opposition to statewide initiative and referendum, the supporters of William Jennings Bryan in Ohio denounced him as a "reactionary," and his support dwindled with each convention ballot. Eventually, Woodrow Wilson was selected as the Democratic nominee. Harmon returned to the practice of law in Cincinnati when his term ended in 1913. He refused to reenter active politics, preferring to continue as a successful corporation attorney and a professor at the Cincinnati Law School. He died in Cincinnati on February 22, 1927. Bibliography: The Judson Harmon Executive Records and Correspondence of Ohio Governors are on deposit in the Ohio Historical Society, Columbus, Ohio; Judson Harmon, *Messages and Other Official Papers of Judson Harmon Governor of Ohio, 1909-1913* (Columbus, 1913); A. C. Harmon, *The Harmon Genealogy, Comprising All Branches in New England* (1920); T.E. Powell, *The Democratic Party in Ohio,* vol. 1 (1913); James M. Cox, "Governor Judson Harmon," *Independent*, LXXI (November 2, 1911).

COX, James Middleton, 1913-1915, 1917-1921

Born near Jacksonburg, Butler County, Ohio, on March 31, 1870, the son of a farmer. Married twice; father of six children. Member of United Brethren, later an Episcopalian. Attended Butler county schools and Amanda (Ohio) High School. After two years of high school passed the teachers' examination and began teaching school at the age of sixteen. Later became a printer's devil, newspaper reporter, and then secretary to Congressman Paul Sorg from 1894 to 1897. Owner and publisher of the Dayton *Daily News* in 1898, and the Springfield *Daily News* in 1903. Elected to the United States Congress as a Democrat, and served from March 4, 1909, to January 12, 1913, when he resigned after being elected Governor of Ohio. In the election, Cox received 439,323 votes to 272,500 for the Republican, Edward Brown, and 217,903 for the Progressive, E. H. Garford. 107,005 votes were scattered among minor party candidates. Cox was elected Governor at the height of Ohio's progressive movement. In his first message to the legislature, he mapped out a fifty-six point program embracing every reform for which there had been a popular demand. By the end of his first term, he had engineered the passage of all of them. Some of the major items of his program included the adoption of a direct primary law; safeguards for the use of initiative and referendum; court reorganization; extension of the civil service law; authorization of a budget commission; centralization of the tax machinery; and creation of a commission to insure unified management of industrial and agricultural policies. He also initiated basic conservation legislation and a good roads program; secured passage of an optional municipal charter law; and encouraged the rewriting of the rural school code. Humanitarian legislation passed during the Cox administration included a model workmen's compensation law, a mothers' pension law, a children's code, the Bureau of Juvenile Research Act, and laws which produced enlightened changes in the state penal system. Cox was renominated in 1914 and received 493,804 votes, but his Republican opponent, Frank Willis, won the election with 523,074 votes. The Progressive candidate, Garfield, trailed in the balloting with 60,904. Two years later Cox ran again, and this time defeated Willis, 568,218 votes to 561,602. The two rivals faced each other for a third time in 1918, and again Cox narrowly beat Willis, this time by a vote of 486,403 to 474,459. During his last two terms, Cox refined but did not introduce any new reform legislation, both because of popular sentiment and because of the United States' entry into World War I three months after his second inauguration. Cox was an unsuccessful candidate for President in 1920; he was later vice chairman of the United States delegation to the World Economic Conference at London in 1933, and President of its Monetary Commission. He refused an appointment to the United States Senate in 1946, preferring to continue as publisher of six newspapers and owner of several radio and television stations. He died in Dayton on July 15, 1957, and was interred in Woodland Cemetery. Bibliography: James M. Cox's Gubernatorial Papers are on deposit in the Ohio Historical Society, Columbus, Ohio; James M. Cox, *Journey Through My Years* (New York, 1946); Roger W. Bobson, *Cox—The Man* (New York, 1920); Hoyt Landon Warner, *Progressivism in Ohio, 1897-1917* (Columbus, 1964); Charles E. Morris, *Progressive Democracy of James M. Cox* (Indianapolis, 1920); Hester E. Hasford, "Ohio's Contribution to Reform; an Interview with Governor James M. Cox," *Independent* (September 4, 1913).

WILLIS, Frank Bartlett, 1915-1917

Born in Lewis Center, Delaware County, Ohio, on November 28, 1871, son of a farmer. Married; father of one daughter, Helen. Attended public schools and high school. Taught school, chopped wood, and did odd jobs to finance his way through Ohio Northern University, from which he graduated in 1894. Studied law and was admitted to the bar in 1901. While studying was professor of history and economics at Ohio Northern. In 1906 became a professor of economics and law, and taught until 1910. Served as a member of Ohio's House of Representatives from 1900-1904. Elected as a Republican to the United States Congress, where he served from March 4, 1911 to January 9, 1915, when he resigned after being elected Governor of Ohio. Willis entered the gubernatorial primary because he correctly judged that the voters wanted a respite from the mass of legislation created during the first term of incumbent Governor James Cox. In the general election, Willis received 523,074 votes to Cox's 493,804, with some 120,000 votes scattered among William Garfield, the Progressive candidate, and others. As governor, Willis stressed economy and retrenchment. He promised a strong campaign against needless and excessive legislative activity. There were some important measures approved by Willis, however, including revision of the road laws; reorganization of the state militia; reorganization of the civil service commission; provisions for the election rather than appointment of land assessment officers; revision of the entire liquor licensing system; and regulations governing the appointment of county agricultural agents. In January 1916, Willis ordered part of the militia to East Youngstown to quell violence which had erupted during a steel strike. When Mexican border trouble took a turn for the worse, he quickly mobilized the entire Ohio National Guard. In 1916 Willis was again the Republican nominee but lost to James Cox, 561,602 votes to 568,218. The election of 1918 featured the same two candidates, with Cox again the victor by a close margin of 486,403 votes to 474,459. As a delegate to the Republican National Convention in 1916, Willis nominated Theodore E. Benton for President; in 1920, he nominated Warren G. Harding. He was elected in 1920 to the United States Senate. He was again a delegate to the Republican National Convention in 1924, and his name was put forward as a presidential candidate in 1928, but on March 30, 1928, Willis died in the midst of a political rally. He was buried in Oak Grove Cemetery near Delaware, Ohio. Bibliography: The Willis Gubernatorial Papers are on deposit in the Ohio Historical Society, Columbus, Ohio: James M. Cox, *Journey Through My Years* (New York, 1946); Joseph B. Foraker, *Notes of a Busy Life* (Cincinnati, 1916); Hoyt Landon Warner, *Progressivism in Ohio, 1897-1917* (Columbus, 1964).

COX, James Middleton, 1913-1915, 1917-1921

DAVIS, Harry L., 1921-1923

Born on January 25, 1878, in Cleveland, Ohio, son of a Welsh immigrant, who worked in the Cleveland steel mills; a Baptist. Married to Lucy V. Forgan on July 16, 1902; father of Harry L. Davis, Jr. Attended public schools until thirteen, when he went to work in the steel mill, and afterwards continued his education in night school and business college. His father was elected to the State Legislature and young Davis was appointed a page, a position which led him to participate actively in Republican politics while still in his early teens. He was elected Treasurer of Cleveland in 1909, and six years later was elected to the first of three successive terms as Mayor. He also continued in the insurance business. Because of Davis's popularity as mayor, he was selected as the Republican candidate for Governor in the 1920 primary. He was carried into the governor's office by the Republican landslide, which also sent Ohio's Warren G. Harding to the White House. Davis's election by a vote of 1,039,835 to 918,962, was the only political defeat ever experienced by his Democratic opponent, A. Victor Donahey. Although Governor Davis had an overwhelmingly Republican legislature to work with, his administration was not a smooth one. Before the end of the first year's session, there were rumors that the Senate wanted to investigate some administrative activities and state contracts. The Senate and House were also at loggerheads over tax legislation and the time of adjournment. The impasse reached a point where the governor, exercising a constitutional prerogative seldom used before, prorogued the General Assembly on May 28, 1921. When Ohio's economy was threatened by a coal miners' work stoppage, however, Davis called the legislature back into special session in September. The lawmakers then passed an emergency law setting up a fuel administrator, with powers to fix the price of coal at the mines and at retail outlets, and with authority to seize and operate the mines if necessary to obtain sufficient fuel for the state's needs. The fuel administration functioned until December 1, 1922, when the office was abolished by executive order. Another piece of legislation which caused some consternation was the state government organization code. After a bitter legislative battle, it was passed as an emergency measure, thus preventing a referendum on it. This resulted in a case before the State Supreme Court, which established that the legislature had the right to determine the emergency character of bills. Davis also pushed through two tax measures which provided building funds for the state's universities and for a welfare institution. Davis refused to be a candidate for reelection in 1922. He ran again against Donahey in 1924, but lost by a vote of 1,064,981 to 888,139. He then returned to his insurance business and spearheaded a campaign to oust the city manager system and to restore the offices of mayor and city councilman to Cleveland. He succeeded, and served another term from 1933 to 1935 as Mayor of Cleveland. He died on May 21, 1950. Bibliography: Charles E. Kennedy, *Fifty Years of Cleveland, 1875-1925* (Cleveland, 1925); James K. Mercer, ed., *Ohio Legislative History*, 6 vols. (Columbus, 1926); Archer H. Shaw, *One Hundred Years in Cleveland* (New York, 1942); Francis R. Aumann, "Ohio Government in the Twentieth Century: From Nash to White (1900-1931)," Harlow Lindley, comp., *Ohio in the Twentieth Century, 1900-1938* (Columbus, 1943).

DONAHEY, Alvin Victor, 1923-1929

Born on July 7, 1873 on a farm near Cadwallader, Tuscarawas County, Ohio, son of John C. Donahey, teacher, farmer, live stock buyer and county clerk, and Catherine (Chaney) Donahey; a member of the Methodist Episcopal Church. Brother of Hal and Will. Married to Mary Edith Harvey on January 5, 1897; father of twelve children. Attended elementary school in West Chester and high school in New Philadelphia, but quit in his junior year to learn the printing trade. Bought his own print shop at the age of twenty. Elected clerk of Goshen Township Board of Trustees in 1898 and served until 1903. From 1905 through 1909, he served as city auditor. From 1902 to 1911 he was a member of the Board of Education. In 1912, he was a delegate to the Fourth Ohio Constitutional Convention and was elected State Auditor, serving until 1921. He ran unopposed in the 1920 Democratic primary but was defeated by Harry Davis. Davis received 1,039,835 votes to Donahey's 918,962. He was again a candidate in 1922, this time defeating the Republican, Thompson 821,948 to 803,300. In 1924, the Republicans nominated Davis again but this time Donahey defeated him by a vote of 1,064,981 to 888,139. When he ran for a third consecutive term against Myers Cooper, Donahey received 707,733 votes to Cooper's 685,597 votes. Donahey became known as "Honest Vic, the Watchdog of the Treasury" while auditor. As governor, he received the title "Veto Vic." As a Republican governor, he had to contend with a heavily Democratic legislature. During his first term alone, he vetoed seventy-six bills and appropriations for $4 million. Although some were eventually passed over his veto, during his tenure as governor, he vetoed every bill which sought to increase taxes. He also vetoed a Ku Klux Klan bill to require daily Bible reading in public schools and the Anti-Saloon League's bill to require public law offenders to serve out unpaid fines by manual labor. On the premise that prohibition enforcement was directed unduly against the poor, he pardoned more than two thousand offenders from jails and work houses. Retiring from the governorship in 1929, Donahey organized and became president of Motorists' Mutual Insurance Company of Columbus. He resided on an island on Indian Lake until nominated for the United States Senate in 1934. He served honorably until he refused to run for reelection and returned to his insurance business in 1941. After several years of failing health, he died in Columbus on April 8, 1946. He was buried in New Philadelphia. Bibliography: Francis R. Aumann, "Ohio Government in the Twentieth Century: From Nash to White (1900-1931)," Harlow Lindley, comp., *Ohio in the Twentieth Century, 1900-1938* (Columbus, 1943); Albert H. Rose, *Ohio Government, State and Local* (St. Louis, 1953); Nelson L. Bosing, "History of Educational Legislation in Ohio from 1851 to 1925," *The Ohio State Archeological and Historical Society Quarterly*, vol. XXXIX (1930); Emory C. Glander, "Tax Administration and Procedure in Ohio," *Ohio State Law Journal*, vol. I (Spring, 1950).

COOPER, Myers Y., 1929-1931

Born on November 25, 1873, near Saint Louisville, Licking County, Ohio, son of Lemuel Cooper, a farmer, and Ann Cooper; Disciple of Christ. Brother of Sanson, James and eight others; married to Martha Kinney; father of Raymond K. and

Martha Ann Judy. Attended country school in Echo and the National Normal University in Lebanon for two years. Entered the real estate business in Cincinnati in 1894. Interest expanded into home construction, lumber distribution and coal mining. Campaigned for Taft in 1908. Joined the Bull Moose movement in 1912, but returned to the regular Republican Party in 1916 and served as state and national party convention delegate regularly until his nomination as governor. Cooper also served as president of the Ohio Fair Managers' Association for eleven years and president for three terms of the Ohio Council of Churches. He was nominated in the Republican primary for Governor in 1926, but lost the election to the Democratic incumbent, Victor Donahey, by a vote of 685,897 to 707,733. Again nominated in the primaries of 1928, he was this time more successful against a lesser-known Democrat, Martin L. Davey. Cooper received 1,355,526 votes to Davey's 1,106,739. As governor, Cooper enjoyed a harmonious relationship with the State Legislature. He vetoed twenty-two bills and permitted three to become law without his signature. All of his vetoes were upheld by the legislature, a sharp contrast to the manner in which the lawmakers had overruled his immediate predecessor. In addition, all of the eleven recommendations which Cooper made to the legislature became law. These included closer regulations of the utility companies; revision of the General Corporation Act and of the state's criminal procedure code; strengthening of the election and banking laws; revision of the highway code; and enaction of a law for the conservation of natural resources. He also implemented the financial provisions of the Reorganization Act of 1921. Cooper was a candidate for re-election in 1930, but lost to the Democrat, George White, by a vote of 923,538 to 1,033,168. After leaving the governor's office, Cooper returned to his business activities in Cincinnati. In 1932 he again offered himself as a gubernatorial candidate, but was defeated in the primaries. He then resumed his party, community and private activities. He died in Cincinnati on December 7, 1958. Bibliography: Myers Cooper's Official Correspondence and Executive Records are on deposit in the Ohio Historical Society, Columbus, Ohio; Harvey Walker, *Constructive Government in Ohio; The Story of the Administration of Governor Myers Y. Cooper, 1929-1931* (Columbus, 1948); Francis R. Aumann, "Ohio Government in the Twentieth Century: From Nash to White (1900-1931)," Harlow Lindley, comp., *Ohio in the Twentieth Century, 1900-1938* (Columbus, 1943).

WHITE, George, 1931-1935

Born in Elmira, New York on August 21, 1872, one of two children of Charles W. White, jeweler, and Mary (Black) White; a Presbyterian. Married to Charlotte McKelvy on September 25, 1900; father of three sons and two daughters; remarried to Mrs. Agnes Hofmann Baldwin in April, 1936; father of one son. Moved with his parents to Titusville, Crawford County, Pennsylvania in 1874; attended the common schools and graduated from the local high school in 1891 and from Princeton College in 1895. Worked in a lumber camp, as a roustabout in the oil fields of northwestern Pennsylvania, and as a school teacher. Mined in the Klondike from 1898 to 1901. Moved to Washington County, Ohio in 1902, settling in Marietta. Entered the oil business in Ohio and West Virginia and later in Oklahoma. Served in the Ohio House of Representatives as a Democrat, 1905-1908. After two unsuccessful attempts, he was elected to Congress in 1910 and 1912.

He lost his reelection bid in 1914, won in 1916, and lost in 1918. He was selected the Democratic National Chairman to manage Cox's presidential campaign
in 1920 and served until November 1921. He won the Democratic gubernatorial
primary in 1930 and defeated the incumbent Republican, Myers Cooper, by a vote
of 1,033,168 to 923,538. Two years later, he made a successful bid for reelection
against the Republican Ingalls, by a vote of 1,356,518 to 1,151,933. As governor,
White's primary concerns resulted from the nationwide economic depression. He
reduced salaries and state expenditures by supplanting real estate taxes, which he
felt bore unfairly on the rural population, with a series of new taxes on intangibles
including cigarettes, beer, cosmetics, an excise tax on public utilities and, most
controversial of all, a general retail sales tax of three percent. He also created a
State Highway Patrol and provided for a system of liquor controls. He concurred
with New Deal policies, although it was widely assumed that he was not a New
Dealer at heart. He announced himself for the Senate in January of 1934, but President Roosevelt and other influential leaders endorsed another candidate, Charles
West and a third candidate, Vic Donahey, was the nominee. White finished his
term as governor. In 1938, White again sought the senatorial nomination, but again
the New Dealers opposed him. Although White was chairman of the Northwest
Territory Commission which sponsored a celebration at Marietta, President
Roosevelt in his address, failed to mention White. White lost the nomination and
consequently campaigned for Wendell Willkie in 1940. He then withdrew from politics and devoted himself to his business affairs. He died in West Palm Beach, Florida
on December 15, 1953 and was interred in Oak Grove Cemetery in Marietta, Ohio.
Bibliography: Larry D. O'Brien, "The Ohio National Guard in the Coal Strike of
1932," *Ohio History*, 84 (Summer, 1975); Mary White, "Autobiography of an Ohio
First Lady," *Ohio History*, 82 (1973); Ohio Historical Society *Governors of Ohio*
(Columbus, 1969); Francis R. Aumann, "Ohio Government in the Twentieth Century: From Nash to White (1900-1931)," in Harlow Lindley, comp., *Ohio in the
Twentieth Century, 1900-1938* (Columbus, 1943).

DAVEY, Martin Luther, 1935-1939

Born in Kent, Portage County, Ohio on July 25, 1884, son of John Davey, a tree surgeon; joined the Church of Christ. Married to Berenice Chrisman and father of two
children. Attended public schools and graduated from Oberlin Academy in 1906
and later attended Oberlin College. Associated with his father in tree surgery in
1906. Organized and became general manager of the Davey Tree Expert Co., Inc.
in 1909 and became president in 1923. Elected Mayor of Kent in 1913 and served
until 1918. Elected in 1913 as a Democrat to Congress and served until March 3,
1921. Elected again to Congress and served from March 4, 1923 to March 3, 1929,
when his term expired. He chose not to run again for Congress, but instead
opposed Myers Cooper, the Republican incumbent for the governorship. Cooper received 1,355,526 votes to Davey's 1,106,739 votes. In 1929 Davey entered the real
estate business and became treasurer of the Davey Compressor Company. In 1934,
Davey again won the Democratic primary and opposed the Republican C. Brown.
Davey received 1,118,257 votes to Brown's 1,052,851 votes. In his reelection bid
against John Bricker, Davey won by a vote of 1,539,461 to Bricker's 1,412,773.
Davey's terms as Governor were marked by feuds both with the legislature and Presi-

dent Roosevelt. When Davey asked the legislature to appropriate money for a new rug and a new limousine, it refused. Davey solicited contributions for the first and bought the latter with National Guard funds. He also used the National Guard to assist a penitentiary warden who displeased him and to break a strike in the Mahoning Valley; thereby incurring the undying enmity of John L. Lewis and the CIO. Davey's feud with Roosevelt began when Davey charged that Federal administration of relief in Ohio was "cruel, inhuman and wasteful." In retaliation Harry Hopkins charged that Davey's campaign committee had extracted contributions from persons doing business with the Federal Relief Administration. A legislative investigation cleared Davey and his managers and Davey countered by taking out an arrest warrant for Hopkins on a charge of criminal libel. Davey also vetoed $10,000,000 in appropriations for Ohio State University. At the end of his first term, Davey asked the legislature to repeal the sales tax on food. When they declined to act Davey organized a petition drive and put the question on the ballot as a legislative amendment. The proposal to repeal the sales tax passed overwhelmingly. Because of scandals associated with his administration and New Deal maneuvering, Davey was defeated in the primary of 1938. He obtained the nomination in 1940 but was defeated in the general election by the Republican incumbent, John Bricker by a vote of 1,460,396 to Bricker's 1,824,863. After this defeat, Davey retired to his home and business. He died of a heart attack in Kent, Ohio on March 31, 1946 and was buried in Standing Rock Cemetery. Bibliography: John F. Shine, "The 1937 Steel Labor Dispute and the Ohio National Guard," *Ohio History*, vol. 84 (Autumn, 1975); Ralph J. Donaldson, "Martin L. Davey," *The Governors of Ohio* (Columbus, 1969); Francis R. Aumann, "Ohio Government in the Twentieth Century: From White to Bricker (1931-1940)." vol. VI of Carl Wittke, ed., *The History of the State of Ohio* (Columbus, 1942); Francis R. Aumann and Harvey Walker, *The Government and Administration of Ohio* (New York, 1956).

BRICKER, John William, 1939-1945

Born on September 6, 1893 in Madison County, Ohio, son of Lemuel Spencer Bricker, a farmer, and Laura (King) Bricker. Brother of Ella (Bricker) Masney. Married to Harriet Day on September 4, 1920; father of John Day. Attended rural schools, Mt. Sterling High School and Ohio State University and graduated with an A.B. in 1916, an LL.B. in 1920 and an LL.D. in 1939. After being rejected by all branches of the military, by special ordination of the Christian Church he entered the Army Chaplain Corps. He was mustered out of the service as a First Lieutenant. He was admitted to the Ohio Bar in 1917; elected solicitor of Grandview Heights from 1920-1928; was appointed Assistant Attorney General of Ohio in 1923 and served until 1927, when he became an unsuccessful candidate for Attorney General. From 1929 to 1932, he served on the Public Utilities Commission. He received the Republican nomination for Attorney General in 1932 and was elected in spite of the fact that Ohio voted heavily for a Democratic Governor and President. While in his second term as Attorney General in 1936, he became the Republican nominee to oppose the Democratic incumbent governor, Martin L. Davey. In a general Democratic sweep, Bricker was defeated by a vote of 1,412,773 to Davey's 1,539,461. Two years later, a year dominated by Republican victories, Bricker, again the Republican gubernatorial nominee, received 1,265,548 votes to Charles Sawyer's 1,147,328. In 1940 Bricker received 1,824,863 to former Governor Davey's 1,460,396 votes. In 1942, he garnered an even larger share of the votes, 1,086,937 to the Democratic candidate's, McSweeney, 709,599 and thus became Ohio's first three term Republican governor. When Bricker assumed the governorship, he inherited a $40 million deficit. He immediately instituted strict economic measures; by the end of his governorship, the state had a surplus in excess of $90 million. He also oversaw Ohio's preparations for World War II, so that it was not even necessary to call a special session of the legislature after Pearl Harbor. In 1944, Governor Bricker was mentioned as a presidential candidate and was selected as the Republican vice-presidential candidate. His candidacy failed at the polls. Bricker returned to Ohio and completed his term as governor. In 1946, Bricker was elected to the United States Senate. He served until he was defeated in 1959. Afterwards, he resumed the practice of law and is still associated with the firm of Bricker, Evatt, Barton, Eckler, and Neikoff. Bibliography: *Bricker of Ohio* (New York, 1944); Francis R. Aumann, "Ohio Government in the Twentieth Century: From White to Bricker, 1931-1946," Carl Wittke, ed., *The History of the State of Ohio*, vol. VI (Columbus, 1942); Albert H. Rose, *Ohio Government, State and Local* (St. Louis, 1953); Francis R. Aumann and Harvey Walker, *The Government and Administration of Ohio* (New York, 1956).

LAUSCHE, Frank John, 1945-1947, 1949-1957

Born in Cleveland on November 14, 1895, son of Louis Lausche, a steel mill worker, and Frances (Milavec) Lausche, both of whom were Roman Catholic. One of ten children. Married in 1928 to Jane Sheal; had no children. Attended Central Institute Prep School,1915-1916, and graduated from John Marshall School of Law in 1920, and received his LL.M. in 1936. Began selling newspapers and employed as a lamplighter at the age of twelve. Played semi-professional baseball. Joined the Army in 1918 as a private and was discharged at the end of World War I as a Second Lieutenant. Admitted to the Cleveland Bar in 1920. Ran as a Democrat for the State Legislature in 1922 but was defeated. In 1924 he was defeated for the State Senate. He was first appointed and then elected Judge of the Municipal Court from 1932-1937. From 1937 until he resigned to run for mayor, Lausche was Judge of the Court of Common Pleas. He served as Mayor of Cleveland from 1941-1944. In 1944, he won the Democratic nomination for Governor. His Republican opponent was James Garfield Stewart, who was Mayor of Cincinnati. Lausche defeated Stewart by a vote of 1,603,809 to 1,491,450. Two years later, however, he received only 1,125,997 votes to the Republican, Thomas Herbert's 1,166,550. After that Lausche was a successful gubernatorial candidate for four more terms. In 1948, he received 1,619,775 votes to Thomas Herbert's 1,398,514. In 1950, he defeated Don Ebright by a vote of 1,522,249 to 1,370,570. In 1952, Charles Taft received 1,590,058 votes to Lausche's 2,015,110 and in 1954 Lausche defeated James Rhodes, by a vote of 1,405,262 to 1,192,528. As governor, Lausche began by vetoing raises for himself and for civil service employees, while greatly expanding the state's welfare system. He developed a program for the conservation and preservation of the state's natural resources which included legislation requiring strip-mine operators to reclaim spoil banks and the governor's voluntary "Plant Ohio" campaign. He set up and personally supervised a state-wide civil defense organization. In 1950, he was elected chairman of the Governors' Conference of the United States. He oversaw the development and construction of the Ohio Turnpike and the creation of a state Board of Education. Lausche resigned as governor in January 1957 to take his seat in the United States Senate, serving until 1968. He was opposed for reelection by the Democratic Central Committee and because of his conservative voting record lost in the primaries. After his defeat, Lausche retired to private life. Bibliography: Albert A. Waldman, "Frank J. Lausche," *Governors of Ohio* (Columbus, 1969); *American Magazine*, vol. 137 (March, 1944); *Newsweek*, vol. 25 (January 8, 1945); *Nation*, vol. 159 (July 22, 1944).

HERBERT, Thomas J., 1947-1949

Born in Cleveland on October 28, 1894, son of John T. and Jane (Jones) Herbert; a Methodist. Married to Mildred Stevenson on January 3, 1948; father of Rosemary Jane. Attended public schools, Adelbert College, Western Reserve University and graduated in 1915. Attended Western Reserve University Law School and received his law degree in July 1920. Served as First Lieutenant in the United States Air Force, attached to the 56th British Royal Air Force Squadron; shot down on his third mission and returned to law school while still hospitalized. Admitted to the bar in December 1920, and in 1921 began his public career as Assistant Director of Law for the City of Cleveland. Appointed in 1922 and 1923 Assistant Prosecuting Attorney for Cuyahoga County. From 1929 to 1933, served as Assistant Attorney General of Ohio and assigned as attorney for the Public Utilities Commission. In 1936 ran as Republican for Attorney General but lost. Elected Attorney General in 1938 for the first of three consecutive terms, and elected president of the National Association of Attorneys General. Candidate for Governor in 1944 but lost in the Republican primary. Two years later, won the nomination and the election over the Democrat incumbent, Frank Lausche, by a vote of 1,166,550 to 1,125,977. Two years later, the results between the two men were reversed and Lausche received 1,619,775 votes to Herbert's 1,398,514. As governor, Herbert sponsored six bills which reduced or eliminated taxes including the sales tax on purchases of less than forty-one cents. He also supported two bills which appropriated $45 million from treasury surplus to compensate veterans of World War II. Herbert oversaw the creation of a state tuberculosis hospital; improvements in the animal and disease control program; the increase of school appropriations; and the paving and resurfacing of more miles of road than in any other term. Also he placed liquor inspectors under classified civil service and vetoed the popular Van Aken labor bill. At the close of his term, he returned to the private practice of law in Cleveland. In May 1953, President Eisenhower appointed him a member of the Subversive Activities Control Board. He was made chairman of the board, and served until he resigned in 1957. Herbert was elected in 1951 to the Ohio Supreme Court and served until 1962 when he retired from public life. He lived in Upper Arlington with his daughter until his death on October 27, 1974. Bibliography: S. Winford Smith, "Thomas J. Herbert," *Governors of Ohio* (Columbus, 1969); Francis R. Aumann and Harvey Walker, *The Government and Administration of Ohio* (New York, 1956); "Thomas James Herbert," *New York Times* (October 28, 1974); *Biographical News* (January, 1975).

LAUSCHE, Frank John, 1945-1947, 1949-1957

BROWN, John William, 1957

Born on December 28, 1913 in Athens, Ohio, son of James A., a coal miner, and Daisy (Foster) Brown; a Methodist. Married to Violet A. Helman in July 1943; father of Rosalie (Brown) Angelus. Attended public schools in Athens and Fairfield Counties and graduated from Lancaster High School in 1932. He was a member of the Ohio Highway Patrol in 1941, and during World War II was a Commander in the United States Coast Guard. He engaged in merchandising, real estate, and the insurance business in Medina. From 1950 to 1953 was Mayor of Medina. Elected Lieutenant Governor, as a Republican, in 1952. When Governor Lausche resigned on January 3, 1957 to accept a seat in the United States Senate to which he had been elected in November, Brown became Governor. During his eleven days as governor, Brown addressed the legislature and, stressed the need for additional school funds; conservation of resources; and urban planning. He brought about a cessation of hostilities and secured an agreement for negotiations in a strike against the Ohio Consolidated Telephone Company at Portsmouth. Brown was defeated in the 1956 Republican gubernatorial primary. In 1959 and 1960, Brown was a member of the Ohio House of Representatives and served as president and director of Investors Heritage Life Insurance Company of Ohio. In 1961 and 1962, he served in the Ohio State Senate and again was elected Lieutenant Governor in 1962 and served until 1975. From 1965 to 1972, he chaired the Ohio Commission on Interstate Cooperation and was Commander-in-Chief of the Ohio Military and Naval Forces from 1969 to 1975. In 1975 Ashland College awarded him the LL.D. degree. He is now living in Medina. Biblography: S. Winford Smith, "John W. Brown," *The Governors of Ohio* (Columbus, 1969).

O'NEILL, Crane William, 1957-1959

Born in Marietta, Ohio on February 14, 1916, son of Charles T., attorney and Justice of the Peace, and Jessie (Arnold) O'Neill; member of the First Community Baptist Church. Brother of Daniel A. T. Married to Betty Hewson on July 29, 1945; father of Charles William and Peggy. Attended the public schools and was a member of a debate team which won a national tournament in 1933. He received his A. B. degree from Marietta College in 1938 and an L.H.D. in 1953. He graduated from Ohio State University Law School in 1942. He was awarded Doctor of Letters degree from, among others, Defiance College in 1953, Ohio University in 1957, and West Virginia University in 1957. After graduation, he entered his father's law firm as a partner. He was elected as a Republican to the Ohio House of Representatives in 1938 and served until 1950. He was chairman of the State Republican Convention in 1948. He served as Speaker in 1947-48 and Minority Leader in 1949-50. In 1944, he was reelected even though he was actively serving with the army in Europe. He entered the war as a private, in the 976th Engineers Company, and was honorably discharged in 1946 as a Sergeant. In 1948 and 1950, O'Neill was an instructor in political science at Marietta College. The United States Junior Chamber of Commerce named O'Neill as one of the outstanding young men in the country in 1950, and also in that year, he was elected Attorney General of Ohio. He was the Republican nominee for Governor in 1956 over Lieutenant Governor John W. Brown, and in the November election, defeated the Democratic candidate, Michael V. DiSalle, by a heavy majority (1,984,988 to 1,557,103). While governor, O'Neill changed the concept of highway construction from maintaining short sections to the development of freeways and divided highways, and changed the term of the director of the Department of Mental Health and Correction from indefinite to a six year term. A proposed "right-to-work" constitutional amendment was introduced, and the governor campaigned vigorously for it, but it was defeated by about a million votes. Because of this and Republican alienation due to lack of patronage and indecision in administrative matters, O'Neill was defeated by DiSalle, 1,414,874 to 1,869,260 in 1958. At the close of his term, O'Neill resumed the private practice of law. In 1959-1960, he was a distinguished professor of public affairs at Bethany College in West Virginia. In 1960 he was elected a Judge of the Ohio Supreme Court and from 1970 to the present, has served as Chief Justice. In 1971, he added the responsibility of being a professor of law at Capitol University. His home is in Columbus. Bibliography: "People of the Week," *U. S. News* (May 16, 1958); S. Winford Smith,"C. William O'Neill," *Governors of Ohio* (Columbus, 1969).

DiSALLE, Michael Vincent, 1959-1963

Born in New York City on January 6, 1908, son of Anthony and Assunta (Arcangelo) DiSalle, both of whom were Catholic. Oldest of seven children. Married to Myrtle Eugene England on December 19, 1929; father of Antoinette, Barbara, Constance, Diane and Michael. Attended the public schools of Toledo, and Central Catholic High School; and attended college and law school at Georgetown University and graduated in 1931. He was admitted to the Ohio Bar in 1932 and began practice in Toledo. The following year he became assistant district counsel of the Home Owners' Loan Corporation. He was elected for one term to the House of Representatives in 1936 and sixty days after being seated he was named one of five outstanding members of the House. He served in the National Guard during World War II. Two years later he served in the State House but was defeated later in a Republican landslide. From 1939 to 1941 he held the post of assistant city law director of Toledo. He was elected to the City Council and served from 1942 to 1947. He was vice-mayor from 1944-1948. Originated in 1945 and chaired the Toledo Labor-Management Citizens Committee. Called for the Toledo Plan, which became a model for other cities, and which brought DiSalle into the national spotlight. In 1946, he ran unsuccessfully for Congress. He was more successful running for Mayor in 1948 and served two terms. He resigned to become Director of Price Stabilization and later Director of Economic Stabilization in the middle of his second term. In 1952, he resigned to run for the U.S. Senate but was defeated. In 1956 he won the Democratic primary election for governor, but was defeated by C. William O'Neill 1,557,103 to 1,984,988. He returned two years later to defeat O'Neill 1,869,260 to 1,444,874. As governor, DiSalle secured nearly half a billion dollars for increased expenditures in spite of strong Republican opposition. The bulk of the new money came from increased taxes on cigarettes, beer, gasoline, corporation franchises, and sales taxes. DiSalle again submitted a budget calling for an increase of $150 million for 1961. He believed the expenditures were justified to upgrade the educational programs; improve institutional conditions; expand the state highway patrol; and to provide for additional capital improvements. During these years, DiSalle served on the President's Advisory Commission on Inter-governmental Affairs. The legislature was not as impressed with his suggestions as the President however, and his last two years in office were marked by serious budget disputes. When DiSalle ran for reelection the voters soundly rejected (1,280,521 to 1,836,190) his record and promise of increased governmental services, in favor of Republican candidate James A. Rhodes' platform of economy in state expenditures. When his term expired, DiSalle practiced law in Columbus until 1966 and then joined the firm of Chapman, Duff and Lenzini in Washington, D.C. Bibliography: Michael V. DiSalle, *The Power of Life and Death;* S. Winford Smith, "Michael V. DiSalle," *Governors of Ohio* (Columbus, 1969); *Pathfinder,* volume 57 (December 13, 1950); *Saturday Evening Post,* volume 223 (March 17, 1951).

RHODES, James A., 1963-1971, 1975-

Born in Coalton, Jackson County, Ohio on September 13, 1909, son of James Allen Rhodes, coal miner who died in 1917, and Susan (Howe) Rhodes; a Methodist. Brother of two sisters. Married to Helen Rawlins; father of Suzanne, Saundra and Sharon. He attended South High School in Springfield and Ohio State University, but was forced to leave before graduation to support his mother and sisters, which he did by opening a restaurant near the campus. He began his political career as a member of the Columbus Board of Education from 1937 to 1939; was elected Auditor of the city of Columbus, 1939, serving until 1944; became Mayor in 1948; was selected to represent the United States at the Olympic Games in London. He was elected Auditor of the state in 1953 and during his ten years in office gained a reputation for efficiency and economy in handling the state's finances. In May of 1950, Rhodes lost the Republican primary for governor. Four years later, he won the primary but lost the election to Frank Lausche, by a vote of 1,192,528 to 1,405,262. Eight years later he was again the Republican nominee. On a platform of economy in government, he defeated (1,836,190 to 1,280,521) the Democratic incumbent, Michael DiSalle. Four years later, he was easily reelected, defeating Frazier Reams by a vote of 1,795,277 to 1,092,054. After his second term, he retired from public life for four years and then returned to defeat John Gilligan, 1,493,679 to 1,482,191. The race was contested with a delay of several days before Rhodes was declared the victor for the four year term, which will expire in 1979. On becoming governor, Rhodes immediately set about keeping his campaign promises. He instituted an austerity program in an effort to wipe out a deficit of $83 million; cut DiSalle's proposed budget; and required state departments to trim expenditures, which resulted in the unemployment of 4,000 state employees. These and other measures enabled Rhodes to balance the budget and turn the deficit into a surplus. He has established an Ohio Youth Commission to deal with juvenile crime. He originated Ohio's Teenage Hall of Fame and wrote a book, *Teenage Hall of Fame.* He is also the author of *Johnny Shiloh, The Trial of Mary Todd Lincoln,* and *The Court Martial of Commodore Perry.* His interest in sports continues. He is a member of the Professional Golfers Association; founder of the National Caddie Association, and serves on the United States Olympic Committee. His interest in the young has led him to promote a series of events and organizations for youth. He has also increased state aid to education including state teachers' salaries. Bibliography: S. Winford Smith, "James A. Rhodes," *Governors of Ohio* (Columbus, 1969); Office of the Secretary of State, *Ohio Blue Book* (Columbus, 1964-77); Edward J. Mowery, "James Allen Rhodes: Taxpayer's Governor," *Bookmailer* (1963); D. Hess, "Rhodes Ninth Inning Optimist," *Biographical News* (January, 1975); "No Place for Fortas," *Time,* vol. 93 (May 19, 1969).

GILLIGAN, John Joyce, 1971-1974

Born on March 22, 1921 in Cincinnati, Ohio, son of Harry J. Gilligan, a businessman, and Blanche Joyce Gilligan, both of whom were Catholic. Brother of a twin sister Jeane, and Francis and Harry Joseph Jr. Married to Mary Kathryn Dixon on June 28, 1945; father of Kathleen, Donald, John and Ellen. Attended St. Xavier High School in Cincinnati. Entered military service in 1942 and served as a destroyer gunnery officer until his discharge in 1945 with the rank of Lieutenant in the United States Naval Reserve. Received his M.A. degree in literature from the University of Cincinnati in 1947 and became an instructor in English at Xavier University from 1948 to 1953. In 1953 he was elected a member of the Cincinnati City Council and served until 1967. He was elected to the United States Congress and served from 1964 through 1966, when Robert Taft Jr. defeated him. From 1968 to the present, he has been a partner in Sauter, Gilligan and Associated Insurance. In 1965 he was an unsuccessful candidate for the United States Senate against William B. Saxbe. After his defeat for reelection, he was a John F. Kennedy Fellow at the Institute of Politics, Harvard in 1969 and also at the Adlai Stevenson Institute of International Studies at the University of Chicago. He won the Democratic primary for Governor in 1970 and faced Roger W. Clawd, the Republican. Gilligan received 1,725,560 votes to Clawd's 1,382,749. As governor, Gilligan sought with limited success to bring the level of taxing and services to the proportions of the DiSalle administration and to undo all of the cutbacks and layoffs James Rhodes had introduced during his administration. In 1974, former Governor Rhodes himself ran against Gilligan in the gubernatorial election. The election was one of the closest in Ohio's history. The results were disputed, and only after several days and a partial recount which showed Rhodes with a total of 1,493,679 votes to Gilligan's 1,482,191, was Rhodes declared the winner. After his defeat, Gilligan returned to his business and educational interests. Bibliography: D. S. Broder, "Forty-Eight Freshmen Build their Fences," *New York Times Magazine* (December 12, 1965); *Guardian* (October 22, 1968); *Time* (October 21, 1966); "People," *Time*, vol. 103 (February 4, 1974); "Democrats: Who's Almost Who," *Newsweek*, vol. 84 (October 7, 1974).

RHODES, James A., 1963-1971, 1975-

OKLAHOMA

OKLAHOMA

HASKELL, Charles Nathaniel, 1907-1911

Born on March 13, 1860 in Leipsic, Ohio, son of George Haskell, a cooper, and Jane Reeves; a Methodist. Brother of Reuel, Helen, Clara, Mary and George. Married Lucy Pomeroy on October 11, 1881, and father of Norman, Murray and Lucy; first wife died in March 1888; married Lillian Elizabeth Gallup in September 1889, and father of Frances, Joe and Jane. Privately educated; became a teacher; studied law privately; admitted to the Ohio Bar on December 6, 1880, but continued teaching until March 4, 1881, before opening a law office in Ottawa, Ohio. He later engaged in railroad building and other construction work. Moved to Muskogee, Oklahoma, on April 18, 1901; organized the Territorial Trust and Banking Company and acquired the *New State Tribune*. Haskell first became politically prominent in Oklahoma in 1905 as a member of the Sequoyah Constitutional Convention. In 1906 he was elected to the Oklahoma Constitutional Convention. In 1907 Haskell won the Democratic gubernatorial primary, and on September 17, 1907, he was elected the first Governor of Oklahoma by gaining 134,162 votes to beat Republican Frank Frantz, who polled 106,507 votes. On November 16, 1907, Haskell took office. Haskell oversaw the organization of most of the state's institutions and signed much progressive legislation—including an extensive labor code, a bank guaranty law and a graduated income tax. His administration also produced Oklahoma's "Jim Crow Code" and "Grandfather Clause." His most important action was the transfer of the state capital from Guthrie to Oklahoma City. On the night of June 11, 1910, after an election had decided in favor of Oklahoma City, Haskell moved the state seal to the Lee-Huckins Hotel there and declared it to be the new State Capitol. Though this violated the Oklahoma Enabling Act, both the Oklahoma Supreme Court and the United States Supreme Court upheld the move. Because of a provision in the original Oklahoma Constitution prohibiting governors from serving successive terms, Haskell left office on January 9, 1911. After being defeated for the Democratic nomination for United States Senator in 1912, Haskell became an investor in the oil business. Haskell died on July 5, 1933, and is buried in Muskogee, Oklahoma. Bibliography: Wilbur Johnson, ed., *Directory of Oklahoma* (Oklahoma City, 1975); Oscar P. Fowler, *The Haskell Regime* (Oklahoma City, 1933); Charles N. Haskell, "Charles N. Haskell Tells of Two Conventions," *The Chronicles of Oklahoma*, vol. XIV, no. 2 (Summer, 1936); Governor Charles N. Haskell, Administration Files, Oklahoma State Library, Oklahoma City, Oklahoma.

CRUCE, Lee, 1911-1915

Born on July 8, 1863, near Marion, Kentucky, son of James Winlock Cruce, a farmer, and Jane Hill; a Presbyterian. Brother of Richard, William, Lafayett, Cabel, Lawrence and Kirby. Married Chickie LaFlore on June 21, 1893, and father of Lorena Cruce. Attended Marion Academy and Vanderbilt University, but was forced to leave because of poor health; studied law privately; admitted to the Kentucky Bar in 1888, but did not practice law until moving to Ardmore, Oklahoma in 1891. Attorney, 1891-1901; cashier, Ardmore National Bank, 1901-1903; President, Ardmore National Bank, 1903-1910; President, Oklahoma Federated Clubs and Industrial Organization, 1905; Trustee, Hargrove College; member, University of Oklahoma Board of Regents; Mason; Beta Theta Pi. Elected as an alderman for the city of Ardmore in 1899. In August 1910 Cruce won the Democratic gubernatorial primary, and in November 1910 he was elected governor, with 120,218 votes against the 99,527 polled by his Republican opponent, J. W. McNeal. He was sworn into office on January 9, 1911. As governor, Cruce attempted to reduce the cost of state government, and clashed with the legislature over his higher education policies. Cruce and the legislature also differed over congressional reapportionment, when he threatened to veto a legislative attempt at gerrymandering. During his administration the State Highway Department was established and two new counties—Cotton and Harmon—were created. Opposed to capital punishment, Cruce refused to allow any executions. He also supported a series of "Blue Laws" and resorted to martial law to prevent prize fighting, gambling, bootlegging and horse racing. Cruce's refusal to call a special legislative session and his interference with local interest projects and gerrymandering resulted in a break with his party. The 1912 legislature investigated the governor's office, and an impeachment resolution was defeated by a single vote. Oklahoma's constitution originally prohibited governors from serving successive terms, and Cruce left office on January 11, 1915. After being defeated in the Democratic primary election for United States Senator in 1930, he invested in oil and real estate. Cruce died on January 16, 1933, and is buried in Ardmore, Oklahoma. Bibliography: Wilbur Johnson, ed., *Directory of Oklahoma* (Oklahoma City, 1975); Rex F. Harlow, *Makers of Government in Oklahoma* (Oklahoma City, 1930); O. P. Sturm, ed., "Lee Cruce," *Sturm's Oklahoma Magazine*, vol. IV, no. 1 (April, 1907); Orben J. Casey, "Governor Lee Cruce," *The Chronicles of Oklahoma* vol. LII, no. 4 (Winter, 1974-1975); Governor Lee Cruce, Administration Files, Oklahoma State Library, Oklahoma City, Oklahoma.

WILLIAMS, Robert Lee, 1915-1919

Born on December 20, 1868 in Brundidge, Alabama, son of Jonathan Williams, a merchant, and Sarah Julia (Paul) Williams; a Methodist. Brother of Mary, Arrie and Simeon; unmarried. Attended Southern University and was graduated in 1894. Became a teacher for one year and then studied law privately; admitted to the Alabama Bar on September 26, 1891. Practiced law in Troy, Alabama, before moving to Guthrie, Oklahoma, in 1893; returned briefly to Alabama and entered the Methodist ministry; moved to Atoka, Oklahoma, in 1896 and six months later settled in Durant, Oklahoma. Member, Democratic National Committee, 1904-1908; member, Oklahoma Constitutional Convention, 1906; elected as Chief Justice of the Oklahoma Supreme Court, 1907-1914, but resigned on March 10, 1914, to run for governor; member, Oklahoma Bar Association; Alpha Tau Omega; Mason. On August 14, 1914, Williams won the Democratic gubernatorial primary, and on November 3, 1914, he was elected governor, receiving 100,597 votes to Republican John Fields' 95,904 and Socialist Fred W. Holt's 52,703. Williams took office on January 11, 1915. During his term the number of state agencies was reduced, the State Board of Affairs created, and the new Capitol opened. In an effort to lower state indebtedness, Williams raised taxes, lowered appropriations, and closed several state institutions. In 1915, the United States Supreme Court declared Oklahoma's "Grandfather Clause" unconstitutional; however, a special legislative session called by Williams adopted a new registration law designed to handicap black voters. With the outbreak of World War I some Oklahomans violently opposed the draft. Called the "Green Corn Rebellion," the uprising was quickly crushed under Williams' direction. Oklahoma's constitution originally prohibited governors from serving successive terms, and Williams left office on January 13, 1919. Williams was United States Judge for the Eastern District of Oklahoma from 1919 to 1937, United States Circuit Judge of the Tenth Circuit Court from 1937 to 1939, and president of the Oklahoma Historical Society from 1938 to 1948. Williams died on April 10, 1948, and is buried in Durant, Oklahoma. Bibliography: Wilbur Johnson, ed., *Directory of Oklahoma* (Oklahoma City, 1975); Edward E. Dale and James D. Morrison, *Pioneer Judge* (Cedar Rapids, 1958); Baxter Taylor, "Robert Lee Williams," *The Chronicles of Oklahoma*, vol. XXXI, no. 4 (Winter, 1953-1954); Robert L. Williams Papers, Library, Oklahoma Historical Society, Oklahoma City, Oklahoma; Governor Robert L. Williams, Administration Files, Oklahoma State Library, Oklahoma City, Oklahoma.

ROBERTSON, James Brooks Ayers, 1919-1923

Born on March 15, 1871 in Keokuk County, Iowa, son of J. B. A. Robertson, a dry goods merchant, and Clarissa M. (Wright) Robertson; a Methodist. Brother of John H., Anna M., George A., Maggie C., Mary E., Meda F., Martha A. and Warren K. Married Olive Stubblefield on April 27, 1900, and father of Olive Frances and James Brooks Ayers, Jr.; first wife died on June 1, 1914; married Isabel Butler in 1917. Received a public education and taught school from 1887 to 1897. Moved to Chandler, Oklahoma, in 1893. Privately studied law and was admitted to the Oklahoma Bar in 1898. Elected County Attorney of Lincoln County, 1900-1902; member, State Democratic Committee, 1905; delegate, Democratic National Convention, 1908 and 1920; Judge, Tenth Judicial District of Oklahoma, 1909-1910; member, Capitol Commission, 1911; member, Oklahoma Supreme Court Commission, 1911-1914; unsuccessful candidate in the Democratic gubernatorial primary, 1914; Mason; Odd Fellow; K. P.; Elk. On August 6, 1918, Robertson won the Democratic gubernatorial primary, and on November 5, 1918, he was elected governor, receiving 104,132 votes to Republican Horace G. McKeever's 82,865. Robertson assumed office on January 13, 1919. The first governor inaugurated in the new Capitol, Robertson's greatest achievements were the construction of 1,300 miles of highways, the appointment of independent regents for state colleges, and the securing of legislative approval for the 18th and 19th amendments. In verdicts handed down between 1920 and 1921, the United States Supreme Court settled the Red River boundary dispute by awarding the entire river to Oklahoma. During Robertson's term the state also underwent a severe postwar depression, witnessed a revival of Ku Klux Klan activity, saw the state electoral vote become Republican for the first time, crushed a coal miner strike with the National Guard, and survived the Tulsa race riot. The Eighth Legislature investigated the governor's office, and an impeachment resolution was defeated by one vote. In 1922, Robertson was indicted for bribery; however, he avoided conviction on a demurrer. Oklahoma's constitution originally prohibited governors from serving successive terms, and Robertson left office on January 8, 1923. Robertson returned to his law practice after his term as governor, but was later an unsuccessful candidate for the 1930 Democratic gubernatorial nomination. He was also a Democratic Presidential Elector-at-Large in 1932, and Chief Council for the Oklahoma Corporation Commission from 1935 to 1938. Robertson died on March 7, 1938, and is buried in Chandler, Oklahoma. Bibliography: Wilbur Johnson, ed., *Directory of Oklahoma* (Oklahoma City, 1975); Rex F. Harlow, *Makers of Government in Oklahoma* (Oklahoma City, 1930); J. B. A. Robertson Collection, "Vertical File," Library, Oklahoma Historical Society, Oklahoma City, Oklahoma; Governor J. B. A. Robertson, Administration Files, State Library, Oklahoma City, Oklahoma.

WALTON, John C., 1923

Born on March 6, 1881, near Indianapolis, Indiana, son of Louis Walton, a farmer, and Callaway Walton; a Catholic. Brother of Robert. Married Madeliene Cecile, and father of Madelynne and Bena. Moved to Nebraska in 1885 and Arkansas in 1889. Educated in public schools and was graduated from Fort Smith, Arkansas Commercial College in 1898. Served in the Field Artillery during the Spanish-American War; studied engineering in Mexico; moved to Oklahoma City, Oklahoma, in 1903. Served as a Colonel in the Engineering Corps during World War I. Delegate to county, state, and national Democratic conventions; member, American Institute of Electrical Engineers; president, Oklahoma Chapter American Association of Engineers; Mason; Shriner; K. P.; Odd Fellow; Modern Woodmen of America. Elected Oklahoma City Commissioner of Public Works, 1917-1919; elected Mayor of Oklahoma City, 1919-1923. Walton won the Democratic gubernatorial primary in August 1922, and in November of the same year he was elected governor, receiving 280,206 votes to Republican John Fields' 230,469. He was sworn into office on January 8, 1923. During Walton's administration he became unpopular with many members of the legislature. In addition, there was a revival of Ku Klux Klan activity. To halt Klan violence, Walton placed Tulsa County under martial law and suspended habeas corpus — thereby violating Oklahoma's constitution. Attempting to prevent a grand jury from investigating his actions, he placed the entire state under martial law, and later used the National Guard to stop the legislature from meeting. However, after the passage of an initiative petition allowing the legislators to call themselves into session, Walton was forced to convene a special session. On October 23, 1923, impeachment charges were brought against Walton, he was suspended from office, and Lieutenant

Governor Martin E. Trapp became Acting Governor. On November 19, Walton was convicted and removed from office. Walton won the Democratic nomination for United States Senator in 1924, but lost the general election. He was defeated for Mayor of Oklahoma City in 1931, although he was elected to the Oklahoma Corporation Commission from 1932 until 1939. He was an unsuccessful candidate for the Democratic nomination for governor in 1934 and 1938. Walton died on November 24, 1949, and is buried in Oklahoma City. Bibliography: Wilbur Johnson, ed., *Directory of Oklahoma* (Oklahoma City, 1975); Sheldon Neuringer, "War on the Ku Klux Klan," *The Chronicles of Oklahoma*, vol. XLV, no. 2 (Summer, 1967); Governor John C. Walton, "Vertical file," Library, Oklahoma Historical Society, Oklahoma City, Oklahoma; Governor John C. Walton, Administration Files, Oklahoma State Library, Oklahoma City, Oklahoma.

TRAPP, Martin Edwin, 1923-1927

Born on April 18, 1877 in Robinson, Kansas, son of Charles Franklin Trapp, a farmer, and Mary Capps Trapp; a member of the Disciples of Christ. Brother of William, Neri, Mary, John, Francis, Alex, Horace, Emma, Martha, Fannie and Belle. Married Lou Strang on November 7, 1907, and father of Martin Edwin, Jr. Moved to Oklahoma Territory in 1889. Educated in the public schools and was graduated from Capitol City College, Guthrie, Oklahoma, in 1898. Studied law privately and was admitted to the Oklahoma Bar in 1912. Elected County Clerk of Logan County, Oklahoma Territory, 1904-1907; elected State Auditor of Oklahoma, 1907-1911; elected Lieutenant Governor of Oklahoma, 1914-1923. Member, Oklahoma Historical Society; Mason; Odd Fellows; Elk. Delegate and Chairman of the Oklahoma delegation to the 1924 Democratic National Convention. Became Acting Governor on October 23, 1923, when impeachment charges were placed against Governor John C. Walton. On November 19, 1923, Walton was convicted and removed from office, and Trapp became Governor of Oklahoma. Trapp's administration was marked by the repeal of over $10,000,000 of proposed "reform legislation." At the same time, the state gasoline tax was increased and used to finance an extensive highway construction program. The Forestry Commission, the Conservation Commission and the Fish and Game Commission were also established during his term in office. To reduce the power of the Ku Klux Klan, an "antimask law" was passed under Trapp. A very popular chief executive, Trapp refused to consider himself anything other than "Acting Governor" in the hope that he could be elected governor in 1926. However, the Oklahoma constitution still prohibited governors from serving consecutive terms, and after the Oklahoma Supreme Court ruled in *Fitzpatrick vs. McAlister* that he was governor, Trapp left office on January 10, 1927. In 1930 he was defeated in the Democratic gubernatorial primary, and turned to a career as a dealer in investment securities. Trapp died on July 26, 1951, and is buried in Oklahoma City, Oklahoma. Bibliography: Wilbur Johnson, ed., *Directory of Oklahoma* (Oklahoma City, 1975); Rex F. Harlow, *Makers of Government in Oklahoma* (Oklahoma City, 1930); Governor Martin E. Trapp, "Vertical File," Library, Oklahoma Historical Society, Oklahoma City, Oklahoma; Governor Martin E. Trapp, Administration Files, Oklahoma State Library, Oklahoma City, Oklahoma.

JOHNSTON, Henry Simpson, 1927-1929

Born on December 30, 1867, near Evansville, Indiana, son of Matthew Simpson Johnston, a farmer, and Mary Jane Lodge Johnston; a member of the Christian Church. Brother of Amy B. and Will W. Married Ethel L. Littleton, in 1910, and adopted father of Robin, Reba, Nell and Gertrude. His family moved to Kansas while Johnston was a child; later, in 1891, he migrated to Colorado. Educated in public schools, Baker University and Methodist College in Kansas. Studied law privately and admitted to the Colorado Bar in 1891. Moved to Perry, Oklahoma Territory, in 1893. Member, Oklahoma Territorial Council, 1897-1904; elected County Attorney, Noble County, Oklahoma Territory, 1901-1904; member, Oklahoma Constitutional Convention, 1906; Chairman, Democratic caucus, Oklahoma Constitutional Convention; Presiding Officer, Oklahoma Constitutional Convention; State Senator, 1907-1908; President Pro Tempore, Oklahoma Senate, 1907-1908; delegate, Democratic National Convention, 1912; Mason. In August 1926 Johnston won the Democratic gubernatorial primary, and in November, 1926, he was elected Governor, receiving 213,167 votes to Republican Omar K. Benedict's 170,714. He was sworn into office on January 10, 1927. Johnston clashed with the legislature over the number of members to be named to the State Highway Commission, and over his reputed inaccessibility to legislators due to the actions of his private secretary, Mrs. O. O. Howard. At the end of its regular session the Eleventh Legislature planned to call itself into session to investigate the governor's office. In spite of an Oklahoma Supreme Court ruling prohibiting the meeting, the lawmakers issued a call to convene. When Johnston prevented this by enforcing martial law, they gathered at the Huckins Hotel in Oklahoma City and voted impeachment charges; however, concerned over the legality of the action the Senate failed to concur with the House. The 1928 Republican sweep of Oklahoma was blamed on Johnston, and in January 1929 the Twelfth Legislature voted impeachment charges, making Lieutenant Governor William J. Holloway acting governor. On March 20, 1929, Johnston was removed from office. Johnston was elected to the Oklahoma Senate from 1932 until 1936, and then returned to his law practice. Johnston died on January 28, 1970, and is buried in Perry, Oklahoma. Bibliography: Wilbur Johnson, ed., *Directory of Oklahoma*, (Oklahoma City, 1975); Henry S. Johnston Collection, Library, Oklahoma State University, Stillwater, Oklahoma; Governor Henry S. Johnston, "Vertical File," Library, Oklahoma Historical Society, Oklahoma City, Oklahoma; Governor Henry S. Johnston, Administration Files, Oklahoma State Library, Oklahoma City, Oklahoma.

HOLLOWAY, William Judson, 1929-1931

Born on December 15, 1888 in Arkadelphia, Arkansas, son of Stephen Lee Holloway, a Baptist minister, and Molly Horne Holloway; a Baptist. Brother of Stephen. Married Amy Arnold on June 10, 1917; father of William Judson, Jr. Educated in the public schools; received a B.A. degree from Ouachita College in 1910. Moved to Hugo, Oklahoma, in 1910 and served as principal of Hugo High School from 1911 until 1914. Studied at the University of Chicago, 1911; received an LL.B. degree from Cumberland University in 1915 and was admitted to the

Oklahoma Bar that same year. Elected County Attorney, Choctaw County, Oklahoma, 1916-1918; United States Army, Officers Training School, 1918; practiced law, 1918-1920; elected to Oklahoma Senate, 1920-1926; President Pro Tempore, Oklahoma Senate, 1925-1926; acting Lieutenant Governor, 1925-1926; elected Lieutenant Governor, 1927-1929; Mason; Woodmen of the World; American Legion. The Twelfth Oklahoma Legislature voted impeachment charges against Governor Henry S. Johnston in January 1929, and Holloway became acting governor. On March 20, 1929, Johnston was removed from office, and Holloway assumed the office of governor. During Holloway's term Oklahoma's child labor laws were expanded, a new mining code was adopted, and the State Highway Commission was reorganized. However, the most important legislation enacted during his administration provided for the adoption of a runoff primary election system. Holloway was in office in 1929 when the Great Depression struck the state with disastrous consequences. The depression had a particularly severe impact on the people of Oklahoma, and the resulting migration of those attempting to escape "dust bowl" conditions gave rise to the "Okie" image. Apparently many people turned to politics in an attempt to find jobs, for in 1930, 103 candidates filed for fifteen elective offices. Because Oklahoma's original constitution prohibited governors from serving consecutive terms, Holloway left office on January 12, 1931. At the end of his term, Holloway returned to his law practice in Oklahoma City, Oklahoma. He also served as Oklahoma's representative on the Interstate Oil Compact Commission. Holloway died on January 28, 1970, and is buried in Oklahoma City. Bibliography: Wilbur Johnson, ed., *Directory of Oklahoma* (Oklahoma City, 1975); Joseph B. Thoburn and Muriel H. Wright, *Oklahoma: The State and Its People*, 4 vols. (New York, 1929); Governor William J. Holloway, "Vertical File," Oklahoma Historical Society, Oklahoma City, Oklahoma; Governor William J. Holloway, Administrative Files, Oklahoma State Library, Oklahoma City, Oklahoma.

MURRAY, William Henry, 1931-1935

Born on November 21, 1869 in Spring Creek, Texas, son of Uriah Murray, a farmer, and Bertha Elizabeth Jones Murray; a Methodist. Brother of John S., George T. and Robert. Married Mary Alice Hearrell on July 19, 1899; father of Massena B., Johnston, William H., Jr., Jean and Burbank. Self-educated and was graduated from College Hill Institute, Springtown, Texas, 1889. Taught school and became a newspaper publisher in Texas. Studied law privately and was admitted to the Texas Bar in 1895. Moved to Tishomingo, Chickasaw Nation, 1898. Citizen by inter-marriage of the Chickasaw Nation; author, Atoka Agreement, 1898; personal attorney of Chickasaw Governor Douglas Johnston; delegate, Sequoyah Convention, 1905; delegate, Oklahoma Constitutional Convention, 1906; president, Oklahoma Constitutional Convention, 1906; Oklahoma House of Representatives, 1907-1908; Speaker, Oklahoma House of Representatives, 1907-1908; United States House of Representatives, 1914-1918; unsuccessful candidate, Democratic gubernatorial primary, 1910, 1918. Murray moved to Bolivia and attempted to establish a colony in 1924, but returned to Oklahoma in 1929. In the summer of 1930 Murray won the Democratic gubernatorial primary and runoff elections, and in November

1930, he was elected governor, receiving 301,921 votes to Republican Ira Hill's 208,575. He was sworn into office on January 12, 1931. The Great Depression continued to plague Oklahoma during Murray's administration. This was partially the result of his dislike of President Franklin D. Roosevelt and many New Deal programs. As a result Murray faced a $5,000,000 deficit, mass foreclosures and numerous bank failures. After obtaining money from the Oklahoma Legislature for aid to indigents, he called for a National Council on Relief to study the problem. During his term the State Tax Commission was established to make taxes more equitable throughout the state. In addition, Murray used the National Guard to enforce a bank moratorium, maintain segregation, close toll bridges and limit oil production. In 1932, he was a candidate for the Democratic presidential nomination. It was during Murray's regime that the 18th Amendment was repealed; however, Oklahoma voted to remain dry and only permit 3.2 percent beer. Because Oklahoma's original constitution prohibited governors from serving consecutive terms, Murray left office on January 14, 1935. After leaving office, Murray returned to his farm in Johnston County, Oklahoma. In 1942, he unsuccessfully attempted to become the Democratic nominee for the United States Senate from Oklahoma. Murray died on October 15, 1956, and is buried in Tishomingo, Oklahoma. Bibliography: Wilbur Johnson, ed., *Directory of Oklahoma* (Oklahoma City, 1975); Gordon Hines, *Alfalfa Bill* (Oklahoma City, 1932); William H. Murray, *Memoirs,* 4 vols. (Boston, 1945); William H. Murray, "The Constitutional Convention," *The Chronicles of Oklahoma*, vol. IX, no. 2 (June, 1931).

MARLAND, Earnest Whitworth, 1935-1939

Born on May 8, 1874 in Pittsburgh, Pennsylvania, son of Alfred Marland, a businessman, and Sarah MacCleod Marland; an Episcopalian. Brother of Ignatia and Charlotte. Married Mary Virginia Collins on November 5, 1903, who died in 1926; married Lydie Miller Roberts on July 14, 1928, and became the adopted father of George R. and Lydie Miller Roberts. Received preparatory education at Park Institute, Pittsburgh; graduated with an LL.B. degree from the University of Michigan in 1893. Entered into law practice in Pittsburgh, but soon abandoned law in favor of the oil business. Moved to Ponca City, Oklahoma, in 1908 and engaged in oil production, refining and marketing. Later he founded the Marland Oil Company and various subsidiary companies in both the United States and Mexico. Elected to the United States House of Representatives, 1933-1935. Mason. Marland won the Democratic gubernatorial primary and runoff elections in the summer of 1934, and in November, 1934, he was elected governor, receiving 365,992 votes to Republican William B. Pine's 243,843. He was sworn into office on January 15, 1935. Marland's administration stressed rehabilitation of the state's economy and the creation of jobs for the unemployed. To accomplish this he proposed a "Little New Deal," which called for establishing 115,000 subsistence homesteads, developing a system of conservation, increasing hydroelectric power, upgrading educational levels, reducing state indebtedness, and organizing a planning board to attract industry. However, the Oklahoma Legislature was more economy-minded during the Depression, and most of Marland's proposals were not adopted. Nonetheless, some reforms were passed during his term—the state sales tax was raised to two percent and used for relief, ad valorem taxes were reduced, and school aid was increased. The State Planning and Resources Board was established in 1937 to help attract new industry to the state; Marland also initiated the Interstate Oil Compact between petroleum producing states to encourage oil conservation and assure a stable petroleum price. Because Oklahoma's constitution prohibited governors from serving consecutive terms, Marland left office on January 9, 1939. After leaving office Marland returned to his oil investments. Marland died on October 3, 1941, and is buried at Ponca City. Bibliography: Wilbur Johnson, ed., *Directory of Oklahoma* (Oklahoma City, 1975); John J. Mathews, *Life and Death of an Oilman* (Norman, 1951); Daughters of the American Revolution, "Earnest W. Marland," *The Last Run* (Ponca City, 1939); Governor E. W. Marland, Administrative Files, Oklahoma State Library, Oklahoma City, Oklahoma.

PHILLIPS, Leon Chase, 1939-1943

Born on December 9, 1890 in Worth County, Missouri, son of Rufus P. Phillips, a farmer, and Bertha Bressler Phillips; a Methodist. Brother of Mary Lois, Leon, Wesley, Bertha and Dorothea. Married Myrtle Ellenberger on June 19, 1916, and became the adopted father of Robert Rowe and Lois Ann. In 1892 Phillips' family moved to near Arapaho, Custer County, Oklahoma Territory. Educated in public schools; taught school, 1908-1909; attended Epworth University; received an LL.B. degree from the University of Oklahoma, 1916. Opened a law office at Okemah, Oklahoma, in 1916, and served in Artillery Officers' Training School, 1917-1918. Special member, Oklahoma Supreme Court, 1927-1928; member, Oklahoma House of Representatives, 1933-1938; Speaker, Oklahoma House of Representatives, 1935; Democratic Minority Leader, Oklahoma House of Representatives, 1937. Mason; Elk; American Legion. On July 12, 1938, Phillips won the Democratic gubernatorial primary, and, since the runoff election system had been abolished in 1937, he became the Democratic nominee in the general election. In November 1938 he was elected governor, receiving 355,740 votes to Republican Ross Rizley's 148,861. Phillips was sworn into office on January 9, 1939. Phillips proposed both to cut appropriations and reduce state indebtedness, and during his term bonds were issued to remove the outstanding debt and a budget balancing amendment added to Oklahoma's constitution. Phillips also opposed the construction of multiple purpose dams in the state, and used the National Guard to hinder completion of the Grand River Dam Project; however, he was overruled by a federal court injunction. The latter portion of Phillips' term was chiefly concerned with mobilizing the state for World War II, a mobilization which helped to bring Oklahoma out of the Great Depression. Because of a schism within the Democratic Party over Franklin D. Roosevelt's New Deal programs, Phillips broke with the Democratic leaders and supported the Republican ticket in the 1942 election. Phillips left office on January 11, 1943, due to the provision in Oklahoma's constitution which prohibited governors from serving two consecutive terms. After leaving office he returned to his law practice in Okemah. Phillips died on March 27, 1958, and is buried in Weleetka, Oklahoma. Bibliography: Wilbur Johnson, ed., *Directory of Oklahoma* (Oklahoma City, 1975); Rex F. Harlow, *Makers of Government in*

Oklahoma (Oklahoma City, 1930); Leon C. Phillips Collection, "Vertical File," Library, Oklahoma Historical Society, Oklahoma City, Oklahoma; Governor Leon C. Phillips, Administrative Files, Oklahoma State Library, Oklahoma City, Oklahoma.

KERR, Robert Samuel, 1943-1947

Born on September 11, 1896, near Ada, Chickasaw Nation, present-day Pontotoc County, Oklahoma, son of William Samuel Kerr, a farmer, and Margaret Wright Kerr; a Baptist. Brother of Lois, Mildred, Aubrey, Travis and Billy. Married Reba Shelton on December 5, 1919; she died on February 12, 1924; married Grace Breene on December 26, 1925; father of Robert Samuel, Jr., Breene, Kay and William. Educated in public schools; attended East Central Normal School, 1909-1911 and 1912-1915; attended Oklahoma Baptist University, 1911-1912; attended the University of Oklahoma, 1915-1916. Taught school, 1916-1917; Second Lieutenant, United States Army Field Artillery, 1917-1919; studied law privately and was admitted to the Oklahoma Bar, 1922. Formed an oil well drilling company in 1926, which became Kerr-McGee Oil Industries, Inc., in 1946. Special Justice, Oklahoma Supreme Court, 1931; president, Oklahoma County Juvenile Council, 1935-1936; president, Kansas-Oklahoma Division, Mid-Continent Oil and Gas Association, 1936-1941; member, Democratic National Committee, 1940, 1944, 1948; Keynote Speaker, Democratic National Convention, 1944; United States Senator, 1948-1963. Mason; American Legion. Kerr won the Democratic gubernatorial primary in August 1942, and because the runoff election system had been abolished in 1937, he became the Democratic nominee in the general election. In November, 1942, he was elected governor, polling 196,565 votes to Republican William J. Otjen's 180,454. Kerr was sworn into office on January 11, 1943. During Kerr's administration a Ballot Separation Law was passed to protect state Democrats from an anticipated Republican sweep in 1944. In addition, a constitutional amendment was adopted which established a sinking fund to retire state bonds. Other constitutional amendments passed during his term created a State Pardon and Parole Board, removed the various college boards of regents from politics, reestablished the primary runoff system, and provided free textbooks for public schools. During World War II forty-one military installations were opened across Oklahoma, as well as nine P.O.W. camps. In spite of state opposition to Franklin D. Roosevelt's fourth term, Kerr remained loyal to the national Democratic Party and delivered the 1944 keynote address at the national convention. Because Oklahoma's constitution prohibited governors from serving consecutive terms, Kerr left office on January 13, 1947. Kerr was elected United States Senator on November 2, 1948, and held the office until his death. Kerr died on January 1, 1963, and is buried at his birthplace near Ada. Bibliography: Wilbur Johnson, ed., *Directory of Oklahoma* (Oklahoma City, 1975); Robert S. Kerr, *Land, Wood and Water* (New York, 1960); Robert S. Kerr Papers, Western History Collections, University of Oklahoma, Norman, Oklahoma; Robert S. Kerr, "Vertical File," Library, Oklahoma Historical Society, Oklahoma City, Oklahoma.

TURNER, Roy Joseph, 1947-1951

Born on November 6, 1894, in Lincoln County, Oklahoma Territory, son of Reason Turner, a farmer, and Etta Louise Rogers Turner; a Methodist. Brother of Lena and Viola. Married Jessica E. Grimm on August 11, 1937, and adopted father of Betty and Bill. Educated in public schools; moved to Oklahoma City, Oklahoma, after graduating from high school; attended Hill's Business College. Bookkeeper, 1911-1915; salesman, 1916; served as a Private in the United States Army during W.W. I; real estate dealer, 1920-1928; organized Harper-Turner Oil Company, 1928; founded 10,000 acre Turner Ranch, 1933; established Turner purebred Hereford cattle herd, 1935. Member, Oklahoma City Board of Education, 1939-1946. President, American Hereford Association, 1939, 1945, 1946; Mason; American Legion. Turner won the Democratic gubernatorial primary and runoff elections in the summer of 1946—the runoff election was reestablished in Oklahoma in 1945 after having been abandoned eight years earlier. On November 5, 1946, Turner was elected governor, receiving 259,491 votes to Republican Olney F. Flynn's 227,426. He was sworn into office on January 13, 1947. During Turner's administration the State Highway Department and the State Planning and Resources Board were reorganized; a Board of Regents for State Colleges was created; the Oklahoma Turnpike Authority was established; and segregation in higher education was ended in the state. Turner was less successful in his efforts to provide a state merit system for employees and to reform public education financing, both of which failed to pass the legislature. In addition, an attempt to revise Oklahoma's constitution during his term also foundered when it was rejected by the state's voters. When the national Democratic Party split over the 1948 election, Turner ignored all efforts to support the Dixiecrats and remained loyal to the national Democratic Party. Because Oklahoma's original constitution prohibited governors from serving consecutive terms, Turner left office on January 8, 1951. After leaving office, Turner returned to his oil and cattle investments, although he did serve on the State Highway Commission from 1959 until 1963. Turner died on June 11, 1973, and is buried in Oklahoma City. Bibliography: Wilbur Johnson, ed., *Directory of Oklahoma* (Oklahoma City, 1975); Roy P. Stewart, *The Turner Ranch* (Oklahoma City, 1961); Roy J. Turner Collection, "Vertical File," Library, Oklahoma Historical Society, Oklahoma City, Oklahoma; Governor Roy J. Turner, Administrative Files, Oklahoma State Library, Oklahoma City, Oklahoma.

MURRAY, Johnston, 1951-1955

Born on July 21, 1902 in Emet, Chickasaw Nation, present-day Johnston County, Oklahoma, son of William Henry "Alfalfa Bill" Murray, farmer, lawyer and governor of Oklahoma, and Mary Alice Hearrell Murray; a Methodist. Brother of Massena B., William H., Jr., Jean and Burbank. Married Willie Roberta Emerson on May 1, 1933, and father of Johnston, Jr. Educated in public schools; graduated from Murray State School of Agriculture in 1924; received an LL.B. from Oklahoma City University in 1946. Newspaperman; accompanied his father to Bolivia, 1924-1930; worked in Oklahoma oil fields, 1930-1942; Douglas Aircraft Company, 1942-1944; investigator, trial lawyer, and clerk, 1944-1946; opened a law office in

Oklahoma City, Oklahoma, 1946. Chairman, Eighth Oklahoma Congressional District, 1932-1933; member, Kay County, Oklahoma, Democratic Central Committee, 1940; Chairman, Oklahoma Electoral College, 1940; member, State Election Board, 1941; member, Oklahoma County, Democratic Central Committee, 1948-1949; member, Oklahoma Electoral College, 1948. Mason; K. P.; Odd Fellow. In the summer of 1950 Murray won the Democratic gubernatorial primary and runoff elections, and on November 7, 1950, he was elected governor, receiving 329,308 votes to Republican Jo O. Ferguson's 313,205. He was sworn into office on January 8, 1951. Murray's administration was committed to a program calling for no new taxes and greater economy in state government. In an attempt to implement these policies, Murray established the Governor's Joint Committee on Reorganization of State Government to study various methods to eliminate waste and streamline state administration. As a means of accomplishing these goals, Murray turned to the veto, which he used forty times in four years. During his term Oklahoma lost two congressional seats because of its declining population, and the legislature was forced to reapportion the state's congressional districts. Murray's administration was also marked by an amendment to Oklahoma's constitution allowing women to serve on juries. Because Oklahoma's first constitution prohibited governors from serving consecutive terms, Murray left office on January 10, 1955. Afterwards Murray practiced law in Texas and Oklahoma and served as a consulting attorney for the Oklahoma Department of Welfare. Murray died on April 16, 1974, and is buried at Tishomingo, Oklahoma. Bibliography: Wilbur Johnson, ed., *Directory of Oklahoma* (Oklahoma City, 1975); Gaston Litton, *History of Oklahoma*, 4 vols. (New York, 1957); Johnston Murray Collection, "Vertical File," Library, Oklahoma Historical Society, Oklahoma City, Oklahoma; Governor Johnston Murray, Administrative Files, Oklahoma State Library, Oklahoma City, Oklahoma.

GARY, Raymond D., 1955-1959

Born on January 21, 1908 in Marshall County, Oklahoma, son of Daniel Remus Gary, a farmer, and Winnie Edith Roman Gary; a Baptist. Brother of Joe F., Anna, Ruby and May. Married Emma Mae Purser on September 1, 1928, and father of Mona Mae and Raymond Jerdy. Educated in public schools; attended Southeastern State College, 1928-1932. Taught school, 1928-1932; elected Marshall County Superintendent of Schools, 1932-1936; proprietor, Gary Furniture Manufacturing Company, 1936-1941; president, Sooner Oil Company, 1946-present; elected Oklahoma Senate, 1940-1954; President Pro Tempore, Oklahoma Senate, 1952-1954. Oklahoma Baptist General Convention; Trustee, Oklahoma Baptist University; Rotary; Lions; Boy Scouts of America. In the summer of 1954 Gary won the Democratic gubernatorial primary and runoff elections, and on November 2, 1954, he was elected governor. He received 357,386 votes to Republican Reuben K. Sparks' 251,808, and was sworn into office on January 10, 1955. During Gary's administration Oklahoma's public schools were integrated, and a constitutional amendment was adopted abolishing state financing of segregated schools. Gary also led the way toward eliminating the remaining racial restrictions throughout the state. As a result, Oklahoma avoided much of the violence that erupted over integration elsewhere across the United States. During Gary's term the state celebrated its fiftieth birthday under the direction of the Oklahoma Semi-Centennial Commission. Gary was greatly interested in improving the state's roads, and between 1955 and 1959 over 3,500 miles of new highways were constructed and approximately 800 miles of the new interstate system planned. He also established the Department of Commerce and Industry which promotes new industrial development, and the Water Study Commission, which monitors Oklahoma's water supply and needs. Because Oklahoma's original constitution prohibited governors from serving consecutive terms, Gary left office on January 8, 1959. Afterward he returned to his oil and cattle interests; he currently resides on his Aberdeen Angus cattle ranch near Madill, Oklahoma. Bibliography: Wilbur Johnson, ed., *Directory of Oklahoma* (Oklahoma City, 1975); Gaston Litton, *History of Oklahoma*, 4 vols. (New York, 1957); Raymond D. Gary Collection, "Vertical File," Library, Oklahoma Historical Society, Oklahoma City, Oklahoma; Governor Raymond D. Gary, Administrative Files, Oklahoma State Library, Oklahoma City, Oklahoma.

EDMONDSON, James Howard, 1959-1963

Born on September 27, 1925 in Muskogee, Oklahoma, son of Edmond Augustus Edmondson, a politician, and Esther Pullen Edmondson; a Presbyterian. Brother of Edmond Augustus, Jr., Ann and Molly. Married Jeannette Bartleston on May 15, 1946; father of James Howard, Jr., Jeanne and Patty. Educated in public schools; received an LL.B. degree from the University of Oklahoma in 1948. Flight Officer Training, United States Army Air Corps, 1942-1945; private law practice, 1948-1953; Chief Prosecutor, Tulsa County Attorney's Office, 1953; Tulsa County Attorney, 1954-1958. American Legion; Phi Gamma Delta; Mason; Rotarian. Edmondson won the Democratic gubernatorial primary and runoff elections in the summer of 1958, and on November 4, 1958, he was elected governor, receiving 399,504 votes to Republican Phil Ferguson's 107,485. He was sworn into office on January 12, 1959. Edmondson clashed repeatedly with the legislature during his term. One of his main campaign promises had been an early vote on the repeal of prohibition, and to encourage this he vigorously enforced Oklahoma's liquor law. As a result, the state became truly "dry." The predictable reaction occurred, and by state referendum prohibition was repealed and an Alcoholic Beverage Control Board established to govern the new liquor outlets. Also during Edmondson's administration, the State Industrial Finance Authority and a state merit system were created. Edmondson, already at odds with state Democratic leaders over prohibition and interference in partisan politics, completed the break by supporting John F. Kennedy for the 1960 Democratic presidential nomination. On January 1, 1963, Oklahoma's United States Senator, Robert S. Kerr died; on January 6, 1963, Edmondson resigned from office, and Lieutenant Governor George P. Nigh became governor. According to Oklahoma's constitution, Nigh was to appoint a successor to Kerr's position until the next general election. Nigh appointed Edmondson to the vacant senatorial seat. On May 26, 1964, Edmondson lost the Democratic runoff election to fill Kerr's unexpired term. Later he opened a law office in Oklahoma City, Oklahoma. Edmondson died on November 17, 1971, and is buried in Edmond, Oklahoma. Bibliography: Wilbur Johnson, ed., *Directory of*

Oklahoma (Oklahoma City, 1975); J. Leland Gourley, *The Best of J. Howard Edmondson* (Oklahoma City, 1963); J. Howard Edmondson Collection, "Vertical File," Library, Oklahoma Historical Society, Oklahoma City, Oklahoma; Governor J. Howard Edmondson, Administrative Files, Oklahoma State Library, Oklahoma City, Oklahoma.

NIGH, George Patterson, 1963

Born on June 9, 1927 in McAlester, Oklahoma, son of Wilbur R. Nigh, owner of a grocery store, and Irene Crockett Nigh; a Baptist. Brother of Wilbur, Bill, Sam and Mary. Married Donna Skinner Mashburn on October 19, 1963; father of Michael Mashburn and Georgeann. Educated in public schools; attended Eastern Oklahoma Agricultural and Mechanical College, 1946-1947; received a B.A. degree from East Central State College in 1950. Seaman Third Class, United States Navy, 1945-1946; taught school, 1952-1958; partner, Nigh Grocery, McAlester, 1956-1960. Elected to the Oklahoma House of Representatives, 1950-1958; Lieutenant Governor of Oklahoma, 1958-1962, 1966-present. On January 6, 1963, Governor James Howard Edmondson resigned, and Lieutenant Governor Nigh became governor. Nigh only served as governor for nine days; however, he quickly appointed former Governor Edmondson to fill the U.S. Senatorial seat left vacant by the death of Robert S. Kerr on January 1, 1963. Because Oklahoma's constitution prohibited governors from serving consecutive terms, Nigh left office on January 14, 1963. After he left the governor's office, Nigh was reelected Lieutenant Governor in 1966, 1970 and 1974. He is currently serving in that office. Bibliography: Wilbur Johnson, ed., *Directory of Oklahoma* (Oklahoma City, 1975); Oklahoma Department of Libraries, *Governors of Oklahoma* (Oklahoma City, 1975); George Nigh Papers, Lieutenant Governor's Office, State Capitol, Oklahoma City, Oklahoma; George P. Nigh Collection, "Vertical File," Library, Oklahoma Historical Society, Oklahoma City, Oklahoma.

BELLMON, Henry Louis, 1963-1967

Born on September 3, 1921 in Tonkawa, Oklahoma, son of George Bellmon, a farmer, and Edith Caskey Bellmon; a Presbyterian. Brother of Randall and George. Married Shirley Osborn on January 24, 1947; father of Patricia, Gail and Ann. Educated in public schools; received a B.S. degree in Agriculture from Oklahoma State University in 1942; graduate study at Colorado State University. First Lieutenant, United States Marine Corps, 1942-1946; received the Legion of Merit for action in the invasion of Saipan; received the Silver Star for bravery in the invasion of Iwo Jima. At the end of World War II, he returned to his farm in Noble County, Oklahoma; elected to the Oklahoma House of Representatives, 1946-1948; Chairman, Oklahoma Republican Committee, 1960-1962. On May 1, 1962, Bellmon won the Republican gubernatorial primary, and on November 6, 1962, he was elected governor, receiving 392,316 votes to Democrat W. P. "Bill" Atkinson's 315,357. He was sworn into office on January 14, 1963. Bellmon was the first Republican Governor of Oklahoma, and in spite of having a Democratic-dominated legislature he remained on good terms with that branch of the government. During Bellmon's term the legislature was reapportioned, under United States Supreme Court pressure, and the urban areas were given a larger share of representation. Bellmon proposed a "Giant Stride" plan for improving the state's educational system; however, a shortage of tax revenue hindered the proposed reforms. As a result, the National Education Association imposed sanctions on the state. During Bellmon's administration, two members of Oklahoma's Supreme Court were accused of accepting bribes—one resigned, the other was impeached and removed from office. In addition, a district attorney system was established in the state, a higher education code was adopted, and the Industrial Development and Park Commission was created. Also, Oklahoma's constitution was amended to allow governors to serve consecutive terms; previously they had not been allowed to succeed themselves. Though the constitution had been altered, the consecutive term provision did not apply to Bellmon, and he left office on January 9, 1967. Afterward he returned to his farming interests, but on November 5, 1968, he was elected to the United States Senate. Reelected in 1974, he currently holds this position. Bibliography: Wilbur Johnson, ed., *Directory of Oklahoma* (Oklahoma City, 1975); Henry L. Bellmon Collection, "Vertical File," Library, Oklahoma Historical Society, Oklahoma City, Oklahoma; Governor Henry Bellmon, Administrative Files, Oklahoma State Library, Oklahoma City, Oklahoma; Henry Bellmon Papers, Library, Oklahoma State University, Stillwater, Oklahoma.

BARTLETT, Dewey Follett, 1967-1971

Born on March 28, 1919 in Marietta, Ohio, son of David Albert Bartlett, who was engaged in the petroleum industry, and Jessie B. Follett Noll Bartlett; a Roman Catholic. Brother of David. Married Ann Chilton Smith on April 2, 1945; father of Dewey Follett, Jr., Joan Chilton and Michael Hopkins. Educated in public schools; received a B.S. degree in Geological Engineering from Princeton University in 1942. Worked in Oklahoma oil fields while attending college; Captain, United States Marine Corps Aviation, 1942-1945; moved to Tulsa, Oklahoma, in 1945 and entered the family petroleum business; partner, Keener Oil Company, Tulsa, 1951-present; president, Dewey Supply Company, 1953-1956; rancher, 1958-present. Member, Executive Committee, Oklahoma Independent Petroleum Association; directory, Independent Petroleum Association; Board of Advisors, Salvation Army. Elected to the Oklahoma Senate, 1963-1965. In May, 1966, Bartlett won the Republican gubernatorial primary and runoff elections, and on November 8, 1966, he was elected governor, receiving 377,078 votes to Democrat Preston J. Moore's 296,328. He was sworn into office on January 9, 1967. During Bartlett's administration Oklahoma's judicial system was reformed so that state judges had to win the approval of voters to retain their positions. In addition, the Justice of the Peace court system was abolished. Also during Bartlett's term Oklahoma's constitution was amended to allow educational funds to be deposited in public banks and trusts, a Legislative Conflict of Interest Law was enacted, the Board of Legislative Compensation was established, and a method for reviewing legislative compensation every two years was created. Bartlett was successful in reforming the state's tax laws and removing the tax on intangible personal property. Bartlett was

Oklahoma's first governor who was eligible to succeed himself in office—Oklahoma's constitution was amended to allow successive terms in 1966. However, on November 3, 1970, he was defeated in his bid for reelection by Democrat David Hall by 2,181 votes. Bartlett left office on January 11, 1971. Afterward he returned to his oil and ranching investments. In August, 1972, Bartlett won the Republican nomination for the United States Senate, and on November 7, 1972, he was elected United States Senator, a position he currently holds. Bibliography: Wilbur Johnson, ed., *Directory of Oklahoma* (Oklahoma City, 1975); Oklahoma Department of Libraries, *Governors of Oklahoma* (Oklahoma City, 1975); Dewey F. Bartlett Collection, "Vertical File," Library, Oklahoma Historical Society, Oklahoma City, Oklahoma; Governor Dewey F. Bartlett, Administrative Files, Oklahoma State Library, Oklahoma City, Oklahoma.

HALL, David, 1971-1975

Born on October 20, 1930 in Oklahoma City, Oklahoma, son of William A. "Red" Hall, a corporate executive, and Audrey Nell Hall; a Presbyterian. Brother of Wendall A. Married to Jo Evans Hall on June 9, 1956; father of Nancy Leigh, Douglas David and Julie Beth. Attended public schools; received a B.A. degree in Government and History from the University of Oklahoma in 1952; attended Harvard University, 1955-1956; received an LL.B. degree from the University of Tulsa in 1959. Served in the United States Air Force, 1952-1954; Captain, United States Air Force Reserve, Judge Advocate General Division; Assistant County Attorney, Tulsa County, Oklahoma, 1959-1962; County Attorney, Tulsa County, 1962-1966; established private law practice, 1966; unsuccessful candidate for the Democratic gubernatorial nomination, 1966; Professor of Law, University of Tulsa, 1968. Author, *Oklahoma Criminal Information Form Book*; Phi Beta Kappa; Boy Scouts of America; Mason; Shriner. In August and September, 1970, Hall won the Democratic gubernatorial primary runoff elections, and on November 3, 1970, he was elected governor after a recount, receiving 338,338 votes to incumbent Republican Governor Dewey F. Bartlett's 336,157. He was sworn into office on January 11, 1971. Hall campaigned on a platform calling for improved law and order techniques, increased narcotics control, and greater education expenditures; he was elected by the closest margin in state history to that date. During his administration the state's Grand Jury system was reorganized, the voting age was lowered to eighteen, and the "silent vote" was eliminated on constitutional amendments proposed by initiative petitions. Also during Hall's term, Oklahoma's tax system was reformed, and an extensive building program was implemented to provide additional space for state agencies. Hall was eligible to succeed himself in office—Oklahoma's constitution had been amended in 1966 to allow successive terms. However, he was defeated in the August, 1974, Democratic gubernatorial primary election. After Hall left office on January 13, 1975, he was indicted and convicted in federal court of extortion and bribery while in office. After losing his appeal, he began serving a three year sentence at the federal prison camp in Safford, Arizona. Bibliography: Wilbur Johnson, ed., *Directory of Oklahoma* (Oklahoma City, 1975); Oklahoma Department of Libraries, *Governors of Oklahoma* (Oklahoma City, 1975); David Hall Collection, "Vertical File,"

Library, Oklahoma Historical Society, Oklahoma City, Oklahoma; Governor David Hall, Administrative Files, Oklahoma State Library, Oklahoma City, Oklahoma.

BOREN, David Lyle, 1975-

Born on April 21, 1941 in Washington, D.C., son of Lyle H. Boren, a politician and five time United States Congressman, and Christine McKown Boren; a Methodist. Brother of Susan. Married Janna Lou Little on September 7, 1968; divorced in 1976; father of Carrie Christine and David Daniel. Attended public schools; received a B.A. degree, summa cum laude, from Yale University in 1963; received an M.A. degree with honors from Oxford University, England, in 1965; received a J.D. degree from the University of Oklahoma in 1968. Assistant to the Director of Liaison, Office of Civil and Defense Mobilization, 1960-1962; Propaganda Analyst, Soviet Affairs, United States Information Agency, London, England, 1962-1963; member, Residential Counseling Staff, University of Oklahoma, 1965-1966; Professor of Political Science, Oklahoma Baptist University, 1969-1974; Chairman, Social Studies Division, Oklahoma Baptist University, 1969-1974; Oklahoma House of Representatives, 1967-1974. Ranking Scholars, Yale University; Rhodes Scholar, Oxford University; Phi Beta Kappa; Sigma Delta Rho; member, Board of Governors, College of Law, University of Oklahoma. In August and September, 1974, Boren won the Democratic gubernatorial primary and runoff elections, and on November 5, 1974, he was elected governor, receiving 514,686 votes to Republican Jim Inhofe's 290,459. He was sworn into office on January 13, 1975. Boren campaigned on a promise to reorganize state government and eliminate waste and costly overlapping of duties. As a result, early in his administration the Department of Transportation was formed from the Highway Department, Highway Safety Office, Aeronautics Commission, Railroad Maintenance Authority and a part of the Department of Economics and Urban Affairs. Boren's current term will end on January 9, 1979. [Governor Boren remarried on November 27, 1977 to Molly W. Shi.] Bibliography: Wilbur Johnson, ed., *Directory of Oklahoma* (Oklahoma City, 1975); Oklahoma Department of Libraries, *Governors of Oklahoma* (Oklahoma City, 1975); David L. Boren Collection, "Vertical File," Library, Oklahoma Historical Society, Oklahoma City, Oklahoma; Governor David L. Boren, Governor's Office, State Capitol, Oklahoma City, Oklahoma.

OREGON

OREGON

WHITEAKER, John, 1859-1862

Born on May 4, 1820 in Dearborn County, Indiana, son of John, a farmer, and Nancy (Smales) Whiteaker, Brother of James, Elizu, Douglas and Catherine. Married to Nancy Jane Hargrave on August 22, 1847; father of Francis, John Charles, Anne, James, Estelle and Benjamin. Almost entirely self-educated, Whiteaker attended school for less than six months as a youth. Volunteered for military service during the war with Mexico, but his company was not called to duty. Worked as a carpenter and later as cabinetmaker, before succumbing to "gold fever" in 1849. Earned enough in California to move his family to Oregon over the Oregon Trail in 1852. Became a farmer in Lane County, Oregon, and was soon active in the Democratic Party. Elected Judge of the Probate Court for Lane County in 1856 and to the Territorial Legislature in 1857. A state constitution was adopted in 1857 and Whiteaker was nominated for governor by one of two factions of the Democratic Party. The Republican candidate withdrew before the election in June 1858, leaving E. M. Barnum, another Democrat, as Whiteaker's opponent. Whiteaker won by a majority of 1,138 and was inaugurated on July 8, 1858. Eight months later Congress admitted Oregon to statehood and Whiteaker assumed office. His pro-slavery position alienated him from a substantial number of the citizens of Oregon at the outbreak of the Civil War. Whiteaker was vilified as a traitor, but continued to serve until the end of his term in September 1862. As governor he urged development of home industries, citing soap, socks and pickles as products Oregonians could make for themselves. His frequent nickname was "Honest John," but was also known as "Old Soap, Socks and Pickles." Although Whiteaker was not nominated to run for a second term, he did not retire from politics. He was elected to three successive terms in the lower branch of the State Legislature in 1866, 1868, and 1870, and to the State Senate in 1876; he also served as presiding officer of both bodies. Elected in 1878 to the 46th Congress, he attracted national attention when Democrats chartered a train to take him to Washington, D.C. in time to vote for a Democratic Speaker of the House. He introduced a congressional bill to authorize negotiations with the Umatilla, Warm Springs and certain other Indian tribes, with the intention of extinguishing their title to reservation lands and removing them to reservations outside Oregon. Appointed Collector of Internal Revenue in Oregon in 1885, he retired in 1889 to Eugene, where he died on October 2, 1902. Bibliography: George S. Turnbull, *Governors of Oregon* (Portland, 1959); Nellie Banfield, "The Public Career of John Whiteaker," B.A. thesis, University of Oregon, 1912; Lucia Wilkins Moore, "John Whiteaker, First Governor of Oregon," *Lane County Historian*, vol. IV, no. 1 (February, 1959); Harrison Rittenhouse Kincaid. *Political and Official History and Register of Oregon* (Appendix to 20th biennial report of Oregon Secretary of State,

1897-98: Salem, Oregon, 1899). The John Whiteaker Papers are on deposit in the Lane County Historical Museum, Eugene, Oregon.

GIBBS, Addison C., 1862-1866

Born on July 9, 1825 in East Otto, New York, son of Abraham, a farmer, and Rachel Scobey Gibbs; a Methodist. Married to Margaret M. Watkins; father of seven children, including William, Lizzie, Charles W. and Katie. As a youth he attended Springville Academy, and in 1848 he entered the State Normal School in Albany. Taught school while studying law in the evenings; was admitted to the New York Bar in May, 1849. Went to California in search of gold but left for Oregon in September, 1850, to manage affairs of the Umpqua Town-site and Colonization Land Company; sold land along the Umpqua River in southern Oregon. He was instrumental in bringing milling machinery and zinc houses, made in Boston, to a site at the mouth of the Umpqua. He also took a claim north of the Umpqua and began and developed the town of Gardiner. In 1853 he volunteered for and participated in the Rogue River Indian War. That same year he was appointed Collector of Customs for southern Oregon, which was then an active mining region. Moved to Portland in 1858; entered into law partnership with George H. Williams, who later became United States Attorney General, 1873-77. Gibbs actively supported the Free Soil Party in New York in 1848. He was elected as a Democrat to the lower house of the Oregon Territorial Legislature in 1852, and served in the 1852-53 session; he was elected to that same body in 1860. When the Union-Republican Party was formed in Oregon in 1862, Gibbs was one of the first to join. He received the gubernatorial nomination of that party at its April 1862 convention, and was elected governor, by a vote of 7,029 to 3,450, over the Democrat, John F. Miller. Inaugurated on September 10, 1862, Gibbs supported Lincoln and his administration during the Civil War. Designated by the legislature to superintend the penitentiary, he effected a revision of the management of the institution, by introducing a system of manufacturing, whose operating costs could be partially met by convict labor. In 1866 he was nominated by the Republicans to the United States Senate but was narrowly defeated. Elected Prosecuting Attorney for the Fourth Judicial District in Oregon in 1868 and reelected in 1870; appointed United States District Attorney for the District of Oregon by President Ulysses S. Grant in 1872; practiced law in Portland. Gibbs died on December 29, 1886 in London, where, for the last two years of his life, he represented American parties selling land in the United States. His remains were returned by an act of the Oregon Legislature to Portland, where he was buried in the Riverview Cemetery on July 9, 1887. Bibliography: *Oregonian* [Portland] (December 31, 1886); Harvey K. Hines, *An Illustrated History of the State of Oregon* (Chicago, 1893); *Republican League Register* (Portland, 1896) *History of the Bench and Bar of Oregon* (Portland, 1910). The Addison Crandall Gibbs Papers are on deposit in the Oregon Historical Society Library in Portland.

WOODS, George Lemuel, 1866-1870

Born on July 30, 1832, in Boone County, Missouri, son of Caleb and Margaret McBride Woods; a Christian; one of four sons. Married to Louisa A. McBride, his cousin, in 1853; father of two sons. Came to Yamhill County, Oregon, with his family in 1847; attended a log cabin school and McMinnville College. Worked on his father's farm; was a carpenter; later was a gold miner in California in 1852-53, Member of an expedition to find gold in eastern Oregon in 1857, but was driven back by Indians. Studied law and admitted to the Oregon Bar in 1858. Practiced law in Walla Walla, Washington Territory, and in The Dalles, Oregon. Was one of the founders of the Republican Party in Oregon; active in party organization in Yamhill County in 1856 and throughout the Willamette Valley in 1857; promoted a free-state movement as Oregon prepared to adopt a state constitution. Appointed Wasco County Judge in 1863, and, in 1864 was nominated as a presidential elector for Abraham Lincoln. Travelled widely in Oregon campaigning for Lincoln. Appointed to the Idaho Territory Supreme Court in 1865 and, in 1866, nominated by the Republican Party State Convention as its candidate for governor of Oregon. He received 10,316 votes to 10,039 for his Democratic opponent, James K. Kelley. At the time of his inauguration on September 12, 1866, Woods was involved in plans to build a railroad from Portland to California with a federal land grant. When the Oregon Central Railroad was organized in November 1866, Woods was an incorporator. In April 1867, he joined a rival company backed by California interests. A bitter contest followed. He also was involved in controversy with the United States War Department over Indian policy in Oregon; Woods argued for a war of extermination against the Snake Indians east of the Cascade Mountains. His position prevailed. A State Legislature dominated by Democrats unsuccessfully attempted to remove Woods from office in 1868 by challenging the validity of his 1866 election. The Republican Party State Convention in April 1870, nominated Joel Palmer for the governorship and Woods campaigned with him in the company of the Democratic candidate, LaFayette Grover. In 1871 President Grant appointed Woods as Governor of Utah, a position he held until 1875. For ten years he practiced law in California and Nevada, returning to Oregon in 1885. He died on January 1, 1890 in Portland. Bibliography: *Oregonian* [Portland] (January 9, 1890); Herbert Lang, *History of the Willamette Valley* (Portland, 1885), *Republican League Register* (Portland, 1896); *Oregon Native Son* (Portland, 1899-1901); Harrison Kincaid, *Political and Official History and Register of Oregon* (Salem, 1899). The papers of George Woods apparently have not survived, but two letters from him are in the library of the University of Oregon, Eugene, Oregon.

GROVER, LaFayette, 1870-1877

Born on November 29, 1823, in Bethel, Maine, son of John, a surgeon and among those who helped frame the constitution of Maine in 1819, and Fanny (Woodman) Grover. Brother of Abernethy, Talleyrand, Cuvier and of two sisters who died early in life. Married to Elizabeth Carter in 1865; father of John Cuvier. Educated at Gould's Academy in Bethel, and at Bowdoin College in Brunswick, Maine. Studied law in Philadelphia and was admitted to the Pennsylvania Bar in March,

1850. In the autumn of that year, Grover sailed around Cape Horn to San Francisco, arriving in July, 1851. He soon proceeded to Oregon, where he began a law practice in Salem. Served for six months as clerk of the United States District Court, resigning in 1852 to resume his law practice. Held rank of First Lieutenant in a company of volunteers which he had helped to recruit to fight in the Rogue River Indian War of 1853-54. Appointed by the Department of the Interior to serve on a committee to assess losses sustained by white settlers in the Indian wars of 1853 and 1857. He was instrumental in the organization of the Willamette Woolen Manufacturing Company in Salem and supervised its growth as director of the company for fifteen years. He directed the completion of Salem Flouring Mills, which were the first exporters of Oregon flour to foreign ports. Grover was elected Prosecuting Attorney of the Second Judicial District in Oregon in 1852; representative to the Territorial Legislature in 1853; reelected in 1855, and was Speaker of the House during the 1855-56 session; elected delegate to the State Constitutional Convention in 1857; chosen as the first representative of Oregon to the United States Congress, but served for only seventeen days until the conclusion of the 35th Congress in March, 1859. In 1870 Grover was the Democratic nominee for governor and was elected by a vote of 11,726 to 11,095 over his Republican opponent, Joel Palmer. Reelected Governor in 1874, holding office until 1877 when he resigned to become a United States Senator, having been chosen for that office by the Oregon Legislature in 1876. Throughout his career as governor and senator, Grover worked to exclude Chinese workers from Oregon and to modify the Burlingame Treaty of 1868, which encouraged Chinese immigration to the United States. He supported the construction of locks at Willamette Falls in Oregon City, which, when completed, allowed river traffic from the lower to the upper Willamette and stimulated farm production by lowering freight rates. He promoted the organization of a state university, an agricultural college, and institutions for deaf mutes and the blind. Also the state capitol building and penitentiary were erected during his term of office. Grover served in the United States Senate from 1877 to 1883; he then retired to Portland, Oregon, where he sold real estate until his death on May 10, 1911. Bibliography: LaFayette Grover, "Notable Things in a Public Life in Oregon," Ms. in Bancroft Library, University of California, Berkeley, typescript in University of Oregon Library. Date, 1878; Elwood Evans, *History of the Pacific Northwest* (Portland, 1889); Harvey K. Hines, *An Illustrated History of the State of Oregon* (Chicago, 1893); Harrison Rittenhouse Kincaid, *Political and Official History and Register of Oregon* (Salem, 1899); *Portrait and Biographical Record of the Williamette Valley, Oregon* (Chicago,1903). The LaFayette Grover Papers are in the Oregon Historical Society Library, Portland.

CHADWICK, Stephen Fowler, 1877-1878

Born on December 25, 1825, in Middletown, Connecticut, son of Ezekiel and Eliza Chadwick. Brother of Henry. Married to Jane A. Smith; father of four children, Stephen J., Pitzer F., Ella P. and Mary. Chadwick received his elementary education in Connecticut; read law in New York City; and was admitted to the New York Bar on May 30, 1850. Sailed for Oregon via Panama on March 13, 1851; also aboard ship was Zenas Moody, who became the seventh governor of Oregon. Chadwick arrived in Oregon on April 21 of that year and settled in Scottsburg, where he set up a law practice and became the first postmaster of the town. Moved from Scottsburg to Roseburg, where he was elected the first Judge of Douglas County. Served as Assistant United States District Attorney for the Southern District of Oregon. In 1866 he was one of the original directors of a Salem corporation, the Oregon Central Railroad Company, which subsequently became part of the Southern Pacific Railroad. Represented Douglas County at Oregon's Constitutional Convention in 1857; was a Democratic presidential elector in 1864 and 1868; elected Secretary of State in 1870 and reelected to that office in 1874. Chadwick succeeded to the office of governor on February 1, 1877, after the resignation of **Governor LaFayette Grover,** who had been elected to the United States Senate. He served simultaneously as Governor and Secretary of State until the expiration of his term on September 11, 1878. The most dramatic event of his short term in office was a personal appearance which he made in eastern Oregon in 1878, during a period of general disorder caused by a series of raids conducted by the Bannock Indians. Chadwick was credited with aiding and encouraging the white settlers during the conflict and with insisting upon the punishment of the Indians responsible for starting the conflict. When the brief war was over, he insisted that friendly Indian chiefs surrender the instigators for prosecution by the state of Oregon; nine Indians were subsequently hung. The Governor's participation in the Indian war contributed to his fame more than did his other activities while in office. Chadwick did not seek reelection to a second term as governor. He resumed his law career in Salem and was particularly active in the Grand Lodge of Masons. He died in Salem on January 15, 1895. Bibliography: *Oregonian* [Portland] (January 16, 1895); Elwood Evans, *History of the Pacific Northwest* (Portland, 1889); Harvey K. Hines, *An Illustrated History of the State of Oregon* (Chicago, 1893); Harrison Rittenhouse Kincaid, *Political and Official History and Register of Oregon* (Salem, 1899). Correspondence from Chadwick is in the Joseph Lane Papers, Oregon Historical Society, Portland, and in the O. C. Applegate Papers and the Asahel Bush Papers, located in the University of Oregon Library, Eugene.

THAYER, William Wallace, 1878-1882

Born on a farm near Lima, New York on July 15, 1827, son of Gideon and Annie Dodge Thayer, whose children included five sons and two daughters. Married to Samantha C. Vincent on November 11, 1852; father of an only child, Claude. Educated in the common schools and through private study of the law; admitted to the New York Bar in 1851 and practiced with a brother, E. Thayer, in Buffalo, New York. Also practiced in Tonawanda, New York, before moving to Oregon in 1862 to practice law with Andrew J. Thayer, another of his brothers. Attracted to Idaho in 1863 by the mining excitement in that territory; opened a law office in Lewiston, where he remained until 1867. Elected District Attorney for the Third Judicial District, Idaho Territory, in 1866; elected to the 1866-67 session of the Idaho Territorial House of Representatives. Moved back to Oregon in 1867, settling in East Portland, where he entered into a law partnership. In 1876 he was one of fifteen persons challenging the certification of J. W. Watts, a Republican presidential elector committed to Rutherford B. Hayes, on grounds that Watts, as postmaster of Lafayette, Oregon, was ineligible to be an elector. Had the challenge been sustained, Samuel J. Tilden would have won the election. It was not. Thayer was nominated by the state Democratic convention in 1878 as its gubernatorial candidate and defeated his Republican opponent, C. C. Beekman, by fifty-nine votes, 16,206 to 16,147. Inaugurated on September 11, 1878, Thayer served a single term. During that time the state debt was paid, and construction of a state insane asylum, accommodating 400 to 500 persons, was almost completed. A significant change in the judiciary was effected by statute, substituting elected justices on the Oregon Supreme Court for the Circuit Court Judges, who, up to that time, had constituted the state's Supreme Court. Thayer did not run for reelection in 1882, but two years later was his party's nominee for a seat on the State Supreme Court. He served in that position for six years, and from 1888 to 1890 was the court's Chief Justice. He died in Portland on October 15, 1899. Bibliography: *Oregonian* [Portland] (October 16, 1899); H. H. Bancroft, *History of Oregon* (San Francisco, 1886-88); Elwood Evans, *History of the Pacific Northwest* (Portland, 1889); Harrison Rittenhouse Kincaid, *Political and Official History and Register of Oregon* (Salem, 1899); Harvey K. Hines, *An Illustrated History of the State of Oregon* (Chicago, 1893), *History of the Bench and Bar of Oregon* (Portland, 1910). The papers of Thayer appear not to have been preserved.

MOODY, Zenas Perry, 1882-1887

Born in Granby, Massachusetts, on May 27, 1832, son of Thomas Hovey, a farmer, and Hannah (Ferry) Moody, both of whom were members of the Congregational Church. Had three brothers, Thomas Hovey, William Ferry and Gideon Webster, and one sister, Mary. Spent his first sixteen years in Granby, where he attended local schools; then lived in Chicopee, Massachusetts for three years, where he attended the Union School. Married to Mary Stephenson on November 19, 1853; father of Malcolm A., Zenas A., William Hovey, Ralph E. and Edna. Sailed from New York on March 13, 1851 for Oregon via Panama. In Oregon worked on the early stages of the United States government survey of western Oregon; kept a store in Brownsville, Oregon from 1853 to 1856, when he was appointed Inspector of United States Surveys in California. From California he went to Illinois for four years, then to Washington, D.C., where he was living in 1861, as the Civil War began; joined a company of volunteers to protect Washington until regular troops arrived, but returned to Oregon in 1862. Established himself as a merchant at The Dalles and then in Umatilla, serving the booming gold mining districts of Oregon, Washington and Idaho. From 1867 to 1869, Moody was in business in Boise, Idaho Territory, then returned to The Dalles to manage affairs for Wells, Fargo and Company until 1873. From 1873 through 1875, he operated a steamboat line between Portland and The Dalles, having gained the contract for carrying the mail between those points. Politically, Moody was a Whig, then a Republican. He was also an officer in the secretive "Know-Nothing Party" in Linn County in 1855. In 1872 he was an unsuccessful candidate for the State Senate from Wasco County. In 1880 he was elected to the State Legislature and was chosen Speaker of the House. **He was the Republican gubernatorial candidate in 1882, defeating Democrat J.** S. Smith, 21,481 votes to 20,029. During his administration the state capitol building was completed, except for its dome; a portion of a new state hospital for the care of the mentally ill was completed and occupied; and the state debt was entirely paid, apart from outstanding road warrants in the amount of $50,000.

Moody encouraged immigration to Oregon, although his welcome did not extend to the Chinese. The Governor applauded an 1882 federal law prohibiting Chinese immigration for twenty years since it would end "the flooding of our fair state with a Chinese population." Oregon was also disturbed by a strident anti-Chinese campaign in the Portland area early in 1886. Moody did not run for a second term, but was succeeded in office by a Democrat, who had attracted public attention by his even more outspoken bigotry against the Chinese in the demonstrations preceding the June 1886 election. After leaving office in 1887, Moody returned to eastern Oregon, where he became a leading wool shipper. He died in Salem, Oregon on March 14, 1917. Bibliography: *Oregonian* [Portland] (March 15, 1917); Frank E. Hodgkin and J. J. Galvin, *Pen Pictures of Representative Men of Oregon* (Portland, 1882); H. H. Bancroft, *History of Oregon* (San Francisco, 1886-88); *Portrait and Biographical Record of the Willamette Valley, Oregon* (Chicago, 1903). The Moody Papers are on deposit in the library of the Oregon Historical Society, Portland.

PENNOYER, Sylvester, 1887-1895

Born on July 6, 1831 in Groton, New York, son of Justus P., a prosperous farmer and state legislator, and Elizabeth (Howland) Pennoyer; the youngest of nine children. Married to Mrs. Mary A. Allen in 1856; father of five children, four of whom died early in life, only Gertrude Elizabeth still survived at the time of Pennoyer's death. Educated at Home Academy, New York and at Harvard Law School, where he graduated in 1854. Travelled to Oregon in 1855 by steamer, and arrived in Portland on July 10. Soon began to teach, rising to become superintendent of Multnomah County schools from 1860 to 1862. Entered the lumber business in 1862 and became a partner in the successful Portland Lumbering and Manufacturing Company. Contributed editorials to Oregon newspapers and became editor of the leading Democratic newspaper in Portland, the *Oregon Herald*, in 1868. Became owner of that paper in 1869. Articles by Pennoyer on the American judicial system were published in 1895 and 1899 in *American Law Review*. Pennoyer was a man of strong conviction whose prejudices sometimes coincided with those of the voters of Oregon. Popular recollection of his sympathy for the Confederacy may have contributed to his defeat in an election to become mayor of Portland in 1885. Anti-Chinese agitation was just then reaching a climax, however, and Pennoyer's leadership in that cause probably gained for him the Democratic nomination for governor in 1886. He was elected by a vote of 27,901 to 24,199, over Republican opponent T. E. Cornelius. In his inaugural address, Pennoyer asserted that the accumulation of wealth by a few, and the growth and arrogance of monopolies, led to the social unrest then on the rise in Oregon as in the rest of the nation. When a group of Knights of Labor, Grangers, and Prohibitionists in Oregon formed the Union Party in 1889, they received the endorsement of the Governor. Both the Union Party and the Democrats nominated him as their candidate for reelection in 1890 and he won, 38,920 votes to 33,765, over his Republican opponent, D. P. Thompson. The Populist Party was organized in Cincinnati in May 1891, and, in October 1892, Pennoyer joined the Populists. The Panic of 1893 increased unemployment, and Jacob S. Coxey organized a massive protest march to Washington, D.C. to demand relief from

Congress. One company of "Coxey's Army" left Portland on April 25, 1894, but, having tired of marching, commandeered a train at Troutdale, Oregon. The United States Cavalry soon caught them and returned the 469 demonstrators to Portland, where they received a stern lecture from the United States District Judge, but the sympathetic support of the Governor. Pennoyer, who by this time had become something of a national figure, retired from office early the following year. He campaigned vigorously for Bryan and the silver standard in the 1896 election. Nominated by both the Populist and Democratic parties for the office of Mayor of Portland in 1896, and won. Retired from that position in 1898, and devoted his attention primarily to the management of his ranch near Portland. He died in Portland on May 30, 1902. Bibliography: *Oregonian* [Portland] (May 31, 1902); Maude Davis Chapman, "Sylvester Pennoyer, Governor of Oregon, 1887-1895," Unpublished Master's Thesis, University of Oregon, 1943; "Scrapbook of letters, printed messages, speeches, and clippings, 1852-1902, relating to Governor Pennoyer of Oregon," Mss. in University of Oregon Library, Eugene, Oregon; Harvey W. Scott, *History of the Oregon Country* (New York, 1924). In addition to the scrapbook noted above, there are some letters from Pennoyer in the Papers of Robert Aubrey Miller at the library of the University of Oregon. Other papers apparently have not survived.

LORD, William Paine, 1895-1899

Born on July 1, 1839, in Dover, Delaware, son of Edward and Elizabeth (Paine) Lord. Married to Juliette Montague on January 14, 1880; father of William P., Jr., Montague and Elizabeth Lord. Attended a Quaker school in Dover and studied with private tutors before entering Fairfield College in New York in 1857. Graduated in 1860 and started the study of the law but the Civil War intervened. Lord enlisted in the Union Army in 1862 and was commissioned a Captain, advancing to the rank of Major in his Delaware Cavalry Regiment by the end of the war. Returned to study law, graduating from Albany Law College, Albany, New York in 1866. Admitted to the New York Bar in that year, but again entered military service, serving in California, Washington and Alaska. When Alaska was purchased by the United States in 1867, Lord was sent to Sitka as the army took formal possession. Resigned in 1868 to take up the practice of law in Salem, Oregon. Became attorney for the city of Salem. Elected State Senator as a Republican in 1878, but resigned to accept the Republican nomination for Justice of the Oregon Supreme Court, a position which he won in 1880. Lord retained a place on the court until 1894, serving as Chief Justice twice during that period. In 1914 the State Bar Association named him the "Greatest of Oregon Chief Justices," to that date. Nominated by the Republican Party in 1894 for governor of Oregon, and, although handicapped by partial deafness and only moderate speaking ability, Lord received 41,139 votes to 26,723 for the People's Party candidate, Nathan Pierce, and 17,865 for the Democrat, William Galloway. Lord was inaugurated on January 16, 1895. The legislative session of 1895 was a disappointment to him because it devoted almost all of its attention to the election of a United States Senator. However, it did find time to provide for a State Land Agent to investigate losses sustained by the state in securing public lands to which it was entitled, and to secure title to land to which the state had a legal claim. Lord, who had encouraged creation of the office, appointed the first state land agent. He did not run for a second term, having been challenged successfully by another Republican, T. T. Geer, in a very close primary race. In 1899 Lord was appointed United States Minister to Argentina. He returned to Oregon in 1902 to practice law. He also codified the laws of Oregon in *Lord's Oregon Laws*, which appeared in three volumes in 1910. He died a year later on February 17, 1911 in a San Francisco hospital. Bibliography: *Oregonian* [Portland] (February 18, 1911); Frank E. Hodgkin and J. J. Galvin, *Pen Pictures of Representative Men of Oregon* (Portland, 1959); Theodore T. Geer, *Fifty Years in Oregon* (New York, 1912). The William Paine Lord Papers are in two libraries. Miscellaneous official correspondence and personal papers are in the library of the Oregon Historical Society, Portland. Other papers relating to his official duties are at the Oregon State Library, Salem.

GEER, Theodore T., 1899-1903

Born on March 12, 1851, near Salem, Oregon, son of Heman J., a farmer, nurseryman and occasional miner, and Cynthia Ann Eoff Geer; a Unitarian; one of five children. Married to Mrs. Nancy (Duncan) Batte, June 16, 1870; father of Maude, Theodosia and Frederick; after his wife's death in 1898, remarried to Isabelle Trullinger. Attended public schools in Silverton and Salem, and, from 1863 to 1865, studied at the Oregon Institute, in Salem, a lower division of Willamette University. Joined a local militia company, the "Marion Rifles," for a brief time in 1864. In 1866 moved to his father's farm in the Grand Ronde Valley in northeastern Oregon. There at age seventeen his first political essay, a vigorous defense of the Republican Party during the 1868 Grant campaign, was published by the *Blue Mountain Times* (La Grande). Moved to a farm near Salem in 1877, where for twenty years Geer composed political articles as he plowed his fields. Known to the public through letters to editors, he was elected to the Oregon Legislature in 1880; reelected in 1888, 1890 and 1892, and Speaker of the House in the 1891 session; nominated as a Republican Presidential Elector in 1896, Geer campaigned across the state on behalf of McKinley and the gold standard. He expected to be rewarded with a federal appointment, but was disappointed in that hope. Political friends offered to support him as candidate for governor instead. He was nominated by the State Republican Convention in 1898 and defeated W. R. King, nominee of both the Democrats and the Populists, by 45,093 votes to 34,542. Inaugurated on January 10, 1899. Oregon volunteers were among the first United States soldiers to see action in the Philippines in 1899, and Governor Geer went to San Francisco to greet them upon their return late in that year. The most significant legislative achievement of the period occurred when the 1899 and 1901 sessions of the Oregon Legislature prepared and presented to the voters of Oregon a constitutional amendment instituting the initiative and referendum. With the support of Governor Geer and other prominent leaders of different political persuasions, the amendment was approved in 1902, and Oregon became one of the first states to enact these reforms. Geer was not renominated for a second term by the Republicans due to friction within the party. Geer later became editor of the Salem *Daily Statesman* in 1903, and in 1905 purchased the *Pendleton Tribune*, which he also published until 1908. He then moved to Portland, where he devoted much of the rest of his life to developing his real estate holdings. In 1911 Geer wrote *Fifty Years in Oregon*, a book of reminiscences. He died in Portland on February 21, 1924. Bibliography: *Oregonian* [Portland] (February 22, 1924); Theodore T. Geer, *Fifty Years in Oregon* (New York, 1912); *Portrait and Biographical Record of the Willamette Valley, Oregon* (Chicago, 1903); Alfred Powers, *History of Oregon Literature* (Portland, 1936). The Theodore Thurston Geer Papers are on deposit in the Oregon Historical Society Library, Portland.

CHAMBERLAIN, George Earle, 1903-1909

Born on January 1, 1854 in Natchez, Mississippi, to Charles T., a physician, and Pamela (Archer) Chamberlain, both of whom were Presbyterians. Brother of Charles, Laura, Josephine and Kate. Married to "Sallie" Newman Welch on May 21, 1879; father of six children, Charles Thomson, Lucie, Marguerite, Carrie Lee, George Earle, Jr., and Fannie. Attended the public schools in Natchez; entered Washington and Lee University in 1872, receiving the degrees of Bachelor of Arts and Law in 1876. Journeyed to Oregon in December 1876 and soon found a teaching position near Albany. Admitted to the Oregon Bar in 1877. The following year Chamberlain served as Second Sergeant in "The Linn County Rifles," a group of volunteer soldiers sent to eastern Oregon to combat hostile Indians. Helped to organize the first temperance society in Albany; was Deputy Clerk of Linn County, 1878-79, and then joined L. Flynn in a law partnership. While continuing his law practice, he became editor of the Albany *States Rights Democrat* in 1882. Chamberlain served in the Oregon House of Representatives, 1880-84; was District Attorney for the Third Judicial District in Oregon, 1884-86; and acted as chairman of the Linn County Democratic Central Committee in 1890. He was appointed the first Attorney General of the state by Governor Pennoyer in 1891 and was elected to a full term the following year, serving until 1895. In 1900 he moved to Portland and became District Attorney of Multnomah County. Chamberlain received the gubernatorial nomination in 1902. Aided by the Republican factionalism and a bipartisan effort to elect a candidate who endorsed the initiative and referendum amendment, Chamberlain, a Democrat, became Governor on January 15, 1903, defeating his nearest rival, W. J. Furnish, by a vote of 41,857 to 41,611. At the end of his first term of office, an article in the May 10, 1906, *Oregon Journal*, praised Governor Chamberlain's administration as probably the "cleanest" that Oregon had ever had. He was reelected to a second term in 1906 over his Republican opponent, James Withycombe, 46,002 votes to 43,508. As governor of a state in which Republicans outnumbered Democrats by a three to one margin, Chamberlain maintained a non-partisan stance. A skillful political strategist, he supported popular causes such as the initiative and referendum amendment, and saved it from Republican legislative attacks. He protected the salmon industry by tighter enforcement of the open and closed fishing seasons; advocated river development to lower freight rates through enhanced competition with railroads; and conducted a determined campaign against fraudulent land dealers. During his term of office, the State Land Board cancelled illegal land certificates for 250,000 acres. Chamberlain resigned as governor in 1909 to take office as a United States Senator after his election by the Oregon Legislature. President Theodore Roosevelt had urged the election of Chamberlain because he supported Roosevelt's conservation policy. As a **senator**, Chamberlain helped to devise the World War I selective service draft and also helped to develop food control procedures. He left office on March 3, 1921. Chamberlain acted as a member of the United States Shipping Board from 1921 to 1923, and practiced law in Washington, D.C., from 1923 until his death on July 9, 1928. He was buried in Arlington National Cemetery. Bibliography: Gene Harper McIntyre, "The Pre-Senatorial Career of George Earle Chamberlain," Unpublished Master's Thesis, University of Oregon, 1965; Harvey Scott, *History of the Oregon Country*, vol. V. (Cambridge, 1924); *Portrait and Biographical Record of the Willamette Valley, Oregon* (Chicago, 1903); Robert E. Burton, *Democrats of Oregon: the Pattern of Minority Politics, 1900-1956* (Eugene, 1970).

BENSON, Frank W., 1909-1910

Born on March 20, 1858 in San Jose, California, son of Henry Clarke Benson, a minister sent to California in 1852 by the Methodist Episcopal Church with his wife, Matilda M. (Williamson) Benson and his three children. Married to Harriet Ruth Benjamin on November 4, 1883; father of two sons, Clifford and Wallace. Moved to Portland in 1864 when his father became editor of the *Pacific Christian Accord*; attended the Portland Academy, then returned to California to study at the College of the Pacific, receiving his A.B. degree in 1877 and later his A.M. degree. In 1880 assumed charge of the Umpqua Academy, a Methodist school in Wilbur, Oregon. Elected County Superintendent of Schools in 1882, serving in that capacity until 1886, when he became President of a Normal School in Drain, Oregon. In 1892 Benson was elected Douglas County Clerk; reelected to that office in 1896, and admitted to the Oregon Bar in the same year. From 1898 until assuming the office of Secretary of State, Benson practiced law in Roseburg. He conducted a vigorous campaign for the Republican nomination for Secretary of State in the 1906 primary election, winning both the primary and general elections. He became Governor after the resignation of George Earle Chamberlain, who had been elected to the United States Senate. Benson was sworn in as governor on March 1, 1909, and retained the office of Secretary of State as well, receiving salaries for both positions. Shortly after becoming Secretary of State, Benson became ill; however by the time he took on the governor's office, he had almost regained his normal vigor. As Secretary of State and Governor, Benson held considerable appointive power, but he did not effect a wholesale removal of Chamberlain appointees. One of his first official acts was to call a special session of the State Legislature to remedy defects in laws passed by the previous session of that body. A two-day special session provided funding for building improvements and for some new facilities at state institutions, including the penitentiary, insane asylum, reform school, and retired soldiers' home. He cooperated with the governor of the State of Washington in an effort to solve a boundary dispute between Oregon and Washington, but was forced to relinquish his office before the issue was settled. Having gone to California for extended treatment of a recurring illness, Benson telephoned C. N. McArthur, his private secretary, on June 15, 1910, directing that Jay Bowerman, President of the Senate, should "assume the duties of the governorship." Bowerman came to Salem and was sworn in on Thursday, June 16, as Acting Governor. Benson soon reported improving health and indicated his intention to return about July 20, 1910, to resume the duties of the office of governor. He did not do so, and did not run for reelection as governor, although he successfully ran for reelection as Secretary of State in 1910. Benson's health continued to fail and he died in Redlands, California on April 14, 1911. Bibliography: *Statesman* [Salem] (April 15, 1911); *Oregonian* [Portland] (April 19, 1911); *History of the Bench and Bar of Oregon* (Portland, 1910). The Papers of Frank W. Benson are in the library of the Oregon Historical Society, Portland.

BOWERMAN, Jay, 1910-1911

Born on August 15, 1876 in Hesper, Iowa, son of Daniel and Lydia (Battey) Bowerman; brother of Ralph, Martha and Mary Bowerman. Married to Elizabeth Hoover in 1903; father of William, Daniel and Elizabeth; after the dissolution of his first marriage, remarried to Wayfe Hockett in 1914; father of Sally and Jayne. Received his early education in public schools of Hesper, then moved to Salem, Oregon in 1893. Entered Willamette University that same year and graduated with a law degree in 1896 at the age of twenty. Admitted to the Oregon Bar the following year, he practiced law in Salem until 1899. Moved to Condon, in Gilliam County, Oregon, where he lived for the next twelve years. There he became a law partner of H. H. Henricks. Service in the Spanish-American War briefly interrupted his practice of the law. Bowerman, a Republican, was elected to the State Senate from Gilliam County in 1904. Reelected four years later, he served as president of that body from 1909 to 1911. When Governor Frank W. Benson was incapacitated by ill health in June, 1916, he asked Bowerman, as President of the Senate, to assume the gubernatorial responsibilities. On June 16, 1910, at age thirty-three, Bowerman became Acting Governor. Mindful of bureaucratic economy, he advocated establishment of a Board of Control to administer the state institutions, which would permit fiscal savings by combined purchasing for state institutions through the office of a single purchasing agent. However the Board of Control was not established until the administration of his successor. Bowerman acted to reduce the risk of loss through bank failure, by prohibiting Oregon bankers from the use of speculative stock as assets, if they had actively promoted that stock. In 1904 the citizens of Oregon adopted a direct primary law prohibiting party nominating conventions. But establishment Republicans, unwilling to relinquish party control over nominations, held an "assembly" in 1910, at which they nominated Bowerman as their candidate for governor. He was therefore cast in the role of opponent of the "Oregon System" of direct government by his Democratic gubernatorial rival, Oswald West. Bowerman campaigned on a platform supporting modernized highway systems; increased economies in the administration of government; and continued tight control of state land management. West defeated him, however, 54,853 votes to 48,751. After leaving the office of governor on January 8, 1911, Bowerman moved to Portland, where he resumed the practice of law. He was reelected President of the State Senate, but retired following the 1911 session. As a private citizen, he actively supported Oregon's first statewide bond issue for highway construction, a $6,000,000 proposal. He also served as an active lobbyist for years at the State Legislature. Bowerman died in Portland on October 25, 1957. Bibliography: *Oregonian* [Portland] (October 26, 1957 and October 31, 1957); *An Illustrated History of Central Oregon* (Spokane, 1905);

Robert E. Burton, *Democrats of Oregon: The Pattern of Minority Politics, 1900-1956* (Eugene, 1970). Newspaper clippings related to Bowerman's term in office are to be found in the library of the Oregon Historical Society (Portland) in scrapbooks 54:45, 67:146, and 276:216, 219. The Bowerman Papers are privately held by members of the family.

WEST, Oswald, 1911-1915

Born in Guelph, Ontario, Canada, on May 20, 1873, son of John Gulliver and Sarah (McGregor) West. One of seven children. Married to Mabel Hutton on September 22, 1897; father of Helen, Gordon and Jean. The West family came to Oregon when Oswald (Os) was four years old. Educated in Salem public schools, he quit in 1889 to work in a Salem bank. Became a teller in 1892, continuing in that capacity until 1899. In 1899 West spent six months in Alaska in search of gold. Governor Chamberlain appointed him State Land Agent in September 1903, and in that capacity he was responsible for the recovery of some 900,000 acres of Oregon school lands fraudulently obtained by land speculators. In 1907 he was appointed to a four-year term on the Oregon Railroad Commission. Having gained a reputation as an effective reformer, West won the primary election and became the Democratic candidate for governor in 1910. He conducted a non-partisan campaign, defending the "Oregon System" of government, including the initiative and referendum and the direct primary. West defeated his Republican opponent, Acting Governor Jay Bowerman, 54,853 votes to 48,751. Determined to advance a progressive legislative program, despite a legislature dominated by Republicans, West gained their cooperation after he vetoed no less than sixty-three bills enacted by the 1911 legislature. What he could not persuade them to enact into law directly, he sought to obtain through skillful use of the initiative and referendum. Women's suffrage and prohibition were both achieved through the initiative. Banks, loan sharks, stock brokers, and most public service corporations were placed under tighter state regulation by the legislature. Wages, hours, pensions and working conditions were more strictly controlled. A workmen's compensation act was passed by referendum, and a state Industrial Accident Commission was set up to administer it. Prison reform was advanced and a State Board of Control, created with administrative authority over state institutions, implemented a unified purchasing system. Also important to West was the preservation of Oregon's natural resources. Under his administration the beaches bordering the Pacific Ocean were protected for public use; the office of State Forester and the Bureau of Forestry were established; and the Fish and Game Commission was created. An ardent advocate of prohibition, he attracted national attention when he mobilized the state militia and sent his secretary, Miss Fern Hobbs, to close down illegal saloons and gambling establishments in Copperfield, an eastern Oregon resort town. Years later West described himself accurately, if not modestly, as the one who "banished dullness from the Oregon Governorship . . . and brought worthwhile laws to benefit the commonwealth." Despite a substantial record of achievement during his single term as governor, he decided not to seek reelection in 1914. West retired from office in March, 1915, moving to Portland to practice law, but he continued to be at the center of political controversy for decades. He wrote dozens of articles for Oregon newspapers and journals on topics ranging from pioneer life in Oregon to horse racing. West died on August 22, 1960, in Portland. Bibliography: Oswald West, ". . . Memoirs of the One and Only Os West," *Oregonian* [Portland] (October 3, 10, 17, 24, 31, November 7 and 14, 1937). Chester H. Case, *The Oregon System and Oswald West*, Unpublished B.A. Thesis, Reed College, 1952. Robert E. Burton, *Democrats of Oregon: The Pattern of Minority Politics, 1900-1956*, (Eugene, 1970). The Papers of Oswald West are on deposit in the library of the Oregon Historical Society, Portland.

WITHYCOMBE, James, 1915-1919

Born in Devonshire, England, on March 21, 1843, son of Thomas and Mary Ann (Spurr) Withycombe. Married to Isabel Carpenter on June 6, 1875; father of Mabel, Harry, Robert, Earl and one other. Attended school in Tavistock, England, and moved to the United States in 1871, when his parents settled on a farm near Hillsboro, Oregon. On April 17, 1900, Withycombe became a citizen of the United States. He was a farmer and a teacher of farmers. Spent four years on his father's farm before buying his own 100 acre farm, which later expanded to 256 acres. Established a reputation as a successful scientific farmer, and in 1898 was recruited by Oregon Agricultural College (now Oregon State University) to instruct Oregon's farmers in advanced agricultural methods. He was soon appointed Director of the College Experiment Station, from which he supervised the agricultural extension program of O.A.C. In 1906 Withycombe was the Republican candidate challenging incumbent Governor George Chamberlain; he lost, 43,508 votes to 46,002. The Republicans turned to him again in 1914, and he defeated Democrat Charles Smith, 121,037 votes to 94,595. He was inaugurated on January 12, 1915. Governor Withycombe promoted the development of a flax industry in Oregon by successfully encouraging the State Legislature to subsidize the raising and processing of flax as a potential prison industry to provide work for inmates. He also encouraged road-building in Oregon, claiming early in his administration that money spent for roads was "the best investment" a state could make, and later claiming that good roads were vital to national defense. During World War I, Withycombe vigorously encouraged the people of Oregon to support the war effort and took great pride in the state's war industry. When the Industrial Workers of the World (I.W.W., or "Wobblies") threatened to disrupt production in Oregon in 1917, the governor alerted the citizens of the state to the danger as he perceived it, claiming that the "Wobblies" threatened to cripple industry and terrorize labor. He instructed Klamath Falls authorities to jail members of the I.W.W. after a mill and elevator fire; encouraged public safety committees in eastern Oregon; and sent the National Guard to Astoria to prevent a strike at the shipyard there. For the further protection of the state; he organized veterans of the Spanish-American War and of the insurrection in the Philippines as an Oregon State Defense Force. When he ran for reelection in 1918, Withycombe described himself as a war Governor active in the nation's defense. He defeated Democrat Walter M. Pierce, 81,067 votes to 65,440, but died on March 3, 1919, after serving only two months of his second term. Bibliography: *Oregonian* [Portland] (April 18, 1915); *Statesman* [Salem] (January 1, 1918 and May 17, 1918); George Turnbull, *Governors of Oregon* (Portland, 1959); *Portrait and Biographical Record of The Willamette Valley*

(Chicago, 1903). The Papers of James Withycombe are in the Library of the Oregon Historical Society, Portland.

OLCOTT, Ben, 1919-1923

Born on October 15, 1872, in Keithsburg, Illinois, son of Hiram Wallace, a banker, and Mary (Wilson) Olcott; a Protestant. Married to Miss Lena Hutton, sister of the wife of Os West, on December 25, 1912; father of Chester, Gordon and Richard. Attended grade school in Keithsburg and a business college in Dixon, Illinois; then worked as a clerk in Chicago. Moved to Salem, Oregon in 1891, where he roomed with Oswald (Os) West, governor of Oregon, 1911-15, who was to become a major influence in his political life. For a decade and a half, Olcott savored the relative freedom of a bachelor in the far west, working as farmhand, bricklayer, hop picker, shoe salesman, sewer digger, bookkeeper, homesteader and clerk, and interrupting these more prosaic occupations to prospect for gold in southern Oregon, British Columbia and Alaska. Drove his own dog team 1,000 miles in winter up the Yukon and Tanana Rivers to Fairbanks in 1904, eventually working as a gold dust teller and buyer, then as branch manager of a bank. Back in Salem, Oregon, he worked for Os West in the State Land Office, and in 1907 was appointed by Governor George Chamberlain to represent the interests of the state when a Portland bank, in which the state had deposited substantial school funds, failed. In 1910, when the Democrat West opened his campaign for governor, Olcott, a Republican, ran his campaign headquarters. West appointed Olcott Secretary of State in April, 1911 and he was later elected to that office twice, in 1912 and 1916. He became Governor on March 3, 1919, when James Withycombe died in office. During his first summer in office, Olcott took extended trips in United States Army planes across Oregon, Washington, and California and persuaded the army to patrol the forests of Oregon for fires by air during 1919-20. His interest in protecting the forests led to enactment of state legislation to protect forested areas along the highways of the state. Olcott asked the Oregon Legislature to prohibit Japanese persons from holding land in the state. Ironically, his opposition to nativism in another form led to his defeat when he ran for Governor in 1922. Fearful of lawlessness associated with a fast growing Ku Klux Klan in Oregon, he jeopardized gaining the Republican nomination by denouncing the Klan on May 13, 1922, just six days before the primary election. He won the primary by a few votes, but in the general election faced Democrat Walter Pierce, who advocated a Klan supported anti-Catholic Compulsory School Bill and who was also the K.K.K. candidate. Olcott opposed the school bill; denounced the Klan; and lost the election 99,164 votes to Pierce's 133,392. Olcott left Oregon to become manager of the Long Beach, California branch of the Bank of Italy. In 1924 he became a director of the Oregon Mutual Savings Bank in Portland. He died in Portland on July 21, 1952, and was buried in Salem. Bibliography: *Statesman* [Salem] (April 15, 1911); *Journal* [Portland] (July 22, 1952); *Oregonian* [Portland] (July 22, 1952). Charles H. Carey, *History of Oregon*, 3 vols. (Chicago, 1922); Malcom Clark, Jr., "The Bigot Disclosed: 90 Years of Nativism," *Oregon Historical Quarterly*, LXXV (June, 1974). The Papers of Ben Olcott are on deposit in the library of the University of Oregon, Eugene, and in the library of the Oregon Historical Society, Portland.

PIERCE, Walter Marcus, 1923-1927

Born on May 30, 1861, near Morris, Illinois, to Charles M. and Charlotte L. (Clapp) Pierce. Brother of Charles, George, Mary and Minnie. Pierce grew up in a Jacksonian Democrat farm home and journeyed west as a young man, settling in 1883 near Milton in northeastern Oregon. He married one of his students, Clara R. Rudio, in 1887, who died in childbirth in 1890; on September 3, 1893, married Clara's sister Laura, who bore him five children: Lloyd, Lucille, Helen, Edith and Lorraine; Laura Pierce died of cancer in **March** 1925; in December 1928, married Cornelia Marvin, first State of Oregon Librarian (1905). After serving as teacher and Superintendent of Schools for Umatilla County from 1886 to 1890 and as County Clerk from 1890 to 1894, during which time he prospered from fees paid for land transactions, he returned to Illinois with his family to seek a law degree. In 1896 he received a Bachelor of Laws degree from Northwestern University at Evanston. Returning to Oregon, he practiced law for a decade in Pendleton; speculated in land; owned and operated the Grande Ronde Electric Company; and became one of the state's best known and most successful breeders of Hereford cattle. In 1902 Pierce won election to a four-year term in the Oregon State Senate, winning passage of a $6.00 per child state support for educational purposes and supporting the unsuccessful effort at prohibition. Defeated for reelection in 1906, Pierce helped organize the Oregon **Farmers'** Union; became President of the State **Taxpayers'** League; organized the Public Power League; and served on the Board of Regents of Oregon Agricultural College from 1905 to 1927. Urging the use of the Columbia River for electrical power, a policy he endorsed throughout his public career, Pierce unsuccessfully sought the Democratic nomination for United States Senator in 1912, losing to Harry Lane, the general election winner. In 1916 Union and Wallowa county voters elected him to the Oregon Senate. A progressive, Pierce challenged Republican incumbent James Withycombe for the governorship in 1918, losing 65,440 votes to 81,067. In 1920 he lost his senate seat by twenty-seven votes. Undaunted, Pierce won the governorship (133,392 to 99,164) in 1922 with the aid of the Ku Klux Klan, by supporting the Compulsory School Bill, and winning many Republican votes because of Governor Olcott's presumed Catholicism. He championed prohibition and a law banning alien land ownership, pressed for adoption of Oregon's first income tax, for liberal labor measures, prison reform, state-owned and operated hydro-electric projects and other progressive measures; many of these proposals were blocked by the overwhelmingly Republican Legislature. Seeking to overcome that disadvantage by joining forces with Republican progressives, Pierce further fragmented his party by supporting Robert M. La Follette for President in 1924. Although he failed to strengthen his party, opponents acknowledged that he was one of Oregon's strongest governors. Nonetheless, in 1926, with emotions reduced, Republicans (who composed 70 percent of Oregon's voters) elected I. L. Patterson (120,073 to 93,470) over Pierce. After his governorship, Pierce failed in 1928 to win Oregon's Second District Congressional seat. Choosing not to run for governor in 1930, Pierce again ran for Congress in 1932 and, with Franklin Roosevelt's landslide victory, won. A loyal New Dealer, he represented the Second District for the next five terms until his defeat in 1942 at age eighty-one. He retired near Salem, Oregon, and died on March 27, 1954. Bibliography: Gerald Schwartz, "Walter M. Pierce and the Tradition of Progressive Reform: A Study of Eastern Oregon's Great Democrat," Unpublished Ph.D.

dissertation, Washington State University, 1969; Robert E. Burton, *Democrats of Oregon: The Pattern of Minority Politics, 1900-1956* (Eugene, Oregon, 1970); George S. Turnbull, *Governors of Oregon* (Portland, Oregon, 1959). The Walter Pierce Papers are scattered: extant gubernatorial papers are in the University of Oregon Library in Eugene; those for the Congressional years in Special Collections, University of Oregon Library, Eugene; others are located in Multnomah County Library and the Oregon State Historical Society, Portland, and in the Walter M. Pierce Library, Eastern Oregon College, La Grande.

PATTERSON, Isaac Lee, 1927-1929

Born on September 17, 1859, on his family's "King's Valley" farm in Benton County, to Francis A., an emigrant from Belleville, Illinois, and Caroline (Tatum) Patterson; a Methodist Episcopalian. He had seven brothers and one sister. Married to Mary E. Woodworth of Salem; raised two sons, Lee and Philip. While growing up Patterson worked as a farm laborer and as a grocery clerk in Independence. He attended the Christian College at Monmouth for one year. In time he became part owner of a grocery. From that modest start he parlayed his mercantile training and his political skills into a successful wool and hide business in Portland after 1905. He later established a brokerage business and also became a gentleman farmer in Eola, Polk County, near Salem, raising peaches, hops, sheep and hogs. A lifelong Republican, Patterson served from 1895 to 1899 as a State Senator for Marion County. In 1898 President McKinley named him Collector of Customs, Portland District, and Theodore Roosevelt reappointed him in 1902, where he remained through the fiscal year 1906. Party work thereafter replaced office holding until Patterson's election to the Oregon State Senate from Benton and Polk counties in 1918. A candidate for governor in 1922, Patterson lost in a five-man race for his party's nomination, scoring a poor third behind the incumbent Olcott and Charles Hall of Coos Bay. However, because of his close ties with Old Guard leaders, he became chairman of the Republican Central Committee in 1924, and later served as chairman of Calvin Coolidge's successful presidential campaign in Oregon. This brought him statewide recognition, the Republican nomination for governor, and election to that office in 1926 when he garnered 120,073 votes to Democrat Walter Pierce's 93,470. As governor, Patterson followed Coolidge's executive style. After an initial effort to reestablish the state income tax in order to relieve property taxes, he "championed no special program to the legislature and contented himself with letting it drift without executive guidance," as reported by the Salem *Capital Journal.* Known for his vetoes more than for his proposals, Patterson did improve administrative efficiency in the state agencies; pressed passage of a bill to provide a single board to control all the institutions of higher education; and secured the transfer of control of the state penitentiary from the governor to the State Board of Control (which also served as the state's central purchasing agent). He continued the expansion of the highway system and sought reforms in the boys' training school. A generally popular and admired figure, he suddenly died from pneumonia on December 21, 1929. Bibliography: None of Patterson's personal papers appear to have survived. His career can be traced through contemporary newspapers, particularly the Portland *Oregonian,* in sketches offered in volumes such as George T. Turnbull's *Governors of Oregon* (Portland, Oregon, 1959) from official documents of the State of Oregon and from bits and pieces gathered in the manuscript materials of other political figures of the time.

NORBLAD, Albin Walter, 1929-1931

Born on March 19, 1881, to Peter and Bessie (Anderson) Youngberg in Malmo, Sweden; a Presbyterian. The Swedish government changed the family name to avoid confusion in the army's files. He had a brother and a sister. Married Edna Lyle Cates in 1906 in Escanaba, Michigan; father of Walter, Jr., and Eleanor Lyle. His father, a brick mason, moved the family to Grand Rapids, Michigan when Albin was a small boy. At age twelve, young Norblad left home to make his own way, pursuing a variety of jobs. Eventually he took classes at the Grand Rapids Business College and subsequently entered the Chicago Law School, graduating and passing the bar exam in 1902. Returning to practice law in Michigan, Norblad soon won election as District Attorney of Delta County. In 1908, while on a business trip to the West, he visited a friend in Astoria, Oregon. The following year Norblad moved there with his family. He practiced law, served as Astoria's City Attorney (1910-15), was a member of the local school board, and joined various local service and fraternal groups. Norblad, a Republican, won election to the Oregon Senate in 1918 and again in 1926, but failed to win the Republican nomination for Congress (First District) in 1922. He served as President of the Senate in 1929, and was elevated to the governorship with the death of Isaac Patterson on December 22, 1929. Within thirty minutes after taking the oath of office, he declared himself a candidate for the gubernatorial nomination in May, 1930. Although seen by some as a tactical error, Norblad needed, and sought to develop, a statewide identity through a variety of public relations techniques. Perceived as a progressive by conservative leaders who controlled his party, Norblad failed to rally strong support for action to cope with the rising rate of unemployment and the economic crisis facing the state. He called for a tax equalization measure, for ways to improve the lot of delinquent youths, and he organized a meeting of business leaders in February 1930 to discuss economic conditions and measures to cope with them; these efforts were for the most part ineffective. Six candidates sought the Republican nomination for governor in 1930. Norblad came in second, receiving 46,074 votes to George W. Joseph's winning total of 50,545 vtoes. Within a month Joseph died. Norblad, who had won a 9,000 vote majority in the primary outside of Multnomah County, refused further consideration. The Republican State Central Committee named Phil Metschan, who had not run in the primary, as its candidate, and Norblad loyally supported the committee's choice. Freed from campaigning, Norblad acted more vigorously to meet the economic crisis, organizing a labor commission with himself as chairman, that dispersed $2,000,000 on road construction, which succeeded in putting 5,000 men to work. He successfully sought federal assistance in settling a feud in Eastern Oregon between cattle and sheep men; organized a State Pardons Board and personally visited the prison and interviewed inmates; called a conference of leaders of Oregon industries to discuss means of improving safety devices on machinery; and gave his support to the Reed-Wainwright Bill, a national proposal for a universal military draft. After leaving office on January 12, 1931, Norblad returned to his law practice and community activities in Astoria, residing there until his death on Easter Sunday, April 17, 1960. Bibliography: To date no theses, dissertations or biographies have focused on Norblad. His career must be traced through contemporary publications such as the Portland *Oregonian, Journal*, and *Telegram*, the Salem *Oregon Statesman* and *Capital Journal*, and in the *Oregon Voter*, as well as in Oregon State Senate documents. A small collection of personal and official papers is at the Library, University of Oregon. Other pertinent materials are in the Chandler Percy Brown Papers, Oregon Historical Society, Portland.

MEIER, Julius L., 1931-1935

Born in Portland, Oregon, on December 31, 1874, to German immigrants, Aaron, a merchant and founder of Oregon's largest department store, and Jeannette (Hirsch) Meier. There were four children in the family; Jewish. Married Grace Mayer on December 25, 1901; father of Jean Ellen, Elsa Francis, and Julius L., Jr. Meier attended public schools and graduated from the University of Oregon Law School in 1895. For four years he practiced law with a partner, George W. Joseph, then went into the family's business. He served as the firm's general manager from 1910 to 1930 and then became its president. During the period of the first World War, Meier headed Liberty Loan drives, served as regional director of the Council of National Defense, and subsequently aided in the rehabilitation of France after the war. He also headed the Oregon Commission of the Pan-Pacific International Exposition in San Francisco. Although a contributor to political campaigns, Meier eschewed political office until 1930 upon the death of his close friend and former associate, George W. Joseph, who had won the Republican nomination for governor on a platform committed to state rather than private development of hydroelectric power on the Columbia River. When the Republican State Central Committee failed to nominate any of the primary candidates and instead selected Phil Metschan, an opponent of public power, Meier agreed to run as an independent candidate. Both major parties were badly split over the power issue, resulting in Meier's easy victory. He won 54.5 percent of the total vote, besting his nearest competitor, the Democratic candidate, Edward F. Bailey, 135,608 votes to 62,434. Ironically, Meier could not fulfill the campaign promise upon which he was elected, as the national government undertook the development of the Columbia River. Still his administration was deemed successful as he reduced budgets and placed the state on a firm financial basis. This was due in large part, to voter approval of a state income tax by the initiative procedure in 1930. Meier promoted the Knox Law, which regulated the liquor traffic; helped create a State Board of Agriculture and State Unemployment Commission; pressed for the adoption of a non-partisan judicial system; and established the Oregon State Police with the assistance of General Smedley Butler. He worked effectively with Oregon's congressional delegation to secure aid for the state's economic problems and the development of its resources. In 1932 he resisted pressure to run for the United States Senate and in 1934 both Republicans and Democrats sought his candidacy in their respective gubernatorial primaries. He declined all offers, in part because of poor health, and retired from office in January 1935. Meier went into semi-retirement until his death at his estate, "Menucha," on the Columbia River, July 14, 1937. He was interred at Beth Israel Cemetery in Portland. Bibliography: George M. Joseph, "George W. Joseph and the Oregon Progressive Tradition," Unpublished B.A. Thesis, Reed College, 1952; George S. Turnbull, *Governors of Oregon* (Portland, 1959); Robert E. Burton, *Democrats of Oregon: The Pattern of Minority Politics, 1900-1956* (Eugene, 1970). Useful manuscript collections are those of Henry M. Hanzen and George W. Joseph at the Oregon Historical Society, Portland, and Henry M. Hanzen's papers in Special Collections, University of Oregon Library, Eugene.

MARTIN, Charles Henry, 1935-1939

Born in White County, Illinois to Samuel H., a local politician, lawyer and judge, and Mary Jane (Hughes) Martin on October 1, 1863; an Episcopalian. Married Louise J. Hughes of Portland, Oregon in 1897; father of Ellis, Samuel, Louise and Jane. Although young Martin showed interest in following his father's career, after a year at Ewing College, his father induced him to accept an appointment to West Point. Graduating in 1887, Martin was assigned to Ft. Vancouver, Washington. Martin's military career took him to the Philippines, China, Mexico, France, Germany, Panama and to stations within the United States. He rose to the rank of Major General in the regular army before his retirement in 1927. Martin had maintained a residence in Oregon through the years. Although a registered Republican prior to 1930, he won two elections to Congress from Oregon's Third Congressional District as a Democrat. Running as a write-in candidate in 1930, he defeated Republican Franklin Korrell, 49,316 votes to 35,483. In 1932 he polled 74,397 votes against 40,650 for Republican Home Angell. In 1934, at the urging of former Governor Oswald West and others, Martin sought and won the Democratic nomination for governor. Ostensibly a supporter of the national administration, Martin soon made it clear that he was no friend of a number of programs, particularly the development of the Columbia River by the national government to provide cheap public power. Republicans also had split bitterly over the public power issue. When Joe E. Dunn, whose position on the issue was at best ambiguous, won the Republican nomination, State Senator Peter Zimmerman, a zealous proponent of public power development, announced himself as an independent candidate. Benefitting from the dissension within the majority party, Martin won, receiving 116,677 votes to Zimmerman's 95,519 and Dunn's 86,923. As governor, Martin loudly, and sometimes profanely, voiced the criticisms of conservatives and reactionaries about the economic and social programs of the New Deal. A zealous believer in a law and order regime, he largely ignored the economic and social plight of large numbers of Oregonians and fought efforts by the national administration to intercede on their behalf. His administration proved to be disastrous for the aspirations of younger and more liberal Democrats who hoped to build a strong and winning party in the state. Martin's actions led to bitter internecine strife that left the party in a shambles, and resulted in his repudiation by the national administration in the primary election in 1938, which saw Martin defeated in a bid for another nomination for governor by Henry L. Hess, a state senator, 59,620 votes to 52,642. Martin campaigned against Hess in the general election and the Democrats lost the governorship, control of the lower house of the State Legislature, and the congressional seat in the Third District. Martin, recurrently honored by his powerful supporters, lived in Portland until his death on September 22, 1946. He was interred in Riverview Cemetery after a ceremony with full military honors at Trinity Episcopal Church on September 26, 1946. Bibliography: George S. Turnbull, *Governors of Oregon* (Portland, 1959); Robert E. Burton, *Democrats of Oregon: The Pattern of Minority Politics, 1900-1956* (Eugene, 1970). Valuable source materials are those of Charles H. Martin and William L. Joslin at the Oregon Historical Society, Portland, and Milton A. Miller at the Oregon State Library, Salem; also Wallace S. Wharton, Oregon State Archives, Salem.

SPRAGUE, Charles Arthur, 1939-1943

Born in Lawrence, Kansas, on November 12, 1887 to Charles Allen and Alice Caroline (Glasgow) Sprague; a Presbyterian. Married to Blanche Chamberlain, a teacher from Umatilla County, Oregon, on August 8, 1912; father of Martha and Wallace Arthur. Young Charles grew up with his brother, Robert Wyatt, in southeast Iowa, where he attended public schools and worked in his father's grain elevator. After attending Monmouth College in Illinois where he received his A.B. degree in 1910, he taught in Iowa; Sprague migrated to Washington State in 1910. At Waitsburg he served as Superintendent of Schools from 1910-1913; he was Assistant Superintendent of Public Instruction for Washington from 1913 to 1915. In 1915 Sprague became editor and publisher of the weekly *Journal-Times* in Ritzville, Washington; a connection he maintained until 1925. Desiring to operate a daily, Sprague became the business manager of the Corvallis Oregon *Gazette-Times* from 1925 to 1937. In 1929 he bought controlling interest in the Salem *Oregon Statesman*, and served as Editor and Manager until 1939, when he became sole owner and publisher. He held control of the paper until his death. Sprague established himself as one of the leading editorialists and public commentators of the Northwest. A declared Republican, he nonetheless took an independent position on the issues of the time, reflecting a progressive view which was often at odds with leaders of his party. In 1938, when the Democrats were badly split between the conservative incumbent, Charles Martin, and those sympathetic to the New Deal, Sprague easily won the Republican nomination for governor in a field of eight candidates. His 62,275 votes nearly equalled those of all of his opponents. Despite warm support by New Dealers for his opponent, Henry L. Hess, Sprague carried 32 of the 36 counties in the general election, winning 214,062 votes to Hess' 158,744. Republicans won control of the State Senate, 21 to 9, and the House, 50 to 10. Republicans expected smooth sailing legislatively and politically. However, Sprague proved himself more progressive than his predecessor and equally independent. He vetoed so many special interest bills passed by his fellow Republicans that opponents initiated a recall move. It failed, but his own effectiveness had been reduced. Sprague began to eliminate state taxes on real property; reduced the state debt by more than $12 million; organized state employment services; and helped bring peace to the labor scene. Perhaps his most enduring achievement was the introduction of state regulations of logging operations to protect and rehabilitate state forest lands. After Pearl Harbor, Sprague devoted his energies to organizing civilian defense units, and cooperating with national officials in expanding Oregon's war efforts. Despite his forward-looking views and general acclaim as a moderate who had led quietly but well, Sprague was challenged for the Republican nomination in May 1942 by Secretary of State, Earl Snell, an astute professional politician. With but 30 percent of the voters participating, Snell beat Sprague 79,696 votes to 56,285. Sprague returned to his job as editor and publisher in January 1943. He served his community, state and nation in a. variety of capacities—including a period as alternate delegate to the United Nations in 1952—before he died of lung cancer in Salem on March 13, 1969. He was interred in Mt. Crest Abbey Mausoleum. Bibliography: Sprague's career can be followed by surveying the major newspapers of the state, particularly his own *Oregon Statesman*. His daily column, "It Seems to Me." is a rich resource. Sprague's gubernatorial files are found in the Oregon State Archives, Salem. Personal papers concerning other activities are in Oregon Historical Society, Portland, of which Sprague was president at the time of his death.

SNELL, Earl Wilcox, 1943-1947

Born on July 11, 1895 in Gilliam County, Oregon, son of William M., a farmer, and Mattie M. Snell; Episcopalian. Brother of four sisters. Married Edith Welshons of Condon after returning from World War I; father of William Earl. Attended public schools in Arlington and Condon, and for a time the Oregon Institute of Technology in Portland. Snell had tried newspaper work briefly, then turned to the automobile business. From 1915 to 1945, he operated a successful dealership with a partner, and eventually extended his interests into wheat ranching and banking. A Republican, Snell served on Arlington's City Council, then won election to the State House of Representatives from 1927 through 1933. Elected Speaker in 1933, he presided over one regular and two special sessions. In 1934 he successfully overcame the Democratic groundswell and won a statewide election as Secretary of State, a post he filled until January 4, 1943. Constitutionally restricted from serving another term, Snell challenged the incumbent Republican Governor, Charles A. Sprague, for his party's nomination for governor. Supported strongly by the state's automobile dealers' organization, Snell overwhelmed Sprague 79,696 to 56,285 in a primary election where only 30 percent of the voters cast a ballot. Snell won 78 percent of the votes in the general election over the Democratic candidate, Lew Wallace. In 1946, with Douglas McKay, a fellow auto dealer, as manager, Snell won reelection as governor over Democrat Carl C. Donough 237,681 votes to 106,474. Most observers predicted a United States Senatorship for Snell either in 1948 or 1950, but Snell died on October 28, 1947 in an airplane crash that also killed Secretary of State Robert S. Farrell, Jr. and Marshall E. Cornett, President of the Oregon State Senate. As governor, Snell had an almost untarnished record of success with the legislature, which was overwhelmingly Republican. Always politically acute, he moved the legislature toward moderate changes that were consistent with numerous New Deal measures which had won public acceptance. Aware of the import of demographic changes and the likely political impact of returning servicemen, Snell initiated several measures of direct benefit to them. While keeping a close rein on public expenditures, he sought assistance for

Oregon's important economic interests, including the wood-products industry. He continued to expand the state's highway system, wherever possible by attracting federal funds to underwrite the programs. His death and that of Farrell and Cornett threatened his party's dominant position in the state, and appeared to offer Democrats an unusual opportunity to reorganize and offer strong challengers for state offices for the first time within a decade. Funeral services for the three state officers were held in Salem after which Snell was buried in Belcrest Memorial Park near that city. Bibliography: Snell's life and career is not chronicled in any separate work. Much can be gleaned from the full accounts recorded in the Portland *Oregonian* and *Oregon Journal*, the Salem *Capital Journal*, *Capital Press*, and *Oregon Statesman* for October 30, 1947 and following. Manuscript collections are on deposit in the Oregon Historical Society, Portland, and the Oregon State Archives, Salem.

HALL, John Hubert, 1947-1949

Born in Portland, Oregon on February 7, 1899 to Jessie E. (Belcher) and John H. Hall, prominent attorney and United States District Attorney for Oregon during William McKinley's and Theodore Roosevelt's presidencies; an Episcopalian. Brother of Jean and Marjorie. Married to Elizabeth Walch on December 28, 1926; father of John III and Mary Elizabeth; after his wife's death in 1937 remarried to Alyce Johnson on December 31, 1941; father of Diane. Hall attended Culver Military Academy (Indiana) and Portland's Lincoln and Jefferson high schools. He served as a naval medical corpsman on the troop transport *Florida* during World War I; attended Oregon State College, taking a degree in business administration in 1923. After a variety of jobs, he began the study of law at Northwestern College of Law, Portland, and was admitted to the bar in September 1926. Hall joined his father's firm until the elder Hall retired in 1932, then joined Jay Bowerman's firm, one of the continuing political centers of the **Republican Party**. Hall's political career began in 1932 when he was elected to the Oregon House of Representatives. He won election to that body again in 1938, then successive terms in 1942, 1944, and 1946. In the 1947 session his colleagues chose him Speaker. It was from that position that he succeeded to the governorship upon the death of Earl Snell, officially taking office on October 30, 1947. Little known beyond his own intimate political circle, Hall immediately sparked a controversy by pressing for the resignation of the Oregon Liquor Control Commission. In his representation of clients before the Commission, he had found it to be arbitrary and non-judicial, and he believed it to be uncooperative with the legislature as well. Almost at the same moment a major challenger appeared for the Republican nominaton for governor the following May in the announced candidacy of State Senator Douglas McKay, a friend of the late governor and leader of the state's automobile dealers' association. Hall had little time to gain statewide recognition or approval for his views or actions. Without a strong organization such as McKay's, his showing was surprisingly strong, but his opponents portrayed him as an immoral spokesman who had served as counsel to nightclub owners and racing groups. He lost the Republican nominaton to McKay in May 1948, 103,224 votes to 107,993. After leaving the governor's chair, Hall moved to Lincoln County, where he practiced law, overcame cancer of the throat, won election to a term as District Court Judge and lived out the rest of his years in semi-retirement. He died at age seventy-one, on November 14, 1970 in Newport, Oregon. Bibliography: Hall's life and career is pieced together from newspapers and from materials in manuscript collections of other individuals. The limited gubernatorial papers are located in Oregon State Achives, Salem.

McKay, James Douglas, 1949-1952

Born on June 24, 1893 in Portland, Oregon, son of Edwin D., a carpenter, and Minnie A. (Musgrove) McKay; a Presbyterian. Married to a Portland stenographer, Mabel Christine Hill, March 31, 1917; father of one son, killed in an auto accident in 1939, and two daughters, Shirley Evelyn and Mary Lou. His father died when he was young and Douglas, as he later preferred to be called, rose from rags to riches, while supporting his mother and younger sister. He finished his high school courses at night while working; entered Oregon Agricultural College and received a B.S. in Agriculture in 1917; and saw action as an infantry officer in World War I, which nearly cost him his life in the Meuse-Argonne in October, 1918. He was discharged sixty-six percent disabled. His dream of becoming a county farm agent ended, he turned to salesmanship, first insurance and then automobiles. In the time between 1927 and 1955, he built one of the state's most successful Chevrolet dealerships in Salem, and served as a leader and once president, of the Oregon Automobile Dealers Association. A personable man with avid social interests, McKay joined a legion of organizations and groups. After moving to Salem, he became politically active, serving as Mayor from January, 1933 to January, 1935. Marion County voters elected him their State Senator in 1934, 1938, and again in 1946 when he returned from three-and-a-half years of **service in the army at Oregon's Camp Adair during World War II. After 1937 he** chaired the vital Road and Highways Committee, where his primary interests lay. He also chaired the Willamette Basin Project Committee, which appealed to his interest in flood control and river resource utilization. Although influential Republicans asked him to oppose Charles Sprague in the 1942 primary, McKay refused. Returning to the Senate in 1947, he could have been named president, but declined until he reacquainted himself with affairs. When Governor Snell died and John Hall succeeded to the governorship, McKay made his move. Supported and financed by the powerful automobile dealers group and the wealthy Arlington Club of Portland, as well as veterans organizations, he defeated Hall in the May 21, 1948 primary and won the governorship over Democrat Lew Wallace, 271,295 votes to 226,958, earning the right to serve the remainder of Snell's unexpired term. In November 1950, after having been unopposed in the Republican primary, he won a four-year term of his own over the Democrat Austin F. Flegel, 334,160 votes to 171,750. While governor, McKay faced few problems in a period of expanding state revenues and general prosperity. He refused to take funds from the state's considerable financial reserve, accumulated from wartime taxation, to expand educational facilities or highway construction. He instead relied upon a pay-as-you-go program. He sought federal funds for state needs where feasible, particularly for improvements and dams on the Willamette River. However, he supported the view that private local groups should help plan, control, and profit from such additions. An early supporter of Dwight Eisenhower for the Republican nomination for **President** in 1952, McKay was chosen in November to became Eisenhower's

Secretary of the Interior. McKay resigned the governorship on December 26, after the Oregon Supreme Court ruled that Paul Patterson, president of Oregon's Senate at its last session, would succeed McKay, rather than his political adversary, Earl T. Newberry, the Secretary of State. McKay had limited success in heading the Interior Department with its 50,000 employees and huge budget. In 1956 he made a late entry into the Republican primary for the United States Senate, and won but then lost a bitter contest in the general election to Wayne Morse. Eisenhower named McKay to chair the United States Section of the International Joint Commission to settle resource problems with Canada along the Columbia River, a post he held until his death in Salem, Oregon of aggravated heart disease on July 22, 1959. He was buried in Bellcrest Memorial Park. Bibliography: Franklyn Daniel Mahar, "Douglas McKay and the Issues of Power Development in Oregon, 1953-1956," Unpublished Ph.D. dissertation, University of Oregon, 1968; "The Politics of Power; The Oregon Test for Partnership," *Pacific Northwest Quarterly*, vol. 65, no. 1 (January, 1974). Manuscript materials valuable for the gubernatorial years are found in Special Collections, University of Oregon Library, Eugene; Oregon State Archives, Salem; and the Oregon Historical Society, Portland.

PATTERSON, Paul Linton, 1952-1956

Born in Kent, Ohio on July 18, 1900, son of George A., a minister, and Ada L. (Linton) Patterson; a Congregationalist. Married to Georgia Searle Benson, daughter of a prominent Portland family, on May 16, 1927; father of Paul Linton, Jr., Georgia S. and Virginia Lee. After 1908 his parents resided in Portland, where Paul and his sister attended school. After a brief service in the army during World War I, he entered the University of Oregon, taking a bachelor's degree in business administration in 1923 and a law degree in 1926. Patterson established a private law practice which he maintained until 1952. He also served as Deputy District Attorney for Washington County under E. B. Tongue from 1926 to 1933. For many years he served as City Attorney for Hillsboro and surrounding communities. He was substantially involved in social, fraternal and service groups through the years. Patterson's political career began in 1944, when, as local chairman of the Republican Party, he found no candidate for the state senate seat from his county, and so agreed to seek it himself. He served in the Senate from 1945 until 1952; on December 17 of that year, as president of the body, he succeeded to the governorship upon the resignation of Douglas McKay. Patterson, though not widely known statewide, proved to be a popular Governor. Guided by the skillful Ted Gamble of the powerful Arlington Club of Portland, Patterson easily overwhelmed Earl I. Newbry, his challenger for the Republican gubernatorial nomination in 1954, by 146,211 votes to 51,991. He went on to defeat the old-line Democrat, Joseph K. Carson, Jr., in the general election, 322,522 to 244,179. As governor, Patterson continued the pattern of recent Republican governors. He maintained a close scrutiny of state expenditures, and guarded the state's reserve funds, while seeking federal funds to meet the water, reclamation and unemployment problems that faced the state. He aided in 1955 in establishing a Water Resources Board to monitor and regulate the development and use of the state's water. He continued to lend strong support to the national highway program in Oregon, as he had while chairman of the Senate's Roads and Highway Committee, and president of the Oregon State Motor Association. Although he did not initiate new or expand old social programs in the state, he did support the national administration's partnership approach to hydroelectric projects. Clearly acceptable to the ruling interests of his party and the national leadership, Patterson challenged Wayne Morse for the United States Senate in 1956. Two days after his formal announcement, on January 31, 1956, while conferring with three advisors at the Arlington Club in Portland, he collapsed and died from a coronary occlusion. After services at the state capitol on February 3, his remains were cremated in Mt. Crest Abbey, Salem, Oregon. Bibliography: Much information is found in the state's newspapers following McKay's resignation and Patterson's death. The changing political conditions are described in Robert E. Burton, *Democrats of Oregon: The Pattern of Minority Politics, 1900-1956* (Eugene, 1970). Also see Franklyn D. Mahar, "Douglas McKay and the Issues of Power Development in Oregon, 1953-1956," Unpublished Ph.D. dissertation, University of Oregon, 1968. Manuscript materials are located in Oregon State Archives, Salem. Also useful is Microfilm 9, Oregon Historical Society, Portland.

SMITH, Elmo Everett, 1956-1957

Born near Grand Junction, Colorado, to Wilmer E. and Katie (Mohler) Smith, on November 19, 1909; Presbyterian. Brother to four sisters and two brothers. Married to Dorothy Leininger of Fayette, Idaho on October 8, 1933; father of Dennis and Janice. He grew up on an uncle's ranch near Wilder, Idaho, after his mother and father died when he was 10 and 13, respectively. After working his way through the College of Idaho and receiving a B.A. in History in 1932, he moved to Ontario, Oregon, where he successfully established himself as a newspaper owner and publisher. Voters twice elected him Mayor of Ontario before World War II. He resigned in 1943 to enlist in the navy. After two years in the South Pacific, where he commanded a naval air transport base, he once again became Mayor. In 1948 he won election to the Oregon State Senate from Grant, Harney and Malheur counties, By that time he had sold his Ontario newspaper and purchased the John Day *Blue-Mountain Eagle* and an interest in the Madras *Pioneer*. As senator, he pushed hard for an equitable weight-mile tax for highway usage, and secured its passage in the legislature and approval by the voters in a referendum, defeating the trucking and logging interests who opposed it. He chaired the Roads and Highways Committee after Patterson became Governor. In 1955 his colleagues chose him President of the Senate. Patterson's death in 1956 elevated Smith to the governorship. Almost immediately he faced a campaign to retain the office, and although he won the Republican primary easily, he was unable to defeat Democrat Robert Holmes in the general election in November, losing by a vote of 361,840 to 369,439. After leaving the governorship, Smith expanded his publishing activities, purchasing the Albany *Democrat-Herald* and several smaller weeklies. He sought office again upon the death of United States Senator Richard Neuberger, but lost to Neuberger's widow, Maureen. In 1964 Smith failed in his effort to become Republican National Committeeman; instead he was selected State Chairman of the Republican Party (March 1964-June 1965). By 1967, gravely ill with cancer, Smith's political activities had ended. He died on July 15, 1968, in Albany and was buried at Willamette Memorial Park Mausoleum. Bibliography: Smith's career can be traced through his own newspapers and those in Salem and Portland. The Elmo Everett Smith Papers are located in the Oregon State Archives, Salem, Oregon.

HOLMES, Robert Denison, 1957-1959

Born in Canisteo, New York on May 11, 1909, to stockbroker George H. and Amy (Crary) Holmes; a Christian Scientist. Brother of two sisters and three brothers. Married to Marie Hoy of Portland in 1934. After graduation from Rochester's West High School in 1925, Holmes' family moved to Oregon. Following a brief period of work with Portland's newspapers, he enrolled at the University of Oregon in 1928, graduating in 1932. Moved to Clatsop County in 1937; engaged in advertising and radio work; became manager of Astoria's station KAST from 1943 to 1957. He showed an interest in improving education and served on both the Gearhart City and the Clatsop County rural boards before 1948. Changing his party affiliation from Republican to Democrat, Holmes was elected to the State Senate in 1948, the first Democrat from Clatsop County in sixty-four years. He won reelection in 1952. In 1953, he was named chairman of the Education Committee by Republican Governor Patterson and won statewide recognition for his efforts to strengthen the state's system of education. Also, he was actively involved in the transformation of the Democratic Party from a tool of conservative patriarchs into a viable organization offering a liberal response to Eisenhower Republicanism. Just days after Governor Patterson's death in 1956, Holmes declared his candidacy for the Democratic nomination and defeated the conservative champion, Lew Wallace, 112,307 votes to 108,822. Strengthened by Wayne Morse's Senate campaign against Douglas McKay, Holmes won a slim victory over Elmo Smith in the general election, 369,439 votes to 361,840. Democrats won three of the four races for Congress, and Morse beat McKay. More importantly, the Democratic Party now had an organization built upon a solid majority of registered voters, reflected in Democratic control of the State Legislature for the first time since 1878. In his two years as governor, Holmes sought, with partial success, to revise state government to make it more efficient and responsive. He secured the first Department for Economic Planning. He reduced the bloated state reserve, by reducing taxes some sixteen percent, and by adopting social welfare and education measures that Republicans had ignored. He pressed for improved conditions and wages for workers, for public power development, and for the abolition of capital punishment in Oregon. In 1958, Holmes dispatched his primary opposition easily, but he faced a formidable young Republican candidate, Mark Hatfield, in the general election. Hurt by campaign tactics of others, criticized for commuting three death sentences to life imprisonment, attacked for cancelling the hunting season because of dry weather just before the election, and most of all, incapable of matching the adroit performance of his opponent, Holmes lost thirty-one of the thirty-six counties, gaining only 267,934 votes to Hatfield's 331,900. Holmes returned to consulting, public relations, and public service. He conducted Portland's KOIN-TV program, "Let's Face It," discussing issues of the day. Later, he was named to the State Board of Higher Education. He resigned in 1974 as a protest against what he saw as legislative interference with the institutions. He also served on the commission to draft a revision of the Oregon Constitution. Holmes died of cancer in an Astoria hospital on June 6, 1976. After public services in Seaside, private services were held at Greenwood Crematorium in Astoria. Bibliography: Robert C. Burton, *Democrats of Oregon: The Pattern of Minority Politics, 1900-1956* (Eugene, 1970). Manuscript materials for Holmes' governorship are in the Oregon State Archives, Salem. Correspondence and documents for the 1958 campaign are in Special Collections, University of Oregon Library, Eugene.

HATFIELD, Mark, 1959-1967

Born in The Dalles, Oregon, on July 12, 1922, son of Charles Dolen and Dovie Odem Hatfield; a Baptist. Married to **Antoinette** Kuzmanich on July 8, 1958; father of Mark, Elizabeth, Theresa, and Charles. Graduated with an A.B. degree from Willamette University in 1943; graduated with an M.A. degree from Stanford University in 1948. Ensign junior grade, United States Naval Reserve, 1943-1946. Teacher; instructor, Willamette University in 1949; dean of students and associate professor of political science, Willamette University from 1950 to 1956. Member, Oregon House of Representatives, 1951-1955; member, Oregon Senate, 1955-1957; Secretary of State, Oregon from 1957-1959; delegate to Republican National Convention from 1952 to 1968. A Republican, Hatfield was elected Governor of Oregon in 1958 with 331,900 votes to defeat Democrat incumbent Robert D. Holmes, who had 267,934. He took office on January 17, 1959. Among the major accomplishments of Hatfield's administration were the passage of a tax cut in 1959; the establishment of a state-backed birth control system; the prohibition of capital punishment in the state; and the reapportionment of the state's congressional districts. Also during Hatfield's tenure, Oregon was struck by several damaging earthquakes and tremors; and the major urban areas were struck by social discontent over racial issues and the war in Vietnam. Hatfield was reelected in 1962 with 345,497 votes, defeating Democratic challenger Robert Y. Thornton, who had 265,359. Hatfield did not seek a third term of office in 1966. He left office on January 9, 1967. After leaving office Hatfield entered the United States Senate in 1967, and currently serves in that position. Bibliography: Oregon, Secretary of State, *Oregon Blue Book* (Portland, published biennially); Howard Corning, *Dictionary of Oregon History* (Portland, 1973); Iris Noble, *Oregon* (Portland, 1966); Neil M. Howison, *Oregon: A Report* (Portland, 1968).

McCALL, Thomas Lawson, 1967-1975

Born in Egypt, Massachusetts, on March 22, 1913, son of Henry and Dorothy (Lawson) McCall; an Episcopalian. Married to Audrey Owen on May 20, 1939; father of Thomas Lawson and Samuel Walker McCall. Graduated with a B.A. degree from the University of Oregon in 1936. Correspondent and a member of the United States Naval Reserve, 1944-1946. Journalist; political analyst, Portland, Oregon from 1944 to 1964. Administrative assistant to Governor Douglas McKay from 1949 to 1952; Secretary of State, Oregon, 1965-1966. Phi Delta Theta; Alpha Delta Sigma. A Republican, McCall was elected Governor of Oregon in 1966 with

377,346 votes to defeat Democrat Robert W. Straub, who received 305,008. He took office on January 9, 1967. One of McCall's first actions as governor was to name himself chairman of the State Sanitary Authority and initiate efforts to clean the pollution from the Willamette River. By 1969 the river was cleared of pollutants and the salmon had returned. Throughout his administration, McCall was a firm supporter of ecological measures and led the fight to keep polluting industries out of Oregon. In 1971 McCall created the State Office of Energy Research and Planning, to find new sources of energy and methods to save existing energy in Oregon. In 1970 he was reelected with 369,964 votes, again defeating Democrat Straub, who received 293,892. In 1974 he did not seek reelection, leaving office on January 13, 1975. Returning to private life, McCall became professor journalism at Oregon State University in Corvallis, where he presently lives. Bibliography: Oregon, Secretary of State, *Oregon Blue Book* (Portland, published biennially); Howard Corning, *Dictionary of Oregon History* (Portland, 1973); Iris Noble, *Oregon* (Portland, 1966); **Neil M.** Howison, *Oregon: A Report* (Portland, 1968).

STRAUB, Robert William, 1975-

Born in San Francisco, California, on May 6, 1920, son of Thomas J. and Mary (Tulley) Straub; a Catholic. Married to Patricia S. Stroud on September 12, 1943; father of Jefferson, Michael, Jane, Patricia, Margaret and William Straub. Attended public school in San Francisco; graduated with a B.A. degree from Dartmouth in 1943; M.A. degree in 1947. Corporal, United States Army, 1944-1945. Businessman; executive, **Weyerhaeuser** Timber Corporation, Springfield, Oregon from 1947 to 1950; building contractor, Springfield, Oregon, from 1950 to 1953. Commissioner, Lane County, Oregon 1955-1959; member, Oregon Senate 1959-1963; State Treasurer, Oregon, 1965-1974. A Democrat, Straub was elected Governor of Oregon in 1974 after failing to achieve that office in 1966 and 1970. He received 444,812 votes to defeat Republican Victor **Atiyeh**, who received 324,751. He took office on January 13, 1975. The major accomplishments of Straub's administration were renewed state interest in the rights of its native people; passage of laws protecting the state's ecology; and attempts to control the growth of the state's population. Straub presently remains in office. Bibliography: **Oregon** Secretary of State, *Oregon Blue Book* (Portland, published biennially); Howard Corning, *Dictionary of Oregon History* (Portland, 1973); Iris Noble, *Oregon* (Portland, 1966); Neil M. Howison, *Oregon: A Report* (Portland, 1968).

PENNSYLVANIA

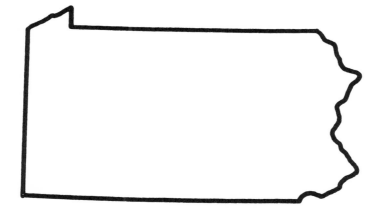

PENNSYLVANIA

MIFFLIN, Thomas, 1790-1799

Born on January 10, 1744 in Philadelphia, son of John, a prosperous merchant, and Elizabeth (Bagnell) Mifflin, both of whom were early Quaker settlers. Brother of George. Received the best education then available; attended a Quaker school in Philadelphia, and then the new College of Philadelphia in 1760. He toured Europe in 1764 and after his return married his cousin, Sarah Morris, on March 4, 1765. Shortly thereafter, he entered the mercantile business with his brother. As the revolutionary crisis approached, Mifflin became a popular Whig orator and was a member of the Pennsylvania Assembly from 1772 to 1776. He was a fiery member of the First Continental Congress and was elected to the Second Congress, but the events at Lexington forced him into active military duty. In May 1775, he was appointed a Major; in June became Washington's aide-de-camp; and in August was designated Quartermaster-General of the Continental Army. His participation in military activities caused his Quaker Meeting to dismiss him. Except for a brief period Mifflin served as quartermaster-general until 1778, although he spent most of his time in the field. He saw action at Lechmire's Point on November 9, 1775, and at the Battles of Long Island, Trenton and Princeton in 1776-1777. On May 16, 1776 he was promoted to Brigadier-General. Washington's difficulties in the winter of 1777-1778 while the British occupied Philadelphia induced Mifflin to become involved in the plot to have General Horatio Gates supplant Washington. The eventual result of this affair was Mifflin's resignation from both his staff and his line commands. Philadelphia elected Mifflin to the State Assembly in 1778-1779 as one of the moderate Whigs who hoped for revisions in the ultra-democratic and largely unworkable new state constitution of 1776. He sat as a member of Congress, 1782-1784, and was its President in 1783. Mifflin was a member of the federal Constitutional Convention of 1787. He was President of the Pennsylvania Supreme Executive Council from 1788 to 1790, and chairman of the Pennsylvania Constitutional Convention of 1789-1790. Personalities dominated the choice of candidates for Governor in the first elections under the new State Constitution of 1790. Mifflin's many friends and the new Federalist Party placed his name before the voters in opposition to General Arthur St. Clair. Mifflin won handily with 27,725 votes against 2,802 for St. Clair. In the new Federalist era, Mifflin held the state government in tight control and was reelected twice: in 1793 over Frederick A. Muhlenberg by a vote of 19,950 to 10,700, and in 1796 with a vote of 30,020 to Muhlenberg's 1,011 and Issac Wayne's 139 votes. Mifflin's nine years in the governorship saw Pennsylvania swing from a strongly Federalist state to an even more powerful Jeffersonian stronghold. The cause lay partly in Federalist foreign policy, but primarily the change was due to the Federalist excise tax on whiskey of 1791 and the window tax of 1798. The former angered the western Scotch-Irish and the latter the Germans in eastern Pennsylvania. As governor, Mifflin had to handle some of the first clashes between the state and national governments under the new federal system. He declined to call up the Pennsylvania Militia at President Washington's request in 1794 to put down the Whiskey Rebellion, setting a precedent that a president could not require a governor, in the absence of any local request, to call up state militia in peacetime. A second conflict arose when President Washington asked Mifflin to suspend the operation of a state law which interfered with federal military operations against western Indians around Presqu'-Isle in 1795. The Pennsylvania Legislature later repealed the controversial law, but Mifflin upheld his position that a president could not require a governor to suspend the operation of a state law. Mifflin's administration saw the initiaton of experimental political procedures for the choosing of federal officials, the beginning of organized state political parties, and the tentative entry of state government into areas of banking and transportation. After giving up the governorship to Thomas McKean in 1799, Mifflin entered the State Legislature where he served until his death on January 2, 1800 at the age of fifty-six. His demise was hastened by a suit brought by his creditors in 1799 which exposed him as a bankrupt and threatened him with imprisonment for debt. The legislature was required to pay the expenses of his burial in the graveyard of Trinity Lutheran Church in Lancaster. Bibliography: W.C. Armor, *Lives of Governors of Pennsylvania* (Harrisburg, 1872); Kenneth Rossman, *Thomas Mifflin and the Politics of the American Revolution* (Chapel Hill, N.C., 1952); Harry M. Tinkcom, *Republicans and Federalists in Pennsylvania, 1790-1801* (Harrisburg, 1950); E. Bruce Thomas, *Political Tendencies in Pennsylvania 1784-1794* (Philadelphia, 1939); *Pennsylvania Archives,* "Colonial Records," ser. I vol. XII (Harrisburg, 1856); "Papers relating to the Establishment at Presqu'Isle, 1794," ser. 2 vol. VI (Harrisburg, 1876); "Papers of the Governors," ser. 4, vol. IV (Harrisburg, 1902); and "Executive Minutes of the Governors," ser. 9, vol. 1 (pt. 1) and vol. II (pt. 1) (Harrisburg, 1935). The Mifflin Papers are in many collections of the Historical Society of Pennsylvania, Philadelphia, and in the "Governors' Papers" in the State Archives Building of the Pennsylvania Historical and Museum Commission, Harrisburg.

McKEAN, Thomas, 1799-1808

Born on March 19, 1734 (O.S.), in New London Township, Chester County, Pennsylvania, son of William and Letitia (Finney) McKean. McKean's father, a Scotch-Irish Presbyterian farmer and tavern keeper, had emigrated from Londonderry; his mother brought wealth and social standing to the family. Brother of Robert, Dorothea and William. On July 21, 1763, married to Mary Borden, a famous beauty from Bordentown, N.J.; father of two sons and four daughters; after his first wife's death in 1773, he married Sarah Armitage of New Castle on September 3, 1774 and fathered five more children. Attended the New London Academy, and was taught by the Rev. Francis Allison; began to study law in 1750 under his cousin, David Finney, in New Castle, Delaware; was admitted to the bar there in 1754. Continued his legal training at Middle Temple, London, in 1758. Began his long political career in Delaware with appointments to a series of minor court positions starting in 1752. In 1756 became Deputy Attorney General for Sussex County; made clerk of the Delaware Assembly in 1757. Elected to the

Assembly in 1762, and returned annually until 1779; served as Speaker in 1772-1773. Justice of the Court of Common Pleas in the 1760s, and appointed Collector of the Port of New Castle, in 1771. A strong proponent of colonial rights, McKean was Delaware's delegate to the Stamp Act Congress in 1765; as a judge, he refused to use stamped paper. He served as a delegate throughout the revolutionary crisis and the war, 1774-83, and played a conspicuous role in the adoption of the Declaration of Independence. In 1776 he also had a dominant part in the creation of Delaware's first state constitution; later, as Colonel of a Pennsylvania militia regiment, he took an active military role in the war. On July 28, 1777, the new government of Pennsylvania commissioned him Chief Justice of the state, a position he held until 1799. McKean was also President of Congress in 1781, raising questions of conflict of interest. He supported the Articles of Confederation, but later became a staunch Federalist. He was a delegate to the Pennsylvania convention which ratified the U.S. Constitution in 1787, and to the Pennsylvania Constitutional Convention of 1789-90, where he supported the concept of a strong executive branch. McKean broke with the Federalist Party over foreign policy, disapproving of any appearance of compromise with England, and by 1796 he had become an outspoken Republican. In the meantime, the Republicans, led by Thomas Jefferson, had begun to make strong inroads into Federalist strength in Pennsylvania, particularly when the Germans in the state rebelled against the Federalist window tax of 1798. In the gubernatorial election of 1799, the Republicans nominated McKean, who convincingly defeated his Federalist rival, James Ross of Pittsburgh, by a vote of 38,036 to 36,643. Pennsylvania's powerful support of Jefferson for President in 1800 secured the hold of that party over the state, and in 1802 McKean again defeated Ross for Governor, 47,879 to 17,037—a fair indication of the relative strength of the parties in that year. The wide patronage power of the governor, along with the large majority enjoyed by the Jeffersonians by 1802, made a split in that party inevitable. McKean hastened the break by appointing Federalists to office, by defending Federalist judges whom the Pennsylvania Assembly was trying to impeach, and by speaking with contempt of the poor and unschooled. McKean's enemies vilified him, calling in 1805 for revisions in the Pennsylvania Constitution which would curtail the powers of the governor. The Assembly in a gesture of defiance nominated Simon Snyder, Speaker of the Assembly and a former tanner's apprentice, as a gubernatorial candidate. McKean, faced by opposition from his own party, was forced into a coalition with the Federalists in 1805. Nevertheless, McKean won his third term, defeating Snyder by a vote of 43,644 to 38,438, in an election which deepened the Republican split. Duane of the Philadelphia *Aurora* mounted a violent newspaper attack against McKean, and persuaded the legislature to bring impeachment proceedings, but the attempt failed. At the end of his term, McKean returned to Philadelphia, where he occupied himself with writing and discussions on political affairs. He died on June 24, 1817, at the age of eighty-three. Bibliography: W.C. Armor, *Lives of the Governors of Pennsylvania* (Philadelphia, 1872); Roberdeau Buchanan, *Genealogy of the McKean Family with a Biography of the Hon. Thomas McKean* (Philadelphia, 1890); John M. Colman, *Thomas McKean, Forgotten Leader of the Revolution* (Rockaway, N.J., 1975); J.H. Peeling, "The Public Life of Thomas McKean, 1734-1817," Ph.D. Thesis University of Chicago, 1929; Gail S. Rowe, "The Life of Thomas McKean, 1734-1817," Unpublished Ph.D. Thesis, Stanford University, 1969; Harry M. Tinkcom, *Republicans and Federalists in Pennsylvania, 1790-1801* (Harrisburg, 1950); S.W. Higginbotham, *Keystone of the Democratic Arch,*

Pennsylvania Politics, 1800-1816 (Harrisburg, 1952); *Pennsylvania Archives,* "Papers of the Governors," ser. 4, vol. IV (Harrisburg, 1902) and "Executive Minutes of the Governors," ser. 9, vols. III, IV (Harrisburg, 1935); Thomas McKean MSS., Historical Society of Pennsylvania, Philadelphia.

SNYDER, Simon, 1808-1817

Born November 5, 1759 in Lancaster, Pennsylvania, the son of Anthony Snyder, an immigrant mechanic from Germany, and his wife, Mary Elizabeth (Knippenberg). Snyder was the fourth of the Moravian couple's five children. Married to Elizabeth Michael of Lancaster in 1790; father of Amelia and John; after his first wife's death in 1794, remarried Catherine Antes on June 12, 1796 and had five more children, Philip and Frederick, who died in their youth, and Henry W., George A. and Antes, who survived their father; after his second wife's death in 1810, remarried on October 16, 1814 to Mary Slough Scott. After his father's death in 1774, he moved to York, Pennsylvania, under a four year apprenticeship to learn tanning and currying. He received a good education there in a night school taught by John Jones, a Quaker. In 1784 he moved to Selinsgrove in Northumberland (now Snyder) County, where he opened a store and operated a grist mill. He was elected Justice of the Peace, a position in which he developed a reputation as a fairminded magistrate with a great concern for the poor. Snyder was sent as a delegate to the State Constitutional Convention of 1789-1790 and was elected continuously to the State Assembly from 1797 to 1807, except for 1805 when he ran for Governor. He served as Speaker of the House in 1804, 1805 and 1807. In the legislature he co-sponsored the $100 Act which expanded the jurisdiction of justices of the peace from $20 damage suits to claims up to $100, saving minor litigants the expense and risk of a court trial. The Jeffersonian Party of Pennsylvania, which had elected Thomas McKean as governor in 1799 and 1802, had split by 1805 because McKean would not sustain the "judge-breaking" efforts of the radical Jeffersonians. Behaving like the aristocrat that he was, McKean made an enemy of William J. Duane, editor of the powerful Philadelphia *Aurora.* In a tactless, letter, McKean deplored the hiring of incompetents for public office, and contemptuously referred to common folks as "clodpoles." Opposition newspapers made this the campaign cry of the 1805 election, and the legislature in April nominated Simon Snyder for Governor, publicizing him as a true "clodpole" and dedicated man of the people. McKean had to arrange a coalition with the Federalists to achieve his own renomination, an alliance called the "Quids" by his enemies. McKean beat Snyder in 1805, 43,644 votes to 38,438, partly because a very distinguished incumbent was opposed by a relatively obscure man, and partly because the Snyder Jeffersonians had unwisely demanded a revision of the State Constitution of 1790 to reduce the powers of the governor and the courts. In 1808, after McKean had served his three-term limit, the Jeffersonians united behind Snyder for Governor and Madison for President, and succeeded in electing him over his Federalist opponent, John Ross, whose followers wanted DeWitt Clinton in the White House. Snyder thus became the first of a long line of Pennsylvania-German governors. He was reelected in 1811 with only token opposition over Federalist William Tilghman, and again in 1814 over Issac Wayne. His party was called the "New School" Democrats. Snyder proved himself to be a strong governor, a kind of precursor of Andrew Jackson on the state level. He freed himself from the influence of the two strongest political editors, Binns of the *Democratic Press* and Duane of the *Aurora*. He mobilized Pennsylvania for the War of 1812 with efficiency. One of his less successful ventures concerned the finale of the Olmsted case in 1809, when Snyder, despite the lessons of the Whiskey Rebellion and Fries Rebellion, tried to uphold Pennsylvania's sovereignty against the federal government. He ordered up the state militia to meet a federal force, with each army defending a decree from its highest court. Snyder was forced to back down at the last moment. The strong support that Snyder's administration gave to Jefferson kept the Republican Party from becoming a sectional party of the south and west, and helped to establish its firm hold north of the Mason-Dixon Line. In 1817 the legislature approved Snyder's recommendation of William Findlay, State Treasurer, as the next candidate for Governor, and further demonstrated its appreciation by electing Snyder to the U.S. Senate. He had just started his term when he became ill and died in Selinsgrove on November 9, 1819, aged sixty. Bibliography: W.C. Armor, *Lives of the Governors of Pennsylvania* (Philadelphia, 1872); J.B. Linn, *Annals of the Buffalo Valley* (Harrisburg, 1877); "Autobiographical Notes by Simon Snyder," *Pennsylvania Magazine of History and Biography,* vol. VI (Philadelphia, 1880); S.W. Higginbotham, *Keystone of the Democratic Arch: Pennsylvania Politics, 1800-1816* (Harrisburg, 1952); G.W. Wagonseller, comp., *Snyder County Annals* (Selinsgove, 1919); "Papers of the Governors," ser. 4, vol. IV (Harrisburg, 1902) and "Executive Minutes of the Governors," ser. 9, vols IV-VI (Harrisburg, 1935); "Simon Snyder Correspondence," 1808-1817, in the Historical Society of Pennsylvania, Philadelphia; Emerson L. Derr, "Simon Snyder, Governor of Pennsyvania, 1800-1817," Unpublished Ph.D. Thesis, Pennsylvania State University, 1960.

FINDLAY, William, 1817-1820

Born on June 20, 1768 in Mercerburg, Pennsylvania, son of Samuel, a storekeeper and farmer, and Jane (Smith) Findlay; a Presbyterian. Brother of John, James, Jonathan, Samuel and Robert; of these, John and James served in the United States Congress. On December 17, 1791, married to Nancy Irwin, daughter of a local farmer whose estate he inherited in 1799; father of Jane. William Findlay received his basic education at home and in local schools; after reading law he was admitted to the Franklin County Bar. An enthusiastic Jeffersonian, Findlay was elected to the Pennsylvania Assembly in 1797; reelected in 1803 and 1807. He was chosen Brigade Inspector of Pennsylvania Militia, with the rank of Major. Elected by the State Legislature in 1807 as State Treasurer, an office to which he was annually reelected until he became Governor in 1817. Governor Simon Snyder had served his constitutional limit of three terms by 1817, and wanted Findlay as his successor. He accomplished this by letting the legislature know his preference, after which his supporters in that body made the nomination in a legislative caucus. The selection of Findlay by this procedure in 1817 raised the major issue of the campaign—the issue of "King Caucus." The Jeffersonians in Pennsylvania comprised a great majority of the voters, and the party had split into two factions: the friends of Governor Snyder, known as the "New School" Democrats, who favored a protective tariff, a federally chartered bank, and publicly funded internal improvements, and the "Old School" or "Independent" faction, who had called for curtailment of governmental functions and had entered into a coalition with the Federalist minority. The "Old School" or faction challenged Findlay's election by nominating Federalist Joseph Hiester in a popularly-chosen convention, from which office-holders were excluded. After a bitter campaign, Findlay won 66,420 votes to Hiester's 59,415. The defeated party then held a legislative investigation of Findlay's years as State Treasurer, and in 1819 began full-scale impeachment proceedings. The move failed, but the testimony of Findlay's enemies magnified by innuendo in the opposition press, had a strong impact on the voters. The Panic of 1819 further eroded his political support. In the 1820 campaign, the "New School" men did not risk another nomination by "King Caucus," but renominated Findlay in a popularly-chosen convention in which, however, legislators could sit as delegates. The "Old School" faction again nominated Hiester, and on this occasion Hiester defeated Findlay, 67,905 votes to 66,308. During his years as governor, political infighting rendered Findlay's administration nearly futile. Construction of a new state capitol building was begun, and there was much exploration of ways to promote canal and turnpike building, but these were never implemented because of the financial panic. Wild land speculation and unregulated state banking could have been curbed, but the state government took no restraining action. In 1821 the State Legislature elected Findlay to the U.S. Senate, where he served until 1827. Shortly afterwards, President Jackson appointed him Director of the U.S. Mint in Philadelphia, a position he held until 1841. He later returned to Harrisburg to be near his daughter, Mrs. F.R. Shunk, and died there on November 12, 1846, at the age of seventy-eight. Bibliography: W.C. Armor, *Lives of the Governors of Pennsylvania* (Philadelphia, 1872); *Old Mercerburg,* 3rd ed. (Williamsport, 1975); Philip S. Klein, "John Binns and the Impeachment of Governor William Findlay," Northumberland County Historical Society, *Proceedings*, vol. II (1939); "Papers of the Governors," *Pennsylvania Archives*, ser. 4, vol. V (1902); "Executive Minutes of the Governors," *Pennsylvania Archives*, ser. 9, vols. VI-VII (1935); P.S. Klein, *Pennsylvania Politics, 1817-1832* (Philadelphia, 1840).

HIESTER, Joseph, 1820-1823

Born on November 18, 1752 in Bern Township, Berks County, Pennsylvania, son of John, a farmer, and Mary Barbara (Epler) Hiester; member of the German Reformed Church. Brother of Catherine and two siblings who died young. In 1771 married Elizabeth Witman, the daughter of his employer; father of Catherine, John Sylvanus, Elizabeth, Rebecca, Adam and Mary Elizabeth. He had some schooling at the local Union Church, but spent most of his youth working on his father's farm; later worked in a general store. Hiester raised a militia company in 1775, and acted as its Captain; attended the Pennsylvania Provincial Conference of June 1776, which seized power from the colonial Assembly; joined Washington's Flying Camp, was captured by the British in August 1776, and was confined on the British prison ships *Jersey* and *Mentor* until exchanged. Promoted to Colonel in the Continental Army and served with distinction in the field until, in 1779, he was put on the Commission for Prisoner Exchange. Retiring from active service in 1780, Hiester entered into partnership with his father-in-law, but was soon diverted from business by his political ambitions. He was elected to the State Assembly for five terms in the late 1780s. In 1787 he was a delegate to the state convention called to ratify the proposed U.S. Constitution, and in 1789-1790 he was a member of the convention which framed the new State Constitution of 1790. Running as a Federalist, he was elected to the State Senate, 1790-1794, served as a Presidential Elector in 1792 and 1796 and was a U.S. Congressman from 1797 to 1805 and again from 1815 to 1820. In 1807 Hiester was commissioned a Major General of the Pennsylvania Militia. After 1810, he joined that state faction of the Jeffersonians known as the "Old School" or "Independent" wing, which opposed nomination by the dictatorial legislative caucus system, and welcomed a coalition with the Federalist minority. This coalition nominated Hiester for the governorship at Carlisle in 1817 at the first nominating convention—a method of nomination which became the main issue of the campaign. Hiester lost the election to William Findlay, the "New School" candidate who had been nominated by legislative caucus. The vote was: Findlay, 66,420 and Hiester, 59,415. During Findlay's term the opposition raised a continual clamor about the corruption inherent in legislative nominations, and in 1819 brought damaging impeachment proceedings against Governor Findlay. In the campaign of 1820, both factions made nominations in state conventions, the same candidates ran again, and the people this time elected Hiester by a vote of 67,905 to 66,308. The Panic of 1819, impeachment disclosures against Findlay, and the tacit admission by the "New School" people that caucus nominations were wrong, since they had abandoned the system, led to Hiester's victory. Nostalgic regard for the old general as a Revolutionary War veteran also played a part. While he was governor, Hiester's non-partisan distribution of the patronage simultaneously achieved administrative efficiency and political disaster. He reduced the powers of the governor by curtailing government expenditures and by appointing men on their merits without regard to private or party advantage, thus earning the animosity of professional politicians. He left few specific accomplishments as governor. However, he did encourage the use of Lancastrian schools as a way to extend education with little cost, and presided over the dedication of a new state capitol building in Harrisburg. Hiester later returned to Reading, where he managed several mercantile businesses and farms. He died on June 10, 1832, at the age of seventy-nine, leaving an estate of nearly half a million dollars. Bibliography: W.C. Armor, *Lives of the Governors of Pennsylvania* (Philadelphia, 1872); H.M.M. Richards, "Governor Joseph Hiester," and "The Hiester Family," in Pennsylvania German Society *Proceedings*, vol. XVI (1907); David M. Gregg, "Governor Joseph Hiester," in *Berks County Historical Review*, vol. I (1936); Richard Vaux, *Sketch of the Life of Joseph Hiester* (Philadelphia, 1887); Philip S. Klein, *Pennsylvania Politics, 1817-1832* (Philadelphia, 1940); "Papers of the Governors," *Pennsylvania Archives*, ser. 4, vol. V (1902); "Executive Minutes of the Governors," *Pennsylvania Archives*, ser. 9, vols. VI-VII (1935); *American Sentinel* [Philadelphia] (June 13, 1832).

SHULZE, John Andrew, 1823-1829

Born on July 19, 1775 in Stouchsberg, Tulpehocken Township, Berks (now Lebanon) County, Pennsylvania, son of the Reverend Christopher Emmanuel and Eve Elizabeth (Muhlenberg) Shulze. Brother of Anna Maria Margaretta, Henry L.,

Frederick Augustus, John Peter Gabriel, Catherine G., Christina Salome, Mary Magdalene and Elizabeth. Married to Susan Kimmell in 1804 or 1805; father of Augustus Emanuel, Wilhelmine, Maria, Louisa and Francis Swaine. Tutored in English by Francis Swaine, his aunt's husband; trained for the ministry by his father and by eminent Lutheran divines at Franklin College, Lancaster, Pennsylvania, where his father was a trustee and his uncle, Henry E. Muhlenberg, was the principal; also studied under the Reverend F.V. Melsheimer and another uncle, the Reverend John Christopher Kunze, in New York. Ordained a Lutheran clergyman in 1796, Shulze served several charges in Berks County, until a rheumatic illness brought his ministry to an end in 1802. After some years of recuperation, he opened a store in Myerstown and within a decade became wealthy. Entering politics as a Jeffersonian, Shulze was elected to the Pennsylvania Assembly for three terms, 1806-1808. He declined an appointment as Surveyor General of Pennsylvania in 1813, but accepted the multiple post of prothonotary, recorder, register, and clerk of the courts of newly-created Lebanon County, which he held from 1813 to 1821. He was elected to the Pennsylvania Assembly again in 1821, and to the Pennsylvania Senate in 1822 from the Eighth District. In 1823 the Democratic faction favoring John C. Calhoun for President in 1824, then known as the "New School" or "Family" Party in Pennsylvania, pressed Shulze to run for Governor against former U.S. Senator Andrew Gregg, a member of the "Old School" wing of Jeffersonians who had allied with the Federalists. Shulze won by a decisive majority, 89,907 votes to 64,100. As the only serious gubernatorial candidate in 1826, Shulze was reelected, polling 72,710 votes, although John Sergeant of Philadelphia did stand for the Federalists and drew a token 1,175 votes. The most important development during Shulze's six years as governor was the redrawing of party lines. The governor refused to become a puppet of the Jackson-Calhoun leadership in the state and, although courted vigorously by both local branches of the new Jackson Party, he remained officially neutral during the heated presidential campaign of 1828. Nevertheless, Shulze's appointments indicated that he preferred the friends of John Quincy Adams to those of Jackson. After Jackson's election in 1828, Shulze declined to be considered for renomination in 1829, and he soon joined the Whigs. His most important contribution to state affairs was to preside over the beginning of the "State Works of Pennsylvania," the huge railway and canal network connecting Philadelphia with Pittsburgh, and New York and Baltimore with both of these—a project the legislature authorized in 1826. Within three years the governor had supervised the expenditure of $6 million dollars of state funds for this vast internal improvements system. Shulze's appeals for legislation to create a public school program failed to bring results, but did stimulate widespread interest which enabled his successor to establish a system at the elementary level. In 1825 Shulze was the state's official host to the Marquis de Lafayette during his ceremonial tour. After leaving the governorship, Shulze moved to Montoursville, Lycoming County, where he bought and farmed a 500 acre tract. He was a delegate to the Whig National Convention of December, 1839 at Harrisburg, and in 1840 he was president of the Electoral College which named William Henry Harrison the ninth President of the United States. In 1846, Shulze moved to Lancaster with many unpaid judgements outstanding against him. He died there on November 18, 1852, at the age of seventy-seven. Bibliography: W.C. Armor, *Lives of the Governors of Pennsylvania* (Philadelphia, 1872); H.M.M. Richards, "Lebanon County's Distinguished Governor, J.A. Shulze," Lebanon

County Historical Society Papers, no. 6 (1914); H.M.M. Richards, "Descendants of H.M. Muhlenberg," Pennsylvania German Society *Proceedings,* vol. 10 (1900); Paul A. W. Wallace, *The Muhlenbergs of Pennsylvania* (Philadelphia, 1950); Eugene P. Bertin "John Andrew Shulze," *Now and Then,* vol. 15 (1965-68); Philip S. Klein, *Pennsylvania Politics, 1817-1832* (Philadelphia, 1940); Philip S. Klein, "John Andrew Shulze, Dark Horse," *Berks County Historical Review,* vol. 7 (1942); "Papers of the Governors," *Pennsylvania Archives,* ser. 4, vol. V (1902); "Executive Minutes of the Governors," *Pennsylvania Archives,* ser. 9, vols. VIII and IX (1935).

WOLF, George, 1829-1835

Born on August 12, 1777 in Allen Township, Northampton County, Pennsylvania, the son of George, a Lutheran emigrant from Lower Alsace, a farmer and a Revolutionary War veteran, and Maria Margaretta Wolf. Brother of Maria Catherina, Elizabeth, Philip and Christina. On June 5, 1798, married Mary Erb; father of Charles E., George Washington, Horace E., Ann M., William A., John Philip, Edward L., Henry A., and Luther. Attended the Allen Township Classical Academy, later becoming principal of the school. After reading law with John Ross of Easton, was admitted to the Northampton County Bar in 1798. An early Jeffersonian, Wolf became clerk to the prothonotary and postmaster in Easton in 1801; was clerk of the Northampton County Orphans Court, 1804-1809; was elected to the Pennsylvania Assembly in 1814; and was defeated for the Pennsylvania Senate in 1815. Conducted an extensive law practice in Easton until he was elected to Congress in 1824; and reelected in 1826 and 1828, resigning in 1829 to become Governor. Wolf became a Jacksonian Democrat, but that party in Pennsylvania in 1828 was split into two factions: an "Amalgamation" section which wanted to support Henry Clay for President after Jackson had served one term, and a "Family" faction which hoped to make John C. Calhoun president in 1832. These factions had united behind Jackson in 1828, but fought to capture the governorship in 1829 in order to use state patronage to promote their own presidential favorites in 1832. Wolf, the candidate of the Calhoun group, won the nomination in March 1829 by trickery, which widened the Democratic split. He went on to win the governorship against Anti-Mason Joseph Ritner, 78,219 votes to 51,776. Wolf praised Jackson's strong stand against nullification in 1832, but opposed the President's attack on the Second Bank of the United States, whose funds Pennsylvania needed to complete its public transportation system. Jackson's bitter fight with Calhoun, resulting in his decision to run for a second term in 1832, brought the Pennsylvania "Family" faction to its knees and greatly weakened Governor Wolf's political power. Nonetheless, he managed some noteworthy achievements. In 1830 he inaugurated a general revision of the statute law of Pennsylvania, the first since 1700. He backed new taxes to underwrite repayment of the massive borrowing needed to finance the state's growing public canal and railway system, and brought this 1,000 mile enterprise near to completion by 1835. Also, he led the movement for passage of the Common School Law of 1834, which marked the start of publicly finanaced education. Wolf ran for a second term against Joseph Ritner in 1832 and won again by a vote of 91,144 to 88,072. The Democrats nominated him for a third term in 1835, but the lingering party split had widened and Wolf's Democratic enemies held a second convention to nominate a rival candidate, Henry A. Muhlenberg. The schism cost the Democrats the election. The Anti-Masonic nominee, Ritner, won with 94,023 votes; Wolf polled 65,804, and Muhlenberg, 40,586. President Jackson later created a new post, Comptroller of the U.S. Treasury, and appointed Wolf to it in 1836. In 1838 Van Buren made Wolf Collector of Customs in Philadelphia, a position he held until his death in 1840 at the age of sixty-two. Bibliography: W.C. Armor, *Lives of the Governors of Pennsylvania* (Philadelphia, 1872); C.A. Beck, *Kith and Kin of George Wolf* (Easton, 1930); H.J. Steele, "The Life and Public Services of Governor Wolf," Pennsylvania German Society, *Proceedings*, vol. XXXIX (1930); P.S. Klein, *Pennsylvania Politics, 1833-1848* (Harrisburg, 1958); "Papers of the Governors," *Pennsylvania Archives*, ser. 4, vols. V and VI (1902); "Executive Minutes of the Governors," *Pennsylvania Archives*, ser. 9, vols. IX and X (1934-1935); George Wolf Papers, Historical Society of Pennsylvania, Philadelphia; George Wolf Papers, Pennsylvania State Archives Building, Harrisburg.

RITNER, Joseph, 1835-1839

Born on March 25, 1780, in Berks County, Pennsylvania of a poor Pennsylvania German farm family. His father, Michael (some sources say John), came to America from Alsace. On May 26, 1801, married Susanna Alter; father of Abraham, Joseph, Henry, Margaret, Peter, Rachel and Emma. Had only six months of rudimentary schooling. At the age of sixteen he moved to Newville, Cumberland County to work as a farm hand for Jacob Myers. Later set up as a farmer for his wife's uncle, David Alter, a scholarly man with a fine library which Ritner used to educate himself. Served briefly in the War of 1812 as a private. Eventually acquired his own farm. A Jeffersonian, Ritner was named local road supervisor in Washington County and then, in 1820, elected to the State Assembly, a post he held for five successive terms, the last two as Speaker. He became involved in the rising Anti-Masonic movement in 1828, and the new party nominated him for Governor in 1829. He lost to George Wolf, a Democrat, who polled 78,219 votes to Ritner's 51,776. The Anti-Masons nominated him again in 1832 to run against Wolf, who defeated him a second time, 91,144 votes to 88,072. Finally, in 1835 Ritner defeated Wolf in his third try for the governorship, polling 94,023 votes to Wolf's 65,804; Ritner's success resulted from a divided Democratic Party which had cast 40,586 votes for Henry A. Muhlenberg, a second Democratic candidate. During Ritner's administration, Thaddeus Stevens, the Anti-Masonic leader in the legislature, used the state rail and canal system as a source of political funds and patronage, and thereby brought the governor's administration into disrepute. Also damaging politically was the massive gerrymandering of legislature districts for Anti-Masonic benefit. After President Jackson and Congress had destroyed the Second Bank of the United States, Ritner signed the state bill giving a Pennsylvania charter to Nicholas Biddle's "monster," in exchange for a $4.5 million payment by the bank to the state, and a $7.5 million loan. Ritner's term was also marked by his strong efforts to preserve free schools in the state. He appointed T.H. Burrows as Secretary of the Commonwealth, with special duties as superintendent of common schools. When a strong movement developed in 1835 to repeal the Public School

Law of 1834, Ritner, Stevens and others worked harmoniously together to prevent repeal, and achieved the passage of an improved law in 1836. At the end of Ritner's term, state aid to public schools had grown from $75,000 dollars annually to $500,000. In his annual message of 1836, Ritner came out strongly against slavery, an issue then becoming a national crisis. His bold stand inspired John Greenleaf Whittier, then a Pennsylvanian, to write one of his early poetic jeremaids against slavery entitled "Ritner." The administration also saw the burning of Pennsylvania Hall in May 1838 by riotous Philadelphia anti-abolitionists. Ritner was the last governor to serve under the Pennsylvania Constitution of 1790. In 1838 Pennsylvania adopted a new constitution framed by a convention which had been authorized in the same election that made Ritner Governor. It limited governors to two terms and restricted the franchise to "white freemen," reflecting an anti-black sentiment which crossed party lines. Ritner was renominated to run against D.R. Porter in 1838 but lost, receiving 122,325 votes to Porter's 127,821. Ritner's partisans challenged the validity of the vote in an episode known as the "Buckshot War," but without success. Ritner then returned to Cumberland County, settling on a farm at Mountain Rock. In 1848 President Taylor appointed him Director of the U.S. Mint in Philadelphia, but because of Taylor's death, the Senate never confirmed him. He was a delegate to the Republican National Convention of 1856 in Philadelphia, but in his later years took more interest in farming and the growth of the state public school system than in politics. He died on October 7, 1869 at the age of eighty-nine.
Bibliography: W.C. Armor, *Lives of the Governors of Pennsylvania* (Philadelphia, 1872); J.W. Jordan, *et al., Encyclopedia of Pennsylvania Biography* (New York, 1914-1952); Alfred Nevin, *Men of Mark in the Cumberland Valley* (Philadelphia, 1876); A.K. McClure, *Old Time Notes of Pennsylvania,* vol. I (Philadelphia, 1905); E.W. Biddle, *Governor Joseph Ritner, 1780-1869* (Carlisle, 1919); H.R. Mueller, *The Whig Party in Pennsylvania* (New York, 1922); C.M. Snyder, *The Jacksonian Heritage: Pennsylvania Politics, 1833-1848* (Harrisburg, 1958); J.W. Norman, "Political Career of Joseph Ritner," M.A. Thesis, University of Pittsburgh, 1949; "Papers of the Governors," *Pennsylvania Archives,* ser. 4, vol. VI (1902); "Executive Minutes of the Governors," *Pennsylvania Archives,* ser. 9, vol. X (1905).

PORTER, David Rittenhouse, 1839-1845

Born on October 31, 1788 near Norristown, Pennsylvania, son of Andrew, a Scotch-Irish Presbyterian who had a notable career in the Revolutionary War, and his second wife, Elizabeth (Parker) Porter. By his first wife, Elizabeth (McDowell) Porter, Andrew Porter had five children: Robert, Elizabeth, Mary, Andrew and William; by his second wife he had eight: John E., Charlotte, Anne Maria, Alexander P., Harriet, David R., George B. and James M.; remarried to Josephine McDermott in 1820; father of Horace, who rose to the rank of General during the Civil War. Received a classical education at Norristown Academy and was ready to enter Princeton when a fire forced it to close. Went to Harrisburg in 1809 as clerk for his father, who was then Surveyor General of Pennsylvania. Upon his father's death in 1813, moved to Huntingdon, working as a clerk and later manager of Barree Forges, part of the Dorsey brothers' iron plantation of Spruce Creek. In 1814 he became part owner of the Sligo Iron Works with Edward Patton, a venture that failed in 1819. During these years Porter studied law with Edward Shippen in Huntingdon, but never sought admission to the bar. He also began farming, specializing in breeding horses and Durham cattle. Porter entered the Pennsylvania Assembly for Huntingdon County in 1819 and was reelected in 1820 and 1822. In 1823 he was appointed prothonotary and clerk of the Huntingdon County courts, and in February, 1827 to the additional posts of Recorder of Deeds and Register of Wills. He entered the Pennsylvania Senate from the Eighth District on January 2, 1836. The Democrats nominated him for Governor in 1838 as a compromise to heal the schism of 1835 between the friends of Governor George Wolf and Henry A. Muhlenberg. Porter ran against the Whig Anti-Masonic incumbent, Joseph Ritner, whose administration had been marred by Anti-Masonic witch-hunting and scandal in the state works. The election resulted in a fight known as the "Buckshot War," when the Ritner people in the legislature vainly tried to win by disqualifying part of the Porter vote. In this first election under the new Pennsylvania Constitution of 1838, Porter was certified by the legislature only a few days before the inauguration. The vote, as finally settled, was Porter, 127,821 and Ritner, 122,325. Assuming office at the height of the depression following the Panic of 1837, Porter faced financial troubles throughout his two terms. He pressed for the passage of a law in 1840 to require interest on the state debt to be paid in specie, in order to sustain faith in the state bonds. He also asked that banks be compelled to redeem their notes in specie or forfeit their charters. He had to reverse himself on this "hard money" stand when the state found itself dependent upon the banks to loan money to the government to meet interest payments. Despite these difficulties, he was renominated and reelected in 1841 in a quiet contest against Whig John Banks. Porter polled 136,504 votes, Banks, 113,473. During his second term, Porter achieved the abolition of imprisonment for debt and acted strongly to suppress the serious nativist riots in Philadelphia in May, 1844. Throughout his term, Porter tried to maintain the separation of powers by curbing legislative encroachments on the executive and judicial branches. He aroused such animosity that enemies in the Assembly tried vainly to impeach him. Partly because of his harrassment as governor and partly because he favored a protective tariff while the Democrats were moving in the opposite direction, Porter withdrew from politics after his gubernatorial service. He did, however, support James Buchanan's progress toward the presidency in 1856, and lobbied for the building of a transcontinental railroad, collaborating with Governor Sam Houston of Texas in promoting the southern route just before the Civil War. During that conflict, he was a War Democrat. Also, he established an iron business in Harrisburg, and experimented with one of the first furnaces to use anthracite coal as a smelting fuel. He died there on August 6, 1867, at the age of seventy-eight. Bibliography: W.C. Armor, *Lives of the Governors of Pennsylvania* (Philadelphia, 1872); J.C. Runk, *Commemorative Biography Cyclopedia of the Juniata Valley*, 2 vols. (Chamersburg, 1897); H.R. Mueller, *The Whig Party in Pennsylvania* (New York, 1922); A.K. McClure, *Old Time Notes of Pennsylvania*, vol. I (Philadelphia, 1905); C.M. Snyder, *The Jacksonian Heritage: Pennsylvania Politics, 1833-1848* (Harrisburg, 1958); "Papers of the Governors," *Pennsylvania Archives*, ser. 4, vol. VI; *The Press* [Philadelphia] (August 7, 8, 1867); W.W. Porter Papers, Historical Society of Pennsylvania, Philadelphia.

SHUNK, Francis Rawn, 1845-1848

Born on August 7, 1788 in Trappe, Montgomery County, Pennsylvania, the son of John, a farmer, and Elizabeth (Rawn) Shunk; a Lutheran. Brother of Isaac. Married to Jane Findlay on December 20, 1820; father of Nancy, James R. and Elizabeth. Attended the common schools; taught at the Trappe School at the age of fifteen, and continued there until 1818. Studied law under Thomas Elder; admitted to the bar in 1816. In 1812, General Andrew Porter, Surveyor General of Pennsylvania, appointed him as clerk. In 1814 Shunk served briefly as private in the Pennsylvania emergency force sent to the defense of Baltimore during the War of 1812. During the governorship of William Findlay he became clerk of the Pennsylvania House of Representatives, a post he held until 1829. From 1829 to 1839, Shunk served as clerk of the Pennsylvania Canal Commission, and in 1839 was named Secretary of the Commonwealth by Governor D.R. Porter, serving until January 25, 1842. He then moved to Pittsburgh, where he practiced law. The Democrats nominated Shunk for Governor in 1844, for he had become familiar to many Democratic leaders during his two decades of service in Harrisburg, and had steered a middle course between the friends of George Wolf and Henry Muhlenberg, whose rivalry for the governorship in 1835 had badly split the state Democratic Party. He opposed involving the nearly bankrupt state in further expenditures for internal improvements, whereas his opponent for the Democratic nomination, Muhlenberg, was a strong "improvements" man. Shunk defeated the Whig candidate, Joseph Markle, by a vote of 160,322 to 156,040. As governor, he mobilized the Pennsylvania quota of volunteers for the Mexican War, but devoted most of his first term to restoring the impaired credit of the state and achieving a balanced budget. He strongly resisted bills giving special advantages to business and promoting the concentration of wealth. He vetoed many such bills, but signed the act incorporating the Pennsylvania Railroad Company in April 1846. Also, he greatly curtailed the large number of legislative divorces. Shunk ran for reelection in 1847 as a supporter of the Democratic friends of James Buchanan. He defeated his Whig rival, James Irvin, by 146,081 votes to 128,148. A Native American candidate, Emanuel Reigart polled 11,247 votes. Shunk had hardly begun his second term when he became so ill from tuberculosis that he had to resign on July 9, 1848. His constitutional successor, Speaker of the Senate William F. Johnston, a Whig, then took office. Shunk died on July 20, 1848, at the age of fifty-nine. He was buried in the cemetery of the Trappe Lutheran Church, where he had been a member.
Bibliography: W.C. Armor, *Lives of the Governors of Pennsylvania* (Philadelphia, 1872); Moses Auge, *Lives of the Eminent Dead...of Montgomery County* (Norristown, 1879); C.M. Snyders, *The Jacksonian Heritage: Pennsylvania Politics 1833-1848* (Harrisburg, 1958); "Papers of the Governors," *Pennsylvania Archives,* ser. 4, vol. VII (1902); "Shunk MSS." Historical Society of Pennsylvania (Philadelphia); "Shunk Folder," Historical Society of Montgomery County (Norristown, Pa.); *Norristown Herald and Free Press* (July 26, 1848).

JOHNSTON, William Freame, 1848-1852

Born on November 29, 1808, in Greensburg, Pennsylvania, to Alexander, a Presbyterian ironmaster, sheriff, and magistrate in Westmoreland County, who lived to the age of 100, and Elizabeth (Freame) Johnston. Brother of nine, including Edward, John W., and Richard. Married Mary Montieth on April 12, 1832; father of five sons and two daughters. Johston had a common school education and then studied law under Major J.B. Alexander. Admitted to the Westmoreland County Bar in 1829, he moved to Armstrong County, and in the same year received an appointment as District Attorney there, a position he held until his election to the Pennsylvania Assembly in 1835. He was at first a high-tariff Democrat, but in the 1840s became a Whig with Free Soil leanings and in the 1850s joined the American Party. Johnston was reelected to the State Assembly in 1838 and 1841. In 1847 he entered the State Senate and was elected its Speaker in 1848. As Senate Speaker, he succeeded Democratic Governor Francis R. Shunk, who resigned on July 9, 1848 because of illness. Johnston, who became Governor on July 26, 1848, could legally have postponed an election until October, 1849, but he chose to hold the popular canvass in October, 1848. The Whigs nominated him, and the Democrats chose Morris Longstreth after a bitter intra-party battle. Johnston triumphed in one of the closest elections in the history of Pennsylvania, polling 168,522 votes to Longstreth's 168,225. His administration brought financial stability to a state which had been on the verge of bankruptcy for a decade. He initiated the editing and printing of the documents of Pennsylvania's early history in twenty-eight volumes of the *Colonial Records*, a project continued as the *Pennsylvania Archives*. Disapproving of the federal Fugitive Slave Law of 1850, Johnston took the position that the federal authorities had exclusive responsibility for enforcement without any assistance from state officers. The Whigs renominated him in 1851 to run against Democrat William Bigler. The "Christiana Riot," over the attempted capture of fugitive slaves, occurred just a few weeks before the election and contributed to Johnston's defeat. He polled 178,034 votes to Bigler's 186,499. In 1856 he was nominated by the North American Party to run for Vice President on a ticket with John C. Fremont, but Johnston later withdrew. Retiring to Kittanning, he engaged in iron making, salt manufacturing and oil refining. He was president of the Allegheny Railroad from Kittanning to Pittsburgh. President Johnson appointed him Collector of the Port of Philadelphia, but after serving a few months he had to leave the office because the Senate would not confirm him. He died on October 25, 1872 at the age of sixty-three. Bibliography: William C. Armor, *Lives of the Governors of Pennsylvania* (Philadelphia, 1872); J.H. Beers, *Armstrong County, Pennsylvania,* 2 vols. (Chicago, 1914); "Papers of the Governors," *Pennsylvania Archives*, ser. 4, vol. VIII (1902); H.R. Mueller, *Whig Party in Pennsylvania* (New York, 1922); Charles M. Snyder, *The Jacksonian Heritage: Pennsylvania Politics, 1833-1848* (Harrisburg, 1958); Sister T. Geary, *History of Third Parties in Pennsylvania, 1840-1860* (Washington, D.C., 1938); John F. Coleman, *Disruption of Democracy in Pennsylvania, 1840-1860* (Harrisburg, 1975).

BIGLER, William, 1852-1855

Born in Shearman's Valley, Cumberland (now Perry) County, Pennsylvania, on January 1, 1814, son of Jacob and Susan (Dock) Bigler, both of German descent. His father speculated in Mercer County land, lost his capital, and died poor in 1827. Brother of John, who became Governor of California in 1852, Samuel and Washington. Married Maria J. Reed on March 23, 1836; father of Reed, John W., William Dock, Edmund A. and Harry Fred. Worked for his brother, John, editor of the *Centre County Democrat*, Bellefonte, Pennsylvania, from 1829 to 1833; in 1833, moved to Clearfield, Pennsylvania, where he started the *Clearfield Democrat*; went into partnership with his father-in-law, lumber merchant Alexander B. Reed, in 1836. During two terms in the Pennsylvania Senate, 1841-1847, Bigler twice held the speakership. In 1849 he became Pennsylvania Revenue Commissioner. Nominated for Governor by the Democrats in 1851, he defeated the Whig incumbent, William F. Johnston, 186,499 votes to 178,034, in a contest largely influenced by excitement over the Christiana fugitive slave riot shortly before the election. As governor, Bigler emphasized economy and fiscal responsibility. By threatening to veto essential public bills to which private interest riders had been attached, he forced the outlawing of the "omnibus" bills which then dominated legislative activity. Suspicious of a rash of applications for new state bank charters, he vetoed many of these bills. He insisted upon rigid state enforcement of the Fugitive Slave Law of 1850 as an obligation imposed by the U.S. Constitution. He endorsed the Kansas-Nebraska Bill of 1854 as a party measure, though he personally disapproved the abrogation of the Missouri Compromise. Renominated for Governor in 1854, he was defeated by Whig James Pollock because of public antipathy to the Kansas-Nebraska Act, and because Pollock was favored by temperance people and nativists. He polled 167,001 votes to Pollock's 204,008. Bigler became president of the Philadelphia and Erie Railroad shortly after leaving the governorship; from January 1856 to March 1861, he served as a Democrat in the United States Senate. He supported President Buchanan's policy on Kansas, and the president's efforts to prevent a military confrontation with the South. He voted for the Crittenden compromise proposals, and served on the Senate Committee of Thirteen which considered them. Bigler was a delegate to the Democratic National Conventions of 1860, 1864 and 1868, and to the Union National Convention of 1866. Retiring to Clearfield, he devoted his time to business, especially the Tyrone and Clearfield Railroad. He played an important role in the Centennial of 1876, persuading Congress to finance an international rather than a national exhibit in Philadelphia. He was a member of the U.S. Centennial Commission and financial officer of the Centennial Board of Finance, and travelled throughout the country to promote the enterprise. Bigler campaigned widely for Samuel J. Tilden in 1876, and was chosen to go to New Orleans to witness the vote recount there after the disputed election of that year. Late in his career, he joined the Presbyterian Church. He died in Clearfield on August 8, 1880. Bibliography: W.C. Armor, *Lives of the Governors of Pennsylvania* (Philadelphia, 1872); Mary M. Bird, "William Bigler," Unpublished M.A. Thesis, University of Pittsburgh, 1937; J.A. Caldwell, *Caldwell's...Atlas of Clearfield County, Pennsylvania* (Pittsburgh, 1878); John F. Coleman, *Disruption of the Pennsylvania Democracy, 1848-1860* (Harrisburg, 1975); A.K. McClure, *Old Time Notes of Pennsylvania*, vol. 1 (Philadelphia, 1905); "Papers of the Governors, *Pennsylvania Archives*, ser. 4, vol. VII (1902); *Philadelphia Press* (August 10, 1880).

Some Bigler MSS are in the Historical Society of Pennsylvania (Philadelphia) and the Pennsylvania Historical and Museum Commission Archives Building, Harrisburg.

POLLOCK, James, 1855-1858

Born on September 11, 1810 in Milton, Pennsylvania, the son of William, a merchant, and Sarah (Wilson) Pollock; a Presbyterian. Brother of Fleming Wilson, Thomas Caldwell, Samuel, Sarah, Margaret and Mary Wilson. Married Sarah Ann Hepburn on December 19, 1837; father of Samuel Hepburn, William Curtis, Louisa Ann, Emily Clara, James Crawford, Mary Agnes, Sarah Margaret and Emily. Attended the local school of Joseph D. Biles, and then the Milton Classical Academy, received an A.B. degree from the College of New Jersey (Princeton) in 1831, and an M.A. degree from the same institution in 1835. Read law with Samuel Hepburn of Milton. Pollock served as District Attorney for Northumberland County from 1836 to 1838, and then as Judge of the Court of Common Pleas. He was elected as a Whig to the Twenty-eighth Congress in 1844 from the Thirtieth District, and was reelected in 1846 and 1848. Pollock was made chairman of the Select Committee on the building of a railroad to the Pacific, and served on the Standing Committees on Territories and on Ways and Means. He befriended Samuel F. B. Morse and strongly urged Congress to provide funds to build the first telegraph line in 1844. In 1850 he was appointed President Judge of the Eighth Pennsylvania Judicial District. The Whigs nominated him for Governor in 1854, and he won the additional support of the nativist "Know-Nothings," the anti-Kansas-Nebraska Bill voters, and the temperance people. He defeated the Democratic incumbent, William Bigler, by a vote of 204,008 to 167,001. Pollock supported the legislative drive to end the state's costly involvement in public transportation, and presided over the sale of the Main Line properties of the Pennsylania State Works to the Pennsylvania Railroad. With this burden removed, he was able to achieve a reduction of the state debt. He set up a special department to implement public school legislation. After the Panic of 1857, he devised means to prevent the total collapse of state-chartered banks. Declining renomination in 1858, he returned to the practice of law. He was chairman of the Pennsylvania delegation to the Washington Peace Convention of 1861. From May until October 1866, he served as Director of the Mint in Philadelphia. Reappointed as director of the mint in 1869, he served until 1873 when he was elevated to a newly-created position, Superintendent of the Mint. He became Naval Officer of Customs (Philadelphia), 1879-1883, and Federal Chief Supervisor of Elections in 1886. Pollock was a trustee of Lafayette College and a founder and trustee of the Pennsylvania Military College. He died in Lock Haven, Pennsylvania on April 19, 1890, at the age of seventy-nine. Bibliography: W.C. Armor, *Lives of the Governors of Pennsylvania* (Philadelphia, 1872); A.K. McClure, *Old Time Notes of Pennsylvania,* vol. I (Philadelphia, 1905); Fred A. Godcharles, "Governor James Pollock," in Northumberland County Historical Society *Proceedings*, vol. VIII (1936); Dorothy Roughton, "James Pollock," M.A. Thesis, Pennsylvania State University, 1956; John F. Coleman, *Disruption of the Pennsylvania Democracy, 1848-1860* (Harrisburg, 1975); "Papers of the Governors," *Pennsylvania Archives*, ser. 4, vol. VII (1902).

PACKER, William Fisher, 1858-1861

Born on April 2, 1807 in Howard, Centre County, Pennsylvania, son of James who died in 1814, and Charity (Bye) Packer; a Quaker. Brother of Hezekiah B., John P., Sarah B. and James. Married to Mary W. Vanderbilt on December 24, 1829; father of ten, six of whom reached maturity: Boyd C., Albert, Mary, Sarah B., Anne and Ellen. Became a printer's apprentice at the Sunbury *Public Inquirer* in 1820, at the *Bellefonte Patriot*, 1821-1825, and was a journeyman with the *Pennsylvania Intelligencer*, Harrisburg, from 1826 to 1827. Studied law in Williamsport for two years but never undertook practice; instead purchased an interest in the *Lycoming Gazette*, Williamsport, in 1829, a strong Jacksonian paper which he served until becoming co-founder in 1836 of the *Keystone Gazette*, the Democratic administration newspaper in Harrisburg. From 1832 to 1835, served as superintendent of the West Branch Division of the Pennsylvania Canal; later promoted the incorporation of the Susquehanna Railroad Company, of which he became president. His effective campaigning for the election of Governor David R. Porter brought him appointment as Canal Commissioner, 1839-1842, and then as state Auditor General, 1842-1845. He was elected to the Pennsylvania Assembly, 1846-1849, from the Lycoming, Clinton, and Potter County District, and served as Speaker of the House during his last two terms. In 1849 he was elected to the State Senate from the district comprising Lycoming, Clinton, Centre and Sullivan Counties. Packer attended the Democratic National Convention which nominated Buchanan for President in 1856 and worked hard for his election. In March, 1857, the Buchanan Democrats nominated him for Governor of Pennsylvania, a post he won with 188,846 votes against 146,139 for Republican David Wilmot, and 28,168 for Isaac Hazlehurst of the American Party. As governor, Packer concentrated on matters of finance and transportation. He achieved the passage of acts requiring state banks to limit their note issues to amounts covered by real security deposited with the state, hastening the end of fifty years of "shinplaster" currency emissions. Also, he presided over the sale of the remnants of the state-owned canal system—the Delaware, North Branch, West Branch, and Susquehanna Divisions. The Sunbury and Erie Railroad, which purchased these holdings, became a main beneficiary of the transaction. Packer also gave his support to the new public school department which had just been set up by his predecessor. He broke with President Buchanan over his Kansas policy, joining the Douglas Democrats for a time, but after Lincoln's election, he encouraged efforts to call a constitutional convention or to seek some other peaceful mode of compromise. Packer retired to Williamsport, where he died on September 27, 1870. Bibliography: H.M. Jenkins, ed., *Pennsylvania: Colonial and Federal*, vol. II; G.P. Donehoo, *Pennsylvania: A History*, vol. III (1926); *Philadelphia Public Ledger* (September 28, 1870); William P. Clarke, *Life and Times of the Honorable William F. Packer* (1937); John F. Coleman, *Disruption of the Pennsylvania Democracy, 1848-1860* (1975); Homer T. Rosenberger, *The Philadelphia and Erie Railroad* (1976); W.B. Wilson, *History of the Pennsylvania Railroad Company*, vol. I (1899).

CURTIN, Andrew Gregg, 1861-1867

Born on April 22, 1815, in Bellefonte, Pennsylvania, the first-born of seven children of Roland Curtin, an ironmaster, and his second wife, Jane Gregg; a Presbyterian. Brother of Constans, Martha Marie, Ellen Honora, Margery Gregg, Nancy Hale and Julia. Married to Katherine Irvine Wilson on May 30, 1844; father of Mary Wilson, Jane Gregg, Martha Irvin, William Wilson, Myron Stanley, Kate Wilson, and Bessie Elliot. Attended the academy of Reverend David Kirkpatrick in Milton, Pennsylvania; studied law with W. W. Potter of Bellefonte, and with Judge John Reed at Dickinson College, Carlisle, Pennsylvania. Admitted to the bar of Centre County, Pennsylvania in 1839, and practiced in partnership with John Blanchard. A fine public speaker, Curtin entered politics as a Whig, actively supporting the presidential campaigns of Harrison, Clay, Taylor and Scott from 1840 to 1852. Governor James Pollock (1855-1858) appointed him Secretary of the Commonwealth and Superintendent of Public Instruction, a post in which he initiated the state system of teacher-training (normal) schools. Curtin became the nominee of the "People's Party" for Governor in 1860. This name incorporated both Republicans and those Whigs and Democrats who favored Republican economic policies (high tariff, free public land) but feared radical abolitionism. His election in October against Democrat Henry D. Foster foreshadowed Lincoln's success in the November presidential canvass, as Lincoln's victory required the electoral vote of Pennsylvania. Curtin defeated Foster by a vote of 262,346 to 230,230. The new governor's state party was split between his supporters and those of U. S. Senator Simon Cameron, later to become Lincoln's Secretary of War, who laid claim to control of the party. This feud continued actively until 1872, when Curtin became an Independent Republican and later a Democrat. In his inaugural address, Curtin placed Pennsylvania, a critical state bordering on slave territory, firmly on the side of the Union. When Lincoln called for mobilization of state troops after the firing on Fort Sumter, Curtin had already established procedures which rapidly produced far more men than the assigned quota. He wisely declined to reduce this force as requested by Secretary of War Cameron, and the Pennsylvania Reserves became a major factor in protecting Washington, D. C., after the unexpected defeat of Union troops at Bull Run. Calling a conference of northern governors at Altoona in September, 1862, Curtin achieved decisive support for Lincoln in two areas of widespread public disagreement—the military draft, and the impending Emancipation Proclamation. Although in poor health, Curtin reluctantly accepted renomination and was re-elected governor against Democrat George Woodward in 1863, by a vote of 269,506 to 254,171. Curtin devoted most of his effort during his second term to logistic military problems: transport, supplies, personnel, and care of troops in the field. Known as "The Soldier's Friend," he instituted state schools for war orphans after the Civil War ended. Within the state, he contributed to the repeal of the State Tonnage Tax, which greatly benefited the Pennsylvania Railroad and aided it in becoming the nation's largest transport system. Curtin ran for the United States Senate after leaving the governorship, but lost to his rival, Simon Cameron. In 1869, President Grant named him Minister to Russia, where he remained until 1872. He condemned the corruption of the Grant era, supported Horace Greeley for President, and served three terms as a Democratic Congressman, 1881-1887. He then retired to Bellefonte, where he died on October 7, 1894. Bibliography: W. H. Egle, ed., *Andrew Gregg Curtin: His Life and Services* (1895); A. K. McClure,

Abraham Lincoln and Men of War Times (1892); A. K. McClure, *The Life and Services of Andrew G. Curtin, An Address* (1895); A. K. McClure, *Old Time Notes of Pennsylvania*, 2 vols. (1905); *Times* [Philadelphia] (October 8, 1894); Erwin S. Bradley, *The Triumph of Militant Republicanism, A Study of Pennsylvania and Presidential Politics, 1860-1872* (1964); William H. Russell: "A Biography of Alexander K. McClure," Ph.D. Dissertation, University of Wisconsin, 1953; Rebecca G. Albright, "The Civil War Career of Andrew G. Curtin," *Western Pennsylvania Historical Magazine*, vol. 48 (April, 1965).

GEARY, John White, 1867-1873

Born on December 30, 1819, near Mount Pleasant, Westmoreland County, Pennsylvania, son of Richard Geary, an ironmaster and schoolmaster, and Margaret (White) Geary; a Methodist. In 1843 married Margaret Ann Logan, who died in 1853; remarried to Mrs. Mary Henderson in 1858; father of several sons by his first wife. Attended local schools and graduated from Jefferson College in 1841; studied civil engineering and law; was admitted to the bar; taught school. Secured a position as assistant superintendent and engineer of the Allegheny Portage Railroad; attained the rank of Colonel in the Mexican War; appointed Postmaster of San Francisco and General Mail Agent for the Pacific coast by President James Polk in 1849; in 1850 elected first Alcalde and later first Mayor of San Francisco; appointed Military Governor of Savannah, Georgia, on December 22, 1864; became Major-General, 1865. An ardent Republican, Geary ran for Governor of Pennsylvania in 1866, supported in his attempt by Simon Cameron, the dominant leader of that party in the state. Geary defeated his Democratic opponent, Hiester Clymer, 307,274 votes to 290,096; he was inaugurated on January 15, 1867, the first of a line of Civil War generals to become governor. In 1869 Geary stood for reelection, and received 290,552 votes against the 285,956 cast for his Democratic opponent, Asa Packer. During Governor Geary's tenure, Pennsylvania enjoyed a period of rapid development in business and industry, and the state debt was reduced by ten million dollars. The power of the railroads was increasing, and Geary supported a constitutional convention to deal with the influence of lobbyists who were petitioning the Assembly for favors. Governor Geary also appointed a commission to adjudicate the claims of those citizens who had lost property during the Confederate invasions of Pennsylvania. Geary left office on January 21, 1873, and died suddenly in Harrisburg on February 8, 1873. Bibliography: Sylvester K. Stevens, *Pennsylvania, Birthplace of a Nation* (New York, 1964); Sylvester K. Stevens, *Pennsylvania, the Keystone State* (New York, 1956); Harry W. Tinkcom, *John White Geary, Soldier-Statesman, 1819-1873* (Philadelphia, 1940); Roy Glashan, *American Governors and Gubernatorial Elections, 1775-1975* (Stillwater, Minnesota, 1975); Congressional Quarterly, Inc., *Guide to U. S. Elections* (Washington, D. C., 1975).

HARTRANFT, John Frederick, 1873-1879

Born December 16, 1830, in New Hanover, Montgomery County, Pennsylvania, son of Samuel Engle, a landowner, and Lydia (Bucher) Hartranft; a Schwenkfeldian. Married to Sallie Sebring on January 26, 1854; father of one son and two daughters. Attended local schools and Marshall College (Pennsylvania) and graduated from Union College (New York) in 1853; secured employment as a civil engineer with the Mauch Chunk and Wilkes-Barre Railroad; studied law with James Boyd of Norristown; admitted to the bar in 1860; Colonel of the 4th Pennsylvania Regiment, 1861, and the 51st Pennsylvania Regiment, 1862; promoted to Brigadier-General, May 1864; brevetted Major-General, March 1865. A Republican, Hartranft was elected Deputy Sheriff of Montgomery County in 1854, and served in this office until the outbreak of the Civil War. After the war Hartranft was elected state Auditor General. Reelected to this post in 1868, he served until he first ran for Governor in 1872. Hartranft won 353,287 votes; his Democratic opponent, Charles B. Buckalew, received 317,700; and minor candidates got 1,250. Governor Hartranft was inaugurated on January 21, 1873. He won his bid for reelection in 1875, defeating Cyrus L. Pershing, his Democratic rival, 304,175 votes to 292,145. Minor hopefuls drew 13,244. During Governor Hartranft's tenure, the industrial boom following the Civil War ended, and the resulting economic depression and unemployment caused serious civil disturbances. Hartranft was forced to call out the state militia on several occasions, and in 1877 asked for federal troops to suppress the violence and loss of property which accompanied the striking railroaders in Reading and Pittsburgh. After peace was restored, he proposed recognition of labor unions and arbitration of claims. He advocated technical training, municipal reform, regulation of banking, and the reorganization of the Pennsylvania National Guard. During his administration the revision of the State Constitution was completed, and a series of geological surveys was begun. Leaving office on January 21, 1879, Hartranft moved to Philadelphia, where he became Postmaster and Commander of the Pennsylvania National Guard. From 1881 to 1885 he was Collector of the Port of Philadelphia. Hartranft died on October 17, 1889. Bibliography: Sylvester K. Stevens, *Pennsylvania, Birthplace of a Nation* (New York, 1964); Sylvester K. Stevens, *Pennsylvania, the Keystone State* (New York, 1956); Roy Glashan, *American Governors and Gubernatorial Elections, 1775-1975* (Stillwater, Minnesota, 1975); Congressional Quarterly, Inc., *Guide to U. S. Elections* (Washington, D. C., 1975).

HOYT, Henry Martyn, 1879-1883

Born on June 8, 1830, in Kingston, Luzerne County, Pennsylvania, son of Ziba, a farmer, and Nancy (Hurlbut) Hoyt; a Presbyterian. Married Mary Loveland on September 25, 1855; father of one son and two daughters. Attended local schools, the Wilkes-Barre Academy, the Wyoming Seminary (Kingston, Pa.), Lafayette College; graduated from Williams College (Mass.) in 1849; taught school at Towanda, Pennsylvania, and the Wyoming Seminary; studied law; admitted to the bar, 1853. Became Lieutenant-Colonel of the 52nd Regiment of Pennsylvania Volunteers, 1861; promoted to Colonel, 1863; brevetted Brigadier-General, 1865; honorary LL.D. from the University of Pennsylvania and from Lafayette College, 1881.

After the close of the Civil War, Hoyt returned to his law practice in Wilkes-Barre. Governor John White Geary appointed him in 1867 to the temporary post of Additional Judge of Luzerne County, and in 1869 he became Collector of Internal Revenue for Luzerne and Susquehanna counties, but resigned in 1873. A staunch Republican, Hoyt was the Chairman of the Republican State Committee from 1875 to 1876. The culmination of Hoyt's political career was his election to the governor's chair in 1878. Voters cast 319,567 ballots for Hoyt; 297,060 for Andrew H. Dill, his Democratic opponent; and 85,411 for minor candidates. Governor Hoyt was inaugurated on January 21, 1879. Hoyt's administration reduced the state debt by a million and a half dollars; collected delinquent taxes; prosecuted railroads for discriminatory freight rates; annulled the charters of "diploma mill" medical schools; and established a state medical board. Interested in penal reform, Hoyt built a new reformatory for first offenders between the ages of fifteen and twenty-five, where young men were taught a trade and given a chance to further their education. Governor Hoyt left office on January 16, 1883, to return to his law practice. A man of many interests, Governor Hoyt in 1879 published *Controversy Between Connecticut and Pennsylvania*, a study of the land claims of seventeen townships in the Wyoming Valley. In 1885 he published *Protection Versus Free-Trade*. His final years were spent in retirement, and he died in Wilkes-Barre, Pennsylvania, in December 1892. Bibliography: Sylvester K. Stevens, *Pennsylvania, Birthplace of a Nation* (New York, 1964); Sylvester K. Stevens, *Pennsylvania, the Keystone State* (New York, 1956); Roy Glashan, *American Governors and Gubernatorial Elections, 1775-1975* (Stillwater, Minnesota, 1975); Congressional Quarterly, Inc., *Guide to U. S. Elections* (Washington, D. C., 1975).

PATTISON, Robert Emory, 1883-1887, 1891-1895

Born on December 8, 1850, in Quantico, Maryland, son of Robert Henry Pattison, a Methodist Episcopalian minister, and Catherine (Woolford) Pattison; a Methodist Episcopalian. Unmarried. Attended public schools in Philadelphia, Pennsylvania; studied law with Lewis C. Cassidy; was admitted to the bar in 1872, and began private practice; received an honorary LL.D. from Dickinson College in 1884. An ardent Democrat, Pattison entered public life in 1878 as City Controller of Philadelphia, a position he held until 1881, when he was reelected for a second term. Having reformed the controller's office and rescued the city from the threat of bankruptcy, Pattison enjoyed great popularity among the people and the Democratic leadership. Consequently, in 1882, he was nominated to run for Governor against James Addams Beaver, the Republican candidate. Pennsylvanians cast 355,791 votes for Pattison, 315,589 for Beaver, and 72,423 for minor candidates. Governor Pattison took office on January 16, 1883, determined to bring reform and fiscal responsibility to the state. He advocated an end to patronage, graft and corruption. He also endeavored to check the rising power of corporations, the growing rift between labor and capital, and the monopolistic tendencies of the state's railroads. Unable to succeed himself, Governor Pattison left office on January 18, 1887, to return to his private law practice in Philadelphia. In April of 1887 he became president of the Chestnut Street National Bank, and later that year President Grover Cleveland appointed him to the Pacific Railroad Commission. After his work with the commission had ended, Pattison turned his attention to banking and church affairs. In 1890 Pattison ran for Governor on a reform platform. He defeated George W. Delamater, his Republican opponent, 464,209 votes to 447,655, with minor candidates receiving 16,332 votes. In his inaugural address on January 20, 1891, Governor Pattison demanded "purification of elections, involving ballot reform, personal registration, and the prevention of the misuses of money in politics; the equalization of the burdens of taxation; and the correction of abuses prevailing in the government of municipalities." He secured the adoption of the secret ballot on June 19, 1891, but he was not as successful in reducing tensions between labor and capital in the state. When the Homestead Strike broke out in 1892, he had to call in the state militia to restore order. Pattison left office for the final time on January 15, 1895, and resumed his private law practice. Pattison died on August 1, 1904. Bibliography: Sylvester K. Stevens, *Pennsylvania, Birthplace of a Nation* (New York, 1964); Sylvester K. Stevens, *Pennsylvania, the Keystone State* (New York, 1956); Roy Glashan, *American Governors and Gubernatorial Elections, 1775-1975* (Stillwater, Minnesota, 1975); Congressional Quarterly, Inc., *Guide to U. S. Elections* (Washington, D. C., 1975).

BEAVER, James Addams, 1887-1891

Born on October 21, 1837, in Millerstown, Perry County, Pennsylvania, son of Jacob, a merchant, and Ann Eliza (Addams) Beaver; a Presbyterian. Married to Mary Allison McAllister on December 26, 1865; father of five sons. Attended local schools in Perry and Mifflin counties and Pine Grove Academy (Center County); graduated from Jefferson College (Canonsburg, Pennsylvania), 1856; studied law with Hugh Nelson McAllister; admitted to Center County Bar, January 1859. Became First Lieutenant of Company H of the 2nd Pennsylvania Volunteer Infantry, 1861; promoted to Lieutenant-Colonel, 45th Pennsylvania Infantry, 1861; promoted to Colonel, 148th Pennsylvania Regiment, September 1862; brevetted Brigadier-General of Volunteers on November 10, 1864; medical discharge from service, December 22, 1864. Beaver returned home to Bellefonte after the Civil War, and built a lucrative law practice. In 1867 Governor John White Geary commissioned him Major-General of the 5th Division of the Pennsylvania National Guard, and Beaver continued to serve until 1887. Beaver, an avid Republican, entered political life in 1882, but was defeated in the governor's race that year by Robert E. Pattison, the Democratic candidate. Voters cast 315,589 ballots for Beaver and 355,791 for Governor Pattison. In 1886 Beaver again entered the gubernatorial contest, and this time defeated Chauncey F. Black, the Democratic candidate, 412,285 votes to 369,634. Minor candidates received 37,293 votes. Beaver was inaugurated on January 18, 1887. Governor Beaver's administration made substantial improvements to the state's roads and education. He was also a strong advocate of temperance legislation, and a proponent of new and better uses for Pennsylvania's forests and waterways. Beaver refused to use the state military except in extraordinary cases; reduced the state debt by three million dollars; and provided quick relief to the flood victims of 1889. Governor Beaver left office on January 20, 1891, to return to his private law practice. Later that year he became president of the Blubacker Coal Company in Cambria County; he also served as a Judge of the First Superior Court of Pennsylvania from 1895 until his death in 1914. In 1889 Dickinson College (Pennsylvania) and Hanover College of Indiana awarded him the honorary degree of

LL.D. General Beaver died in Bellefonte, Pennsylvania, on January 31, 1914. Bibliography: Sylvester K. Stevens, *Pennsylvania, Birthplace of a Nation* (New York, 1964); Sylvester K. Stevens, *Pennsylvania, the Keystone State* (New York, 1956); Frank A. Burr, *Life and Achievements of James Addams Beaver* (Philadelphia, 1882); Roy Glashan, *American Governors and Gubernatorial Elections, 1775-1975* (Stillwater, Minnesota, 1975); Congressional Quarterly, Inc., *Guide to U. S. Elections* (Washington, D.C., 1975).

PATTISON, Robert Emory, 1883-1887, 1891-1895

HASTINGS, Daniel Hartman, 1895-1899

Born on February 26, 1849, in Salona, Clinton County, Pennsylvania, son of William, a farmer, and Sarah (Hartman) Hastings; a Presbyterian. Unmarried. Attended local schools in Clinton County; taught school in the winter and worked on his father's farm in the summer; principal of the Bellefonte High School from 1867 to 1875; studied law; admitted to the bar in 1875. Hastings, a Republican, quickly became prominent in legal and political affairs as an associate of Matthew S. Quay. In 1888 Hastings, as delegate-at-large to the Republican National Convention, nominated Senator John Sherman for the presidency. From 1880 to 1885 he was a Colonel in the Pennsylvania National Guard. He looked after his interests in coal mines and banking from 1886 to 1890, and during this period served as Governor James A. Beaver's Adjutant-General. During the flood of 1889 in Johnstown, Hastings took charge of the relief measures and became a state hero. Hastings desired the Republican nomination in the gubernatorial race of 1890, but his associate, Quay, preferred George W. Delmater, a wealthy banker and a friend of Standard Oil interests. Many Republicans who would have voted for Hastings either did not vote or voted for Robert Pattison, the former Democratic governor, thus enabling Pattison to win the election. By 1894 Hastings had won Quay's support and became the Republican candidate for governor. Hastings defeated William M. Singerly, the Democratic standard bearer, 574,801 votes to 333,404, while minor candidates received 44,812 votes. Inaugurated on January 15, 1895, Governor Hastings was Pennsylvania's leader during the Spanish-American War. He directed the Assembly to support the war effort with men, supplies and money. Hastings left office on January 17, 1899, to return to his private law practice. Hastings died in Bellefonte on January 9, 1903. Bibliography: Sylvester K. Stevens, *Pennsylvania, Birthplace of a Nation* (New York, 1964); Sylvester K. Stevens, *Pennsylvania, the Keystone State* (New York, 1956); Roy Glashan, *American Governors and Gubernatorial Elections, 1775-1975* (Stillwater, Minnesota, 1975); Congressional Quarterly, Inc., *Guide to U. S. Elections* (Washington, D. C., 1975).

STONE, William Alexis, 1899-1903

Born on April 18, 1846, in Delmar, Tioga County, Pennsylvania, son of Israel, a farmer, and Amanda (Howe) Stone; a Presbyterian. Married to Ellen Stevens on August 18, 1870; father of Harriet and Stephen; after his first wife's death in 1878, remarried Elizabeth White, by whom he had six children—Robert Graham, Allen Bache, Jean, Margaret, Isabel and John. Attended local schools and the state normal school; served as a private in the Civil War from 1862 to 1865; admitted to the bar in 1870; began his law practice in Wellsboro. A Republican, Stone entered public life in 1874 as District Attorney of Tioga County, serving in this capacity until 1877. He then moved to Pittsburgh, where he served as U. S. District Attorney for western Pennsylvania from 1877 until 1886. President Grover Cleveland eventually removed him from that office for his public support of Governor James A. Beaver's bid for reelection. In 1890 Stone ran for the U. S. Congress. Elected, he served from 1891 to 1898, when he ran for Governor. In the gubernatorial election of 1898, Stone was involved in a feud between Republican boss Matthew S. Quay and Philadelphia merchant John Wanamaker. Quay secured the nomination of Stone, defeating Wanamaker's candidate for nomination, Charles W. Stone (no relation). Wanamaker and the Philadelphia *North American* called for freedom from Quay's "corrupt and sinister spirit," but William Stone went on to defeat George A. Jenks, the Democratic candidate, 476,206 votes to 358,300. Dr. Silas Swallow, the Prohibition standard bearer, received 132,931 votes, and several minor candidates drew 4,305. Inaugurated on January 17, 1899, Governor Stone successfully overcame the state's deficit of three million dollars through careful management. He caused a scandal by appointing his supporter, Quay, to the United States Senate, at a time when Quay was under indictment for misappropriation of state funds. Stone left office on January 20, 1903, to join his son Stephen in a law practice. He later served as Prothonotary of the Supreme Court in 1915, and of the Superior Court in 1916. Stone died in Philadelphia on March 1, 1920. Bibliography: Sylvester K. Stevens, *Pennsylvania, Birthplace of a Nation* (New York, 1964); Sylvester K. Stevens, *Pennsylvania, the Keystone State* (New York, 1956); Roy Glashan, *American Governors and Gubernatorial Elections, 1775-1975* (Stillwater, Minnesota, 1975); Congressional Quarterly, Inc., *Guide to U. S. Elections* (Washington, D. C., 1975).

PENNYPACKER, Samuel Whitaker, 1903-1907

Born on April 9, 1843, in Phoenixville, Chester County, Pennsylvania, son of Isaac Anderson, physician and professor at the Philadelphia College of Medicine, and Anna Maria (Whitaker) Pennypacker; a Lutheran. Unmarried. Attended the Grovemont Seminary in Phoenixville and the West Philadelphia Institute; served as a private in the 26th Pennsylvania Emergency Regiment, 1863-1865; studied law with Peter McCall and attended the University of Pennsylvania Law School; admitted to the bar in 1866; began his law practice shortly thereafter. From 1867 until 1902, Pennypacker concerned himself with his career in law and his interests in history and education. In 1868 he became president of the Law Academy of Philadelphia. His works on law include *Digest of the English Common Law Reports*, four volumes of *Pennypacker's Supreme Court Cases*, and a book on Pennsylvania colonial cases. He also authored thirty-seven books and papers on the early history of Philadelphia and the surrounding area. From 1886 to 1889 he served on the Board of Education for Philadelphia and acted as Controller of Public Schools for the 29th Ward. In 1889 Governor James A. Beaver appointed him to the Court of Common Pleas, where he served until 1900. He received an LL.D. from Franklin and Marshall College in 1917. In the gubernatorial election of 1902, Pennypacker won the Republican nomination with the support of Matthew S. Quay's political machine. He defeated the Democratic hopeful, Robert Pattison, 593,328 votes to 450,978, while minor candidates received 50,465 votes. Inaugurated on January 20, 1903, Governor Pennypacker advocated political reform. When the Assembly refused to act on his measures, he called a special session, and the legislature eventually adopted a personal registration-of-voters act; heavier penalties for election abuses; and provisions for civil service examinations for some offices in Philadelphia. The lawmakers also established the Pennsylvania State Police to curb abuses by the police forces employed by the state's coal and iron companies. Leaving office on January 15, 1907, Governor Pennypacker returned to his law practice and other interests. He died in Philadelphia on September 2, 1916. Bibliography: Samuel Pennypacker, *The Autobiography of a Pennsylvanian* (Winston, 1918); Sylvester K. Stevens, *Pennsylvania, Birthplace of a Nation* (New York, 1964); Sylvester K. Stevens, *Pennsylvania, the Keystone State* (New York, 1956); Roy Glashan, *American Governors and Gubernatorial Elections, 1775-1975* (Stillwater, Minnesota, 1975); Congressional Quarterly, Inc., *Guide to U. S. Elections* (Washington, D. C., 1975).

STUART, Edwin Sydney, 1907-1911

Born on December 28, 1853, in Philadelphia, Pennsylvania, son of Hugh, a small farmer, and Anna (Newman) Stuart; a Presbyterian. Unmarried. Stuart attended the Philadelphia public schools until he was fourteen, and then took a job as a clerk in Leary's Bookstore. He soon rose to head clerk, later became a partner, and eventually bought out Mr. Leary. A staunch Republican, Stuart was deeply interested in the political affairs of the day. In 1880 he became president of the Young Republicans of Philadelphia, and in 1882 he was elected state president, serving in that capacity until he resigned in 1891. He helped to organize the State League of Republican Clubs in 1884, and became its first president, serving until 1886. In 1891 Stuart won the Republican nomination for Mayor of Philadelphia and was elected by a large majority. During his period as mayor, Stuart led the investigation into John Bardsley's embezzlement of large sums of money from the city. Bardsley, a city trustee, and others implicated in the scandal were prosecuted, convicted and sent to prison. Stuart was elected to the Select Council of Philadelphia in 1896, representing the 26th Ward. Stuart had the support of Boies Penrose, leader of the Pennsylvania Republican organization since Matthew S. Quay's death, in his 1906 bid for the governorship, and he defeated his Democratic opponent, Lewis Emery, Jr., by 506,418 votes to 458,054 in the general election. Minor candidates accounted for 42,105 votes. Inaugurated on January 15, 1907, Governor Stuart was soon confronted by another scandal. William H. Berry, the state treasurer, discovered that the thirteen million dollar new state capitol building should have cost much less, and that the state had been misled by several key officials who had inflated the actual cost and billed the state for unjustified charges. Although Governor Stuart aided in the investigation and prosecution of the guilty parties, Pennsylvania's political reputation greatly suffered. In other areas, Stuart was influential in Pennsylvania's campaign against tuberculosis, and lent his considerable support to the state's common school system, which later received fifteen million dollars biannually. Governor Stuart left office on January 17, 1911, and returned to his business interests. He died in Philadelphia on March 21, 1937. Bibliography: Sylvester K. Stevens, *Pennsylvania, Birthplace of a Nation* (New York, 1964); Sylvester K. Stevens, *Pennsylvania, the Keystone State* (New York, 1956); Roy Glashan, *American Governors and Gubernatorial Elections, 1775-1975* (Stillwater, Minnesota, 1975); Congressional Quarterly, Inc., *Guide to U. S. Elections* (Washington, D. C., 1975).

TENER, John Kinley, 1911-1915

Born on July 25, 1863, in County Tyrone, Ireland, son of George Evans, who brought his family to Pittsburgh, Pennsylvania, in 1873, and Susan (Wallis) Tener; an Episcopalian. On October 29, 1889, married Harriet Day, who died in 1935; on August 11, 1936, remarried Leone Evans. Attended public schools in Pittsburgh; in 1881 secured employment as a clerk with Oliver Brothers & Phillips; became an officer in the Chartiers Valley Gas Company in 1887, later working for the Chambers & McKee Glass Company; moved to Charleroi, Pennsylvania, in 1891, where he became president of the First National Bank in 1897; gradually became involved with many phases of Charleroi's financial and industrial life. Tener, a Republican, entered politics in 1908, when he was elected to the United States Congress, an office he filled until 1911. In 1910 he ran for Governor, defeating D. Webster Grim, the Democratic candidate, by a count of 415,614 to 129,395. William H. Berry, Tener's "Keystone Party" opponent, received 382,127 votes, while minor candidates accounted for 71,302. Inaugurated on January 17, 1911, Governor Tenor proved a resourceful and capable administrator. Developments during his years as chief executive included the modernization of the state highway system; the creation of the State Public Service Commission to regulate public utilities; the institution of a state school code introducing vocational training into the public schools; inauguration of a new agency to supervise labor and industrial affairs; provisions for state-wide primaries for nomination to all public offices; and passage of a pure food law, a mothers' pension act, and a prison reform act. Also enacted into law were a plan for expanding the capital area, and a bill creating the Pennsylvania Historical Commission to recognize and preserve the state's history. Governor Tener left office on January 19, 1915, to return to his business interests. A professional baseball player as a young man, Tener was president of the National Baseball League from 1913 to 1918. He was also president of the W. J. Tener Insurance Company, and of Tener, Lowry & Company of Pittsburgh. Tener died in Charleroi on May 19, 1946. Bibliography: Sylvester K. Stevens, *Pennsylvania, Birthplace of a Nation* (New York, 1964); Sylvester K. Stevens, *Pennsylvania, the Keystone State* (New York, 1956); Roy Glashan, *American Governors and Gubernatorial Elections, 1775-1975* (Stillwater, Minnesota, 1975); Congressional Quarterly, Inc., *Guide to U. S. Elections* (Washington, D. C., 1975).

BRUMBAUGH, Martin Grove, 1915-1919

Born on April 14, 1862, in Huntingdon County, son of George Boyer, a farmer, and Martha (Peightal) Brumbaugh; a Dunker. Married to Anna Konigmacher on July 30, 1884; father of two children. Attended public schools in Huntingdon County; graduated from Juniata College in Huntingdon in 1881; studied higher mathematics at the State Normal School in Millersville in 1882; did postgraduate work at Harvard from 1891 to 1892, and at the University of Pennsylvania from 1892 to 1894; received an A.D. in 1893 and a Ph.D. in 1894; received an honorary LL.D. from Franklin and Marshall College in 1902 and from Pennsylvania College in 1900, and an honorary Litt.D. from Lafayette College in 1915; did post-doctoral work at the University of Jena, Germany, in 1895. Brumbaugh was a professor at the State Normal School from 1882 to 1883, and Superintendent of Huntingdon County schools from 1884 to 1890. He declined the presidency of Juniata College to accept the Chair of Pedagogy at the University of Pennsylvania in 1894. From 1886 to 1891 he conducted teachers' institutes for Louisiana, and lectured in Ohio, Pennsylvania, New Jersey, Maryland, Delaware, Kentucky and Indiana. Elected president of the Pennsylvania State Teachers' Association, Dr. Brumbaugh held membership in the Pennsylvania Historical Society and the Pennsylvania German Society. He was the author of several books on pedagogy and German religious sects, and was appointed the first Commissioner of Education for Puerto Rico, serving from 1900 to 1902. In 1914 Brumbaugh ran for Governor on the Republican ticket. He defeated his Democratic opponent, Vance C. McCormick, by a vote of 588,705 to 453,380, with minor candidates receiving 68,667 votes. Inaugurated on January 19, 1915, Governor Brumbaugh established a conservative, *laissez-faire* tone for his administration. Accordingly, he vetoed over four hundred bills in two sessions of the Assembly. Measures which did pass dealt with child labor, conservation, and workmen's compensation. When World War I broke out, Brumbaugh organized the Council of Defense to coordinate the state's war effort. Brumbaugh's term expired on January 21, 1919, and he returned to private life. He died on March 14, 1930. Bibliography: Sylvester K. Stevens, *Pennsylvania, Birthplace of a Nation* (New York, 1964); Sylvester K. Stevens, *Pennsylvania, the Keystone State* (New York, 1956); Roy Glashan, *American Governors and Gubernatorial Elections, 1775-1975* (Stillwater, Minnesota, 1975); Congressional Quarterly, Inc., *Guide to U. S. Elections* (Washington, D. C., 1975).

SPROUL, William Cameron, 1919-1923

Born on September 16, 1870, in Octoraro, Lancaster County, Pennsylvania, son of William Hall, who was connected with the iron industry, and Deborah Dickinson (Slokom) Sproul; a Quaker. Married Emeline Roach on January 21, 1892; father of two children—Dorothy Wallace and John Roach. Attended local schools and graduated from Swarthmore College in 1891. Interested in journalism, Sproul bought a half interest in the Chester *Times*, which he later purchased outright. He subsequently owned and published both the *Times* and the Chester *Morning Republican*. His business affairs soon extended to shipbuilding, when he became director of the Roach shipyards in 1898, and to the iron industry, when he organized the

Seaboard Steel Casting Company in 1900 and established a plant in Chester. Other business ventures with which he became involved included railroads, land, coal, banking, fire-brick manufacturing and bridge building. A Republican, Sproul's political career began in 1896 with his election to the Pennsylvania State Senate, a position he held for the next twenty-two years. In the gubernatorial election of 1918, Sproul defeated his Democratic opponent, Eugene C. Bonniwell, by a vote of 552,537 to 305,315, while minor candidates received 47,173. Inaugurated on January 21, 1919, Governor Sproul was a constructive, progressive administrator. During his tenure as the state's chief executive, the Assembly endorsed the eighteenth and nineteenth amendments to the United States Constitution. Other legislation adopted included a reorganization of the public school system, provision for the relief and care of disabled World War I veterans, a massive road building program, and the establishment of a public welfare department. In the steel strike of 1919 and in the coal strike of 1922, Governor Sproul averted disorder and loss of property by quickly sending National Guard units and sheriffs to the affected areas. His appointment of a fuel commission to arbitrate the disagreements ultimately helped to settle these strikes. From 1912 to 1920, Sproul received the honorary LL.D. from nine institutions: Franklin and Marshall College in 1912; Gettysburg College in 1918; the University of Pennsylvania, the University of Pittsburgh, Lafayette College, Pennsylvania Military College, and Swarthmore College in 1919; Allegheny College and Grove City College in 1920. Governor Sproul left office on January 16, 1923, to devote himself to his business and humanitarian interests. He died in Chester, Pennsylvania, on March 21, 1928. Bibliography: Sylvester K. Stevens, *Pennsylvania, Birthplace of a Nation* (New York, 1964); Sylvester K. Stevens, *Pennsylvania, the Keystone State* (New York, 1956); Roy Glashan, *American Governors and Gubernatorial Elections, 1775-1975* (Stillwater, Minnesota, 1975); Congressional Quarterly, Inc., *Guide to U. S. Elections* (Washington, D. C., 1975).

PINCHOT, Gifford, 1923-1927, 1931-1935

Born on August 11, 1865, in Simsbury, Connecticut, son of James, a New York City merchant, and Mary (Eno) Pinchot; an Episcopalian. Married to Cornelia Elizabeth Bryce on August 15, 1914; father of one son, Gifford Bryce Pinchot. Attended public schools in Simsbury and Phillips Exeter Academy; graduated from Yale in 1889; studied forestry at the Ecole National Forestiére, Nancy, France, and in the French Alps and the Vosges; toured Switzerland, Germany and Austria with students of the English Forest School. Among Pinchot's many honors were degrees from the following institutions: M.A. from Yale in 1901 and Princeton in 1904; Sc.D. from Michigan Agricultural College in 1907; and LL.D. from McGill University, 1909, Pennsylvania Military College, 1923, Yale, 1925, and Temple University, 1931. Returning to the United States in 1891, Pinchot surveyed forests for the Phelps-Dodge Company, and in 1892 for George W. Vanderbilt. In 1892 he opened an office in New York City as a consulting forester. From 1893 to 1895, he worked for the Vanderbilts, and from 1895 to 1896, he was a forest consultant for New Jersey. He became a member of the National Forest Commission in 1896, serving until 1898; from 1898 to 1905 he was Chief of the Division of Forestry under James Wilson, Secretary of Agriculture; and from 1905 to 1910 served as Chief Forester on the National Conservation Commission. From 1920 to 1922, he was Forester of Pennsylvania. Pinchot, a Republican, ran for Governor in 1922, defeating his Democratic opponent, John A. McSparran, by 831,696 votes to 581,625, while minor candidates received 51,351. Governor Pinchot was inaugurated on January 16, 1923. His was a progressive administration, which reorganized state government; wiped out a three million dollar deficit; revised laws for care and treatment of the insane and retarded; devised a retirement system for state employees; and established an old age pension system. Since a Pennsylvania governor cannot succeed himself, Pinchot left office on January 18, 1927. In 1930 Pinchot won his bid for re-election. He received 1,068,874 votes; his Democratic opponent, John M. Hemphill, drew 1,036,605; minor candidates accounted for only 26,367. Inaugurated on January 20, 1931, Governor Pinchot continued his program of progressive reform: 20,000 miles of improved rural roads; laws to correct abuses by corporations, bankers, and building and loan associations; laws to stop unfair use of labor injunctions; a reduction in utility rates; and pensions for the blind. Governor Pinchot left office on January 15, 1935, to continue his work in conservation. Pinchot died in New York City on October 4, 1946. Bibliography: Nelson McGeary, *Gifford Pinchot, Forester-Politician* (Princeton, 1960); Martin Fausold, *Gifford Pinchot, Bull Moose Progressive* (Syracuse, 1961); Gifford Pinchot, *Breaking New Ground* (New York, 1947); Sylvester K. Stevens, *Pennsylvania, Birthplace of a Nation* (New York, 1964); Sylvester K. Stevens, *Pennsylvania, the Keystone State* (New York, 1956); Roy Glashan, *American Governors and Gubernatorial Elections, 1775-1975* (Stillwater, Minnesota, 1975); Congressional Quarterly, Inc., *Guide to U. S. Elections* (Washington, D. C., 1975).

FISHER, John Stuchell, 1927-1931

Born on May 25, 1867, in South Mahoning Township, Pennsylvania, son of Samuel Royer, a farmer, and Mariah (McGaughey) Fisher; a Presbyterian. Married to Hapsie Miller on October 11, 1893; father of two children—Robert Miller and Mary Miller Fisher. Attended district schools; graduated from Pennsylvania State Normal School in 1886; taught school and was principal of schools in Plumville and Indiana, Pennsylvania, from 1886 to 1893; studied law with Samuel Cunningham; admitted to the bar in 1893; became a partner in the firm of Cunningham & Fisher, and practiced law from 1893 until 1927; received honorary LL.D. degrees from many institutions, including the following: Lafayette College in 1926; Franklin and Marshall College and Westminster College in 1927; the University of Pennsylvania and Juniata College in 1928; Pennsylvania Military College and Temple University in 1929. A Republican, Fisher became interested in state affairs at the beginning of his law career. From 1900 to 1909, he served as a State Senator, and became prominent for his prosecution of those involved in the frauds connected with the construction of the new State Capitol in Harrisburg. He was a member of the Commission on Constitutional Revision, and served as State Commissioner of Banking from 1919 until 1922. In the gubernatorial election of 1926, Fisher defeated Eugene C. Bonniwell, the Democratic standard bearer, 1,102,823 votes to 365,280. Minor candidates received 35,565 votes. Inaugurated on January 18, 1927, Governor Fisher was especially interested in a sound fiscal policy, public works construction, conservation, and voting reform. He set up a Department of Revenue, and used the money saved to improve normal schools and state highways; to build 4,000 miles of new roads; and to construct a new hospital for the insane, two state office buildings, the state farm show building, and the Soldiers and Sailors Memorial Bridge. About 450,000 acres were added to the state forests, and the use of voting machines was adopted during Fisher's administration. On January 20, 1931, Governor Fisher, known as "the builder," left office to return as consultant to his son's law firm and to attend to his business interests. He was also chairman of the board of the National Union Fire Insurance Company in Pittsburgh; Director of the Forbes National Bank and of the Savings & Trust Company in Indiana, Pennsylvania; and a member of the boards of Indiana (Pennsylvania) Hospital, the State Normal School, and Pennsylvania State College. Fisher died in Pittsburgh, Pennsylvania, on June 25, 1940. Bibliography: Sylvester K. Stevens, *Pennsylvania, Birthplace of a Nation* (New York, 1964); Sylvester K. Stevens, *Pennsylvania, the Keystone State* (New York, 1956); Roy Glashan, *American Governors and Gubernatorial Elections, 1775-1975* (Stillwater, Minnesota, 1975); Congressional Quarterly, Inc., *Guide to U. S. Elections* (Washington, D. C., 1975).

PINCHOT, Gifford, 1923-1927, 1931-1935

EARLE, George Howard, 1935-1939

Born on December 5, 1890, in Devon, Pennsylvania, son of George H. Jr., businessman, and Catharine Hansell (French) Earle; an Episcopalian. Brother of Frances van Lohr, Edith, Ralph, Catharine Ann, Gladys Howard, Hansell French and three others. Married to Huberta F. Potter on January 20, 1916; later married Jacqueline Sacre in December 1945; father of George Howard IV, Hubert, Lawrence Ralph and Jacqueline Anthony. Attended Harvard, 1909-1911; received his LL.B. degree from Temple University, 1935; also LL.D. and LH.D. degrees from Waynesburg College, 1935. Served in 2nd Pennsylvania Infantry in 1916, and on the Mexican border as 2nd Lieutenant in 1917; Earle also commanded a submarine chaser in World War I, 1917-1918. Awarded the Navy Cross for bravery, and again served in the Navy during World War II. Earle worked with his father for the Pennsylvania Sugar Company after the first World War, and later founded the Flamingo Sugar Mills in Philadelphia. He was appointed U. S. Minister to the Republic of Austria in 1933, but resigned in 1934 to become a candidate for Governor of Pennsylvania. A Democrat. As the Democratic candidate for Governor, Earle defeated Republican William A. Schnarder on November 6, 1934, by a vote of 1,476,467 to 1,410,138. He was inaugurated on January 15, 1935. During his administration, which was known as "Pennsylvania's Little New Deal," the legislature passed the state's first gasoline and cigarette tax and its first civil rights bill. Other legislation passed while Earle served as governor included a law which permitted the showing of Sunday movies, a highway bill which cleared the way for the construction of the Pennsylvania Turnpike, and a law ridding company mining towns of "coal and iron police." Governor Earle left office on January 17, 1939. Governor Earle lost in his bid for election to the United States Senate in 1938. He was appointed United States Minister to Bulgaria in 1940, Associate Naval Attaché to Turkey, in 1943, and Assistant Governor of Samoa in 1945. He then returned to his business interests. George H. Earle died on December 30, 1974, at Bryn Mawr, Pennsylvania. Bibliography: Roy Glashan, *American Governors and Gubernatorial Elections, 1775-1975* (Stillwater, Minnesota, 1975); Congressional Quarterly, Inc., *Guide to U. S. Elections* (Washington, D. C., 1975); Sylvester K. Stevens, *Pennsylvania, Birthplace of a Nation* (New York, 1964); Philadelphia *Evening Bulletin* (December 31, 1974).

JAMES, Arthur Horace, 1939-1943

Born on July 14, 1883, in Plymouth, Luzerne County, Pennsylvania, son of James David, a coal miner, and Rachel (Edwards) James; a Methodist. On October 23, 1912, married Ada Morris, who died in 1935; later married Emily (Radcliffe) Case, a widow, on October 1, 1941; father of two children by his first wife—Dorothy Rachel and Arthur Horace James. Attended Plymouth public schools; graduated from the law school of Dickinson College, Carlisle, Pennsylvania, in 1904; admitted to the bar and began to practice law in Plymouth in 1904. Honorary degrees include: LL.D. degree from Susquehanna University, 1927; Dickinson College, 1938; Temple University and Jefferson Medical, Pennsylvania Military, Muhlenberg, Franklin and Marshall, and Washington and Jefferson Colleges, 1939; University of Pennsylvania, 1940; Moravian and Lafayette Colleges, 1941; and Gettysburg and Grove City Colleges and Bucknell University, 1942; also an honorary D.C.L. degree from Hahnemann Medical College, 1939. Moving to Wilkes-Barre to open a new law office in 1905, James became involved in politics. As a Republican, he was elected District Attorney of Luzerne County in 1920, and reelected in 1923, serving in this capacity until 1926. From 1926 to 1930, he was Lieutenant Governor of the state; he was also Judge of the Superior Court of Pennsylvania from 1932 to 1939. In the 1938 gubernatorial race, James received 2,035,340 votes, while his Democratic opponent, Charles Alvin Jones, drew 1,756,192. Minor candidates got 20,435 votes. He was inaugurated on January 17, 1939. Governor James created the state's Department of Commerce; extended the Pennsylvania Turnpike; enacted a bill which banned the "sit-down" strike and another which modified the anti-injunction law; strengthened the civil service; advocated milk-price supports; reinforced liquor control laws; provided for the retirement of much of Pennsylvania's bonded debt; and created the Anthracite Emergency Commission. He also mobilized the state's efforts during World War II by creating the State Council of Defense and the Selective Service Board. When the National Guard was federalized, he set up the Pennsylvania Reserve Defense Corps for home defense, and he organized the Citizens' Defense Corps to guard against possible air raids. James left office on January 19, 1943, and returned to his private law practice. James died April 27, 1973. Bibliography: Sylvester K. Stevens, *Pennsylvania, Birthplace of a Nation* (New York, 1964); Sylvester K. Stevens, *Pennsylvania, the Keystone State* (New York, 1956); Roy Glashan, *American Governors and Gubernatorial Elections, 1775-1975* (Stillwater, Minnesota, 1975); Congressional Quarterly, Inc., *Guide to U. S. Elections* (Washington, D. C., 1975).

MARTIN, Edward, 1943-1947

Born on September 18, 1879, in Washington, Greene County, Pennsylvania, son of Joseph T., a farmer, and Hannah M. (Bristor) Martin; a Presbyterian. Married to Charity Scott in December 1908; father of two children—Edward and Mary. Attended local schools; graduated from Waynesburg College in 1901; admitted to the bar in 1905 and began practice in Waynesburg. A military man, Martin spent forty-four years in the service. In 1898 he enlisted as a private and later became a corporal, seeing action in the Philippines. Mustered out of the army in 1899, he joined the Pennsylvania National Guard as a Sergeant in January 1900. He received his commission as First Lieutenant in 1901; he was made a Captain in 1905 and a Major in 1910. In 1917 Martin served in France as a Major, and was promoted to Lieutenant Colonel in September 1918. Before World War I ended, he had received four decorations: the Distinguished Service Cross, the Oak Leaf Cluster, and a Purple Heart with an Oak Leaf Cluster. In 1920 he was promoted to Colonel, and he became a Brigadier General in August 1922. In June 1939, he was raised to Major General of the Pennsylvania National Guard, which was federalized in 1941 and sent south on maneuvers. In 1942 he was released from the army. Martin, a Republican, was also active in politics. He was Auditor General of Pennsylvania from 1925 to 1929, State Treasurer from 1930 to 1934, and Adjutant General from 1939 to 1943, except for the period between February 17, 1941, and April 1, 1942, when he was in the army. Supported by the political machine of Joseph Newton Pew, Jr., Martin ran for Governor in 1942. Pennsylvanians cast 1,367,531 votes for Martin; 1,149,897 for F. Clair Ross, his Democratic opponent; and 30,643 for minor candidates. He was inaugurated on January 19, 1943. Governor Martin urged more funds for unemployment compensation and liberalized insurance benefits for occupational diseases. He insisted upon safety inspections of mines and factories, and advocated new low-cost housing and an end to discrimination. Martin was elected to the United States Senate in 1946, and resigned the governorship on January 2, 1947, in order to be seated at the opening session. Reelected for a second term in the Senate, Martin served from 1947 to 1959. Active in numerous veterans', church and educational organizations, and the Elk and Masonic lodges, Martin also received many honorary degrees: LL.D. degrees from Washington and Jefferson College, 1938; the University of Pittsburgh, 1941; Temple University, Pennsylvania Military College, Villanova College, Drexel Institute of Technology, 1943; Gettysburg College, 1944; and Grove City College, Lebanon Valley College, and Westminster College, 1945. In 1940 Waynesburg College awarded him a Doctor of Military Science degree, and Hahnemann Medical College and the Hospital of Philadelphia honored him with a Doctor of Humane Letters degree in 1945. For his military services, he received the Pennsylvania Reilly Medal in 1937. Martin died on March 19, 1967. Bibliography: Sylvester K. Stevens, *Pennsylvania, Birthplace of a Nation* (New York, 1964); Sylvester K. Stevens, *Pennsylvania, the Keystone State* (New York, 1956); Roy Glashan, *American Governors and Gubernatorial Elections, 1775-1975* (Stillwater, Minnesota, 1975); Congressional Quarterly, Inc., *Guide to U. S. Elections* (Washington, D. C., 1975).

BELL, John Cromwell, 1947

Born on October 25, 1892, in Philadelphia, Pennsylvania, son of John Cromwell, lawyer and Attorney-General of Pennsylvania, and Fleuretta deBenneville (Myers) Bell; an Episcopalian. Brother of Bert. Married to Sarah Andrews Baker on June 29, 1918; father of John Cromwell, Louis Baker, George deBenneville, Sarah and Sophie Shepley. Graduated from the University of Pennsylvania with an LL.D. in 1937; admitted to the Pennsylvania Bar, 1917. Served as Assistant Solicitor for the city of Philadelphia, 1919-1922; Assistant District Attorney, 1922-1925. Appointed State Secretary of Banking by Governor Arthur H. James in 1938, and served until 1943. Lieutenant Governor of Pennsylvania, 1943-1947. Served as President of the State Senate and Chairman of the State Board of Pardons, 1943-1947. A Republican, John C. Bell became Governor of Pennsylvania after the resignation of Governor Edward Martin on January 2, 1947, and served until the newly-elected governor, James H. Duff, took office on January 21, 1947. Governor James Duff appointed Bell to the State Supreme Court in 1950; Bell eventually became Chief Justice of the Supreme Court in 1961 and served until his retirement in 1972. He was also appointed special consultant to the district attorney's office in 1972, and served until his death. John Cromwell Bell, Jr., died on March 18, 1974, and was buried in Wynnewood, Pennsylvania. Bibliography: Roy Glashan, *American Governors and Gubernatorial Elections, 1775-1975* (Stillwater, Minnesota, 1975); Congressional Quarterly, Inc., *Guide to U. S. Elections* (Washington, D. C., 1975); Sylvester K. Stevens, *Pennsylvania, Birthplace of a Nation* (New York, 1964); Philadelphia *Evening Bulletin* (March 19, 1974).

DUFF, James Henderson, 1947-1951

Born on January 21, 1883, in Carnegie, Pennsylvania, son of Joseph Miller, a farmer, and Margaret (Morgan) Duff; a Presbyterian. Married to Jean Taylor on October 26, 1909; no children. Attended Carnegie public schools; received his B.A. from Princeton in 1904; studied at the University of Pennsylvania Law School from 1905 to 1906; studied for his LL.B. at the University of Pennsylvania Law School from 1905 to 1906; received his LL.B. from the University of Pittsburgh in 1907. For the next thirty-six years, Duff was associated with the law firm of Duff, Scott and Smith in Pittsburgh. A Republican, Duff served as a delegate to the Republican National Conventions of 1932, 1936 and 1939; he was also Governor Edward Martin's Attorney General from 1943 to 1947. In the gubernatorial election of 1946, Duff defeated his Democratic opponent, John S. Rice, by a vote of 1,828,462 to 1,270,947. Minor candidates received 24,585 votes. Inaugurated on January 21, 1947, Governor Duff presided over a particularly active period in Pennsylvania's history. During his tenure, he sought greater revenue for conservation, building and public health, without having to raise taxes on real estate. Accordingly, he increased the tax on cigarettes, taxed soft drinks, and reinstated a tax on capital stocks. A measure in 1947 also empowered local communities to tax anything not taxed by the state. Duff developed the Philadelphia port area; initiated a program to rid the Schuylkill River of contamination; erected new bridges over the Delaware River; expanded the overcrowded mental hospitals; and increased the salary of Pennsylvania teachers. Concerned that labor-management conflicts often overrode the public welfare, Duff signed a law forbidding strikes by essential public utilities, and another law forbidding an individual to picket a plant where he did not work. In July 1947, Duff also approved a bill providing women with equal pay for equal work. The permissible work week for women was extended from forty-four to forty-eight hours a week. On January 16, 1951, Duff left office to take a seat in the United States Senate, where he served until 1956. He received numerous honorary degrees, including LL.D. degrees in 1947 from Duquesne University, Albright College, Pennsylvania Military College, Lafayette College, Franklin and Marshall College, Washington and Jefferson College, the University of Pennsylvania, Temple University, and St. Francis College. In June 1948, Villanova College awarded him the degree of Doctor of Humane Letters. Duff died December 20, 1970. Bibliography: Sylvester K. Stevens, *Pennsylvania, Birthplace of a Nation* (New York, 1964); Sylvester K. Stevens, *Pennsylvania, the Keystone State* (New York, 1956); Roy Glashan, *American Governors and Gubernatorial Elections, 1775-1975* (Stillwater, Minnesota, 1975); Congressional Quarterly, Inc., *Guide to U. S. Elections* (Washington, D. C., 1975).

FINE, John Sydney, 1951-1955

Born on April 10, 1893, near Nanticoke, Pennsylvania, son of Jacob W., a coal miner, and Margaret (Croop) Fine; an Episcopalian. Married to Helene Pennebecker Morgan on December 5, 1939; father of two children—John Sydney, Jr., and Donald. Attended public schools in Nanticoke; received his LL.B. degree from Dickinson School of Law in 1914; admitted to the Luzerne County Bar in 1915, and began his law practice in Wilkes-Barre. Fine served as a sergeant in World War I from 1917 to 1919. While on duty in Ireland, he did postgraduate study at Trinity College, University of Dublin. Discharged from the service in August 1919, Fine resumed his law practice and became a partner in the firm of Coughlin and Fine. Fine, a Republican, became active in politics and served as Secretary of the Luzerne County Republican Committee. He was also an alternate delegate to the Republican National Convention in 1920, and was elected Republican County Chairman in 1922. In 1927 Governor Gifford Pinchot appointed him Judge of the Court of Common Pleas of Luzerne County. Reelected to this post in November 1939, Fine served until June 17, 1947, when Governor James Duff appointed him to a vacancy on the Pennsylvania Superior Court. Fine was reelected in November 1948, and served on the court until he resigned on March 1, 1950, to run for Governor. In a close race, Fine won 1,796,070 votes to Richard Dilworth's 1,710,355. Minor candidates received 33,585 votes. After his inauguration on January 16, 1951, Governor Fine faced a financial crisis and the problem of governmental reorganization. Needing over one billion dollars for the first two years, Fine tried to get a one percent income tax. Although it opposed any form of income tax, the Assembly eventually granted a one percent selective sales and use tax. Fine initiated the Chesterman Committee to study governmental structure; the committee's recommendations, while made during Fine's tenure, were not carried out until after he had left office. Fine also reorganized the Department of Health, and continued Pennsylvania's efforts to improve its educational and mental health programs, clean the state's streams, and expand its highway programs. Fine left office on January 18, 1955, to return to his law practice and other interests. Bibliography: Sylvester K. Stevens, *Pennsylvania, Birthplace of a Nation* (New York, 1964); Sylvester K. Stevens, *Pennsylvania, the Keystone State* (New York, 1956); Roy Glashan, *American Governors and Gubernatorial Elections, 1775-1975* (Stillwater, Minnesota, 1975); Congressional Quarterly, Inc., *Guide to U. S. Elections* (Washington, D. C., 1975).

LEADER, George Michael, 1955-1959

Born on January 17, 1918, in York County, Pennsylvania, son of Guy Alvin, a poultry breeder, and Beulah (Boyer) Leader; a Lutheran. Married Mary Jane Strickler on September 17, 1939; father of four children—George Michael, Frederick Milton, Jane Ellen and Charles David. Attended public schools in York; received his B.S. from the University of Pennsylvania in 1939; and in 1942 did graduate work there; secured employment as Secretary-Treasurer of his father's firm, Guy A. Leader & Sons; served in World War II as an Ensign in the United States Navy, 1942; honorably discharged in 1946 as a Lieutenant. A staunch Democrat, Leader was a member, later the secretary, and finally the chairman of the York County Democratic Committee. From 1950 to 1954, he served as a State Senator. Elected Governor in the election of 1954, Leader defeated his Republican opponent, Lloyd H. Wood, 1,996,266 votes to 1,717,070. Minor candidates received only 7,121 votes. Inaugurated on January 18, 1955, Governor Leader faced a financial dilemma, needing $1,273,164,930 for his first two years in office. Educational and public assistance expenses accounted for about eighty percent of the amount required. To meet the challenge, Governor Leader levied new taxes and increased others. He then initiated programs for industrial redevelopment, and urged mental-health, clean-streams, and water-conservation programs. He also implemented several recommendations of the Chesterman Committee, begun under Governor John Fine. Leader created the Office of Administration, and made the Secretary of Administration a cabinet member in order to coordinate a more efficient operation of state government. Moreover, Leader placed several thousand state employees under the merit system, thus weakening the traditional spoils policy of previous political leaders. Governor Leader left office on January 20, 1959, to return to his business and community interests. Among his numerous honors are the following degrees: L.H.D. degree from Gettysburg College, 1956; LL.D. degrees from Temple University in 1955, Elizabethtown College in 1956, and Lincoln University and LaSalle College in 1957. Bibliography: Sylvester K. Stevens, *Pennsylvania, Birthplace of a Nation* (New York, 1964); Roy Glashan, *American Governors and Gubernatorial Elections, 1775-1975* (Stillwater, Minnesota, 1975); Congressional Quarterly, Inc., *Guide to U.S. Elections* (Washington, D.C., 1975).

LAWRENCE, David Leo, 1959-1963

Born on June 18, 1889, in Pittsburgh, Pennsylvania, son of Charles B., a teamster, and Catherine (Conwell) Lawrence; a Roman Catholic. Married Alice Golden on June 8, 1921; father of five children—two sons who died in an automobile accident in 1942, and Mary, Anna May and Gerald. Attended parochial schools and a two-year commercial school; secured work at fourteen as an office boy for William J. Breunem, Democratic party leader of Pittsburgh; served as an enlisted man in the office of the Judge Advocate General in Washington, D. C., during World War I, and worked for Woodrow Wilson at the 1912 Democratic National Convention as a page. Lawrence, a Democrat, served that party in some official capacity from 1912. A member of the Pittsburgh Registration Commission between 1914 and 1924, he became Collector of Internal Revenue for the Western District of Pennsylvania from 1933 to 1934. He resigned this post in 1934 to become chairman of the Democratic State Committee. From 1935 to 1939, Lawrence was Secretary of the Commonwealth under Governor George Earle. Lawrence then headed the Harris-Lawrence Company, Inc., an insurance firm, and continued as an influential Pittsburgh Democratic leader. In 1945 he ran for Mayor of Pittsburgh and was reelected to four terms, serving from 1946 to 1958. Finally, in 1958, he won the governorship, defeating his Republican opponent, Arthur T. McGonigle, 2,024,852 votes to 1,948,769. Minor candidates received only 13,297 votes. He was inaugurated on January 20, 1959. Governor Lawrence inherited a deficit from his predecessor, George Leader. He consequently increased the sales tax to four percent in order to balance the budget. Governor Lawrence also supported and continued many of Leader's programs. He retained nearly all of Leader's cabinet and his executive civil service, and relied on the Office of Administration for improved management programs. Building programs, including the William Penn Memorial Museum and the Archives Building, were strongly encouraged by the Lawrence administration, as were projects for improvements to other aspects of the state's history. Governor Lawrence left office on January 15, 1963, and returned to private business. In 1959 the University of Pennsylvania conferred upon him an honorary LL.D. Lawrence died on November 21, 1966. Bibliography: Sylvester K. Stevens, *Pennsylvania, Birthplace of a Nation* (New York, 1964); Roy Glashan *American Governors and Gubernatorial Elections, 1775-1975* (Stillwater, Minnesota, 1975); Congressional Quarterly, Inc., *Guide to United States Elections* (Washington, D. C., 1975).

SCRANTON, William Warren, 1963-1967

Born on July 19, 1917, in Madison, Connecticut, son of Worthington Scranton, president of the family-controlled Scranton Gas and Water Company, and Marion Margery (Warren) Scranton; a Presbyterian. Married Mary Lowe Chamberlin on July 6, 1942; father of four children—Susan, William Worthington, Joseph Curtis and Peter Kip. Attended local Scranton schools, Fessenden School in West Newton, Massachusetts, the Hotchkiss School in Lakeville, Connecticut, Yale University, receiving his B.A. in 1939, and the Yale Law School, obtaining his LL.B. in 1946. Served as a Lieutenant in the Army Air Force during World War II; discharged in 1945 as a Captain; now a Major in the Air Force Reserve; admitted to the Pennsylvania Bar, and joined the firm of O'Malley, Harris, Warren & Hill in

1947. An active Republican, Scranton was a member of the personal staffs of Secretaries of State John Foster Dulles and Christian A. Herter from 1959 to 1960. In 1960 Scranton was elected to the United States Congress, serving from 1961 to 1962, when he ran for Governor. He defeated the Democratic standard bearer, Richardson Dilworth, 2,424,918 votes to 1,938,627. Minor candidates received 14,497 votes. After his inauguration on January 15, 1963, Governor Scranton called for realignment of the state's legislative districts, creation of a Department of Mental Health and a State Board of Education, extension of the civil service merit system, and funding for the Pennsylvania Industrial Development Authority. He also advocated technical training programs and the creation of a Council of Science and Technology, and he endeavored to interest foreign investors in Pennsylvania. Moreover, he authorized the Department of Mines and Minerals to search for new markets and uses for coal. Since Scranton left office on January 17, 1967, he has served the nation in numerous capacities: member of the President's Price Commission, 1971-1972; member of the President's General Advisory Commission on Arms Control and Disarmament, 1972 to the present; consultant to the President, 1974-1976; Ambassador to the United Nations, 1976 to the present; Vice chairman of the President's Panel for Riot Torn Areas, 1967; United States Ambassador and Chairman of the United States delegation INTELSAT, 1969; Chairman, President's Commission on Campus Unrest, 1970; member, Price Commission, 1971; Chairman, National Conference on Government, 1971; and member, Executive Committee on Trilateral Commission, 1971. Bibliography: Sylvester K. Stevens, *Pennsylvania, Birthplace of a Nation* (New York, 1964); Roy Glashan, *American Governors and Gubernatorial Elections, 1775-1975* (Stillwater, Minnesota, 1975); Congressional Quarterly, Inc., *Guide to U. S. Elections* (Washington, D. C., 1975).

SHAFER, Raymond Philip, 1967-1971

Born on March 5, 1917, in New Castle, Pennsylvania, son of David Philip, a farmer, and Mina Belle (Miller) Shafer; a Presbyterian. Married to Jane Harris Davies on July 5, 1941; father of three children, Diane Elizabeth, Raymond Philip and Jane Ellen. Attended local schools and Allegheny College, receiving his A.B. cum laude in 1938; received his LL.B. from Yale in 1941; admitted to both the New York and Pennsylvania Bars. He became associated with the law firm of Withrop, Stimson, Putnam & Roberts in New York City, and also practiced law in Meadville, Pennsylvania. Shafer served with the United States Naval Reserve from 1942 to 1945. Shafer, a Republican, served as District Attorney of Crawford County from 1948 to 1956. From 1959 to 1963, he was a State Senator from the Fiftieth District. Shafer became Lieutenant Governor in 1963, and at the end of his term ran for Governor. In the gubernatorial election of 1966, Shafer defeated Milton Shapp, the Democratic standard bearer, 2,110,349 votes to 1,868,719, while minor candidates drew 71,600 votes. Inaugurated on January 17, 1967, Governor Shafer continued former Governor Scranton's efforts to interest foreign investors in locating plants in Pennsylvania. To further industrial development, Governor Shafer reiterated the need for more liberal depreciation allowances for research, manufacturing and development companies. He also supported President Richard Nixon's efforts to wind down the war in Vietnam. On January 19, 1971, Governor Shafer left office to return to his private law practice and to his efforts on behalf of community charities.

Shafer has been active in many areas since his return to private life. He was chairman of the National Commission on Marijuana and Drug Abuse, and chairman of the Board of Trustees of Allegheny College. Member of Phi Beta Kappa and Phi Kappa Psi, Shafer holds membership in the American, the Pennsylvania, and the Crawford County Bar associations. Bibliography: Roy Glashan, *American Governors and Gubernatorial Elections, 1775-1975* (Stillwater, Minnesota, 1975); Congressional Quarterly, Inc., *Guide to U. S. Elections* (Washington, D. C., 1975).

SHAPP, Milton Jerrold, 1971-

Born Milton Jerrold Shapiro on June 25, 1912, in Cleveland, Ohio, son of Aaron, a hardware wholesaler, and Eva (Smelsey) Shapiro; a Jew. Married to Muriel Matzkin on May 20, 1947; father of three children, Richard, Joanne and Dolores. Attended public schools in Cleveland, Ohio, and Case Institute of Technology, receiving his B.S. in electrical engineering in 1933; worked as a truck driver and as a salesman in Philadelphia. Had his name legally changed to Shapp. Served in the United States Army Corps during World War II, and discharged from the service in 1946 as a Captain. In 1948 Shapp founded the Jerrold Electronics Corporation. Shapp, a Democrat, served as consultant to the Peace Corps, the Department of Commerce, and the National Public Advisory Committee on Area Redevelopment during President John F. Kennedy's administration. In 1966 he unsuccessfully ran for governor, when Raymond P. Shafer, the Republican standard bearer, defeated him by a vote of 2,110,349 to 1,868,719. In 1970, however, Shapp was victorious, winning 2,043,029 votes against the 1,542,854 cast for Raymond J. Broderick, his Republican opponent. Minor candidates received 114,177 votes. Under a new law, a Pennsylvania governor can now succeed himself, and Shapp ran again in 1974. The Republican candidate, Andrew L. Lewis, Jr., received 1,578,917 of the ballots cast, while Shapp won 1,878,252 votes, and minor candidates got 34,065. Inaugurated on January 19, 1971, Governor Shapp promised that he would be "the people's advocate." His Insurance Commissioner, Dr. Herbert S. Denenberg, sought to improve the cost and quality of service in hospitalization and in life and auto insurance. Although the State Legislature refused Shapp's proposed graduated income tax bill, the governor did get a 2.3 percent tax; he also instituted a state-wide lottery designed to yield a yearly $60,000,000, thirty percent of which was to be used to reduce the property taxes of poor elderly citizens. Among Governor Shapp's many honors are the B'nai B'rith's Reuben J. Miller Award, the Pennsylvania AFL-CIO's 1963 Man of the Year Award, and the humanitarian awards of the National Business League and the Pennsylvania State Baptist Convention. Moreover, Shapp was elected Chairman of the Mid-Atlantic Governors' Conference in 1973. Bibliography: Roy Glashan, *American Governors and Gubernatorial Elections, 1775-1975* (Stillwater, Minnesota, 1975); Congressional Quarterly, Inc., *Guide to U.S. Elections* (Washington, D.C., 1975).

INDEX

Each Governor's name is followed by a two-letter state abbreviation, a roman numeral (I, II, III, IV) denoting the volume in which the entry appears, and page number.

A

Index

Ames, Oliver, MA, II, 716
Ammons, Elias Milton, CO, I, 141
Ammons, Teller, CO, I, 147
Andersen, Elmer Lee, MN, II, 794
Anderson, C. Elmer, MN, II, 793
Anderson, Charles, OH, III, 1210
Anderson, Forrest Howard, MT, III, 885
Anderson, Hugh Johnson, ME, II, 605
Anderson, John, KS, II, 499
Anderson, Sigurd, SD, IV, 1457
Anderson, Victor Emanuel, NE, III, 913
Anderson, Wendell Richard, MN, II, 796
Andrew, John Albion, MA, II, 707
Andrews, Charles Bartlett, CT, I, 182
Andrus, Cecil Dale, ID, I, 360
Ansel, Martin Frederick, SC, IV, 1427
Anthony, George Tobey, KS, II, 465
Anthony, Henry Bowen, RI, IV, 1344
Apodaca, Jerry, NM, III, 1064
Ariyoshi, George Ryoichi, HI, I, 332
Armstrong, Samuel Turell, MA, II, 700
Arn, Edward F., KS, II, 495
Arnall, Ellis Gibbs, GA, I, 319
Arnold, Lemuel Hastings, RI, IV, 1338
Aronson, J. Hugo, MT, III, 882
Arthur, Harold John, VT, IV, 1612
Ashe, Samuel, NC, III, 1113
Askew, Reubin O'Donovan, FL, I, 275
Atkinson, George Wesley, WV, IV, 1697
Atkinson, William Yates, GA, I, 308
Austin, Horace, MN, II, 777
Avery, William Henry, KS, II, 500
Aycock, Charles Brantley, NC, III, 1148
Ayers, Roy Elmer, MT, III, 880

B

Babbitt, Bruce, AR, I, 60
Babcock, Tim, MT, III, 884
Bachelder, Nahum Josiah, NH, III, 982
Bacon, Walter W., DE, I, 242
Badger, William, NH, III, 952
Bagby, Arthur Pendleton, AL, I, 11
Bagley, John Judson, MI, II, 750
Bailey, Carl Edward, AR, I, 90
Bailey, Thomas L., MS, II, 828

Index

Index

Index

Index

Index

Buckner, Simon Bolivar, KY, II, 530
Buckson, David Penrose, DE, I, 244
Budd, James Herbert, CA, I, 114
Bulkeley, Morgan Gardner, CT, I, 185
Bullock, Alexander Hamilton, MA, II, 708
Bullock, Rufus Brown, GA, I, 301
Bulow, William John, SD, IV, 1453
Bumpers, Dale Leon, AR, I, 96
Burke, Andrew H., ND, III, 1171
Burke, John, ND, III, 1176
Burleigh, Edwin C., ME, II, 622
Burnett, Peter Hardeman, CA, I, 101
Burney, Dwight Willard, NE, III, 915
Burnquist, Joseph Alfred Arner, MN, II, 786
Burns, Haydon William, FL, I, 274
Burns, John Anthony, HI, I, 331
Burnside, Ambrose Everett, RI, IV, 1351
Burroughs, John, NM, III, 1061
Burton, Hutchins Gordon, NC, III, 1123
Burton, William, DE, I, 228
Busbee, George Dekle, GA, I, 326
Bushfield, Harlan John, SD, IV, 1456
Bushnell, Asa S., OH, III, 1221
Busiel, Charles Albert, NH, III, 979
Butler, Benjamin Franklin, MA, II, 714
Butler, David C., NE, III, 889
Butler, Ezra, VT, IV, 1567
Butler, Pierce Mason, SC, IV, 1402
Byrd, Harry Flood, VA, IV, 1659
Byrd, Richard C., AR, I, 65
Byrne, Brendan Thomas, NJ, III, 1045
Byrne, Frank M., SD, IV, 1451
Byrnes, James Francis, SC, IV, 1438

C

Cabell, Wiliam Henry, VA, IV, 1628
Cahill, William Thomas, NJ, III, 1045
Caldwell, Millard Fillmore, FL, I, 270
Caldwell, Tod Robinson, NC, III, 1140
Cameron, William, Evelyn, VA, IV, 1650
Campbell, David, VA, IV, 1638
Campbell, James Edwin, OH, III, 1219
Campbell, John M., NM, III, 1062
Campbell, Thomas Edward, AZ, I, 50
Campbell, Thomas Mitchell, TX, IV, 1531

Index

Index

Index

Index

D

Index

Index

E

Index

Emerson, Frank Collins, WY, IV, 1775
Emerson, Lee E., VT, IV, 1613
Emmerson, Louis L., IL, I, 385
English, James Edward, CT, I, 179
Erbe, Norman A., IA, II, 452
Erickson, John Edward, MT, III, 878
Eustis, William, MA, II, 697
Evans, Daniel Jackson, WA, IV, 1686
Evans, John Gary, SC, IV, 1424
Everett, Edward, MA, II, 701
Ewing, William Lee Davidson, IL, I, 368
Exon, John James, NE, III, 917

F

Fairbanks, Erastus, VT, IV, 1576
Fairbanks, Horace, VT, IV, 1586
Fairchild, Lucius, WI, IV, 1728
Fairfield, John, ME, II, 602
Fancher, Frederick Bartlett, ND, III, 1174
Fannin, Paul Jones, AZ, I, 57
Farnham, Roswell, VT, IV, 1588
Farnsworth, Daniel Duane Tompkins, WV, IV, 1692
Farrar, Frank Leroy, SD, IV, 1460
Farwell, Leonard James, WI, IV, 1718
Faubus, Orval Eugene, AR, I, 94
Felch, Alpheus, MI, II, 744
Felker, Samuel Demeritt, NH, III, 987
Fenner, Arthur, RI, IV, 1334
Fenner, James, RI, IV, 1335
Fenton, Reuben Eaton, NY, III, 1085
Ferguson, James Edward, TX, IV, 1532
Ferguson, Miriam A., TX, IV, 1535
Fernald, Bert Manfred, ME, II, 625
Ferris, Woodbridge, N., MI, II, 758
Ferry, Elisha Peyre, WA, IV, 1675
Fielder, James Fairman, NJ, III, 1033
Fields, William Jason, KY, II, 539
Fifer, Joseph Wilson, IL, I, 379
Finch, Charles Clifton, MS, II, 834
Findlay, William, PA, III, 1297
Fine, John Sydney, PA, III, 1326
Fish, Hamilton, NY, III, 1080
Fishback, William M., AR, I, 79
Fisher, John Stuchell, PA, III, 1321

Index

Index

G

Index

Index

H

Index

Index

Index

Index

I

J

K

Index

L

Index

Index

Low, Frederick Ferdinand, CA, I, 107
Lowden, Frank O., IL, I, 384
Lowe, Enoch Louis, MD, II, 665
Lowe, Ralph P., IA, II, 431
Lowndes, Lloyd, MD, II, 676
Lowry, Robert, MS, II, 819
Lubbock, Francis Richard, TX, IV, 1520
Lucas, Franklin Earl, WY, IV, 1774
Lucas, Robert, OH, III, 1199
Luce, Cyrus G., MI, II, 753
Lucey, Patrick J., WI, IV, 1760
Ludington, Harrison, WI, IV, 1732
Ludlow, George C., NJ, III, 1025
Lumpkin, Wilson, GA, I, 290
Lynch, Charles, MS, II, 804

M

McAlister, Harry Hill, TN, IV, 1503
MacArthur, Arthur, WI, IV, 1720
McArthur, Duncan, OH, III, 1198
McBride, Henry, WA, IV, 1678
McCall, Samuel Walker, MA, II, 725
McCall, Thomas Lawson, OR, III, 1288
McCarty, Daniel Thomas, FL, I, 271
McClellan, George, NJ, III, 1024
McClelland, Robert, MI, II, 745
McClung, Joseph W., MO, II, 849
McConaughy, James Lukens, CT, I, 202
McConnell, William John, ID, I, 338
McCord, Jim Nance, TN, IV, 1506
MacCorkle, William Alexander, WV, IV, 1697
McCray, Warren T., IN, I, 415
McCreary, James Bennett, KY, II, 528
McCuish, John Berridge, KS, II, 497
McCullough, John Griffith, VT, IV, 1597
McDaniel, Henry D., GA, I, 305
McDonald, Charles James, GA, I, 292
McDonald, Jesse Fuller, CO, I, 138
McDonald, William C., NM, III, 1049
McDougal, John, CA, I, 101
McDowell, James, VA, IV, 1641
McDuffie, George, SC, IV, 1401
McEnery, Samuel Douglas, LA, II, 575
McFarland, Earnest William, AZ, I, 56
McGill, Andrew Ryan, MN, II, 780

Index

Index

Index

Index

Morehead, John Henry, NE, III, 904
Morehead, John Motley, NC, III, 1130
Morehouse, Albert P., MO, II, 855
Morgan, Edwin Denison, NY, III, 1084
Morgan, Ephriam Franklin, WV, IV, 1703
Morley, Clarence J., CO, I, 144
Morril, David Lawrence, NH, III, 947
Morrill, Anson Peaslee, ME, II, 607
Morrill, Edmund Needham, KS, II, 473
Morrill, Lot Myrick, ME, II, 610
Morris, Luzon Burritt, CT, I, 186
Morrison, Cameron, NC, III, 1153
Morrison, Frank Brenner, NE, III, 915
Morrison, John T., ID, I, 341
Morrow, Edwin Porch, KY, II, 539
Morrow, Jeremiah, OH, III, 1197
Morton, Levi Parsons, NY, III, 1092
Morton, Marcus, MA, II, 698
Morton, Oliver P., IN, I, 405
Moseley, William Dunn, Fl, I, 251
Moses, Franklin J., SC, IV, 1417
Moses, John, ND, III, 1183
Moultrie, William, SC, IV, 1388
Mount, James A., IN, I, 411
Mouton, Alexandre, LA, II, 562
Murphree, Herron Dennis, MS, II, 826
Murphy, Francis Parnell, NH, III, 995
Murphy, Frank, MI, II, 763
Murphy, Franklin, NJ, III, 1030
Murphy, Isaac, AR, I, 70
Murphy, John, AL, I, 7
Murrah, Pendleton, TX, IV, 1521
Murray, Johnston, OK, III, 1251
Murray, William Henry, OK, III, 1247
Muskie, Edmund S., ME, II, 637

N

Nance, Albinus, NE, III, 892
Nash, George Kilbon, OH, III, 1222
Neely, Matthew Mansfield, WV, IV, 1707
Neff, Pat Morris, TX, IV, 1534
Nelson, Gaylord Anton, WI, IV, 1757
Nelson, Knute, MN, II, 782
Nestos, Ragnvald Anderson, ND, III, 1178

Index

Neville, M. Keith, NE, III, 905
Newbold, Joshua G., IA, II, 435
Newell, William Augustus, NJ, III, 1020
Nice, Harry Whinna, MD, II, 680
Nicholas, Wilson Cary, VA, IV, 1631
Nicholls, Francis Redding Tillou, LA, II, 573
Nigh, George Patterson, OK, III, 1254
Nobel, Patrick, SC, IV, 1403
Noble, Noah, IN, I, 398
Noe, James Albert, LA, II, 585
Noel, Edmond Favor, MS, II, 822
Noel, Philip William, RI, IV, 1382
Norbeck, Peter, SD, IV, 1451
Norblad, Albin Walter, OR, III, 1278
Norris, Edwin L., MT, III, 875
Northen, William J., GA, I, 307
Notte, John A., RI, IV, 1379
Noyes, Edward F., OH, III, 1213
Nunn, Louie B., KY, II, 549
Nutter, Donald Grant, MT, III, 883

O

Oates, William Calvin, AL, I, 24
O'Callaghan, Mike, NV, III, 935
O'Conor, Herbert Romulus, MD, II, 681
O'Daniel, Wilbert Lee, TX, IV, 1538
Oddie, Tasker Lowndes, NV, III, 927
Odell, Benjamin Baker, NY, III, 1094
O'Ferrall, Charles Triplett, VA, IV, 1652
Ogden, Aaron, NJ, III, 1011
Ogilvie, Richard Buell, IL, I, 390
Ogle, Benjamin, MD, II, 649
Oglesby, Richard James, IL, I, 374
Olcott, Ben, OR, III, 1275
Olden, Charles Smith, NJ, III, 1021
Oldham, William, AR, I, 84
Olson, Culbert L., CA, I, 122
Olson, Floyd Bjornstjerne, MN, II, 789
Olson, Ole H., ND, III, 1181
O'Neal Edward Asbury, AL, I, 22
O'Neal, Emmet, AL, I, 29
O'Neill, Crane William, OH, III, 1235
Orman, James Bradley, CO, I, 137
Ormsbee, Ebenezer Jolls, VT, IV, 1591

Index

P

Index

Index

Plumer, William, NH, III, 944
Poindexter, George, MS, II, 801
Poletti, Charles, NY, III, 1102
Polk, Charles, DE, I, 221
Polk, James Knox, TN, IV, 1472
Polk, Trusten, MO, II, 845
Pollard, John Garland, VA, IV, 1660
Pollock, James, PA, III, 1308
Pond, Charles Hobby, CT, I, 173
Ponder, James, DE, I, 230
Porter, Albert G., IN, I, 408
Porter, David Rittenhouse, PA, III, 1303
Porter, James Davis, TN, IV, 1484
Pothier, Aram, RI, IV, 1367
Powell, Lazarus Whitehead, KY, II, 521
Powell, Wesley, NH, III, 1000
Powers, Llewellyn, ME, II, 623
Powers, Ridgley Ceylon, MS, II, 818
Poynter, William Amos, NE, III, 898
Prall, Horace Griggs, NJ, III, 1039
Pratt, Thomas George, MD, II, 664
Prescott, Benjamin Franklin, NH, III, 971
Preston, James Patton, VA, IV, 1632
Preus, Jacob Aall Ottesen, MN, II, 787
Price, James Hubert, VA, IV, 1662
Price, Rodman McCauley, NJ, III, 1019
Price, Sterling, MO, II, 844
Proctor, Fletcher Dutton, VT, IV, 1598
Proctor, Mortimer R., VT, IV, 1610
Proctor, Redfield, VT, IV, 1587
Proctor, Redfield, Jr., VT, IV, 1605
Prouty, George Harrison, VT, IV, 1599
Pryor, David, AR, I, 97
Pyle, John Howard, AZ, I, 55

Q

Quinby, Henry Brewer, NH, III, 985
Quinn, Robert Emmet, RI, IV, 1373
Quinn, William Francis, HI, I, 331
Quitman, John Anthony, MS, II, 806

Index

R

Rabun, William, GA, I, 286
Ralston, Samuel, IN, I, 414
Rampton, Calvin Lewellyn, UT, IV, 1556
Ramsdell, George Allen, NH, III, 980
Ramsey, Alexander, MN, II, 774
Randall, Alexander Williams, WI, IV, 1723
Randolph, Beverly, VA, IV, 1623
Randolph, Peyton, VA, IV, 1630
Randolph, Theodore Fitz, NJ, III, 1023
Randolph, Thomas Mann, VA, IV, 1632
Ransom, Epaphroditus, MI, II, 745
Ratner, Payne Harry, KS, II, 490
Ray, Dixy Lee, WA, IV, 1687
Ray, James Brown, IN, I, 397
Ray, Robert D., IA, II, 454
Reagan, Ronald Wilson, CA, I, 126
Rector, Henry Massey, AR, I, 68
Reed, Clyde Martin, KS, II, 486
Reed, Harrison, FL, I, 256
Reed, John H., ME, II, 640
Reid, David Settle, NC, III, 1133
Rennebohm, Oscar, WI, IV, 1754
Reynolds, John, IL, I, 367
Reynolds, John W., WI, IV, 1758
Reynolds, Robert John, DE, I, 232
Reynolds, Thomas, MO, II, 841
Rhodes, James A., OH, III, 1237
Ribicoff, Abraham Alexander, CT, I, 205
Rice, Alexander Hamilton, MA, II, 712
Rich, John T., MI, II, 755
Richards, DeForest, WY, IV, 1768
Richards, John Gardiner, SC, IV, 1432
Richards, Wiliam Alford, WY, IV, 1767
Richardson, Friend William, CA, I, 120
Richardson, James Burchill, SC, IV, 1391
Richardson, John Peter, SC, IV, 1404
Richardson, John Peter, Jr., SC, IV, 1423
Rickards, John Ezra, MT, III, 874
Ridgeley, Charles Carnan, MD, II, 654
Riley, Bob Cowley, AR, I, 96
Ritchie, Albert Cabell, MD, II, 680
Ritner, Joseph, PA, III, 1302
Rivers, Eurith Dickinson, GA, I, 318
Roane, Archibald, TN, IV, 1466
Roane, John Selden, AR, I, 66

Index

Index

S

Index

Index

Index

Index

Index

Index

Index

Index

Index